Modern Leaders
Being A Series Of
Biographical Sketches

by

JUSTIN McCARTHY

Double 9
BOOKS

Modern Leaders
Being A Series Of Biographical Sketches
by JUSTIN McCARTHY

Copyright © 2023

All Rights reserved.

ISBN: 978-93-59959-23-8

Published by

DOUBLE 9 BOOKS

2/13-B, Ansari Road
Daryaganj, New Delhi – 110002
info@double9books.com
www.double9books.com
Tel. 011-40042856

ABOUT THE AUTHOR

Justin A. McCarthy is an American demographer who was born on October 19, 1945, and used to teach history at the University of Louisville in Louisville, Kentucky. He was given the Order of Merit of Turkey in 1998 and has an honorary doctorate from Bogazici University in Turkey. He is also on the boards of the Institute of Turkish Studies and the Center for Eurasian Studies (AVIM). He knows a lot about the history of the last few years of the Ottoman Empire. Many experts are very critical of McCarthy's work. They say that McCarthy's views supporting Turkish crimes against Armenians are the same thing as denying genocide. Hans-Lukas Kieser thinks McCarthy has "an indefensible bias toward the official perspective of Turkey." He taught at Middle East Technical University and Ankara University while in the Peace Corps in Turkey from 1967 to 1969. His PhD was from the University of California, Los Angeles, and it was given to him in 1978. After that, Boğazici University gave him an honors doctorate. He is also on the board of the Institute of Turkish Studies.

CONTENTS

INTRODUCTION 7

QUEEN VICTORIA AND HER SUBJECTS 9

THE REAL LOUIS NAPOLEON 23

EUGENIE, EMPRESS OF THE FRENCH 33

THE PRINCE OF WALES.. 47

THE KING OF PRUSSIA 60

VICTOR EMANUEL, KING OF ITALY............................. 73

LOUIS ADOLPHE THIERS 88

PRINCE NAPOLEON 103

THE DUKE OF CAMBRIDGE.. 113

BRIGHAM YOUNG 128

THE LIBERAL TRIUMVIRATE OF ENGLAND 142

THE ENGLISH POSITIVISTS... 155

ENGLISH TORYISM AND ITS LEADERS....................... 168

"GEORGE ELIOT" AND GEORGE LEWES...................... 181

GEORGE SAND 193

EDWARD BULWER, LORD LYTTON 207

"PAR NOBILE FRATRUM—THE TWO NEWMANS" 222

ARCHBISHOP MANNING... 233

JOHN RUSKIN... 243

CHARLES READE... 254

THE EXILE-WORLD OF LONDON................................. 267

THE REVEREND CHARLES KINGSLEY 279

MR. JAMES ANTHONY FROUDE.................................... 293

SCIENCE AND ORTHODOXY IN ENGLAND 307

INTRODUCTION

The sketches which make up this volume are neither purely critical nor merely biographical. They endeavor to give the American reader a clear and just idea of each individual in his intellect, his character, his place in politics, letters, and society. In some instances I have written of friends whom I know personally and well; in others of men with whom I have but slight acquaintance; in others still of persons whom I have only seen. But in every instance those whom I describe are persons whom I have been able to study on the spot, whose character and doings I have heard commonly discussed by those who actually knew them. In no case whatever are the opinions I have given drawn merely from books and newspapers. This value, therefore, these essays may have to an American, that they are not such descriptions as any of us might be enabled to put into print by the mere help of study and reading; descriptions for example such as one might make of Henry VIII. or Voltaire. They are in every instance, even when intimate and direct personal acquaintance least assist them, the result of close observation and that appreciation of the originals which comes from habitual intercourse with those who know them and submit them to constant criticism.

I have not made any alteration in the essays which were written some years ago. Let them stand as portraits bearing that date. If 1872 has in any instance changed the features and the fortunes of 1869 and 1870, it cannot make untrue what then was true. What I wrote in 1869 of the Prince of Wales, for example, will probably not wholly apply to the Prince of Wales to-day. We all believe that he has lately changed for the better. But what I wrote then I still believe was true then; and it is a fair contribution to history, which does not consent to rub out yesterday because of to-day. I wrote of a "Liberal Triumvirate" of England when the phrase was an accurate expression. It would hardly be accurate now. To-day Mr. Mill does not appear in political life and Mr. Bright has been an exile, owing to his health, for nearly two years from the scenes of parliamentary debate and triumph. But the portraits of the men do not on that account need any change. Even where some reason has been shown me for a modification of my own judgment I have still preferred to leave the written letter as it is. A distinguished Italian friend has impressed on me that King Victor Emanuel is personally a much more ambitious man than I have painted him. My friend has had far better opportunities of judging than I ever could have had; but I gave the best opinion I could, and still holding to it prefer to let it stand, to be taken for what it is worth.

I think I may fairly claim to have anticipated in some of the political sketches, that of Louis Napoleon, for instance, the judgment of events and history, and the real strength of certain characters and institutions.

These sketches had a gratifying welcome from the American public as they appeared in the "Galaxy." I hope they may be thought worth reading over again and keeping in their collected form.

Justin McCarthy.

48 Gower Street, Bedford Square, London, July 31, 1872.

QUEEN VICTORIA AND HER SUBJECTS

"And when you hear historians tell of thrones, and those who sat upon them, let it be as men now gaze upon the mammoth's bones, and wonder what old world such things could see."

So sang Byron half a century ago, and great critics condemned his verse, and called him a "surly Democrat" because he ventured to put such sentiments and hopes into rhyme. The thrones of Europe have not diminished in number since Byron's day, although they have changed and rechanged their occupants; and the one only grand effort at the establishment of a new Republic—that of France in 1848—went down into dust and ashes. Naturally, therefore, the tendency in Europe is to regard the monarchical principle as having received a new lease and charter of life, and to talk of the republican principle as an exotic forced for a moment into a premature and morbid blossom upon European soil, but as completely unsuited to the climate and the people as the banyan or the cocoa tree.

I do not, for myself, quite agree in this view of the aspect of affairs. Of course, if one were inclined to discuss the question fairly, he must begin by asking what people mean when they talk of the republican principle. What is the republican principle? When you talk of a Republic, do you mean an aggressive, conquering, domineering State, ruled by faction and living on war, like the Commonwealth of Rome? or a Republic like that planned by Washington, which should repudiate all concern in foreign politics or foreign conquest? Do you mean a Federal Republic, like that of the United States, or one with a centralized power, like the French Republic of 1848? Do you mean a Republic like that of Florence, in which the people were omnipotent, or a Republic like that of Venice, in which the people had no power at all? Do you mean a Republic like that of Switzerland, in which the President is next to nobody, or a Republic like that of Poland, which was ornamented by a King? In truth, the phrase "republican principle" has no set meaning. It means just what the man who uses it wishes to express. If, however, we understand it to mean, in this instance, the principle of popular self-government, then it is obvious that Europe has made immense progress in that direction since Byron raged against the crimes of Kings. If it means the opposite to the principle of Divine Right or Legitimacy, or even personal loyalty—loyalty of the old-time, chivalric, enthusiastic fashion—then it must be owned that it shows all over Europe the mark of equal progress. The ancient, romantic, sentimental loyalty; the loyalty which reverenced the Sovereign and was proud to abase itself before him; the loyalty of the Cavaliers; the loyalty which went wild over "Oh, Richard! Oh, mon Roi!" is dead and gone—its relics a thing to be stared at, and wondered over, and preserved for a landmark in the progress of the world—just like the mammoth's bones.

The model Monarchy of Europe is, beyond dispute, that of Great Britain. In England there is an almost absolute self-government; the English people can have anything whatever which they may want by insisting on it and agitating a little for it. The Sovereign has long ceased to interfere in the progress of national affairs. I can only recollect one instance, during my observation, in which Queen Victoria put her veto on a bill passed by Parliament, and that was on an occasion when it was discovered, at the last moment, that the Lords and Commons had passed a bill which had a dreadful technical blunder in it, and the only way out of the difficulty was to beg of the Queen to refuse it her sanction, which her Majesty did accordingly, and the blunder was set right in the following session. If a Prime Minister were to announce to the House of Commons, to-morrow, that the Queen had boxed his ears, it would not create a whit more amazement than if he were to say, no matter in what graceful and diplomatic periphrasis, that her Majesty was unwilling to agree to some measure which her faithful Commons desired to see passed into law.

Nothing did Mr. Disraeli more harm, nothing brought greater contempt on him than his silly attempts last session to induce the Commons to believe, by vague insinuations and covert allusions, that the Queen had a personal leaning toward his policy and himself. So long ago as the time of the free trade struggle, the Tories, for all their hereditary loyalty, complained of and protested against the silent presence of Prince Albert in the Peers' gallery of the House of Commons, on the ground that it was an attempt to influence the Parliament improperly, and to interfere with the freedom of debate. No one has anything to say against the Queen which carries any weight or is worth listening to. She is undoubtedly a woman of virtue and good sense. So good a woman, I venture to think, never before reigned over any people, and that she is not a great woman, an Elizabeth, a Catherine of Russia, or even an Isabella of Castile, is surely rather to the advantage than otherwise of the monarchical institution in its present stage of existence. Here, then, one might think, if anywhere and ever, the principle of personal loyalty has a fair chance and a full justification. A man might vindicate his loyalty to Queen Victoria in the name of liberty itself; nay, he might justify it by an appeal to the very principle of democracy. Yet one must be blind, who, living in England and willing to observe, does not see that the old, devoted spirit of personal loyalty is dead and buried. It is gone! it is a memory! You may sing a poetic lament for it if you will, as Schiller did for the gods of Hellas; you may break into passionate rhetoric, if you can, over its extinction, as Burke did for the death of the age of Chivalry. It is gone, and I firmly believe it can never be revived or restored.

I do not mean to say that there are many persons in England who feel any strong objection to the Monarchy, or warmly desire to see a Republic substituted for it. I know in England several theoretical republicans—they are to be met with in almost any company. I have never met with any one Englishman living in England, who showed any anxious, active interest in the abolition of the Monarchy. I do not know any one who objects to drink the usual loyal toasts at a public dinner, or betrays any conscientious reluctance to listen to the unmeaning eulogy which it is the stereotyped fashion for the chairman of every such banquet to heap on "Her Majesty and the rest of the Royal Family." But this sort of thing, if it ever had any practical meaning, has now none. It has reached that stage at which profession and practice are always understood to be quite different things. Every one says at church that he is a miserable sinner; no one is supposed really to believe anything of the sort. Every one has some time or other likened women to angels, but we are not therefore supposed seriously to ignore the fact that women wear flannel petticoats, and have their faults, and are mortal. So of loyal professions in England now. They are understood to be phrases, like "Your obedient servant," at the bottom of a letter. They do not suggest hypocrisy or pretence of any kind. There is apparently no more inconsistency now in a man's loyally drinking the health of the Queen, and proceeding immediately after (in private conversation) to abuse or ridicule her and her family, than there would be in the same man beginning with "Dear Sir," a missive to one whom he notoriously dislikes. Every one who has been lately in London must have heard an immense amount of scandal, or at all events of flippant joking at the expense of the Queen herself; and of more serious complaint and distrust as regards the Prince of Wales. Yet the virtues of the Queen, and the noble qualities of the Prince of Wales are panegyrized and toasted, and hurrah'd at every public dinner where Englishmen gather together.

The very virtues of Queen Victoria have contributed materially toward the extinction of the old-fashioned sentiment of living, active loyalty. The English people had from the time at least of Anne to our own day a succession of bad princes. Only a race patient as Issachar could have endured such a line of sovereigns as George II., George III., and George IV. Then came William IV., who being a little less stupidly obstinate than George III., and not so grossly corrupt as George IV., was hailed for a while as the Patriot King by a people who were only too anxious not to lose all their hereditary and traditional veneration. Do what they would, however, the English nation could not get into any sincere transports of admiration about the Patriot King; and they soon found that any popular reform worth having was to be got rather in spite of the Patriot King, than by virtue of any wisdom or patriotism in the monarch. Great popular demonstrations and tumults, and threats of marching on London; and O'Connell meetings at Charing Cross, with significant allusion by the great demagogue to the King who lost his head at Whitehall hard by; the hanging out of the black flag at Manchester, and a general movement of brickbats everywhere—these seem to have been justly regarded as the persuasive influences which converted a Sovereign into the Patriot King and a Reformer. Loyalty did not gain much by the reforms of that reign. Then followed the young Victoria; and enthusiasm for a while wakened up fresh and genuine over the ascension of the comely and simple-hearted girl, who was so frank and winning; who ran down stairs in her night-dress, rather than keep her venerable councillors waiting when they sought her out at midnight; who openly acknowledged her true love for her cousin, and offered him her hand; who was at once queenly and maidenly, innocent and fearless.

But this sort of thing did not last very long. Prince Albert was never popular. He was cold; people said he was stingy; his very virtues, and they were genuine, were not such as anybody, except his wife and family, warmly admires in a man; he was indeed misunderstood, or at all events misprized in England, up to the close of his life. Then the gates of the convent, so to speak, closed over the Queen, and royalty ceased to be an animating presence in England.

The young men and women of to-day—persons who have not passed the age of twenty-one—can hardly remember to have ever seen the Sovereign. She is to them what the Mikado is to his people. Seven years of absolute seclusion on the part of a monarch must in any case be a sad trial to personal loyalty, at least in the royal capital. A considerable and an influential section of Queen Victoria's subjects in the metropolis have long been very angry with their Sovereign. The tailors, the milliners, the dressmakers, the jewellers, the perfumers, all the shopkeepers of the West End who make profit out of court dinners and balls and presentations, are furious at the royal seclusion which they believe has injured their business. So, too, are the aristocratic residents of the West End, who do not care much about a court which no longer contributes to their season's gayety. So, too, are all the flunkey class generally. Now, I am sure there are no three sections of the population of London more influential in the spreading of scandal and the nursing of this discontent than the shopkeepers, the aristocrats, and the flunkeys of the West End. These are actively and demonstratively dissatisfied with the Queen. These it is who spread dirty scandals about her, and laugh over vile lampoons and caricatures of which she is the object.

Every one knows that there is a low, mean scandal afloat about the Queen—and it is spread by the clubs, the drawing-rooms, the shops, and the servants'-halls of the West End. I am convinced that not one of those who spread the scandal really believes it; but they like to spread it because they dislike the Queen. There can be no doubt, however, that much dissatisfaction at the Queen's long seclusion is felt by persons who are incapable of harboring any motives so mean or spreading any calumnies so unworthy. Most of the London papers have always found fault rather sharply and not over decently with the royal retirement. Mr. Ayrton, representative of the Tower Hamlets—the largest constituency in England—openly expressed this sentiment at a public meeting; and though his remarks were at once replied to and condemned by Mr. Bright, they met with a more or less cordial response from most of his audience.

There is or was in the House of Commons (the general election has got happily rid of him), a foolish person named Reardon, a Piccadilly auctioneer, who became, by what we call in England "a fluke," a member of the House of Commons. This person moved last session a resolution, or something of the kind, calling on the Queen to abdicate. The thing was laughed down— poor Mr. Reardon's previous career had been so absurd that anything coming from him would have been hooted; and the House of Commons is fiercely intolerant of "bores" and men with crotchets. But I have reason to believe that Mr. Reardon's luckless project was concocted by a delegation of London tradesmen, and had the sympathy of the whole class; and I know that many members of the House which hooted and laughed him down had in private over and over again grumbled at the Queen's retirement, and declared that she ought to abdicate.

"What on earth does it matter," I asked of a member of Parliament—one of the most accomplished scholars and sharp logicians in the House—"What on earth does it matter whether or not the Queen gives a few balls to a few thousand West End people in the season? How can rational people care, one way or the other?" "My dear fellow," was the answer, "I don't care; but all that sort of thing is her business, and she is paid to do it, and she ought to do it. If she were a washerwoman with a family, she would have to do her work, no matter what her grief." Now this gentleman—who is utterly above any sympathy with scandal or with the lackey-like grumblings of the West End—did, undoubtedly, express fairly enough a growing mood of the public dissatisfaction.

Beyond all this, however, is the fact that people—the working-class especially—are beginning to ask whether we really want a Sovereign at all, seeing that we get on just as well during the eclipse of royalty as in its brightest meridian splendor. This question is being very often put; and it is probably more often thought over than put into words. Now I think nothing worse could possibly happen to royalty in England than that people should begin quietly to ask whether there really is any use in it. If there is a bad King or Queen, people can get or look for, or hope and pray for a good one; and the abuse of the throne will not be accounted a sufficient argument against the use of it. But how will it be when the subjects begin to find that during the reign of one of the best sovereigns possible to have, they can get on perfectly well although the monarch is in absolute seclusion?

George IV. was an argument against bad kings only—Queen Victoria may come to be accepted as an illustration of the uselessness of the very best kind of Sovereign. I think King Log was much better calculated to do harm to the institution of royalty than King Stork, although the frogs might have regretted the placid reign of the former when the latter was gobbling up their best and fattest.

Decidedly the people of England are learning of the Queen how to do without royalty. A small section of her subjects are angry with her and bitter of heart against her; a much larger number find they can do perfectly well without her; a larger number still have forgotten her. On a memorable occasion Prince Albert declared that constitutional government was on its trial in England. The phrase, like many that came from the same well-meaning lips, was unlucky. Constitutional government was not upon its trial then; but Monarchy is upon its trial now.

Do I mean to say that Great Britain is on the verge of a revolution; that the dynasty is about to be overthrown; that a new Cromwell is to make his appearance? By no means. It does not follow that even if the English people were to be convinced to-morrow of the absolute uselessness of a throne, and a sovereignty, they would therefore proceed to establish a republic. No people under the sun are more strongly governed by tradition and "the majesty of custom" than the English. Cobden used to say that they had a Chinese objection to change of any kind. The Lord Mayor's show, long threatened, and for a while partially obscured, has come out again in full gingerbread. There is a functionary who appears every night at the door of the House of Commons just at the moment when the sitting is formally declared to be over, and bawls out to the emptying benches the resonant question, "Who's for home?" I believe the practice originated at a time when Westminster was unpeopled, and midnight roads were dangerous, and members were glad to make up parties to travel home together; and, so a functionary was appointed to issue stentorian appeal to all who were thus willing to combine their strength and journey safely in company. The need of such an arrangement has, I need hardly say, passed away these many generations; but the usage exists. It oppresses no one to have the formal call thundered out; the thing has got to be a regular performance; it is part of the whole business and system; nobody wants it, but nobody heeds it or objects to it, and the functionary appears every night of every session and shouts his invitation to companionship as regularly as if the Mohocks were in possession of Charing Cross, and Claude Duval were coming full trot along Piccadilly.

Now, this may be taken as a sort of illustration of the manner in which the English people are naturally inclined to deal with any institutions which are merely useless, and have the recommendation of old age and long descent. The ordinary Englishman to-day would find it hard to bring up before his mind's eye a picture of an England without a Sovereign. If it were made fully plain to him, and thoroughly impressed upon his mind that he could do just as well without a Sovereign as with, and even that Monarchy never could possibly be of use to him any more, I think he would endure it and pay its cost, and drink its health loyally for all time, providing Monarchy did nothing outrageously wrong; or provided—which is more to my present purpose—that no other changes of a remarkable nature occurred in the meantime to remove ancient landmarks, to disturb the basis of his old institutions and to prepare him for a new order of things. This is indeed the point I wish to discuss just now. I have explained what I believe to be the depth and strength and meaning of the average Englishman's loyal feelings to his Sovereign at the present moment. I should like to consider next how that feeling will, in all probability, be affected by the changes in the English political system, which seem inevitable, and by the accession, or expected accession, of a new Sovereign to the throne.

England has, just now, something very nearly approaching to manhood suffrage; and to manhood suffrage it will probably come before long. The ballot will, doubtless, be introduced. The Irish Church is as good as dead. I cannot doubt that the English State Church will, ultimately, and before very long, succumb to the same fate. Not that this logically or politically follows as a matter of necessity; and nothing could be more unwise in the interest of their own cause than the persistency with which the Tories keep insisting that the doom of the one is involved in the doom of the other. The Irish Church is the foreign church of a miserably small minority; the English Establishment is the Church of the majority, and is an institution belonging to the soil. The very principle which maintains the English Church ought of right to condemn the Irish Church. But it is the fact that an agitation more influential than it seemed to the careless spectator, has long been going on in England for the abolition of the State Church system altogether; and there can be no doubt that the fate of the Irish Establishment will lend immense courage and force to that agitation. Revolutionary movements are always contagious in their nature, and the movement against the Irish Church is in the strictest sense revolutionary. The Dutch or the Scotch would have carried such a movement to triumph across rivers of blood if it were needful; and no man of spirit could say that the end would not be worth the cost. I assume, then, that the overthrow of the Irish Church will inflame to iconoclastic fervor the movement of the English Dissenters against all Church establishments. I do not stop just now to inquire whether the movement is likely to be successful or how long it may take to accomplish the object. To me, it seems beyond doubt that it must succeed; but I do not care to assume even that for the purpose of my present argument. I only ask my readers to consider the condition of things which will exist in England when a movement resting on a suffrage which is almost universal, a movement which will have already overthrown one State Church within Great Britain, proceeds openly and exultingly to attack the English Church itself, within its own dominions. I ask whether it is likely that the institution which is supposed to be bound up inseparably with that Church, the Monarchy which is based upon, and exists by virtue of religious ascendency, is likely to escape all question during such a struggle, and after it? The State Church and the Aristocracy, if they cannot always be called bulwarks of the throne, are yet so completely associated with it in the public mind that it is hard even to think of the one without the others, and yet harder to think of the one as existing serene and uninjured after the decay or demolition of the others.

Now, the Aristocracy have, as Mr. Bright put it so truly and so effectively the other day, already capitulated. They have given up all notion of any longer making the laws of the country in the interest of their own class. One of the first things the Reformed Parliament will do, when it has breathing-time to think about such matters, will be to abolish the purchase system in the army, and throw open promotion to merit, without reference to class. The diplomatic service, that other great stronghold of the Aristocracy, will be thoroughly reorganized and made a real, useful department, doing solid work, and open to talent of whatever caste; or it will be abolished altogether. Something will have to be done with the House of Lords. It, too, must be made a reality, or dismissed into the land of shadows and the past. Efforts at reforming it, while it stands on its present basis, are futile. Its existence is, in its present form, the one great objection to it.

The good-natured, officious Lord Shaftesbury went to work, a few months ago, to prepare a scheme of reform for the House of Lords, in order to anticipate and conciliate the popular movement which he expected. He could think of nothing better than a recommendation that the House should meet an hour earlier every evening, in order, by throwing more time on their hands, to induce the younger Peers to get up debates and take part in them. This, however, is not precisely the kind of reform the country will ask for when it has leisure to turn its attention to the subject. It will ask for some reorganization which shall either abolish or reduce to a comparative nothing the hereditary legislating principle on which the House of Lords now rests. A set of law-makers or law-marrers intrusted with power only because they are born to titles, is an absurd anomaly, which never could exist in company with popular suffrage. "Hereditary law-makers!" exclaimed Franklin. "You might as well talk of hereditary mathematicians!" Franklin expressed exactly what the feeling of the common sense of England is likely to be when the question comes to be raised. I expect then, not that the House of Lords will be abolished, but that the rule of the hereditary principle will be brought to an end—that the Aristocracy there, too, will have to capitulate.

Now, I doubt whether an American reader can have any accurate idea, unless he has specially studied the matter and watched its practical operation in England, of the manner in which the influence of the Peers makes itself felt through the political life of Great Britain. Americans often have some kind of notion that the Aristocracy govern the country directly and despotically, with the high hand of imperious feudalism. There is nothing of the kind in reality. The House of Lords is, as a piece of political machinery, almost inoperative—as nearly as possible harmless. No English Peer, Lord Derby alone excepted, has anything like the political authority and direct influence of Mr. Gladstone, Mr. Disraeli, or Mr. Bright. There are very few Peers, indeed, about whose political utterances anybody in the country cares three straws. But, on the other hand, the traditional *prestige* of the Peers, the tacit, time-honored, generally-conceded doctrine that a Peer has first right to everything—the mediæval superstition tolerated largely in our own time, which allows a sort of divinity to hedge a Peer— all this has an indirect, immense, pervading, almost universal influence in the practical working of English politics. The Peers have, in fact, a political *droit du seigneur* in England. They have first taste of every privilege, first choice of every appointment. Political office is their pasture, where they are privileged to feed at will. There does not now exist a man in England likely to receive high office, who would be bold enough to suggest the forming of a Cabinet without Peers in it, even though there were no Peers to be had who possessed the slightest qualification for any ministerial position.

The Peers must have a certain number of places, because they are Peers. The House of Commons swarms with the sons and nephews of Peers. The household appointments, the ministerial offices, the good places in the army and the church are theirs when they choose—and they generally do choose—to have them. The son of a Peer, if in the House of Commons, may be raised at one step from his place in the back benches to a seat in the Cabinet, simply because of his rank. When Earl Russell, two or three years ago, raised Mr. Goschen, one of the representatives of the city of London and a partner in a great London banking-house, to a place in the Cabinet, the whole country wondered: a very few, who were not frightened out of their propriety, admired; some thought the world must be coming to an end. But when the Marquis of Hartington was suddenly picked out of West End dissipation and made War Secretary, nobody expressed the least wonder, for he was the heir of the House of Devonshire. Indeed, it was perfectly notorious that the young Marquis was presented to office, in the first instance, because it was hoped by his friends that official duties might wean him from the follies and frivolities of a more than ordinarily heedless youth. Sir Robert Peel the present, the *magni nominis umbra*, is not, of course, in the strict sense, an aristocrat; but he is mixed up with aristocrats, and is the son of a Peer-maker, and may be regarded as claiming and having the privileges of the class. Sir Robert Peel was presented with the First Secretaryship as something to play with, because his aristocratic friends, the ladies especially, thought he would be more likely to sow his wild oats if he were beguiled by the semblance of official business. A commoner must, in fact, be supposed to have some qualification for office before he is invited to fill a ministerial place. No qualification is believed necessary for the near relative or connection of a Peer. Even in the most favorable examples of Peers who are regular occupants of office, no special fitness is assumed or pretended. No one supposes or says that Lord Clarendon, or Lord Granville, or Lord Malmesbury has any particular qualification which entitles him, above all other men, to this or that ministerial place. Yet it must be a man of bold imagination indeed, who could now conceive the possibility of a British Cabinet without one of these noblemen having a place in it.

All this comes, as I have said, out of a lingering superstition—the faith in the divine right of Peers. Now, a reform in the constitution of the Upper House, which should purge it of the hereditary principle, would be the first great blow to this superstition. Julius Cæsar, in one of his voyages of conquest, was much perplexed by the priests, who insisted that he had better go back because the sacred chickens would not eat. At last he thought the time had come to prove his independence of the sacred chickens, "If they will not eat," he said, "then let them drink"—and he flung the consecrated fowls into the sea; and the expedition went on triumphantly, and the Roman soldiers learned that they could do without the sacred chickens. I think a somewhat similar sensation will come over all classes of the English people when they find that the hereditary right to make laws is taken from the English Peerage. I do not doubt that the whole fabric of superstition will presently collapse, and that the privilege of the Peer will cease to be anything more than that degree of superior influence which wealth and social rank can generally command, even in the most democratic communities. The law which gives impulse and support to the custom of primogeniture is certain to go, and with it another prop of the mediæval superstition. The Peerage capitulates, in fact—no more expressive word can be found to describe the situation.

Now, in all this, I have been foreshadowing no scheme of wild, vague, far-distant reform. I appeal to any one, Liberal or Tory, who is practically acquainted with English politics, to say whether these are not changes he confidently or timidly looks to see accomplished before long in England. I have not spoken of any reform which is not part of the actual accepted programme of the Radical party. To the reform of the House of Lords, of the military and diplomatic service; to abolition of the law of primogeniture, the whole body of the Liberals stands pledged; and Mr. Bright very recently renewed the pledges in a manner and with an emphasis which showed that change of circumstances has made no change in his opinions, brought no faltering in his resolution. The abolition of the English Church is not, indeed, thus openly sought by so powerful a party; but it is ostentatiously aimed at by that solid, compact, pertinacious body of Dissenters who, after so long a struggle, succeeded at last in getting rid of Church rates; and the movement will go on with a rush after the fall of the Irish establishment. Here then we have, in the not distant future, a prospect of an England without a privileged Aristocracy, and with the State Church principle called into final question. I return to my first consideration—the consideration which is the subject of this paper—how will this affect the great aristocratic, feudal and hierarchical institution of England, the Throne of the Monarch?

The Throne then will stand naked and alone, stripped of its old-time and traditional surroundings and associations. It cannot be like that of France, the throne of a Cæsar, a despotic institution claiming to exercise its despotism over the people by virtue of the will and delegated power of the people. The English Crown never can be an active governing power. It will be the last idol in the invaded sanctuary. It will stand alone, among the pedestals from which popular reform has swept the embodied superstitions which were its long companions. It must live, if at all, on the old affection or the toleration which springs out of custom and habit. This affection, or at least this toleration, may always be looked upon as a powerful influence in England. One can hardly imagine, for instance, anything occurring in our day to dethrone the Queen. However one class may grumble and another class may gibe, the force of habit and old affection would, in this instance, prove omnipotent. But, suppose the Prince of Wales should turn out an unpopular and ill-conditioned ruler? Suppose he should prove to be a man of low tastes, of vulgar and spendthrift habits, a maladroit and intermeddling king? He is not very popular in England, even now, and he is either one of the most unjustly entreated men living, or he has defects which even the excuse of youth can scarcely gloss over.

An illustrated weekly paper in London forced itself lately into a sudden notoriety by publishing a finely-drawn cartoon, in which the Prince of Wales, dressed as Hamlet, was represented as breaking away from the restraining arms of John Bull as Horatio, and public opinion as Marcellus, and rushing after a ghost which bore the form and features of George IV., while underneath were inscribed the words, "Lead on; I'll follow thee!" This was a bold and bitter lampoon; I am far from saying that it was not unjust, but I believe it can hardly be doubted that the Prince of Wales has, as yet, shown little inclination to imitate the example or cultivate the tastes of his pure-minded and intellectual father. Now suppose, for the sake of argument, that the Prince of Wales should turn out a George IV., or suppose, and which would be far worse from a national point of view, he or his son should turn out a George III. And suppose further that, about the same time any great crisis should arise in England—suppose the country entangled in a great foreign war, or disturbed by some momentous domestic agitation—can any one doubt that the Crown, in its then isolated condition, would be really in danger?

We must remember, when the strength of English institutions is boasted, that they have not, since 1815, stood any strain which could fairly be called critical. England has never had her national strength, her political position, or even her *prestige* seriously imperilled since that time. Even the Indian war could not be called a great supreme trial, such as other nations have lately had to bear. No one, even for a moment, could have doubted how that struggle would end. It was bitter, it was bloody; but the life of the nation was not staked upon it, even had its issue been uncertain; and its issue never was uncertain. It would be superfluous to say that England has passed through no ordeal like that to which the United States were lately subjected. She has not even had to confront anything like the crisis which Prussia voluntarily invited, which Austria had to meet, in 1866. It will be time to consider English feudal institutions, or what may remain of them, safe and firmly-rooted, when they have stood the worst result of such a crisis as that, and not been shaken down.

What I contend is that there is nothing in the present condition of the English public mind, and nothing in the prospect of the immediate future to warrant the almost universal assumption that the throne of England is founded on a rock. The stupidity of loyalty, the devotion as of the spaniel to his master, of the idolator to his god, is gone. I doubt if there exists one man in England who feels the sentiment of loyalty as his grandfather would have felt it. The mass of the people have learned satisfactorily that a sovereign is not a part of the necessary machinery of the government. The great problem which the Duke of Wellington used to present for solution— "How is the Queen's Government to be carried on?" has been solved in one and an unexpected sense. It can be carried on without a queen. Here then we have the institution proving itself superfluous, and falling into public indifference at the very same moment that some other institutions which seemed always involved with it as its natural and necessary companions, are about to be broken to pieces and thrown away. He must, indeed, be full of a verily transcendental faith in the destinies and divinity of royalty who does not admit that at least there is a time of ordeal awaiting it in England, such as it has not encountered before during this century.

To me it seems that the royal principle in England is threatened, not with sudden and violent extinction, but with death by decay. I do not expect any change of any kind to-morrow or the day after, or even the week after next. I do not care to dogmatize, or predict, or make guesses of any kind. I quite agree with my friend Professor Thorold Rogers, that an uninspired prophet is a fool. But I contend that as the evident signs of the times now show themselves, the monarchical principle in England does seem to be decaying; that the national faith which bore it up is sorely shaken and almost gone, and that some of the political props which most nearly supported it are already being cut away. There may, indeed, be some hidden virtue in the principle, which shall develop itself unexpectedly in the hour of danger, and give to the institution that seemed moribund a new and splendid vitality. Such a phenomenon has been manifested in the case of more than one institution that seemed on the verge of ruin—it may be the fortunate destiny of British royalty. But unless in the sudden and timely development of some such occult and unlooked-for virtue, I do not see what is to preserve the monarchical principle in England through the trials of the future.

Let it be remembered, too, that the one great plea hitherto always made in England for monarchy, is that it alone will work on a large scale. "We admit," it was said, "that your republican theory looks better and admits of more logical argument in its favor. But we are practical men, and we find that our system, with all its theoretical disadvantages, will work and stand a strain; and your republican theory, with all its apparent advantages in logic, is not suited for this rough world. Our machinery will stand the hardest trial; yours never did and never will. Don't tell us about Switzerland. Switzerland is a little country. Kept out of the stress and danger of European commotions, and protected by a guarantee of the great powers, any constitution ought to work under such advantages. But a great independent republic never did last; never did stand a sudden strain, and never will." So people thought and argued in England—even very intelligent people, until at last it became one of the British Philistine's articles of faith, that the republican principle never will work on a large scale. When Sir John Ramsden declared in the House of Commons at the beginning of the American civil war, that the republican bubble had burst, and all Philistinism in Britain applauded the declaration, the plaudits were given not so much because of any settled dislike Philistinism had to the United States, as because Philistinism beheld what it believed to be a providential testimony to its own wisdom and foresight. Since then Philistinism has found that after all republicanism is able to bear a strain as great as monarchy has ever yet borne, and can come out of the trial unharmed and victorious.

The lesson has sunk deeply. The mind of something better than Philistinism has learned that republics can be made to work on a large scale. I believe Mr. Gladstone is one of the eminent Englishmen who now openly admit that they have learned from the American war something which they did not know before, of the cohesiveness and durability of the republican system. Up to the time of that war in fact, most Englishmen, when they talked of republican principles, thought only of French republicanism, and honestly regarded such a system as a brilliant empty bubble, doomed to soar a little, and float, and dazzle, and then to burst.

That idea, it is quite safe to say, no longer exists in the English mind. The fundamental, radical objection to republicanism—the objection which, partly out of mere reaction and partly for more substantial reasons, followed the brief and romantic enthusiasm of the days of Fox—is gone. The practical Englishman admits that a republic is practicable. Only those who know England can know what a change in public opinion this is. It is, in fact, something like a revolution. I think the most devoted monarchist will hardly deny that if some extraordinary combination of chances (after all, even the British Throne is but a human institution) were to disturb the succession of the house of Brunswick, Englishmen would be more likely to try the republican system than to hunt about for a new royal family, or endeavor to invent a new scheme of monarchy. Here, then, I leave the subject. Take all this into account, in considering the probabilities of the future, and then say whether, even in the case of England, it is quite certain that Byron's prediction is only the dream of a cynical poet, destined never to be fulfilled among human realities.

THE REAL LOUIS NAPOLEON

"How will it be with him," said Richard Cobden to a friend, one night, as they spoke of a great and successful adventurer whom the friend was striving to defend—"how will it be with him when life becomes all retrospect?" The adventurer they spoke of was not Louis Napoleon; but the inquiry might well apply just now to the Emperor of the French. Life has reached that point with him when little more than retrospect can be left. In the natural course of events, there can be no great triumphs for Louis Napoleon still to achieve. Great blunders are possible, though hardly probable; but the greatest of blunders would scarcely efface the memory of the substantial triumphs. "Not heaven itself," exclaimed an ambitious and profane statesman, "can undo the fact that I have been three times Prime Minister." Well, the Fates—let them do their best—can hardly undo the fact that the despised outcast of Constance, and Augsburg, and London, and New York, whom Lord Palmerston excused himself to Guizot for tolerating, on the ground that really nobody minded the dull, harmless poor fellow; the Fates cannot undo the fact that this man has elected himself Emperor of the French, has defeated the Russians and the Austrians, and made a friend and ally of England.

So much of the past, then, is secure; but there are hardly any triumphs to be won in the future. If one may venture to predict anything, he may venture to predict that the Emperor of the French will not live to be a very old man. He has already led many lives—fast, hard, exhausting lives, "that murder the youth in a man ere ever his heart has its will." Exile, conspiracy, imprisonment, hard thinking, hard working, wild and reckless dissipation, prolonged to the very outer verge of middle life, the brain, the nerves, the muscles, the whole physical and mental constitution always strained to the utmost—these are not the ways that secure a long life. Louis Napoleon is already an "*abgelebter mann*"—an outworn, used-up, played-out man. The friends and familiars with whom he started in life are nearly all gone. Long since laid in earth is the stout form of the wild Marquis of Waterford, who was a wonder to our fathers (his successor to the title ran away with somebody's wife the other day; and I thought Time had turned back by thirty years when I read of the *escapade*, with the name, once so famous, of the principal performer), and who rode by Louis Napoleon's side at the

Modern Leaders Being A Series Of Biographical Sketches | 23

celebrated, forgotten Eglintoun Tournament, and was, like Louis Napoleon, one of the Knights Challengers in that piece of splendid foolery. Dead, lang syne, is Eglintoun himself, the chivalrous Earl of the generous instincts and the florid, rotund eloquence, reminding one of Bulwer Lytton diluted. I do not know whether the Queen of Beauty of that grand joust is yet living and looking on the earth; but if she be, she must be an embodied sermon on the perishableness of earthly charms. De Morny is dead, the devoted half-brother, son of Louis Napoleon's mother, the chaste Hortense, and the Count de Flahault—De Morny, the brilliant, genial, witty, reckless gambler in politics and finance, the man than whom nobody ever, perhaps, was more faithful to friendship and false to morality, more good-natured and unprincipled. I have seen tears in men's eyes when De Morny died—in the eyes of men who owned all the time, smiling through their tears like Andromache, that the lost patron and friend was the most consummate of *roués* and blacklegs. Walewski is dead—Walewski of romantic origin, born of the sudden episode of love between the great Napoleon and the Polish lady—Walewski, who, like Prince Napoleon-Jerome, carried his pedigree stamped upon his face—Walewski, the lover of Rachel, and, to do him justice, the steady friend of Poland. Old Mocquard is gone, the faithful scribe and confidant: he is dead, and the dramas he would persist in writing are dead with him, nay, died even before him. I do not know whether the faithful, devoted woman who worked for Louis Napoleon, and believed in him when nobody else did; the woman to whose inspirings, exertions, and ready money he owes, in great measure, the fact that he is now Emperor of the French—I do not know whether this woman is alive or dead. I think she is dead. Anyhow, I suppose the dignity of history, as the phrase is, can hardly take account of her. She helped to make an Emperor, and the Emperor, in return, made her a Countess; but then he had to marry—and so we take leave of the woman who made the Emperor, and do our homage to the woman who married him. All those are gone; and St. Arnaud, of the stormy youth, and Pelissier, the bland, sweet-tempered chevalier, who, getting into a dispute (on his way to be governor of Algeria) with the principal official of a Spanish port, invited that dignitary to salute a portion of the Pelissier person which assuredly the foes of France were never allowed to see—all these are gone, and many more, and only a very few, fast fading, of the old friends and followers remain. Life to Louis Napoleon must now, indeed, be nearly all retrospect. His career, his Imperial reign may be judged even now as fairly and securely as as if his body had just been laid beside that of his uncle, under the dome of the Invalides.

Recent events seem specially to invite and authorize that judgment. Within the past twelve months, the genuine character of Louis Napoleon has displayed itself, strikingly, nakedly, in his policy. He has tried, in succession, mild liberalism, severe despotism, reactionary conservatism, antique Cæsarism, and then, in an apologetic, contrite sort of way, a liberalism of a rather pronounced character. Every time that he tried any new policy he was secretly intriguing with some other, and making ready for the possible necessity of having to abandon the former and take up with the latter. He was like the lady in "Le Diable Boiteux," who, while openly coquetting with the young lover, slily gives her hand behind her back to the old admirer. So far as the public could judge, Louis Napoleon has, for many months back, been absolutely without any settled policy whatever. He has been waiting for a wind. Such a course is probably the safest a man in his position can take; but one who, at a great crisis, cannot originate and initiate a policy, will not be remembered among the grand rulers of the world. I do not remember any greater evidence given in our time of absolute incapacity to seize a plan of action and decide upon it, than was shown by the Emperor of the French during the crisis of June and July. So feeble, so vague, halting, vacillating was the whole course of the government, that many who detest Louis Napoleon, but make it an article of faith that he is a sort of all-seeing, omnipotent spirit of darkness, were forced to adopt a theory that the riots in Paris and the provinces were deliberately got up by the police agents of the Empire, for the purpose of frightening the *bourgeois* class out of any possible hankering after democracy. No doubt this idea was widely spread and eagerly accepted in Paris; and there were many circumstances which seemed to justify it. But I do not believe in any such Imperial stage-play. I fancy the riots surprised the Government, first, by their sudden outburst, and next, by their sudden collapse. Probably the Imperial authorities were very glad when the disturbances began. They gave an excuse for harsh conduct, and they seemed, for the time, to put the Government in the right. They restored Louis Napoleon at that moment, in the eyes of timid people, to that position, as a supreme maintainer of order, which for some years he had not had an opportunity effectively to occupy. But the obvious want of stamina in the disturbing force soon took away from the Imperial authorities this opportune *prestige*, and very little political capital was secured for Imperialism out of the abortive barricades, and incoherent brickbats, and effusive chantings of the "Marseillaise." In truth, no one had anything else to offer just then in place of the Empire. The little crisis was no test whatever of the Emperor's hold over his people, or of his power to deal with a popular revolution. To me it seems doubtful whether the elections brought out for certain any fact with which the world might not already have been well acquainted, except the bare fact that Orleanism has hardly any more of vitality in it than Legitimacy. Rochefort, and not Prevost Paradol, is the typical figure of the situation.

The popularity and the success of Rochefort and his paper are remarkable phenomena, but only remarkable in the old-fashioned manner of the straws which show how the wind blows. Rochefort's success is due to the fact that he had the good-fortune to begin ridiculing the Empire just at the time when a general notion was spreading over France that the Empire of late had been making itself ridiculous. Louis Napoleon had reached the turning-point of his career—had reached and passed it. The country saw now all that he could do. The bag of tricks was played out. The anticlimax was reached at last.

The culmen, the crisis, the turning-point of Louis Napoleon's career seems to me to have been attained when, just before the outbreak of the Schleswig-Holstein war—so small a war in itself, so fateful and gigantic in its results—he appealed to the Emperors and Kings of Europe, and proposed that the nations should hold a Congress, to settle, once and forever, all pending disputes. I think the attitude of Louis Napoleon at that moment was dignified, commanding, imperial. His peculiar style, forcible, weighty, measured—I have heard it well described as a "monumental" style—came out with great effect in the language of the appeal. There was dignity, and grace, there was what Edmund Burke so appropriately terms "a proud humility," in Louis Napoleon's allusion to his own personal experience in the school of exile and adversity as an excuse for his presuming to offer advice to the sovereigns of Europe. One was reminded of Henry of Navarre's allusion to the wind of adversity which, blowing so long upon his face, had prematurely blanched his hair. I do not wonder that the proposed Congress never met. I do not wonder that the European governments put it aside— some with courteous phrase and feigned willingness to accept the scheme, like Russia and Austria; some with cold and brusque rejection, like England. Nothing worth trying for could have come of the Congress. Events were brooding of which France and England knew nothing, and which could not have been exorcised away by any resolutions of a conclave of diplomatists. But that was, I think, the last occasion when Louis Napoleon held anything like a commanding, overruling position in European affairs, and even then it was but a semblance. After that, came only humiliations and reverses. In a diplomatic sense, nothing could be more complete than the checkmate which the Emperor of the French drew upon himself by the sheer blundering of his conduct with regard to Prussia. He succeeded in placing himself before the world in the distinct attitude of an enemy to Prussia; and no sooner had he, by assuming this attitude, forced Prussia to take a defiant tone, than he suddenly sank down into quietude. He had bullied to no purpose; he had to undergo the humiliation of seeing Prussia rise in public estimation, by means of the triumph which his unnecessary and uncalled-for hostility had enabled her to win. In fact, he was outgeneralled by his pupil, Bismarck, even more signally than he had previously been outgeneralled by his former pupil, Cavour. More disastrous and ghastly, by far, was the failure of his Mexican policy. That policy began in falsehood and treachery, and ended as it deserved. Poetic and dramatic justice was fearfully rendered. Never did Philip II., of Spain, never did his father, never did Napoleon I., never did Mendez Pinto, or any other celebrated liar, exceed the deliberate monstrosity of the falsehoods which were told by Louis Napoleon or Louis Napoleon's Ministers at his order, to conceal, during the earlier stages of the Mexican intervention, the fact that the French Emperor had a *protégé* in the background, who was to be seated on a Mexican throne. The world is not much affected by perfidy in sovereigns. It laughs at the perjuries of princes as Jove does at those of lovers. But it could not overlook the appalling significance of Louis Napoleon's defeat in that disastrous chapter of his history. Wisdom after the event is easy work; but many, many voices had told Louis Napoleon beforehand what would come of his Mexican policy. Not to speak of the hints and advice he received from the United States, he was again and again assured by the late Marshal O'Donnell, then Prime Minister of Spain; by General Prim, who commanded the allied forces during the earlier part of the Mexican expedition; by Prince Napoleon, by many others—that neither the character of the Mexican people nor the proximity of the United States would allow a French proconsulate to be established in Mexico under the name of an Empire. It is a certain fact that Louis Napoleon frequently declared that the foundation of that Empire would be the great event of his reign. This extraordinary delusion maintained a hold over his mind long after it had become apparent to all the world that the wretched bubble was actually bursting. The catastrophe was very near when Louis Napoleon, in conversation with an English political adventurer, who then was a Member of Parliament, assured him that, however the situation might then look dark, history would yet have to record that he, Louis Napoleon, had established a Mexican Empire. The English member of Parliament, although ordinarily a very shrewd and sceptical sort of person, was actually so impressed with the earnestness of his Imperial interlocutor that he returned to London and wrote a pamphlet, in which, to the utter amazement of his acquaintances, he backed the Empire of Mexico for a secure existence, and said to it *esto perpetua*. The pamphlet was hardly in circulation when the collapse came. If Louis Napoleon ever believed in anything, he believed in the Mexican Empire. He believed, too, in the certain success of the Southern Confederation. No Belgravian Dundreary, no *exaltée* Georgian girl, could have been more completely taken by surprise when the collapse of that enterprise came than was the Emperor Napoleon III., whose boundless foresight and profound sagacity we had all for years been applauding to the echo. "That which is called firmness in a King," said Erskine, "is called obstinacy in a donkey." That which is called foresight and sagacity in an Emperor, is often what we call blindness and blundering in a newspaper correspondent. The question is whether we can point to any great event, any political enterprise, subsequent to his successful assumption of the Imperial crown, in regard to which Napoleon III., if called upon to act or to judge, did not show the same aptitude for rash judgments and unwise actions? Certainly no great thing with which he has had to do came out in the result with anything like the shape he meant it to have. The Italian Confederation, with the Pope at the head of it; the Germany irrevocably divided by the line of the Main; the Mexican Empire; the "rectification" of frontier on the Rhine; the acquisition of Luxembourg; these are some of the great Napoleonic ideas, by the success or failure of which we may fairly judge of the wisdom of their author. At home he has simply had a new plan of government every year. How many different ways of dealing with the press, how many different schemes for adjusting the powers of the several branches of legislation, have been magniloquently announced and floated during the last few years, each in turn to fail rather more dismally than its predecessor? Now, it seems, we are to have at last something like that ministerial responsibility which the Imperial lips themselves have so often described as utterly opposed to the genius of France. Assuredly it shows great mental flexibility to be able thus quickly to change one's policy in obedience to a warning from without. It is a far better quality than the persistent treachery of a Charles I., or the stupid doggedness of a George III. But unless it be a characteristic of great statesmanship to be almost always out in one's calculations, wrong in one's predictions, and mistaken in one's men, the Emperor has for years been in the habit of doing things which are directly incompatible with the character of a great statesman.

Contrasting the Louis Napoleon of action and reality with the Louis Napoleon of the journals, I am reminded of a declaration once made by a brilliant, audacious, eccentric Italian journalist and politician, Petruccelli della Gattina. Petruccelli was, and perhaps still is, a member of the Italian Parliament, and he had occasion to find fault with some office or dignity, or something of the kind, conferred by Count Cavour on the Neapolitan, Baron Poerio, whose imprisonment and chains, during the reign of the beloved Bomba, aroused the eloquent anger of Mr. Gladstone, and through Gladstone's efforts and appeals became the wonder and the horror of the world. Petruccelli insisted that Poerio's undeserved sufferings were his only political claim. "You know perfectly well," he said, in effect, to Cavour, "that there is no such man as the Poerio of the journals. It suited us to invest the poor victim with the attributes of greatness, and therefore, we, the journalists, created a Poerio of our own. This imposed upon the world, but it did not impose upon you, and you have no right to take our Poerio *au serieux*." I do not know whether the journals created an imaginary Poerio, but I am convinced that they have created an imaginary Louis Napoleon. The world in general now so much prefers the imaginary to the real Louis, that it would for the present be as difficult to dethrone the unreal and set up the real, as it would be to induce the average reader to accept Lane's genuine translation of the "Arabian Nights" instead of the familiar translation from a sprightly, flippant, flashy French version, which hardly bears the slightest resemblance to the original. English journalism has certainly created a Disraeli of its own—a dark, subtle, impenetrable, sphinx-like being, who never smiles, or betrays outward emotion, or is taken by surprise, or makes a mistake. This Disraeli is an immense success with the public, and is not in the least like the real Disraeli, who is as good-natured and genial in manner as he is bold and blundering in speech and policy. So, on a wider scale, of Louis Napoleon. We are all more or less responsible for the fraud on the public; and, indeed, are to be excused on the ground that, enamored of our own creation, we have often got the length of believing in it. We have thus created a mysterious being, a sphinx of far greater than even Disraelian proportions, an embodiment of silence and sagacity, a dark creature endowed with super-human self-control and patience and foresight; one who can bend all things, and all men, and destiny itself to his own calm, inexorable will.

I do not believe there is anything of the sphinx about Louis Napoleon. I do not believe in his profound sagacity, or his foresight, or his stupendous self-control. I have grown so heretical that I do not even believe him to be a particularly taciturn man. I am well satisfied that Louis Napoleon is personally a good-natured, good-tempered, undignified, awkward sort of man, ungainly of gesture, not impressive in speech, a man quite as remarkable for occasional outbursts of unexpected and misplaced confidence as for a silence that often is, if I may use such an expression, purely mechanical and unmeaning. I calmly ask my *confrères* of the press, is it not a fact that Louis Napoleon is commonly made the dupe of shallow charlatans, that he has several times received and admitted to confidential counsel and conference, and treated as influential statesmen and unaccredited ambassadors, utterly obscure American or English busybodies who could hardly get to speech of the Mayor of a town at home; that he has entered into signed and sealed engagements with impudent adventurers from divers countries, under the impression that they could render him vast political service; that he has paid down considerable sums of money to subsidize the most obscure and contemptible foreign journals, and never seemed able for a moment to comprehend that in England and the United States no journal that can be bought for any price, however high, is worth buying at any price, however low; that his personal inclinations are much more toward quacks and pretenders than toward men of real genius and influence; that Cobden was one of the very few great men Louis Napoleon ever appreciated, while impostors, and knaves, and blockheads, of all kinds, could readily find access to his confidence? Of course, a man might possibly be a great sovereign although he had these weaknesses; but the Louis Napoleon of journalism is not endowed with these, or indeed with any other weaknesses.

Those who know Paris well, know that there is yet another Louis Napoleon there, equally I trust a fiction with him of the journals. I speak of the Louis Napoleon of private gossip, the hero of unnumbered *amours* such as De Grammont or Casanova might wonder at. I have heard stories poured into my patient but sceptical ears which ascribed to Louis Napoleon of to-day, adventures illustrating a happy and brilliant combination of Haroun Al Raschid and Lauzun—the disguises of the Caliph employed for the purposes of Don Juan. Now, Louis Napoleon certainly had, and perhaps even still has, his frailties of this class, but I reject the Lauzun or Don Juan theory quite as resolutely as the sphinx theory.

What we all do really know of Louis Napoleon is, that having the advantage of a name of surpassing prestige, and at a moment of unexampled chances not created by him, he succeeded in raising himself to the throne made by his uncle; that when there, he held his place firmly, and by maintaining severe order in a country already weary of disturbance and barren revolution, he favored and stimulated the development of the material resources of France; that he entered on several enterprises in foreign politics, not one of which brought about the end for which it was undertaken, and some of which were ludicrous, disastrous failures; that he strove to compensate France for the loss of her civil liberty, by audaciously attempting to make her the dictator of Europe, and that he utterly failed in both objects; for here toward the close of his rule, France seems far more eager for domestic freedom than ever she was since the *coup d'état*, while her influence over the nations of Europe is considerably less than it was at any period since the fall of Sebastopol. Now, if this be success, I want to know what is failure? If these results argue the existence of profound sagacity, I want to know what would show a lack of sagacity? Was Louis Napoleon sagacious when he entered Lombardy, to set Italy free from the Alps to the sea, and sagacious also when, after a campaign of a few weeks, he suddenly abandoned the enterprise never to resume it? Was he wise when he told Cavour he would never permit the annexation of Naples, and wise also when, immediately after, he permitted it? Was he a great statesman when he entered on the Mexican expedition, and also a great statesman when he abandoned it and his unfortunate pupil, puppet, and victim together? Did it show a statesmanlike judgment to bully Prussia until he had gone near to making her an irreconcilable enemy, and also a statesmanlike judgment then to "cave in," and declare that he never meant anything offensive? Was it judicious to demand a rectification of frontier on the Rhine, and judicious also to abandon the demand in a hurry, when it was received as anybody might have known that a proud, brave nation, flushed with a splendid success, would surely have received it? Did it display great foresight to count with certainty that the Southern Confederation would succeed, and that Austria would win an easy victory over Prussia? Was it judicious to instruct an official spokesman to declare that France had taken steps to assure herself against any spread of Prussian influence beyond the Main, and to have to stand next day, amazed and confounded, before an amazed and amused Europe, when Bismarck made practical answer by contemptuously unrolling the treaties of alliance actually concluded between France and the principal States of South Germany? Was it a proof of a great ruling mind to declare that France could never endure a system of ministerial responsibility, and also a proof of a great ruling mind to declare that this is the one thing needful to her contentment? All this bundle of paradoxes one will have to sustain, if he is content to accept as a genuine being that monstrous paradox, the Louis Napoleon of the press. Of course, I do not deny to Louis Napoleon certain qualities of greatness. But I believe the public was not a whit more gravely mistaken when it regarded the King street exile as a dreamy dunce, than it is now, when it regards Napoleon III. as a ruler of consummate wisdom.

There was much of sound sense as well as wit in the saying ascribed to Thiers, that the second Empire had developed two great statesmen—Cavour and Bismarck. I do not know of any one great idea, worthy of being called a contribution to the science of government, which Louis Napoleon has yet embodied, either in words or actions. The recent elections, and the events succeeding them, only demonstrate the failure of Imperialism or Cæsarism, after a trial and after opportunities such as it probably will never have again in Europe. I certainly do not expect any complete collapse during the present reign. Doubtless the machine will outlast the third Emperor's time. He has sense and dexterity enough to trim his sails to each breeze that passes, and he will, probably, hold the helm till his right hand loses its cunning with its vital power. But I see no evidence whatever which induces me to believe that he has founded a dynasty or created an enduring system of any kind. Some day France will shake off the whole thing like a nightmare. Meantime, however, I am anxious to help in dethroning the Louis Napoleon of the journals rather than him of the Tuileries. The latter has many good qualities which the former is never allowed to exhibit. I believe the true Louis Napoleon has a remarkably kind and generous heart; that he is very liberal and charitable; that he has much affection in him, and is very faithful to his old friends and old servants; that people who come near him love him much; that he is free and kindly of speech; that his personal defects are rather those of a warm and rash, than of a cold and stern nature. But I think it is high time that we were done with the melodramatic, dime-romance, darkly mysterious Louis Napoleon of the journals. He belongs to the race of William Tell, of the Wandering Jew, the Flying Dutchman, the Sphinx to whom he is so often compared, the mermaid, the sea-serpent, Byron's Corsair, and Thaddeus of Warsaw.

EUGENIE, EMPRESS OF THE FRENCH

There are certain men and women in history who seem to have a peculiarity, independent of their merits or demerits, greatness or littleness, virtues or crimes—a peculiarity which distinguishes them from others as great or as little, as virtuous or as criminal. They are, first and above all things, interesting. It is not easy to describe what the elements are which make up this attribute. Certainly genius or goodness, wit or wisdom, splendid public services, great beauty, or even great suffering, will not always be enough to create it. The greatest English king since the First Edward was assuredly William the Third; the greatest military commanders England has ever had were Marlborough and Wellington; but these three will hardly be called by any one interesting personages in the sense in which I now use the word. Why Nelson should be interesting and Wellington not so, Byron interesting and Wordsworth not so, is perhaps easy enough to explain; but it is not quite easy to see why Rousseau should be so much more interesting than Voltaire, Goethe than Schiller, Mozart than Handel, and so on through a number of illustrations, the accuracy of which nearly all persons would probably acknowledge. Where history and public opinion and sentiment have to deal with the lives and characters of women, the peculiarity becomes still more deeply emphasized. What gifts, what graces, what rank, what misfortunes have ever surrounded any queens or princesses known to history with the interest which attaches to Mary Stuart and Marie Antoinette? Lady Jane Grey was an incomparably nobler woman than either, and suffered to the full as deeply as either; yet what place has she in men's feelings and interest compared with theirs? Who cares about Anna Boleyn, though she too shared a throne and mounted a scaffold?

Absit omen! I am about to speak of an illustrious living lady, who has in common with Mary Stuart and Marie Antoinette two things at least: she has a French sovereign for a husband, and she has the fame of beauty. But she has likewise that other peculiarity of which I spoke: she is interesting. It is only speaking by the card to say that by far the most interesting of all the imperial and royal ladies now living is Eugénie, Empress of the French. I think there are princesses in Europe more beautiful and even more graceful than she is, or than she ever could have been; I fancy there are some much more highly gifted with intellect; but there is no woman living in any

European palace in whom the general world feels half so much interest. There is not the slightest reason to believe that she is a woman of really penetrating or commanding intellect, and should she be happy enough to live out her life in the Tuileries and die peacefully in her bed, history will find but little to say about her, good or bad. Yet so long as her memory remains in men's minds, it will be as that of a princess who had above all things the gift of being interesting—the power of attracting toward herself the eyes, the admiration, the curiosity, the wonder of all the civilized world.

"We count time by heart-throbs, not by figures on a dial," says a poet who once nearly secured immortality, Philip James Bailey. There certainly are people whose age seems to defy counting by figures on a dial. Ask anybody what two pictures are called up in his mind when he hears the names of Queen Victoria and the Empress of the French, no matter whether he has ever seen the two illustrious ladies or not. In the case of the former I may safely venture to answer for him that he sees the face and figure of a motherly, homely body; a woman who has got quite beyond the age when people observe how she dresses; to whom personal appearance is no longer of any importance or interest. In the case of the latter he sees a dazzling court beauty; a woman who, though not indeed in her youth, is still in a glorious prime; a woman to captivate hearts, and inspire poets, and set scandal going, and adorn a ball-room or a throne. The first instinctive idea would be, I think, that the Empress of the French belonged positively to a later generation than the good, unattractive, dowdyish Queen of England. Yet I believe the difference in actual years is very slight. To be sure, you will find in any almanac that Queen Victoria was born on the 24th of May, 1819, and is consequently very near to fifty-one years of age; while the fair Eugénie is set down as having been born on May 5th, 1826, and consequently would now appear to be only in her forty-fourth year. But then Queen Victoria was born in the purple, and cannot, poor thing, make any attempt at reducing by one single year the full figure of her age. History has taken an inexorable, ineffaceable note of the day and hour of her birth; and even court flattery cannot affect to ignore the record. Now Eugénie was born in happy obscurity; even the place of her birth is not known by the public with that certainty which alone satisfies sceptics; and I have heard that the date recorded as that of her natal hour is only a graceful fiction, a pretty bit of polite biography. Certainly I have heard it stoutly maintained that if any historian or critic were now to be as ungallant in his researches as John Wilson Croker was in the case of Lady Morgan (was it not Lady Morgan?), he would find that the birth of the brilliant Empress of the French would have to be dated back a few years, and that after all the difference between her and the elderly Queen Victoria is less an affair of time than of looks and of heart-throbs.

About a dozen years, I suppose, have passed away since I saw the Empress Eugénie and Queen Victoria sitting side by side. Assuredly the difference even then might well have been called a contrast, although the Queen was in her happiest time, and has worn out terribly fast since that period. But the quality which above all others Queen Victoria wanted was just that in which the Empress of the French is supreme—the quality of imperial, womanly grace. I have never been a rapturous admirer of the beauty of the Empress; a certain narrowness of contour in the face, the eyes too closely set together, and an appearance of artificiality in every movement of the features, seem to me to detract very much from the charms of her countenance. But her queenly grace of gesture, of attitude, of form, of motion, must be admitted to be beyond cavil, and superb. She looks just the woman on whom any sort of garment would hang with grace and attractiveness; a blanket would become like a regal mantle if it fell round her shoulders; I verily believe she would actually look graceful in Mary Walker's costume, which I consider decidedly the most detestable, in an artistic sense, ever yet indued by mortal woman. Poor Queen Victoria looked awkward and homely indeed by the side of this graceful, noble form; this figure that expressed so well the combination of suppleness and affluence, of imperial dignity and charming womanhood. Time has not of late spared the face of the Empress of the French. Lines and hollows are growing fast there; the bright eyes are sinking deeper into their places; the complexion is fading and clouding; malicious people now say that, like that of the lady in the "School for Scandal," it comes in the morning and goes in the night; and the hair is apparently fast growing thin. But the grace of form and movement is still there, unimpaired and unsurpassed. The whitest and finest shoulders still surmount a noble bust, which, but that its amplitude somewhat exceeds the severe proportions of antique Grecian beauty, might· be reproduced in marble to illustrate the contour of a Venus or a Juno. I have seldom looked at the Empress of the French or at any picture or bust of her without thinking how Mary Wortley Montagu would have gone into bold and eloquent raptures over the superb womanhood of that splendid form.

Well, the face always disappointed me at least. It seems to me cold, artificial, narrow, insincere. It wants nobleness. It does not impress me as being the face of a frivolous woman, a coquette, a court butterfly; but rather that of one who is always playing a part which sometimes wearies. If I were to form my own impressions of the Empress of the French merely from her face, I should set her down as a keen, politic woman, with brains enough to be crafty, not enough to be great. I should set her down as a woman who needs and loves the stimulus of incessant excitement, just as much as a certain class of actress does. Indeed, I think I have seen in the face of more than one actress just such an habitual expression, off the stage, as one may see in the countenance of the French Empress. I fear that sweet and gracious smile, which is said to be so captivating to those for whose immediate and special homage it is put on, changes into sudden blankness or weariness when its momentary business has been done. Sam Slick tells us of a lady whose smile dropped from her face the moment the gazer's eyes were withdrawn "like a petticoat when the strings break;" and if I might apply this irreverent comparison to the smile of an Empress, I would say that I think I have noted just such a change in the expression of the brilliant Eugénie. Indeed, it must be a tiresome part, that which she has had to play through all these resplendent years; a part thrilling with danger, made thorny by many sharp vexations. Were the Empress of the French the mere *belle* of a court, she might doubtless have joyfully swallowed all the bitternesses for the sake of the brightness and splendor of her lot; were she a woman of high, imperial genius, a Maria Theresa, an Anne of Austria, she might have found in the mere enjoyment of power, or in the nobler aspirings of patriotism, abundant compensation for her individual vexations. But being neither a mere coquette nor a woman of genius, being neither great enough to rise wholly above her personal troubles, nor small enough to creep under them untouched, she must have suffered enough to render her life very often a weary trial; and the traces of that weariness can be seen on her face when the court look is dropped for a moment.

The Empress seems to have passed through three phases of character, or at least to have made on the public opinion of France three successive and different impressions. For a long time she was set down as a mere coquette, a creature whose soul soared no higher than the aspiration after a bonnet or a bracelet, whose utmost genius exhausted itself in the invention of a crinoline. Indeed, it may be questioned whether any invention known to modern Europe had so sudden and wonderful a success or made the inventor so talked about as Eugénie's famous *jupon d'acier*. A sour and cynical Republican of my acquaintance once declared that anybody might have known the Empress to be a *parvenue* by the mere fact that she could and did invent a petticoat; for he maintained that no born emperor or empress ever was known to have done even so much in the way of invention. Decidedly, the Empress did a great deal of harm in those her earlier and more brilliant days. To her influence and example may be ascribed the passion for mere extravagance and variety of dress which has spread of late years among all the fashionable and would-be fashionable women of Europe and America. It is not too much to say that the Empress of the French demoralized, in this sense, the womanhood of two generations. How literally debauching her influence was to the women immediately under its control, the women of the fashionable world of Paris, I need not stop to tell. Graceful, gracious, and elegant as she is, she did undoubtedly succeed in branding with a stamp of vulgarity the brilliant court of the Second Empire. It is not wonderful if scandal said coarse and bitter things about the goddess of prodigality who presided over the revels of the Tuileries. The most absurd stories used to be told of the amusements which went on in the private gardens of the palace and in its inner circles; and the levity and occasional flightiness of a vivacious young woman thirsting for fresh gayeties and new excitements were perverted and magnified into reckless and wanton extravagances. Of course it was inevitable that there should be scandal over the birth of the Prince Imperial. Were the Empress Eugénie chaste as ice, pure as unsunned snow, she could not, under the circumstances, escape that calumny.

About the time of her sudden and mysterious escapade to London, the Empress began to emerge a little from the character of a mere woman of fashion, and to become known and felt as a politician. People say that some at least of the influence and control which she began to obtain over her husband was owing to her knowledge of his many infidelities and his reluctance to provoke her into open quarrel. Unless Eugénie was wholly free from the jealousy which is supposed to lie in the heart of every other woman, she must have suffered cruelly in this way for many years. In her own court circles, at her own side, were ladies whom universal report designated as successive *maîtresses en titre* of the Emperor Napoleon. Stories, too, of his indulgence in low and gross amours were told everywhere, and, true or false (charity itself could not well doubt that some of them were true), must have reached the Empress's ears. She suffered severely, and she took to politics—perhaps as a harassed man sometimes takes to drinking. Her political influence was, in its day, simply disastrous. She was always on the wrong side, and she was always impetuous, unreasoning, and pertinacious, as cynical people say is the way of women. She became a devotee of the narrowest kind; and just as Madame de Maintenon's religious bigotry did infinitely more harm to France than the vilest profligacy of a Pompadour or a Dubarry could have done, so the religious fervor of the Empress Eugénie threatened at one time to prove a worse thing for the State and for Europe than if she had really carried on during all her lifetime the palace orgies which her enemies ascribed to her. Reaction, Ultramontanism, illiberalism, superstition, found a patroness and leader in her. She fought for the continued occupation of Rome; she battled against the unity of Italy; she recommended and urged the Mexican expedition. Louis Napoleon is personally a good-natured, easy-going sort of man, averse to domestic disputes, fully conscious, no doubt, of his frequent liability to domestic censure. What wonder if European politics sometimes had to suffer heavily for the tolerated presence of this or that too notorious lady in the inner circles of the French court? "Who is the Countess de — —?" I once asked of a Parisian friend who was attached to the Imperial household—I was speaking of a lady whose beauty and whose audacities of dress were then much talked of in the French capital. "The latest favorite," was the reply. "I shouldn't wonder if her presence at court cost another ten years of the occupation of Rome."

With the Empress's introduction to politics and political intrigue, the era of scandal seems to have closed for her. She dressed as brilliantly and extravagantly as ever, and she would take as much pains about her toilet for the benefit of Persigny and Baroche and Billault at a Council of State as for a ball in the Tuileries. She received the same sort of company, was surrounded by the same ladies and the same cavaliers as ever. But she ceased to be herself a subject of scandal—a fact which is not a little remarkable when one remembers how many bitter enemies she made for herself at this period of her career. She seems to have seriously contemplated the assumption of a great political and religious part—the part of the patroness and protectress of the Papacy. I believe she studied hard to educate herself for this part, and indeed for the work in politics generally which devolved upon her. The position of Vicegerent, assigned to her by the Emperor during his absence in the Lombardy campaign, stirred up political ambition within her, and she seems to have shown a remarkable aptitude for political work. She certainly sustained the opinion expressed by John Stuart Mill in his "Subjection of Women," that the business of politics, from which laws in general shut women out, is just the one intellectual occupation in which, whenever they have had a chance, they have proved themselves the equals of men. When Eugénie was raised to the Imperial throne, she appears to have had no better education than any young Spanish woman of her class, and that certainly is not much. A lady once assured me that she was one of a group who were presented to the Empress at the Tuileries, and that there being in the group two beautiful girls from America, to whom Eugénie desired to be particularly gracious, her Imperial Majesty began to ask them several questions about their native land, and astonished them almost beyond the capacity to reply by kindly inquiring whether they had come from New York "over the sea, or over the land." But the Empress has read up a good deal, and mastered much other knowledge besides that of geography, since those salad days. Meanwhile, she became more and more the divinity of the Ultramontanes; and the French court presented the interesting spectacle of having two rival and extreme parties, one led by the Emperor's wife, and the other by his cousin, Prince Napoleon, between whom the Emperor himself maintained an attitude something like that of the central figure in a game of seesaw. I presume there can be little doubt that the Empress regarded her husband's portly cousin with a cordial detestation. She is not a woman endowed with a keen sense of humor, nor in any case would she be quite likely to enjoy anything which was humorous at her own expense; and Prince Napoleon is credited broadly with having said things concerning her which doubtless made his friends and followers and boon companions laugh, but which, reported to her, as they assuredly would be, must have made her cheek flame and her lips quiver. Moreover, the Red Prince was notoriously in the habit of turning into jest some things more sacred in the eyes of the Imperial devotee than even her own reputation. She feared his tongue, his reckless wit, his smouldering ambition. She feared him for her boy, whose rival and enemy he might come to be; and Prince Napoleon had more sons than one. Therefore the rivalry was keen and bitter. She was for the Pope; he was for Italy and the Revolution. She sympathized with the South in the American civil war; Prince Napoleon was true to his principles and stood by the North. She favored the Mexican enterprise; he opposed it. She was for all manner of repressive action as regarded political speaking and writing; he was for a free platform and free press. Her triumph came when, during the Emperor's visit to Algeria, Prince Napoleon delivered his famous Ajaccio speech—a speech terribly true and shockingly indiscreet— and was punished by an Imperial rebuke, which led him to resign all his political offices and withdraw absolutely from public life for several successive years.

But just when the Empress seemed to have the field all to herself, her political influence began somehow to wane. Perhaps she grew a little weary of the work of statecraft; perhaps she had not been so successful in some of her favorite projects as she had expected to be. The Mexican expedition turned out a dismal, ghastly failure, and that enterprise had always been regarded as the joint work of the two influences which cynical people say have usually been most disastrous in politics—the priest and the petticoat. Then the idea of working out the scheme of European politics from the central point of the Tuileries was suddenly exploded by the unexpected intrusion of Prussia, and the dazzling victory in which the Bonaparte as well as the Hapsburg was overthrown and humbled. The old framework of things was disjointed by this surprising event. A new political centre of gravity had to be sought for Europe. France was rudely pushed aside. The fair Empress, who had been training herself for quite a different condition of things, found herself now confronted by new, strange, and bewildering combinations. One thing is highly to her credit. I have been assured by people who claim to know something of the matter, that her earnest influence was used to induce the French Government to accept, without remonstrance, the new situation. While Louis Napoleon was committing the inexcusable blunder of feeling his way towards a war with Prussia, and thereby subjecting himself to the ignominy of having to draw hastily back, the voice of the Empress, I am assured, was always raised for peace. But I think the new situation was too much for her. She had made up for a game of politics between the Pope and Italy; when other players and other stakes appeared, the Empress was disinclined to undertake a new course of education. She thereupon passed into the third phase—that of philanthropic devotee, Lady Bountiful, and mother of her people; and since then, if she cannot be said to have grown universally popular, she may fairly be described as having got rid of nearly all her former unpopularity. Her good deeds began to be magnified everywhere, and even ancient enemies were content to sing her praises, or, at least, to hear them sung.

Undoubtedly she has a kindly, charitable heart, and can do heroic as well as graceful things. Her famous visitation of the cholera hospitals may doubtless have been done partly for effect, but even in this sense it showed a lofty appreciation of the duties of an Empress, and could not have been conceived or carried out by an ignoble nature. When the cholera appeared in Madrid, the fat, licentious woman who then cumbered and disgraced the throne of Spain, fled in dismay from her capital; and this act of peculiarly unwomanlike cowardice told heavily against her and hurried her deeply down into that public contempt which is so fatal to sovereigns. The Empress Eugénie, on the other hand, dignified and served herself and her husband by her fearless exposure of her own life in the cause of humanity and charity. Kindly and generous deeds of hers are constantly reported in Paris, and these things go far in keeping up the superstition of loyalty. Every one knows how gracious and winning the Empress can be in her personal relations with those who approach her. Sometimes her demeanor and actions come into sharp contrast with those of other sovereigns in matters less momentous than the visiting of death-charged hospital wards. I have heard of an American lady who once made some rich and complete collections of specimens of American foliage, collected them at immense labor, arranged them with exquisite taste in two large and beautiful volumes, and sent one as an offering to Queen Victoria, the other to the Empress of the French. From the British court came back the volume itself, with a formal reply from an official intimating that Her Majesty the Queen made it a rule not to accept such gifts. From Paris came a letter of genial, graceful acceptance, written by the Empress Eugénie herself, full of good taste, good feeling, and courteous, ladylike expression. These are small things, but womanly tact and grace seldom have much opportunity of expressing themselves save in just such small things.

The Empress then has of late years faded a little out of political life. I think it may be taken for granted that although she is a quick, clever woman, with talents far beyond the mere inventing of bonnets and petticoats, she is not gifted with any political genius, not qualified to see quickly into the heart of a difficult question, not endowed with the capacity to surmount a great crisis. I have never heard anything which induces me to think that Eugénie's intellect and power would count for much in the chances of the dynasty should Louis Napoleon die while his son is yet a boy. Like Louis Napoleon himself, she was twice misjudged: first when people set her down as an empty-headed coquette, and next when they cried her up as a woman with a genius for government. So far as one may venture to predict, I think she would not prove strong enough for the place, if evil fortune should throw upon her the task of preserving the throne for her boy.

Recent events seem to me to prove that the imperial system is less strong and more shaky than most of us would have supposed six months ago. I for one do fully believe that the recent disturbances are the genuine indications of a profound and bitter popular discontent. I beg the readers of The Galaxy to be very cautious how they form an estimate of the situation from the correspondence and editorial articles of the London press. If the "Times" believes Bonapartism safe and strong in Paris, I have only to remark that the "Times" believed the same, almost up to the bitter end, of Bonapartism in Mexico. There are very few London journals which can be trusted where the politics of France are concerned. Not that the journals are bribed; everybody knowing anything of the London press knows how absurd the idea of such bribery is; but that all London Philistinism (and Philistinism does a good deal of the writing for the London papers) considers it genteel and respectable, and the right sort of thing generally, to go in for the Empire and sneer at revolution. I have read with no little wonder many of the comments of the London, and indeed some of the New York journals, on Henri Rochefort and his colleagues. One would think that in order to prove a certain revolutionary movement powerless and contemptible, you had only to show that its leaders were themselves contemptible and disreputable persons. Some of the journals here and in London write as if the Empire must be safe because the satire of the "Lanterne" and the "Marseillaise" seems to them coarse and witless, and because they have heard that Henri Rochefort is an insincere man, of doubtful courage and tainted moral character. One longs to ask whether the "Père Duchesne" and the "Vieux Cordelier" were publications fit to be read in the drawing-rooms of virtuous families; whether Mirabeau's private character was quite blameless; whether Marat and Hébert had led reputable lives; whether Camille Desmoulins was habitually received into the highest circles; whether Théroigne de Méricourt was the sort of young woman one's wife would like to invite to tea. The imbecility with which certain journalists go on day after day trying to assure themselves and the world that imperialism has nothing to fear at the hands of a movement led by scurrilous and disreputable men, has something in it at once amusing and provoking. The strength of a revolutionary movement is not exactly to be estimated by the claims of its leaders to carry off the *prix Monthyon* or the Holy Grail. Perhaps if it were to be so estimated, it would be hard to say where the victory should go in the present instance. For the worst of Rochefort's colleagues have never been accused of any profligacies and basenesses so bad as those which universal public opinion ascribes to the leading Bonapartes and some of their most influential supporters. Undoubtedly there is a great deal of scurrility and even worse in the papers conducted by Rochefort. It is not in good taste to go on asking who was the mother of De Morny, who was the father of Walewski; how the present Walewski, Walewski *fils*, comes to be called a count, and who was his mother, and so on; and the direct and libellous attacks on the Empress are utterly indefensible. If one were making up a memoir of Henri Rochefort, or engaged in a debating society's controversy on his character, one would have to admit that he is by no means a model demagogue, a pattern patriot. But one might at the same time hint that, judging by historical precedent, he is probably all the more formidable as a revolutionary leader for that very reason. His literary attacks on the Government are by no means all vulgar, or scurrilous, or contemptible. There was fresh and genuine humor as well as telling satire in the "Lanterne's" early declaration of allegiance to the Napoleons, the purport of which was that, feeling bound to express his devotion to a Napoleon, Rochefort had selected as the object of his loyal homage Napoleon the Second, the sovereign who never coerced the press, or corrupted the Senate, or robbed the nation of its liberty, or exiled its patriots, or carried on a Mexican expedition, or impoverished the country to maintain a gigantic army. But there is one thing certain—that whether Rochefort is witty or not, wise or not, he has waked an echo throughout France and Europe in general which even very wise and undeniably witty enemies of the Empire did not succeed in creating. Nothing he has written will compare in artistic strength of satire or invective with Victor Hugo's "Châtimens" or "Napoléon le Petit." Eugène Pelletan's "Nouvelle Babylone" was a prolonged outpouring of indignant eloquence by a gentleman, a scholar, and a thinker. Rogeard's "Propos de Labienus" was a piece of really fine sarcasm. But not the most celebrated of these attacks on the Empire created anything like the sensation which Rochefort has succeeded in creating by the constant "pegging away" of his bitter, envenomed, and unscrupulous pen. Indeed, the reason is obvious—at least to those who, like me, believe that the great mass of the Parisian population (the army, the officials, and the priests not counted) are heartily sick of Bonapartism, and would get rid of it if they could. Rochefort assails the Empire and the Emperor in a style which they can understand. He is a master of a certain kind of coarse, rasping ridicule, which delights the disaffected *ouvrier*; and he has no scruple about assailing any weak place he can find in his enemy, even though in doing so the heart of a woman has likewise to be wounded. An angry and disaffected populace delights in this kind of thing. The fact that Rochefort has created such a sensation is the best proof in the world that the Parisian populace is angry and disaffected. Rochefort has a happy gift of epithets, which goes a long way with admirers and followers such as his. I doubt whether a whole chapter could have described more accurately and vividly the person, character, and career of Prince Pierre Bonaparte than Rochefort did when he branded him as "a social bandit." Personally, Rochefort is not qualified to be a demagogue in the sense that Danton was a demagogue, and he can make no pretension to be a revolutionary leader of a high class. But he can incite a populace, madden the hearts of disaffected crowds, as the bitter tongue of a shrill woman might do, and as the tongue of a great orator might perhaps fail to do. Doubtless Rochefort and his literary sword-and-buckler men are not strong enough to create a serious disturbance of themselves alone. But if a moment of general uncertainty and unsettlement came, they might prove a dangerous disturbing force. If, for example, there should come a crisis which of itself rendered change of some kind necessary, when all the chances of the future might depend upon a single hour or perhaps a single decisive command, and when it was not certain who had the right, who would assume the responsibility to give the command, then indeed the bitter screams, and jeers, and invectives of these reckless literary bravos might have much to do with the ordering of the situation. If, for example, the Emperor were to die just now, who shall venture to say how much the chances of the Empress and her son might not be affected at that moment of terrible crisis by the pens and the tongues of Rochefort and his followers?

Some time, in the natural course of things, the Empress may expect to have to face such a crisis. It is highly probable that the time will come while yet her boy is young and dependent upon her guardianship and care. Has she won for herself the affection, confidence, and loyalty of France, to such an extent that she could count upon national support? I am convinced that she has not. She is much liked and even loved by those who know her. They have countless anecdotes to tell of her affectionate ways as a mother, of her generosity and kindness as a woman. But although she has outlived many of the early prejudices against her, she is still regarded with distrust and dislike by the older families of France; and I am confident that a large proportion of the working classes in Paris and the large towns delight to believe the worst things that malice and slander can say to her detriment. The priests and the shopkeepers are probably her best friends; but I am not aware that priests and shopkeepers have ever proved themselves very powerful bulwarks against sudden popular revolution. The generals and the army might of course remain perfectly loyal to her; probably would if they had no time to consider the situation, and there were no favorite rival in the way (if Prince Napoleon, for example, were a brilliant soldier, she would not have a ghost of a chance against him); but it must be remembered that the loyalty of an army is something like the epigrammatic description of the honor of a woman: when there is any deliberation, it is likely to be lost; and the claims of the Empress are certainly not such as absolutely to forbid deliberation and render it impossible. Much of course would depend on the woman herself. There was a moment when Catharine of Russia's unfortunate husband might have carried all before him if he had only seized the chance; and he did not seize it, and so lost all. There was a moment when Catharine might have utterly failed if she had not risen to the height of the crisis, and seized the opportunity with both hands; and she did rise to the height of the crisis, did seize the opportunity, and so won all. Place Eugénie in such a position, and is she a woman to win? Is she in fact a woman of genius? I think not. Nothing that I have ever heard of her—and I have known many who were her intimate friends—has led me to believe her endowed with a quick, strong, commanding intellect. Mentally she seems to be narrow and shallow; in temper she is quick, capricious, full of warm personal affections and almost groundless personal dislikes. I have a strong idea that no matter what the urgency of the crisis, she would stay to make herself picturesque before taking any public action; and I venture to think she would be guided by counsel only where she happened to have a personal liking for the counsellor. She cannot, I fancy, be trusted at a great crisis to make the fortune of her son. Enough if she do not mar it at such a time.

Political considerations apart, one can only wish her well. Her face is one which ought to smile sweetly and gracefully through history. If fate and France will endure the Bonapartes for another generation or so, there will be some consolation to gallant and romantic souls in the thought that thereby this gracious, queenly woman will be allowed to make a happy end of her brilliant, not untroubled life. Thus far we may, in summing up her career, describe her, first, as a bright, vivacious young coquette, with a dash of the adventuress about her, ranging the world in search of a husband; then a woman suddenly and surprisingly raised to the dazzling rank of an Empress, and a little bewildered by the change; then a splendid leader of the world's fashion, magnificently frivolous and heedless; then a political *intrigante*, the supreme patroness of Ultramontanism; and now a quiet, queenly mother, verging toward that kind of devoteeism in which some satirical person declares that coquetry in France is sure to end. She is not a woman to make any deep impression on history. She has neither gifts enough nor faults enough. As a politician she has been a failure, and perhaps worse than a failure; but she has been fortunate enough to escape from all public responsibility for her mistakes, and may get quietly into history as merely an intelligent, good-natured, and beautiful woman. Posterity will probably see her and appreciate her sufficiently in her portrait by Winterhalter: a name, a vague memory, and a smooth fair picture with bright complexion, shining hair, and noble shoulders, alone carrying down to other times the history of the Third Napoleon's wife. Only great misfortunes could redeem her from this destiny of half oblivion; and history has names enough that are burnt by misfortune into eternal memory, and may well spare hers. One great claim she has to a liberal construction of her character: her personal enemies are those who do not know her well; her intimates seem to be always her friends. She has one good quality, which her husband with all his faults likewise possesses: she has never in her imperial splendor forgotten or neglected or been ashamed of old acquaintances and friends. I have heard scores of anecdotes from people who know her well—I have heard one such anecdote since I began writing this article—which prove her to be entirely above the mean and vulgar weakness of the *parvenu*, who shrinks in her magnificence from any acquaintanceship or association likely to remind her of less brilliant days. Taken on the whole, the Empress Eugénie is better than her fortunes and her surroundings might have made her. She is, I think, a woman much more deserving of respect than Josephine Beauharnais, whose misfortunes, joined with the quiet pathetic dignity of her retirement and her later years, have made the world forget the levities, frivolities, and follies of her earlier life. She has shown a quicker and better appreciation of the duties and difficulties of her station, and the temper of the people among whom she had to live, than was at any time shown by Marie Antoinette. Whether she could ever under the most favorable conditions prove an Anne of Austria may well be doubted; and we must all hope for her own sake that she may never be put to the proof. She has at least made it clear that she is no mere Reine Crinoline; she has shown that she possesses some heart, some courage, and some brains; she has had sense enough to retrieve blunders, and merit enough to live down calumny. The best thing one can hope for her is that she may never again be placed in a position which would tempt and allow her to make political influence the instrument of religious bigotry. The greatest woman her native country ever produced, Isabella of Castile, became with all her virtues and genius a curse to Spain, because of her bigotry and her power; and there was a time when it seemed as if the Empress Eugénie was likely to make for herself an odious fame as the chief patroness of a conspiracy against the religious and political liberties of the south of Europe. Let us hope that in her future career she may be saved from any such temptation, and that she may be kept as much as possible out of all political complications where religion interferes; and if she be thus graced by fortune, it is all but certain that whatever her future years may bring, she will deserve and receive a genial record in the history of France.

THE PRINCE OF WALES

"It is now sixteen or seventeen years," says Edmund Burke, in that famous passage to which one is almost ashamed to allude any more, so hackneyed has it been, "since first I saw the Queen of France, then the Dauphiness, at Versailles; and surely never lighted on this orb, which she hardly seemed to touch, a more delightful vision." That glowing, impassioned apostrophe did more to make partisans and admirers for poor Marie Antoinette among all English-speaking peoples, probably for all time, than any charms, or virtues, or misfortunes of the Queen and the woman could have done. I can never of late read or recall to mind the burning words of Burke, without thinking of a certain day in March some seven years ago, when I stood on a platform in Trafalgar Square, London, and saw a bright, beautiful young face smiling and bending to a vast enthusiastic crowd on either side, and I, like everybody else, was literally stricken with admiration of the beauty, the sweetness, and the grace of the Princess Alexandra of Denmark. In truth, I am not in general an enthusiast about princes or princesses; I do not believe that the king's face usually gives grace. In this instance the beauty of the Princess Alexandra had been so noisily trumpeted by literary lacqueys already, that one's natural instinct was to feel disappointed, and to say so, when the Princess herself came in sight. But it was impossible to feel disappointment, or anything but admiration, at the sight of that bright, fair face, so transparent in the clearness of its complexion, so delicate and refined in its outlines, so sweet and gracious in its expression. I think something like the old-fashioned, chivalric, chimerical feeling of personal loyalty must have flamed up for the moment that day in the hearts of many men, who perhaps would have been ashamed to confess that their first experience of such an emotion was due to a passing glimpse of the face of a pretty, tremulous girl.

If ours were days of augury, men might have shuddered at the omens which accompanied the wedding ceremonies of the Prince and Princess of Wales. When Goethe, then a youth, surveyed the preparations for the reception of Marie Antoinette at Strasbourg, on her way to Paris, he observed significantly on the inauspicious fact that in the grand chamber adorned for her coming, the tapestry represented the wedding of Jason and Medea. The civil authorities of London certainly did not greet the fair stranger with any such grisly and ghastly emblazonings; but there were other and even more inauspicious omens offered by chance and the hour. The sky darkened, a dreary wind whistled; presently the rain came down in drenching streams that would not abate. There was a mourning-garb at the wedding—the black dress of the Queen, who would not lay aside her widow's-weeds even for that hour; and the night of the wedding, when the streets of London were illuminated, the crowd was so great that, as on a memorable occasion in the early married life of Marie Antoinette, people were crushed and trampled to death amid the universal jubilation.

Well, we defy augury, with Hamlet. But I think some at least in the crowd who welcomed Alexandra felt a kind of doubt and pity as to her future, which needed no inspiration from omens and superstition. No foreign princess has ever been so popular in England as Alexandra; and assuredly some at least of the affection felt for her springs from a pity which, whether called for or not, is genuine and universal. The last time I saw the Princess of Wales was within a very few days of my leaving England to visit the United States. It was in Drury Lane Theatre, then fitted up as an opera house in consequence of the recent burning of Her Majesty's Theatre. The Prince of Wales, his wife, and one of his sisters were in their box. I had not seen the Princess for some time, and I was painfully impressed with the change which had come over her. Remembering, as it was easy to do, the brightness of her beauty during the early days of her marriage, there was something almost shocking in the altered appearance of her face. It looked wasted and haggard; the complexion, which used to be so dazzlingly fair, had grown dull, and, if I may say so, discolored; and I must be ungracious enough to declare bluntly that, to my eyes at least, there seemed little trace indeed of the beauty of a few years before left in that dimmed and worn countenance. "Only the eyes remained—they would not go." Of course, it must be remembered that the Princess was then only just recovering from a long, painful, and exhausting illness; and she may have—I truly hope she has—since then regained all her brightness and beauty. In any case, it would be unjust indeed to assume that the wasted look of the Princess was to be attributed to domestic unhappiness. But even a very matter-of-fact and unsentimental person, looking at her then, and remembering what she so lately was, might be excused if he fancied that some of the unpropitious omens which surrounded the Princess's marriage had already begun to justify themselves in practical fulfilment.

For even at the time of the marriage of the Prince and Princess there were not wanting prophets of evil who predicted that this royal union would not prove much happier than state-made marriages commonly are. Even then there were stories and reports afloat which ascribed to the Prince habits and tendencies not likely to promote the domestic happiness of a delicate and refined young wife, hardly more than a mere child in years. Indeed, there was already considerable doubt in the public mind as to the personal character of the Prince of Wales. He certainly did not look a very intellectual or refined sort of person even then, and some at least were inclined to think him, as Steerforth says of little Em'ly's lover, "rather a chuckle-headed kind of fellow," to get such a girl. There was, certainly, a breath of serious distrust abroad. On the Prince's coming of age, and again, I think, on the announcement of his approaching marriage, the London daily papers had set themselves to preaching sermons at him; and a very foolish chorus of sermons that was which broke out from all those tongues together. The only marked effect of this outburst of lay-preaching was, I fancy, to impress the public mind with the idea that the Prince was really a very much more dreadful young man than there was any good reason to believe him. People naturally imagined that the writers who poured forth such eloquent, wise, and suggestive admonitions must know a great deal more than they felt disposed to hint at; whereas, I venture to think that, in truth, the majority of the writers were disposed to hint at a great deal more than they knew. For, indeed, almost all that is generally and substantially known of the Prince of Wales has been learned and observed since his marriage.

Still, even before, and long before the marriage, there were ominous rumors. Those that I mention I give simply as rumors—not, indeed, the mere babble of the streets, but as the kind of thing which people told you who professed to know—the talk of the House of Commons, and the clubs, and the fashionable drawing-rooms and smoking-rooms. People told you that the Prince and his father had had many quarrels arising out of the extravagance, dissipation, and wrong-headedness of the former; and there was even a painful and cruel report thus whispered about that the death of Prince Albert was the result of a cold he had taken from walking incautiously in a heavy rain during excitement caused by a quarrel with his son. Stories were told of this and that *amour* and *liaison* in Ireland when the Prince of Wales was with the camp on the Curragh of Kildare; of his excesses when he was a student at the University; of his escapades at many other times and places. Certain actresses of a low class, and other women of a still lower class, were pointed out in London as special favorites of the Prince of Wales. Of course every man of sense knew, first, that stories of this kind must be taken with a large amount of allowance for exaggeration; and, next, that the public must not expect all the virtues of a saint to belong to the early years of a prince of the family of Guelph. In England public opinion, although it has grown much more exacting of late years on the score of decorum than it used to be, is still disposed to look over without censure a good deal of extravagance and dissipation in young and unmarried men, especially if they be men of rank. Therefore, if the rumors which attended the early career of the Prince of Wales had not followed him into his married years, the world would soon have forgotten all about his youthful indiscretions. But it became a serious question for the whole nation when it began to be whispered everywhere that the Prince was growing worse instead of better during his married life, and when to the suspicion that he was wasting his own youth and his own credit came to be added the belief that he was neglecting and injuring the young and beautiful woman whom state reasons had assigned to him as a wife. In good truth, it is really a question of public and historical interest whether the Queen of England is likely to be succeeded by an Albert the Good or another George the Fourth; and I am not therefore inviting the readers of The Galaxy to descend to the useless discussion of a mere piece of idle court scandal when I ask them to consider with me the probabilities of the future from such survey as we can take of the aspects of the present.

Those who saw the Prince of Wales when he visited this country, would surely fail to recognize the slender, fair-haired, rather graceful youth of that day in the heavy, fat, stolid, prematurely bald, elderly-young-man of this. It would not be easy to see in any assembly a more stupid-looking man than the Prince of Wales is now. On horseback he shows to best advantage. He rides well, and the pleasure he takes in riding lends something of animation to his usually inexpressive face. But when his eyes and features lapse into their habitual condition of indolent, good-natured, stolid repose, all light of intellect seems to have been banished. The outline of the head and face, and the general expression, seemed to me of late to be growing every day more and more like the head and face of George the Third. Anybody who may happen to have a shilling or half-crown of George the Third's time, can see on the coin a very fair presentment of the countenance of the present heir-apparent of the English throne. Whether the Prince of Wales resembles George the Fourth in character and tastes or not, he certainly does not resemble him in face. Even a court sycophant could not pretend to see beauty or grace in our present Prince.

I think that to the eye of the cynic or the satirist the Prince of Wales shows to greatest advantage when he sits in his box at an advanced hour of some rather heavy classic opera, or has to endure a long succession of speeches at a formal public dinner. The heavy head droops, the heavy jaws hang, the languid eyes close, the heir-apparent sinks into a doze. Loyalty itself can see nothing dignified or kingly in him then. I have watched him thus as he sat in his box during some high-class, and to him, doubtless, very heavy performance at the Italian opera, and have thought that at times he might remind irreverent and disloyal observers of Pickwick's immortal fat boy. I have sometimes observed that his little dozes appeared to afford innocent amusement to his sisters, if any of them happened to be in the box; and occasionally one of the Princesses would playfully poke her slumbering brother in the princely ribs, and the Heir of all the Ages would open his eyes and smile languidly, and try to look at the stage and listen to the music; and then, after a while, the heavy head would sink once more on the vast expanse of shirt-front in which the Prince seems to delight, and the fat boy would go to sleep again. But this would only happen at certain performances. There were times when the Prince had eyes and ears open and attentive, even in the opera house. His tastes in general, however, are not for high art in music or the drama. He is very fond of the little theatres where the vivacious blondes display their unconcealed attractions. There are, as everybody knows, several minor theatres in London where the audience, or, I should say more properly, the spectators, will be found to consist chiefly of men, while, on the other hand, the performers are chiefly women. These are the temples of the leg drama. "*Pièce aux jambes? Pièce aux cuisses!*" indignantly exclaims Eugene Pelletan, denouncing such performances in his "Nouvelle Babylone"; and he goes on to add some cumulative illustrations which I omit. Well, the Prince of Wales loves the *pièce aux jambes*, and the theatres where it flourishes. He constantly visits theatres at which his wife and sisters are never seen, and in which it would be idle to deny that there are actresses who have made themselves conspicuous objects of popular scandal.

Now, I am far from saying that this necessarily implies anything worse than a low taste on the part of the Prince of Wales. But there are stations in life which render private bad taste a public sin. In London, of late, there has been a just outcry against a certain kind of theatrical performance. It is held to be demoralizing and degrading that the stage should be made simply a show-place for the exhibition of half-naked women, for the audacious display of legs and bosoms. Now, I beg to say for myself that I have entire faith in the dramatic as in every other art; that I believe it always when truthfully pursued vindicates itself, and that I think any costume which the true and legitimate needs of the drama require is fitting, proper, and modest. I regard the ballet, in its place, as a graceful and delightful entertainment; and I do not believe that any healthy and pure mind ought to be offended by the kind of costume which the dance requires. But artists and moralists in London alike objected, and justly objected, to performances the whole purpose, and business, and attraction of which was the exhibition of a crowd of girls as nearly naked as they could venture to show themselves in public.

Now this was undoubtedly the kind of exhibition which the Prince of Wales especially favored and patronized. Night after night, even during the long and lamentable illness of his young wife, he visited such theatres, and gazed upon "those prodigies of myriad nakednesses." Likewise did he much delight in the performances of Schneider—that high priestess of the obscene, rich with the spoils of princes. I say emphatically that there were actions, gestures, *bouffonneries* performed amid peals of laughter and thunders of applause by this fat Faustina in the St. James's Theatre, London, which were only fit to have gladdened the revels of Sodom and Gomorrah. And this woman was, artistically at least, the prime favorite of the Prince of Wales; and when his brother, the Duke of Edinburgh, reached England for the first time after his escape from the Fenian bullet in Sydney, the *par nobile fratrum* celebrated the auspicious event by hastening to the theatre where Schneider kicked and wriggled and helped out the point of lascivious songs by a running accompaniment of obscene gestures.

So much at least has to be said against the Prince of Wales, and cannot be gainsaid. All that he could do by countenance and patronage to encourage a debauching and degrading style of theatric entertainment, he has done. He is said to be fond of the singing of the vulgar and low buffoons of the music-halls, and to have had such persons brought specially to his residence, Marlborough House, to sing for him. I have been assured of this often by persons who professed to know; but I do not know anything of it myself, nor is it indeed a matter of any importance. The other facts are known to everybody who reads the London papers. The manager or manageress of a theatre takes good care to announce in the journals when a visit from the Prince of Wales has taken place, and we all thus come to know how many times a week the little theatric temples of nakedness have been honored by his presence.

Am I attaching too much importance to such matters as this? I think not. The social influence and moral example of a royal personage in England are now almost the only agencies by which the royal personage can affect us for good or evil. I hold that no man thoughtful or prudent enough, no matter what his morals, to be fit to occupy the position assigned to the Prince of Wales, would be guilty of lending his public and constant patronage to such exhibitions and amusements as those which he especially patronizes. Moreover, the Prince has often shown a disregard, either cynical or stupid—probably the latter—for public opinion, a heedlessness of public scandal, in other matters as well. He has made companionship for himself among young noblemen conspicuous for their debauchery. At a time, not very long ago, when the Divorce Court was occupied with the hearing of a scandalous cause, in which a certain young duke figured most prominently and disgracefully, this young duke was daily and nightly to be seen the close companion of the Prince of Wales.

Let me touch upon another subject, of a somewhat delicate nature. I have said that there were times when our Prince was always wide awake at the opera house. There is a certain brilliant and capricious little singer whom all England and Germany much admire, and who in certain operatic parts has, I think, no rival. Now, public scandal said that the Prince of Wales greatly admired this lady, and paid her the most marked attentions. Public scandal, indeed, said a great deal more. I hasten to record my conviction that, so far as the fair artiste was concerned, the scandal was wholly unfounded, and that she is a woman of pure character and honor. But the Prince was credited with a special admiration for her; and I am sure the Prince's father under such circumstances would have taken good care to lend no foundation, afford no excuse, for scandal to rest upon. Now, I speak of what I have myself observed when I say that the Prince of Wales, whenever he had an opportunity, always demeaned himself as if he really desired to give the public good reason for believing the scandal, or as if he was too far gone in infatuation to be able to govern his actions. For he was always at the opera when this lady sang; and he always conducted himself as if he wished to blazon to the world his ostentatious and demonstrative admiration. When the prima donna went off the stage, the Prince disappeared from his box; when she came on the stage again, he returned to his seat; he lingered behind all his party at the end, that he might give the last note of applause to the disappearing singer; he made a more pertinacious show of his enthusiasm than even the military admirer of Miss Snevellicci was accustomed to do. Now, all this may have been only stolidity or silliness, and may not have denoted anything like cynicism or coarse disdain of public opinion; but whatever it indicated, it certainly did not, I think, testify to the existence of qualities likely to be found admirable or desirable in the heir to a throne.

Of the truth or falsehood of the private scandals in general circulation concerning the Prince of Wales I know nothing whatever. But everybody in England is aware that such stories are told, and can name and point out this or that titled lady as the heroine of each particular story. It need hardly be said that when a man acquires the sort of reputation which attaches to the Prince of Wales, nothing could be more unjust or unreasonable than to accept, without some very strong ground of belief, any story which couples his name with that of any woman belonging to the society in which he moves. Obviously, it would be enough, in the eyes of an English crowd, that the Prince should now pay any friendly attention to any handsome duchess or countess in order to convert her into an object of scandal. I am myself morally convinced that some of the titled ladies who are broadly and persistently set down by British gossip as mistresses of the Prince of Wales are as innocent of such a charge as if they had never been within a thousand miles of a court. But the Prince is a little unlucky wherever he goes, for scandal appears to pursue him as Horace's black care follows the horseman. When the Prince of Wales happens to be in Paris, he seems to be surrounded at once by the same atmosphere of suspicion and evil report. Some two years ago I chanced to be in Paris at the time the Prince was there, and I can answer for it that observers who had never heard or read of the common gossip of London formed the same impression of his general character that the public of London had already adopted. The Prince was then paying special attention to a brilliant and beautiful lady moving in the court circles of the French capital, a lady who had but very recently distinguished herself by appearing at one of the fancy balls of the Tuileries in the character of the Archangel Michael or Raphael—it does not much matter which—and attired in a costume which left the company no possibility of doubting the symmetry of her limbs and the general shapeliness of her person. Malicious satirists circulated thereupon an announcement that the lady was to appear at the next fancy ball as "La Source," the beautiful naked nymph so exquisitely painted by Ingres. This lady received the special attentions of the Prince of Wales. He followed her, people said, like her shadow; and a smart pun was soon in circulation, which I refrain from giving because it contrives ingeniously to blend with his name the name of the lady in question, and I am not writing a scandalous chronicle. This was the time when the Prince made his royal mother so very angry by attending the Chantilly races on a Sunday. When he came back to London he had to take part in some public ceremonial—I forget now what it was—at which the Queen had consented to be present. Her Majesty was present, and I have been assured by a friend who stood quite near that a sort of little scene was enacted which much embarrassed those who had to take part in the official pageantry of the occasion. Up came the Prince, who had travelled in hot haste from Paris, and with a somewhat abashed and sheepish air approached his royal mother. She looked at him angrily, and turned away. The Duke of Cambridge, her cousin, made an awkward effort to mend matters by bringing up the Prince again, and with the action of a friendly and deprecating intercessor presenting the delinquent. This time, I am assured, the Queen, with determined and angry gestures, and some words spoken in a low tone, repelled intercessor and offender at once; and the Prince of Wales retired before the threatened storm. The Duke of Edinburgh, who had been lingering a little in the background—he, too, had just come from Paris, and he had been to Chantilly—anxious to see what kind of reception would be accorded to his brother, thought, apparently, that he had seen enough to warrant him in keeping himself at a modest distance on that occasion, and not encountering the terrors of what Thackeray, in "The Rose and the Ring," describes as "the royal eye."

I have little doubt that Queen Victoria is a somewhat rigorous and exacting mother, and I should be far from accepting her frown as decisive with regard to the delinquencies of one of her sons. Cigar-smoking alone would probably be accounted by the Queen a sin hardly allowing of pardon. Her husband, Prince Albert, was a man so pure of life, so free from nearly all the positive errors of manhood, so remarkably endowed with at least all the negative virtues, that his companionship might easily have spoiled her for the toleration of natures less calm and orderly. I suspect that the Queen is one of that class of thoroughly good women who, from mere lack of wide sympathies and genial toleration, are not qualified to deal to the best advantage with children who show a little inclination for irregularity and self-indulgence. Nor do I believe that the Prince of Wales is the wicked and brutal profligate that common libel makes him out. The shocking story which one sees so often alluded to in the London correspondence of certain American papers, and which attributes the long illness of the Princess of Wales to the misconduct of her husband, I believe to be utterly unfounded and unjustifiable. One of the London medical journals, the "Lancet" I think it was, had the courage to refer directly to this monstrous statement, and to give it an emphatic and authoritative refutation. If the worst things said of the Prince of Wales with any appearance of foundation were true, it is certain that he would still not be any worse than many other European princes and sovereigns. I have never heard anything said of the Prince of Wales half so bad as the stories which are believed everywhere in Paris of the enormous profligacies of Prince Napoleon; and it would be hardly possible for charity itself to doubt that up to a very recent period the private life of the Emperor of the French himself was stained with frequent and reckless dissipation. Those who were in Vienna anywhere about the autumn of 1866, will remember the stories which were told about the fatal results of the exalted military command given by the imperial will to certain favored generals, and the kind of influence by which those generals had acquired imperial favor. Common report certainly describes the Empress of Austria as being no happier in her domestic relations than the Princess of Wales. Everybody knows what Victor Emanuel's private character is, and what sort of hopeful youth is his eldest son, Umberto. Therefore, the Prince of Wales could doubtless plead that he is no worse than his neighbors; and even in his own family he might point to other members no better than himself. The Duke of Cambridge, for instance, has often been accused of profligacy and profligate favoritism. I wish I could venture to repeat here, for the sake of the genuine wit and keen satire of it, a certain epigram in Latin, composed by an English military officer, to describe the influence which brought about the sudden and remarkable promotion of another officer who was not believed to be personally quite deserving of the rank conferred on him by the Duke of Cambridge, commander-in-chief of the British army. But the position of the Prince of Wales is very different from that of the Duke of Cambridge, and he has to face a public opinion quite unlike that which surrounds Prince Napoleon or the Emperor of the French. People in France are not inclined to make any very serious complaint about the amours of a prince, or even of an emperor. I do not venture to say that there is much more of actual immorality in Paris than in London; but, assuredly, a man may, without harm to his public and political influence, acknowledge an amount of immorality in Paris which would be utterly fatal to his credit and reputation in London. Moreover, some of the illustrious profligates I have mentioned are distinguished by other qualities as well as profligacy; but I cannot say that I have ever heard any positively good quality, either of heart or intellect, ascribed to the Prince of Wales.

Unless his face, his head, his manners in public, and the tastes he so conspicuously manifests wholly belie him, the heir to the British throne is a remarkably dull young man. He cannot even deliver with any decent imitation of intelligence the little speeches which Arthur Helps or somebody else usually gets up for him when the exigencies of the situation compel the Prince to make a speech in public. He is reputed to be parsimonious even in his pleasures, and has managed to get himself deeply into debt without being supposed to have wasted any of his substance in obedience to a generous impulse. The Prince inherited a splendid property. His prudent father had looked well after the revenues of the duchy of Cornwall, which is the appanage of the Prince of Wales (even in some very dingy parts of London you may if you hire a house find that you have the Prince of Wales for a landlord), and the property of the heir must have been raised to its very highest value. Yet it is notorious that a very few years after he had attained his majority, Albert Edward had contrived to get deeply immersed in debt. There was for some time a scheme in contemplation to apply to Parliament for an addition to the huge allowance made to the Prince of Wales; and the "Times" and other newspapers were always urging the fact that the Queen left the Prince to perform nearly all her social duties for her, as a reason why the nation ought to award him an augmented income. It puzzles people in London, who read the papers and who study, as most Britons do, the occupations and pastimes of royalty, to know where the lavish and regal hospitalities take place which the Prince of Wales is supposed to dispense on behalf of his mother. However, the project for appealing to the generosity of Parliament seems to have been put aside or to have fallen through—I have read somewhere that the Queen herself has agreed to increase her son's allowance out of her own ample and well-hoarded purse—and the English public are not likely to be treated to any Parliamentary debate on the subject just yet. But this much is certain, that the same almost universal rumor which attributes coarse and dissipated habits to the Prince of Wales attributes to him likewise a mean and stingy parsimony where aught save his own pleasure is concerned; and even there, if by any possibility the pleasure can be obtained without superfluous cost.

This then is the character which the son of the Queen of England bears, in the estimation of the vast majority of his mother's subjects. Almost any and every one you meet in London will tell you, as something beyond doubt, that the Prince of Wales is dull, stingy, coarse, and profligate. As for the anecdotes which are told of his habits and tastes by the artists and officials of the theatres which he frequents, I might fairly leave them out of the question, because most of them that I have heard seem to me obvious improbabilities and exaggerations. They have nevertheless a certain value in helping us to a sort of historical estimate of the Prince's character. Half the stories told of the humors and debaucheries of Sheridan and Fox are doubtless inventions or exaggerations; but we are quite safe in assuming that the persons of whom such stories abound were not frugal, temperate, and orderly men. If the Prince of Wales is not a young man of dissipated habits, then a phenomenon is exhibited in his case which is, I fancy, without any parallel in history— the phenomenon of a whole watchful nation, studying the character and habits of one whose position compels him to live as in a house of glass, and coming, after years of observation, to a conclusion at once unanimous and erroneous. But were it proved beyond the remotest possibility of doubt that the Prince is personally chaste as a Joseph, temperate as Father Mathew, tender to his wife as the elder Hamlet, attached to his mother as Hamlet the younger, it would still remain a fact indisputable to all of us in London, who have eyes to see and ears to hear, that the Prince is addicted to vulgar amusements; that he patronizes indecent exhibitions; that he is given to the companionship of profligate men, and lends his helping hand to the success and the popularity of immoral and lascivious women.

What is to be the effect upon England of the reign of the Prince of Wales? Will England and her statesmen endure the rule of a profligate sovereign? No country can have undergone in equal time a greater revolution in public taste and sentiment at least, if not in morals, than England has since the time of George the Fourth. No genius, no eloquence, no political wisdom or merits could now induce the English people to put up with the open and undisguised excesses of a Fox; nor could any English statesman of the rank of Fox be found now who would condescend to pander to the vices of a George the Fourth. Thirty years of decorum in the Court, the Parliament, and the press have created a public feeling in England which will not long bear to be too openly offended by any one. But, although I may seem at first to be enunciating a paradox, I must say that all this is rather in favor of the chances of the Prince of Wales than against them. It will take so small a sacrifice on his part to satisfy everybody, that only the very extravagance of folly could lead him long astray on any unsatisfactory course, when once he has become directly responsible to the nation. We are not exacting in England as regards the private conduct of our great people. We only ask them to be publicly decorous. Everywhere in English society there is a quite unconscious, naive sort of Pharisaism, the unavowed but actual principle of which is that it matters very little if a man does the wrong thing, provided he publicly acts and says the right thing. I am perfectly satisfied that the great bulk of respectable and Philistine society in England would regard Robert Dale Owen, with his pure life and his views on the question of divorce, as a far more objectionable person than the veriest profligate who did evil stealthily, and professed to maintain the theory of a rigid marriage bond. The Prince of Wales will therefore need very little actual improvement in his way of life, in order to be all that his future subjects will expect, or care to ask. No one wants the Prince to be a man of ability; no one wishes him to be a good speaker. If Albert Edward were to rise in the House of Lords some night, and deliver a powerful and eloquent speech, as Prince Napoleon has often done in the French Senate, the English public would be not only surprised but shocked. Such a feat performed by a Prince would seem almost as much out of place, as if he were to follow the example of Caligula or Nero and exhibit himself in the arena as a gladiator. Of course the idea of the Prince of Wales fulminating against the policy of the Crown and the Government, after the fashion of Prince Napoleon, would be simply intolerable to the British mind of to-day—a thing so outrageous as indeed to be practically inconceivable. The Prince of Wales's part during the coming years, whether as first subject or as ruler, is as easy as could well be assigned to man. It is the very reverse of Bottom's; it is to avoid all roaring. He must be decorous, and we will put up with any degree of dulness; he must be decent, and we will all agree to know nothing of any private compensations wherewith he may repay himself for public propriety. All the influences of English statesmanship, rank, religion, journalism, patriotism, Philistinism, and flunkeyism, will instinctively combine to screen the throne against scandal, if only the throne will consent to allow of the possibility of such a protection. I have hardly ever known an Englishman whose hostility to monarchical institutions went so far that he would not be ready to say, "We have got a monarchy; let us try to make the best we can of it." Therefore the Prince of Wales must be the very Marplot or L'Etourdi of princes, if he cannot contrive to make himself endurable to a people who will bear so much rather than be at the trouble of a change. Of course it is possible that his faults may become grosser and more unmanageable with years (indeed, he is quite old enough already to have sown his wild oats long since); and it would be a hard trial upon decorous English statesmen and the English public to endure an openly profligate King. Yet even that nuisance I think would be endured for one lifetime at all events, rather than encounter the danger and trouble of any organic change.

So long as the Prince of Wales keeps out of politics, he may hold his place well enough; the England of to-day could far better endure even a George the Fourth than a George the Third. I have little doubt that the Prince of Wales, when he comes to be King, will be discreet in this matter at least. He has never indeed shown any particular interest in political affairs, so far as I have heard. He seems to care little or nothing about the contests of parties. Some three or four years ago, at the time of the celebrated Adullamite secession from the Liberal party, there was some grumbling among Radicals because it was reported that the Prince of Wales had expressed a wish to make the acquaintance of Robert Lowe, the brilliant, eccentric chief of the secession, and had had Lowe brought to him and spent a long time talking with him; and it was urged that this was done by the Prince to mark his approval of the Adullamites and his dislike of radicalism. But just about the very same time the Prince took some trouble to make the acquaintance of John Bright, and paid what might have been considered very flattering attentions to the great popular tribune. The Prince has more than once visited the Pope, and he has likewise more than once visited Garibaldi. Indeed, he seems to have a harmless liking for knowing personally all people who are talked about; and I fancy he hunted up the Pope, and Garibaldi, and John Bright, and Robert Lowe, just as he sends for Mr. Toole the comic actor, or Blondin, or Chang the giant. Nothing can be safer and better for the Prince in the future than to keep to this wholesome indifference to politics. In England we could stand any length of the reign of King Log. I shall not venture to conjecture what might happen if the Prince of Wales were to develop a perverse inclination to "meddle and muddle" in politics, because I think such a thing highly improbable. My impression is, on the whole, that things will go on under the reign of the next sovereign in England very much as they have been going on under the present; that the Prince of Wales will be induced to pay a little more attention to decorum and public propriety than he has hitherto done; and that the people of England will laugh at him and cheer for him, talk scandal about him and sing God save him, and finally endure him, on somewhat the same principle as that which induces the New York public to endure overcrowded street-cars and miserable postal arrangements—just because it is less trouble to each individual to put up with his share of a defective institution, than to go out of his way for the purpose of endeavoring to organize any combination to get rid of it.

THE KING OF PRUSSIA

Ronsard, in one of his songs addressed to his mistress, tells her that in her declining years she will be able to boast that "When I was young a poet sang of me." In a less romantic spirit the writer of this article may boast in old age, should he attain to such blest condition, that "When I was young a king spoke to me." That was the only king or sovereign of any kind with whom I ever exchanged a word, and therefore I may perhaps be allowed to be proud of the occasion and reluctant to let it sleep in oblivion. The king was William, King of Prussia, and the occasion of my being spoken to by a sovereign was when I, with some other journalists, was formally presented to King William after his coronation, and listened to a word or two of commonplace, good-humored courtesy.

The coronation of King William took place, as many readers of The Galaxy are probably aware, in the old historic town of Königsberg, on the extreme northeastern frontier of Prussia, a town standing on one of the inlets of the Baltic Sea, where once the Teutonic Knights, mentioned by Chaucer, were powerful. Carlyle's "Frederick the Great" had brought Königsberg prominently before the eyes and minds of English-speaking readers, just previously to the ceremony in which King William was the most conspicuous performer. It is the city where Immanuel Kant passed his long and fruitful life, and which he never quitted. It is a picturesque city in its way, although not to be compared with its neighbor Dantzic. It is a city of canals and streams, and many bridges, and quaint, narrow, crooked streets, wherein are frequent long-bearded and gabardined Jews, and where Hebrew inscriptions are seen over many shop-windows and on various door-plates. In its centre the city is domineered over by a Schloss, or castle-palace, and it was in the chapel of this palace that the ceremony of coronation took place, which provoked at the time so many sharp criticisms and so much of popular ridicule.

The first time I saw the King was when he rode in procession through the ancient city, some two or three days before the performance of the coronation. He seemed a fine, dignified, handsome, somewhat bluff old man—he was then sixty-four or sixty-five years of age—with gray hair and gray moustache, and an expression which, if it did not denote intellectual power, had much of cheerful strength and the charm of a certain kind of frank manhood about it. He rode well—riding is one of the accomplishments in which kings almost always excel—and his military costume became him. Certainly no one was just then disposed to be very enthusiastic about him, but every one was inclined to make the best of the sovereign and the situation; to forget the past and look hopefully into the future. The manner in which the coronation ceremony was conducted, and the speech which the King delivered soon after it, produced a terrible shock of disappointment; for in each the King manifested that he understood the crown to be a gift not from his people, but from heaven. To me the ceremonies in the chapel, splendid and picturesque as was the *mise en scène*, appeared absurd and even ridiculous. The King, bedizened in a regal costume which suggested Drury Lane or Niblo's Garden, lifting a crown from off the altar (was it, by the way, an altar?) and, without intervention of human aid other than his own hands, placing it upon his head, to signify that he had his crown from heaven, not from man; then putting another crown upon the head of his wife, to show that *she* derived her dignities from him; and then turning round and brandishing a gigantic sword, as symbolical of his readiness to defend his State and people—all this seemed to me too suggestive of the *opéra comique* to suit the simple dignity of the handsome old soldier. Far better and nobler did he look in his military uniform and with his spiked helmet, as he sat on his horse in the streets, than when, arrayed in crimson velvet cloak and other such stage paraphernalia of conventional royalty, he stood in the castle chapel, the central figure in a ceremonial of mediæval splendor and worse than mediæval tediousness.

But the King's face, bearing, and manner, as I saw him in Königsberg, and immediately afterwards in Berlin, agreeably disappointed me. It was one of the best faces to be seen among all the throng at banquet and ball and pageant during those days of gorgeous and heavy ceremonial. At the coronation performances there were two other personages who may be said to have divided public curiosity and interest with the King. One was the illustrious Meyerbeer, who composed and conducted the coronation ode, which thus became almost his swan-song, his latest notes before death. The other was a man whose name has lately again divided attention with that of the King of Prussia—Marshal MacMahon, Duke of Magenta. MacMahon was sent to represent the Emperor of the French at the coronation, and he was then almost fresh from the glory of his Lombardy battles. There was great curiosity among the Königsberg public to get a glimpse of this military hero; and although even Prussians could hardly be supposed to take delight in a fame acquired at the expense of other Germans, I remember being much struck by the quiet, candid good-humor with which people acknowledged that he had beaten their countrymen. There was, indeed, a little vexation and anger felt when some of the representatives of Posen, the Prussian Poland, cheered somewhat too significantly for MacMahon as he drove in his carriage from the palace. The Prussians generally felt annoyed that the Poles should have thus publicly and ostentatiously demonstrated their sympathy with France and their admiration of the French general who had defeated a German army. But except for this little ebullition of feeling, natural enough on both sides, MacMahon was a popular figure at the King's coronation; and before the ceremonies were over, the King himself had become anything but popular. The foreigners liked him for the most part because his manners were plain, frank, hearty, and agreeable, and to the foreigners it was a matter of little consequence what he said or did in the accepting of his crown. But the Germans winced under his blunt repudiation of the principle of popular sovereignty, and in the minds of some alarmists painful and odious memories began to revive and to transform themselves into terrible omens for the future.

For this pleasant, genial, gray-haired man, whose smile had so much of honest frankness and even a certain simple sweetness about it, had a grim and bloodstained history behind him. Not Napoleon the Third himself bore a more ominous record when he ascended the throne. The blood of the Berliners was purple on those hands which now gave so kindly and cheery a welcome to all comers. The revolutionists of Baden held in bitter hate the stern prince who was so unscrupulous in his mode of crushing out popular agitation. From Cologne to Königsberg, from Hamburg to Trieste, all Germans had for years had reason only too strong to regard William Prince of Prussia as the most resolute and relentless enemy of popular liberty. When the Pope was inspiring the hearts of freemen and patriots everywhere in Europe with sudden and splendid hopes doomed to speedy disappointment, the Prince of Prussia was execrated with the Hapsburgs, the Bourbons, and the Romanoffs. The one only thing commonly said in his favor was that he was honest and would keep his word. The late Earl of Clarendon, one of the most incautious and blundering of diplomatists (whom after his death the English newspapers have been eulogizing as a very sage and prince of statesmen), embodied this opinion sharply in a few words which he spoke to a friend of mine in Königsberg. Clarendon represented Queen Victoria at the coronation ceremonies, and my friend happened in conversation with him to be expressing a highly disparaging opinion of the King of Prussia. "There is just this to be said of him," the British Envoy remarked aloud in the centre of a somewhat miscellaneous group of listeners—"he is an honest man and a man of his word; he is not a Corsican conspirator."

Yes, this was and is the character of the King of Prussia. In good and evil he kept his word. You might trust him to do as he had said. During the greater part of his life the things he promised to do and did were not such as free men could approve. He set out in life with a genuine detestation of liberal principles and of anything that suggested popular revolution. William of Prussia is certainly not a man of intellect or broad intelligence or flexibility of mind. He would be in private life a respectable, steady, rather dull sort of man, honest as the sun, just as likely to go wrong as right in his opinions, perhaps indeed a shade more likely to go wrong than right, and sure to be doggedly obstinate in any opinion which he conceived to be founded on a principle. Horror of revolution was naturally his earliest public sentiment. He was one of the princes who entered Paris in 1815 with the allied sovereigns when they came to stamp out Bonapartism; and he seemed to have gone on to late manhood with the conviction that the mission of honest kings was to prevent popular agitation from threatening the divine right of the throne. Naturally enough, a man of such a character, whose chief merits were steadfastness and honesty, was much disgusted by the vacillation, the weakness, the half-unconscious deceitfulness of his brother, the late Frederick William. Poor Frederick William! well-meaning, ill-doing dreamer, "wind-changing" as Warwick, a sort of René of Anjou placed in a responsible position and cast into a stormy age. What blighted hopes and bloody streets were justly laid to his charge—to the charge of him who asked nothing better than to be able to oblige everybody and make all his people happy! Frederick William loved poetry and poets in a feeble, *dilettante* sort of way. He liked, one might say, to be thought to like the Muses and the Graces. He used to insist upon Tieck the poet reading aloud his new compositions to the royal circle of evenings; and when the bard began to read the King would immediately fall asleep, and nod until he nodded himself into wakefulness again; and then he would start up and say, "Bravo, Tieck! Delightful, Tieck! Go on reading, Tieck!" and then to sleep again. He liked in this sort of fashion the poetic and sentimental aspects of revolution, and he dandled popular movements on his royal knee until they became too demonstrative and frightened him, and then he shook them off and shrieked for the aid of his strong-nerved brother. One day Frederick William would be all for popular government and representative monarchy, and what not; the next day he became alarmed and receded, and was eager to crush the hopes he had himself awakened. He was always breaking his word to his people and his country, and yet he was not personally an untruthful man like English Charles the First. In private life he would have been amiable, respectable, gently æsthetical and sentimental; placed in a position of responsibility amid the seething passions and conflicting political currents of 1848, he proved himself a very

Modern Leaders Being A Series Of Biographical Sketches | 63

dastard and caitiff. Germany could hardly have had upon the throne of Prussia a worse man for such a crisis. He was unlucky in every way; for his vacillation drew on him the repute of hypocrisy, and his whimsical excitable manners procured for him the reproach of intemperance. A sincerely pious man in his way, he was almost universally set down as a hypocrite; a sober man who only drank wine medicinally on the order of his physicians, he was favored throughout Europe with the nickname of "King Clicquot." His utter imbecility before and after the massacre of those whom he called his "beloved Berliners," made him more detestable to Berlin than was his blunt and stern brother, the present King, who gave with his own lips the orders which opened fire on the population. A more unkingly figure than that of poor, weak, well-intentioned, sentimental, lachrymose Frederick William, never in our days at least has been seen under a royal canopy.

It was but natural that such a character or no-character as this should disgust his brother and successor, the present King. Frederick William, as everybody knows, had no son to succeed him. The stout-hearted William would have liked his brother and sovereign to be one thing or the other; a despot of course he would have preferred, but he desired consistency and steadfastness on whatever side. William, it must be owned, was for many years a downright stupid, despotic old feudalist. At one of his brother's councils he flung his sword upon the table and vowed that he would rather appeal to that weapon than consent to rule over a people who dared to claim the right of voting their own taxes. He appears to have had the sincere stupid faith that Heaven directly tells or teaches kings how to rule, and that a king fails in his religious duty who takes counsel of aught save his own convictions. Perhaps a good many people in lowlier life are like William of Prussia in this respect. He certainly was not the only person in our time who habitually accepted his own likings and dislikings as the appointed ordinances of Heaven. In my own circle of acquaintance I think I have known such individuals.

Thus William of Prussia strode through life sword in hand menacing and, where he could, suppressing popular movement. Yet he was saved from utter detestation by the admitted integrity of his character—a virtue so dear to Germans, that for its sake they will pardon harshness and sometimes even stupidity. People disliked or dreaded him, but they despised his brother. There was a certain simplicity, too, always seen in William's mode of living which pleased the country. There was no affectation about him; he was almost as much of a plain, unpretending soldier as General Grant himself. Since he became King, anybody passing along the famous Unter den Linden might see the white-haired, simple old man writing or reading at the window of his palace. He was in this respect a sort of military Louis

Philippe; a Louis Philippe with a strong purpose and without any craft. Therefore, when the death of his brother in 1861 called him to the throne, he found a people anxious to give him credit for every good quality and good purpose, willing to forget the past and look hopefully into the coming time. They only smiled at his renewal of the coronation ceremonies at Königsberg, believing that the old soldier thought there was something of a religious principle somehow mixed up in them, and that it was the imaginary piety, not the substantial pomp, which commended to his mind so gorgeous and costly an anachronism. After the coronation ceremonies, however, came back the old unpopularity. The King, people said, has learned nothing and forgotten nothing since he was Prince of Prussia. Every act he did after his accession to the crown seemed only more and more to confirm this impression. It was, I think, about this time that the celebrated "Diary" of Varnhagen von Ense was published by the niece of the deceased diplomatist; a diary full in itself of the most piquant interest, but made yet more piquant and interesting by the bitter and foolish persecution with which the King's officials endeavored to suppress the work and punish its publishers. I have not read or even seen the book for years, but the impression it made on me is almost as distinct just now as it was when I laid down the last of its many and vivacious volumes.

Varnhagen von Ense was a bitter creature, and the pen with which he wrote his diary seems to have been dipped in gall of special acridity. The diary goes over many years of Berlin court life, and the present King of Prussia is one of its central figures. The author does not seem to have had much respect for anybody; and King William was evidently an object of his particular detestation. All the doings of the days of 1848 are recorded or commented on, and the pages are interspersed with notices of the sharp ungenial things said by one royal personage of another. If the late Frederick William chose to say an ill-natured thing of Queen Victoria of England, down goes the remark in Varnhagen's pages, and it is chronicled for the perusal of all the world. We learn from the book that the present King of Prussia does not live on the most genial terms with his wife Augusta; that Augusta has rather a marked inclination towards Liberalism, and would find nothing more pleasant than a little coquetry with Revolution. Varnhagen intimates that the illustrious lady loved lions and novelties of any kind, and that at the time he writes she would have been particularly glad to make the acquaintance of Louis Blanc; and he more than hints at a decided inclination on her part to *porter le pantalon*—an inclination which her husband was not at all likely to gratify, consciously at least. Of the progressive wife Varnhagen speaks with no whit more respect than of the reactionary husband; and indeed he seems to look with irreverent and cynical eyes on everything royal that comes under his observation. Throughout the whole of the diary, the figure of the present King comes out consistently and distinctly. William is always the blunt, dull, wrong-headed, I might almost say pig-headed soldier-fanatic, who will do and suffer and make others do and suffer anything, in a cause which he believes to be right. With all Varnhagen von Ense's bitterness and scorn, he gives us no worse idea of King William than just this. But judging from the expression of the King's face, from his manner, and from what I have heard of him in Berlin and elsewhere, I should say there was a good deal of individual kindness and bonhomie in him for which the critic did not give him credit. I think he is, on the whole, better than Varnhagen von Ense chose to paint him or see him.

From Alexander Humboldt, as well as from Varnhagen von Ense, we learn a good deal of the inner life of kings and queens and princes in Berlin. There is something almost painful in reflecting on the kind of life which Humboldt must have led among these people, whom he so cordially despised, and whom in his private chroniclings he so held up to scorn. The great philosopher assuredly had a huge treasure of hatred locked up in his heart. He detested and scorned these royal personages, who so blandly patronized him, or were sometimes so rough in their condescending familiarity. Nothing takes the gilt off the life of courts so much as a perusal of what Humboldt has written about it. One hardly cares to think of so great, and on the whole so noble a man, living a life of what seems so like perpetual dissimulation; of his enduring these royal dullards and pert princesses, and doubtless seeming profoundly reverential, and then going home of nights to put down on paper his record of their vulgarity, and selfishness, and impertinence. Sometimes Humboldt was not able to contain himself within the limits of court politeness. The late King of Hanover (father of the now dethroned King George) was a rough brutal trooper, who had made himself odious in England as the Duke of Cumberland, and was accused by popular rumors of the darkest crimes—unjustly accused certainly, in the case where he was charged with the murder of his valet. The Duke did not make a very bad sort of King, as kings then went; but he retained all his roughness and coarseness of manner. He once accosted Humboldt in the palace of the late King of Prussia, and in his pleasant graceful way asked why it was that the Prussian court was always full of philosophers and loose women— describing the latter class of visitors by a very direct and expressive word. "Perhaps," replied Humboldt blandly, "the King invites the philosophers to meet me, and the other persons to please your Majesty!" Humboldt seems to have had little liking for any of the illustrious personages he met under the roof of the King of Prussia. A brief record he made of a conversation with the late Prince Albert (for whom he expressed a great contempt) went far when it was published to render the husband of Queen Victoria more unpopular and even detested in Ireland than another George the Fourth would have been. The Irish people will probably never forget that, according to the statement of Humboldt, the Prince spoke contemptuously of Irish national aspirations, declared he had no sympathy with the Irish, and that they were as restless, idle, and unmanageable as the Poles—a pretty speech, the philosopher remarks, to be made by the husband of the Queen of Great Britain and Ireland. Some attempt was made when this record of Humboldt's came to light to dispute the truth of it; but Humboldt was certainly not a liar—and anyhow the Irish people believed the story and it did no little mischief; and Humboldt in his grave might have had the consolation of knowing that he had injured one prince at least.

What we learn of the King of Prussia through Humboldt is to the same effect as the teaching of Varnhagen's cynical spirit; and I think, if these keen irreverent critics did not do him wrong, his Majesty must have softened and improved with the responsibilities of royalty. In many respects one might be inclined to compare him with the English George the Third. Both were indeed dull, decent, and fanatical. But there are some wide differences. George the Third was obstinate in the worst sense; his was the obstinacy of a stupid, self-conceited man who believes himself wise and right in everything. Now, I fancy the King of Prussia is only obstinate in what he conceives, rightly or wrongly, to be questions of duty and of principle; and that there are many subjects, political and otherwise, of which he does not believe himself to be the most competent judge, and which therefore he is quite willing to leave to the consideration and decision of others. For instance, it was made evident that in the beginning of the transactions which were followed by (although they cannot be said to have caused) the present war, the King more than once expressed himself willing to do certain things, of which, however, Count von Bismarck subsequently disapproved; and the King quietly gave way. "You know better than I do; act as you think best," is, I believe, a quite common sentence on the lips of King William, when he is talking with this or that trusted minister. Then again it has been placed beyond all doubt that George the Third could be, when he thought fit, the most unabashed and unscrupulous of liars; and not even hatred itself will charge King William with any act or word of falsehood or duplicity.

Steadily did the King grow more and more unpopular after his coronation. All the old work of prosecuting newspapers and snubbing, or if possible punishing, free-spoken politicians, came into play again. The King quarrelled fiercely with his Parliament about the scheme of army reorganization. I think he was right as to the scheme, although terribly wrong-headed and high-handed in his way of forcing it down the throats of the people, and, aided by his House of Peers, he waged a sort of war upon the nation's representatives. Then first came to the front that extraordinary political figure, which before very long had cast into the shade every other in Europe, even including that of the Emperor Napoleon; that marvellous compound of audacity and craft, candor and cunning, the profound sagacity of a Richelieu, the levity of a Palmerston; imperturbably good-humored, illimitably unscrupulous; a patriot without lofty emotion of any kind, a statesman who could sometimes condescend to be a juggler; part bully, part buffoon, but always a man of supreme courage, inexhaustible resources of brain and tongue—always in short a man of genius. I need hardly add that I am speaking of the Count von Bismarck.

At the time of the Schleswig-Holstein campaign, there was probably no public man in Europe so generally unpopular as the King of Prussia, except perhaps his Minister, the Count von Bismarck. In England it was something like an article of faith to believe that the King was a bloodthirsty old tyrant, his Prime Minister a combination of Strafford and Sejanus, and his subjects generally a set of beer-bemuddled and servile blockheads. The dislike felt toward the King was extended to the members of his family, and the popular conviction in England was that the Princess Victoria, wife of the King's son, had a dull coarse drunkard for a husband. It is perfectly wonderful how soon an absurdly erroneous idea, if there is anything about it which jumps with the popular humor, takes hold of the public mind of England. The English people regarded the Prussians with utter detestation and contempt. Not only that, but they regarded it as quite a possible and even likely thing that poor brave little Denmark, with a population hardly larger than that of the city of New York, could hold her own, alone, against the combined forces of Austria and Prussia. One might have thought that there never was a Frederick the Great or an Archduke Charles; that the only part ever played in history by Germans was that of impotent braggarts and stupid cowards. When there seemed some prospect of England's drawing the sword for Denmark, "Punch" published a cartoon which was very popular and successful. It represented an English sailor and soldier of the conventional dramatic style, looking with utter contempt at two awkward shambling boobies with long hair and huge meerschaums—one booby supposed to represent Prussia, the other Austria; and Jack Tar says to his friend the redcoat: "They can't expect us to *fight* fellows like those, but we'll kick them, of course, with pleasure." This so fairly represented the average public opinion of England that there was positively some surprise felt in London when it was found that the Prussians really could fight at all. Towards the Austrians there was nothing like the same ill-feeling; and when Bismarck's war against Austria (I cannot better describe it) broke out shortly after, the sympathy of England went almost unanimously with the enemy of Prussia. Ninety-nine men out of every hundred firmly believed that Austria would clutch Italy with one hand and Prussia with the other, and easily choke the life out of both. About the merits of the quarrel nobody in England outside the range of a very few politicians and journalists troubled himself at all. It was settled that Austria had somehow come to represent the cause of human freedom and progress; that the King of Prussia was a stupid and brutal old trooper, hurried to his ruin by the evil counsels of a drunken Mephistopheles; and that the Austrian forces would simply walk over the Prussians into Berlin. There was but one newspaper in London (and it has since died) which ventured to suggest, first, that perhaps the Prussians had the right side of the quarrel, and next, that perhaps they would have the better in the fight.

With the success of Prussia at Sadowa ended King William's personal unpopularity in Europe. Those who were prepared to take anything like a rational view of the situation began to see that there must be some manner of great cause behind such risks, sacrifices, and success. Those who disliked Prussia more than ever, as many in France did, were disposed to put the King out of their consideration altogether, and to turn their detestation wholly on the King's Minister. In fact, Bismarck so entirely eclipsed or occulted the King, that the latter may be said to have disappeared from the horizon of European politics. His good qualities or bad qualities no longer counted for aught in the estimation of foreigners. Bismarck was everything, the King was nothing. Now I wish the readers of The Galaxy not to take this view of the matter. In everything which has been done by Prussia since his accession to the throne, King William has counted for something. His stern uncompromising truthfulness, seen as clearly in the despatches he sent from recent battle-fields as in any other deeds of his life, has always counted for much. So too has his narrow-minded dread of anything which he believes to savor of the revolution. So has his thorough and devoted Germanism. I am convinced that it would have been far more easy of late to induce Bismarck to make compromises with seemingly powerful enemies at the expense of German soil, than it would have been to persuade Bismarck's master to consent to such proposals. The King's is far more of a typical German character (except for its lack of intellect) than that of Bismarck, in whom there is so much of French audacity as well as of French humor. On the other hand, I would ask my readers not to rush into wild admiration of the King of Prussia, or to suppose that liberty owes him personally any direct thanks. King William's subjects know too well that they have little to thank him for on that score. Strange as the comparison may seem at first, it is not less true that the enthusiasm now felt by Germans for the King is derived from just the same source as the early enthusiasm of Frenchmen for the first Napoleon. In each man his people see the champion who has repelled the aggression of the insolent foreigner, and has been strong enough to pursue the foreigner into his own home and there chastise him for his aggression. The blind stupidity of Austria and the crimes of Bonapartism have made King William a patriot King. When Thiers wittily and bitterly said that the Second Empire had made two great statesmen, Cavour and Bismarck, he might have said with still closer accuracy that it had made one great sovereign, William of Prussia. Never man attained such a position as that lately won by King William with less of original "outfit" to qualify him for the place. Five or six years ago the King of Prussia was as much disliked and distrusted by his own subjects as ever the Emperor of the French was by the followers of the Left. Look back to the famous days when "Bockum-Dolff's hat" seemed likely to become a symbol of civil revolution in Germany. Look back to the time when the King's own son and heir apparent, the warrior Crown Prince who since has flamed across so many a field of blood, felt called upon to make formal protest in a public speech against the illiberal, repressive, and despotic policy of his father! Think of these things, and say whether any change could be more surprising than that which has converted King William into the typical champion and patriot of Germany; and when you seek the explanation of the change, you will simply find that the worst enemies of Prussia have been unwittingly the kindest friends and the best patrons of Prussia's honest and despotic old sovereign.

I think the King of Prussia's subjects were not wrong when they disliked and dreaded him, and I also think they are now not wrong when they trust and applaud him. It has been his great good fortune to reign during a period when the foreign policy of the State was of infinitely greater importance than its domestic management. It became the business of the King of Prussia to help his country to assert and to maintain a national existence. Nothing better was needed in the sovereign for this purpose than the qualities of a military dictator, and the King, in this case, was saved all trouble of thinking and planning. He had but to accept and agree to a certain line of policy—a certain set of national principles—and to put his foot down on these and see that they were carried through. For this object the really manly and sturdy nature of the King proved admirably adapted. He upheld manfully and firmly the standard of the nation. His defective qualities were rendered inactive, and had indeed no occasion or chance to display themselves, while all that was good of him came into full activity and bold relief. But I do not believe that the character of the King in any wise changed. He was a dull, honest, fanatical martinet when he turned his cannon against German liberals in 1848; he was a dull, honest, fanatical martinet when he unfurled the flag of Prussia against the Austrians in 1866 and against the French in 1870. The brave old man is only happy when doing what he thinks right; but he wants alike the intellect and the susceptibilities which enable people to distinguish right from wrong, despotism from justice, necessary firmness from stolid obstinacy. But for the wars and the great national issues which rose to claim instant decision, King William would have gone on dissolving Parliaments and punishing newspapers, levying taxes without the consent of representatives, and making the police-officer the master of Berlin. The vigor which was so popular when employed in resisting the French, would assuredly otherwise have found occupation in repressing the Prussians. I see nothing to admire in King William but his courage and his honesty. People who know him personally speak delightedly of his sweet and genial manners in private life; and I have observed that, like many another old *moustache*, he has the art of making himself highly popular with the ladies. There is a celebrated little *prima donna* as well known in London as in Berlin, who can only speak of the bluff monarch as *der süsse König*—"the sweet King." Indeed, there are not wanting people who hint that Queen Augusta is not always quite pleased at the manner in which the venerable soldier makes himself agreeable to dames and demoiselles. Certainly the ladies seem to be generally very enthusiastic about his Majesty when they come into acquaintanceship with him, and to the *prima donna* I have mentioned his kindness and courtesy have been only such as are well worthy of a gentleman and of a king. Still we all know that it does not take a great effort on the part of a sovereign to make people, especially women, think him very delightful. I do not, therefore, make much account of King William's courtesy and *bonhomie* in estimating his character. For all the service he has done to Germany let him have full thanks; but I cannot bring myself to any warmth of personal admiration for him. It is indeed hard to look at him without feeling for the moment some sentiment of genuine respect. The fine head and face, with its noble outlines and its frank pleasant smile, the stately, dignified form, which some seventy-five years have neither bowed nor enfeebled, make the King look like some splendid old paladin of the court of Charlemagne. He is, indeed, despite his years, the finest physical specimen of a sovereign Europe just now can show. Compare him with the Emperor Napoleon, so many years his junior—compare his soldierly presence, his manly bearing, his clear frank eyes, his simple and sincere expression, with the prematurely wasted and crippled frame, the face blotched and haggard, the lack-lustre eyes which seem always striving to avoid direct encounter with any other glance, the shambling gait, the sinister look of the nephew of the great Bonaparte, and you will say that the Prussians have at least had from the beginning of their antagonism an immense advantage over their rivals in the figurehead which their State was enabled to exhibit. But I cannot make a hero out of stout King William, although he has bravery enough of the common, military kind, to suit any of the heroes of the "Nibelungen Lied." He never would, if he could, render any service to liberty; he cannot understand the elements and first principles of popular freedom; to him the people is always, as a child, to be kept in leading strings and guided, and, if at all boisterous or naughty, smartly birched and put in a dark corner. There is nothing cruel about King William; that is to say, he would not willingly hurt any human creature, and is, indeed, rather kind-hearted and humane than otherwise. He is as utterly incapable of the mean spites and shabby cruelties of the great Frederick, whose statue stands so near his palace, as he is incapable of the savage brutalities and indecencies of Frederick's father. He is, in fact, simply a dull old disciplinarian, saturated through and through with the traditions of the feudal party of Germany, his highest merit being the fact that he keeps his word—that he is "a still strong man" who "cannot lie;" his noblest fortune being the happy chance which called on him to lead his country's battles, instead of leaving him free to contend against, and perhaps for the time to crush, his country's aspirations after domestic freedom. Kind Heaven has allowed him to become the champion and the representative of German unity—that unity which is Germany's immediate and supreme need, calling for the postponement of every other claim and desire; and this part he has played like a man, a soldier, and a king. But one can hardly be expected to forget all the past, to forget what Humboldt and Varnhagen von Ense wrote, what Jacobi and Waldeck spoke, what King William did in 1848, and what he said in 1861; and unless we forget all this and a great deal more to the same effect, we can hardly help acknowledging that but for the fortunate conditions which allowed him to prove himself the best friend of German unity, he would probably have proved himself the worst enemy of German liberty.

VICTOR EMANUEL, KING OF ITALY

I have before me just now a little silver coin picked up in Savoy very soon after Italy had become a kingdom, and Savoy had ceased to be part of it. That was in truth the only thing that made the coin in any way specially interesting—the fact that it happened to be in chance circulation through Savoy when Savoy had no longer any claim to it. So, for that little scrap of melancholy interest I have since kept the coin in my purse, and it has made many journeys with me in Europe and America; and I suppose I can never be utterly destitute while it remains in my possession. Now, the head which is displayed upon that coin is not of kingly mould. The mint has flattered its royal master much less than is usual with such portrait painters. An English silver or gold coin of this year's mintage will still represent Her Majesty Queen Victoria as a beautiful young woman of twenty, with features worthy of a Greek statue and a bust shapely enough for Dryden's Iphigenia. But the coin of King Victor Emanuel has little flattery in it. There is the coarse, bulldog cast of face; there are the heavy eye-brows, the unshapely nose, the hideous moustache, the receding forehead, and all the other beauties and graces of the "bloat King's" countenance. Certainly the face on the coin is not bloated enough, and there is too little animalism displayed in the back of the head, to do justice to the first King of Italy. Moreover, the coin gives somehow the idea of a small man, and the King of Italy finds it not easy to get a horse strong enough to bear the load of Antony. But for a coin it is a wonderfully honest and truthful piece of work, quite a model to other mints, and it gave when it was issued as fair an idea as a little piece of silver could well give of the head and face of Europe's most ill-favored sovereign.

What a chance Victor Emanuel had of being a hero of romance! No king perhaps ever had such a chance before, and missed it so persistently. Europe seemed at one time determined, whether he would or no, to make a hero, a knight, a *preux chevalier*, out of the son of Charles Albert. Not Charles Edward, the brilliant, unfortunate Stuart himself, not Gustavus Adolphus even seemed to have been surrounded by such a romantic rainbow of romance and of hope. When, after the crowning disaster of Novara, Victor Emanuel's weak, vacillating, unlucky, and not very trustworthy father abdicated the crown of Sardinia in favor of his son, the latter seemed in the eyes of liberal Europe to represent not merely the hopes of all true Italians, but the best hopes of liberty and progress all over the world. There was even then a vague idea afloat through Europe—although Europe did not know how Cavour had already accepted the idea as a principle of action—that with her tremendous defeats Piedmont had won the right to hoist the standard of one Italy. This then was the cause which the young King was taken to represent. He had been baptized in blood to that cause. He represented Italy united and free—free from Austrian and Pope, from political and religious despotism. He was at all events no carpet knight. He had fought bravely on more than one fearful field of battle; he had looked on death closely and undismayed; he had been wounded in fighting for Italy against the Austrian. It was said of the young sovereign—who was only Duke of Savoy then—that on the night of Novara, when all was over save retreat and humiliation, he shook his dripping sword at the ranks of the conquering Austrians and exclaimed, "Italy shall make herself for all that!" Probably the story is substantially true, although Victor Emanuel may perhaps have used stronger expressions if he spoke at all; for no one ever doubted his courage and coolness in the hour of danger. But true or not, the anecdote exactly illustrated the light in which the world was prepared to regard the young sovereign of Sardinia—as the hope of Italy and of freedom, the representative of a defeat which he was determined and destined to convert into a victory.

Not many years after this, and while the lustre of his misfortunes and the brilliancy of his hopes still surrounded him, King Victor Emanuel visited England. He was welcomed everywhere with a cordiality of personal interest and admiration not often accorded by any people to a foreign king. Decidedly it was a hard thing to look at him and yet retain the thought of a hero of romance. He was not then nearly so bloated and burly as he is now; and he was at least some dozen or fourteen years younger. But even then how marvellously ill-favored he was; how rough and coarse-looking; how unattractive in manner; how brusque and uncouth in gesture and bearing; how liable to fits of an apparently stolid silence; how utterly devoid of grace and dignity! His huge straw-colored moustache, projecting about half a foot on each side of his face, was as unsightly a piece of manly decoration as ever royal countenance displayed. Yet the public tried to forget all those external defects and still regard him as a hero of romance somehow, anyhow. So fully was he believed to be a representative of civil and religious freedom in Italy, that one English religious society of some kind—I forget which it was— actually went the length of presenting an address to him, in which they flourished about the errors of Popery as freely as if they were appealing to an Oliver Cromwell or Frederick the Great. Cavour gave them very neatly and tersely the snub that their ignorance and presumption so well deserved; and their address did not obtain an honored place among Victor Emanuel's memorials of his visit to England.

He was very hospitably entertained by Queen Victoria, who is said to have suffered agonies of martyrdom from her guest's everlasting cigar—the good soul detests tobacco as much as King James himself did—and even more from his occasional outbursts of roystering compliment and canteen love-making toward the ladies of her staid and modest court. One of the household edicts, I think, of Queen Elizabeth's court was that no gallant must "toy with the maids, under pain of fourpence." Poor Victor Emanuel's slender purse would have had to bear a good many deductions of fourpence, people used to hint, if this penal decree had prevailed in his time at Windsor or Osborne. But Queen Victoria was very patient and friendly. Cavour has left some pleasant descriptions of her easy, unaffected friendliness toward himself. Guizot, it will be remembered, has described her as the stiffest of the stiff, freezing into petrifaction a whole silent circle by her invincible coldness and formality. I cannot pretend to reconcile the conflicting accounts of these two eminent visitors, but certainly Cavour has drawn some animated and very attractive pictures of Queen Victoria's almost girlish good-humor and winning familiarity. However that may be, the whole heart of free England warmed to Victor Emanuel, and was ready to dub him in advance the chosen knight of liberty, the St. George of Italy, before whose resistless sword every dragon of despotism and superstition was to grovel in the dust.

So the King went his way, and the next thing the world heard of him was that he was in league with Louis Napoleon against the Austrian, and that the child his daughter was to be married to the obese and elderly Prince Napoleon, whose eccentric genius, varied accomplishments, and thrilling eloquence were then unrecognized and unknown. Then came the triumphs of Magenta and Solferino, and it was made plain once more to the world that Victor Emanuel had the courage of a true soldier. He actually took a personal share of the fighting when the Italians were in action. He did not sit on his horse, far away from the bullets, like his imperial ally, and direct the movements of the army by muttering "C'est bien," when an aide-de-camp galloped up to announce to him as a piece of solemn farce that this or that general had already accomplished this or that operation. No; Victor Emanuel took his share of the fighting like a king. In the affair of San Martino he led an attack himself, and encouraged his soldiers by bellowing in stentorian voice quite a clever joke for a king, just as he was about to charge. A crack regiment of French Zouaves (the French Zouaves were soldiers in those days) was so delighted with the Sardinian King that it elected him a corporal of the regiment on the field of battle—a quite wonderful piece of compliment from a Zouave regiment to a foreign sovereign. Not so long before had Lamoricière declared that "Italians don't fight," and here was a crack Zouave regiment enthusiastic about the fighting capacity of an Italian King. The irony of fate, it will be remembered, decreed soon after that Lamoricière should himself lay down his arms before an Italian general and Italian soldiers.

Out of that war, then, Victor Emanuel emerged still a hero. But the world soon began to think that he was only a hero in the field. The sale of Savoy and Nice much shocked the public sentiment of Europe. The house of Savoy, as an English orator observed, had sprung from the womb of the mountains which the unworthy heir of Savoy sold to a stranger. As the world had given to Victor Emanuel the credit of virtues which he never possessed, it was now ready to lay on him all the burden of deeds which were not his. Whether the cession of Savoy was right or wrong, Victor Emanuel was not to blame, under the hard circumstances, for withdrawing, according to the first Napoleon's phrase, "*sous les draps d'un roi constitutionnel,*" and allowing his ministers to do the best they could. In fact, the thing was a necessity of the situation. Napoleon the Third had to make the demand to satisfy his own people, who never quite "seemed to see" the war for Italy. The Sardinian ministers had to yield to the demand to satisfy Napoleon the Third. Had Prussia been a raw, weak power in September, 1866, she must have ceded some territory to France. Sardinia or Italy was raw and weak in 1860, and had no choice but to submit. There were two things to be said for the bargain. First, Italy got good value for it. Next, the Savoyards and Nizzards never were good Italians. They rather piqued themselves on not being Italians. The Savoy delegates would not speak Italian in the old Turin Parliament. The ministers had to answer their French "interpellations" in French.

Still all this business did an immense harm to the reputation of King Victor Emanuel. He had acted like a quiet, sensible man—not in any way like a hero of romance, and Europe desired to see in him a hero of romance. Then he did not show himself, people said, very grateful to Garibaldi when the latter opened the way for the expulsion of the Bourbons from Naples, and did so much to crown Victor Emanuel King of Italy. Now I am a warm admirer of Garibaldi. I think his very weaknesses are noble and heroic. There is carefully preserved among the best household treasures of my family a vine leaf which Garibaldi once plucked and gave me as a *souvenir* for my wife. But I confess I should not like to be king of a new monarchy partly made by Garibaldi and with Garibaldi for a subject. The whole policy of Garibaldi proceeded on the gallant and generous assumption that Italy alone ought to be able to conquer all her enemies. We have since seen how little Italy availed against a mere fragment of the military power of Austria—that power which Prussia crushed like a nutshell. Events, I think, have vindicated the slower and less assuming policy of Victor Emanuel, or, I should say, the policy which Victor Emanuel consented to adopt at the bidding of Cavour.

But all the same the *prestige* of Victor Emanuel was gone. Then Europe began to look at the man coolly, and estimate him without glamour and without romance. Then it began to listen to the very many stories against him which his enemies could tell. Alas! these stories were not all untrue. Of course there were grotesque and hideous exaggerations. There are in Europe some three or four personages of the highest rank whom scandal delights to assail, and of whom it tells stories which common sense and common feeling alike compel us to reject. It would be wholly impossible even to hint at some of the charges which scandal in Europe persistently heaped on Victor Emanuel, the Emperor Napoleon III., Prince Napoleon, and the reigning King of the Netherlands. If one-half the stories told of these four men were true, then Europe would hold at present four personages of the highest rank who might have tutored Caligula in the arts of recondite debauchery, and have looked down on Alexander the Sixth as a prudish milksop. But I think no reasonable person will have much difficulty in sifting the probable truth out of the monstrous exaggerations. No one can doubt that Victor Emanuel is a man of gross habits and tastes, and is, or was, addicted to coarse and ignoble immoralities. "The manners of a mosstrooper and the morality of a he goat," was the description which my friend John Francis Maguire, the distinguished Roman Catholic member of the House of Commons, gave, in one of his Parliamentary speeches, of King Victor Emanuel. This was strong language, and it was the language of a prejudiced though honest political and religious partisan; but it was not, all things considered, a very bad description. Moreover, it was mildness, it was compliment—nay, it was base flattery—when compared with the hideous accusations publicly and distinctly made against Victor Emanuel by one of Garibaldi's sons, not to speak of other accusers, and privately whispered by slanderous gossip all over Europe. One peculiarity about Victor Emanuel worthy of notice is that he has no luxury in his tastes. He is, I believe, abstemious in eating and drinking, caring only for the homeliest fare. He has sat many times at the head of a grand state banquet, where the rarest viands, the most superb wines were abundant, and never removed the napkin from his plate, never tasted a morsel or emptied a glass. He had had his plain fare at an earlier hour, and cared nothing for the triumphs of cookery or the choicest products of the vine. He has thus sat, in good-humored silence, his hand leaning on the hilt of his sword, through a long, long banquet of seemingly endless courses, which to him was a pageant, a ceremonial duty, and nothing more. He delights in chamois-hunting—in hunting of almost any kind—in horses, in dogs, and in women of a certain coarse and gross description. There is nothing of the Richelieu or Lauzun, or even the Francis the First, about the dull, I had almost said harmless, immoralities of the King of Italy. Men in private and public station have done far greater harm, caused far more misery than ever he did, and yet escaped almost unwhipt of justice. The man has (or had, for people say he is reformed now) the coarse, easily-gratified tastes of a sailor turned ashore after a long cruise—and such tastes are not kingly; and that is about all that one feels fairly warranted in saying either to condemn or to palliate the vices of Victor Emanuel. He absolutely wants all element of greatness. He is not even a great soldier. He has boisterous animal courage, and finds the same excitement in leading a charge as in hunting the chamois. But he has nothing even of the very moderate degree of military capacity possessed by a dashing *sabreur* like Murat. It seems beyond doubt that it was the infatuation he displayed in attempting the personal direction of affairs which led to the breakdown at Custozza. The man is, in fact, like one of the rough jagers described in Schiller's "Wallenstein's Camp"—just this, and nothing more. When Garibaldi was in the zenith of his fortunes and fame in 1860, Victor Emanuel declared privately to a friend that the height of his ambition would be to follow the gallant guerilla leader as a mere soldier in the field. Certainly, when the two men entered Naples together, every one must have felt that their places ought to have been reversed. How like a king, an ideal king—a king of poetry and painting and romance—looked Garibaldi in the superb serenity of his untaught grace and sweetness and majesty. How rude, uncouth, clownish, even vulgar, looked the big, brawny, ungainly trooper whom people had to salute as King. When Garibaldi went to visit the hospitals where the wounded of the short struggle were lying, how womanlike he was in his sympathetic tenderness; how light and noiseless was his step; how gentle his every gesture; what a sweet word of genial compassion or encouragement he had for every sufferer. The burly King strode and clattered along like a dragoon swaggering through the crowd at a country fair. Not that Victor Emanuel wanted good nature, but that his rude *physique* had so little in it of the sympathetic or the tender.

Was there ever known such a whimsical, harmless, odd saturnalia as Naples presented during those extraordinary days? I am thinking now chiefly of the men who, mostly uncalled-for, "rallied round" the Revolution, and came from all manner of holes and corners to offer their services to Garibaldi, and to exhibit themselves in the capacity of freedom's friends, soldiers, and scholars. Hardly a hero, or crackbrain, or rantipole in Europe, one would think, but must have been then on exhibition somewhere in Naples. Father Gavazzi harangued from one position; Alexandre Dumas, accompanied by his faithful "Admiral Emile," directed affairs from another. Edwin James, then a British criminal lawyer and popular member of Parliament, was to be seen tearing round in a sort of semi-military costume, with pistols stuck in his belt. The worn, thoughtful, melancholy face of

Mazzini was, for a short time at least, to be seen in juxtaposition with the cockney visage of an ambitious and restless common councilman from the city of London, who has lived all his life since on the glorious memories and honors of that good time. The House of Lords, the House of Commons, and the Guildhall of London were lavishly represented there. Men like Türr, the dashing Hungarian and Mieroslawski, the "Red" leader of Polish revolution—men to whom battle and danger were as the breath of their nostrils—were buttonholed and advised by heavy British vestrymen and pert Parisian journalists. Hardly any man or woman entered Naples from a foreign country at that astonishing time who did not believe that he or she had some special counsel to give, which Victor Emanuel or Garibaldi or some one of their immediate staff was bound to listen to and accept. Woman's Rights were pretty well represented in that pellmell. There was a Countess something or other—French, they said—who wore short petticoats and trousers, had silver-mounted pistols in her belt and silver spurs on her heels, and was generally believed to have done wonders in "the field"— what field no one would stop to ask. There was Jessie Mario White, modest, pleasant, fair-haired woman, wife of a gallant gentleman and soldier— Jessie White, who made no exhibition of herself, but did then and since faithful and valuable work for Italian wounded, such as Italy ought not soon to forget. There was Mrs. Chambers—Mrs. Colonel Chambers—the Mrs. "Putney Giles" of Disraeli's "Lothair"—very prominent everywhere, sounding the special eulogies of Garibaldi with tireless tongue, and utterly overshadowing her quiet husband, who (the husband I mean) afterwards stood by Garibaldi's side at Aspromonte. Exeter Hall had sent out powerful delegations, in the firm faith apparently that Garibaldi would at their request order Naples forthwith to break up its shrines and images of saints and become Protestant; and that Naples would at once obey. Never was such a time of dreams and madness and fussiness, of splendid aspirations and silly self-seeking vanity, of chivalry and daring, and true wisdom and nonsense. It was a time naturally of many disappointments; and one disappointment to almost everybody was His Majesty King Victor Emanuel. His Majesty seemed at least not much to care about the whole affair from the beginning. He went through it as if he didn't quite understand what it was all about, and didn't think it worth the trouble of trying. People who saw him at that splendid moment when, the forces of Garibaldi joining with the regular Sardinian troops after all had been won, Garibaldi and the King met for the first time in that crisis, and the soldier hailed the sovereign as "King of Italy!"—people who saw and studied that picturesque historic meeting have told me that there was no more emotion of any kind on Victor Emanuel's face than if he were receiving a formal address from the mayor of a country town. "I thank you," were his only words of reply; and I am assured that it

Modern Leaders Being A Series Of Biographical Sketches | 79

was not "I thank *you*," with emphasis on the last word to indicate that the King acknowledged how much he owed to his great soldier; but simply "I thank you," as he might have thanked a groom who opened a stable door for him. Perhaps the very depth and grandeur of the King's emotions rendered him incapable of finding any expression for them. Let us hope so. But I have had the positive assurances of some who saw the scene, that if any such emotions were felt the royal countenance concealed them as completely as though they never had been.

In truth, I presume that the whole thing really was a terrible bore to the royal Rawdon Crawley, who found himself compelled by cursed spite to play the part of a patriot king. The Pope, the ultramontane bishops, and the ultramontane press have always been ringing fierce changes on the inordinate and wicked ambition of Victor Emanuel. I am convinced the poor man has no more ambition than his horse. If he could have chalked out his own career for himself, he would probably have asked nothing better than to be allowed to devote his life to chamois-hunting, with a hunter's homely fare, and the companionship of a few friends (some fat ladies among the number) with whom he could talk and make jokes in the *patois* of Piedmont. This, and perhaps a battle-field and a dashing charge every now and then, would probably have realized his dreams of the *summum bonum*. But some implacable destiny, embodied in the form of a Cavour or a Garibaldi, was always driving on the stout King and bidding him get up and attempt great things—be a patriot and a hero. Fancy Rawdon Crawley impelled, or rather compelled by the inexorable command of Becky his wife, to go forth in quest of the Holy Grail, and one may perhaps be able to guess what Victor Emanuel's perplexity and reluctance were when he was bidden to set out for the accomplishment of the regeneration of Italy. "Honor to those to whom honor is due; honor to old Mother Baubo," says some one in "Faust." Honor on that principle, then, to King Victor Emanuel. He did get up and go forth and undertake to bear his part in the adventure. And here seriously let me speak of the one high merit of Victor Emanuel's career. He is not a hero; he is not a statesman or even a politician; he is not a patriot in any grand, exalted sense. He would like to be idle, and perhaps to be despotic. But he has proved that he understands the true responsibilities and duties of a constitutional King better than many sovereigns of higher intellect and better character. He always did go, or at least endeavor to go, where the promptings of his ministers, the commands of his one imperious minister, or the voice of the country directed. There must be a great struggle in the mind of Victor Emanuel between his duty as a king and his duty as a Roman Catholic, when he enters into antagonism with the Pope. Beyond doubt Victor Emanuel is a superstitious Catholic. Of late years his constitution has once or twice threatened to give way, and he is probably all the more anxious to be reconciled with the Church. Perhaps he would be glad enough to lay down the load of royalty altogether and become again an accepted and devoted Catholic, and hunt his chamois with a quieted conscience. But still, impelled by what must be some sort of patriotism and sense of duty, he accepts his uncongenial part of constitutional King, and strives to do all that the voice of his people demands. It is probable that at no time was the King personally much attached to his illustrious minister Cavour. The genius and soul of Cavour were too oppressively imperial, high-reaching, and energetic for the homely, plodding King. With all his external levity Count Cavour was terribly in earnest, and he must often have seemed a dreadful bore to his sovereign. Cavour knew himself the master, and did not always take pains to conceal his knowledge. He would sometimes adopt the most direct and vigorous language in remonstrating with the King if the latter did not act on valuable advice at the right moment. Sometimes, when things went decidedly against Cavour's wishes, the minister would take the monarch to task more roundly than even the most good-natured monarchs are likely to approve. When Napoleon the Third disappointed Cavour and all Italy by the sudden peace of Villafranca, I have heard that Cavour literally denounced Victor Emanuel for consenting to the arrangement. Count Arrivabene, an able writer, has given a very vivid and interesting description of Cavour's demeanor when he reached the Sardinian headquarters on his way to an interview with the King and learned what had been done. He was literally in a "tearing rage." He tore off his hat and dashed it down, he clenched his hands, he stamped wildly, gesticulated furiously, became red and purple, foamed at the mouth, and grew inarticulate for very passion. He believed that he and Italy were sold—as indeed they were; and it was while this temper was yet on him that he went to see the King, and denounced him, as I have said. Now this sort of thing certainly could not have been agreeable to Victor Emanuel; and yet he patiently accepted Cavour as a kind of glorious necessity. He never sought, as many another king in such *duresse* would have done, to weaken his minister's influence and authority by showing open sullenness and dissatisfaction. Ratazzi, with his pliable ways and his entire freedom from any wearisome earnestness or devotion to any particular cause, was naturally a far more companionable and agreeable minister for the King than the untiring and imperious Cavour. Accordingly, it was well known that Ratazzi was more of a personal favorite; but the King never seems to have acted otherwise than loyally and honestly toward Cavour. Ricasoli was all but intolerable to the King. Ricasoli was proud and stern; and he was, moreover, a somewhat rigid moralist, which Cavour hardly professed to be. The King writhed under the government of Ricasoli, and yet, despite all that was at the time whispered, he cannot, I think, be fairly accused of having done anything personally to rid himself of an obnoxious minister. Indeed, the single merit of Victor Emanuel's character, if we put aside the element of personal courage, is its rough integrity. He is a *galantuomo*, an honest man—in that sense, a man of his word. He gave his word to constitutional government and to Italy, and he appears to have kept the word in each case according to his lights.

But his popularity among his subjects, the interest felt in him by the world, have long been steadily on the wane. Years and years ago he ceased to retain the faintest gleam of the halo of romance that once was, despite of himself, thrown around him. His people care little or nothing for him. Why, indeed, should they care anything? The military *prestige* which he had won, such as it was, vanished at Custozza, and it was his evil destiny, hardly his fault, to be almost always placed in a position of antagonism to the one only Italian who since Cavour's death had an enthusiastic following in Italy. Aspromonte was a calamity for Victor Emanuel. One can hardly blame him; one can hardly see how he could have done otherwise. The greatest citizen or soldier in America or England, if he attempted to levy an army of his own, and make war from American or English territory upon a neighboring State, would surely have seen his bands dispersed and found himself arrested by order of his government; and it would never have occurred to any one to think that the government was doing a harsh, ungrateful, or improper thing. It would be the necessary, rightful execution of a disagreeable duty, and that is all. But the conditions of Garibaldi's case, like the one splendid service he had rendered, were so entirely abnormal and without precedent, the whole thing was from first to last so much more a matter of national sentiment than of political law, that national sentiment insisted on judging Garibaldi and the King in this case too, and at least a powerful, passionate minority declared Victor Emanuel an ingrate and a traitor. Mentana was almost as bad for the King as Custozza. The voice of the country, so far as one could understand its import, seemed to declare that when the King had once ordered the Italian troops to cross the frontier, he should have ordered them to go on; that if they had actually occupied Rome, France would have recognized accomplished facts; that as it was, Italy offended France and the Pope by stepping over the barrier of the convention of September, only to humiliate herself by stepping back again without having accomplished anything. Certainly the policy of the Italian Government at such a crisis was weak, miserable, even contemptible. Then indeed Italy might well have exclaimed, "Oh for one hour of Cavour!" One hour of the man of genius and courage, who, if he had moved forward, would not have darted back again! Perhaps it was unfair to hold the King responsible for the mistakes of his ministers. But when a once popular King has to be pleaded for on that sole ground, it is pretty clear that there is an end to his popularity. So with Victor Emanuel. The world began to forget him; his subjects began to despise him. Even the thrilling events that have lately taken place in Italy, the sudden crowning of the national edifice—the realization of that hope which so long appeared but a dream—which Cavour himself declared would be the most slow and difficult to realize of all Italy's hopes—even the possession of Rome hardly seems to have brought back one ray of the old popularity on the heavy head of King Victor Emanuel. Again the wonderful combination of good luck and bad—the good fortune which brought to the very door of the house of Savoy the sudden realization of its highest dreams—the misfortune which allowed that house no share in the true credit of having accomplished its destiny. What had Victor Emanuel to do with the sudden juncture of events which enabled Italy to take possession of her capital? Nothing whatever. His people have no more reason to thank him for Rome than they have to thank him for the rain or the sunshine, the olive and the vine. The King seems to have felt all this. His short visit to Rome, and the formal act of taking possession, may perhaps have been made so short because Victor Emanuel knew that he had little right to claim any honors or expect any popular enthusiasm. He entered Rome one day and went away the next. I confess, however, that I should not wonder if the visit was made so short merely because the whole thing was a bore to the honest King, and he could only make up his mind to endure a very few hours of it.

Victor Emanuel, King of United Italy, and welcomed by popular acclamation in Rome—his second son almost at the same moment proclaimed King of the Spaniards—his second daughter Queen of Portugal. How fortune seems to have delighted in honoring this house of Savoy. I only say "seems to have." I do not venture yet to regard the accession of King Amadeus to the crown of Spain as necessarily an honorable or a fortunate thing. Every one must wish the poor young prince well in such a situation; perhaps we should rather wish him well out of it. Never king assumed a crown with such ghastly omens to welcome him. Here is the King putting on his diadem; and yonder, lying dead by the hand of an assassin, is the man who gave him the diadem and made him King! But for Juan Prim there would be no Amadeus, King of the Spaniards; and for that reason Juan Prim lies dead. The young King must have needed all his hereditary courage to enable him to face calmly and bravely, as he seems to have done, so terrible a situation. Macaulay justly says that no danger is so trying to the nerves of a brave man as the danger of assassination. Men utterly reckless in battle—like "bonny Dundee" for example—have owned that the knowledge of the assassin's purpose and haunting presence was more than they could endure. The young Italian prince seems to have shown no sign of flinching. So far as anything indeed is known of him, he is favorably known to the world. He bore himself like a brave soldier at Custozza, and obtained the special commendation of the Austrian victor, the gallant old Archduke Albrecht. He married for love a lady of station decidedly inferior to that of a royal prince; the lady had the honor of being sneered at even in her honeymoon for the modest, inexpensive simplicity of her toilet, as she appeared with her young husband at one of the watering-places; he had not made himself before marriage the subject of as much scandal as used to follow and float around the bachelor reputation of his elder brother Humbert. He is believed to be honestly and manfully liberal in his views. He ought to make a good King as kings go—if the murderers of General Prim only give him the chance.

As I have mentioned the name of the man whose varied, brilliant, daring, and turbulent career has been so suddenly cut short, I may perhaps be excused for wandering a little out of the path of my subject to say that I think many of the American newspapers have hardly done justice to Prim. Some of them have written of him, even in announcing his death, as if it were not possible for a man to be honest and yet not to be a republican. In more than one instance the murder of Prim was treated as a sort of thing which, however painful to read of, was yet quite natural and even excusable in the case of a man who endeavored to give his country a King. There was a good deal too much of the "Sic semper tyrannis" tone and temper about some of the journals. Now, I do not believe that Prim was a patriot of that unselfish and lofty group to which William the Silent, and George Washington, and Daniel Manin belong. His was a very mixed character, and ambition had a large place in it. But I believe that he sincerely loved and tried to serve Spain; and I believe that in giving her a King he honestly thought he was doing for her the thing most suited to her tendencies and her interests. If Prim could have made Spain a republic, he could have made himself her President, even perhaps for life; while he could not venture, she being a kingdom, to constitute himself her King. Many times did Prim himself say to me, before the outbreak of his successful revolt, that he believed the republican to be the ultimate form of government everywhere, and that he would gladly see it in Spain; but that he did not believe Spain was yet suited for it, or numbered republicans enough. "To have a republic you must first have republicans," was a common saying of his. New England is a very different sort of place from Old Castile. At all events, Prim is not to be condemned as a traitor to his country and to liberty, even if it were true that he could have created a Spanish republic. We have to show first that he knew the thing was possible and refused to do it, for selfish or ignoble motives. This I am satisfied is not true. I think Prim believed a republic impossible in the Spain of to-day, and simply acted in accordance with his convictions. He came very near to being a great man; he wanted not much of being a great patriot. He was, I think, better than his fame. As Spain has decreed, he "deserved well of his country." It seems hardly reasonable or just to decry him or condemn him because he did not deserve better. Such as he was, he proved himself original. "He walked," as Carlyle says, "his own wild road, whither that led him." In an age very prolific of great political men, he made a distinct name and place for himself. "Name thou the best of German singers," exclaims Heine with pardonable pride, "and my name must be spoken among them." Name the half-dozen really great, originating characters in European politics during our time, and the name of Prim must come in among them.

But I was speaking of Victor Emanuel and his children. All I have heard then of the Duke of Aosta leads me to believe that he is qualified to make a respectable and loyal constitutional sovereign. High intellectual capacity no one expects from the house of Savoy, but there will probably be good sense, manly feeling, and no small share of political discretion. In the Duke of Aosta, too, Spain will have a King who can have no possible sympathy with slave systems and their products of whatever kind, and who can hardly have much inclination for the coercing and dragooning of reluctant populations. If Spain in his day and through his influence can get decently and honorably rid of Cuba, she will have entered upon a new chapter of her national existence, as important for her as that grand new volume which opens upon France when defeat has purged her of her thrice-accursed "militaryism." The dependencies have been a miserable misfortune to Spain. They have entangled her in all manner of complications; they have filled her with false principles; they have created whole corrupt classes among her soldiers and politicians. General Prim himself once assured me that the real revenues of Spain were in no wise the richer for her colonial possessions. Proconsuls made fortunes and spread corruption round them, and that was all. If her new King could only contrive to relieve Spain of this source of corruption and danger, he would be worth all the cost and labor of the revolution which gives him now a Spanish throne.

Why did fate decree that the very best of all the children of Victor Emanuel should have apparently the worst fortune? The Princess Clotilde is an exile from the country and the palace of her husband; and if the sweetness and virtue of one woman might have saved a court, the court of the Tuileries might have been saved by Victor Emanuel's eldest daughter. I have heard the Princess Clotilde talked of by Ultramontanes, Legitimists, Orleanists, Republicans, Red Republicans (by some among the latter who firmly believed that the poor Empress Eugénie was wickeder than Messalina), and

I never heard a word spoken of her that was not in her praise. Every one admitted that she was a pure and noble woman, a patient wife, a devoted mother; full of that unpretending simplicity which, let us own it frankly, is one of the graces which very high birth and old blood do sometimes bring. The Princess must in her secret soul have looked down on some of the odd *coteries* who were brought around her at the court of the Tuileries. She comes of a house in whose genealogy, to quote Disraeli's humorous words, "Chaos was a novel," and she found herself forced into companionship with ladies and gentlemen whose fathers and mothers, good lack! sometimes seemed to have omitted any baptismal registration whatever. I presume she was not ignorant of the parentage of De Morny, or Walewski, or Walewski's son, or the Jerome David class of people. I presume she heard what every one said of the Countess this and the Marchioness that, and so on. Of course the Princess Clotilde did not like these people—how could any decent woman like them?—but she accepted the necessities of her position with a self-possession and dignity which, offending no one, marked the line distinctly and honorably between her and them. Her joy was in her children. She loved to show them to friends, and to visitors even whom she felt that she could treat as friends. Perhaps she is not less happy now that the ill-omened, fateful splendors of the Palais Royal no longer help to make a gilded cage for the darlings of her nursery. Of the whole family, hers may be called the only career which has been doomed to what the world describes and pities as failure. It may well be that she is now happiest of all the children of the house of Savoy.

Meanwhile, Victor Emanuel has been welcomed at the Quirinal, and is indeed, at last, King of Italy. We may well say to him, as Banquo says of Macbeth, "Thou hast it all!" Lombardy, Tuscany, Parma, Modena, the Two Sicilies, Venetia, and Rome—what gathering within less than a fifth of an ordinary lifetime! And on the Quirinal Victor Emanuel may be said to have stood alone. Of all the men who mainly wrought to bring about that grand consummation, not one stood by his side. Daniel Manin, the pure, patient, fearless, patriot hero; Cavour, the consummate statesman; Massimo d'Azeglio, the Bayard or Lafayette of Italy's later days, the soldier, scholar, and lover of his country—these are dead, and rest with Dante. Mazzini is still a sort of exile—homeless, unshaken, seeing his prophecies fulfil themselves and his ideas come to light, while he abides in the gloom and shadow, and the world calls him a dreamer. Garibaldi is lending the aid of his restless sword to a cause which he cannot serve, and a people who never understood him; and he is getting sadly mixed up somehow in ordinary minds with General Cluseret and George Francis Train. Louis Napoleon, who, whatever his crimes, did something for the unity of Italy, is a broken man in captivity. Only Victor Emanuel, least gifted of all, utterly unworthy almost to be named in the same breath with any of them (save Louis Napoleon alone)—only he comes forward to receive the glories and stand up as the representative of one Italy! Let us do him the justice to acknowledge that he never sought the position or the glory. He accepted both as a necessity of his birth and his place, a formal duty and a bore. His was not the character which goes in quest of greatness. As Falstaff says of rebellion and the revolted English lord, greatness "lay in his way, and he found it."

LOUIS ADOLPHE THIERS

Guizot quietly at work in the preparation of a history of France for the instruction of children—Thiers taking his place in a balloon to fly from one seat of government in France to another! Such were the occupations, at a given time in last November, of the two distinguished men whose rivalries and contentions disturbed the politics of France for so many years.

An ill-natured person might feel inclined to say that the adventures in the balloon were a proper crowning of the edifice of M. Thiers's fitful career. Was not his whole political life (*non meus hic sermo*, please to understand—it is the ill-natured person who says this) an enterprise in a balloon, high out of all the regions where common sense, consistency, and statesmanship are ruling elements? Did he not overleap with aëronautic flight when it so suited him, from liberalism to conservatism, from advocating freedom of thought to enforcing the harshest repression? Was not his literary reputation floated into high air by that most inflated and gaseous of all balloons, the "History of the Consulate and the Empire"? Thiers in a balloon is just where he ought to be, and where he ever has been. Condense into one meagre little person all the egotism, all the self-conceit, all the vainglory, all the incapacity for looking at anything whatever from the right point of view, which belong to the typical Frenchman of fiction and satire, and you have a pretty portrait of M. Thiers.

Doubtless, the ill-natured person who should say all this would be able to urge a good many plausible reasons in justification of his assertions. Still, one may be allowed to admire—one cannot help admiring—the astonishing energy and buoyancy which made M. Thiers, despite his seventy-three years, the most active emissary of the French Republic during the past autumn, the aëronautic rival of the vigorous young Corsican Gambetta, who was probably hardly grown enough for a merry-go-round in the Champs Elysées when Thiers was beginning to be regarded as an old fogy by the ardent revolutionists of 1848. About the middle of last September, a few days after the sudden creation of the French Republic, M. Thiers precipitated himself on London. An account in the newspapers described him as "accompanied by five ladies." Thus gracefully escorted, he marched on the English capital. He had interviews with Mr. Gladstone, Lord Granville, the

French Ambassador, and divers other great personages. He was always rushing from diplomatic office to office. He "interviewed" everybody in London who could by any possibility be supposed capable of influencing in the slightest degree the fortunes of France. He never for a moment stopped talking. Great men excel each other in various qualities; but there never was a great man who could talk against M. Thiers. He could have shut up the late Lord Macaulay in no time; and I doubt whether Mr. Seward could have contrived to edge in a word while Thiers was in the same room. M. Thiers stayed in London little more than two days. He arrived, I think, on a Wednesday night, and left on the following Saturday. During that time he managed to do all the interviewing, and was likewise able to take his family to see the paintings in the National Gallery, where he was to be observed keenly eyeing the pictures, and eloquently laying down critical law and gospel on their merits, as if he had come over on a little autumnal holiday from a settled and peaceful country, which no longer needed looking after. Then he started from London in a steam-yacht, cruised about the North Sea and the Baltic, dropped in upon the King of Denmark, sounded the views of Sweden, collected the general opinion of Finland, visited the Emperor of Russia and talked him into semi-bewilderment, and then travelled down by land to Vienna, where he used all his powers of persuasion on the Emperor Francis Joseph, and to Florence, where by the sheer force of argument and fluency he drove Victor Emanuel nearly out of his senses. Since that time, he all but concluded an armistice with Bismarck, and when last I heard of him (previous to this writing) he was, as I have said, going on a mission somewhere in a balloon.

During his recent diplomatic flights, M. Thiers constantly offered to encounter much greater fatigues and responsibilities if needful. He was ready to go anywhere and talk to anybody. He would have hunted up the Emperor of China or the Mikado of Japan, if either sovereign seemed in the remotest degree likely to intervene on the side of France. I believe I can say with confidence, that at the outset of his expedition he had no official authority or mission whatever from the Provisional Government. He told Jules Favre and the rest that he was about to start on a tour of inspection round the European cabinets, and that they had better let him try what he could do; and they did not refuse to let him try, and it would not have mattered in the least whether they refused or not. He came, in the first instance, altogether "on his own hook." Perhaps, at first, the Republican Government was not very anxious to accept the services of M. Thiers as a messenger of peace. No living Frenchman had done half so much to bring about the state of national feeling which enabled Louis Napoleon to precipitate the nation into a war against Prussia. Perhaps they thought the man whose bitterest complaint against the Emperor was that he failed to take advantage of the chance of crushing Prussia in 1866, was not the most likely emissary to conciliate victorious Prussia in 1870. But Thiers was determined to make himself useful, and the Republican Government had to give in at last, and concede some sort of official authority to him. Like the young lady who said she married the importunate suitor to get rid of him, Jules Favre and his colleagues probably accepted M. Thiers for their spokesman as the only way of escaping from his eloquence. His mission was heroic and patriotic, or egotistical and fussy, just as you are pleased to regard it. In certain lights Cardinal Richelieu looks wonderfully like Bottom the weaver. But it is impossible not to admire the energy and courage of the irrepressible, inexhaustible, fragile-looking, shabby old Orleanist. Thiers does not seem a personage capable of enduring fatigue. He appears a sapless, withered, wasted old creature. But the restless, fiery, exuberant, egotistical energy which carried him along so far and so fast in life, has apparently gained rather than lost in strength and resource during the forty years which have elapsed since the subject of this sketch, then editor of the "National," drew up in Paris the famous protest against the five infamous *ordonnances* of Charles the Tenth, and thus sounded the prelude to the Revolution of July.

It must have been no common stock of self-possession and self-complacency which enabled M. Thiers to present himself before the great Prussian Chancellor as a messenger of peace. Bismarck, who has a happy knack of apt Shakespearian quotation, might have accosted him in the words of Beatrice and said, "This is a man's office, but not yours." For M. Thiers, throughout his whole career, devoted his brilliant gifts to the promotion of that spirit of narrow national vainglory which of late years has made France dreaded and detested in Germany. M. Thiers is like Æsop's trumpeter— guilty not of making war himself, but of blowing the blasts which set other men fighting. The very speech in which he protested last summer against the war initiated by the Imperial Government, was inspired by a principle more immoral, and more calculated to inflame Germany with resentment, than the very declaration of war itself. For Thiers only condemned the war on the ground that France was not properly prepared to crush Germany; that she had lost her opportunity by not falling on Prussia while the latter was in the death-grapple with Austria in 1866; and that as France had not done the thing at the right time, she had better not run the risk of doing it incompletely, by making the effort at an inopportune moment.

These considerations, however, did not trouble M. Thiers. He advanced to meet Count von Bismarck with the easy confidence of one who feels that he has a right to be treated as the best of friends and most appropriate of envoys. If, immediately after the conclusion of the American war, John Bright had been sent to Washington by England to endeavor to settle the Alabama dispute, he probably would not have approached the President with anything like the confident assurance of a genial welcome which inspired M. Thiers when he offered himself as a messenger to the Prussian statesman. This very sublimity of egotism is, and always was, one of the sources of the success of M. Thiers. No man could with more perfect composure and self-satisfaction dare to be inconsistent. His was the very audacity and Quixotism of inconsistency. In office to-day, he could advocate and enforce the very measures of repression which yesterday, out of office, he was the foremost to denounce—nay, which he obtained office by opposing and denouncing. He whose energetic action in protesting against the celebrated five *ordonnances* of Charles the Tenth did so much to bring about the Revolution of July, was himself the chief official author of the equally celebrated "laws of September," introduced in Louis Philippe's reign, which might have suited the administration of a Peter the Great, or any other uncompromising despot. In practical politics, of course, almost every minister is occasionally compelled by the force of circumstances to do things which bear a considerable resemblance to acts warmly condemned by him while he sat in opposition. But M. Thiers invariably, when in power, exhibited himself as the author and champion of principles and policy which he had denounced with all the force of his eloquent tongue when he was the opponent of the Government. He seemed in fact to be two men rather than one, so entirely did Thiers in office contrast with Thiers in opposition. But Thiers himself never appeared conscious of inconsistency. Indeed, he was always consistent with his one grand essential principle and creed—faith in the inspiration and the destiny of M. Thiers.

To one other principle too let it be said in justice that this brilliant politician has always been faithful—the principle which maintains the right of France to throw her sword into the scale where every or any foreign question is to be weighed. When, after a long absence from the parliamentary arena, he entered the Imperial Corps Législatif as one of the deputies for Paris, he soon proved himself to be "old Cassius still." Age, study, experience, retirement, reflection, had in no wise dimmed the fire of his ardent nationalism. Eagerly as ever he contended for the sacred right of France to dragoon all Europe into obedience, to chop up the Continent into such symmetrical sections as might seem suitable to the taste and the convenience of French statesmen. Undoubtedly he was a sharp, tormenting thorn in the side of the Imperial Government when he returned to active political life. Louis Napoleon had no minister who could pretend to compare with Thiers in debate. He was an aggravating and exasperating enemy, against whom fluent and shallow men like Billault and Baroche, or even speakers of heavier calibre like Rouher, had no chance whatever. But there were times when to any impartial mind the invectives of Thiers made the Imperial policy look noble and enlightened in comparison with the canons of detestable egotism which he propounded as the true principles of government. I remember thinking more than once that if Louis Napoleon's Ministers could only have risen to the real height of the situation and appealed to whatever there was of lofty unselfish feeling in France, they might have overwhelmed their remorseless and envenomed critic. In 1866 and 1867, for example, Thiers made it a cardinal point of complaint and invective against the French Government that it had not prevented by force of arms the progress of Germany's unity. Nothing could be more pungent, brilliant, bitter, than the eloquence with which he proclaimed and advocated his doctrines of ignoble and unscrupulous selfishness. Why did not the Imperial spokesmen assume a virtue if they had it not, and boldly declare that the Government of France scorned the shallow and envious policy which sees calamity and danger in the union and growing strength of a neighboring people? Such a chord bravely struck would have awakened an echo in every true and generous heart. But the Imperial Ministers feebly tried to fight M. Thiers upon his own ground, to accept his principles as the conditions of contest. They endeavored in a paltering and limping way to show that the French Government had been selfish and only selfish, and had taken every care to keep Germany properly weak and divided. It was during one of these debates, thus provoked by M. Thiers, that occasion was given to Count von Bismarck for one of his most striking *coups de théâtre*. The French Minister (if I remember rightly, it was M. Rouher), tortured and baited by M. Thiers, stood at bay at last, and boldly declared that the Government of France had taken measures to render impossible any political cohesion of North and South Germany. A day or two after, Count von Bismarck effectively and contemptuously replied to this declaration by unfolding in the Prussian Chamber the treaties of alliance already concluded between his Government and the South German States.

It has always been a matter of surprise to me that Thiers did not prove a success at the bar, to which at first he applied his abilities. He seems to have the very gifts which would naturally have made a great pleader. All through his political career he displayed a wonderful capacity for making the worse appear the better cause. The adroitness which contends skilfully that black is white to-day, having argued with equal force and fluency that white was green yesterday, would have been highly appropriate and respectable in a legal advocate. But M. Thiers did not somehow get on at the bar, and having no influential friends (he was, I think, the son of a locksmith), but plenty of ambition, courage, and confidence, he strove to enter political life by the avenue of journalism. Much of Thiers's subsequent success as a debater was probably due to that skill which a practised journalist naturally acquires—the dexterity of arraying facts and arguments so as not to bear too long on any one part of the subject, and not to offer to the mind of the reader more than his patience and interest are willing to accept. Most of the events of his political career, up to his reappearance in public life in 1863, belong wholly to history and the past. His long rivalry with Guizot, his intrigues out of office, and his conduct as a Minister of Louis Philippe, have hardly a more direct and vital connection with the affairs of to-day than the statecraft of Mazarin or the political vicissitudes of Bolingbroke. One indeed of the projects of M. Thiers has now come rather unexpectedly into active operation. The fortifications of Paris were the offspring of the apprehension M. Thiers entertained, thirty years ago, that the Eastern question of that day might provoke another great European war. Since that time many critics sneered and laughed a good deal at M. Thiers's system of fortifications; but the whirligig of time has brought the statesman his revenge. No one could mistake the meaning of the smile of self-satisfaction which used last autumn to light up the unattractive features of the veteran Orleanist, as he made tour after tour of inspection around the defences of Paris. This chain of fortifications alone, one might almost say, connects the Thiers of the present generation with the Thiers of the past. There were malignant persons who did not scruple to say that the author of the scheme of defences was not altogether sorry for the national calamity which had brought them into use, and apparently justified their construction. It is very hard to be altogether sorry for even a domestic misfortune which gives one who is especially proud of his foresight and sagacity an opportunity of pointing out that the precautions which he recommended, and other members of the family scorned, are now eagerly adopted by unanimous concurrence. There certainly was something of the pardonable pride of the author of a long misprized invention visible in the face of M. Thiers as he used to gaze upon his beloved system of fortifications any time in last September. Little did even he himself think when, after Sadowa, he accused the Emperor's Government of having left itself no blunder more to commit, that it had yet to perpetrate one crowning and gigantic mistake, and that one effect at least of this stupendous error would be to compel Paris to treat *au sérieux*, and as a supreme necessity, that system of defences so long regarded as good for little else than to remind the present generation that Louis Adolphe Thiers was once Prime Minister of France.

Thiers was not far short of seventy years old when, in 1863, he entered upon a new chapter of his public life as one of the deputies for Paris in the Imperial Corps Législatif. A new generation had meantime arisen. Men were growing into fame as orators and politicians who were boys when Thiers was last heard as a parliamentary debater. He returned to political life at an eventful time and accompanied by some notable compeers. The elections which sent Thiers to represent the department of the Seine made the venerable and illustrious Berryer one of the delegates from Marseilles. I doubt whether the political life of any country has ever produced a purer, grander figure than that of Berryer; I am sure that an obsolete and hopeless cause never had a nobler advocate. The genius and the virtues of Berryer are indeed the loftiest claims modern French legitimacy can offer to the respect of posterity. I look back with a feeling of something like veneration to that grand and kingly form, to the sweet, serene, unaffected dignity of that august nature. Berryer belonged to a totally different political order from that of Thiers. As John Bright is to Disraeli, as John Henry Newman is to Monsignore Capel, as Montalembert was to Louis Veuillot, as Charles Sumner is to Seward, so was Berryer to Thiers. Of the oratorical merits of the two men I shall speak hereafter; now I refer to the relative value of their political characters. With Thiers and Berryer there came back to political life some men of mark and worth. Garnier-Pagès was one, the impulsive, true-hearted, not very strong-headed Republican; a man who might be a great leader if fine phrases and good intentions could rule the world. Carnot was another, not much perhaps in himself, but great as the son of the illustrious organizer of victory (oh, if France had lately had one hour of Carnot!), and personally very popular just then because of his scornful rejection of Louis Napoleon's offer to bring back the ashes of his father from Magdeburg in Prussia to France. Eugène Pelletan, who had been suffering savage persecution because of his fierce attack on the Empire in his book, "The New Babylon"; Jules Simon, a superior sort of French Tom Hughes—Tom Hughes with republican convictions and strong backbone—and several other men of name and fibre, were now companions in the Corps Législatif. All these, differing widely in personal opinions, and indeed representing every kind of political view, from the chivalrous and romantic legitimacy of Berryer to the republican religion or fetichism of Garnier-Pagès, combined to make up an opposition to the Imperial Government. Up to that time the opposition had consisted simply of five men. For years those five had fought a persevering and apparently hopeless fight against the strength of Imperial arms, Imperial gold, and the lungs of Imperial hirelings. Of the five the leader was Jules Favre. The second in command was Emile Ollivier, whose treason to liberty, truth, and peace has since been so sternly avenged by destiny. The other three were Picard, a member of the Republican

Government of September, and MM. Darimon and Henon. Numerically the opposition, now strengthened by the new accessions, became quite respectable; morally and politically it wholly changed the situation. It was no longer a Leonidas or Horatius Cocles desperately holding a pass; it was an army encountering an army. The Imperialists of course still far outnumbered their opponents; but there were no men among the devotees of Imperialism who could even pretend to compare as orators with Berryer, Thiers, or Favre. Of these three men, it seems to me that Berryer was by far the greatest orator, but Thiers left him nowhere as a partisan leader. Thiers undoubtedly pushed Jules Favre aside and made him quite a secondary figure. Thiers delighted in worrying a ministry. He never needed, as Berryer did, the impulse of a great principle and a great purpose. He felt all the joy of the strife which distinguishes the born gladiator. He soon proved that his years had in no degree impaired his oratorical capacity. It became one of the grand events of Paris when Thiers was to speak. Owing to the peculiar regulations of the French Chamber, which required that those who meant to take part in a debate should inscribe their names beforehand in the book, and speak according to their turn—an odious usage, fatal to all genuine debate—it was always known in advance through Paris that to-morrow or the day after Thiers was to speak. Then came a struggle for places in what an Englishman would call the strangers' gallery. The Palais Bourbon, where the Corps Législatif held its sittings, opposite the Place de la Concorde, has the noble distinction of providing the least and worst accommodation for the public of any House of Assembly in the civilized world. The English House of Commons is miserably defective and niggardly in this respect, but it is liberal and lavish when compared with the French Corps Législatif. Therefore, when M. Thiers was about to speak, there was as much intriguing, clamoring, beseeching, wrangling, storming for seats in the public *tribunes* as would have sufficed to carry an English county election. The trouble had its reward. Nobody could be disappointed in M. Thiers who merely desired an intellectual exercise and treat. Thiers never was heavy or dull. He is, I think, the most interesting of all the great European debaters. I do not know whether I convey exactly the meaning I wish to express when I used the word "interesting." What I mean is that there is in M. Thiers an inexhaustible vivacity, freshness, and variety which never allows the attention to wander or flag. He never dwells too long on any one part of his subject; or if he has to dwell long anywhere, he enlivens the theme by a lavish copiousness of novel argument, application, and illustration, which is irresistibly piquant and fascinating. Reëntering public life in his old age, M. Thiers had physically something like the advantage which I have known to be possessed by certain mature actresses, who, never having had any claim to personal beauty in their youth, were visited with hardly any penalty of time when they began to descend into age. Thiers always had an insignificant presence, a dreadfully bad voice, and an unpleasant delivery. Time added nothing, and probably could add-nothing, to these disadvantages. Already John Bright has lost, already Gladstone is losing, those magnificent qualities of voice and intonation which till lately distinguished both from all other living English orators. One of the only fine passages in Disraeli's "Life of Lord George Bentinck" is that in which he describes the melancholy sensation created in the House of Commons when Daniel O'Connell, feeble and broken down, tried vainly to raise above a mumbling murmur those accents which once could thrill and vibrate to the furthest corner of the most capacious hall. But the voice and delivery of Thiers at seventy were no whit worse than those of Thiers at forty; and in energy, vivacity, and variety, I think the opposition leader of 1866 had rather gained upon the Minister of 1836. In everything that makes a great orator he was far beneath Berryer. The latter had as commanding a presence as he had a superb voice, and a manner at once graceful and dignified. Berryer, too, had the sustaining strength of a profound conviction, pure and lofty as a faith. If Berryer was a political Don Quixote, Thiers was a political Gil Blas. Thiers was all sparkle, antithesis, audacity, sophistry. His *tours de force* were perfect masterpieces of fearless adroitness. He darted from point to point, from paradox to paradox, with the bewildering agility of a squirrel. He flashed through the heavy atmosphere of a dull debate with the scintillating radiancy of a firefly. He propounded sentiments of freedom which would positively have captivated you if you had not known a little of the antecedents of the orator. He threw off concise and luminous maxims of government which would have been precious guides if human politics could only be ruled by epigram. His long experience as a partisan leader, in and out of office, had made him master of a vast array of facts and dates, which he was expert to marshal in such a manner as often to bewilder his opponents. His knowledge of the mechanism and regulations of diplomatic and parliamentary practice was consummate. He was singularly clear and attractive in statement; his mode of putting a case had something in it that was positively fascinating. He was sharp and severe in retort, and there was a cold, self-complacent *hauteur* in his way of putting down an adversary, which occasionally reminded one of a peculiarity of Earl Russell's style when the latter was still a good parliamentary debater. M. Thiers had the great merit of never talking over the heads, above the understandings of his audience. His style of language was of the same character perhaps as that of Mr. Wendell Phillips. Of course no two men could possibly be more unlike in the manner of speaking, but the rhetorical vernacular of both has a considerable resemblance. The diction in each case is clear, incisive, penetrating—never, or hardly ever, rising to anything of exalted oratorical grandeur, never involved in mist or haze of any kind, and with the same habitual acidity and sharpness in it. I presume M. Thiers wrote the greater part of his speeches beforehand, but he evidently had the happy faculty, rare even among accomplished orators, which enables a speaker to blend the elaborately prepared portions of his discourse with the extemporaneous passages originated by the impulses and the incidents of the debate. Some of the cleverest arguments, and especially some of the cleverest sarcastic hits in M. Thiers's recent speeches, were provoked by questions and interruptions which must have been quite unexpected. But a strange peculiarity about the whole body of the speeches, the written parts as well as the extemporaneous, was that they bore no resemblance whatever to the glittering and gorgeous style which is so common and so objectionable in the pages of the author's history of the French Revolution, and of the Consulate and the Empire. I must say that I think M. Thiers's historical works are decidedly heavy reading. I think his speeches are more interesting and attractive to read than those of any political speaker of our day. As an orator I set him below Berryer, below Gladstone and Bright, below Wendell Phillips, and not above Disraeli. But as an interesting speaker—I can think of no better qualification for him—I place M. Thiers above any of those masters of the art of eloquence.

I have not compared M. Thiers with Jules Favre. Any juxtaposition of the two ought rather perhaps to be in the way of contrast than of comparison. Jules Favre is probably the most exquisite and perfect rhetorician practising in the public debates of our time. No one else can lend so brilliant an effect, so delightful an emphasis to words and phrases by the mere modulations of his tone. I once heard a French workingman say that Jules Favre *parlait comme un ange*—talked like an angel; and there was a simple appropriateness in the expression. An angel, if he had to address so unsympathetic and uncongenial an audience as the Imperial Corps Législatif, could hardly lend more musical effect to the meaning of his words than was given by Jules Favre's consummate rhetorical skill. But I must acknowledge that to me at least there never seemed to be much in what Jules Favre said. It seemed to me too often to want marrow and backbone. It was an eloquence of fine phrases and splendid vague generalities. "Flow on, thou shining river," one felt sometimes inclined to say as the bright, broad, shallow stream glided away. If Thiers spoke for half a day, and the discourse covered a dozen columns of the closely-printed "Moniteur," yet the listener or reader came away with the impression that the orator had crammed quite a surprising quantity of matter into his speech, and could have found ever so much more to say on the same subject. The impression produced on me at least by the speeches of Jules Favre was always of the very opposite character. They seemed to be all rhetoric and modulation; they were without depth and without fibre. The essentially declamatory character of Jules Favre's eloquence received its most complete illustration in that remarkable document—so painful and pathetic because of its obvious earnestness, so ludicrous and almost contemptible because of its turgid and extravagant outbursts—the report of his recent interviews with Count von Bismarck at the Prussian headquarters near Versailles. One must keep constantly in mind the awful seriousness of the situation, and the genuine suffering which it must have imposed upon Jules Favre, not to laugh outright or feel disgusted at the inflated, hyperbolical, and melodramatic style in which the Republican Minister describes his interview with the Prussian Chancellor. Now, whatever faults of style M. Thiers might commit, he never could thus make himself ridiculous. He never allows himself to be out of tune with the occasion and the audience. You may differ utterly from him, you may distrust and dislike him; but Thiers, the parliamentary orator, will not permit you to laugh at him.

Thiers was always very happy in his replies and retorts, and he never allowed if he could an interruption to one of his speeches in the Corps Législatif to pass without seizing its meaning and at once dissecting and demolishing it. He rejoiced in the light sword-play of such exercises. He would never have been contented with the superb quietness of contempt by which Berryer in one of his latest speeches crushed Granier de Cassagnac, the abject serf and hireling of Imperialism. While Berryer was speaking, Granier de Cassagnac suddenly expressed his coarse dissent from one of the orator's statements by crying out, "That is not true." Berryer was not certain as to the source of this insolent interruption. He gazed all round the assembly, and demanded in accents of subdued and noble indignation who had dared thus to challenge the truth of his statement. There was a dead pause. Even enemies looked up with reverence to the grand old orator, and were ashamed of the rude insult flung at him. De Cassagnac quailed, but every eye was on him, and he was compelled to declare himself. "It was I who spoke," said the Imperial servant. Berryer looked at him for a moment, and then said, "Oh, it was *you*!—then it is of no consequence," and calmly resumed the thread of his discourse. Nothing could have been finer, nothing more demolishing than the cold, grand contempt which branded De Cassagnac as a creature incapable of meriting, even by insult, the notice of a man of honor. But Thiers would never have been satisfied with such a mode of crushing an adversary; and indeed it needed all the majesty of Berryer's presence and the moral grandeur of his character to give it full force and emphasis. Thiers would have showered upon the head of the Imperial lacquey a whole fiery cornucopia of sarcasm and sharp invective, and De Cassagnac would have gone home rather proud of having drawn down upon his head the angry eloquence of the great Orleanist orator.

Thiers threw his whole soul into his speeches—not merely as to their preparation, but as to their revision and publication. According to the Imperial system, no independent reports of speeches in the Chambers were allowed to appear in print. The official stenographers noted down in full each day's debate, and the whole was published next day in the "Moniteur Universel." These reports professed to give every word and syllable of the speeches—every whisper of interruption. Sometimes, therefore, the "Moniteur" came out with twenty of its columns filled up with the dull maunderings of some provincial blockhead, for whom servility and money had secured an official candidature. Besides these stupendous reports, the Government furnished a somewhat condensed version, in which the twenty-column speech was reduced say to a dozen columns. Either of these reports the public journals might take, but none other; and no journal must alter or condense by the omission of a line or the substitution of a word the text thus officially furnished. When Thiers had spent the whole day in delivering a speech, he was accustomed to spend the whole night in reading over and correcting the proof-sheets of the official report. The venerable orator would hurry home when the sitting was over, change his clothes, get into his arm-chair before his desk, and set to work at the proof-sheets according as they came. Over these he would toil with the minute and patient inspection of a watchmaker or a lapidary, reading this or that passage many times, until he had satisfied himself that no error remained and that no turn of expression could well be improved. Before this task was done, the night had probably long faded and the early sun was already lighting Paris; but when the Corps Législatif came to assemble at noon, the inexhaustible septuagenarian was at his post again. That evening he would be found, the central figure of a group, in some salon, scattering his brilliant sayings and acrid sarcasms around him, and in all probability exercising his humor at the expense of the Imperial Ministers, the Empire, and even the Emperor himself. After 1866 he was exuberant in his *bons mots* about the humiliation of the Imperial Cabinet by Prussia. "Bismarck," he once declared, "is the best supporter of the French Government. He keeps it always in its place by first boxing it on one ear and then maintaining the equilibrium by boxing it on the other."

If one could have been present at the recent interviews between Count Bismarck and M. Thiers, he would doubtless have enjoyed a curious and edifying intellectual treat. Bismarck is a man of imperturbable good humor; Thiers a man of imperturbable self-conceit. Thiers has a tongue which never lacks a word, and that the most expressive word. Bismarck has a rare gift of shrewd satirical humor, and of phrases that stick to public memory. Each man would have regarded the other as a worthy antagonist in a duel of words. Neither would care to waste much time in lofty sentiment and grandiose appeals. Each would thoroughly understand that his best motto would be, "*A corsaire, corsaire et demi.*" Bismarck would find in Thiers no feather-headed Benedetti; assuredly, Thiers would favor Bismarck with none of Jules Favre's sighs and tears, and bravado and choking emotions. Thiers would have the greater part of the talk, that is certain; but Bismarck would probably contrive to compress a good deal of meaning and significance into his curt interjected sentences. Thiers assuredly must have long since worn out any freshness of surprise or thrilling emotion of any kind at the political convulsions of France. To him even the spectacle of the standard of Prussia hoisted on the pinnacles of Versailles could hardly have been an overpowering wonder. He had seen the soldiers of Prussia picketed in Paris; he could remember when a fickle Parisian populace, weary of war, had thronged into the streets to applaud the entrance of the conquering Czar of Russia. He had seen the Bourbon restored, and had helped to overthrow him. He had been twice the chief Minister of that Louis Philippe of Orleans, who in his youth had had to save the Princess his sister by carrying her off in her night-gown, without time to throw a shawl around her, and whose long years of exile had led him, in fulfilment of the prophecy of Danton, to the throne of France at last. He had helped towards the downfall of that same King his master, and had striven vainly at the end to stand between him and his fate. He had seen a second Republic rise and sink; he had now become the envoy of a third Republic. He had refused to serve an Imperial Napoleon, although his own teaching and preaching had been among the most effective agencies in debauching the mind and heart of the nation, and thus rendering a second Empire possible. People say M. Thiers has no feelings, and I shall not venture to contradict them—I have often heard the statement from those who know better than I can pretend to do. It would have been personally unfortunate for him in his interview with Count von Bismarck if he had been burthened with feelings. For he must surely in such a case have felt bitterly the consciousness that the misfortunes which had fallen on his country were in great measure the fruit of his own doctrines and his own labors. If the public conscience of France had not been seared and hardened against all sentiment of obligation to international principle, where French glory and French aggrandizement were concerned; if France had not learned to believe that no foreign nation had any rights which she was bound to respect; if she had not been saturated with the conviction that every benefit to a neighbor was an injury to herself; if she had not accepted these views as articles of national faith, and followed them out wherever she could to their uttermost consequences, then M. Thiers might be said to have written and spoken and lived in vain.

It is probable that a new career presents itself as a possibility to the indomitable energy, and, as many would say, the insatiable ambition of M. Thiers. Certainly, there seems not the faintest indication that the veteran believes himself to lag superfluous on the stage. It is likely that he rushed into the recent peace negotiations with the hope of playing over again the part so skilfully played by Talleyrand at the time of the Congress of Vienna, by virtue of which France obtained so much advantage which might hardly have been expected, and Germany got so little of what she might naturally have looked for. I certainly shall not venture to say whether M. Thiers may not even yet have an important official career before him. His recent enterprises and expeditions give evidence enough that he has nerve and physique for any undertaking likely to attract him, and I see no reason to doubt that his intellect is as fresh and active as it was thirty years ago. Thiers deserves nothing but honor for the unconquerable energy and courage which refuse to yield to years, and will not acknowledge the triumph of time. He would deserve far greater honor still if we could regard him as a disinterested patriot; highest honor of all if his principles were as wise and just as his ambition was unselfish. But charity itself could hardly hope to reconcile the facts of M. Thiers's long and varied career with any theory ascribing to the man himself a pure and disinterested purpose. That a statesman has changed his opinions is often his highest glory, if, as in the case of Mr. Gladstone, he has thereby grown into the light and the right. Nor is a change of views necessarily a reproach to a politician, even though he may have retrograded or gone wrong. But the man who is invariably a passionate liberal when out of office, and a severe conservative when in power; who makes it a regular practice to have one set of opinions while he leads the opposition, and another when he has succeeded in mounting to the lead of a ministry; such a man cannot possibly hope to obtain for such systematic alternations the credit of even a capricious and fantastic sincerity. No one who knows anything of M. Thiers would consent thus to exalt his heart at the expense of his head. When the late Lord Cardigan was, rightly or wrongly, accused of having returned rather too quickly from the famous charge of the Light Brigade at Balaklava, his lordship, among other things, alleged that his horse had run away with him. A bitter critic thereupon declared that Lord Cardigan could not be allowed thus unfairly to depreciate his consummate horsemanship, I am afraid we cannot allow M. Thiers's intelligence and shrewdness to be unjustly depreciated by the assumption that his political tergiversations were the result of meaningless caprice.

M. Thiers is one of the most gifted men of his day. But he is not, in my judgment, a great man. He wants altogether the grand and stable qualities of principle and judgment which are needed to constitute political greatness. His statesmanship is a sort of policy belonging apparently to the school of the Lower Empire; a Byzantine blending of intrigue and impudence. He has never had the faculty of reading the signs of the times, or of understanding that to-day is not necessarily like yesterday. But for the wonderful gifts of the man, there would seem to be something positively childish in the egotism which could believe that it lay in the power of France to maintain, despite of destiny, the petty princes of Germany and Italy, to arrange the political conditions of England, and prescribe to the United States how far their principle of internal cohesion should reach. Victor Hugo is undoubtedly an egotistic Frenchman. Some of his recent utterances have been foolish and ridiculous. But the folly has been that of a great soul; the folly has consisted in appealing, out of all time and place, to sublime and impracticable sentiments of human brotherhood and love which ought to influence all human souls, but do not and probably never will. Far different is the egotism of Thiers. It is the egotism of selfishness, arrogance, and craft. In a sublime world, Victor Hugo's appeals would cease to be ridiculous; but the nobler the world, the more ignoble would seem the doctrines and the policy of Thiers. My own admiration of Thiers extends only to his skill as a debater and his marvellous intellectual vitality. The man who, despite the most disheartening disadvantages of presence, voice, and manner, is yet the most fascinating political debater of his time, the man who at seventy-three years of age can go up in a balloon in quest of a new career, must surely command some interest and admiration, let critical wisdom preach to us never so wisely. But the best days will have arisen for France when such a political character and such a literary career as those of M. Thiers shall have become an anachronism and an impossibility.

PRINCE NAPOLEON

Some few years ago, seven or eight perhaps, a certain sensation was created among artists, and journalists, and literary men, and connoisseurs, and critics, by one of Flandrin's best portraits. Undoubtedly, the portrait was an admirable likeness; no one who had ever seen the original could deny or question that; but yet there was an air, a character, a certain depth of idealized expression about it which seemed to present the subject in a new light, and threw one into a kind of doubt as to whether he had ever truly understood the original before. Either the painter had unduly glorified his sitter, or the sitter had impressed upon the artist a true idea of his character and intellect which had never before been revealed to the public at large. The portrait was that of a man of middle age, with a smooth, broad, thoughtful brow, a character of command about the finely-formed, somewhat sensuous lips; chin and nose beautifully moulded, in fact what ladies who write novels would call "chiselled;" a face degenerating a little into mere flesh, but still dignified and imposing. Everywhere over the face there was a tone of dissatisfaction, of disappointment, of sullenness mingling strangely with the sensuous characteristics, and conveying somehow the idea of great power and daring ambition unduly repressed by outward conditions, or rendered barren by inward defects, or actually frustrated by failure and fate. "A Cæsar out of employment!" exclaimed a celebrated French author and critic. So much there was of the Cæsar in the face that no school-boy, no Miss in her teens could have even glanced at it without saying, "That is the face of a Bonaparte!" Were not the features a little too massive, it might have passed for an admirable likeness of the victor of Austerlitz; or, at all events, of the Napoleon of Leipzig or the Hundred Days. Probably any ordinary observer would at once have set it down as a portrait of the great Napoleon, and never thought there could be any doubt about the matter. It was, in fact, the likeness of Napoleon-Jerome, son of the rattle-pate King of Westphalia— Prince Napoleon, as he is ordinarily called, the Plon-plon whom soldiers jeer at, the "Red Prince" whom priests and Legitimists denounce, the cousin of the Emperor of the French, the son-in-law of the King of Italy.

It was only somewhere about, or a little before the time of the Flandrin portrait, that Prince Napoleon had the honor of becoming a mystery in the eyes of the public. Up to 1860, his character was quite settled in public estimation, just as that of Louis Napoleon had been up to the time of the *coup d'etat*. Public opinion generally settles the characters of conspicuous men at first by the intuitive process—the most delightful and easy method possible, dispensing, as it does, with any necessity for studying the subject, or even knowing anything at all about it. When the intuitive process has once adjusted a man's character, it is not easy to get people to believe in any other adjustment. Still, there are some remarkable instances of a change in popular opinion. The case of Louis Napoleon, the Emperor, is one illustration; that of Prince Napoleon, his cousin, is another, not so remarkable, certainly, but still quite worthy of some attention.

Prince Napoleon had been before the world more or less since he appeared as representative of Corsica, in the Constituent Assembly of 1848. He was made conspicuous, in a negative sort of way, by having had no hand in the *coup d'etat*, or having even opposed it, although he did not scruple to profit by its success and enjoy its golden advantages. He had a command in the Crimean war; he was sent into Tuscany during the Italian campaign. All that time public opinion in Europe was unanimous about him. He was a sensualist, a coward, an imbecile, and a blockhead. He was a fat, stupid, muddle-headed Heliogabalus. Dulness, cowardice, and profligacy were his principal, perhaps his only characteristics. When the young Clotilde, of Savoy, was given to him for a wife, a positive cry of wonder and disgust went up from every country of Europe. In good truth, it was a scandalous thing to marry a young and innocent girl to a man nearly as old as her father; and who, undoubtedly, had been a *mauvais sujet*, and had led a life of dissipation so far. But Europe cried aloud as if three out of every four princely alliances were not made on the same principle and endowed with the same character. Had the Princess Clotilde been affianced to a hog or a gorilla, there could hardly have been greater wonder and horror expressed, so clear was the public mind about the stupidity and brutality of Prince Napoleon.

Certainly, if one looked a little deeper than mere public opinion, he would have found, even then, that here and there some men, not quite incapable of judging, did not accept the popular estimate of the Emperor's cousin. All through the memorable progress of the Congress of Paris—out of which sprang Italy—we find, by the documents subsequently made public, that Cavour was in close and frequent consultation with Prince Napoleon. Once we find Cavour saying that Prince Napoleon complains of his slowness, his too great moderation, and thinks he could serve the cause better by a little more boldness. "Perhaps he is right," says Cavour, in words to that effect; "but I fear I lack his force of character, his daringness of purpose." Richard Cobden makes the acquaintance of Prince Napoleon, and is surprised and delighted with his advanced opinions on the subject of free trade; and deliberately describes him (I heard Cobden use the words) as "one of the best informed, if not the very best informed, of all the public men of Europe." Kinglake observes the Prince during the Crimean campaign—where Napoleon-Jerome got his reputation for cowardice and his nick-name of Plon-plon—and finds in him a genius very like that of his uncle, the great Napoleon, especially a wonderful power of distinguishing at a glance between the essentials and the accidentals of any question or situation—and any one who has ever studied politics and public men will know how rare a faculty that is—and finally declares that he sees no reason to believe him inferior in courage to the conqueror of Marengo! Edmond About, not a very dull personage, and not quite given up to panegyric, bursts into a strain of almost lyrical enthusiasm about the wit, the brilliancy, the culture, the daring ambition of Prince Napoleon, and declares that the Prince is kept as much out of the way as possible, because a man endowed with a soul of such unresting energy, and the face of the great Emperor, is too formidable a personage to be seen hanging about the steps of a throne. To close this string of illustrations, Prince Napoleon is in somewhat frequent and confidential intercourse with Michel Chevalier, a man not likely to cultivate the society of heavy blockheads and dullards, even though these might happen to wear princely coronets. Clearly, public opinion here was even more directly at odds than it often is with the opinion of some whom we may call experts; and the difference was so great that there seemed no possible way of reconciling the two. A man may be a profligate and yet a man of genius, and even a patriot; but one cannot be a profligate blockhead and a man of genius, a Cloten and an Alcibiades, a Cæsar and a Pyrgopolinices at once.

It was in the early part of 1861 that Prince Napoleon contributed something of his own spontaneous motion to help in the solution of the enigma. That was the year when the Emperor removed the restriction which prevented both Chambers of the Legislature from freely debating the address, and the press from fully reporting the discussions. There was a remarkable debate in the Senate, ranging over a great variety of domestic and foreign questions, and one most memorable event of the debate was the brilliant, powerful and exhaustive oration delivered, with splendid energy and rhetorical effect, by Prince Napoleon. *Mon âne parle et même il parle bien*, declares the astonished Joan, in Voltaire's scandalous poem, "La Pucelle." Perhaps there was something of a similar wonder mingled with the burst of genuine admiration which went up first from Paris, then from France, and finally from Europe and America, when that magnificent democratic manifesto came to be read. Certainly, I remember no single speech which, during my time, created anything like the same sensation in Europe. For it took the outer world wholly by surprise. It was not a case like that of the sensation lately created by the florid and fervid eloquence of the young Spanish orator, Castellar. In this latter case the public were surprised and delighted to find that there was a master of thrilling rhetoric alive, and arrayed on the side of democratic freedom, of whose very existence most persons had been previously ignorant. But, in the case of Prince Napoleon, the surprise was, that a man whom the public had long known, and always set down as a stupid sensualist, should suddenly, and without any previous warning, turn out a great orator, whose eloquence had in it something so fresh, and genuine, and forcible that it recalled the memory of the most glorious days of the French Tribune. I write of this celebrated oration now only from recollection; and, of course, I did not hear it spoken. I say "of course," because the rules of the French Senate, unlike those of the Corps Legislatif, forbid the presence of any strangers during the debates. But those who heard it spoke enthusiastically of the force and freedom with which it was delivered; the sudden, impulsive fervor of occasional outbursts; and the wonderful readiness with which the speaker, when interrupted, as he was very frequently, passed from one topic to another in order to dispose of the interruption, and replied to sudden challenge with even prompter repartee. No one could read the speech without admiring the extent and variety of the political knowledge it displayed; the prodigality of illustration it flung over every argument; the thrilling power of some of its rhetorical "phrases;" the tone of sustained and passionate eloquence which made itself heard all throughout; and, perhaps above all, that flexible, spontaneous readiness of language and resource to which every interruption, every interjected question only acted like a spur to a generous horse, calling forth new and greater, and wholly unexpected efforts. In the French Senate I need, perhaps, hardly tell my readers, it is the habit to allow the utmost license of interruption, and Prince Napoleon's audacious onslaught on the reactionists and the *parti prêtre* called out even an unusual amount of impatient utterance. Those who interrupted took little by their motion. The energetic Prince tossed off his assailants as a bull flings the dogs away on the points of his horns. "Our principles are not yours," scornfully exclaims a Legitimist nobleman—the late Marquis de la Rochejaquelein, if I remember rightly. "Your principles are not ours!" vehemently replies the orator. "No, nor are your antecedents ours. Our pride is that our fathers fell on the battle-field resisting the foreign invaders whom your fathers brought in for the subjugation of France!" The speech is studded with sudden replies equally fervid and telling. Indeed, the whole material of the oration is rich, strong, and genuine. There seems to be in the eloquence of the French Chambers, of late, a certain want of freshness and natural power. I do not speak of Berryer—he had no such want. But Thiers—by far the ablest living debater who speaks only from preparation—with all his wonderful science and skill as an artist in debate, appears to be always somewhat artificial and elaborate. Jules Favre, with his exquisitely modulated tones, and his unrivalled choice of words, hardly ever appears to me to rise to that height where the orator, lost in his subject, compels his hearers to lose themselves also in it. Now, I cannot help thinking that the two or three really great speeches made by Prince Napoleon had in them more of the native fibre, force and passion of oratory than those of almost any Frenchman since the days of Mirabeau.

However that may be, the effect wrought on the public mind was unmistakable. Plon-plon had startled Europe. He entered the palace of the Luxembourg on that memorable day without any repute but that of a dullard and a sensualist; he came out of it a recognized orator. I have been told that he lay back in his open carriage and smoked his cigar, as he drove home from the Senate, to all appearance the same indolent, sullen, heavy apathetic personage whom all Paris had previously known and despised.

One notable effect of this famous speech was the reply which a certain passage in it drew from Louis Philippe's son, the Duc d'Aumale. Prince Napoleon had indulged in a bitter sneer or two against former dynasties, and the Duc d'Aumale, a man of great culture and ability, took up the quarrel fiercely. The Duke assailed Prince Napoleon in one of the keenest, most biting pamphlets which the political controversy of our day has produced. Among other things, the Duke replied to a supposed imputation on the weakness of Louis Philippe by admitting, frankly, that the *bourgeois* King had not dealt with enemies, when in his power, as a Bonaparte would have done. "*Et tenez*, Prince," wrote the Duke, "the only time when the word of a Bonaparte may be believed is when he avows that he will never spare a defenceless enemy." The pamphlet bristled with points equally sharp and envenomed. But the Duc d'Aumale was not content with written rejoinder. He sent a challenge to the Prince, and in serious earnest. The Prince, it need hardly be said, did not accept the challenge.

> Yes, like enough, high-battled Cæsar will
>
> Unstate his greatness, and be staged to the show
>
> Against a sworder!

Our Cæsar, though not "high-battled," was by no means likely to consent to be "staged against a sworder." The Emperor hastened to prevent any disastrous consequences, by insisting that the Prince must not accept the challenge—and there was no duel. People winked and sneered a good deal. It is said that the martial King Victor Emmanuel grumbled and chafed at his son-in-law; but there was no fight. Let me say, for my own part, that I think Prince Napoleon was quite right in not accepting the challenge, and that I do not believe him to be wanting in personal courage.

From that moment, Prince Napoleon became a conspicuous figure in European politics, and when any great question arose, men turned anxiously toward him, curious to know what he would do or say. In three or four successive sessions he spoke in the Senate, and even with the impression of the first surprise still strong on the public mind, the speeches preserved abundantly the reputation which the earliest of them had so suddenly created. He might be the *enfant terrible* of the Bonaparte family; he might be utterly wanting in statesmanship; he might be insincere; he might be physically a coward; but all the world now admitted him to be an orator, and, in his way, a man of genius.

Then it became known to the public, all at once, that the Prince, whatever his failings, had some rare gifts besides that of eloquence. He was undoubtedly a man of exquisite taste in all things artistic; he had an intelligent and liberal knowledge of practical science; he had a great faculty of organization; he was a keen humorist and wit. He loved the society of artists, and journalists, and literary men; he associated with them *en bon camarade*, and he could talk with each upon his own subject; his *bon mots* soon began to circulate far and wide. He was a patron of Revolution. In the innermost privacy of the Palais Royal men like Mieroslawski, the Polish Red Revolutionist, men like General Türr, unfolded and discussed their plans. Prince Gortschakoff, in his despatches at the time of the Polish Rebellion, distinctly pointed to the palace of Prince Napoleon as the headquarters of the insurrection. The "Red Prince" grew to be one of the mysterious figures in European policy. Was he in league with his cousin, the Emperor—or was he his cousin's enemy? Did he hope, on the strength of that Bonaparte face, and his secret league with Democracy, to mount one day from the steps of the throne to the throne itself? Between him and the succession to that throne intervened only the life of one frail boy. Was Prince Napoleon preparing for the day when he might play the part of a Gloster (without the smothering), and, pushing the boy aside, succeed to the crown of the great Emperor whom in face he so strikingly resembled?

At last came the celebrated Ajaccio speech. The Emperor had gone to visit Algeria; the Prince went to deliver an oration at the inauguration of a monument to Napoleon I., at Ajaccio. The speech was, in brief, a powerful, passionate denunciation of Austria, and the principles which Austria represented before Sadowa taught her a lesson of tardy wisdom. Viewed as the exposition of a professor of history, one might fairly acknowledge the Prince's speech to have illustrated eloquently some solid and stern truths, which Europe would have done well even then to consider deeply. Subsequent events have justified and illuminated many of what then seemed the most startling utterances of the orator. Austria, for example, practically admits, by her present policy, the justice of much that Prince Napoleon pleaded against her. But as the speech of the Emperor's cousin; of one who stood in near order of succession to the throne; of one who had only just been raised to an office in the State so high that in the absence of the sovereign it made him seem the sovereign's proper representative, it was undoubtedly a piece of marvellous indiscretion. Europe stood amazed at its outspoken audacity. The Emperor could not overlook it; and he publicly repudiated it. Prince Napoleon resigned his public offices—including that of President of the Commissioners of the International Exhibition, which undertaking suffered sadly from lack of his organizing capacity and his admirable taste and judgment—and the Imperial orator of Democracy disappeared from the public stage as suddenly, and amid as much tumult, as he had entered upon it.

Prince Napoleon has, indeed, been taken into favor since by his Imperial cousin, and has been sent on one or two missions, more or less important or mysterious; but he has never, from the date of the Ajaccio speech up to the present moment, played any important part as a public man. He is not, however, "played out." His energy, his ambition, his ability, will assuredly bring him prominently before the public again. Let us, meanwhile, endeavor to set before the readers of The Galaxy a fair and true picture of the man, free alike from the exaggerated proportions which wondering *quid nuncs* or parasites attribute to him, and from the distortions of unfriendly painters. Exaggeration of both kinds apart, Prince Napoleon is really one of the most remarkable figures on the present stage of French history. He is, at least, a man of great possibilities. Let us try to ascertain fairly what he is, and what are his chances for the future.

Born of a hair-brained, eccentric, adventure-seeking, negligent, selfish father, Prince Napoleon had little of the advantages of a home education. His boyhood, his youth, were passed in a vagrant kind of way, ranging from country to country, from court to court. He started in life with great natural talents, a strong tendency to something not very unlike rowdyism, an immense ambition, an almost equally vast indolence, a deep and genuine love of arts, letters, and luxury, an eccentric, fitful temper, and a predominant pride in that relationship to the great Emperor which is so plainly stamped upon his face. Without entering into any questions of current scandal, everybody must know that Napoleon III. has nothing of the Bonaparte in his face, a fact on which Prince Napoleon, in his earlier and wilder days, was not always very slow to comment. Indolence, love of luxury, and a capricious temper have, perhaps, been the chief enemies which have hitherto prevented the latter from fulfilling any high ambition. It would be affectation to ignore the fact that Prince Napoleon flung many years away in mere dissipation.

Stories are told in Paris which would represent him almost as a Vitellius or an Egalité in profligacy—stories some of which simply transcend belief by their very monstrosity. Even to this day, to this hour, it is the firm conviction of the general public that the Emperor's cousin is steeped to the lips in sensuality. Now, rejecting, of course, a huge mass of this scandal, it is certain that Prince Napoleon was, for a long time, a downright *mauvais sujet*; it is by no means certain that he has, even at his present mature age, discarded all his evil habits. His temper is much against him. People habitually contrast the unvarying courtesy and self-control of the Emperor with the occasional brusqueness, and even rudeness, of the Prince. True that Prince Napoleon can be frankly and warmly familiar with his intimates, and even that, like Prince Hal, he sometimes encourages a degree of familiarity which hardly tends to mutual respect. But the outer world cannot always rely on him. He can be undiplomatically rough and hot, and he has a gift of biting jest which is perhaps one of the most dangerous qualities a statesman can cultivate. Then there is a personal restlessness about him which even princes cannot afford safely to indulge. He has hardly ever had any official position assigned to him which he did not sometime or other scornfully abandon on the spur of some sudden impulse. The Madrid embassy in former days, the Algerian administration, the Crimean command—these and other offices he only accepted to resign. He has wandered more widely over the face of the earth than any other living prince—probably than any other prince that ever lived. It used to be humorously said of him that he was qualifying to become a teacher of geography, in the event of fortune once more driving the race of Bonaparte into exile and obscurity. What port is there that has not sheltered his wandering yacht? He has pleasant dwellings enough to induce a man to stay at home. His Palais Royal is one of the most elegant and tasteful abodes belonging to a European prince. The stranger in Paris who is fortunate enough to obtain admission to it—and, indeed, admission is easy to procure—must be sadly wanting in taste if he does not admire the treasures of art and *vertu* which are laid up there, and the easy, graceful manner of their arrangement. Nothing of the air of the show-place is breathed there; no rules, no conditions, no watchful, dogging lacqueys or sentinels make the visitor uncomfortable. Once admitted, the stranger goes where he will, and admires and examines what he pleases. He finds there curiosities and relics, medals and statues, bronzes and stones from every land in which history or romance takes any interest; he gazes on the latest artistic successes—Doré's magnificent lights and shadows, Gérome's audacious nudities; he observes autograph collections of value inestimable; he notices that on the tables, here and there, lie the newest triumphs or sensations of literature—the poem that every one is just talking of, the play that fills the theatres, George Sand's last novel, Rénan's new volume, Taine's freshest criticism: he is impressed everywhere with the conviction that he is in the house of a man of high culture and active intellect, who keeps up with the progress of the world in arts, and letters, and politics. Then there was, until lately, the famous Pompeiian Palace, in one of the avenues of the Champs Elysées, which ranked among the curiosities of Paris, but which Prince Napoleon has at last chosen, or been compelled, to sell. On the Swiss shore of the lake of Geneva, one of the most remarkable objects that attract the eye of the tourist who steams from Geneva to Lausanne, is La Bergerie, the palace of Prince Napoleon. But the owner of these palaces spends little of his time in them. His wife, the Princess Clotilde, stays at home and delights in her children, and shows them with pride to her visitors, while her restless husband is steaming in and out of the ports of the Mediterranean, the Black Sea, or the Baltic. Prince Napoleon has not found his place yet, say Edmond About and other admirers—when he does he will settle firmly to it. He is a restless, unmanageable idler and scamp, say his enemies—unstable as water, he shall not excel. Meanwhile years go by, and Prince Napoleon has long left even the latest verge of youth behind him; and he is only a possibility as yet, and is popular with no political party in France.

Strange that this avowed and ostentatious Democrat, this eloquent, powerful spokesman of French Radicalism, is not popular even with Democrats and Red Republicans. They do not trust him. They cannot understand how he can honestly extend one hand to Democracy, while in the other he receives the magnificent revenues assigned to him by Despotism. One might have thought that nothing would be more easy than for this man, with his daring, his ambition, his brilliant talents, his commanding eloquence, his democratic principles, and his Napoleon face, to make himself the idol of French Democracy. Yet he has utterly failed to do so. As a politician, he has almost invariably upheld the rightful cause, and accurately foretold the course of events. He believed in the possibility of Italy's resurrection long before there was any idea of his becoming son-in-law to a King of Italy; he has been one of the most earnest friends of the cause of Poland; he saw long ago what every one sees now, that the fall of the Austrian system was an absolute necessity to the progress of Europe; he was a steady supporter of the American Union, and when it was the fashion in France, as in England, to regard the independence of the Southern Confederacy as all but an accomplished fact, he remained firm in the conviction that the North was destined to triumph. With all his characteristic recklessness and impetuosity, he has many times shown a cool and penetrating judgment, hardly surpassed by that of any other European statesman. Yet the undeniable fact remains, that his opinion carries with it comparatively little weight, and that no party recognizes him as a leader.

Is he insincere? Most people say he is. They say that, with all his professions of democratic faith, he delights in his princely rank and his princely revenues; that he is selfish, grasping, luxurious, arrogant and deceitful. The army despises him; the populace do not trust him. Now, for myself, I do not accept this view of the character of Prince Napoleon. I think he is a sincere Democrat, a genuine lover of liberty and progress. But I think, at the same time, that he is cursed with some of the vices of Alcibiades, and some of the vices of Mirabeau; that he has the habitual indolence almost of a Vendôme, with Vendôme's occasional outbursts of sudden energy; that a love of luxury, and a restlessness of character, and fretfulness of temper stand in his way, and are his enemies. I doubt whether he will ever play a great historical part, whether he ever will do much more than he has done. His character wants that backbone of earnest, strong simplicity and faith, without which even the most brilliant talents can hardly achieve political greatness. He will probably rank in history among the Might-Have-Beens. Assuredly, he has in him the capacity to play a great part. In knowledge and culture, he is far, indeed, superior to his uncle, Napoleon I.; in justice of political conviction, he is a long way in advance of his cousin, Napoleon III. Taken for all in all, he is the most lavishly gifted of the race of the Bonapartes—and what a part in the cause of civilization and liberty might not be played by a Bonaparte endowed with genius and culture, and faithful to high and true convictions! But the time seems going by, if not gone by, when even admirers could expect to see Prince Napoleon play such a part. Probably the disturbing, distracting vein of unconquerable levity so conspicuous in the character of his father, is the marplot of the son's career, too. After all, Prince Napoleon is perhaps more of an Antony than a Cæsar— was not Antony, too, an orator, a wit, a lover of art and letters, a lover of luxury and free companionship, and woman? Doubtless Prince Napoleon will emerge again, some time and somehow, from his present condition of comparative obscurity. Any day, any crisis, any sudden impulse may bring him up to the front again. But I doubt whether the dynasty of the Bonapartes, the cause of democratic freedom, the destinies of France, will be influenced much for good or evil, by this man of rare and varied gifts—of almost measureless possibilities—the restless, reckless, eloquent, brilliant Imperial Democrat of the Palais Royal, and Red Republican of the Empire— the long misunderstood and yet scarcely comprehended Prince Napoleon.

THE DUKE OF CAMBRIDGE

There used to be a story current in London, which I dare say is not true, to the effect that her gracious Majesty Queen Victoria once demurred to the Prince and Princess of Wales showing themselves too freely in society, and asked them angrily whether they meant to make themselves "as common as the Cambridges."

Certainly the Duke of Cambridge and his sister the Princess Mary, now Princess of Teck, were for a long time, if not exactly "common," if not precisely popular, the most social, the most easily approached, and the most often seen in public pageantry of all members of the royal family. The Princess Mary might perhaps fairly be called popular. The people liked her fine, winsome face, her plump and buxom form. If she has not a kindly, warm, and generous heart, then surely physiognomy is no index of character. But the Duke of Cambridge, although very commonly seen in public, and ready to give his presence and his support to almost any philanthropic meeting and institution which can claim to be fashionable, never seems to have attained any degree of popularity. Like his father, who enjoyed the repute of being the worst after-dinner speaker who ever opened his mouth, the Duke of Cambridge is to be found acting as chairman of some public banquet once a week on an average during the London season. He is president or patron of no end of public charities and other institutions. Yet the people do not seem to care anything about him, or even to like him. His appearance is not in his favor. He is handsome in a certain sense, but he is heavy, stolid, sensual-looking, and even gross in form and face. He has indeed nearly all the peculiarities of physiognomy which specially belong to the most typical members of the Guelph family, and there is, moreover, despite the obesity which usually suggests careless good-humor, something sinister or secret in his expression not pleasant to look upon. He seems to be a man of respectable average abilities. He is not a remarkably bad speaker. I think when he addresses the House of Lords, which he does rarely, or a public meeting or dinner-party, which he does often, he acquits himself rather better than the ordinary county member of Parliament. Judging by his apparent mental capacity and his style as a speaker, he ought to be rather popular than otherwise in England, for the English people like respectable mediocrity and not talent in their princes. "He is so respectable and such an ass," says Thackeray speaking of somebody, "that I positively wonder he didn't get on in England." The Duke of Cambridge is so respectable (in intellectual capacity) and so dull that I positively wonder he has not been popular in England. But popular he never has been. No such clamorous detestation follows him as used to pursue the late Duke of Cumberland, subsequently King of Hanover. No such accusations have been made against him as were familiarly pressed against the Duke of York. Even against the living Prince of Wales there are charges made by common scandal more serious than any that are usually talked of in regard to the Duke of Cambridge. But the English public likes the Duke as little as it could like any royal personage. England has lately been growing very jealous of the manner in which valuable appointments are heaped on members of the Queen's family. The Duke of Cambridge has long enjoyed some sinecure places of liberal revenue, and he holds one office of inestimable influence, for which he has never proved himself qualified, and for which common report declares him to be utterly disqualified. He is Commander-in-Chief of the British army; and that I believe to be his grand offence in the eyes of the British public. Many offences incident to his position are indeed charged upon him. It is said that he makes an unfair use, for purposes of favoritism, of the immense patronage which his office places at his disposal. Some years ago scandal used to charge him with advancing men out of the same motive which induced the Marquis of Steyne to obtain an appointment for Colonel Rawdon Crawley. The private life of the Duke is said to have been immoral, and unluckily for him it so happened that some of his closest friends and favorites became now and then involved in scandals of which the law courts had to take cognizance. But had none of these things been so, or been said, I think the Duke of Cambridge would have lacked popularity just as much as he does. The English people are silently angry with him, mainly because he is an anachronism—a man raised to the most influential public appointment the sovereign can bestow, for no other reason than because he is a member of the royal family. The Duke of Cambridge in the office of Commander-in-Chief is an anachronism at the head of an anomaly. The system is unfit for the army or the country; the man is incompetent to manage any military system, good or bad. As the question of army reorganization, now under debate in England, has a grand political importance, transcending by far its utmost possible military import, and as the position of the Duke of Cambridge is one of the peculiar and typical anomalies about to be abolished, it may surely interest American readers if I occupy a few pages in describing the man and the system. Altering slightly the words of Bugeaud to Louis Philippe in 1848, this reorganization of the army in England is not a reform, but a revolution. It strikes out the keystone from the arch of the fabric of English aristocracy.

The Duke of Cambridge is, as everybody knows, the first cousin of the Queen of England. He is about the same age as the Queen. When both were young it used to be said that he cherished hopes of becoming her husband. He is now himself one of the victims of the odious royal marriage act, which in England acknowledges as valid no marriage with a subject contracted by a member of the royal family without the consent of the sovereign. The Duke of Cambridge, it is well known, is privately married to a lady of respectable position and of character which has never been reproached, but whom, nevertheless, he cannot present to the world as his wife because the royal consent has not ratified the marriage. Many readers of The Galaxy may perhaps remember that only four or five years ago there was some little commotion created in England by the report, never contradicted, that a princess of the royal house had set her heart upon marrying a young English nobleman who loved her, and that the Queen utterly refused to give her consent. Much sympathy was felt for the princess, because, as she was not a daughter of the Queen and was not young enough to be reasonably expected to acknowledge the control of any relative, this rigorous exercise of a merely technical power seemed particularly unjust and odious. It will be seen, therefore, that the objections raised against the Duke and his position in England are not founded on the belief that he is himself as an individual inordinately favored by the sovereign; but on the obvious fact that place and power are given to him because he is a member of the reigning family. The Duke of Cambridge has never shown the slightest military talent, the faintest capacity for the business of war. In his only campaign he proved worse than useless, and more than once made a humiliating exhibition, not of cowardice, but of utter incapacity and flaccid nervelessness. His warmest admirer never ventured to pretend that the Duke was personally the best man to take the place of Commander-in-Chief. While he was constantly accused by rumor and sometimes by public insinuation of blundering, of obstinacy, of ignorance, of gross favoritism, no defence ever made for him, no eulogy ever pronounced upon him, went the length of describing him as a well-qualified head of the military organization. His upholders and panegyrists were content with pleading virtually that he was by no means a bad sort of Commander-in-Chief; that he was not fairly responsible for this or that blunder or malversation; that on the whole there might have been men worse fitted than he for the place. The social vindication of the appointment was that which proved very naturally its worst offence in the eyes of the public—the fact that the sovereign and her family desired that the place should be given to the Duke of Cambridge, and that the ministers then in power either had not the courage or did not think it worth their while to resist the royal inclination.

The Duke, if he never proved himself much of a soldier, had at least opportunity enough to learn all the ordinary business of his profession. He actually is, and always has been, a professional soldier—not nominally an officer, as the late Prince Albert was, or as the Prince of Wales is, or as the Princess Victoria (Crown Princess of Prussia) may be said for that matter to be, the lady holding, I believe, an appointment as colonel of some regiment, and being doubtless just as well acquainted with her regimental duties as her fat and heavy brother. The Duke of Cambridge was made a colonel at the age of eighteen, and he did the ordinary barrack and garrison duties of his place. He used when young to be rather popular in garrison towns. In Dublin, for example, I think Prince George of Cambridge, as he was then called, was followed with glances of admiration by many hundred pairs of bright eyes. On the death of his father (whose after-dinner eloquence used to afford "Punch" a constant subject for mirth) Prince George became in 1850 Duke of Cambridge. He holds some appointments which I presume are sinecures to him; among the rest he is keeper of some of the royal parks (I don't know the precise title of his office), and the name of "George" may be seen appended to edicts inscribed on various placards on the trees and gates near Buckingham Palace. Nothing in particular was known about him as a soldier until the Crimean war. Indeed, up to that time there had been for many years as little chance for an English officer to prove his capacity as there was for a West Point man to show what he was worth in the period between the Mexican war and the attack on Fort Sumter. When the Crimean war broke out the Duke was appointed to the command of the first division of the army sent against the Russians. I believe it is beyond all doubt that he proved himself unfit for the business of war. He "lost his head," people say; he could not stand the sights and sounds of the battle-field. It required on one occasion—at Inkerman, I believe—the prompt and sharp interference of the late Lord Clyde, then Sir Colin Campbell, to prevent his Royal Highness from making a sad mess of his command. It is not likely that he wanted personal courage—few princes do; but his nerves gave way, and as he could be of no further use to anybody he was induced to return home. France and England each sent a fat prince, cousin of the reigning sovereign, to the Crimean war, and each prince rather suddenly came home again with the invidious whispers of the malign unpleasantly criticising his retreat from the field. After the Duke's return the corporation of Liverpool gave him (why, no man could well say) a grand triumphal entry, and I remember that an irreverent and cynical member of one of the local boards suggested that among the devices exhibited in honor of the illustrious visitor, a white feather would be an appropriate emblem. There the Duke's active military career began and ended. He had not distinguished himself. Perhaps he had not disgraced himself; perhaps it was really only ill-health which prevented him from proving himself as genuine a warrior as his relative, the Crown Prince of Prussia. But the English people only saw that the Duke went out to the war and very quickly came back again. Julius Cæsar or the First Napoleon or General Sherman might have had to do the same thing under the same circumstances; but then these more lucky soldiers did not have to do it, and therefore were able to prove their military capacity. One thing very certain is, that without such good fortune and such proof of capacity neither Cæsar, Napoleon, nor Sherman would ever have been made commander-in-chief, and therein again they were unlike the Duke of Cambridge. For it was not long after the Duke's return home that on the death or resignation (I don't now quite remember which) of Viscount Hardinge, our heavy "George" was made Commander-in-Chief of the British army. I venture to think that, taking all the conditions of the time and the appointment into consideration, no more unreasonable, no more unjustifiable instance of military promotion was ever seen in England.

For observe, that the worst thing about the appointment of the Duke of Cambridge is not that an incompetent person obtains by virtue of his rank the highest military position in the State. If this were all, there might be just the same thing said of almost every other European country—indeed, of almost every other country. The King of Prussia was Commander-in-Chief of the armies of North Germany, but no one supposed that he was really competent to discharge all the duties of such a position. Abraham Lincoln was Commander-in-Chief of the Federal army, by virtue of his office of President; but no one supposed that his military knowledge and capacity would ever have recommended him to such a post. The appointment in each case was only nominal, and as a matter of political convenience and propriety. It did not seem wise or even safe that the supreme military authority should be formally intrusted to any one but the ruler or the President. It was thoroughly understood that the duties of the office were discharged by some professional expert, for whose work the King or the President was responsible to the nation. But the office of Commander-in-Chief of the English army is something quite different from this. It is understood to be a genuine office, the occupant actually doing the work and having the authority. In the lifetime of the Duke of Wellington the country had the services of the very best Commander-in-Chief England could have selected. The sound and wise principle which dictated that appointment is really the principle on which the office is based in England. The Commander-in-Chief is not regarded, as on the Continent, in the light of an ornamental president of a great bureau whose duties are done by others, but as the most efficient military officer, the man best qualified to do the work. Marlborough was Commander-in-Chief, and so was Schomberg, and so was General

Seymour Conway. When in 1828 the Duke of Wellington became Prime Minister, and therefore resigned the command of the army, Lord Hill was placed at the head of military affairs. The Duke of Wellington resumed the command in 1842 and held it to his death, when it was given to Viscount Hardinge, a capable man. The title of the office was not, I believe, actually "Commander-in-Chief," but "General Commanding-in-Chief." It was, if I remember rightly, owing to the disasters arising out of military mismanagement in the Crimea, that the changes were made which created a distinct Secretary of War and gave to the office of Commander-in-Chief its present title. Therefore it will be seen that the intrusting the command of the army to the Duke of Cambridge is not even justifiable on the ground that it follows an old established custom. It is, on the contrary, an innovation, and one which illustrates the worst possible principle. There is nothing to be said for it. No necessity justified or even excused it. When Viscount Hardinge died, if the principle adopted in his case—that of appointing the best man to the place—had been still in favor, there were many military generals in England, any one of whom would have filled the office with efficiency and credit. But the superstition of rank prevailed. The Duke of Wellington is believed to have once recommended that on his death Prince Albert, the Queen's husband, should be created Commander-in-Chief. Ridiculous as the suggestion may seem, it would probably have been a far better arrangement than that which was more recently adopted. Prince Albert could hardly have been called a professional soldier at all; and this would have been greatly in his favor. For he would have filled the place merely as the King of Prussia does; he would have intrusted the actual duties to some qualified man, and being endowed with remarkable judgment, temper, and discretion, he would doubtless have found the right man for the work. But the Duke of Cambridge, as a professional soldier, although a very indifferent one, is expected to perform and does perform the duties of his office, after his own fashion. He is too high in rank to be openly rebuked, contradicted, or called to account; he is not high enough to be accepted as a mere official ornament or figurehead. He is too much of a professional general to become willingly the pupil and instrument of a more skilled subordinate; too little of a professional general to render his authority of any real value, or to be properly qualified for any high military position. So the Duke of Cambridge did actually direct the affairs of the army, interfered in everything, was supreme in everything, and I think it is not too much to say mismanaged everything. He stood in the way of all useful reforms; he sheltered old abuses; he was as dictatorial as though he had the military genius of a Wellington or a Von Moltke; he was as independent of public opinion as the Mikado of Japan. The kind of mistakes which were made and abuses which were committed under his administration were not such as to attract much of the attention or interest of the newspapers. In England the press, moreover, is not supposed to be at liberty to criticise princes. Of late some little efforts at daring innovation are made in this direction; but as a rule, unless a prince does something very wrong indeed, he is secure from any censure or even criticism on the part of the newspapers. There was, besides, one great practical difficulty in the way of any one inclined to criticise the military administration of the Duke of Cambridge. The War Department in England had grown to be a kind of anomalous two-headed institution. There is a Secretary of War, who sits in the House of Lords or the House of Commons, as the case may be, and whom every one can challenge, criticise, and censure as he pleases. There is the Commander-in-Chief. Which of these two functionaries is the superior? The theory of course is that the Secretary of War is supreme; that he is responsible to Parliament, and that every official in the department is responsible to him. But everybody in England knows that this is not the actual case. There stands in Pall Mall, not far from the residence of the Prince of Wales, a plain business-like structure, with a statue of the late Lord Herbert of Lea (the Sidney Herbert of Crimean days) in front of it; and this is the War Office, where the Secretary of War is in power. But there is in Whitehall another building far better known to Londoners and strangers alike; an old-fashioned, unlovely, shabby-looking sort of barrack, with a clock in its shapeless cupola and two small arches in its front, in each of which enclosures sits all day a gigantic horseman in steel cuirass and high jack-boots. The country visitor comes here to wonder at the size and the accoutrements of the splendid soldiers; the nursery-maid loves the spot, and gazes with open mouth and sparkling eyes at the athletic cavaliers, and too often, like Hylas sent with his urn to the fountain, *"proposito florem prætulit officio,"* prefers looking at the gorgeous military carnation blazing before her to the duty of watching her infantile charge in the perambulator. This building is the famous "Horse Guards," where the Commander-in-Chief is enthroned. I suppose the theory of the thing was, that while the army system was to be shaped out and directed in the War Office, the actual details of practical administration were to be managed at the Horse Guards. But of late years the relations of the two departments appear to have got into an almost inextricable and hopeless muddle, so that no one can pretend to say where the responsibility of the War Office ends or the authority of the Horse Guards begins. The Duke of Cambridge, it is said, habitually acts upon his own authority and ignores the War Office altogether. Things are done by him of which the Secretary for War knows nothing until they are done. The late Sidney Herbert, a man devoted to the duties of the War Department, over which he presided for some years, once emphatically refused during a debate in the House of Commons to evade the responsibility of some step taken at the Horse Guards, by pleading that it was made without the knowledge of the War Office. He declared that he considered himself, as War Secretary, responsible to Parliament for everything done in any office of the War Department. But it was quite evident from the tone of his speech that the thing had been done without his knowledge or consent, and that if anybody but the Queen's cousin had done it there would have been a "row in the building." Now Sidney Herbert was an aristocrat of high rank, of splendid fortune, of unsurpassed social dignity and influence, of great political talents and reputation. If he then could not attempt to control and rebuke the Queen's cousin, how could such an attempt be expected from a man like Mr. Cardwell, the present War Secretary? Mr. Cardwell is a dull, steady-going, respectable man, who has no pretension to anything like the rank, social influence, or even popularity of Sidney Herbert. In fact, the War Secretaries stand sometimes in much the same relation toward the Duke of Cambridge that a New York judge occasionally holds toward one of the great leaders of the bar who pleads before him and is formally supposed to acknowledge his superior authority. The person holding the position nominally superior feels himself in reality quite "over-crowed," to use a Spenserian expression, by the influence, importance, and dignity of the other. Let any stranger in London who happens to be in the gallery of the House of Lords, observe the astonishing deference with which even a pure-blooded marquis or earl of antique title will receive the greeting of the Duke of Cambridge; and then say what chance there is of a War Secretary, who probably belongs to the middle or manufacturing classes, venturing to dictate to or rebuke so tremendous a *magnifico*. Lately an audacious critic of the Duke has started up in the person of a clever, vivacious young member of Parliament, George Otto Trevelyan, son of one of the ablest Indian administrators and nephew of Lord Macaulay. Trevelyan once held, I think, some subordinate place in the War Department, and he has lately been horrifying the conservatism and veneration of English society by boldly making speeches in which he attacks the Queen's cousin, declares that the latter is an injury and nuisance to the army system, that he stands in the way of all improvement, and that he ought to be abolished. But although most people do profoundly and potently believe what this saucy Trevelyan says, yet his words find little echo in public debate, and his direct motions in the House of Commons have been unsuccessful. The Duke, I perceive, has lately, however, descended so far from his position of supreme dignity as to defend himself in a public speech, and to claim the merit of having always been a progressive and indeed rather daring army reformer. But I do not believe the English Government or Parliament would ever have ventured to take one step to lessen the Duke of Cambridge's power of doing harm to the military service, were it not for the pressure of events with which England had nothing directly to do, and which nevertheless have proved too strong for the resistance even of princes and of vested interests. The practical dethronement of the Duke of Cambridge I hold to be as certain as any mortal event still in the future can well be declared. The anomaly, the inconvenience, the degradation which English Governments and Parliaments would have endured forever if left to themselves, may be regarded as destined to be swept away by the same flood which overwhelmed the military organization of France, and washed the Bonapartes off the throne of the Tuileries. The Duke of Cambridge too had to surrender at Sedan.

For with the overwhelming successes of Prussia and the unparalleled collapse of France, there arose in England so loud and general a cry for the reorganization of the decaying old army system that no Government could possibly attempt to disregard it. Mr. Gladstone's Cabinet had the sense and spirit to see that no middle course of reform would be worth anything. *In medio tutissimus ibis* would never apply to this case. Any reform must count on the obstinate opposition of vested interests—a tremendous power in English affairs; and the only way to bear down that opposition would be by introducing a reform so thorough and grand as to carry with it the enthusiasm of popular support. Therefore the Government have undertaken a new work of revolution, certainly not less bold than that which overthrew the Irish Church, and destined perhaps to have a still more decisive influence on the political organization of English society. One of the many changes this measure will introduce—and it is certain to be carried, first or last—will be the extinction of the anomaly now represented by the position of the Duke of Cambridge. I shall not inflict any of the details of the measure upon my readers in The Galaxy, and shall even give but slight attention to such of its main features as are of purely military character and import. But I shall endeavor briefly to make it clear that some of the changes it proposes to introduce will have a profound influence on the political and social condition of England, and are in fact steps in that great English revolution which is steadily marching on under our very eyes.

First comes the abolition of the purchase system as regards the commissions held by military officers. Except in certain regiments, and certain branches of the service outside England itself, the rule is that an officer obtains his commission by purchase. Promotion can be bought in the same way. A commission is a vested interest. The owner has paid so much for it, and expects to sell it for an equal sum. The regulation price recognized by law and the Horse Guards is by no means the actual price of the article. It is worth ever so much more to the holder, and he must of course have its real, not its regulation value. The pay in the English army is, for the officers, ridiculously small. The habits of the army, among officers, are ridiculously expensive. An officer is not expected to live upon his pay.

Whether expected to do so or not, he could hardly accomplish the feat under any conditions; under the common conditions of an officers' mess-room the thing would be utterly impossible. Now let any reader ask himself what becomes of a department of the public service where you obtain admission by payment, and where when admitted you receive practically no remuneration? Of course it becomes a mere club and association for the wealthy and aristocratic; a brotherhood into which admission is sought for the sake of social distinction. Every man of rank in England will, as a matter of course, have one of his sons in the army. It is the right sort of thing to do, like hunting or going into the House of Commons. Then, on the other hand, every person who has made money sends one of his sons into the army, because thereby he acquires a stamp of gentility. Poverty and merit have no chance and no business there. It certainly is not true, as is commonly believed here, that promotion from the ranks never takes place; but speaking of the system as a whole, one may fairly say that promotion from the ranks is opposed to the ordinary regulation, and occurs so rarely that it need hardly be taken into our consideration here. Therefore the English army became an essentially aristocratic service. To be an officer was the right of the aristocratic, the luxury, ambition, and ornament of the wealthy. One is almost afraid now to venture on saying anything in praise of the French military system; but it had, if I do not greatly mistake, one regulation among others which honorably distinguished it from the English. I believe it was not permitted to a wealthy officer to distinguish himself from his fellows while in barracks by extravagance of expenditure. He had to live as the others lived. But the English system allowed full scope to wealth, and the result was that certain regiments prided themselves on luxury and ostentation, and a poor man, or even a man of moderate means, could not live in them. Add to all this that while the expenses were great and the pay next to nothing, there were certain valuable prizes, sinecures, and monopolies to be had in the army, which favoritism and family influence could procure, and which therefore rendered it additionally desirable that the control of the military organization should be retained in the hands of the aristocracy. John Bright described the military and diplomatic services of England as "a gigantic system of outdoor relief for the broken-down members of the British aristocracy." This was especially true of the military service, which had a large number of rich and pleasant prizes to be awarded at the uncontrolled discretion of the authorities. It might be fairly said that every aristocratic family had at least one scion in the army. Every aristocratic family had likewise one in the House of Commons; sometimes two, or three, or four sons and nephews. The mere numerical strength of the military officers who had seats in the House of Commons was enough to hold up a tremendous barrier in the way of army reform or political reform.

It was as clear as light that a popular Parliament would among its very first works of reformation proceed to throw open the army to the competition of merit, independently of either aristocratic rank or moneyed influence. So the military men in the House of Commons were, with some few and remarkable exceptions, steady Tories and firm opponents of all reform either in the army or the political system. Year after year did gallant old De Lacy Evans bring forward his motion for the abolition of the purchase system in vain. He was always met by the supposed practical authority of the great bulk of the military members and by the dead weight of aristocratic influence and vested interests. The army, as then organized, was at once the fortress and the trophy of the English aristocracy. At last the effort at reform seemed to be given up altogether. Though humane reformers did at last succeed in getting rid of the detestable system of flogging in the army, the practice of trafficking in commissions seemed safer than ever. One difficulty in the way of its abolition was always pressed with special emphasis by persons who otherwise were prodigal enough of the public money—the cost such a measure would entail on the people of England. It would be impossible, of course, to abolish such a system without compensating those who had paid money for the commissions which thenceforward could be sold no more. The amount of money required for such compensation would be some forty millions of dollars. Moreover, when commissions are given away among all classes according to merit, the pay of officers will have to be raised. It would indeed be a cruel mockery to give poor Claude Melnotte an officer's rank if he does not at the same time get pay enough to enable him to live. Therefore for once the English aristocrats and Tories were heard to raise their voices in favor of the saving of public money; but they were only assuming the attitude of economists for the sake of upholding their own privileges and defending their vested interests. There will, of course, be a fierce and long fight made even still against the change, but the change, I take it, will be accomplished. The English army will cease to be an army officered exclusively from among the ranks of the aristocracy and the wealthy. Our time has seen no step attempted in English political affairs more distinctly democratic than this. I can hardly realize to my mind what England will be like when commissions and promotions in its military service are the recognized prizes of merit in whatever rank of life, and are won by open competition.

Next, the English Government, approaching rather delicately the difficulty about the Commander-in-Chief, propose to unite the two departments of the service under one roof. The Commander-in-Chief and his staff and offices will be transferred from the Horse Guards in Whitehall to the War Office in Pall Mall, and placed more directly under the control of the Secretary of War. This change must inevitably bring about the end at which it aims—the abolition of the embarrassing and injurious dualism of system now prevailing. It must indeed reduce the General commanding-in-chief to his proper position as the executive officer of the War Secretary, who is himself the servant of Parliament. Such a position would entail no restriction whatever on the military capacity or genius of the Commander-in-Chief were he another Marlborough; but it would make him responsible to somebody who is himself responsible to the House of Commons. I think it may be taken for granted that this will come to mean, sooner or later, the shelving of the Duke of Cambridge. It may be hoped that he will not consider it consistent with his dignity as a member of the royal family to remain in a position thus made virtually that of a subordinate. Some other place perhaps will be found for the cousin of the Queen. I have already heard some talk about the possibility and propriety of sending his Royal Highness as Lord Lieutenant to govern Ireland. Why not? There is a *vile corpus* convenient and ready to hand for any experiment. It would be quite in keeping with all the traditions of English rule, with the practice which was illustrated only a few years ago when the noisy and brainless scamp Sir Robert Peel, whom "Punch" christened "The Mountebank Member," was made Irish Secretary, if the Duke of Cambridge were allowed to soothe his offended dignity by practising his skilful hand on the government of Ireland.

Finally, the Government propose to introduce measures calculated to weld together as far as possible the regular and irregular forces of the country. There are in England three classes of soldiery—the regular army, the militia, and the volunteers. The militia constitute a force as nearly as possible corresponding with that in whose companionship Sir John Falstaff declined to march through Coventry. Bombastes Furioso or the Grande Duchesse hardly ever marshalled such a body of men as may be seen when a British militia regiment is turned out for exercise. Awkward country bumpkins and beer-swilling rowdies of the poacher class make up the bulk of the privates. They are a terror to any small town where they may happen to be exercising, and where not infrequently they finish up a day's drill by a general smashing of windows, sacking of shops, and plundering of inhabitants. The volunteers are a force composed of a much better class of men, and are capable, I think, of great military efficiency and service if properly organized. Of late the volunteer force has, I believe, been growing somewhat demoralized. The Government never gave it very cordial encouragement, its position was hardly defined, and the national enthusiasm out of which it sprang naturally began to languish. We in England have always owed our volunteer force to some sudden menace or dread of French invasion. It was so in the time of William Pitt. We all remember the famous sarcasm with which that statesman replied to the request of some volunteer regiments not to be sent out on foreign service. Pitt gravely assured them that they never should be sent out of the country unless in case of England's invasion. Erskine was a volunteer, and I think it was as an officer of volunteers that Gibbon said he acquired a practical knowledge of military affairs, which proved useful to him in describing the decline and fall of the Roman empire. Our present volunteer service originated in the last of the "three panics" described by Cobden—the fear of invasion by Louis Napoleon, the panic which Tennyson endeavored to foment by his weak and foolish "Form, form! Riflemen, form!" The volunteer force, however, continued to grow stronger and stronger long after the alarm had died away; and even though recently the progress of improvement seems to have been somewhat checked, and the volunteer body to have become lax in its organization, it appears to me that in its intelligence, its earnestness, and its physical capacity there exists the material out of which might be moulded a very valuable arm of the military service. The War Minister now proposes to take steps which shall render the militia a decent body, commanded by really qualified and responsible officers, which shall give better officers to the volunteers, and place these latter under more effective discipline, and which shall bring militia and volunteers into closer relationship with the regular army. How far these objects may be attained by the measures now under consideration I do not pretend to judge; but I cannot regard the present War Minister as a man highly qualified for the place he holds. Mr. Cardwell is an admirable clerk—patient, plodding, untiring; but I doubt whether he has any of the higher qualities of an administrator or much force of character. He is perhaps the very dullest speaker holding a marked position in the House of Commons. He is fluent, not as Gladstone and a river are fluent, but as the sand in an hour-glass is fluent. That sand itself is not more dull, colorless, monotonous, and dry, than is the eloquence of the War Minister. Mr. Cardwell is not always fortunate in his military prophecies. On the memorable night in last July when the news reached London that France had declared war against Prussia, Mr. Cardwell affirmed that that meant the occupation of Berlin by the French within a month. It must be remembered, however, as an excuse for the War Minister's unlucky prediction, that an English military commission sent to examine the two systems had shortly before reported wholly in favor of the French army organization and dead against that of Prussia.

The English Government, wisely, I think, decline to attempt the introduction of any measure for general and compulsory service, except as a last resource in desperate exigencies. The England of the future is not likely, I trust, to embroil herself much in Continental quarrels; and she may be quite expected to hold her own in the improbable event of any of her neighbors attempting to invade her. For myself, I can recollect no instance recorded by history of any foreign war wherein England took part, from which good temper, discretion, judgment, and justice would not alike have counselled her to hold aloof.

Such then are in substance the changes which are proposed for the reconstruction of the English army. The one grand reform or revolution is the abolition of the purchase system. This change will inevitably convert the army into a practical and regular profession, to which all classes will look as a possible means of providing for some of their children. It will have one advantage over the bar, that admission to the ranks of the officers will not necessarily involve the preliminary payment of any sum of money, however small. The profession will cease to be ornamental and aristocratic. It will no longer constitute one of the great props, one of the grand privileges, of the system of aristocracy. Its reorganization will be another and a bold step toward the establishment of that principle of equality which is of late years beginning to exercise so powerful a fascination over the popular mind of England. Caste had in Great Britain no such illustration and no such bulwark as the army system presented. I should be slow to undertake to limit the possible depth and extent of the influence which the impulse given by this reform may exercise over the political condition of England. I can hardly realize to myself by any effort of imagination the effect which such a change will work in what is called society in England, and in the literature, especially the romantic and satirical literature, of the country. Are we then no longer to have Rawdon Crawley, and Sir Derby Oaks, and "Captain Gandaw of the Pinks"? Was Black-Bottle Cardigan really the last of a race? Will people a generation hence fail to understand what was meant by the intimation that "the Tenth don't dance"? Is Guy Livingstone to become as utter a tradition and myth as Guy of Warwick? Is the English military officer to be henceforward simply a hard-working, well-qualified public servant, who obtains his place in open competition by virtue of his merits? Appreciate the full meaning of the change who can, it is too much for me; I can only wonder, admire, and hope. But it is surely not possible that the Duke of Cambridge, cousin of the Queen, can continue to preside over a service wherein the butcher, the baker, and the candlestick-maker have as good a chance of obtaining commissions for their sons as the marquis or the earl or the great millionaire. Only think of the flood of light which will be poured in upon all the details of the military organization, when once it becomes the direct interest of each of us to see that the profession is properly managed in which his own son, however poor in purse and humble in rank, has a chance of obtaining a commission! I believe the Duke of Cambridge had and has an honest hatred and contempt for the coarse and noisy interference of public and unprofessional criticism where the business of the sacred Horse Guards is concerned. Once, when goaded on to sheer desperation by comments in the papers, his Royal Highness actually wrote or dictated a letter of explanation to the "Times," signed with the monosyllabic grandeur of his name "George," we all held up the hands and eyes of wonder that such things had come to pass, that royal princes condescended to write to newspapers, and yet the world rolled on. I cannot think the Duke will abide the awful changes that are coming. He will probably pass into the twilight and repose of some dignified office, where blundering has no occupation and obstinacy can do no harm. Everything considered, I think we may say of him that he might have been a great deal worse than he was. My own impression is that he is rather better than his reputation. If the popular voice of England were to ask in the words of Shakespeare's "Lucio," "And was the Duke a fleshmonger, a fool, and a coward, as you then reported him to be?" I might answer, in the language of the pretended friar, "You must change persons with me ere you make that my report. You indeed spoke so of him, and much more, much worse."

BRIGHAM YOUNG

Those among us who are not too young to have had "Evenings at Home" for a schoolday companion and instructor will remember the story called "Eyes and No Eyes" and its moral. They will remember that, of the two little boys who accomplished precisely the same walk at the same time, one saw all manner of delightful and wonderful things, while the other saw nothing whatever that was worth recollection or description. The former had eyes prepared to see, and the other had not; and that made all the difference. I have to confess that, during a recent visit to Salt Lake City—a visit lasting nearly as many days as that out of which my friend, Hepworth Dixon, made the better part of a volume—I must have been in the condition of the dull little reprobate who had no eyes to see the wonders which delighted his companion. For, so far as the city itself, its streets and its structures, are concerned, I really saw nothing in particular. A muddy little country town, with one or two tolerably decent streets, wherein a few handsome stores are mixed up with old shanties, is not much to see in any part of the civilized world. Other travellers have seen a wondrous sight on the very same spot. They have seen a large and beautiful city, with spacious, splendid streets, shaded by majestic trees and watered by silvery currents flowing in marble channels; they have seen a city combining the cleanliness and activity of young America with the picturesqueness and dignity of the Orient; a city which would be beautiful and wonderful anywhere, but which, raised up here on the bare bosom of the desert, is a phenomenon of apparently almost magical creation. Naturally, therefore, they have gone into raptures over the energy, and industry, and æstheticism of the Mormons; and, even while condemning sternly the doctrine and practice of polygamy, they have nevertheless been haunted by an uneasy doubt as to whether, after all, there is not some peculiar virtue in the having half a dozen wives together which endows a man with super-human gifts as a builder of cities. Otherwise how comes this beautiful and perfect city, here on the unfriendly and unsheltering waste?

Well, I saw no beautiful and wonderful city, although I spent several days in the Mormon capital, and tramped every one of its streets, and lanes, and roads, scores of times over. Where others beheld the glorious virgin, Dulcinea del Toboso, radiant in beauty and bedight with queenly apparel,

I saw only the homely milkmaid, with her red elbows and her russet gown. In plain words, the Mormon city appeared to me just a commonplace little country town, and no more. I saw in it no evidences of preternatural energy or skill. It has one decent street, wherein may be found, at most, half a dozen well-built and attractive-looking shops. It has a good many comfortable residences in the environs. It has two or three decentish hotels, like the hotels of any other fiftieth-class country town. It has the huge Tabernacle, a gigantic barn merely, a simple covering in and over of so much space—a thing in shape "very like a land turtle," as President George L. Smith, First Councillor of Brigham Young, observed to me. Salt Lake City has no lighting and no draining, except such draining as is done by the little runnels of water to be found in every street, and which remind one faintly and sadly of dear, quaint old Berne in Switzerland. At night you have to trudge along in the darkness and the mud, or slush, or dust, and it is a perilous quest the seeking of your way home, for at every crossing you must look or feel for the plank which bridges over the artificial brooklets already described, or you plunge helpless and hopeless into the little torrent. Decidedly, a "one-horse" place, in my estimation; I don't see how men endowed with average heads and arms could for twenty years have been occupied in the building of a city, and produced anything less creditable than this. I do not wonder at the complacency and self-conceit with which all the Mormon residents talk of the beauty of their city and the wonderful things they have accomplished, when Gentile travellers of credit and distinction have glorified this shabby, swampy, ricketty, common-place, vulgar, little hamlet into a town of sweetness and light, of symmetry and beauty. For my part, and for those who were with me, I can only say that we spent the first day or so in perpetual wonder as to whether this really could be the Mormon city of which we had read so many bewildering and glorious descriptions. And the theatre—oh, Hepworth Dixon, I like you much, and I think you are often abused and assailed most unjustly; but how could you write so about that theatre? Or was the beautiful temple of the drama which *you* saw here deliberately taken down, and did they raise in its place the big, gaunt, ugly, dirty, dismal structure which *I* saw, and in which I and my companions made part of a dreary dozen or two of audience, and blinked in the dim, depressing light of mediæval oil-lamps? I observe that, when driven to bay by sceptical inquiry, complacent Mormons generally fall back on the abundance of shade-trees in the streets. Let them have the full credit of this plantation. They have put trees in the streets, and the trees have grown; and, when we observe to a Mormon that we have seen rows of trees similarly growing in even smaller towns of the benighted European continent, he evidently thinks it is our monogamic perversity and prejudice which force us to deny the wondrous works of Mormonism. Making due allowance for every natural difficulty, remembering how nearly every implement, and utensil, and scrap of raw material had to be brought from across yonder rampart of mountains, and from hundreds of miles away, I yet fail to see anything very remarkable about this little Mormon town. Perhaps no other set of people could have made much more of the place; I cannot help thinking that no other set of people who were not Digger Indians could have made much less.

In fact, to retain the proper and picturesque ideas of Salt Lake City, one never ought to have entered the town at all. We ought to have remained on this hillside, from which you can look across that most lovely of all valleys on earth, cinctured as it is by a perfect girdle of mountains, the outlines of which are peerless and ineffable in their symmetry and beauty. The air is as clear, the skies are as blue, the grass as green as the dream of a poet or painter could show him. There below, fringed and mantled in the clustering green of its trees, you see the city, with the long, low, rounded dome or back of the Tabernacle rising broad and conspicuous. Looking down, you may well believe that the city thus exquisitely placed, thus deliciously shaded and surrounded, is itself a wonder of picturesqueness and symmetry. Why go down into the two or three dirty, irregular, shabby little streets, with their dust or mud for road pavement, their nozzling pigs trotting along the sidewalks, their dung-heaps and masses of decaying vegetable matter, their utterly commonplace, mean and disheartening aspect everywhere? But then we did go down—and where others had seen a fair and goodly, aye, and queenly city, we saw a muddy, uninteresting, straggling little village, disfiguring the lovely plain on which it stood.

Profound disappointment, then, is my first sensation in Salt Lake City. The place is so like any other place! Certainly, one receives a bracing little shock every now and then, which admonishes him that, despite the small, shabby stores and the pigs, and the dunghills, he is not in the regions of merely commonplace dirt. For instance, we learn that the proprietor of the hotel where we are staying has four wives; and it is something odd to talk with a civil, respectable, burgess-like man, dressed in ordinary coat and pantaloons, and wearing mutton-chop whiskers—a sort of man who in England would probably be a church-warden—and who has more consorts than an average Turk. Then again it is startling to be asked, "Do you know Mr. ——?" and when I say "No, I don't," to be told, "Oh, you ought to know him. He came from England, and he has lately married two such nice English girls!" One morning, too, we have another kind of shock. There is a pretty little chambermaid in our hotel, a new-comer apparently, and she happens to find out that my wife and I had lived for many years in that part of the North of England from which she comes herself, whereupon she bursts into a perfect passion and tempest of tears, declares that she would rather be in her grave than in Salt Lake City, that she was deceived into coming, that the Mormonism she heard preached by the Mormon propaganda in England was a quite different thing from the Mormonism practised here, and that her only longing was to get out of the place, anyhow, forever. The girl seemed to be perfectly, passionately sincere. What could be done for her? Apparently nothing. She had spent all her money in coming out; and she seemed to be strongly under the conviction that, even if she had money, she could not get away. An influence was evidently over her which she had not the courage or strength of mind to attempt to resist, or even to elude. Doubtless, as she was a very pretty girl, she would be very soon sealed to some ruling elder. She said her sister had come with her, but the sister was in another part of the city, and since their arrival—only a few days, however—they had not met. My wife endeavored to console or encourage her, but the girl could only sob and protest that she never could learn to endure the place, but that she could not get away, and that she would rather be in her grave. We spoke of this case to one of the civil officers of the United States stationed in the city, and he shook his head and thought nothing could be done. The influence which enslaved this poor girl was not wholly that of force, but a power which worked upon her senses and her superstitions. I should think an underground railway would be a valuable institution to establish in connection with the Mormon city.

I well remember that when I lived in Liverpool, some ten or a dozen years ago, the Mormon propaganda, very active there, always kept the polygamy institution modestly in the background. Proselytes were courted and won by descriptions of a new Happy Valley, of a City of the Blest, where eternal summer shone, where the fruits were always ripe, where the earth smiled with a perpetual harvest, where labor and reward were plenty for all, and where the outworn toilers of Western Europe could renew their youth like the eagles. I remember, too, the remarkable case of a Liverpool family having a large business establishment in the most fashionable street of the great town, who were actually beguiled into selling off all their goods and property and migrating, parents, sons, and daughters, to the land of promise beyond the American wilderness, and how, before people had ceased to wonder at their folly, they all came back, humiliated, disgusted, cured. They had money and something like education, and they were a whole family, and so they were able, when they found themselves deceived, to effect a rapid retreat at the cost of nothing worse than disappointment and pecuniary loss. But for the poor, pretty serving-lass from Lancashire I do not know that there is much hope. Poverty and timidity and superstitious weakness will help to lock the Mormon chains around her. Perhaps she will get used to the place in time. Ought one to wish that she may—or rather to echo her own prayer, and petition that she may find an early grave? The graveyards are densely planted with tombs here in this sacred city of Mormonism.

The place is unspeakably dreary. Hardly any women are ever seen in the streets, except on the Sunday, when all the families pour in to service in the huge Tabernacle. Most of the dwelling houses round the city are pent in behind walls. Most of the houses, too, have their dismal little *sucursales*, one or two or more, built on to the sides—and in each of these additions or wings to the original building a different wife and family are caged. There are no flower gardens anywhere. Children are bawling everywhere. Sometimes a wretched, slatternly, dispirited woman is seen lounging at the door or hanging over the gate of a house with a baby at her breast. More often, however, the house, or clump of houses, gives no external sign of life. It stands back gloomy in the sullen shade of its thick fruit trees, and might seem untenanted if one did not hear the incessant yelling of the children. We saw the women in hundreds, probably in thousands, at the Tabernacle on the Sunday—and what women they were! Such faces, so dispirited, depressed, shapeless, hopeless, soulless faces! No trace of woman's graceful pride and neatness in these slatternly, shabby, slouching, listless figures; no purple light of youth over these cheeks; no sparkle in these half-extinguished eyes. I protest that only in some of the *cretin* villages of the Swiss mountains have I seen creatures in female form so dull, miserable, moping, hopeless as the vast majority of these Mormon women. As we leave the Tabernacle, and walk slowly down the street amid the crowd, we see two prettily-dressed, lively-looking girls, who laugh with each other and are seemingly happy, and we thank Heaven that there are at least two merry, spirited girls in Salt Lake City. A few days after we meet our blithesome pair at Mintah station; and they are travelling with their father and mother on to San Francisco, whither we too are going—and we learn that they are not Mormons, but Gentiles—pleasant lasses from Philadelphia who had come with their parents to have a passing look at the externals of Mormonism.

My object, however, in writing this paper was to speak of the chief, Brigham Young himself, rather than of his city or his system. We saw Brigham Young, were admitted to prolonged speech of him, and received his parting benediction. The interview took place in the now famous house with the white walls and the gilded beehive on the top. We were received in a kind of office or parlor, hung round with oil paintings of the kind which in England we regard as "furniture," and which represented all the great captains and elders of Mormonism. Joseph Smith is there, and Brigham Young, and George L. Smith, now First Councillor; and various others whom to enumerate would be long, even if I knew or remembered their names. President Young was engaged just at the moment when we came, but his Secretary, a Scotchman, I think, and President George L. Smith, are very civil and cordial. George L. Smith is a huge, burly man, with a Friar Tuck joviality of paunch and visage, and a roll in his bright eye which, in some odd, undefined sort of way, suggests cakes and ale. He talks well, in a deep rolling voice, and with a dash of humor in his words and tone—he it is who irreverently but accurately likens the Tabernacle to a land-turtle. He speaks with immense admiration and reverence of Brigham Young, and specially commends his abstemiousness and hermit-like frugality in the matter of eating and drinking. Presently a door opens, and the oddest, most whimsical figure I have ever seen off the boards of an English country theatre stands in the room; and in a moment we are presented formally to Brigham Young.

There must be something of impressiveness and dignity about the man, for, odd as is his appearance and make up, one feels no inclination to laugh. But such a figure! Brigham Young wears a long-tailed, high-collared coat; the swallow-tails nearly touch the ground; the collar is about his ears. In shape the garment is like the swallow-tail coats which negro-melodists sometimes wear, or like the dandy English dress coat one can still see in prints in some of the shops of St. James street, London. But the material of Brigham's coat is some kind of rough, gray frieze, and the garment is adorned with huge brass buttons. The vest and trowsers are of the same material. Round the neck of the patriarch is some kind of bright crimson shawl, and on the patriarch's feet are natty little boots of the shiniest polished leather. I must say that the gray frieze coat of antique and wonderful construction, the gaudy crimson shawl, and the dandy boots make up an incongruous whole which irresistibly reminds one at first of the holiday get-up of some African King who adds to a great coat, preserved as an heirloom since Mungo Park's day, a pair of modern top-boots, and a lady's bonnet. The whole appearance of the patriarch, when one has got over the African monarch impression, is like that of a Suffolk farmer as presented on the boards of a Surrey theatre. But there is decidedly an amount of composure and even of dignity about Brigham Young which soon makes one forget the mere ludicrousness of the patriarch's external appearance. Young is a handsome man—much handsomer than his portrait on the wall would show him. Close upon seventy years of age, he has as clear an eye and as bright a complexion as if he were a hale English farmer of fifty-five. But there is something fox-like and cunning lurking under the superficial good-nature and kindliness of the face. He seems, when he speaks to you most effusively and plausibly, to be quietly studying your expression to see whether he is really talking you over or not. The expression of his face, especially of his eyes, strangely and provokingly reminds me of Kossuth. I think I have seen Kossuth thus watch the face of a listener to see whether or not the listener was conquered by his wonderful power of talk. Kossuth's face, apart from its intellectual qualities, appeared to me to express a strange blending of vanity, craft, and weakness; and Brigham Young's countenance now seems to show just such a mixture of qualities. Great force of character the man must surely have; great force of character Kossuth, too, had; but the face of neither man seemed to declare the possession of such a quality. Brigham Young decidedly does not impress me as a man of great ability; but rather as a man of great plausibility. I can at once understand how such a man, with such an eye and tongue, can easily exert an immense influence over women. Beyond doubt he is a man of genius; but his genius does not reveal itself, to me at least, in his face or his words. He speaks in a thin, clear, almost shrill tone, and with much apparent *bonhomie*. After a little commonplace conversation about the city, its improvements, approaches etc., the Prophet voluntarily goes on to speak of himself, his system, and his calumniators. His talk soon flows into a kind of monologue, and is indeed a curious rhapsody of religion, sentimentality, shrewdness and egotism. Sometimes several sentences succeed each other in which his hearers hardly seem to make out any meaning whatever, and Brigham Young appears a grotesque kind of Coleridge. Then again in a moment comes up a shrewd meaning very distinctly expressed, and with a dash of humor and sarcasm gleaming fantastically amid the scriptural allusions and the rhapsody of unctuous words. The purport of the whole is that Brigham Young has been misunderstood, misprized, and calumniated, even as Christ was; that were Christ to come up to-morrow in New York or London, He would be misunderstood, misprized, and caluminated, even as Brigham Young now is; and that Brigham Young is not to be dismayed though the stars in their courses should fight against him. He protests with especial emphasis and at the same time especial meekness, with eyes half closed and delicately-modulated voice, against the false reports that any manner of force or influence whatever is, or ever was, exercised to keep men or women in Salt Lake City against their will. He appeals to the evidence of our own eyes, and asks us whether we have not seen for ourselves that the city is free to all to come and go as they will. At this time we had not heard the story told by the poor little maid at the hotel; but in any case the evidence of our eyes could go no farther than to prove that travellers like ourselves were free to enter and depart. We have, however, little occasion to trouble ourselves about answering; for the Prophet keeps the talk pretty well all to himself. His manner is certainly not that of a man of culture, but it has a good deal of the quiet grace and self-possession of what we call a gentleman. There is nothing *prononcé* or vulgar about him. Even when he is most rhapsodical his speech never loses its ease and gentleness of tone. He is bland, benevolent, sometimes quietly pathetic in manner. He poses himself *en victime*, but with the air of one who does this regretfully and only from a disinterested sense of duty. I begin very soon to find that there is no need of my troubling myself much to keep up the conversation; that my business is that of a listener; that the Prophet conceives himself to be addressing some portion of the English or American press through my humble medium. So I listen and my companion listens; and Brigham Young talks on; and I do declare and acknowledge that we are fast drifting into a hazy mental condition by virtue of which we begin to regard the Mormon President as a victim of cruel persecution, a suffering martyr and an injured angel!

Time, surely, that the interview should come to a close. We tear ourselves away, and the Prophet dismisses us with a fervent and effusive blessing. "Good-bye—do well, mean well, pray always. Christ be with you, God be with you, God bless you." All this, and a great deal more to the same effect, was uttered with no vulgar, maw-worm demonstrativeness of tone or gesture, no nasal twang, no uplifted hands; but quietly, earnestly, as if it came unaffectedly from the heart of the speaker. We took leave of Brigham Young, and came away a little puzzled as to whether we had been conversing with an impostor or a fanatic, a Peter the Hermit or a Tartuffe. One thing, however, is clear to me. I do not say that Brigham Young is a Tartuffe; but I know now how Tartuffe ought to be played so as to render the part more effective and more apparently natural and lifelike than I have ever seen it on French or English stage.

No one can doubt the sincerity of the homage which the Mormons in general pay to Brigham Young. One man, of the working class, apparently, with whom I talked at the gate of the Tabernacle, spoke almost with tears in his eyes of the condescension the Prophet always manifested. My informant told me that he was at one time disabled by some hurt or ailment; and, the first day that he was able to come into the street again, President Young happened to be passing in his carriage, and caught sight of the convalescent. "He stopped his carriage, sir, called me over to him, addressed me by my name, shook hands with me, asked me how I was getting on, and said he was glad to see me out again." The poor man was as proud of this as a French soldier might have been if the Little Corporal had recognized him and called him by his name. There is no flattery which the great can offer to the humble like this way of addressing the man by his right name, and thus proving that the identity of the small creature has lived clearly in the memory of the great being. Many a renowned commander has endeared himself to the soldiers whom he regarded and treated only as the instruments of his business, by the mere fact that he took care to remember men's names. They would gladly die for one who could be so nobly gracious, and could thus prove that they were regarded by him as worthy to occupy each a distinct place in his busy mind. The niggardliness and selfishness of John, Duke of Marlborough, the savage recklessness of Claverhouse, were easily forgotten by the poor private soldiers whom each commander made it his business, when occasion required, to address correctly by their appropriate names of Tom, Dick, or Harry. Lord Palmerston governed the House of Commons and most of those outside it with whom he usually came into contact, by just such little arts or courtesies as this. In one of Messrs. Erckmann and Chatrian's novels we read of a soldier who declares himself ready to go to the death for Marshal Ney because the Marshal, who originally belonged to the same district as himself, had just recognized his fellow-countryman and called him by his name. But the hero of the novel is somewhat grim and sarcastic, and he thinks it was not so wonderful a condescension that Ney should have recognized an old comrade and called him by his name. Perhaps the hero of the tale had not himself received any such recognition from Ney—perhaps if it had been vouchsafed to him he, too, would have been ready to go to the death. Anyhow, this correct calling of names, and quick recognition has always been a great power in the governing of men and women. "Deal you in words," is the advice of Mephistophiles to the student, in Faust, "and you may leave others to do the best they can with things." I was able to appreciate the governing power of Brigham Young all the better when I had heard the expression of this poor Mormon's gratitude and homage to the great President who had shaken hands with him and addressed him promptly and correctly by his name.

This same Mormon was very communicative. Indeed, as a rule, I found most of the men in Salt Lake City ready and even eager to discuss their "peculiar institution," and to invite Gentile opinion on it. He showed us his two wives, and declared that they lived together in perfect harmony and happiness; never had a word of quarrel, but were contented and loving as two sisters. He delivered a panegyric on the moral condition of Salt Lake City, where, he declared, there was no dishonesty, no drunkenness, and no prostitution. I believe he was correct in his description of the place. From many quite impartial authorities I heard the same accounts of the honesty of the Mormons. There certainly is no drunkenness to be observed anywhere openly, and I believe (although I have heard others assert the contrary) that Salt Lake City is really and truly free from this vice; and I suppose it goes without saying that there is little or no prostitution in a place where a man is expected to keep as many wives as his means will allow him. Intelligent Mormons rely immensely on this absence of prostitution as a justification of their system. They seem to think that when they have said, "We have no prostitutes," all is said; and that the Gentile, with the shames of London, Paris and New York burning in his memory and his conscience, must be left without a word of reply. Brigham Young, in conversation with me, dwelt much on this absence of prostitution. Orson Pratt preached in the Tabernacle during our stay a sermon obviously "at" the Gentile visitors, who were just then specially numerous; and he drew an emphatic contrast between the hideous profligacy of the Eastern cities and the purity of the Salt Lake community. I must say, for myself, that I do not think the question can thus be settled; I do not think prostitution so great an evil as polygamy. If this blunt declaration should shock anybody's moral feelings I am sorry for it; but it is none the less the expression of my sincere conviction. Pray do not set me down as excusing prostitution. I think it the worst of all social evils—except polygamy. I think polygamy the worse evil, because I am convinced that, regarded from a physiological, moral, religious, and even merely poetical and sentimental point of view, the only true social bond to be sought and maintained and justified is the loving union of one man with one woman—at least until death shall part the two. Now, I regard the existence of prostitution as a proof that some men and women fail to keep to the right path. I look on polygamy as a proof that a whole community is going directly the wrong way. No man proposes to himself to lead a life of profligacy. He falls into it. He would get out of it if he only could—if the world and the flesh and the devil were not now and then too strong for him. But the polygamist deliberately sets up and justifies and glorifies a system which is as false to physiology as it is to morals. Observe that I do not say the polygamist is necessarily an immoral man. Doubtless he is often—in Utah I really believe he is commonly—a sincere, devoted, mistaken man, who honestly believes himself to be doing right. But when he attempts to vindicate his system on the ground that it banishes prostitution, I, for myself, declare that I believe a society which has to put up with prostitution is in better case and hope than one which deliberately adopts polygamy. I am emphatic in expressing this opinion because, as I am opposed to any stronghanded or legal movement whatever to put down Brigham Young and his system, I desire to have it clearly understood that my opinions on the subject of polygamy are quite decided, and that no one who has clamored, or may hereafter clamor, for the uprooting of Mormonism by fire and sword, can have less sympathy than I have with Mormonism's peculiar institution.

Let me return to Brigham Young. I saw the Prophet but twice—once in the street and once in his own house, where the interview took place which I have described. The day after that on which I last saw him he left Salt Lake City and went into the country—some people said to avoid the necessity of meeting Mr. Colfax, who was just then expected to arrive with his party from the West. My impressions, therefore, of Brigham Young and his personal character are necessarily hasty, and probably superficial. I can only say that he did not impress me either as a man of great genius, or as a mere *charlatan*. My impression is that he is a sincere man—that is to say, a man who sincerely believes in himself, accepts his own impulses, prejudices and passions as divine instincts and intuitions to be the law of life for himself and others, and who, therefore, has attained that supreme condition of utterly unsparing and pitiless selfishness when the voice of self is listened to as the voice of God. With such a sincerity is quite consistent the adoption of every craft and trick in the government of men and women. Nobody can doubt that Napoleon I. was perfectly sincere as regards his faith in himself, his destiny, and his duty; and yet there was no trick of lawyer, or play-actor, or priest, of which he would not condescend to avail himself if it served his purpose. This is not the sincerity of a Pascal, or a Garibaldi, or a Garrison; but it is just as genuine and infinitely more common. It is the kind of sincerity which we meet every day in ordinary life, when we see some dogmatic, obstinate father of a family or sense-carrier of a small circle trying to mould every will and conscience and life under his control according to his own pedantic standard, and firmly confident all the time that his own perverseness and egotism are a guiding inspiration from heaven. After all, the downright, conventional stage-hypocrite is the rarest of all beings in real life. I sometimes doubt whether there ever was *in rerum naturâ* any one such creature. I suppose Tartuffe had persuaded himself into self-worship, into the conviction that everything he said and did must be right. I look upon Brigham Young as a man of such a temperament and character. Cunning and crafty he undoubtedly is, unless all evidences of eye, and lip, and voice belie him; but we all know that many a fanatic who boldly and cheerfully mounted the funeral pile or the scaffold for his creed had over and over again availed himself of all the tricks of craft and cunning to maintain his ascendancy over his followers. The fanatic is often crafty just as the madman is: the presence of craft in neither case disproves the existence of sincerity.

I believe Brigham Young to be simply a crafty fanatic. That he professes and leads his creed of Mormonism merely to obtain lands and beeves and wives, I do not believe, although this seems to be the general impression among the Gentiles who visit his city. I am convinced that he regards himself as a prophet and a heaven-appointed leader, and that this belief prevents him from seeing how selfish he is in one sense and how ridiculous in another. Any man who can deliberately put on such a coat in combination with such a pair of boots, as Brigham Young displayed during my interview with him, must have a faith in himself which would sustain him in anything. No human creature capable of looking at any two sides of a question where he himself was concerned, ever did or could present himself in public and expect to be reverenced when arrayed in such uncouth and preposterous toggery.

I cannot pretend to have had any extraordinary revelations of the inner mysteries or miseries of Mormonism made to me during my stay at Salt Lake City. Other travellers, nearly all other travellers indeed, have apparently been more fortunate or more pushing and persevering. I fancy it is rather difficult just now to get to know much of the interior of Mormon households; and I confess that I never could quite understand how people, otherwise honorable and upright, can think themselves justified in worming their way into Mormon confidences, and then making profit one way or another by revelations to the public. But one naturally and unavoidably hears, in Salt Lake City, of things which are deeply significant and which he may without scruple put into print. For example—there was a terrible pathos to my mind in the history of a respectable and intelligent woman who, years and years ago, when her life, now fading, was in its prime, married a man now a shining light of Mormonism, whose photograph you may see anywhere in Salt Lake City. She has been superseded since by divers successive wives; she is now striving in a condition far worse than widowhood to bring up her seven or eight children, and she has not been favored with even a passing call for more than a year and a half by the husband of her youth, who lives with the newest of his wives a few hundred yards away. I am told that such things are perfectly common; that the result of the system is to plant in Utah a number of families which may be described practically as households without husbands and fathers. I believe the lady of whom I have just spoken accepts her destiny with sad and firm resignation. Her faith in the religion of Mormonism is unshaken, and she regards her forlorn and widowed life as the heaven-appointed cross, by the bearing of which she is to win her eternal crown. Of course the Indian widows regard their bed of flames, the Russian women-fanatics behold their mutilated and mangled breasts with a similar enthusiasm of hope and superstition. But none the less ghastly and appalling is the monstrous faith which exacts and glorifies such unnatural sacrifices. These dreary homes, widowed not by death, seem to be the saddest, most shocking birth of Mormonism. After all, this is not the polygamy of the East, bad as that may be. "Give us," exclaimed M. Thiers in the French Chamber, three or four years ago, when Imperialism had reached the zenith of its despotic power—"give us liberty as in Austria!" So I can well imagine one of these superseded and lonely wives in Salt Lake City, crying aloud in the bitterness of her heart, "Give us polygamy as in Turkey!"

That the thing is a religion, however hideously it may show, I do not doubt. I mean that I feel no doubt that the great majority of the Mormon men are drawn to and kept in Mormonism by a belief in its truth and vital force as a religion. I do not believe that conscious and hypocritical sensuality is the leading impulse in making them or keeping them members of the Mormon church. I never heard of any community where a sensual man found any difficulty in gratifying his sensuality; nor are the vast majority of the Mormons men belonging to a class on whom a severe public opinion would bear so directly that they must necessarily wander thousands of miles away across the desert in order to be able comfortably to gratify their immoral propensities. To me, therefore, the possibility which appears most dangerous of all is the chance of any sudden crusade, legal or otherwise, being set on foot against this perverted and unfortunate people. Left to itself, I firmly believe that Mormonism will never long bear the glare of daylight, the throng of witnesses, the intelligent rivalry, the earnest and active criticism, poured in and forced in upon it by the Pacific railroads. But if it can bear all this then it can bear anything whatever which human ingenuity or force can put in arms against it; and it will run its course and have its day, let the Federal Hercules himself do what he may. Meanwhile it would be well to bear in mind that Mormonism has thus far cumbered the earth for comparatively a very few years; that all its members there in Utah counted together would hardly equal the population of a respectable street in London; and that at this moment the whole concern is ricketty and shaky, and threatens to tumble to pieces. I know that some of the ruling elders are panting for persecution; that they are openly doing their very best to "draw fire;" that they are daily endeavoring to work on the fears or the passions of Federal officials resident at Salt Lake by threats of terrible deeds to be done in the event of any attempt being made to interfere with Mormonism. Many of these Mormon apostles, dull, vulgar and clownish as they seem, have foresight enough to see that their system sadly needs just now the stimulus of a little persecution, and have fanatical courage enough to put themselves gladly in the front of any danger for the sake of sowing by their martyrdom the seed of the church. "That man," said William the Third of England, speaking of an inveterate conspirator against him "is determined to be made a victim, and I am determined not to make him one." I hope the United States will deal with the Mormons in a similar spirit. At the same time, I would ask my brothers of the pen whether those of them who have visited Salt Lake City have not made the place seem a good deal more wonderful, more alluringly mysterious, more grandly paradoxical in its nature, than it really is? I feel convinced that if people in Lancashire and Wales and Sweden had all been made distinctly aware that Salt Lake City is only a dusty or muddy little commonplace country hamlet, where labor is not less hard and is not any better paid than in dozens or scores of small hamlets this side the Missouri, one vast temptation to emigrate thither, the temptation supplied by morbid curiosity and ignorant wonder, would never have had any conquering power, and Mormonism would have been deprived of many thousand votaries. For, regarded in an artistic point of view, the City of the Saints is a vulgar sham; a trumpery humbug; and I verily believe that it has swelled into importance not more through the fanatical energy of its governing elders and the ignorance of their followers, than through the extravagant exaggeration and silly wonder of most of its hostile visitors and critics.

THE LIBERAL TRIUMVIRATE OF ENGLAND

A year ago I happened to be talking with some French friends at a dinner-table in Paris, about the Reform agitation then going on in England. "We admire your great orators and leaders," said an enthusiastic French gentleman; "your Bright, your Beales" —and he was warming to the subject when he saw that I was smiling, and he at once pulled up, and asked me earnestly whether he had said anything ridiculous. I endeavored to explain to him gently that in England we did not usually place our Bright and our Beales on exactly the same level—that the former was our greatest orator, our most powerful leader, and the latter a respectable, earnest gentleman of warm emotions and ordinary abilities whom chance had made the figurehead of a passing and vehement agitation, and who would probably be forgotten the day after to-morrow or thereabouts.

My French friend did not seem convinced. He had seen Mr. Beales's name in the London papers quite as often and as prominently for some months as Mr. Bright's; and, moreover, he had met Mr. Beales at dinner, and did not like to be told that he had not thereby made the acquaintance of a great tribune of the British people. So I dropped the subject and allowed our Bright and and our Beales to rank together without farther protest.

Here in New York, where English politics are understood infinitely better than in Paris, I have noticed not a little of this "Bright and Beales" classification when people talk of the leaders of English Liberalism. I have heard, with surprise, this or that respectable member of Parliament, who never for a moment dreamed of being classed among the chiefs of his party, exalted to a place of equality with Gladstone or Bright. In truth the English Liberal party (I mean now the advancing and popular party—not the old Whigs) has only three men who can be called leaders. After Gladstone, Bright, and Mill there comes a huge gap—and then follow the subalterns, of whom one might name half a dozen having about equal rank and influence, and of whom you may choose any favorite you like. Take, for example, Mr. W. E. Forster, Mr. Stansfeld, Mr. Thomas Hughes, the O'Donoghue, Mr. Coleridge (who, however, is marked out for the judicial bench, and therefore need hardly be counted), and one or two others, and you have the captains of the advanced Liberal party. The Liberals are not rich in rising talent; at least there seems no man of the younger political generation who gives any promise of commanding ability. They have many good debaters and clever politicians, but I see no "pony Gladstone" to succeed him who used to be called the "pony Peel;" and the man has yet to show himself in whom the House of Commons can hope for a future Bright. The great Liberals of our day have apparently not the gift of training disciples in order that the latter may become apostles in their time. Like Cavour, they are too earnest about the work and do too much of it themselves to have leisure or inclination for teaching and pushing others.

Officially Mr. Gladstone has been, of course, for several years the leader of the party. He is formally invested with all the insignia of command. He is indeed the only possible leader; for he is the only man who has the slightest chance just now of commanding the allegiance of the old Whigs with their dukes and earls, and the young Radicals with their philosophers, their Comtists, their Irish Nationalists, and their working men. But the true soul and voice and heart of the Liberal party pay silent allegiance to John Bright. He is, by universal acknowledgment, the maker of the Reform agitation and the Reform Bill.

Mr. Disraeli has over and over again flung in the face of Mr. Gladstone the fact that Bright, and not he, is the master spirit of Radicalism. Of late the Tories have taken to praising and courting Bright incessantly and ostentatiously, and contrasting his calm, consistent wisdom with Gladstone's impetuosity and fitfulness. Of course both Bright and Gladstone thoroughly understand the meaning of this, and smile at it and despise it. The obvious purpose is to try to set up a rivalry between the two. If Gladstone's authority could be damaged that would be quite enough; for it would be impossible at present to get the Whig dukes and earls to follow Bright, and the dethronement of Gladstone would be the break-up of the party. The trick is an utter failure. Bright is sincerely and generously loyal to Gladstone, and is a man as completely devoid of personal vanity or self-seeking as he is of fear. No personal question will ever divide these two men.

Gladstone is beyond doubt the most fluent and brilliant speaker in the English Parliament. No other man has anything like his inexhaustible flow and rush of varied and vivid expression. His memory is as surprising as his fluency. Grattan spoke of the eloquence of Fox as "rolling in resistless as the waves of the Atlantic." So far as this description conveys the idea of a vast volume of splendid words pouring unceasingly in, it may be applied to Gladstone. A listener new to the House is almost certain to prefer him to any other speaker there, and to regard him as the greatest English orator of the present generation. I was myself for a long time completely under the spell, and a little impatient of those who insisted on the superiority of

Bright. But when one becomes accustomed to the speaking of the two men it is impossible not to find the fluency, the glitter, the impetuous volubility, the involved and complicated sentences, the Latinized, sesquipedalian words of Gladstone gradually losing their early charm and influence, just as the pure noble Saxon, the unforced energy, the exquisite simplicity, the perfect "fusion of reason and passion" which are the special characteristics of Bright's eloquence, grow more and more fascinating and commanding. Perhaps the same effect may be found to arise from a study or a contrast (if one must contrast them) between the political characters of the two men.

It is a somewhat singular fact that one English county has produced the three men who undoubtedly rank beyond all others in England as Parliamentary orators. The Earl of Derby, Mr. Gladstone, and Mr. Bright are all Lancashire men. But Gladstone is only Lancashire by birth. His shrewd old Scotch father came to Liverpool from across the Tweed, and made his money and founded his family in the great port of the Mersey. The Gladstones had, and have, large West Indian property; and when England emancipated her slaves by paying off the planters, the Gladstones came in for no small share of the national purchase-money. When the great Liberal orator came out so impetuously and unluckily with his celebrated panegyric on Jefferson Davis, a few years ago, some people shook their heads and remarked that the old planter spirit does not quite die out in the course of one generation; and I heard bitter allusion made to the celebrated declaration flung by Cooke, the great tragedian, in the face of an indignant theatre in Liverpool, that there was not a stone in the walls of that town which was not "cemented by the blood of Africans." But, indeed, Gladstone's outburst had no traditional, or hereditary, or other such source. It came straight from the impulsive heart and nature of the speaker. His strength and his weakness are alike illustrated by that sudden, indiscreet, unjustifiable, and repented outburst. Thus he every now and then disappoints his friends and shakes the confidence of his followers. A keen, intellectual, cynical member of the Liberal party, Mr. Grant Duff, not long since publicly reproached Mr. Gladstone with this trick of suddenly "turning round and firing his revolver in the face of his followers." Certain it is that there is little or no enthusiasm felt toward Gladstone personally, by his party. Admirers of Mr. Disraeli are usually devotees of the man himself. Young men, especially, delight in him and adore him. Mr. Gladstone is followed as a leader, admired as an orator; but I have heard very few of his followers ever express any personal affection or enthusiasm for him; but it is quite notorious in London that some of his adherents can hardly control their dislike of him. Mr. Bright, although a man of somewhat cold and reserved demeanor, and occasionally *brusque* in manner, is popular everywhere in the House. Mr. Gladstone is not personally popular even among his own followers. What is the reason? His enemies say that he has a bad temper and an unbending intellectual pride, which is as untrue as if they were to say he had a hoarse voice and a stammer. The obscurest man in the House of Commons is not more modest; and there is nothing ungenial in his manner or his temper. But the truth is that people cannot rely upon him, or think they cannot, which, so far as they are concerned, amounts to the same thing. His strongest passion in life—stronger than his love of figures, or of Homer, or even of liberty—is a love of argument. He is always ready to sacrifice his friend, or his party, or even his cause, to his argument. Add to this that he has a conscience so sensitive that it can hardly ever find any cause or deed smooth enough to be wholly satisfactory; add, moreover, that he has an eloquence so fluent as to flow literally away from him, or with him, and the wonder will be how such a man ever came to be the successful leader of a great party at all. He is always reconsidering what he has done, always penitent for something he has said, always turning up to-day the side of the question which everybody supposed was finally put away and done with yesterday.

You can read all this in his face. Furrowed with deep and rigid lines, it proclaims a certain self-torturing nature—the nature of the penitent, self-examining ascetic, whose heart is always vexed by doubts of his own worth and purity, and past and future. Decidedly, Gladstone wants force of character, and force of intellect as well. He is not a man of great thought. Every such man settles a question, so far as he is himself concerned, finally, one way or the other, before long; sees and accepts what the human limitations of thinking are; recognizes the necessity of being done with mere thinking about it, and so decides and is free to act. There is intellectual weakness in Gladstone's interminable consideration and reconsideration, qualification and requalification of every subject and branch of a subject. But there is also a strong, genuine, unmingled delight in mere argument— perhaps as barren a delight as human intellect can yield to.

Last year there were three Fenian prisoners lying under sentence of death in Manchester. Their crime was such as undoubtedly all civil governments are accustomed to punish by death. But there was considerable sympathy for them, partly because of their youth, partly because the deed they had done—the killing of a policeman in order to rescue a political conspirator— did not seem to be a mere base and malignant murder. Some eminent Liberals, Mr. Bright among the rest, endeavored to obtain a mitigation of the sentence. The Tory Government refused; then a point of law was raised on their behalf, and argued in the House of Commons. The point was new, the Tory law-officers, dull men at the best, were taken by surprise, and broke down in reply. Yet there was a reply, and legally, a sufficient one.

Mr. Gladstone saw it; saw where the point raised was defective, and how it might be disposed of. He sprang to his feet, pulled the Tory law-officers out of their difficulty, and upset the case for the Fenians. Now this must have seemed to a conscientious man quite the right thing to do. To a lover of argument the temptation of upsetting a defective plea was irresistible. But most of Mr. Gladstone's Irish followers, on whom he must needs rely, were surprised and angry, and even some of his English friends thought he might have left the Tories unaided to hang their own political prisoners. Gladstone's conduct was eminently characteristic. No impartial man could honestly say that he had done a wrong thing; but no one acquainted with political life could feel surprised that a leader who habitually does such things, is almost always being grumbled at by one or other section of his followers.

There is an obvious lack of directness as well as of robustness in the whole intellectual and political character of the man. I think it was Nathaniel Hawthorne who said of General McClellan that if he could only have shut one eye he might have gone straight into Richmond almost at any time during his command of the Army of the Potomac. I am sure if Gladstone would only close one eye now and then he might lead his party much more easily to splendid victory. With all his great, varied, comprehensive faculties, he is not a man to make a deep mark on the history of his country. He has to be driven on. Somebody must stand behind him. He is not self-sufficing. His style of eloquence is not straightforward, cleaving its way like an arrow. It goes round and round a subject, turning it up, holding it to the light, now this way, now that, examining and re-examining it. Even his reform speeches are as Disraeli once said very happily of Lord Palmerston, rather speeches about Reform than orations on behalf of it. He is indeed the brilliant Halifax of his age—at least he is a complete embodiment of Lord Macaulay's Halifax. A leader with so many splendid gifts and merits, no English parliamentary party of modern times has ever had. Taking manner, voice, elocution and all into account, as is but right in judging of a speaker, I think he is the most splendid of all English orators. Burke's manner and accent were terribly against him; Fox was full of repetition, and often stammered and stuttered in the very rush and tumult of his thoughts; Sheridan's glitter was sometimes tawdriness; both the Pitts were given to pompousness and affectation; Bright has neither the silver voice nor the varied information of Gladstone; Disraeli I do not rank among orators at all. Gladstone has none of the special defects of any of these men, yet I am convinced that Fox was a *greater* orator than Gladstone; I know that Bright is; while Burke's speeches are, as intellectual studies, incomparably beyond anything that Gladstone will ever bequeath to posterity; and as instruments to an end, some of Disraeli's speeches have been more effective and triumphant than anything ever spoken by his present rival.

In brief, Gladstone is not, to my thinking, a *great* orator; and I do not believe he is a great statesman. A great statesman, I presume, is tested by a crisis, and is greatest at a crisis. Such was Chatham; such was Washington; such was Napoleon Bonaparte; such was Cavour; such is Bismarck. All I have seen of Gladstone compels me to believe that he is not such a man. He is just the man to lead the Liberal party at this time; but I should despair of the triumph of that party for the present generation, if there were not stronger and simpler minds behind his to keep him in the right way, to drive him on—and, above all, to prevent him from recoiling after he has made an effective stride forward.

One of the great questions likely to arise soon in English political discussion is that of national education. On educational questions I fancy Mr. Gladstone is rather narrow-minded and old-fashioned; taking too much the tone and view of a college Don. His recent severance from the political representation of Oxford may have done something to release his mind from tradition and pedantry; but I much doubt whether he will not be found sadly wanting when a serious attempt is made to revolutionize the principles and the system of the English universities, and to substitute there (I quote again the language of Grant Duff) "the studies of men for the studies of children." Gladstone is a devotee of classical study; and his whole nature is under the influence of æstheticism, or of what is commonly called "sentiment." The sweet and genial traditions of the past have immense influence over him. His love of Greek poetry and of Italian art follow him into politics. With the Teuton, his poetry and his politics he has little or no sympathy; and I think the question to be decided shortly as regards the university system in England maybe figuratively described as a question between Classic and Teuton. Gladstone is a profound Greek and Latin scholar—a master of Italian, a connoisseur of Italian art; he does not, I believe, know or care much about German literature. Accordingly, he was a devoted Philhellene and a passionate champion of Italian independence; while the outbreak of the recent struggle between the past and the present in Germany found him indifferent, and probably even ignorant. So it was in regard to the American crisis the other day. He knew little of American politics and national life; and the whole thing was a bewilderment and a surprise to him. If the Laocoon had been the work of a New England artist I think the North would have found at once a warm advocate in Mr. Gladstone.

Of a mould utterly different is John Bright, at the very root of whose character are found simplicity and straightforwardness. By simplicity I do not mean freedom from pretence or affectation; for no man can be more thoroughly unaffected and sincere than Gladstone. I mean that purely intellectual attribute which frees the judgment from the influence of complex emotions; which distinguishes at once essentials from non-essentials; which sees at a glance the true end and the real way to it, and can go directly onward. Men supremely gifted with this great practical quality are commonly set down as men of one idea. In this sense, undoubtedly, John Bright is a man of one idea; but the phrase does not justly describe him, or men like him, who are peculiar merely in having an accurate appreciation of what I may call political perspective, and thus knowing what proportion of public consideration certain objects ought, under certain circumstances, to obtain.

So far as ideas are the offspring of information, Mr. Bright has undoubtedly fewer ideas than some of his contemporaries. He is not a profound classical scholar like Gladstone; he has had nothing like the varied culture of Lowe; he makes, of course, no pretence to the attainments of Mill, who is at once a master of science, of classics, and of *belles-lettres*. But given a subject, almost any subject, coming at all within the domain of politics or economics, and time to think over it, and he is much more likely to be right in his judgment of it than any of the three men I have named. He is gifted beyond any Englishman now living with the rare and admirable faculty of seeing right into the heart of a subject, and discerning what it means and what it is worth. Nor is this ever a lucky jump at a conclusion. Bright never gives an opinion at random or off-hand. Some new policy is announced; some new subject is broached in the House of Commons; and Bright sits silent and listens. Friends and followers come round him and ask him what he thinks of it. "Wait until to-morrow and I will tell you," is almost invariably, in whatever form of words, the tenor of his reply—and to-morrow's judgment is certain to be right. I can remember no great public question coming up in England for the past dozen years in regard to which Mr. Bright's deliberate judgment did not prove itself to be just.

This quality of sagacious judgment, however valuable and uncommon, would not of itself make a man a great statesman or even a great party leader; but it is only one of many remarkable attributes which are found harmoniously illustrated in the character of Mr. Bright. I do not mean, however, to dwell at any length here on the place John Bright holds in English political life or the qualities which have won him that place. He has lately been the subject of an article in this magazine, and he is indeed better known to American readers than any other English political man now living. One or two observations are all that just now seem necessary to make.

Men who have not heard Bright speak, and who only know him by repute as a powerful tribune of the people, a demagogue ("John of Bromwicham," Carlyle calls him, classing him with John of Leyden), are naturally apt to think of him as an impetuous, passionate, stormy orator, shaking people's souls with sound and fury. Almost anybody who only knew the two men vaguely and by rumor, would be likely to assume that the style of the classical Gladstone was stately, calm, and regular; that of the popular orator and democrat, impetuous, rugged, and vehement. Now, the great characteristic of Gladstone, after his fluency, is his impetuosity; that of Bright is his magnificent composure and self-control. Intensity is his great peculiarity. He never foams or froths or bellows, or wildly gesticulates. The heat of his oratorical passion is a white heat which consumes without flash or smoke or sputter. Some of his greatest effects have been produced by passages of pathetic appeal, of irony, or of invective, which were delivered with a calm intensity that might almost have seemed coldness, if the fire of genius and of eloquence did not burn beneath it. Another remark I should make is that Mr. Bright is the greatest master of pure Saxon English now speaking the English language. As the blind commonly have their sense of sound and of touch intensified, so it may be that Mr. Bright's comparative indifference to classic and foreign literature has tended to concentrate all his attention upon the culture of pure English, and given him a supreme faculty of appreciating and employing it. Certain it is that his unvarying choice of the very best Saxon word in every case seems to come from an instinct which is in itself something like genius.

Finally, let me remark, that the extent of Mr. Bright's democratic tendencies would probably disappoint some Americans. I may say now what I should probably have been laughed at for saying two or three years ago, that there is a good deal of the conservative about John Bright; that he is by nature disposed to shrink from innovation; that change for the mere sake of change is quite abhorrent to him; and that he is about the last man in England who would care to make political war for an idea. He seems to me to be the only one Englishman I have lately spoken with who retains any genuine feeling of personal loyalty toward the sovereign of England. But for his eloquence and his power, I fancy Mr. Bright would seem rather a slow sort of politician to many of the younger Radicals. The "Times" lately attributed Mr. Bright's conservatism to his advancing years. This was merely absurd. Mr. Bright is little older now than O'Connell was when he began his Parliamentary career. He is considerably younger than Disraeli, or Gladstone, or Mill. What Bright now is he always was. A dozen years ago he was defending the Queen and Prince Albert against the attacks of Tories and of some Radicals. He never was a Democrat in the French or Italian sense. He has always been wanting even, in sympathy, with popular revolution abroad. He never showed the slightest interest in speculative politics. I doubt if he ever talked of the "brotherhood of peoples." He has been driven into political agitation only because, like Schiller's Wilhelm Tell, he saw positive, practical, and pressing grievances bearing down upon his neighbors, which he felt called by duty to make war against. I have many times heard Mr. Bright say that he detests the House of Commons, and would be glad if it were permitted him never to mount a platform again.

But if Mr. Bright had little natural inclination for a Parliamentary career, what is one to say of Mr. John Stuart Mill's natural disinclination for such a path of life?

Physical constitution, intellectual peculiarities, temperament, habits—all seemed to mark out Mr. Mill as a man destined to close his career, as he had so long conducted it—in almost absolute seclusion. He is a silent, shy, shrinking man, of feeble frame and lonely ways. Until the general election of three years back, Mr. Mill was to his countrymen but as an oracle—as a voice—almost as a myth. The influence of his writings was immense. Personally he was but a name. He never came into any public place; he knew nobody. When the promoters of the movement to return him to Parliament came to canvass the Westminster electors, the great difficulty they had to contend with was, that three out of every four of the honest traders and shopkeepers had never heard of him; and the few who knew anything of his books had a vague impression that the author was dead years before. The very men who formed the executive of his committee could not say that they knew him, even by sight. Half in jest, half for a serious purpose, some of the Tories sent abroad over Westminster an awful report that there was no such man in existence as John Stuart Mill. "Did you ever see him?" was the bewildering question constantly put to this or that earnest canvasser, and invariably answered with an apologetic negative. I believe the services of my friend Dr. Chapman, editor of the "Westminster Review," were brought into pressing requisition, because he was one of the very few who really could boast a personal acquaintance with Stuart Mill. The day when the latter first entered the House of Commons was the first time he and Bright ever saw each other. I believe Cobden and Mill never met. Mill had no university acquaintances—he had never been to any university. He had no school friends—he had never been to a school. Perhaps the best educated man of his time in England, he owes his education to the personal care and teaching of his distinguished father, James Mill, who would have been illustrious if his son had not overshadowed his fame. Assuredly, to know James Mill intimately was, if I may thus apply Leigh Hunt's saying, in itself a liberal education. Following his father's steps at the India House, John Mill worked there methodically and quietly, until he rose to the highest position his father had occupied; and then he resigned his office, declined an offer of a seat at the Indian Council Board, subsequently made by Lord Stanley, and lapsed wholly into private life. Of late he rarely met even his close and early friends. Some estrangement, not necessary to dwell on, had taken place, I believe, between him and his old friend Thomas Carlyle, and I suppose they ceased to meet. After the death of the wife whom he so loved and revered, Mill lived almost always at Avignon, in the south of France, where she died, and where he raised a monument over her remains, which he visits and tends with a romantic devotion and constancy worthy of a Roland.

Only a profound sense of duty could drag such a man from his scholarly and sacred seclusion into the stress and storm of a parliamentary life. But it was urged upon Mill that he could do good to the popular cause by going into Parliament; and he is not a man to think anything of his personal preference in such a case. He accepted the contest and won. Some of his warmest admirers regretted that he had ever given his consent. They feared not so much that he might damage his reputation as that he might weaken the influence of his authority, and with it the strength of every great popular cause. Certainly those who thought thus, and who met Mr. Mill for the first time during the progress of the Westminster contest, did not feel much inclined to take a more encouraging view of the prospect.

Mr. Mill seems cut out by nature not to be a parliamentary success. He has a thin, fragile, awkward frame; he has a nervous, incessant twitching of the lips and eyes; he has a weak voice and a sort of stammer; he is over sixty years of age; he had never, so far as I know, addressed a political meeting of any kind up to the time of the Westminster contest. Yet with all these disadvantages, Mill has, as a political leader and speaker, been an undoubted success with the country, and a sort of success in the House. An orator of any kind he never could be. One might call him a wretchedly bad speaker, if his speaking were not so utterly unlike anybody else's, as to refuse to be classified with any other speaking, good or bad. But, so far as the best selection of words, the clearest style, the most coherent and convincing argument can constitute eloquence, Mill's speeches are eloquent. They are, of course, only spoken essays. They differ in no wise from the speaker's writings; and I need hardly say that a speech, to be effective, must never be just what the speaker would have written if it were to be consigned at once to print as a letter or an essay. As speeches, therefore, Mr. Mill's utterances in the House have little or no effect. Indeed, they are only listened to by a very few men of real intelligence and judgment on both sides. Some of the more boisterous of the Tories made many attempts to cough and laugh Mill into silence; indeed, there was obviously a deliberate plan of this kind in operation at one time. But Mill is a man whom nothing can deter from saying or doing what he thinks right. A more absolutely fearless being does not exist. He is even free from that fear which has sometimes paralyzed the boldest spirits, the fear of becoming ridiculous. So the Tory trick failed. Mill went on with patient, imperturbable, proud good-humor, despite all interruption—now and then paying off his Tory enemies by some keen contemptuous epigram or sarcasm, made all the more pungent by the thin, bland tone in which it was uttered. So the Tories gave up shouting, groaning and laughing; the more quickly because one at least of their chiefs, the Marquis of Salisbury (then in the House of Commons as Lord Cranbourne) had the spirit and sense to express openly and loudly his anger and disgust at the vulgar and brutal behaviour of some of his followers. Therefore Mr. Mill ceased to be interrupted; but he is not much listened to. That supreme, irrefutable evidence that a man fails to interest the House—the fact that a hum and buzz of conversation may be heard all the time he is speaking—is always fatally manifest when Mr. Mill addresses the Commons. But the House, after all, is only a platform from which a man endeavors to speak to the country, and if Mill does not always get the ear of the House, he never fails to be heard by the nation. I have no doubt that even the Tory members of the House read Mill's speeches when they appear in print; assuredly all intelligent Tories do. These speeches, in any case, are never lost on the country. They form at once a part of the really successful literature of each session. They always excite controversy of some kind—not even the great orations of Bright and Gladstone are more talked of.

So far they are a success, and there is something in the personal character of Mr. Mill himself, which makes him specially popular with the working classes of England. I doubt if there is now any Englishman whose name would be received with a more cordial outburst of applause at a popular meeting. Working-men, in fact, are very proud of Mr. Mill's scholarship, culture, and profundity. They can perceive easily enough that he is remarkable for just those intellectual qualities which the conventional demagogue never has. Tory newspapers and the "Saturday Review" sometimes affect to regard Mr. Bright as a man of defective education, but it is impossible to pretend to think that Mill is ignorant of Greek or superficial in his knowledge of history. When such a man makes himself especially the champion of working-men, the working-men think of him very much as the Irish peasants of '98 and '48 did of Edward Fitzgerald and Smith O'Brien, the aristocrats of birth and rank, who stepped down from their high places and gave themselves up to the cause of the unlettered and the poor.

There is something fascinating, moreover, about the singular blending of the emotional, and even the romantic, with the keen, vigorous, logical intellect, which is to be observed in Mill. Even political economy, in Mill's mind, is strangely guided and governed by mere feeling. Somebody said he was a combination of Ricardo and Tom Hughes—somebody else said, rather more happily, I think, that he is Adam Smith and Fénélon revived and rolled into one. The "Pall Mall Gazette" found his picture well painted in Lord Macaulay's analysis of the motives which influenced Edmund Burke, when he flung his soul into the impeachment of Warren Hastings. The mere eccentricities, the very defects of such a nature have in them something captivating. The admirers of Mr. Mill are therefore not unusually somewhat given to exalting admiration into idolatry. The classes who most admire him are the scholarly and adventurous young Radicals, who have a dash of Positivism in them; the extreme Radicals, who are prepared to go any and all lengths for the mere sake of change; and the working-men.

This is the Triumvirate of the English Liberal Party. Combined they represent, guide, and govern every section and fraction of that party that is worth taking into any consideration. Mr. Gladstone represents official Liberalism; Mr. Bright speaks for and directs the old-fashioned, robust, popular Liberalism of which Manchester was the school; Mr. Mill is the exponent of the new Liberalism, the Liberalism of Idea and Logic. Bright's programme is a little ahead of Gladstone's, but Gladstone will probably be easily pulled up to it. Mill goes far beyond either, far beyond any point at which either is ever likely to arrive. Indeed, Mr. Mill may be fairly described by a phrase, which I believe is German, as a man in advance of every possible future—at least in England. But he is quite prepared to act loyally and steadily with his party and its leader on all momentous issues. On some minor questions he has lately gone widely away from them, and given thereby much offence; and indeed I am sure there are not a few of the old-fashioned Liberals and the Manchester men who would rather Mr. Mill had never come into Parliament and sat at their side. But on nearly all questions of Parliamentary Reform, and on that of the Irish Church, Mill and his Liberal colleagues will pull cordially together. So, too, on most economic questions, reduction of taxation, imposition of duties and the like. Where a sharp difference is likely to arise will only be in relation to some subject having an idea behind it—some question of foreign policy perhaps, something not at present imminent; and, let us hope, not destined in any case to be vital to the interests of the party. Only where an idea is involved will Mr. Mill refuse to allow his own judgment to bend to the general necessities of the party. It was his objection (a very unwise one, I think) to the idea behind the system of the ballot, which led him to separate himself sharply from Bright and other Liberals on that subject; it was the idea which lies at the bottom of a representation of minorities, which beguiled him into lending his advocacy to that most chimerical, awkward, and absurd piece of political mechanism which we know in England as the three-cornered constituency. The cohesion of Gladstone and Bright is decidedly more close and likely to endure than that between Bright and Mill. But on all immediate questions of great importance, these two men are sure to be found side by side. Mill has a deep and earnest admiration for Bright, who is sometimes, perhaps, a little impatient of the Politics of Idea.

During the session of 1868, I attended a meeting of a few representative Liberals of all classes, brought together to decide on some course of agitation with regard to Ireland. Mr. Mill was there, so were Professor Fawcett, Mr. Thomas Hughes, Lord Amberley, and other members of Parliament; Mr. Frederick Harrison, with some of his Positivist colleagues, and several representative working men. Mr. Bright was unable to attend. A certain course of action being recommended, Mr. Mill expressed his own approval of it, but emphatically declared that he considered Mr. Bright's judgment was entitled to be regarded as authoritative, and that should Mr. Bright recommend the meeting not to go on, the scheme had better be given up. Mr. Bright subsequently discouraged the scheme, and it was, on Mr. Mill's recommendation, at once abandoned. I mention this fact to illustrate the loyalty which Mr. Mill, with all his tendency to political eccentricity, usually displays toward the men whom he regards as the leaders of the party.

Mill and Bright are alike warm admirers of Gladstone and believers in him. Indeed one sometimes feels ashamed to doubt for a moment the steadfastness of a man in whom Bright and Mill put so full a faith.

Certainly the English Liberal has reason to congratulate himself, and feel proud when he remembers what sort of men his party's leaders used to be, and sees what men they are to-day. It will not do to study too closely the private characters of the chiefs of any political band in the House of Commons, from the days of Bolingbroke to those of Fox. The man who was not a sinecurist or a peculator was pretty sure to be a profligate or a gambler. Not a few eminent men were sinecurists, peculators, profligates, and gamblers. The political purity of the English Liberal leaders to-day is absolutely without the faintest shade of suspicion—it never even occurs to any one to suspect them, while their private lives, it may be said without indelicacy, are in pure and perfect accord with the noble principles they profess. Not often has there been a political triumvirate of greater men; of better men, never.

THE ENGLISH POSITIVISTS

Some few months ago, a little bubble of interest was made on the surface of London life, by a course of Sunday lectures of a peculiar kind.

These lectures were given in a small room in Bouverie street, off Fleet street—Bouverie street, sacred to publishing and newspaper offices—and only a very small stream of persons was drawn to the place. There was something very peculiar, however, about the lectures, the lecturer, and the audience, which might well have repaid a stranger in London for the trouble of going there. I doubt whether such a proportion of intellectual faces could have been seen among the congregation of any London church on these Sunday mornings; and I know one, at least, who attended the lectures, less for the sake of what he heard than because such listeners as the authoress of "Romola" were among the audience. The lecturer was Mr. Richard Congreve, and the subject of his discourses was the creed of Positivism.

I do not know how familiar Mr. Congreve and his writings and his doctrines are to the American public. In London, Mr. Congreve is, in a quiet way, a sort of celebrity or peculiarity. He is the head of the small, compact band of English Positivists. It is understood that he goes as far in the direction of the creed which was the dream of Auguste Comte's later years as any sane human creature can well go. I have, however, very little to say here of Mr. Congreve, individually; and I take his recent course of Sunday lectures only as a convenient starting point from which to begin a few remarks on the political principles, character, and influence of that small, resolute, aggressive body of intellectual, highly-educated and able men who are beginning to be known in the politics and society of England as the London Positivists.

A discourse on the principles of Positivism would be quite out of place here; but even those who understand the whole subject will, perhaps, allow me, for the benefit of those who do not, to explain very briefly what an English Positivist is. Positivism, it is known to my readers, is the name given to the philosophy which Auguste Comte, more than any other man, helped to reduce to a system. Regarded as a philosophy of history and human society, its grand and fundamental doctrine merely is that human life evolves itself in obedience to certain fixed laws, of which we could obtain a knowledge if only we applied ourselves to this study as we do to all other studies in practical science, by the patient observation of phenomena. Auguste Comte's reduction of this philosophical theory to a scientific system is undoubtedly one of the grandest achievements of human intellect. The philosophy did not begin with him or his generation, or, indeed, any generation of which we have authentic record. Whenever there were men capable of thinking at all, there must have been some whose minds were instinct with this doctrine; but Comte made it a system at once simple, grand, and fascinating, and he will always remain identified with its development, in the memory of the modern world. Unfortunately, Comte, in his later years, set to founding a *religion* also—a religion which has, perhaps, called down upon its founder and its followers more ridicule, contempt, and discredit than any vagary of human imagination in our day. I speak of all this only to explain to my readers that there is some little difficulty in defining what is meant by a Positivist. If we mean merely a believer in the philosophical theory of history, then Positivists are, indeed, to be named as legion, and their captains are among the greatest intellects of the world to-day. In England, we regard Mr. John Stuart Mill as, in this sense, the greatest Positivist, and undoubtedly he is so regarded here. But Mill utterly rejects and ridicules the fantastic religion which Comte, in his days of declining mental power, sought to graft on his grand philosophy. In his treatise on Comte, Mr. Mill showed no mercy to the Positivist religion, and, indeed, bitterly offended many of its votaries by his contemptuous exposure of its follies. What is said of Mill may be said of nineteen out of every twenty, at least, of the English followers of Comte. They accept the philosophy as grand, scientific, inexorable truth; they reject the religion with pity or with scorn, as a fantastic and barren chimera. Mr. Congreve is, in London, the leader of the small school who go for taking all or nothing, and to whom Auguste Comte is the prophet of a new and final religion, as well as the teacher of a new philosophy. Now this little school is the nucleus of the body of Englishmen of whom I write.

When I speak, therefore, of English Positivists, I do not mean the men who go no farther than John Stuart Mill does. These men are to be found everywhere; they are of all schools, and all religions. I mean the much smaller body of votaries who go, or feel inclined to go, much farther, and accept Comte's religious teaching as a law of life. It is quite probable that, even among the men who are now identified more or less, in the public mind, with Mr. Congreve and his school, there may be some who do not adopt, or even concern themselves about the religion of Positivism. A community of sentiment on historical and political questions, the habit of meeting together, consulting together, writing for publication together, might naturally bring into the group men who may not go the length of adopting the Comte worship. It is quite possible, therefore, that, in mentioning the names of English Positivists, I may happen to speak of some who have no more to do with that worship than I have.

I mean, then, only the group of men, most of whom are young, most of whom are highly cultured, many of whom are endowed with remarkable ability, who are to be found in a literary and political phalanstery with Mr. Congreve, and of whom the majority are understood to be actual votaries of the religion of Comte. Of course I have nothing to do here with their faith or their practices. If they adopt the worship of woman I think they do a better thing after all than the increasing and popular class of writers, whose principal business in life is to persuade us that our wives and sisters are all Messalinas in heart and nearly all Messalinas in practice. If, when they pray, they touch certain cranial bumps at certain passages of the prayer, I do not see that they institute anything worse than the genuflections of the Ritualist or the breast-beating of the Roman Catholics. If, finally, one is sometimes a little puzzled when he receives a letter from a Positivist friend, and finds it dated "5th Marcus Aurelius," or "12th Auguste Comte," instead of July or December, as the case may be, one must remember that there never yet was a young sect which did not delight in puzzling outsiders by a new and peculiar nomenclature. I never heard anything worse charged against the Positivists than that they worship woman, touch their foreheads when they pray, and arrange the calendar according to a plan of their own invention; except, of course, the general charge of Atheism; but as that is made in England against anybody whom all his neighbors do not quite understand, I hardly think it worth discussing in this particular instance. We are all Atheists in England in the estimation of our neighbors, whose political opinions are different from our own.

The English Positivists, then, are beginning to stand out sharply against the common background of political life. They are a little school; as distinctly a school for their time and chances as the Girondists were, or the Manchester school, or the Massachusetts Abolitionists, or the Boston Transcendentalists. They are Radical, of course, but their Radicalism has a curious twist in it. On any given question of Radicalism they go as far as any practical politician does; but then they also go in most cases so very much farther that they often alarm the practical politician out of his ordinary composure. They are generally incisive of speech, aggressive of purpose, defiant of political prudery, and even of political prudence. Their politics are always politics of idea.

Some three or four years ago the Positivists published a large and ponderous volume of essays on subjects of international policy. Each man who contributed an essay signed his name, and although a general community of idea and principle pervaded the book, it was not understood that everybody who wrote necessarily adopted all the views of his associates. The book, in fact, was constructed on the model of the famous "Essays and Reviews" which had sent such a thrill through the religious world a few years before. The political essays naturally failed to create anything like the sensation which was produced by their theological predecessors; but they did excite considerable attention, and awoke the echoes. They astonished a good many Liberal politicians of the steady old school, and they set many men thinking. What surprised people at first was the singular combination of literary culture and ultra-Radical opinion. Literary young men in England, of late, are generally to be divided into two classes—the smart writers for periodicals, the minor novelists and dramatists, and so forth, who know no more and care no more about politics than ballet girls do, and the University men, the men of "culture," who affect Toryism as something fine and distinguished, and profess a patrician horror of democracy and the "mob." If at the time this volume was published one had taken aside some practical politician in London and said, "Here is a collection of practical essays written by a cluster of young men who all have University degrees after their names—will you read it?" the answer would certainly have been—"Not I, it's sure to be some contemptible sham Tory rubbish; some 'blood-and-culture' trash; some schoolboy impertinence about demagoguism and the mob." Therefore the surprise was not slight to such men when they read the book and found that its central idea, its connecting thread, was a Radicalism which might well be called thorough; a Radicalism which made Bright look like a steady old Conservative; invited Mill to push his ideas a little farther; and poured scorn upon the Radical press for its slowness and its timidity. A simple, startling foreign policy was prescribed to England. Its gospel, after all, was but an old one—so old that it had been forgotten in English politics. It was merely—Be just and fear not. Renounce all aggression; give back the spoils of conquest. Give Gibraltar back to the Spaniards who own it; prepare to cast loose your colonial dependencies; prepare even to quit your loved India; ask the Irish people fairly and clearly what they want, and if they desire to be free of your rule, bid them go and be free and Godspeed. All the old traditional policies seemed to these men only obsolete and odious superstitions. They would have England, the State, to stand up and act precisely as an Englishman of honor and conscience would do, and they treated with utter contempt any policy of expediency or any policy whatever that aimed at any end but that of finding out the right thing to do and then doing it at once. This seemed to me, studying the school quite as an outside observer, its one great central idea; and it would of course be impossible not to honor the body of writers who proposed to show how it was to be accomplished.

But no school lives on one grand idea; and this school had its chimeras and crotchets—almost its crazes. For example, the leader of the Positivist band took great trouble to argue that Europe ought to form herself into a noble federation of States, to the exclusion of Russia, which was to be regarded as an Oriental, barbarous, unmanageable, intolerable sort of thing, and pushed out of the European system altogether. Then a good many of the leading minds of the school are imbued with a passionate love for a sort of celestial despotism, an ideal imperialism which the people are first to create and then to obey—which is to teach them, house them, keep them in employment, keep them in health, and leave them nothing to do for themselves, while yet securing to them the most absolute freedom. To some of these men the condition of New York, where the State does hardly anything for the individual, would seem as distressing and objectionable as that of despotic Paris or even Constantinople. A distinguished member of the school declared that nothing was to him more odious than any manner of voluntaryism, and that he hoped to see State operation introduced into every department of English social organization. The connection of this theory with the principle of Positivism, which would mould all men into a sort of hierarchy, is natural and obvious enough, and there is, to support it, a certain reaction now in England against the voluntary principle, in education and in public charities. But, as it is put forward and argued by men of the school I describe, it may be taken as one of the most remarkable points of departure from the common tendency of thought in England. The Positivists are all, indeed, un-English, in the common use of a phrase which is ceasing of late to be so dreaded a stigma as it once used to be in British politics. They are, as I have already said, a somewhat aggressive body, and are imbued with a contempt, which they never care to conceal, for the average public opinion of the British Philistine, whether he present himself as a West End tradesman or a West End Peer.

The Positivists are almost always to be found in antagonism with this sort of public opinion. They attack the Philistine, and they attack no less readily the dainty scholar and critic who lately gave the Philistine his name, and whose over-refining love of sweetness and light is so terribly offended by the rough and earnest work of Radical politics. Whatever way average opinion tends, the influence of the Positivists is sure to tend the other way.

There was a time, nearly two years ago, when the average English mind was suddenly seized with a passion of blended hate, fear, and contempt for Fenianism. The thing was first beginning to show itself in a serious light and it had not gone far enough to show what it really was. It looked more formidable than it proved to be, and it seemed less like an ordinary rebellious organization than like some mysterious and demoniacal league against property and public security. When I say it seemed, I mean it seemed to the average English mind, to the ordinary swell and the ordinary shopkeeper. Just at this time the Positivists drew up a petition to be presented to the House of Commons, in which they called upon the House to insist that lenity should be shown to all Fenian prisoners, that they should be regarded as men driven into rebellion by a deep sense of injustice, and that measures should be taken to prevent the British troops from committing such excesses in Ireland as had been perpetrated in the suppression of the Indian mutiny, and more lately in Jamaica. Now, if there was anything peculiarly calculated to vex and aggravate the House of Commons and the English public generally, it was such a view of the business as this. Fenianism had not acquired the solemn and tragic interest which it obtained a few months afterward. It is only just to say that Englishmen in general began to look with pity and a sort of respect on Fenianism, once it became clear that it had among its followers men who, to quote the language of one of the least sympathetic of London newspapers, "knew how to die." But, at the time I speak of, Fenianism was a vague, mystic, accursed thing, which it was proper to regard as utterly detestable and contemptible. Imagine then what the feeling of the English county member must have been when he learned that there were actually in London a set of educated Englishmen, nearly all trained in the universities and nearly all moving in good society, who regarded the Fenians just as he himself regarded rebels against the Emperor of Austria or the Pope of Rome, and who not merely asked that consideration should be shown toward them, but went on to talk of the necessity of protecting them against the brutality of the loyal British soldier! The petition was signed by all who had a share in its preparation. Such men as Richard Congreve, T. M. Ludlow, Frederick Harrison and Professor Beesly, were among the petitioners who risked their admission into respectable society by signing the document. The petitioners did not feel quite sure about getting any one of mark to present their appeal; and it is certain that a good many professed Liberals, of advanced opinions and full of sympathy with foreign rebels of any class or character, would have promptly refused to accept the ungenial office. The petitioners, however, applied to one who was not likely to be influenced by any considerations but those of right and justice, and whom, moreover, no body in the House of Commons would think of trying to put down. They asked Mr. Bright to present their petition, and there was, of course, no hesitation on his part. Mr. Bright not merely presented the petition, but read it amid the angry and impatient murmurs of an amazed and indignant House; and he declared, in tones of measured and impressive calmness, that he entirely approved of and adopted the sentiments which the petitioners expressed. There was, of course, a storm of indignation, and some members went the length of recommending that the petition should not even be received—an extreme and indeed extravagant course in a country where the right of petition is supposed to be held sacred, and which the good sense even of some Tory members promptly repudiated. Mr. Disraeli did his very best to aggravate the feeling of the House against the petitioners. During the Indian mutiny he had himself loudly protested against the spirit of vengeance which our press encouraged; asked whether we meant to make Nana Sahib the model for a British officer, and whether Moloch or Christ was our divinity. Yet he now declared that the language of the petition was a libel on the Indian army, and that nothing had ever occurred during the Bengal outbreak to warrant the imputations cast on the humanity of our soldiers.

I suppose it is not easy to convey to an American reader a correct idea of the degree of boldness involved in the presentation of this celebrated petition. It really was a very bold thing to do. It was running right in the very teeth of the public opinion of all the classes which are called respectable in England. It was, however, strictly characteristic of the men who signed it. Most, if not all of them, took a prominent part in the prosecution of Governor Eyre of Jamaica, for the lawless execution of George William Gordon and the wholesale and merciless floggings and hangings by which order was made to reign in the island. Most of them, indeed, have a pretty spirit of contradiction of their own, and a pretty gift of sarcasm. I think I hardly remember any man who received, during an equal length of time, a greater amount of abuse from the press than Professor Beesly drew down on himself not very long ago. It was at the time when the public mind was in its wildest thrill of horror at the really fearful revelations of organized murder in connection with the Sawgrinders' Union in Sheffield. The whole question of trades' union organization had been under discussion; and even before the Sheffield revelations came out, the general voice of English respectability was against the workmen's societies altogether. But when the disclosures of organized murder in connection with one union came out, a sort of panic took possession of the public mind. The first, and not unnatural impulse was to assume that all trades' unions must be very much the same sort of thing, and that the societies of workmen were little better than organized Thuggism. Now, Professor Beesly, Mr. Frederick Harrison and other signers of the petition for the Fenians, had long been prominent and influential advocates of the trades' union principle. They had been to the English artisan something like what the Boston Abolitionist was so long to the negro. The trades' union bodies, who felt aggrieved at the unjust suspicion which made them a party to hideous crimes they abhorred, began to hold public meetings to repudiate the charge, and record their detestation of the Sheffield outrages. Professor Beesly attended one of these meetings

Modern Leaders Being A Series Of Biographical Sketches | 161

in London. He made a speech, in which he told the working men that he thought enough had been done in the way of disavowing crimes which no one had a right to impute to them; that there was no need of their further humiliating themselves; and that it was rather odd the English Aristocracy had such a horror of murderers among the poorer classes, seeing how very fond they were of men like Eyre, of Jamaica! In fact, Professor Beesly uplifted his voice very honestly, but rather recklessly and out of time, against the social hypocrisy which is the stain and curse of London society, and which is never so happy as when it can find some chance of denouncing sin or crime among Republicans, or Irishmen, or workingmen. There was nothing Professor Beesly said which had not sense and truth in it; but it might have been said more discreetly and at a better time; and it was said with a sarcastic and scornful bitterness which is one of the characteristics of the speaker. For several days the London press literally raged at the professor. "Punch" persevered for a long time in calling him "Professor Beastly;" a a strong effort was made to obtain his expulsion from the college in which he has a chair. He was talked of and written of as if he were the advocate and the accomplice of assassins, instead of being, as he is, an honorable gentleman and an enlightened scholar, whose great influence over the working classes had always been exerted in the cause of peaceful progress and good order. It was a common thing, for days and weeks, to see the names of Broadhead and Beesly coupled with ostentatious malignity in the leading columns of London newspapers.

I give these random illustrations only to show in what manner the school of writers and thinkers I speak of usually present themselves before the English public. Now Mr. Harrison devotes himself to a pertinacious, powerful series of attacks on Eyre, of Jamaica, at a time when that personage is the hero and pet martyr of English society; now Professor Beesly horrifies British respectability by pointing out that there are respectable murderers who are quite as bad as Broadhead; now Mr. John Morley undertakes even to criticise the Queen; now Mr. Congreve assails the anonymous writers of the London press as hired and masked assassins; now the whole band unite in the defence of Fenians. This sort of thing has a startling effect upon the steady public mind of England; and it is thus, and not otherwise, that the public mind of England ever comes to hear of these really gifted and honest, but very antagonistic and somewhat crochetty men. Several of them are brilliant and powerful writers. Professor Beesly writes with a keen, caustic, bitter force which has something Parisian in it. I know of no writer in English journalism who more closely resembles in style a certain type of the literary gladiator of French controversy. He has much of Eugene Pelletan in him, and something of Henri Rochefort, blended with a good deal that reminds one of Jules Simon. Frederick Harrison is fast becoming a power in the Radical politics and literature of England. John Morley is a young man of great culture, and who writes with a quite remarkable freshness and force. I could mention many other men of the same school (I have already said that I do not know whether each and every one of these is or is not a professed Positivist) who would be distinguished as scholars and writers in the literature of any country. However they may differ on minor points, however they may differ in ability, in experience, in discretion, they have one peculiarity in common: they are to be found foremost in every liberal and radical cause; they are always to be found on the side of the weak, and standing up for the oppressed; they are inveterate enemies of cant; they hate vulgar idolatry and vulgar idols. Looking back a few years, I can remember that almost, if not quite, every man I have alluded to was a fearless and outspoken advocate of the cause of the North, at a time when it was *de rigueur* among men of "culture" in London to champion the cause of the South. Some of the men I have named were indefatigable workers at that time on the unfashionable side. They wrote pamphlets; they wrote leading articles; they made speeches; they delivered lectures in out-of-the-way quarters to workingmen and poor men of all kinds; they hardly came, in any prominent way, before the public, in most of this work. It brought them, probably, no notoriety or recognition whatever on this side of the ocean; but their work was a power in England. I feel convinced that, in any case, the English workingmen would have gone right on such a question as that which was at issue between North and South. As Mr. Motley truly said in his address to the New York Historical Society, the workers and the thinkers were never misled; but I am bound to say that the admirable knowledge of the realities of the subject; the clear, quick, and penetrating judgment, and the patient, unswerving hope and confidence which were so signally displayed by the London workingmen from first to last of that great struggle, were in no slight degree the result of the teaching and the labor of men like Professor Beesly and Frederick Harrison.

If I were to set up a typical Positivist, in order to make my American reader more readily and completely familiar with the picture which the word calls up in the minds of Londoners, I should do it in the following way: I should exhibit my model Positivist as a man still young for anything like prominence in English public life, but not actually young in years—say thirty-eight or forty. He has had a training at one of the great historical Universities, or at all events at the modern and popular University of London. He is a barrister, but does not practise much, and has probably a modest competence on which he can live without working for the sake of living, and can indulge his own tastes in literature and politics. He has immense earnestness and great self-conceit. He has an utter contempt for dull men and timid or half-measure men, and he scorns Whigs even more than Tories. He devotes much of his time generously and patiently to the political and other instruction of working men. He writes in the "Fortnightly Review," and sometimes in "MacMillan," and sometimes in the "Westminster Review." He plunges into gallant and fearless controversy with the "Pall Mall Gazette," and he is not easily worsted, for his pen is sharp and his ink very acrid. Nevertheless, is any great question stirring, with a serious principle or a deep human interest at the heart of it, he is sure to be found on the right side. Where the controversy is of a smaller kind and admits of crotchet, then he is pretty sure to bring out a crotchet of some kind. He is perpetually giving the "Saturday Review" an opportunity to ridicule him and abuse him, and he does not care. He writes pamphlets and goes to immense trouble to get up the facts, and expense to give them to the world, and he never grudges trouble or money, where any cause or even any crotchet is to be served. He is ready to stand up alone, against all the world if needs be, for his opinions or his friends. Benevolent schemes which are of the nature of mere charity he never concerns himself about. I never heard of him on a platform with the Earl of Shaftesbury, and I fancy he has a contempt for all patronage of the poor or projects of an eleemosynary character. He is for giving men their political rights and educating them—if necessary compelling them to be educated; and he has little faith in any other way of doing good. He has, of course, a high admiration for and faith in Mr. Mill. His nature is not quite reverential—in general he is rather inclined to sit in the chair of the scorner; but if he reverenced any living man it would be Mill. He admires the manly, noble character of Bright, and his calm, strong eloquence. I do not think he cares much about Gladstone—I rather fancy our Positivist looks upon Gladstone as somewhat weak and unsteady—and with him to be weak is indeed to be miserable. Disraeli is to him an object of entire scorn and detestation, for he can endure no one who has not deeply-rooted principles of some kind. He has a crotchet about Russia, a theory about China; he gets quite beside himself in his anger over the anonymous leading articles of the London press. He is not an English type of man at all, in the present and conventional sense. He cares not a rush about tradition, and mocks at the wisdom of our ancestors. The bare fact that some custom, or institution, or way of thinking has been sanctioned and hallowed by long generations of usage, is in his eyes rather a *prima facie* reason for despising it than otherwise. He is pitilessly intolerant of all superstitions—save his own—that is to say, he is intolerant in words and logic and ridicule, for the wildest superstition would find him its defender, if it once came to be practically oppressed or even threatened. He is "ever a fighter," like one of Browning's heroes; he is the knight-errant, the Quixote

164 | Modern Leaders Being A Series Of Biographical Sketches

of modern English politics. He admires George Eliot in literature, and, I should say, he regards Charles Dickens as a sort of person who does very well to amuse idlers and ignorant people. I do not hear of his going much to the theatre, and it is a doubt to me if he has yet heard of the "Grande Duchesse." Life with him is a very earnest business, and, although he has a pretty gift of sarcasm, which he uses as a weapon of offence against his enemies, I cannot, with any effort of imagination, picture him to myself as in the act of making a joke.

A small drawing-room would assuredly hold all the London Positivists who make themselves effective in English politics. Yet I do not hesitate to say that they are becoming—that they have already become—a power which no one, calculating on the chances of any coming struggle, can afford to leave out of his consideration. Their public influence thus far has been wholly for good; and they set up no propaganda that I have ever seen or heard of, as regards either philosophy or religion. The course of lectures I have already mentioned was the nearest approach to any public diffusion of their peculiar doctrines which I can remember, and it created little or no sensation in London. Indeed, little or no publicity was sought for it. I have read lately somewhere that a newspaper, specially devoted to the propagation and vindication of Positivism, is about to be, or has been started in London. I do not know whether this is true or not; but for any such journal I should anticipate a very small circulation, and an existence only to be maintained by continual subsidy.

So quietly have these men hitherto pursued their course, whatever it may be, in religion or religious philosophy, that it was long indeed before any idea got abroad that the cluster of highly-educated, ultra-radical thinkers, who were to be found sharpshooting on the side of every great human principle and every oppressed cause, and who seemed positively to delight in standing up against the vulgar rush of public opinion, were anything more than chance associates, or were bound by any tie more close and firm than that of general political sympathy. Even now that people are beginning to know them, and to classify them, in a vague sort of way, as "those Positivists," they make so little parade of any peculiarity of faith that, without precise and personal knowledge, it would be rash to say for certain that this or that member of the group is or is not an actual professor of the Comtist religion. I read a few days ago, in one of the few sensible books written on America by an Englishman, some remarks made about a peculiar view of Europe's duty to Egypt, which was described as being held by "the Comtists." I do not know whether the men referred to hold the view ascribed to them or not; but, assuredly, if they do, the fact has no more direct connection with their Comtism than Bright's free-trade views have with Bright's Quakerism. An illustration, however, will serve well enough as an example of the vague and careless sort of way in which doctrines and the men who profess them get mixed up together insolubly in the public mind. The Sultan of a generation back, who told the European diplomatist that if he changed his religion at all he would become a Roman Catholic, because he observed that Roman Catholic people always grew the best wine, was not more unreasonable in his logic than many well-informed men when they are striving to connect cause and effect in dealing with the religion of others.

I do not myself make any attempt to explain why a follower of Comte's worship should, at least in England, be always on the side of liberty and equality and human progress. Indeed, if inclined to discuss such a question at all, I should rather be disposed to put it the other way and ask how it happens that men so enlightened and liberal in education and principles should yield a moment's obedience to the ghostly shadow of Roman Catholic superstition, which Auguste Comte, in the decaying years of his noble intellect, conjured up to form a new religion. But I am quite content to let the question go unanswered—and should be willing, indeed, to leave it unasked. I wish just now to do nothing more than to direct the attention of American readers to the fact that a new set or sect has arisen to influence English politics, and that their influence and its origin are different from anything which, judging by the history of previous generations, one might naturally have been led to expect. "Culture" in England has, of late years, almost invariably ranked itself on the side of privilege. The Oxford undergraduate shouts himself hoarse in cheering for Disraeli and groaning for Bright. Oxford rejects Gladstone the moment he becomes a Liberal. The vigorous Radicalism of Thorold Rogers costs him his chair as professor of political economy, although no man in England is a more perfect master of some of the more important branches of that science. The journals which are started for the sake of being read by men of "culture" are sure to throw their influence, nine times out of ten, into the cause of privilege and class ascendency. The "Saturday Review" does this deliberately; the "Pall Mall Gazette" does it instinctively. Suddenly there comes out from the bosom of the universities themselves a band of keen, acute, fearless gladiators, who throw themselves into the van of every great movement which works for democracy, equality and freedom. They invade the press and the platform; they write in this journal and in that; they are always writing, always printing; they are ready for any assailant, however big, they are willing to work with any ally, however small; they shrink from no logical consequence or practical inconvenience of any argument or opinion; they take the working man by the hand and talk to him and tell him all they know—and it is something worth studying, the fact that their scholarship and his no-scholarship so often come to the same conclusion. They will work with anybody, because they go farther than almost anybody; and they will allow anybody the full swing of his own crotchet, even though he be not so willing to give them scope enough for theirs. Thus they are commonly associated with Goldwin Smith, who has a perfect horror of French Democracy and French Imperialism, and who sees in Mirabeau only a "Voltairean debauchee;" with Tom Hughes, who is a sturdy member of the Church of England, and does not, I fancy, care three straws about the policy of ideas; with Bright, whose somewhat Puritanical mind draws back with a kind of dread from anything that savors of free-thinking; with Auberon Herbert, the mild young aristocrat, converted from Toryism by pure sentimentalism and philanthropy; with Connolly, the eloquent Irish plasterer, whose vigorous stump oratory aroused the warm admiration of Louis Blanc. It would be impossible that such a knot of men, so gifted and so fearless, so independent and so unresting, so keen of pen, and so unsparing of logic, should be without a clear and marked influence on the politics of England. It is quite a curious phenomenon that such a group of men should be found in close and constant co-operation with the English artisan, his trades' union organizations, and his political cause. Frederick Harrison represented the working men in the Parliamentary commission lately held to inquire into the whole operation of the trades' unions. Professor Beesly writes continually in the "Beehive," the newspaper which is the organ of George Potter and the trades' societies. I cannot see how the cause of Democracy can fail to derive strength and help from this sort of alliance, and I therefore welcome the influence upon English politics of the little group of Positivist penmen, believing that it will have a deeper reach than most people now imagine, and that where it operates effectively at all, it will be for good.

ENGLISH TORYISM AND ITS LEADERS

Sir John Mandeville tells a story of a man who set out on a voyage of discovery, and sailing on and on in a westerly direction, at last touched a land where he was surprised to find a climate the same as his own; animals like those he had left behind; men and women not only having the same dress and complexion, but actually speaking the same language as the people of his own country. He was so struck with this unexpected and wonderful discovery, that he took to his ship again without delay, and sailed back eastward to impart to his own people the news that in a far-off, strange, western sea he had found a race identical with themselves. The truth was that the simple voyager had gone round the world, reached his own country without recognizing it, and then went round the world again to get home.

If the voyage were made in our time, and the explorer were a British Tory who had left England in the opening of the year 1867, and after unconsciously sailing round the world had fallen in with British Tories again in the autumn of the same year, one could easily excuse his failing to recognize his own people. For in the interval of time from February to August, British Toryism underwent the most sudden and complete transformation known outside the sphere of Ovid's Metamorphoses. If any of my American readers will try to imagine a whole political party, great in numbers, greater still in wealth, station and influence, suddenly performing just such a turn-round as the "New York Herald" accomplished at a certain early crisis of the late civil war, he will have some idea of the marvellous and unprecedented feat which was executed by the English Tories, when, renouncing all their time-honored traditions, watchwords and principles, they changed a limited and oligarchical franchise into household suffrage. It is singular, indeed, that such a thing should have been done. It is more singular still that it should have been done, as it most assuredly was done, in order that one man should be kept in power. It is even more singular yet that it should have been done by a party of men individually high principled, honorable, unselfish, incapable of any deliberate meanness—and of whom many if not most actually disliked and distrusted the man in whose interest and by whose influence the surrender of principle was made.

Perhaps when I have said a little about the leadership of the English Tories, the phenomenon will appear less wonderful or at least more intelligible. It was not a mere epigram which Mr. Mill uttered when he described the Tories as the stupid party. An average Tory really is a stupid man. He is a gentleman in all the ordinary acceptation of the word. He has been to Oxford or Cambridge; he has received a decent classical education; he has travelled along the beaten tracks—made what would have been called in Mary Wortley Montague's day "the grand tour;" he has birth and high breeding; he is a good fellow, with manly, honorable ways, and that genial consideration for the feelings of others which is the fundamental condition, the vital element of gentlemanly breeding. But he is, with all this, stupid. His mind is narrow, dull, inflexible; he cannot connect cause with effect, or see that a change is coming, or why it should come; with him *post hoc* always means *propter hoc*; he cannot account for Goodwin Sands otherwise than because of Tenterden steeple. You cannot help liking him, and sometimes laughing at him. It may seem paradoxical, but I at least am unable to get out of my mind the conviction that there is a solid basis of stupidity in the mind of the great Conservative Chief, Lord Derby. Let me explain what I mean. The Earl of Derby is in one sense a highly accomplished man. He is a good classical scholar, and can make a speech in Latin. He has produced some very spirited translations from Horace; and I like his version of the Iliad better on the whole than any other I know. He is a splendid debater—Macaulay said very truly that with Lord Derby the science of debate was an instinct. He will roll out resonant, rotund, verbose sentences by the hour, by the yard; he is great at making hits and points; he has immense power of reply and repartee—of a certain easy and obvious kind; his voice is fine, his manner is noble, his invective is powerful. But he has no ideas. The light he throws out is a polarized light. He adds nothing new to the political thought of the age. I have heard many of his finest speeches; and I can remember that they were then very telling, in a Parliamentary point of view; but I cannot remember anything he said. He is always interpreting into eloquent and effective words the commonplace Philistine notions, the hereditary conventionalities of his party—and nothing more. His mind is not open to new impressions, and he is not able to appreciate the cause, the purpose or the tendency of change. This I hold to be the essential characteristic of stupidity; and this is an attribute of Lord Derby, with all his Greek, his Latin, his impetuous rhetoric, his debating skill and his audacious blunders, which sometimes almost deceive one into thinking him a man of genius. Now the Earl of Derby is the greatest Tory living; and if I have fairly described the highest type of Tory, one can easily form some conception of what the average Tory must be. Every one likes Lord Derby, and I fully believe it to be the fact that those who know him best like him best. I cannot imagine Lord

Derby doing a mean thing; I cannot imagine him haughty to a poor man, or patronizingly offensive to a timid visitor of humble birth. Look at Lord Derby through the wrong end of the intellectual telescope and you have the average British Tory. The Tory's knowledge is confined to classics and field sports—when he knows anything. Even Lord Derby has been guilty of the most flagrant mistakes in geography and modern history. People are never tired of alluding to a famous blunder of his about Tambov in Russia. It is also told of him that he once spoke in Parliament of Demerara as an island; and when one of his colleagues afterward remonstrated with him on the mistake, he asked with ingenuousness and *naïvete* "How on earth was I to know that Demerara was not an island?" He once, at a public meeting, spoke of himself very frankly as having been born "in the pre-scientific period"— the period but too recently closed, when English Universities and high class schools troubled themselves only about Greek and Latin, and thought it beneath their dignity to show much interest in such vulgar, practical studies as chemistry and natural history, to say nothing of that ungentlemanly and ungenerous study, the science of political economy. The average British Tory is a Lord Derby without eloquence, brains, official habits and political experience.

How, then, do the Tories exist as a party? How do they continue to believe themselves to be Tories, and speak of themselves as Tories, when they have surrendered all, or nearly all, the great principles which are the creed and faith, and business of Toryism? Because they have, in our times, never had Tories for leaders. A man is not a Tory merely because he fights the Tory battles, any more than a captain of the Irish Brigade was a Frenchman because he fought for King Louis, or Hobart Pasha is a Turk because he commands the Ottoman navy. The Tory party has always, of late years, had to call in the aid of brilliant outsiders, political renegades, refugees from broken-down agitations, disappointed and cynical deserters from the Liberal camp, or mere adventurers, to fight their battles for them. It used to be quite a curious sight, some three or four years ago, when the Tories were, as they are now again, in opposition, to look down from the gallery of the House of Commons and see the men who did gladiatorial duty for the party. Along the back benches, above and below the "gangway," were stretched out huge at length the stalwart, handsome, manly country gentlemen, the bone and sinew of the Tory party—the only real Tories to be found in the House. But *they* did not bear the brunt of debate. They could cheer splendidly, and vote in platoons; but you don't suppose they were just the sort of men to confront Gladstone, and reply to Bright? Not they; and they knew it. There sat Disraeli, the brilliant renegade from Radicalism, who was ready to think for them and talk for them: and who were his lieutenants? Cairns, the successful, adroit, eloquent lawyer, a North of Ireland man, with about as much of the genuine British Tory in him as there is in Disraeli himself; Seymour Fitzgerald, the clever, pushing Irishman, also a lawyer; Whiteside, the voluble, eloquent, rather boisterous advocate, also a lawyer, and also an Irishman; smart, saucy Pope Hennessy, a young Irish adventurer, who had taken up with Toryism and ultramontanism as the best way of making a career, and who would, at the slightest hint from his chief, have risen, utterly ignorant of the subject under debate, and challenged Gladstone's finance or Roundel Palmer's law. These men, and such men—these and no others—did the debating and the fighting for the great Tory party of England at a most critical period of that party's existence. Needless to say that the party who were compelled by their own poverty of idea, their own stupidity, to have these men for their representatives, were stupid enough to be led anywhere and into anything by the force of a little dexterity and daring on the part of the one man into whose hands they had confided their destinies.

In speaking, therefore, of the leaders of Toryism, I must distinctly say that I am not speaking of Tories. The rank and file are Tories; the general and officers belong to another race. Mr. Disraeli is so well known on this side of the Atlantic that I need not occupy much time or space in describing him. He is the most brilliant specimen of the adventurer or political soldier of fortune known to English public life in our days. I do not suppose anybody believes Mr. Disraeli's Toryism to be a genuine faith. This is not merely because he has changed his opinions so completely since the time when he came out as a Radical, under the patronage of O'Connell, and wrote to William Johnson Fox, the Democratic orator, a famous letter, in which he, Disraeli, boasted that "his forte was revolution." Men have changed their views as completely, and even as suddenly, and yet obtained credit for sincerity and integrity. It is not even because, in all of Mr. Disraeli's novels, a prime and favorite personage is a daring political adventurer, who carries all before him by the audacity of his genius and his unscrupulousness; it is not even that Mr. Disraeli, in private life, frequently speaks of success in politics as the one grand object worth striving for or living for. "What do you and I come to this House of Commons night after night for?" said Mr. Disraeli once to a great Englishman, and when the latter failed to reply very quickly, he answered his own question by saying, "You know we come here for fame." The man to whom he spoke declared, in all truthfulness, that he did not follow a political career for the sake of fame. But Disraeli was quite incredulous, and probably could not, by any earnestness and apparent sincerity of asseveration, be got to believe that there lives a being who could sacrifice time, and money, and intellect, and eloquence merely for the sake of serving the public. Yet it is not alone this cynical avowal of selfishness which makes people so profoundly sceptical as to Mr. Disraeli's Toryism. It is the fact that he always escapes into Liberalism whenever he has an opportunity; that he lives by hawking Toryism, not by imbibing it himself; that he is ready to sell it, or betray it, or drag it in the dirt whenever he can safely serve himself by doing so; that he can become the most ardent of Freetraders, the most uncompromising champion of a Popular Suffrage to-day, when it is for his interest, after having fought fiercely against both yesterday, when to fight against them was for his interest. Mr. Disraeli is decidedly a man without scruple. Those who have read his "Vivian Grey" will remember with what zest and unction he describes his hero bewildering a company and dumbfoundering a scientific authority by extemporizing an imaginary quotation from a book which he holds in his hand, and from which he pretends to read the passage he is reciting. It is not long since Mr. Disraeli himself publicly ventured on a bold little experiment of a somewhat similar kind. The story is curious, and worth hearing; and it is certain that it cannot be contradicted.

Three or four years ago, a bitter factious attack was made in the House of Commons upon Mr. Stansfeld, then holding office in the Liberal government, because of his open and avowed friendship for, and intimacy with Mazzini. This was at a time when the French government were endeavoring to connect Mazzini with a plot to assassinate the Emperor Napoleon. Mr. Disraeli was very stern in his condemnation of Mr. Stansfeld for his friendship with one who, twenty odd years before, had encouraged a young enthusiast (as the enthusiast said) in a design to kill Charles Albert, King of Sardinia. Mr. Bright, in a moderate and kindly speech, deprecated the idea of making unpardonable crimes out of the hotheaded follies of enthusiastic men in their young days; and he added that he believed there would be found in a certain poem, written by Disraeli himself some twenty-five or thirty years before, and called "A Revolutionary Epick," some lines of eloquent apostrophe in praise of tyrannicide. Up sprang Mr. Disraeli, indignant and excited, and vehemently denied that any such sentiment, any such line, could be found in the poem. Mr. Bright at once accepted the assurance; said he had never seen the poem himself, but only heard that there was such a passage in it; apologized for the mistake—and there most people thought the matter would have ended. In truth, the volume which Mr. Disraeli had published a generation before, with the grandiloquent title, "A Revolutionary Epick" (not "epic," in the common way, but dignified, old-fashioned "epick"), was a piece of youthful, bombastic folly long out of print, and almost wholly forgotten. But Disraeli chose to attach great importance to the charge he supposed to be made against him; and he declared that he felt himself bound to refute it utterly by more than a mere denial. Accordingly, in a few weeks, there came out a new edition of the Epick, with a dedication to Lord Stanley, and a preface explaining that, as the first edition was out of print, and as a charge founded on a passage in it had been made against the author, said author felt bound to issue this new edition, that all the world might see how unfounded was the accusation. Sure enough, the publication did seem to dispose of the charge effectually. There was only one passage which in any way bore on the subject of tyrannicide, and that certainly did not express approval. What could be more satisfactory? Unluckily, however, the gentleman on whose hint Mr. Bright spoke, happened to possess one copy of the original edition. He compared this, to make assurance doubly sure, with the copy at the British Museum, the only other copy accessible to him, and he found that the passage which contained the praise of tyrannicide had been partly altered, partly suppressed, in the new edition specially issued by Mr. Disraeli, in order to prove to the world that he had not written a line in the poem to imply that he sanctioned the slaying of a tyrant. Now, this was a small and trifling affair; but just see how significant and characteristic it was! It surely did not make much matter whether Mr. Disraeli, in his young, nonsensical days, had or had not indulged in a burst of enthusiasm about the slaying of tyrants, in a poem so bombastical that no rational man could think of it with any seriousness. But Mr. Disraeli chose to regard his reputation as seriously assailed; and what did he do to vindicate himself? He published a new edition, which he trumpeted as not merely authentic, but as issued for the sole purpose of proving that he had not praised tyrannicide, and he deliberately excised the lines which contained the passage in question! The controversy turned on some two lines and a half; and of these Mr. Disraeli cut out all the dangerous words and gave the garbled version to the world as his authoritative reply to the charge made against him! This, too, after the famous "annexation" of one of Thiers's speeches, and the delivery of it as a panegyric on the memory of the Duke of Wellington, and after the appropriation of a page or two out of an essay by Macaulay, and its introduction wholesale, as original, into one of Mr. Disraeli's novels.

The truth is that Disraeli is so reckless a gladiator that he will catch up any weapon of defence, use any means of evasion and escape; will fight anyhow, and win anyhow. In political affairs, at least, he has no moral sense whatever; and the public seems to tolerate him on that understanding. Certainly, escapades and practices which would ruin the reputation of any other public man do not seem to bring Disraeli into serious disrepute. The few high-toned men of his own party and the other who hold all trickery in detestation, had made up their minds about him long ago; and nothing could hurt him more in their esteem—the great majority of politicians laugh at the whole thing, and take no thought. The feeling seems to be, "We don't expect grave and severe virtue from this man; we take him as he is. It would be ridiculous to apply a grave moral test to anything he may say or do." In Lockhart's "Life of Walter Scott," it is told that the great novelist went one morning very early to call on a certain friend. The friend was in bed, and Scott, pushing into the room familiarly, found that his friend was— not alone, as he expected him to be. Scott was a highly moral man, and he would have turned his back indignantly on any other of his friends whom he found guilty of vice; but his biographer says that he took the discovery he had made very lightly in this instance; and he afterward explained that the delinquent was so ridiculously without depth of character it would be absurd to find serious fault with anything he did. Perhaps it is in a similar spirit that the British public regard Mr. Disraeli. He delivered a memorable peroration one night last year in the House of Commons, the utterance and the language of which were so peculiar that charity itself could not affect to be ignorant of the stimulating cause which sent forth such extraordinary eloquence. Yet hardly anybody seemed to regard it as more than a good joke; and the newspapers which were most indignant and most scandalized over Andrew Johnson's celebrated inaugural address made no allusion whatever to Mr. Disraeli's bewildering outburst. One reason, probably, is that Disraeli, in private, is much liked. He is very kindly; he is a good friend; he is sympathetic in his dealings with young politicians, and is always glad to give a helping hand to a young man of talent. Personal ambition, which, in Mr. Bright's eyes, is something despicable, and which Mr. Gladstone probably regards as a sin, is, in Disraeli's acceptation, something generous and elevating, something to be fostered and encouraged. Therefore, young men of talent admire Disraeli, and are glad and proud to gather round him. The men who have any brains in the Tory ranks are usually of the adventurer class; and they form a phalanx by the aid of which Disraeli can do great things. No matter how the honest, dull bulk of his party may distrust him, they cannot do without him and his phalanx; and they allow him to win his battles by the force of their votes, and they think he is winning their battles all the time.

One young man of brains there was on the Tory side of the House of Commons, who did not like Disraeli, and never professed to like him. This was Lord Robert Cecil, who subsequently became Viscount Cranbourne, and now sits in the House of Lords as Marquis of Salisbury. Lord Robert Cecil was by far the ablest scion of noble Toryism in the House of Commons. Younger than Lord Stanley he had not Lord Stanley's solidity and caution; but he had much more of original ability; he had brilliant ideas, great readiness in debate, and a perfect genius for saying bitter things in the bitterest tone. The younger son of a wealthy peer, he had, in consequence of a dispute with his father, manfully accepted honorable poverty, and was glad, for no short time, to help out his means by the use of his pen. He wrote in the "Quarterly Review," the time-honored organ of Toryism; and after a while certain political articles regularly appearing in that periodical became identified with his name. One great object of these articles seemed to be to denounce Mr. Disraeli and warn the Tory party against him as a traitor, certain in the end to sell and surrender their principles. Lord Robert Cecil was an ultra-Tory—or at least thought himself so—I feel convinced that his intellect and his experience will set him free one day. He was a Tory on principle and would listen to no compromise. People did not at first see how much ability there was in him—very few indeed saw how much of genuine manhood and nobleness there was in him. His tall, bent, awkward figure; his prematurely bald crown, his face with an outline and a beard that reminded one of a Jew pedler from the Minories, his ungainly gestures, his unmelodious voice, and the extraordinary and wanton bitterness of his tongue, set the ordinary observer strongly against him. He seemed to delight in being gratuitously offensive. Let me give one illustration. He assailed Mr. Gladstone's financial policy one night, and said it was like the practice of a pettifogging attorney. This was rather coarse and it was received with loud murmurs of disapprobation, but Lord Robert went on unheeding. Next night, however, when the debate was resumed, he rose and said he feared he had used language the previous evening which was calculated to give offence, and which he could not justify. There were murmurs of encouraging applause—nothing delights the House of Commons like an unsolicited and manly apology. Yes, he had, on the previous night, in a moment of excitement, compared the policy of the Chancellor of the Exchequer to the practice of a pettifogging attorney. That was language which on sober consideration he felt he could not justify and ought not to have used, "and therefore," said Lord Robert, "I beg leave to offer my sincere apology"—here Mr. Gladstone half rose from his seat, with face of eager generosity, ready to pardon even before fully asked—"I beg leave to tender my sincere apology—to the attorneys!" Half the House roared with laughter, the other half with anger—and Gladstone threw himself back in his seat with an expression of mingled disappointment, pity and scorn, on his pallid, noble features.

There was something so wanton, something so nearly approaching to outrageous buffoonery, in conduct like this, on the part of Lord Robert Cecil, that it was long before impartial observers came to recognize the fine intellect and the manly character that were disguised under such an unprepossessing exterior. When the Tories came into power, the great place of Secretary for India was given to Lord Robert, who had then become Viscount Cranbourne, and the responsibilities of office wrought as complete a change in him as the wearing of the crown did in Harry the Fifth. No man ever displayed in so short a time greater aptitude for the duties of the office he had undertaken, or a loftier sense of its tremendous moral and political responsibility, than did Lord Cranbourne during his too brief tenure of the Indian Secretaryship. The cynic had become a statesman, the intellectual gladiator an earnest champion of exalted political principle. The license of tongue, in which Lord Cranbourne had revelled while yet a free lance, he absolutely renounced when he became a responsible minister. He extorted the respect and admiration of Gladstone and Bright, and indeed of every one who took the slightest interest in the condition and the future of India. The manner of his leaving office became him, too, almost as much as his occupation of it. He was sincerely opposed to a sudden lowering of the franchise, and he insisted that his party ought to think nothing of power when compared with principle. He found that Disraeli was determined to surrender anything rather than power, and he withdrew from the uncongenial companionship. He resigned office, and dropped into the ranks once more, never hesitating to express his conviction of the utter insincerity of the Conservative leader. He would have been a sharp and stinging thorn in Disraeli's side, only that death intervened and took away, not him, but his father. The death of his elder brother had made Lord Robert Cecil, Viscount Cranbourne; the death of his father now converted Viscount Cranbourne into the Marquis of Salisbury, and condemned him to the languid, inert, lifeless atmosphere of the House of Peers. The sincere pity of all who admired him followed the brilliant Salisbury in his melancholy descent. I should despair of conveying to an American reader unacquainted with English politics any adequate idea of the profundity and hopelessness of the fall which precipitates a young, ardent and gifted politician from the brilliant battle-ground of the House of Commons into the lifeless, Lethean pool of the House of Lords.

Still, the Tory party may be led, as it has been, by a chief in the House of Lords, although its great and splendid fights must be fought in the Commons. If then, in our time, Toryism ever should again become a principle which a man of genius and high character could fairly fight for, it has a leader ready to its hand in the Marquis of Salisbury. For the present it has Lord Cairns. The Earl of Derby's health no longer allows him to undertake the serious and laborious duties of party leadership. When he withdrew from the front, an attempt was made to put up with Lord Malmesbury. But Malmesbury is stupid and muddle-headed to a degree which even Tory peers cannot endure in a Tory peer; and it has somehow been "borne in upon him" that he had better leave the place to some one really qualified to fill it. Now, the Tories in the House of Commons, the country gentlemen of England, the men whose ancestors came over, perhaps, with the Conqueror, the men who imbibed family Toryism from the breasts of their mothers, are driven, when they want a capable leader, to follow a renegade Radical, the son of a middle-class Jew. In like manner the Tory Lords, also sadly needing an efficient leader, are compelled to take up with a lawyer from Belfast, the son of middle-class parents in the North of Ireland, who has fought his way by sheer talent and energy into the front rank of the bar, into the front bench of the Parliamentary Opposition, and at last into a peerage. Lord Cairns is a very capable man; his sudden rise into high place and influence proves the fact of itself, for he was not a young man when he entered Parliament, obscure and unknown, and he is now only in the prime of life, while he leads the Opposition in the House of Lords. He is one of the most fluent and effective debaters in either House; he has great command of telling argument; his training at the bar gives him the faculty of making the very most, and at the shortest notice, of all the knowledge and all the facts he can bring to bear on any question. He has shown more than once that he is capable of pouring forth a powerful, almost indeed, a passionate invective. An orator in the highest sense he certainly is not. No gleam of the poetic softens or brightens his lithe and nervous logic; no deep feeling animates, inspires and sanctifies it. He has made no speeches which anybody hereafter will care to read. He has made, he will make, no mark upon his age. When he dies, he wholly dies. But living, he is a skilful and a capable man—far better qualified to be a party leader than an Erskine or a Grattan would be. A North of Ireland Presbyterian, he has made his way to a peerage, and now to be the leader of peers, with less of native genius than that which conducted Wolfe Tone, another North of Ireland Presbyterian, to rebellion and failure and a bloody death. He has, above all things, skill and discretion; and he can lead the Tory party well, so long as no great cause has to be vindicated, no splendid phantom of a principle maintained. His name and his antecedents are useful to us now, inasmuch as they serve still farther to illustrate the fact that Toryism is not led by Tories.

In speaking of Tory leaders one ought not, of course, to leave out the name of Lord Stanley. But Lord Stanley is only a Tory *ex officio*, and by virtue of his position as the eldest son and heir of the great Earl of Derby. I have never heard of Lord Stanley's uttering a Tory sentiment, even when he had to play a Tory part. His speeches are all the speeches of a steady, respectable, thoughtful sort of Liberal, inclined to study carefully both or all sides of a question, and opposed to extreme opinions either way. He will never, it is quite clear, be guilty of the audacity of openly breaking with his party while his father lives; and perhaps when he becomes Earl of Derby, there may be nothing distinctively Tory worth fighting about. Lord Stanley is indeed totally devoid of that generous ardor which makes men open converts. He is no longer young, and he will probably remain all his life where he stands at present. But a genuine Tory he is not. I confess that at one time I looked to him with great hope, as a man likely to develop into statesmanship of the highest order, and to announce himself as a votary of political and intellectual progress. Some years ago I wrote an article in the "Westminster Review," the object of which was to point to Lord Stanley as the future colleague of Gladstone in a great and a really liberal government. I have changed my opinion since. Lord Stanley wants, not the brains, but the heart for such a place. He has not the spirit to step out of his hereditary way. He is one of the sort of men of whom Goethe used to say, "If only they would commit an extravagance even, I should have some hope for them." He seems to care for little beyond accuracy of judgment and propriety; and I do not suppose accuracy of judgment and propriety ever made a great statesman. There is nothing venturesome about Lord Stanley—therefore there is nothing great. A man to be great must brave being ridiculous; and I do not remember that Lord Stanley has ever run the risk of being ridiculous. One of the finest and most celebrated passages of modern Parliamentary eloquence is that in which George Canning, vindicating his recognition of the South American republics, proclaimed that he had called in the New World to redress the balance of the Old. I once heard a member of the House of Lords, now dead, who sat in the House of Commons near Canning, when Canning spoke that famous speech, say that when the orator came to the great climax the House was actually breaking into a titter, so absurd then did any grandiloquence about South American republics seem; and it was only the earnestness and resolve of his manner that commanded a respectful attention, and thus compelled the House to recognize the genuine grandeur of the idea, and to break into a tempest of applause. I have heard something the same told of one of the grandest passages in any of Bright's speeches— that in one of his orations against the Crimean War, in which he declared that he already heard, during the debate, the beating of the wings of the Angel of Death. The House was under the influence of a war fever, and disposed to scoff at all appeals to prudence or to pity; and it was just on the verge of a laugh at the orator's majestic apostrophe, when his earnestness conquered, the grandeur of the moment was recognized, and a peal of irrepressible applause proclaimed the triumph of his eloquence. Now, these are the risks that a man like Lord Stanley never will run. Only genius makes such ventures. He is always safe: great statesmen must sometimes brave terrible hazards. In England he has received immense praise for the part he took in averting a war between France and Prussia on the Luxembourg question. Now, it is quite true that he did much; that, in fact, he lent all the influence of England to the mode of arrangement by which both the contending Powers were enabled to back decently out of a dangerous and painful position. But the idea of such a mode of settlement did not come from him. It was originated by Baron von Beust, the Austrian Prime Minister, and it was quietly urged a good deal before Lord Stanley saw it. Von Beust, who has a keener wit than Stanley, knew that if the proposition came directly from him it would, *ipso facto*, be odious to Prussia; and he was, therefore, rejoiced when Lord Stanley took it up and adopted it as his own and England's. Von Beust was well content, and so was Lord Stanley—just as Cuddie Headrigg, in "Old Mortality," is content that John Gudyill shall have the responsibility and the honor of the shot which the latter never fired. The one original thing which Lord Stanley did during the controversy was to write a dispatch to Prussia recommending her to come to terms, because of the superior navy of France, and the certainty, in the event of war, that France would have the best of it at sea.

Now, this was a capital argument to influence a man like Lord Stanley himself—calm, cold-blooded, utterly rational. But human ingenuity could hardly have devised an appeal less likely to influence Prussia in the way of peace. Prussia, flushed with her splendid victories over Austria, and deeply offended by the arrogant and dictatorial conduct of France, was much more likely to be stung by such an argument, if it affected her at all, into flinging down the gauntlet at once, and inviting France to come if she dared. The use of such a mode of persuasion is, indeed, an adequate illustration of the whole character of Lord Stanley. Cool, prudent, and rational, he is capable enough of weighing things fairly when they are presented to him; but he can neither create an opportunity nor run a risk. Therefore, he remains officially a Tory, mentally a Liberal, politically neither the one nor the other. His bones are marrowless, his blood is cold. He can forfeit his own career, and hazard his reputation for his party; but that is all. He cannot give his mind to it, and he cannot redeem himself from his futile bondage to it. He is a respectable speaker, despite his defective articulation and his lifeless manner; he will be a respectable politician, despite his want of faith in, or zeal for the cause he tries to follow. That is his career; that is the doom to which he voluntarily condemns himself.

I do not know that there are any other Tory chiefs worth talking about. Sir Stafford Northcote looks like a Bonn or Heidelberg professor, and has a fair average intellect, fit for commonplace finance and elementary politics; there is not a ghost of an idea in him. Walpole is a pompous, well-meaning, gentlemanlike imbecile. Gathorne Hardy is fluent, as the sand in an hourglass is fluent—he can pour out words and serve to mark the passing of time. Sir John Pakington is an educated Dogberry, a respectable Justice Shallow. Not upon men like these do the political fortunes of the Tory party of our day depend, although Walpole and Pakington fairly represent the sincerity, the manhood, and the respectability of Toryism.

I come back to the point from which I started—that Toryism, in itself, is only another word for stupidity, and that any triumphs the party have won or may win are secured by the surrender of the principle they profess to be fighting for, and by the skilful management of men whose conscience permits them to adapt the means unscrupulously to the end. Were the Tory party led by genuine Tories it would have been extinct long ago. It lives and looks upon the earth, it has its triumphs and its gains, its present and its future, only because by very virtue of its own dulness it has allowed itself to be led by men whom it ought to detest, whom it sometimes does distrust, but who have the wit to sell principle in the dearest market, and buy reputation in the cheapest.

"GEORGE ELIOT" AND GEORGE LEWES

Literary reputations are, in one respect, like wines—some are greatly improved by a long voyage, while others lose all zest and strength in the process of crossing the ocean. There ought to be hardly any difference, one would think, between the literary taste of the public of London and that of the public of New York; and yet it is certain that an author or a book may be positively celebrated in the one city and only barely known and coldly recognized in the other. Every one, of course, has noticed the fact that certain English authors are better known and appreciated in New York than in London; certain American writers more talked of in London than in New York. The general public of England do not seem to me to appreciate the true position of Whittier and Lowell among American poets. The average Englishman knows hardly anything of any American poet but Longfellow, who receives, I venture to think, a far more wholesale and enthusiastic admiration in England than in his own country. Robert Buchanan, the Scottish poet, lately, I have read, described "Evangeline" as a far finer poem than Goethe's "Hermann und Dorothea," a judgment which I presume and hope it would be impossible to get any American scholar and critic to indorse or even to consider seriously. On the other hand, it is well known that both the Brownings—certainly Mrs. Browning—found quicker and more cordial appreciation in America than in England. Lately, we in London have taken to discussing and debating over Walt Whitman with a warmth and interest which people in New York do not seem to manifest in regard to the author of "Leaves of Grass." Charles Dickens appears to me to have more devoted admirers among the best class of readers here than he has in his own country. Of course, it would be hardly possible for any man to be more popular and more successful than Dickens is in England; but New York journals quote him and draw illustrations from him much more frequently than London papers do—I do not think any day has passed since first I came to this country, six or seven months ago, that I have not seen at least two or three allusions to Dickens in the leading articles of the daily papers—and I question whether, among critics standing as high in London as George William Curtis does here, Dickens could find the enthusiastic, the almost lyrical devotion of Curtis's admiration. Charles Reade, again, is more generally and warmly admired here than in England.

Am I wrong in supposing that the reverse is the case with regard to the authoress of "Romola" and "The Mill on the Floss?" All American critics and all American readers of taste, have doubtless testified practically their recognition of the genius of this extraordinary woman; but there seems to me to be relatively less admiration for her in New York than in London. The general verdict of English criticism would, I feel no doubt, place George Eliot on a higher pedestal than Charles Dickens. We regard her as belonging to a higher school of art, as more nearly affined to the great immortal few whose genius and fame transcend the fashion of the age and defy the caprice of public taste. So far as I have been able to observe, I do not think this is the opinion of American criticism.

In any case, the mere question will excuse my writing a few pages about a woman whom I regard as the greatest living novelist of England; as, on the whole, the greatest woman now engaged in European literature. Only George Sand and Harriet Martineau could fairly be compared with her; and, while Miss Martineau, of course, is far inferior in all the higher gifts of imagination and the higher faculties of art, George Sand, with all her passion, her rich fancy, and daring, subtle analysis of certain natures, has never exhibited the serene, symmetrical power displayed in "Romola" and in "Silas Marner." Mrs. Lewes (it would be affectation to try to assume that there is still any mystery about the identity of "George Eliot") is what George Sand is not—a great writer, merely as a writer. Few, indeed, are the beings who have ever combined so many high qualities in one person as Mrs. Lewes does. Her literary career began as a translator and an essayist. Her tastes seemed then to lead her wholly into the somewhat barren fields where German metaphysics endeavor to come to the relief or the confusion of German theology. She became a contributor to the "Westminster Review;" then she became its assistant editor, and worked assiduously for it under the direction of Dr. John Chapman, the editor, with whose family she lived for a time, and in whose house she first met George Henry Lewes. She is an accomplished linguist, a brilliant talker, a musician of extraordinary skill. She has a musical sense so delicate and exquisite that there are tender, simple, true ballad melodies which fill her with a pathetic pain almost too keen to bear; and yet she has the firm, strong command of tone and touch, without which a really scientific musician cannot be made. I do not think this exceeding sensibility of nature is often to be found in combination with a genuine mastery of the practical science of music. But Mrs. Lewes has mastered many sciences as well as literatures. Probably no other novel writer, since novel writing became a business, ever possessed one tithe of her scientific knowledge. Indeed, hardly anything is rarer than the union of the scientific and the literary or artistic temperaments. So rare is it, that the exceptional, the almost solitary instance of Goethe comes up at once, distinct and striking, to the mind. English novelists are even less likely to have anything of a scientific taste than French or German. Dickens knows nothing of science, and has, indeed, as little knowledge of any kind, save that which is derived from observation, as any respectable Englishman could well have. Thackeray was a man of varied reading, versed in the lighter literature of several languages, and strongly imbued with artistic tastes; but he had no care for science, and knew nothing of it but just what every one has to learn at school. Lord Lytton's science is a mere sham. Charlotte Bronté was all genius and ignorance. Mrs. Lewes is all genius and culture. Had she never written a page of fiction, nay, had she never written a line of poetry or prose, she must have been regarded with wonder and admiration by all who knew her as a woman of vast and varied knowledge; a woman who could think deeply and talk brilliantly, who could play high and severe classical music like a professional performer, and could bring forth the most delicate and tender aroma of nature and poetry lying deep in the heart of some simple, old-fashioned Scotch or English ballad. Nature, indeed, seemed to have given to this extraordinary woman all the gifts a woman could ask or have—save one. It will not, I hope, be considered a piece of gossipping personality if I allude to a fact which must, some day or other, be part of literary history. Mrs. Lewes is not beautiful. In her appearance there is nothing whatever to attract admiration. Hers is not even a face like that of Charlotte Cushman, which, at least, must make a deep impression, and seize at once the attention of the gazer. Nor does it seem, like that of Madame de Staël or Elizabeth Barrett Browning, informed and illuminated by the light of genius. Mrs. Lewes is what we in England call decidedly plain—what people in New York call homely; and what persons who did not care to soften the force of an unpleasant truth would describe probably by a still harder and more emphatic adjective.

This woman, thus rarely gifted with poetry and music and imagination —thus disciplined in man's highest studies and accustomed to the most laborious of man's literary drudgery—does not seem to have found out, until she had passed what is conventionally regarded as the age of romance, that she had in her, transcendent above all other gifts, the faculty of the novelist. When an author who is not very young makes a great hit at last, we soon begin to learn that he had already made many attempts in the same direction, and his publishers find an eager demand for the stories and sketches which, when they first appeared, utterly failed to attract attention. Thackeray's early efforts, Trollope's, Charles Reade's, Nathaniel Hawthorne's, all these have been lighted into success by the blaze of the later triumph. But it does not seem that Miss Marion Evans, as she then was, ever published anything in the way of fiction previous to the series of sketches which appeared in "Blackwood's Magazine," and were called "Scenes of Clerical Life." These sketches attracted considerable attention, and were much admired; but I do not think many people saw in them the capacity which produced "Adam Bede" and "Romola." With the publication of "Adam Bede" came a complete triumph. The author was elevated at once and by acclamation to the highest rank among living novelists. I think it was in the very first number of the "Cornhill Magazine" that Thackeray, in a gossiping paragraph about novelists of the day, whom he mentioned alphabetically and by their initials, spoke of "E" as a "star of the first magnitude just risen on the horizon." Thackeray, it will be remembered, was one of the first, if not, indeed, the very first, to recognize the genius manifested in "Jane Eyre." The publishers sent him some of the proof sheets for his advice, and Thackeray saw in them the work of a great novelist.

The place which Mrs. Lewes thus so suddenly won, she has, of course, always maintained. Her position of absolute supremacy over all other women writers in England is something peculiar and curious. She is first— and there is no second. No living authoress in Britain is ever now compared with her. I read, not long since, in a New York paper, a sentence which spoke of George Eliot and Miss Mulock as being the greatest English authoresses in the field of fiction. It seemed very odd and funny to me. Certainly, an English critic would never have thought of bracketing together such a pair. Miss Mulock is a graceful, true-hearted, good writer; but Miss Mulock and George Eliot! Robert Lytton and Robert Browning! "A. K. H. B." (I think these are the initials) and John Stuart Mill! Mark Lemon's novels and Charles Dickens's! Mrs. Lewes has made people read novels who perhaps never read fiction from any other pen. She has made the novel the companion and friend and study of scholars and thinkers and statesmen. Her books are discussed by the gravest critics as productions of the highest school of art. Men and journals which have always regarded, or affected to regard, Thackeray as a mere cynic, and Dickens as little better than a professional buffoon, have discussed "The Mill on the Floss" and "Romola" as if these novels were already classic. Of course it would be a very doubtful kind of merit which commanded the admiration of literary prigs or pedants; but that is not the merit of George Eliot. Her books find their way to all hearts and intelligences, but it is their peculiarity that they compel, they extort the admiration of men who would disparage all novels, if they could, as frivolous and worthless, but who are forced even by their own canons and principles to recognize the deep clear thought, the noble culture, the penetrating, analytical power, which are evident in almost every chapter of these stories. Most of our novelists write in a slipslop, careless style. Dickens is worthless, if regarded merely as a prose writer; Trollope hardly cares about grammar; Charles Reade, with all his masculine force and clearness, is terribly irregular and rugged. The woman writers have seldom any style at all. George Eliot's prose might be the study of a scholar anxious to acquire and appreciate a noble English style. It is as luminous as the language of Mill; far more truly picturesque than that of Ruskin; capable of forcible, memorable expression as the robust Saxon of Bright. I am not going into a criticism of George Eliot, who has been, no doubt, fully criticised in America already. I am merely engaged in pointing out the special reasons why she has won in England a certain kind of admiration which, it seems to me, hardly any novelist ever has had before. I think she has infused into the novel some elements it never had before, and so thoroughly infused them that they blend with all the other materials, and do not form anywhere a solid lump or mass distinguishable from the rest. There are philosophical novels—"Wilhelm Meister," for example—which are weighed down and loaded with the philosophy, and which the world admires in spite of the philosophy. There are political novels—Disraeli's, for instance—which are only intelligible to those who make politics and political personalities a study, and which viewed merely as stories would not be worth speaking about. There are novels with a great direct purpose in them, such as "Uncle Tom's Cabin," or "Bleak House," or Charles Reade's "Hard Cash;" but these, after all, are only magnificent pamphlets, splendidly illustrated diatribes. The deep philosophic thought of George Eliot's novels suffuses and illumines them everywhere. You can point to no sermon here, no lecture there, no solid mass interposing between this incident and that, no ponderous moral hung around the neck of this or that personage. Only you feel that you are under the control of one who is not merely a great story-teller but who is also a deep thinker.

It is not, perhaps, unnecessary to say to American readers that George Eliot is the only novelist who can paint such English people as the Poysers and the Tullivers just as they really are. She looks into the very souls of these people. She tracks out their slow peculiar mental processes; she reproduces them fresh and firm from very life. Mere realism, mere photographing, even from the life, is not in art a very great triumph. But George Eliot can make her dullest people interesting and dramatically effective. She can paint two dull people with quite different ways of dulness—say a dull man and a dull woman, for example—and you are astonished to find how utterly distinct the two kinds of stupidity are—and how intensely amusing both can be made. Look at the two pedantic, pompous, dull advocates in the later part of Robert Browning's "The Ring and the Book." How distinct they are; how different, how unlike, and how true, are the two portraits. But then it must be owned that the poet is himself terribly tedious just there. His pedants are quite as tiresome as they would be in real life, if each successively held you by the button. George Eliot never is guilty of this great artistic fault. You never want to be rid of Mrs. Poyser or Aunt Glegg, or the prattling Florentines in "Romola." It is almost superfluous to say that there never was or could be a Mark Tapley, or a Sam Weller. We put up with these impossibilities and delight in them, because they are so amusing and so full of fantastic humor. But Mrs. Poyser lives, and I have met Aunt Glegg often; and poor Mrs. Tulliver's cares and hopes, and little fears, and pitiful reasonings, are animating scores of Mrs. Tullivers all over England to-day. I would propose a safe and easy test to any American or other "foreigner" (I am supposing myself now again in England), who is curious to know how much he understands of the English character. Let him read any of George Eliot's novels—even "Felix Holt," which is so decidedly inferior to the rest—and if he fails to follow, with thorough appreciation, the talk and the ways of the Poysers and such like personages, he may be assured he does not understand one great phase of English life.

Are these novels popular in England? Educated public opinion, I repeat, ranks them higher than the novels of any other living author. But they are not popular—that is, as Wilkie Collins or Miss Braddon is popular; and I do not mean to say anything slighting of either Wilkie Collins or Miss Braddon, both of whom I think possess very great talents, and have been treated with quite too much of the *de haut en bas* mood of the great critics. George Eliot's novels certainly are not run after and devoured by the average circulating library readers, as "The Woman in White," and "Lady Audley's Secret" were. She has, of course, nothing like the number of readers who follow Charles Dickens; nor even, I should say, nearly as many as Anthony Trollope. When "Romola," which the "Saturday Review" justly pronounced to be, if not the greatest, certainly the noblest romance of modern days, was being published as a serial in the "Cornhill Magazine," it was comparatively a failure, in the circulating library sense; and even when it appeared in its complete form, and the public could better appreciate its artistic perfection, it was anything but a splendid success, as regarded from the publisher's point of view. Perhaps this may be partly accounted for by the nature of the subject, the scene and the time; but even the warmest admirer of George Eliot may freely admit that "Romola" lacks a little of that passionate heat which is needed to make a writer of fiction thoroughly popular. When a statue of pure and perfect marble attracts as great a crowd of gazers as a glowing picture, then a novel like "Romola" will have as many admirers as a novel like "Consuelo" or "Villette."

I am not one of the admirers of George Eliot who regret that she ventured on the production of a long poem. I think "The Spanish Gypsy" a true and a fine poem, although I do not place it so high in artistic rank as the best of the author's prose writings. But I believe it to be the greatest story in verse ever produced by an Englishwoman. This is not, perhaps, very high praise, for Englishwomen have seldom done much in the higher fields of poetry; but we have "Aurora Leigh;" and I think "The Spanish Gypsy," on the whole, a finer piece of work. Most of our English critics fell to discussing the question whether "The Spanish Gypsy" was to be regarded as poetry at all, or only as a story put into verse; and in this futile and vexatious controversy the artistic value of the work itself almost escaped analysis. I own that I think criticism shows to little advantage when it occupies itself in considering whether a work of art is to be called by this name or that; and I am rather impatient of the critic who comes with his canons of art, his Thirty-Nine articles of literary dogma, and judges a book, not by what it is in itself, but by the answer it gives to his self-invented catechism. I do not believe that the art of man ever can invent—I know it never has invented—any set of rules or formulas by which you can decide, off-hand and with certainty, that a great story in verse, which you admit to have power and beauty and pathos and melody, does not belong to true poetry. One great school of critics discovered, by the application of such high rules and canons that Shakespeare, though a great genius was not a great poet; a later school made a similar discovery with regard to Schiller; a certain body of critics now say the same of Byron. I don't think it matters much what you call the work. "The Spanish Gypsy" has imagination and beauty; it has exquisite pictures and lofty thoughts; it has melody and music. Admitting this much, and the most depreciating critics did admit it, I think it hardly worth considering what name we are to apply to the book. Such, however, was the sort of controversy in which all deep and true consideration of the artistic value of "The Spanish Gypsy" evaporated. I am not sorry Mrs. Lewes published the poem; but I am sorry she put her literary name to it in the first instance. Had it appeared anonymously it would have astonished and delighted the world. But people compared "The Spaniel Gypsy" with the author's prose works, and were disappointed because the woman who surpassed Dickens in fiction did not likewise surpass Tennyson and Browning in poetry. Thus, and in no other sense, was "The Spanish Gypsy" a failure. No woman had written anything of the same kind to surpass it; but some men, even of our own day, had—and no man of our day has written novels which excel those of George Eliot. Mrs. Lewes will probably not write any more long poems; but I think English poetry has gained something by her one venture.

Mrs. Lewes's mind is of a class which, however varied its power, is not fairly described by the word "versatile." Versatility is a smaller kind of faculty, a dexterity of intellect and capacity—the property of a mind of the second order. If we want a perfect type and pattern of versatility, we may find it very close to the authoress of "Silas Marner," in the person of her husband, George Henry Lewes. What man of our day has done so many things and done them so well? He is the biographer of Goethe and of Robespierre; he has compiled the "History of Philosophy," in which he has something really his own to say of every great philosopher, from Thales to Schelling; he has translated Spinoza; he has published various scientific works; he has written at least two novels; he has made one of the most successful dramatic adaptations known to our stage; he is an accomplished theatrical critic; he was at one time so successful as an amateur actor that he seriously contemplated taking to the stage as a profession, in the full conviction, which he did not hesitate frankly to avow, that he was destined to be the successor to Macready. He did actually join a company at one of the Manchester theatres, and perform there for some time under a feigned name; but the amount of encouragement he received from the public did not stimulate him to continue on the boards, although I believe his confidence in his own capacity to succeed Macready remained unshaken. Mr. Lewes was always remarkable for a frank and fearless self-conceit, which, by its very sincerity and audacity, almost disarmed criticism. Indeed, I do not suppose any man less gifted with self-confidence would have even attempted to do half the things which George Henry Lewes has done well. Margaret Fuller was very unfavorably impressed by Lewes when she met him at Thomas Carlyle's house, and she wrote of him contemptuously and angrily. But these were the days of Lewes's Bohemianism; days of an audacity and a self-conceit unsubdued as yet by experience and the world, and some saddening and some refining influences; and Margaret Fuller failed to appreciate the amount of intellect and manliness that was in him. Charlotte Bronté, on the other hand, was quite enthusiastic about Lewes, and wrote to him and of him with an almost amusing veneration. Indeed, he is a man of ability and versatility that may fairly be called extraordinary. His merit is not that he has written books on a great variety of subjects. London has many hack writers who could go to work at any publisher's order and produce successively an epic poem, a novel, a treatise on the philosophy of the conditioned, a handbook of astronomy, a farce, a life of Julius Cæsar, a history of African explorations, and a volume of sermons. But none of these productions would have one gleam of genuine native vitality about it. The moment it had served its purpose in the literary market it would go, dead, down to the dead. Lewes's works are of quite a different style. They have positive merit and value of their own, and they live. It was a characteristically audacious thing to attempt to cram the history of philosophy into a couple of medium-sized volumes, polishing off each philosopher in a few pages—draining him, plucking out the heart of his mystery and his system, and stowing him away in the glass jar designed to exhibit him to an edified class of students. But it must be avowed that Lewes's has been a marvellously clever and successful attempt. He certainly crumples up the whole science of metaphysics, sweeps away transcendental philosophy, and demolishes *a priori* reasoning, in a manner which strongly reminds one of Arthur Pendennis upsetting, in a dashing criticism and on the faith of an hour's reading in an encyclopædia, some great scientific theory of which he had never heard previously, and the development of which had been the life's labor of a sage. But Lewes does, somehow or other, very often come to a right conclusion, and measure great theories and men with accurate estimate; and the work is immensely interesting, and it is not easy to see how anybody could have done it better. His "Life of Goethe" is undoubtedly a very successful, symmetrical, and comprehensive piece of biography. Some of his scientific studies have a genuine value, and they are all fascinating. One of his pieces—adapted from the French, of course, as most so-called English pieces are—will always be played while Charles Mathews lives, or while there are actors who can play in Charles Mathews's style. I wonder whether any of the readers of The Galaxy read, or having read remember, Lewes's novels? I only recollect two of them, and I do not know whether he wrote any others. One was called "Ranthorpe," and it had, in its day, quite a sort of success. How long ago was it published? Fully twenty years, I should think: I remember quite well being thrown into youthful raptures with it at the time. But I do not go upon my boyish admiration for it. I came across it somewhere much more recently, and read it through. There was a good deal of inflation, and audacity, and nonsense in it; but at the same time it showed more of brains and artistic impulse and constructive power than nine out of every ten novels published in England to-day. It was all about a young poet, who came to London and made, for a moment, a great success, and was dazzled by it, and became intoxicated with love for a lustrous beauty of high rank, who only played with him; and how he forgot, for a time, the modest, delightful, simple girl to whom he was pledged at home; and how he did not get on, and the public and the *salons* grew tired of him; and he became miserable, and was going to drown himself (I think), but was prevented by some wise and timely person; and how, of course, it all came right in the end, and he was redeemed. This outline, probably, will not suggest much of originality to any reader; but there was a great deal of freshness and thought in the book, some of the incidents and one or two of the characters had a flavor of originality about them; and the style was, for the most part, animated and attractive. It was

Modern Leaders Being A Series Of Biographical Sketches | 189

the work of a man of brains, and culture, and taste; and one felt this all through, and was not ashamed of the time spent in reading it. The other of Lewes's novels was called "Rose, Blanche, and Violet." It charmed me a good deal when I read it; but I have not read it lately, and so I forbear giving any decided opinion as to its merits. It is, of course, quite settled now that George Lewes had not in him the materials to make a successful novelist; but men of far less talent have produced far worse novels than his, and been, in their way, successful.

Lewes first became prominent in literature as a contributor to the "Leader," a very remarkable weekly organ of advanced opinions on all questions, which was started in London seventeen or eighteen years ago, and died, after much flickering and lingering, in 1861 or thereabouts. The "Leader," in its early and best days, fairly sparkled all over with talent, originality and audacity. It was to extreme philosophical radicalism, (with a dash of something like atheism) what the "Saturday Review" now is to cultured swelldom and Belgravian Sadduceeism. Miss Martineau wrote for it. Lewes and Thornton Hunt (they were then intimates, unfortunately for Lewes) were among its principal contributors; Edward Whitty flung over its pages the brilliant eccentric light which was destined to immature and melancholy extinction. Lewes's theatrical criticisms, which he used to sign "Vivian," were inimitable in their vivacity, their wit, and their keenness, even when their soundness of judgment was most open to question. Poor Charles Kean was an especial object of Lewes's detestation, and was accordingly pelted and peppered with torturingly clever and piquant pasquinades in the form of criticism. Lewes has got wonderfully sober and grave in style since those wild days, and his occasional contributions in the shape of dramatic criticism to the "Pall Mall Gazette" are doubtless more generally accurate, are certainly much more thoughtful, but are far less amusing than the admirable fooling of days gone by. It was in the "Leader," I think, that Lewes carried on his famous controversy with Charles Dickens on the possibility of such spontaneous combustion as that of the old brute in "Bleak House," and it was in the "Leader" that he made an equally famous exposure of a sham spiritualist medium, about whom London was then much agitated. The "Leader," probably, never paid; it was far too iconoclastic and eccentric to be a commercial success, but it made quite a mark and will always be a memory. It did not succeed in its object; but, like the arrow of the hero in Virgil, it left a long line of sparkles and light behind it. Lewes has abandoned Bohemia long since, and Edward Whitty is dead, and Thornton Hunt has come to nothing—and there is another "Leader" now in London which bears about as much resemblance to the original and real "Leader" as Richard Cromwell did to Oliver, or Charles Kean to Edmund.

Bohemianism, and novel-writing, and amateur acting, and persiflage, and epigram, are all gone by now with Lewes. He has settled into a grave and steady writer, for the most part of late confining himself to scientific subjects. A few years ago he started the "Fortnightly Review," in the hope of establishing in England a counterpart of the "Revue des Deux Mondes." The first number was enriched by one of the most thoughtful, subtle, beautiful essays lately contributed to literature; and it bore the signature of George Eliot. Lewes himself wrote a series of essays on "The Principles of Success in Literature," very good, very sound, but not very lively reading. A great English novelist was pleased graciously to say, *apropos* of these essays, "Success in literature! What does Lewes know about success in literature?" and the small devotees of the great successful novelist laughed and repeated the joke. It is certain that the "Fortnightly Review" was not a success under the editorship of George Henry Lewes; and people said, I do not know how truly, that a good deal of the nobly-earned money paid for "Silas Marner" and the "Mill on the Floss" disappeared in the attempt to erect a British "Revue des Deux Mondes." The "Fortnightly" lives still, and is called "Fortnightly" still, although it now only comes out once a month, but Lewes has long ceased to edit it. I think the present editor, John Morley, a young man of great ability and promise, is better suited for the work than Lewes was—indeed I doubt whether Lewes, with all his varied gifts and acquirements, possesses the peculiar qualities which make a man a genuine editor. But, the difference between wild Hal, the Prince of Gadshill, and grave, wise Henry the Fifth, could hardly be greater than that between the Vivian of the "Leader" and the late editor of the solemn, ponderous "Fortnightly Review."

Lewes wrote at one time a great deal for the "Westminster Review." It was during his connection with it that he became acquainted, at Dr. Chapman's house, with Marion Evans. There was a great similarity between their tastes. Both loved the study of languages, and of philosophical thought, and of literature and science generally. Both were splendid in conversation, brilliant in epigram; both loved music and were intensely susceptible to its influence. The mind of the woman was, I need hardly say, far the stronger, wider, deeper of the two; but the affinity was clear and close. A great misfortune had fallen on Lewes; and he was probably in that condition of mind which makes a man not unlikely to lose his faith in everything and drift into hopeless, perpetual cynicism. From this, if this impended over him, Lewes was saved by his intercourse with the rarely-gifted woman he had met in so timely an hour. The result is, as every one knows, a companionship and union unusual indeed in literary life. Very seldom has a distinguished author had for wife a distinguished authoress, or *vice versa*; indeed, it used to be one of the dear delightful theories of blockheads that such unions, if they could take place, would be miserably unhappy. This theory, so soothing to complacent dulness, was hardly borne out in the instance of the Brownings; it is just as little corroborated by the example of "George Eliot" and George Lewes. I believe, too, the example of George Eliot is highly unsatisfactory to the devotees of that other theory, so long cherished by dolts of both sexes, that a woman of talent and culture can never do anything in the way of mending or making, of cooking a chop or ordering a household. People tell us they can trace the influence of Lewes's varied scholarship and critical judgment in the novels of George Eliot. It is hardly possible to doubt that some such influence must be there, but I certainly never saw it anywhere distinctly and openly evident. It would be poor art which allowed a thin stream of Lewes to be seen sparkling through the broad, deep, luminous lake which mirrors the genius of George Eliot. I am, however, rather inclined to fancy that Lewes, in general, abstains from critical *surveillance* or restraint over the productions of his greater companion, believing, perhaps, that the higher mind had better be a law to itself. If this be so, I think it is a wholesome principle pushed sometimes too far, for one can hardly believe that the calm judgment of any sincere and qualified adviser would not have discouraged and condemned the painful, unnecessary underplot of past intrigue and sin which is so great a blot in "Felix Holt," or suggested a rapider dramatic movement in some passages of "The Spanish Gypsy." Lewes once wrote to Charlotte Bronté that he would rather be the author of Miss Austen's stories than of the whole of the Waverley Novels. I certainly do not agree with him in that opinion; but it is strange that one who held it should not have endeavored to prevent an authoress greater than Miss Austen, and far more directly under his influence than Charlotte Bronté, from sinking, in one or two instances, into faults which neither Miss Austen nor Miss Bronté would ever have committed. Many things are strange about this literary and domestic companionship; this comparatively trifling fact seems to me not the least strange.

Finally let me say that I fully expect George Eliot yet to give to the world some work of art even greater than any she has already produced. She is not a woman to close with even a comparative failure. Her maxim, I feel confident, would be that of the Emperor Napoleon—offer terms of peace and repose after a great victory; never otherwise.

GEORGE SAND

We are all of us probably inclined now and then to waste a little time in vaguely speculating on what might have happened if this or that particular event had not given a special direction to the career of some great man or woman. If there had been an inch of difference in the size of Cleopatra's nose; if Hannibal had not lingered at Capua; if Cromwell had carried out his idea of emigration; if Napoleon Bonaparte had taken service under the Turk—and so on through all the old familiar illustrations dear to the minor essayist and the debating society. I have sometimes felt tempted thus to lose myself in speculating on what might have happened if the woman whom all the world knows as George Sand had been happily married in her youth to the husband of her choice. Would she ever have taken to literature at all? Would she, loving as she does, and as Frenchwomen so rarely do, the changing face of inanimate nature—the fields, the flowers, and the brooks—have lived a peaceful and obscure life in some happy country place, and been content with home, and family, and love, and never thought of fame? Or if, thus happily married, she still had allowed her genius to find an expression in literature, would she have written books with no passionate purpose in them—books which might have seemed like those of a good Miss Mulock made perfect—books which Podsnap might have read with approval and put without a scruple into the hands of that modest young person, his daughter? Certainly one cannot but think that a different kind of early life would have given a quite different complexion to the literary individuality of George Sand.

Bulwer Lytton, in one of his novels, insists that true genius is always quite independent of the individual sufferings or joys of its possessor, and describes some inspired youth in the novel as sitting down while sorrow is in his heart and hunger gnawing at his vitals, to throw off a sparkling and gladsome little fairy tale. Now this is undoubtedly true in general of any high order of genius; but there are at least some great and striking exceptions. Rousseau and Byron are, in modern days, remarkable illustrations of genius, admittedly of a very high rank, governed and guided almost wholly by the individual fortunes of the men themselves. So too must we speak of the genius of George Sand. Not Rousseau, not even Byron, was in this sense more egotistic than the woman who broke the chains of her ill-assorted marriage with a crash that made its echoes heard at last in every civilized country in the world. Just as people are constantly quoting *nous avons changé tout cela* who never read a page of Molière, or *pour encourager les autres* without even being aware that there is a story of Voltaire's called "Candide," so there have been thousands of passionate protests uttered in America and Europe for the last twenty years by people who never saw a volume of George Sand, and yet are only echoing her sentiments and even repeating her words.

In a former number of The Galaxy I expressed casually the opinion that George Sand is probably the most influential writer of our day. I am still, and deliberately, of the same opinion. It must be remembered that very few English or American authors have any wide or deep influence over peoples who do not speak English. Even of the very greatest authors this is true. Compare, for example, the literary dominion of Shakespeare with that of Cervantes. All nations who read Shakespeare read Cervantes: in Stratford-upon-Avon itself Don Quixote is probably as familiar a figure in people's minds as Falstaff; but Shakespeare is little known indeed to the vast majority of readers in the country of Cervantes, in the land of Dante, or in that of Racine and Victor Hugo. In something of the same way we may compare the influence of George Sand with that of even the greatest living authors of England and America. What influence has Charles Dickens or George Eliot outside the range of the English tongue? But George Sand's genius has been felt as a power in every country of the world where people read any manner of books. It has been felt almost as Rousseau's once was felt; it has aroused anger, terror, pity, or wild and rapturous excitement and admiration; it has rallied around it every instinct in man or woman which is revolutionary; it has ranged against it all that is conservative. It is not so much a literary influence as a great disorganizing force, riving the rocks of custom, resolving into their original elements the social combinations which tradition and convention would declare to be indissoluble. I am not now speaking merely of the sentiments which George Sand does or did entertain on the subject of marriage. Divested of all startling effects and thrilling dramatic illustrations, these sentiments probably amounted to nothing more dreadful than the belief that an unwedded union between two people who love and are true to each other is less immoral than the legal marriage of two uncongenial creatures who do not love and probably are not true to each other. But the grand, revolutionary idea which George Sand announced was that of the social independence and equality of woman—the principle that woman is not made for man in any other sense than as man is made for woman. For the first time in the history of the world woman spoke out for herself with a voice as powerful as that of man. For the first time in the history of the world woman spoke out as woman, not as the servant, the satellite, the pupil, the plaything, or the goddess of man.

Now I intend at present to write of George Sand rather as an individual, or an influence, than as the author of certain works of fiction. Criticism would now be superfluously bestowed on the literary merits and peculiarities of the great woman whose astonishing intellectual activity has never ceased to produce, during the last thirty years, works which take already a classical place in French literature. If any reputation of our day may be looked upon as established, we may thus regard the reputation of George Sand. She is, beyond comparison, the greatest living novelist of France. She has won this position by the most legitimate application of the gifts of an artist. With all her marvellous fecundity, she has hardly ever given to the world any work which does not seem at least to have been the subject of the most elaborate and patient care. The greatest temptation which tries a story-teller is perhaps the temptation to rely on the attractiveness of story-telling, and to pay little or no attention to style. Walter Scott's prose, for example, if regarded as mere prose, is rambling, irregular, and almost worthless. Dickens's prose is as bad a model for imitation as a musical performance which is out of tune. Of course, I need hardly say that attention to style is almost as characteristic of French authors in general, as the lack of it is characteristic of English authors; but even in France, the prose of George Sand stands out conspicuous for its wonderful expressiveness and force, its almost perfect beauty. Then of all modern French authors—I might perhaps say of all modern novelists of any country—George Sand has added to fiction, has annexed from the worlds of reality and of imagination, the greatest number of original characters—of what Emerson calls new organic creations. Moreover, George Sand is, after Rousseau, the one only great French author who has looked directly and lovingly into the face of Nature, and learned the secrets which skies and waters, fields and lanes, can teach to the heart that loves them. Gifts such as these have won her the almost unrivalled place which she holds in living literature, and she has conquered at last even the public opinion which once detested and proscribed her. I could therefore hope to add nothing to what has been already said by criticism in regard to her merits as a novelist. Indeed, I think it probable that the majority of readers in this country know more of George Sand through the interpretation of the critics than through the pages of her books. And in her case criticism is so nearly unanimous as to her literary merits, that I may safely assume the public in general to have in their minds a just recognition of her position as a novelist. My object is rather to say something about the place which George Sand has taken as a social revolutionist, about the influence she has so long exercised over the world, and about the woman herself. For she is assuredly the greatest champion of woman's rights, in one sense, that the world has ever seen; and she is, on the other hand, the one woman out of all the world who has been most commonly pointed to as the appalling example to scare doubtful and fluttering womanhood back into its sheepfold of submissiveness and conventionality. There is hardly a woman's heart anywhere in the civilized world which has not felt the vibration of George Sand's thrilling voice. Women who never saw one of her books, nay, who never heard even her *nom de plume*, have been stirred by emotions of doubt or fear or repining or ambition, which they never would have known but for George Sand, and perhaps but for George Sand's uncongenial marriage. For indeed there is not now, and has not been for twenty years, I venture to think, a single "revolutionary" idea, as slow and steady-going people would call it, afloat anywhere in Europe or America, on the subject of woman's relations to man, society, and destiny, which is not due immediately to the influence of George Sand, and to the influence of George Sand's unhappy marriage upon George Sand herself.

The world has of late years grown used to this extraordinary woman, and has lost much of the wonder and terror with which it once regarded her. I can quite remember — younger people than I can remember — the time when all good and proper personages in England regarded the authoress of "Indiana" as a sort of feminine fiend, endowed with a hideous power for the destruction of souls and an inextinguishable thirst for the slaughter of virtuous beliefs. I fancy a good deal of this sentiment was due to the fearful reports wafted across the seas, that this terrible woman had not merely repudiated the marriage bond, but had actually put off the garments sacred to womanhood. That George Sand appeared in men's clothes was an outrage upon consecrated proprieties far more astonishing than any theoretical onslaught upon old opinions could be. Reformers indeed should always, if they are wise in their generation, have a care of the proprieties. Many worthy people can listen with comparative fortitude when sacred and eternal truths are assailed, who are stricken with horror when the ark of propriety is never so lightly touched. George Sand's pantaloons were therefore regarded as the most appalling illustration of George Sand's wickedness. I well remember what excitement, scandal, and horror were created in the provincial town where I lived some twenty years ago, when the editor of a local Panjandrum (to borrow Mr. Trollope's word) insulted the feelings and the morals of his constituents and subscribers by polluting his pages with a translation from one of George Sand's shorter novels. Ah me, the little novel might, so far as morality was concerned, have been written every word by Miss Phelps, or the authoress of the "Heir of Redcliffe"; it had not a word, from beginning to end, which might not have been read out to a Sunday school of girls; the translation was made by a woman of the purest soul, and in her own locality the highest name; and yet how virtue did shriek out against the publication! The editor persevered in the publishing of the novel, spurred on to boldness by some of his very young and therefore fearless coadjutors, who thought it delightful to confront public opinion, and liked the notion of the stars in their courses fighting against Sisera, and Sisera not being dismayed. That charming, tender, touching little story! I would submit it to-day cheerfully to the verdict of a jury of matrons, confident that it would be declared a fit and proper publication. But at that time it was enough that the story bore the odious name of George Sand; public opinion condemned it, and sent the magazine which ventured to translate it to an early and dishonored grave. I remember reading about that time a short notice of George Sand by an English authoress of some talent and culture, in which the Frenchwoman's novels were described as so abominably filthy, that even the denizens of the Paris brothels were ashamed to be caught reading them. Now this declaration was made in all good faith, in the simple good faith of that class of persons who will pass wholesale and emphatic judgment upon works of which they have never read a single page. For I need hardly tell any intelligent person of to-day, that whatever may be said of George Sand's doctrines, she is no more open to the charge of indelicacy than the authoress of "Romola." I cannot myself remember any passage in George Sand's novels which can be called indelicate; and indeed her severest and most hostile critics are fond of saying, not without a certain justice, that one of the worst characteristics of her works is the delicacy and beauty of her style, which thus commends to pure and innocent minds certain doctrines that, broadly stated, would repel and shock them. Were I one of George Sand's inveterate opponents, this, or something like it, is the ground I would take up. I would say: "The welfare of the human family demands that a marriage, legally made, shall never be questioned or undone. Marriage is not a union depending on love or congeniality, or any such condition. It is just as sacred when made for money, or for ambition, or for lust of the flesh, or for any other purpose, however ignoble and base, as when contracted in the spirit of the purest mutual love. Here is a woman of great power and daring genius, who says that the essential condition of marriage is love and natural fitness; that a legal union of man and woman without this is no marriage at all, but a detestable and disgusting sin. Now the more delicately, modestly, plausibly she can put this revolutionary and pernicious doctrine, the more dangerous she becomes, and the more earnestly we ought to denounce her." This was in fact what a great many persons did say; and the protest was at least consistent and logical.

But horror is an emotion which cannot long live on the old fuel, and even the world of English Philistinism soon ceased to regard George Sand as a mere monster. Any one now taking up "Indiana," for example, would perhaps find it not quite easy to understand how the book produced such an effect. Our novel-writing women of to-day commonly feed us on more fiery stuff than this. Not to speak of such accomplished artists in impurity as the lady who calls herself Ouida, and one or two others of the same school, we have young women only just promoted from pantalettes, who can throw you off such glowing chapters of passion and young desire as would make the rhapsodies of "Indiana" seem very feeble milk-and-water brewage by comparison. Indeed, except for some of the descriptions in the opening chapters, I fail to see any extraordinary merit in "Indiana"; and toward the end it seems to me to grow verbose, weak, and tiresome. "Leone Leoni" opens with one of the finest dramatic outbursts of emotion known to the literature of modern fiction; but it soon wanders away into discursive weakness, and only just toward the close brightens up into a burst of lurid splendor. It is not those which I may call the questionable novels of George Sand—the novels which were believed to illustrate in naked and appalling simplicity her doctrines and her life—that will bear up her fame through succeeding generations. If every one of the novels which thus in their time drew down the thunders of society's denunciation were to be swept into the wallet wherein Time, according to Shakespeare, carries scraps for oblivion, George Sand would still remain where she now is, at the head of the French fiction of her day. It is true, as Goethe says, that "miracle-working pictures are rarely works of art." The books which make the hair of the respectable public stand on end, are not often the works by which the fame of the author is preserved for posterity.

It is a curious fact that at the early time to which I have been alluding, little or nothing was known in England (or, I presume, in America) of the real life of Aurore Amandine Dupin, who had been pleased to call herself George Sand. People knew, or had heard, that she had separated from her husband, that she had written novels which depreciated the sanctity of legal marriage, and that she sometimes wore male costume in the streets. This was enough. In England, at least, we were ready to infer any enormity regarding a woman who was unsound on the legal marriage question, and who did not wear petticoats. What would have been said had people then commonly known half the stories which were circulated in Paris; half the extravagances into which a passionate soul and the stimulus of sudden emancipation from restraint had hurried the authoress of "Indiana" and "Lucrezia Floriani"? For it must be owned that the life of that woman was, in its earlier years, a strange and wild phenomenon, hardly to be comprehended perhaps by American or English natures. I have heard George Sand bitterly arraigned even by persons who protested that they were at one with her as regards the early sentiments which used to excite such odium. I have heard her described by such as a sort of Lamia of literature and passion; a creature who could seize some noble, generous, youthful heart, drain it of its love, its aspirations, its profoundest emotions, and then fling it, squeezed and lifeless, away. I have heard it declared that George Sand made "copy" of the fierce and passionate loves which she knew so well how to awaken and to foster; that she distilled the life-blood of youth to obtain the mixture out of which she derived her inspiration. The charge so commonly (I think unjustly) made against Goethe, that he played with the girlish love of Bettina and of others in order to obtain a subject for literary dissection, is vehemently and deliberately urged in an aggravated form, in many aggravated forms, against George Sand. Where, such accusers ask, is that young poet, endowed with a lyrical genius rare indeed in the France of later days, that young poet whose imagination was at once so daring and so subtle; who might have been Béranger and Heine in one, and have risen to an atmosphere in which neither Béranger nor Heine ever floated? Where is he, and what evil influence was it which sapped the strength of his nature, corrupted his genius, and prepared for him a premature and shameful grave? Where is that young musician, whose pure, tender, and lofty strains sound sweetly and sadly in the ears, as the very hymn and music of the Might-Have-Been—where is he now, and what was the seductive power which made a plaything of him and then flung him away? Here and there some man of stronger mould is pointed out as one who was at the first conquered, and then deceived and trifled with, but who ordered his stout heart to bear, and rose superior to the hour, and lived to retrieve his nature and make himself a name of respect; but the others, of more sensitive and perhaps finer organizations, are only the more to be pitied because they were so terribly in earnest. Seldom, even in the literary history of modern France, has there been a more strange and shocking episode than the publication by George Sand of the little book called "Elle et Lui," and the rejoinder to it by Paul de Musset called "Lui et Elle." I can hardly be accused of straying into the regions of private scandal when I speak of two books which had a wide circulation, are still being read, and may be had, I presume, in any New York bookstore where French literature is sold. The former of the two books, "She and He," was a story, or something which purported to be a story, by George Sand, telling of two ill-assorted beings whom fate had thrown together for a while, and of whom the woman was all tenderness, love, patience, the man all egotism, selfishness, sensuousness, and eccentricity. The point of the whole business was to show how sublimely the woman suffered, and how wantonly the man flung happiness away. Had it been merely a piece of fiction, it must have been regarded by any healthy mind as a morbid, unwholesome, disagreeable production; a sin of the highest æsthetic kind against true art, which must always, even in its pathos and its tragedy, leave on the mind exalted and delightful impressions. But every one in Paris at once hailed the story as a chapter of autobiography, as the author's vindication of one episode in her own career—a vindication at the expense of a man who had gone down, ruined and lost, to an early grave. Therefore the brother of the dead man flung into literature a little book called "He and She," in which a story, substantially the same in its outlines, is so told as exactly to reverse the conditions under which the verdict of public opinion was sought. Very curious indeed was the manner in which the same substance of facts was made to present the two principal figures with complexions and characters so strangely altered. In the woman's book, the woman was made the patient, loving, suffering victim; in the man's reply, this same woman was depicted as the most utterly selfish and depraved creature the human imagination could conceive. Even if one had no other means whatever of forming an estimate of the character of George Sand, it would be hardly possible to accept as her likeness the hideous picture sketched by Paul de Musset. No woman, I am glad to believe, ever existed in real life so utterly selfish, base, and wicked as his bitter pen has drawn. I must say that the thing is very cleverly done. The picture is at least consistent with itself. As a character in romance it might be pronounced original, bold, brilliant, and, in an artistic sense, quite natural. There is something thoroughly French in the easy and delicate force of the final touch with which de Musset dismisses his hideous subject. Having sketched this woman in tints that seem to flame across the eyes of the reader; having described with wonderful realism and power her affectation, her deceit, her reckless caprices, her base and cruel coquetries, her devouring wantonness, her soul-destroying arts, her unutterable selfishness and egotism; having, to use a vulgar phrase, "turned her inside out," and told her story backwards, the author calmly explains that the hero of the narrative in his dying hour called his brother to his bedside, and enjoined him, if occasion should ever arise, if the partner of his sin should ever calumniate him in his grave, to vindicate his memory and avenge the treason practised upon him. "Of course," adds the narrator, "the brother made the promise—and I have since heard that he has kept his word." I can hardly hope to convey to the reader any adequate idea of the effect produced on the mind by these few simple words of compressed, whispered hatred and triumph, closing a philippic, or a revelation, or a libel of such extraordinary bitterness and ferocity. The whole episode is, I believe and earnestly hope, without precedent or imitation in literary controversy. Never, that I know of, has a living woman been publicly exhibited to the world in a portraiture so hideous as that which Paul de Musset drew of George Sand. Never, that I know of, has any woman gone so near to deserving and justifying such a measure of retaliation.

For if it be assumed—and I suppose it never has been disputed—that in writing "Elle et Lui" George Sand meant to describe herself and Alfred de Musset, it is hard to conceive of any sin against taste and feeling, against art and morals, more flagrant than such a publication. The practice, to which French writers are so much addicted, of making "copy" of the private lives, characters, and relationships of themselves and their friends, seems to me in all cases utterly detestable. Lamartine's sins of this kind were grievous and glaring; but were they red as scarlet, they would seem whiter than snow when compared with the lurid monstrosity of George Sand's assault on the memory of the dead poet who was once her favorite. The whole affair indeed is so unlike anything which could occur in America or in England, that we can hardly find any canons by which to try it, or any standard of punishment by which to regulate its censure. I allude to it now because it is the only substantial evidence I know of which does fairly seem to justify the worst of the accusations brought against George Sand; and I do not think it right, when writing for grown men and women, who are supposed to have sense and judgment, to affect not to know that such accusations are made, or to pretend to think that it would be proper not to allude to them. They have been put forward, replied to, urged again, made the theme of all manner of controversy in scores of French and in some English publications. Pray let it be distinctly understood that I am not entering into any criticism of the morality of any part of George Sand's private life. With that we have nothing here to do. I am now dealing with the question, fairly belonging to public controversy, whether the great artist did not deliberately deal with human hearts as the painter of old is said to have done with a purchased slave— inflicting torture in order the better to learn how to depict the struggles and contortions of mortal agony. In answer to such a question I can only point to "Lucrezia Floriani" and to "Elle et Lui," and say that unless the universal opinion of qualified critics be wrong these books, and others too, owe their piquancy and their dramatic force to the anatomization of dead passions and discarded lovers. We have all laughed over the pedantic surgeon in Molière's "Malade Imaginaire," who invites his *fiancée* as a delightful treat to see him dissect the body of a woman. I am afraid that George Sand did sometimes invite an admiring public to an exhibition yet more ghastly and revolting—the dissection of the heart of a dead lover.

But in truth we shall never judge George Sand and her writings at all if we insist on criticising them from any point of view set up by the proprieties or even the moralities of Old England or New England. When the passionate young woman, in whose veins ran the wild blood of Marshal Saxe, found herself surrendered by legality and prescription to a marriage bond against which her soul revolted, society seemed for her to have resolved itself into its original elements. Its conventionalities and traditions contained nothing which she held herself bound to respect. The world was not her friend, nor the world's law. By one great decisive step she sundered herself forever from the bonds of what we call society. She had shaken the dust of convention from her feet; the world was all before her where to choose. No creature on earth is so absolutely free as the Frenchwoman who has broken with society. There, then, stood this daring young woman, on the threshold of a new, fresh, and illimitable world; a young woman gifted with genius such as our later years have rarely seen, and blessed or cursed with a nature so strangely uniting the most characteristic qualities of man and woman as to be in itself quite unparalleled and unique. Just think of it—try to think of it! Society and the world had no longer any laws which she recognized. Nothing was sacred; nothing was settled. She had to evolve from her own heart and brain her own law of life. What wonder if she made some sad mistakes? Nay, is it not rather a theme for wonder and admiration that she did somehow come right at last? I know of no one who seems to me to have been open at once to the temptations of woman's nature and man's nature except this George Sand. Her soul, her brain, her style may be described, from one point of view, as exuberantly and splendidly feminine; yet no other woman has ever shown the same power of understanding and entering into the nature of a man. If Balzac is the only man who has ever thoroughly mastered the mysteries of a woman's heart, George Sand is the only woman, so far as I know, who has ever shown that she could feel as a man can feel. I have read stray passages in her novels which I would confidently submit to the criticism of any intelligent men unacquainted with the text, convinced that they would declare that only a man could have thus analyzed the emotions of manhood. I have in my mind just now especially a passage in the novel "Piccinino" which, were the authorship unknown, would, I am satisfied, secure the decision of a jury of literary experts that the author must be a man. Now this gift of entire appreciation of the feelings of a different sex or race is, I take it, one of the rarest and highest dramatic qualities. Especially is it difficult for a woman, as our social life goes, to enter into the feelings of a man. While men and women alike admit the accuracy of certain pictures of women drawn by such artists as Cervantes, Molière, Balzac, and Thackeray, there are few women—indeed, perhaps there are no women but one—by whom a man has been so painted as to challenge and compel the recognition and acknowledgment of men. In The Galaxy some months ago I wrote of a great Englishwoman, the authoress of "Romola," and I expressed my conviction that on the whole she is entitled to higher rank as a novelist than even the authoress of "Consuelo." Many, very many men and women, for whose judgment I have the highest respect, differed from me in this opinion. I still hold it, nevertheless; but I freely admit that George Eliot has nothing like the dramatic insight which enables George Sand to enter into the feelings and the experiences of a man. I go so far as to say that, having some knowledge of the literature of fiction in most countries, I am not aware of the existence of any woman but this one who could draw a real, living, struggling, passion-tortured man. All other novelists of George Sand's sex—even including Charlotte Brontë—draw only what I may call "women's men." If ever the two natures could be united in one form, if ever a single human being could have the soul of man and the soul of woman at once, George Sand might be described as that physical and psychological phenomenon. Now the point to which I wish to direct attention is the peculiarity of the temptation to which a nature such as this was necessarily exposed at every turn when, free of all restraint and a rebel against all conventionality, it confronted the world and the world's law, and stood up, itself alone, against the domination of custom and the majesty of tradition. I claim, then, that when we have taken all these considerations into account, we are bound to admit that Aurora Dudevant deserves the generous recognition of the world for the use which she made of her splendid gifts. Her influence on French literature has been on the whole a purifying and strengthening power. The cynicism, the recklessness, the wanton, licentious disregard of any manner of principle, the debasing parade of disbelief in any higher purpose or nobler restraint, which are the shame and curse of modern French fiction, find no sanction in the pages of George Sand. I remember no passage in her works which gives the slightest encouragement to the "nothing new, and nothing true, and it don't signify" code of ethics which has been so much in fashion of late years. I find nothing in George Sand which does not do homage to the existence of a principle and a law in everything. This daring woman, who broke with society so early and so conspicuously, has always insisted, through every illustration, character, and catastrophe in her books, that the one only reality, the one only thing that can endure, is the rule of right and of virtue. Nor has she ever, that I can recollect, fallen into the enfeebling and sentimental theory so commonly expressed in the works of Victor Hugo, that the vague abstraction society is always to bear the blame of the faults committed by the individual man or woman. Of all persons in the world Aurora Dudevant might be supposed most likely to adopt this easy and complacent theory as her guiding principle. She had every excuse, every reason for endeavoring to preach up the doctrine that our errors are society's and our virtues our own. But I am not aware that she ever taught any lesson save the lesson that men and women must endeavor to be heroes and heroines for themselves, heroes and heroines though all the world else were craven and weak and selfish and unprincipled. Even that wretched and lamentable "Elle et Lui" affair, utterly inexcusable as it is when we read between the lines its secret history, has at least the merit of being an earnest and powerful protest against the egotistical and debasing indulgence of moral weaknesses and eccentricities which mean and vulgar minds are apt to regard as the privilege of genius. "Stand upon your own ground; be your own ruler; look to yourself, not to your stars, for your failure or success; always make your standard a lofty ideal, and try persistently to reach it, though all the temptations of earth and all the power of darkness strive against you"—this and nothing else, if I have read her books rightly, is the moral taught by George Sand. She may be wrong in her principle sometimes, but at least she always has a principle. She has a profound and generous faith in the possibilities of human nature; in the capacity of man's heart for purity, self-sacrifice, and self-redemption. Indeed, so far is she from holding counsel with wilful weakness or sin, that I think she sometimes falls into the noble error of painting her heroes as too glorious in their triumph over temptation, in their subjugation of every passion and interest to the dictates of duty and of honor. Take, for instance, that extraordinary book which has just been given to the American public in Miss Virginia Vaughan's excellent translation, "Mauprat." If I understand that magnificent romance at all, its purport is to prove that no human nature is ever plunged into temptation beyond its own strength to resist, provided that it really wills resistance; that no character is irretrievable, no error inexpiable, where there is sincere resolve to expiate and longing desire to retrieve. Take again that exquisite little story, "La Dernière Aldini"; I do not know where one could find a finer illustration of the entire sacrifice of man's natural impulse, passion, interest, to what might almost be called an abstract idea of honor and principle. I have never read this little story without wondering how many men one ever has known who, placed in the same situation as that of Nello, the hero, would have done the same thing; and yet so simply and naturally are the characters wrought out and the incidents described, that the idea of pompous, dramatic self-sacrifice never enters the mind of the reader, and it seems to him that Nello could not do otherwise than as he is doing. I speak of these two stories particularly, because in both of them there is a good deal of the world and the flesh; that is, both are stories of strong human passion and temptation. Many of George Sand's novels, the shorter ones especially, are as absolutely pure in moral tone, as entirely free from even a taint or suggestion of impurity, as they are perfect in style. Now, if we cannot help knowing that much of this great woman's life was far from being irreproachable, are we not bound to give her all the fuller credit because her genius at least kept so far the whiteness of its soul? Revolutions are not to be made with rose water; you cannot have omelettes without breaking of eggs. I am afraid that great social revolutionists are not often creatures of the most pure and perfect nature. It is not to patient Griselda you must look for any protest against even the uttermost tyranny of social conventions. One thing I think may at least be admitted as part of George Sand's vindication—that the marriage system in France is the most debased and debasing institution existing in civilized society, now that the buying and selling of slaves has ceased to be a tolerated system. I hold that the most ardent advocates of the irrevocable endurance of the marriage bond are bound by their very principles to admit that in protesting against the so-called marriage system of France George Sand stood on the side of purity and right. Assuredly she often went into extravagances in the other direction. It seems to be the fate of all French reformers to rush suddenly to extremes; and we must remember that George Sand was not a Bristol Quakeress or a Boston transcendentalist, but a passionate Frenchwoman, the descendant of one of the maddest votaries of love and war who ever stormed across the stage of European history.

Regarding George Sand then as an influence in literature and on society, I claim for her at least four great and special merits. First, she insisted on calling public attention to the true principle of marriage; that is to say, she put the question as it had not been put before. Of course, the fundamental principle she would have enforced is always being urged more or less feebly, more or less sincerely; but she made it her own question, and illuminated it by the fervid, fierce rays of her genius and her passion. Secondly, her works are an exposition of the tremendous reality of the feelings which people who call themselves practical are apt to regard with indifference or contempt as mere sentiments. In the long run the passions decide the life-question one way or the other. They are the tide which, as you know or do not know how to use it, will either turn your mill and float your boat, or drown your fields and sweep away your dwellings. Life and society receive no impulse and no direction from the influences out of which the novels of Dickens or even of Thackeray are made up. These are but pleasant or tender toying with the playthings and puppets of existence. George Sand constrains us to look at the realities through the medium of her fiction. Thirdly, she insists that man can and shall make his own career; not whine to the stars and rail out against the powers above, when he has weakly or wantonly marred his own destiny. Fourthly—and this ought not to be considered her least service to the literature of her country—she has tried to teach people to look at nature with their own eyes, and to invite the true love of her to flow into their hearts. The great service which Ruskin, with all his eccentricities and extravagances, has rendered to English-speaking peoples by teaching them to use their own eyes when they look at clouds, and waters, and grasses, and hills, George Sand has rendered to France.

I hold that these are virtues and services which ought to outweigh even very grave personal and artistic errors. We often hear that this or that great poet or romancist has painted men as they are; this other as they ought to be. I think George Sand paints men as they are, and also not merely as they ought to be, but as they can be. The sum of the lesson taught by her books is one of confidence in man's possibilities, and hope in his steady progress. At the same time she is entirely practical in her faith and her aspirations. She never expects that the trees are to grow up into the heavens, that men and women are to be other than men and women. She does not want them to be other; she finds the springs and sources of their social regeneration in the fact that they are just what they are, to begin with. I am afraid some of the ladies who seem to base their scheme of woman's emancipation and equality on the assumption that, by some development of time or process of schooling, a condition of things is to be brought about where difference of sex is no longer to be a disturbing power, will find small comfort or encouragement in the writings of George Sand. She deals in realities altogether; the realities of life, even when they are such as to shallow minds may seem mere sentiments and ecstasies; the realities of society, of suffering, of passion, of inanimate nature. There is in her nothing unmeaning, nothing untrue; there is in her much error, doubtless, but no sham.

I believe George Sand is growing into a quiet and beautiful old age. After a life of storm and stress, a life which, metaphorically at least, was "worn by war and passion," her closing years seem likely to be gilded with the calm glory of an autumnal sunset. One is glad to think of her thus happy and peaceful, accepting so tranquilly the reality of old age, still laboring with her unwearied pen, still delighting in books, and landscapes, and friends, and work. The world can well afford to forget as soon as possible her literary and other errors. Of the vast mass of romances, stories, plays, sketches, criticisms, pamphlets, political articles, even, it is said, ministerial manifestoes of republican days, which she poured out, only a few comparatively will perhaps be always treasured by posterity; but these will be enough to secure her a classic place. And she will not be remembered by her writings alone. Hers is probably the most powerful individuality displayed by any modern Frenchwoman. The influence of Madame Roland was but a glittering unreality, that of Madame de Staël only a boudoir and coterie success, when compared with the power exercised over literature, human feeling, and social law, by the energy, the courage, the genius, even the very errors and extravagances of George Sand.

EDWARD BULWER, LORD LYTTON

Ten years ago an important political question was agitating the English House of Commons and the English public. It was the old question of Parliamentary Reform in a new shape. Thirty years before Lord John Russell had pleaded the right of the middle classes to have a voice in the election of their Parliamentary representatives; this time he was asserting a similar right for the working population. Then he had to contend against the opposition of the aristocracy only; this time he had to fight against the combined antagonism of the aristocracy and the middle classes, the latter having made common cause with their old enemies to preserve a monopoly of their new privileges. The debate in the House of Commons on the proposed Reform Bill of 1860 was long and bitter. When it was reaching its height, a speaker arose on the Tory side of the House whose appearance on the scene of the debate lent a new and piquant interest to the night's discussion. He sat on the front bench of the Opposition, quite near to Disraeli himself. The moment he rose, every head craned forward to see him; the moment he began to speak, every ear was strained with keen curiosity to hear him. The ears were for a while sorely tried and perplexed. What was he saying—nay, what language was he speaking? What extraordinary, indescribable sounds were those which were heard issuing from his lips? Were they articulate sounds at all? For some minutes certainly those who like myself had never heard the speaker before were utterly bewildered. We could only hear what seemed to us an incoherent, inarticulate guttural jabber, like the efforts at speech of somebody with a mutilated tongue or excided palate. Anything like it I never heard before or since; for no subsequent listening to the same speaker ever produced nearly the same impression: either he had greatly improved in elocution, or his listener had grown used to him. But the night of this famous speech, nothing could have exceeded the extraordinary nature of the sensations produced on those who heard the orator for the first time. After a while we began to detect articulate sounds; then we guessed at and recognized words; then whole sentences began to shape themselves out of the guttural fag; and at last we grew to understand that, with an elocution the most defective and abominable ever possessed by mortal orator, this Tory speaker was really delivering a speech of astonishing brilliancy, ingenuity, and power. The sentences had a magnificent, almost majestic rotundity, energy, and power; they reminded one of something cut out of solid and glittering marble, at once so dazzling and so impressive. The speech was from first to last an aristocratic argument against the fitness of the working man to be anything but a political serf. In the true fashion of the aristocrat, the speaker was for patronizing the working man in every possible way; behaving to him as a kind and friendly master; seeing that he had a decent home to live in and coals and blankets in winter; but all the time insisting that the ruin of England must follow any successful attempt to place political power in the hands of "poverty and passion." The speech overflowed with illustration, ingenious analogy, felicitous quotation, brilliant epigram, and political paradoxes that were made to sound wondrously like maxims of wisdom. Despite all its hideous defects of delivery, this speech was, beyond the most distant comparison, the finest delivered on the Tory side during the whole of that long and memorable debate. For a time one was almost cheated into the belief that that elaborate and splendid diction, now so stately and now so sparkling, was genuine eloquence. Yet to the last the listener was frequently baffled by some uncouth, semi-articulate, hardly intelligible sound. "What on earth does he mean," asked a puzzled and indeed agonized reporter of some laboring brother, "by talking so often about the political authority of Joe Miller?" Careful inquiry elicited the fact that the name of the political authority to which the orator had been alluding was John Mill. Fortunately for his readers and his fame, the speaker had taken good care to write out his oration and send the manuscript to the newspapers.

Now this inarticulate orator, this Demosthenes without the pebble-training, was, as my readers have already guessed, Edward Bulwer-Lytton, then a baronet and a member of the House of Commons, now a peer. Undoubtedly he succeeded, by this and one or two other speeches, in securing for himself a place among the few great Parliamentary debaters of the day. Despite of physical defects which would have discouraged almost any other man from entering into public life at all, he had succeeded in winning a reputation as a great speaker in a debate where Palmerston, Gladstone, Bright, and Disraeli were champions. So deaf that he could not hear the arguments of his opponents, so defective in utterance as to become often almost unintelligible, he actually made the House of Commons doubt for a while whether a new great orator had not come among them. It was not great oratory after all; it was not true oratory of any kind; but it was a splendid imitation of the real thing—the finest electroplate anywhere to be found. "If it is not Bran, it is Bran's brother," says a Scottish proverb. If this speech of Bulwer-Lytton's was not true oratory, it was oratory's illegitimate brother.

Nearly a whole generation before the winning of that late success, Bulwer-Lytton had tried the House of Commons, and miserably, ludicrously failed. The young Tory members who vociferously cheered his great anti-reform speech of 1860, were in their cradles when Bulwer-Lytton first addressed the House of Commons, and having signally failed withdrew, as people supposed, altogether from Parliamentary life. His failure was even more complete than that of his friend Disraeli, and he took the failure more to heart. Rumor affirms that the first serious quarrel between Bulwer and his wife arose out of her vexation and disappointment at his break-down, and the bitter, provoking taunts with which she gave vent to her anger. I know no other instance of a rhetorical triumph so long delayed, and at length so completely effected. Nor can one learn that it was by any intervening practice or training that Bulwer in his declining years atoned for the failure of his youth. He was never that I know of a public speaker; he won his Parliamentary success in defiance of Charles James Fox's famous axiom, that a speaker can only improve himself at the expense of his audiences. Between his failure and his triumph Bulwer-Lytton may be said to have had no political audience.

A statesman Bulwer-Lytton never became, although he held high office in a Tory Cabinet. He did little or nothing to distinguish himself, unless there be distinction in writing some high-flown, eloquent despatches, such as Ernest Maltravers might have penned, to the discontented islanders of Ionia; and it was he, if I remember rightly, who thought of sending out "Gladstone the Philhellene" on that mission of futile conciliation which only misled the Ionians and amused England. It always seemed to me that in his political career Bulwer acted just as one of the heroes of his own romances might have done. Having suffered defeat and humiliation, he vowed a vow to wrest from Fate a victory upon the very spot which had seen his discomfiture; and he kept his word, won his victory, and then calmly quitted the field forever. A more prosaic explanation might perhaps be found in the fact that weak physical health rendered it impossible for Bulwer to encounter the severe continuous labor which English political life exacts. But I prefer for myself the more romantic and less commonplace explanation, and I hope my readers will do likewise. I prefer to think of the great romancist retrieving after thirty years of silence his Parliamentary defeat, and then, having reconciled himself with Destiny, retiring from the scene contented, to struggle in that arena no more. In all seriousness, there must be some quality of greatness in the man who, after bearing such a defeat for so many years, can struggle with Fate again, and accomplish so conspicuous a success.

Now this is in fact one grand explanation of Bulwer-Lytton's rank in English literature. He has the self-reliance, the patience, the courage so rare among literary men, by which one is enabled to extract their full and utter value from whatsoever intellectual endowments he may possess. Bulwer-Lytton alone among all famous English authors of our days has apparently done all that he could possibly do—obtained from his faculties their entire tribute. Readers of the letters of poor Charlotte Brontë may remember the impatience with which she occasionally complained that her idol Thackeray would not put forth his whole strength. No such fault could possibly be found with Bulwer-Lytton. Sooner or later he always put forth his whole strength. He had many failures, but, as in the case of his political discomfiture, he had always the art of learning from failure the way how to succeed, and accordingly succeeding. When he wrote his wretched "Sea Captain," the critics all told him he could not produce a successful drama. Bulwer thought he could. He thought the very failure of that attempt would show him how to succeed another time. He was determined not to give in until he had satisfied himself as to his fitness, one way or the other, and so he persevered. Now observe the character of the man, and see how much superior he himself is to his works, and how much of their success the works owe to the man's peculiar temper. We all know what authors usually are, and how they receive criticism. In ordinary cases, when the critics declare some piece of work a failure, the author either is crushed for the time by the fiat, or he insists that the critics are idiots, hired assassins, personal enemies, and so forth; he defiantly adheres to his own notions and his own method—and he probably fails. Bulwer-Lytton looked at the matter in quite a different light. He said, apparently, to himself: "The critics only know what I have done; I know what I can do. From their point of view they are quite right—this thing is a failure. But I know that it is a failure only because I went to work the wrong way. I *can* do something infinitely better. Their experience and their comments have given me some valuable hints; I will forthwith go to work on a better principle." So Bulwer-Lytton wrote "Richelieu," "Money," and the "Lady of Lyons"—the last probably the most successful acting drama produced in England since the days of Shakespeare, and the first hardly below it in stage success. Of course I am not claiming for either of these plays a high and genuine dramatic value. They probably bear the same resemblance to the true drama that their author's Parliamentary speech-making does to true eloquence. But of their popularity and their transcendent technical success there cannot be the slightest doubt. Bulwer-Lytton proved to his critics that he could do better than any other living man the very thing they said he could never do—write a play that should conquer the public and hold the stage. So to those who affirmed that, whatever else he might do, he never could be a Parliamentary speaker, he replied by standing up when approaching the very brink of old age, and delivering speeches which won the willing and generous applause of Disraeli, and extorted the reluctant but manly and frank recognition of such an opponent as John Bright.

Bulwer-Lytton once insisted, in an address delivered to some English literary institution, that the word "versatile" is generally used wrongly when we speak of men who do a great many things well; that it is a comprehensive, not merely a versatile mind, each of these men has; not a knack of adroitly turning himself to many heterogeneous labors, but a capacity so wide that it unfolds quite naturally many fields of labor. In this sense Bulwer-Lytton has undoubtedly a more comprehensive mind than any of his English contemporaries. He has written the most successful dramas and some of the most successful novels of his day; and he has so varied the method of his novel-writing that he may be said to have at least three distinct and separate principles of construction. Some of his poetic translations seem to me almost absolutely the best done in England of late years; many of his essays approach a true literary value, while all or nearly all of them are attractive reading; his satire, "The New Timon," is the only thing of the kind which is likely to outlive his age; and his political speeches are what I have already described. Now, to estimate the personal value of these successes, let us not fail to remember that their author never was placed in a condition to make literary or other labor a necessity, and that for nearly a whole generation he has been in the enjoyment of actual wealth; that in England literature adds little or no social distinction to a man of Bulwer-Lytton's rank; and that during a considerable portion of his life the author of "The Caxtons" and "My Novel" has been tortured by almost incessant ill-health. Almost everything that could tend to make a man shun continuous and patient labor (opulence and ill-health would be quite enough to make most of us shun it) combined to render Bulwer-Lytton an idle or at least an indolent man. Yet almost all the literary success he attained was due to a patient toil which would have wearied out a penny-a-liner, and a laborious self-study and self-culture which might have overtaxed the nerves of a Königsberg professor. "Easy writing is cursed hard reading," is a maxim which Bulwer-Lytton fully understood, and of which he showed his appreciation in his personal practice.

Bulwer-Lytton was born on the fringe of the aristocratic region. He can hardly be said to belong to the genuine aristocracy, although of late, thanks to his political opinions and his peerage, he has come to be ranked among aristocrats. He is the brother of a distinguished diplomatist, Sir Henry Bulwer, and the father of a somewhat promising diplomatist, not quite unknown to Washington people, Robert Lytton, "Owen Meredith." Bulwer-Lytton had advanced tolerably far upon his career when he inherited through his mother a magnificent estate, which enabled him to set up for an aristocrat. His baronetcy had been conferred upon him by the Crown, as his peerage lately was. He started in political life, like Mr. Disraeli, as a Liberal; indeed, it was, if I am not greatly mistaken, on the introduction of Bulwer-Lytton that Disraeli obtained the early patronage of Daniel O'Connell, which he so soon forfeited by the political tergiversation that drew down from the great Agitator the famous outburst of fierce and savage scorn wherein, alluding to Disraeli's boasted Jewish origin, he proclaimed him evidently descended in a right line from the blasphemous thief who died impenitent on the cross. Disraeli's apostasy was sudden and glaring, and he kept the field. Bulwer-Lytton soon faded out of politics altogether for nearly thirty years, and when he reappeared in the House of Commons and wore the garb of a Tory, his old friend and political patron O'Connell had long become a mere tradition. Nearly all of those who listened with curiosity to Bulwer-Lytton's speeches in 1859 and 1860, were curious only to hear how a great romancist and dramatist would acquit himself in a part which, so far as they were concerned, was entirely a new appearance. They had no personal memory of his former efforts; no recollection of the time when the young author of the sparkling, piquant, and successful "Pelham" endeavored to take London by storm as a political orator, and failed in the enterprise.

In one peculiarity, at least, Bulwer-Lytton the novelist surpassed all his rivals and contemporaries. His range was so wide as to take in all circles and classes of English readers. He wrote fashionable novels, historical novels, political novels, metaphysical novels, psychological novels, moral-purpose novels, immoral purpose novels. "Wilhelm Meister" was not too heavy nor "Tristram Shandy" too light for him. He tried to rival Scott in the historical romance; he strove hard to be another Goethe in his "Ernest Maltravers"; he quite surpassed Ainsworth's "Jack Sheppard," and the general run of what we in England call "thieves' literature," in his "Paul Clifford"; he became a sort of pinchbeck Sterne in "The Caxtons," and was severely classical in "The Last Days of Pompeii." One might divide his novels into at least half a dozen classes, each class quite distinct and different from all the rest, and yet the one author, the one Bulwer-Lytton, showing and shining through them all. Bulwer is always there. He is masquerading now in the garb of a mediæval baron, and now in that of an old Roman dandy; anon he is disguised as a thief from St. Giles's, and again as a full-blooded aristocrat from the region of St. James's. But he is the same man always, and you can hardly fail to recognize him even in his cleverest disguise. It may be questioned whether there is one spark of true and original genius in Bulwer. Certain ideas commonly floating about in this or that year he collects and brings to a focus, and by their aid he burns a distinct impression into the public mind. Just as he expressed the thin and spurious classicism of one period in his Pompeian romance, so he made copy out of the pseudoscience and bastard psychology of a later day in his "Strange Story." Never was there in literature a more masterly and wonderful mechanic. Many-sided he never was, although probably the fame of many-sidedness (if one may use so ungraceful an expression) is the renown which he specially coveted and most strenuously strove to win. Only genius can be many-sided, and Bulwer-Lytton's marvellous capability never can be confounded with genius. The nearest approach to genius in all his works may be found in their occasional outbursts and flashes of audacious, preposterous absurdity. The power which could palm off such outrageous nonsense as in some instances he has done on two or three generations of novel-readers, which could compel the public to swallow it and delight in it, despite all that the satire of a Thackeray or a Jerrold could do, must surely, one would almost say, have had something in it savoring of a sort of genius. For there are in some even of the very best and purest of Bulwer's novels whole scenes and characters which it seems almost utterly impossible that any reader whatever could follow without laughter. I protest that I think the author of "Ernest Maltravers" owed much of his success to the daring which assumed that anything might be imposed on the public, and to the absence of that sense of the ludicrous which might have made a man of a different stamp laugh at his own nonsense. I assume that Bulwer wrote in perfect faith and seriousness, honestly believing them to be fine, the most ridiculous, bombastic, fantastic passages in all his novels. I take it for granted that Mr. Morris's sad hero, "The Man who never Laughed Again," must have been frivolity itself when compared with Bulwer-Lytton at work upon a novel. The sensitive distrust of one's own capacity, the high-minded doubt of the value of one's own works, which is probably the companion, the Mentor, the tormentor often, and not unfrequently the conqueror and destroyer of true genius, never seems to have vexed the author of "Eugene Aram" and "Godolphin." Bulwer-Lytton won a great name partly because he was not a man of genius. The kind of thing he tried to do could not have been done truly and successfully, in the high artistic sense, by any one with a capacity below that of a Shakespeare, or at least a Goethe. A man of genius, but inferior genius, would have made a wretched failure of it. Between the two stools of popularity and art, of time and eternity, he must have fallen to the ground. But where genius might fail to achieve a splendid success, talent and audacity might turn out a magnificent sham. This is the sort of success, this and none other, which I believe Bulwer-Lytton to have achieved. He is the finest *faiseur* in the literature of to-day. His wax-work gallery surpasses Madame Tussaud's; or rather his sham art is as much superior to that of a

James or an Ainsworth as Madame Tussaud's gallery is to Mrs. Jarley's show. That sort of sentiment which lies somewhere down in the heart of every one, however commonplace, or busy, or cynical—the sentiment which is represented by the applause of the galleries in a popular theatre, and which cultivated audiences are usually ashamed to acknowledge—was the feeling which Bulwer-Lytton could always reach and draw forth. He had so much at least of the true artistic instinct as to recognize that the strongest element of popularity is the sentimental; and he knew that out of ten persons who openly laugh at such a thing, nine are secretly touched by it. Bulwer-Lytton found much of his stock and capital in the human emotions which sympathize with youthful ambition and youthful love, just as Dickens makes perpetual play with the feelings which are touched by the death of children. When Claude Melnotte, transfigured into the splendid Colonel Morier, rushes forward just at the critical moment, outbids yon sordid huckster for his priceless jewel Pauline, flings down the purse containing double the needful sum, declares that he has bought every coin of it in the cause of nations with a Frenchman's blood, and sweeps away his ransomed bride amid the thunder of the galleries, of course we all know that sort of thing is not poetry, or high art, or anything but splendiferous rubbish. Yet it does touch most of us somehow. I know I always feel divided between laughter and enthusiastic sympathy even still, when I see it for the hundred and fiftieth time or so. In the same way, when Paul Clifford charges on society the crimes of his outlaw career; when Rienzi vows vengeance for his brother's blood; when Zanoni resigns his immortal youth that "the flower at his feet may a little longer drink the dew"; when Ernest Maltravers silently laments amid all his splendor of success the obscure Arcadia of his boyish love, we can all see at a glance how bombastic, gaudy, melodramatic, is the style in which the author works out his ideas; how utterly unlike the simple, strong majesty of true art the whole thing is; but yet we must acknowledge that the author understands thoroughly how to touch a certain vein of what may be called elementary emotion, common almost to all minds, which it is the object of society to repress or suppress, and the object of the popular artist to stir up into activity. Preach, advise, remonstrate, demonstrate as you will, the majority of us will always feel inclined to give alms to beggar-women and whining little children in the snowy streets. We know we are doing unwisely, and perhaps even wrongly; we know that the misery which touches us is probably a trumped-up and sham misery; we know that whatever we give to the undeserving and the insincere is practically withdrawn from the deserving and the sincere; we are ashamed to be seen giving the money, and yet we do give it whenever we can. Because, after all, our common emotion of sympathy with the more obvious, intelligible, and I would almost say vulgar forms of human suffering, are far too strong for our moderating maxims and our more refined mental conditions. So of the sympathies which heroes and heroines, aspirations and agonies of the style of Bulwer-Lytton awaken in us. Virtue cannot so inoculate our old stock but we shall relish it; and is not he something of an artist who recognizes this great fact in human nature, and plays upon that vibrating, imperishable chord, and compels it to give him back such an applauding echo? After all, I think there is just as much of sham and of Madame Tussaud, and of the beggar-child in the snow, about Paul Dombey's deathbed and Little Dorrit's filial devotion, as about the mock heroics of Claude Melnotte or the domestic virtues of the Caxtons. Of course I am not comparing Bulwer-Lytton with Dickens. The latter was a man of genius, and one of the greatest humorists known at least to modern literature. But nearly all the pathetic side of Dickens seems to me of much the same origin as the heroic side of Bulwer-Lytton, and I question whether the greater part of the popularity won by the author of "Bleak House" has not been gained by a mastery of the very same kind of art as that which sets galleries applauding for Claude Melnotte, and young women in tears for Eugene Aram.

There are, moreover, two points of superiority in artistic purpose which may be claimed for Bulwer-Lytton over either Dickens or Thackeray. They do not, perhaps, "amount to much" in any case; but they are worth mentioning. Bulwer-Lytton has more than once drawn to the best of his power a gentleman, and he has often drawn, or tried to draw, a man possessed by some great, impersonal, unselfish object in life. The former of these personages Dickens never seemed to have known or believed in; the latter, Thackeray never even attempted to paint. Why has Dickens never drawn a gentleman? I am not using the word in the artificial, conventional, snobbish sense. I mean by a gentleman a creature with intellect as well as heart, with refined and cultivated tastes, with something of personal dignity about him. I do not care from what origin he may have sprung, or to what class he may have belonged: there is no reason, even in England, why a man born in a garret might not acquire all the ways, and thoughts, and refinements of a gentleman. Among the class to which most of Dickens's heroes are represented as belonging, have we not all in England known gentlemen of intellect and culture? Yet Dickens has never painted such a being. Nicholas Nickleby is a plucky, honest, good-hearted blockhead; Tom Pinch is a benevolent idiot; Eugene Wrayburn is a low-bred, impertinent snob—a mere "cad," as Londoners would say. I have had no sympathy with the "Saturday Review" in its perpetual accusations of vulgarity against Dickens; and I think a recent English critic was pleasantly and purposely extravagant when he charged the author of the "Christmas Carol" with having no loftier idea of human happiness than the eating of plum pudding and kissing girls under the mistletoe. But I do say that Dickens never drew a cultivated English gentleman or lady—a cultivated and refined English man or woman, if you will; and yet I know that there are such personages to be found without troublesome quest among the very classes of society which he was always describing.

Now Thackeray could draw and has drawn English gentlemen and gentlewomen; but has he ever drawn a high-minded, self-forgetting man or woman devoted to some, to any, great object, or cause, or purpose of any kind in life—absorbed by it and faithful to it? Is it true that even in London society men are wholly given up to dining, and paying visits, and making and spending money? Is it true that all men, even in London society, pass their lives in a purposeless, drifting way, making good resolves and not carrying them out; doing good things now and then out of easy, generous impulse; loving lightly, and recovering from love quickly? Are there in London society, on the one hand, no passions; on the other hand, no simple, strong, consistent, unselfish, high-minded lives? Assuredly there are; but Thackeray, the greatest painter of English society England has ever had, chose, for some reason or another, to ignore them. Only when he comes to speak of artists, more especially of painters, does he ever hint that he is aware of the existence of men whose lives are consistent, steadfast, and unselfish. Surely this is a great omission. One does not care to drag into this discussion the names of living illustrations; but I should like to have pointed Thackeray's attention to this and that and the other man whom, to my certain knowledge, he knew and warmly, fully appreciated, and asked him, "Why, when you were painting with such incomparable fidelity such illustrations of English life as you chose to select, did you not think fit to picture such a simple, strong, consistent, magnanimous, self-forgetting, self-devoting nature as that, or that, or that?"—and so on, through many examples which I or anybody could have named. I suppose the honest answer would have been, "I cannot draw that kind of character; I cannot quite enter into its experiences and make it look life-like as I see it; it is not in my line, and I prefer not to attempt it." Now, I think it to the credit of Bulwer-Lytton, as a mere artist, that he did include such figures even in his wax-work gallery. He could not make them look like life; but he showed at least that he was aware of their existence, and that he did his best to teach the world to recognize them.

Thus then, using with inexhaustible energy and perseverance his wonderful gifts as an intellectual mechanician, Edward Bulwer-Lytton went on from 1828 to 1860 grinding out of his mill an almost unbroken succession of novels and romances to suit all changes in public taste. I do not believe he changed his themes and ways of treating them purposely, to suit the changes of public taste; but rather that, being a man of no true original and creative power, his style and his views were modified by the modifying conditions of successive years. Some new idea, some new way of looking at this or that question of human life came up, and it attracted him who was always a close and diligent student of the world and its fashions; and he made it into a romance. Whatever new schools of fiction came into existence, Bulwer-Lytton, always directing the new ideas into the channel where popular and elementary sympathies flowed freely, succeeded in turning each change to advantage, and keeping his place. Dickens sprang up and founded a school; and yet Bulwer-Lytton held his own. Thackeray arose and established a new school, and Bulwer-Lytton, whom no human being would have thought of comparing with either as a man of genius, did not lose a reader. Charlotte Brontë came like a shadow, and so departed; George Eliot gave a new lift and life to romance; the realistic school was followed by the sensational school; the Literature of Adultery ran its vulgar course—and Bulwer-Lytton remained where he always had been, and moulted no feather.

It is not likely that any true critic ever thought very highly of him, or indeed took him quite seriously; but for many, many years criticism, which had so scoffed and girded at him once, had only civil words and applauding smiles for him. How Thackeray once did make savage fun of "Bullwig," and more lately how Thackeray praised him! Charles Dickens—what an enthusiastic admirer of the genius of his friend Lytton he too became! And Tennyson—what a fierce passage of arms that was long ago between Bulwer and him; and now what cordial mutual admiration! Fonblanque and Forster, the "Athenæum" and "Punch," Tray, Blanche, and Sweetheart—how they all welcomed in chorus each new effort of genius by the great romancist who was once the stock butt of all lively satirists. How did this happy change come about? Nobody ever had harder dealing at the hands of the critics than Bulwer when his powers were really most fresh and forcible; nobody ever had more general and genial commendation than shone of late years around his sunny way. How was this? Did the critics really find that they had been mistaken and own themselves conquered by his transcendent merit? Did he "win the wise who frowned before to smile at last"? To some extent, yes. He showed that he was not to be written down; that no critical article could snuff him out; that he really had some stuff in him and plenty of mettle and perseverance; and he soon became a literary institution, an accomplished fact which criticism could not help recognizing. But there was much more than this operating towards Bulwer-Lytton's reconciliation with criticism. He became a wealthy man, a man of fashion, a sort of aristocrat, with yet a sincere love for the society of authors and artists, with a taste for encouraging private theatricals and endowing literary institutions, and with a splendid country house. He became a genial, golden link between literature and society. Even Bohemia was enabled by his liberal and courteous goodwill to penetrate sometimes into the regions of Belgravia. The critics began to fall in love with him. I do not believe that Lord Lytton made himself thus agreeable to his literary brethren out of any motive whatever but that of honest goodfellowship and kindness. I have heard too many instances of his frank and brotherly friendliness to utterly obscure writers, who could be of no sort of service to him or to anybody, not to feel satisfied of his unselfish good-nature and his thorough loyalty to that which ought to be the *esprit de corps* of the literary profession. But it is certain that he thus converted enemies into friends, and stole the gall out of many an inkstand, and the poison from many a penman's feathered dart. Not that the critics simply sold their birthright of bitterness for an invitation to dinner or the kindly smile of a literary Peer. But you cannot, I suppose, deal very rigidly with the works of a man who is uniformly kind to you; who brings you into a sort of society which otherwise you would probably never have a chance of seeing; who, being himself a lord, treats you, poor critic, as a friend and brother; and whose works, moreover, are certain to have a great public success, no matter what you say or leave unsaid. The temptation to look for and discover merit in such books is strong indeed—perhaps too strong for frail critical nature. Thus arises the great sin of English criticism. It is certainly not venal; it is hardly ever malign. Mere ill-nature, or impatience, or the human delight of showing one's strength, may often induce a London critic to deal too sharply with some new and nameless author; but although we who write books are each and all of us delighted to persuade ourselves that any disparaging criticism must be the result of some personal hatred, I cannot remember ever having had serious reason to believe that a London critic had attacked a book because of his personal ill-will to the author. The sin is quite of another kind—a tendency to praise the books of certain authors merely because the critic knows the men so intimately, and likes them so well, that he is at once naturally prejudiced in their favor, and disinclined to say anything which could hurt or injure them. Thus of late criticism has had hardly anything to say of Lord Lytton, except in the way of praise. He is the head, and patron, and ornament of a great London literary "Ring." I use this word because none other could so well convey to a reader in New York a clear idea of the friendly professional unity of the coterie I desire to describe; but I wish it to be distinctly understood that I do not attribute anything like venality or hired partisanship of any kind to the literary Ring of which Lord Lytton is the sparkling gem. Of course it has become, as such cliques always must become, somewhat of a Mutual Admiration Society; and it is certain that a place in that brotherhood secures a man against much disparaging criticism. There are indeed literary cliques in London, of a somewhat lower range than this, where the influence of personal friendships does operate in a manner that closely borders upon a sort of literary corruption. But Lord Lytton and his friends and admirers are not of that sort. They are friends together, and they do admire each other, and I suppose everybody (save one person) likes Lord Lytton now; and so it is only in the rare case of a fresh, independent outsider, like the critic who wrote in the "Westminster Review" some two years ago, that a really impartial, keen, artistic survey is taken of the works of him that was "Bullwig." When Lytton published his "Caxtons," the reviewer of the "Examiner," even up to that time a journal of great influence and prestige, having nearly exhausted all possible modes of panegyric, bethought himself that some unappreciative and cynical persons might possibly think there was a lack of originality in a work so obviously constructed after the model of "Tristram Shandy." So he hastened to confute or convince all such persons by pointing out that in this very fact consisted the special claim of "The Caxtons" to absolute originality. The original genius of Lytton was proved by his producing so excellent a copy. Don't you see? You don't, perhaps. But then if you were intimate with Lord Lytton, and were liked by him, and were a performer in the private theatricals at Knebworth, his country seat, you would probably see it quite clearly, and agree with it, every word.

There was one person indeed who had no toleration for Lord Lytton, or for his friendly critics. That was Lord Lytton's wife. There really is no scandal in alluding to a conjugal quarrel which was brought so persistently under public notice by one of the parties as that between Bulwer-Lytton and his wife. I do not know whether I ought to call it a quarrel. Can that be called a fight, piteously asks the man in Juvenal, where my enemy only beats and I am merely beaten? Can that be called a quarrel in which, so far as the public could judge, the wife did all the denunciation, and the husband made no reply? Lady Lytton wrote novels for the purpose of satirizing her husband and his friends—his parasites, she called them. Bulwer-Lytton she gracefully described as having "the head of a goat on the body of a grasshopper"—a description which has just enough of comical truthfulness in its savage ferocity to make it specially cruel to the victim of the satire, and amusing to the unconcerned public. Lady Lytton attributed to her husband the most odious meannesses, vices, and cruelties; but the public, with all its love of scandal, seems to have steadfastly refused to take her ladyship's word for these accusations. Dickens she denounced and vilified as a mere parasite and sycophant of her husband. At one time she poured out a gush of fulsome eulogy on Thackeray because he apparently was not one of Lytton's friends; afterwards, when the relationship between "Pelham" and "Pendennis" became friendly, she changed her tune and tried to bite the file, to satirize the great satirist. Disraeli she caricatured under the title of "Jericho Jabber." This sort of thing she kept always going on. Sometimes she issued pamphlets addressed to the women of England, calling on them to take up her quarrel—which somehow they did not seem inclined to do. Once when Lord Lytton, then only Sir Edward, was on the hustings, addressing his constituents at a county election, her ladyship suddenly mounted the platform and "went for" him. Sir Edward and his friends prudently and quietly withdrew. I do not know anything of the merits of the quarrel, and have always been disposed to think that something like insanity must have been the explanation of much of Lady Lytton's conduct. But it is beyond doubt that her husband's demeanor was remarkable for its quiet, indomitable patience and dignity. Lately the public has happily heard little of Lady Lytton's complaints. I did not even know whether she was still living, until I saw a little book announced the other day by some publisher, which bore her name. Let her pass—with the one remark that her long succession of bitter attacks upon her husband does not seem to have done him any damage in the estimation of the world.

It is not likely that posterity will preserve much of Lord Lytton's writings. They do not, I think, add to literature one original character. Even the glorified murderer or robber, the Eugene Aram or Paul Clifford sort of person, had been done and done much better by Schiller, by Godwin, and by others, before Bulwer-Lytton tried him at second hand. As pictures of English society, those of them which profess to deal with modern English life have no value whatever. The historical novels, the classical novels, are glaringly false in their color and tone. Some of the personages in "The Last Days of Pompeii" are a good deal more like modern English dandies than most of the people who are given out as such in "Pelham." The attempts at political satire in "Paul Clifford," at broad humor in "Eugene Aram" (the Corporal and his cat for example), are feeble and miserable. There is hardly one touch of refined and genuine pathos—of pathos drawn from other than the old stock conventional sources—in the whole of the romances, plays, and poems. The one great faculty which the author possessed was the capacity to burnish up and display the absolutely commonplace, the merely conventional, the utterly unreal, so that it looked new, original, and real in the eyes of the ordinary public, and sometimes even succeeded, for the hour, in deceiving the expert. Bulwer-Lytton's romance is only the romance of the London "Family Herald" or the "New York Ledger," plus high intellectual culture and an intimate acquaintance with the best spheres of letters, art, and fashion. I own that I have considerable admiration for the man who, with so small an original outfit, accomplished so much. So successful a romancist; occasionally almost a sort of poet; a perfect master of the art of writing plays to catch audiences; so skilful an imitator of oratory that, despite almost unparalleled physical defects, he once nearly persuaded the world that his was genuine eloquence—who shall say that the capacity which can do all this is not something to be admired? It is a clever thing to be able to make ornaments of paste which shall pass with the world for diamonds; mock-turtle soup which shall taste like real; wax figures which look at first as if they were alive. Of the literary art which is akin to this, our common literature has probably never had so great a master as Lord Lytton. Such a man is especially the one to stand up as the appropriate representative of literature in such an assembly as the English House of Lords. I should be sorry to see a Browning, a Thackeray, a Carlyle, a Tennyson, a Dickens there; but I think Lord Lytton is in his right place—a splendid sham author in a splendid sham legislative assembly.

"PAR NOBILE FRATRUM— THE TWO NEWMANS"

"The truth, friend," exclaims Mr. Arthur Pendennis, debating some question with his comrade Warrington; "where is the truth? Show it me. I see it on both sides. I see it in this man who worships by act of Parliament, and is rewarded with a silk apron and five thousand a year; in that man who, driven fatally by the remorseless logic of his creed, gives up everything, friends, fame, dearest ties, closest vanities, the respect of an army of churchmen, the recognized position of a leader, and passes over, truth-impelled, to the enemy in whose ranks he is ready to serve henceforth as a nameless private soldier; I see the truth in that man as I do in his brother, whose logic drives him to quite a different conclusion, and who, after having passed a life in vain endeavors to reconcile an irreconcilable book, flings it at last down in despair, and declares, with tearful eyes and hands up to heaven, his revolt and recantation."

Perhaps many American readers, meeting with this passage, may have supposed that the two brothers here described were merely typical figures, invented almost at random by Thackeray to enable Pendennis to point his moral. But in England people know that the two brothers are real personages, and still live. I saw one of them a few nights ago, the one last mentioned by Arthur Pendennis. I saw him, as he is indeed often to be seen, the centre and leader of a little group or knot, a hopeless minority, vainly striving by force of argument and logic, of almost unlimited erudition, and a keen bright intellect, to obtain public attention for something which the public persisted in regarding as an idle crotchet, an impotent craze. The other brother, the elder, is a man whose secession from the Church of England has lately been described by Disraeli, in the preface to the collected edition of his works, as having "dealt a blow to the Church under which it still reels." "That extraordinary event," says Disraeli, "has been 'apologized for' but has never been explained. It was a mistake and a misfortune." Probably no reader of "The Galaxy" will now need to be told that the typical brothers alluded to by Pendennis are John Henry and Francis W. Newman.

The Atlantic deals curiously and capriciously with reputations. Both these brothers Newman seem to me to be less known in America than they deserve to be. John Henry in especial I found to be thus comparatively ignored in the United States. He is beyond doubt one of the greatest, certainly one of the most influential Englishmen of our time. He has engraved his name deeply on the history of his age. He has led perhaps the most remarkable religious movement known to England for generations. He is one of the very few men whose lofty and commanding intellect has been acknowledged and admired by all sects and parties. Gather together any company of eminent Englishmen, however select in its composition, however splendid in its members, and John Henry Newman will be among the few especially conspicuous.

Perhaps most of my readers will be of opinion that Newman's intellect has been sadly misused; that his influence has been for the most part disastrous. But no one who knows anything of the subject can deny the greatness alike of the intellect and of the influence. Let me add, too, that no enemy ever yet called into question the simple sincerity, the blameless purity of John Henry Newman's purposes and character. Of later years he has been rarely seen in London, for his duties keep him in Birmingham, where he is at the head of a religious and educational institution. I have heard that years are telling heavily on him, and that when he now preaches he is listened to with the kind of half-melancholy reverence which hangs on the words of a great man who is already beginning to be a portion of the past. But his influence was a power almost unequalled in its day, and that day has not yet wholly faded.

The Newman brothers are Londoners by birth, sons of a wealthy banker of Lombard street—the British Wall street. Both were educated at Ealing school, and both went to the University of Oxford. John Henry is by some four years the senior of Francis, who was born in 1805, and who now looks at least a dozen or fifteen years younger than his distinguished brother. Both men were endowed with remarkable gifts; both had a splendid faculty of acquiring knowledge. John Henry Newman became a clergyman of the Established Church. He was a close and intimate friend of Keble, of Pusey, and of Manning. He grew to be regarded as one of the rising stars of Protestantism. No name, soon, stood higher than his. His friends loved him, and Protestant England began to revere him. Now observe the change that came on these two brothers, alike so gifted and earnest, alike so wooed by the promise of brilliant worldly career. Two movements of thought, having perhaps a common origin in the dissatisfaction with the existing intellectual stagnation of the Church, but tending in widely different directions, carried the brothers along with them—"seized," to use the words of Richter, "their bleeding hearts and flung them different ways." The younger brother found himself drawn toward rationalism. He could not subscribe the Thirty-Nine Articles for his degree as a Master; he left Oxford. He wandered for years in the East, endeavoring, not very successfully, to teach Christianity on its broadest basis to the Mohammedans; and he finally returned to England to take his place among the leaders of that school of free thought which the ignorant, the careless, or the malignant set down as infidelity. In the mean time his brother became one of the pioneers of a still more unexpected movement. In the English Church for a long time every thing had seemed to be settled and at rest. The old controversy with Rome appeared out of date, unnecessary, and perhaps vulgar. Everything was just as it should be—stable and respectable. But it suddenly occurred to some earnest, unresting souls, like that of Keble—souls "without haste and without rest," like Goethe's star—to insist that the Church of England had higher claims and nobler duties than those of preaching harmless sermons and enriching bishops. Keble could not bear to think of the Church taking pleasure since all is well. He urged on some of the more vigorous and thoughtful minds around him that they should reclaim for the Church the place which ought to be hers as the true successor of the Apostles. He claimed for her that she, and she alone, was the real Catholic Church, authorized to teach all nations, and that Rome had wandered away from the right path, foregone the glorious mission which she might have maintained. One of Keble's closest and dearest friends was John Henry Newman, and Keble regarded Newman as a man qualified beyond all others to become the teacher and leader of the new movement. Keble preached a famous sermon in 1833, and inaugurated the publication of a series of tracts designed to vindicate the real mission of the Church of England. This was the Tractarian movement, which had early, various, and memorable results. John Henry Newman wrote the most celebrated of all the tracts, the famous "No. 90," which drew down the censure of the University authorities on the ground that it actually tended to abolish all difference between the Church of England and the Church of Rome. Yet a little, and the gradual workings of Newman's mind became evident to all the world. The brightest and most penetrating intellect in the English Protestant Church was publicly and deliberately withdrawn from her service, and John Henry Newman became a priest of the Church of Rome. To this had the inquiry conducted him which led his friend Dr. Pusey merely to endeavor to incorporate some of the mysticism and the symbols of Rome with the practice and the progress of the English Church; which had led Dr. Keble only to a more liberal and truly Christianlike temper of Protestant faith; which had sent Francis Newman into radical rationalism. The two brothers were intellectually divided forever. Each renounced a career rich in promise for mere conscience' sake; and the one went this way, the other that.

Disraeli has in no wise exaggerated the depth and painfulness of the sensation produced among English Protestants by the secession of John Henry Newman. It was of course received upon the opposite side with corresponding exultation. No man, indeed, could be less qualified than Mr. Disraeli to understand the tremendous, the irresistible force of conviction in a nature like that of Newman. The brilliant master of political tactics has made it evident that he did not understand the motive of Newman's secession any more than he did the meaning of the title of Newman's celebrated book, "Apologia pro Vitâ suâ." "That extraordinary event," says Disraeli, speaking of the secession, "has been apologized for, but has never been explained." Evidently Disraeli believed that the English word "apology" is the correct translation of the Latinized Greek word "apologia," which it most certainly is not. Nothing could have been further from Newman's mind or from the purpose, or indeed from the title of his book, than to apologize for his secession. On the contrary, the book is sharply and pertinaciously aggressive. It was called forth by an attack made on Dr. Newman by the Rev. Charles Kingsley. I think Kingsley was in the main right in his views, but he was rough and blundering in his expression of them, and he is about as well qualified to carry on a controversy with John Henry Newman as Governor Hoffman would be to undertake a rhetorical competition with Mr. Wendell Phillips. Kingsley's bluff, rude, illogical way of fighting, his "wild and skipping spirit," were placed at ludicrous and fearful disadvantage. Newman "went for him" unsparingly, and literally tore him with the beak and claws of logic, satire, and invective. One was reminded of Pascal's attacks on the Jesuits—only that this time the wit and power were on the side which might fairly be called Jesuitical. Out of this merciless onslaught on Kingsley came the "Apologia pro Vitâ suâ," in which Newman endeavored to vindicate and glorify, not excuse or apologize for, his strange secession. The book is well worth reading, if only as a curious illustration of the utter inadequacy of human intellect and human logic to secure a soul from the strangest wandering, the saddest possible illusion. You cannot read a page of it without admiration for the intellect of the author, and without pity for the poverty even of the richest intellectual gifts where guidance is sought in a faith and in things which transcend the limits of human logic.

John Henry Newman threw his whole soul, energy, genius, and fame into the cause of the Roman Catholic Church. Rome welcomed him with that cordial welcome she always gives to a new-comer, and she utilized him and set work for him to do. Macaulay has shown very effectively in one of his essays how the Roman Church seldom loses any one it has gained, because it is so skilful in finding for everybody his proper place, and assigning him in her service the task he is best qualified to do, so that her ambition becomes his ambition, her interest his interest, her conquests his conquests. Newman appears to have been made a sort of missionary from Rome to the intellect and culture of the English people. Within the Church to which he had gone over he became an immense influence and almost unequalled power. The Catholics delighted to have a leader whose intellect no one could pretend to despise, whose gifts and culture had been panegyrized in the most glowing terms, over and over again, by the foremost statesmen and divines of the Protestant Church. Newman was appointed head of the oratory of St. Philip Neri at Birmingham, and was for some years rector of the Roman Catholic University of Dublin. He rarely came before the public. In all the arts that make an orator or a great preacher he is strikingly deficient. His manner is constrained, awkward, and even ungainly; his voice is thin and weak. His bearing is not impressive. His gaunt, emaciated figure, his sharp, eagle face, his cold, meditative eye, rather repel than attract those who see him for the first time. The matter of his discourse, whether sermon, speech, or lecture, is always admirable, and the language is concise, scholarly, expressive— perhaps a little overweighted with thought; but there is nothing there of the orator. It is as a writer, and as an "influence"—I don't know how better to express it—that Newman has become famous. I doubt if we have many better prose writers. He is full of keen, pungent, satirical humor; and there is, on the other hand, a subtle vein of poetry and of pathos suffusing nearly all he writes. One of the finest and one of the most frequently quoted passages in modern English literature is Newman's touching and noble apostrophe to England's "Saxon Bible." He has published volumes of verse which I think belong to the very highest order of verse-making that is not genuine poetry. They are full of thought, feeling, pathos, tenderness, beauty of illustration; they are all that verse can be made by one who just fails to be a poet. An English critical review not long since classed the poetical works of Dr. Newman and George Eliot together, as the nearest approach which intellect and culture have made in our days toward the production of genuine poetry. When Newman made his famous attack on Dr. Achilli, an Italian priest who had renounced the Roman Church, and whom Newman publicly accused of many crimes, the judge who had to sentence the accuser to the payment of a fine for libel pronounced a panegyric on his intellect and his character such as is rarely heard from an English judgment seat. Not long after, when the subject came up somehow in the House of Commons, Mr. Gladstone broke into an encomium of John Henry Newman which might have seemed poetical by hyperbole to those who did not know the merits of the one man and the conscientious truthfulness of the other. We have heard the testimony borne by Mr. Disraeli to the importance of Newman's intellect as a support of the English Church, and the shock which was caused by his withdrawal. Seldom, indeed, has a man seceded from one church and become the aggressive, unsparing, intolerant champion of its enemy, and yet retained the esteem and the affection of those whom he abandoned, as this good, great, mistaken Englishman has done.

The two brothers then are hopelessly divided. One consorts with the Pope and Cardinal Wiseman and Archbishop Manning, and is the idol and saint of the Ultramontanes, and devotes his noble intellect to the task of making the Irish Catholic a more bigoted Catholic than ever. The other falls in with the little band, that once seemed a forlorn hope, of what we may call the philosophical radicals of England. He becomes a professor of the rationalistic University of London, and a contributor to the free-thinking "Westminster Review." Judging each brother's success merely by what each sought to do, I suppose the career of the Catholic has been the more successful. Not that I think he has made much way toward the conversion of England to Catholicism. With all its Puseyism and ritualism, England seems to have little real inclination toward the doctrines of Rome. There is indeed a distinguished "convert" every now and then—the Marquis of Bute some two years ago, Lord Robert Montagu last year; but the great mass of the English people remain obstinately anti-papal. The tendency is far more toward Rationalism than toward Romanism; with the Newman who withdrew from all churches rather than with the Newman who renounced one church to enter another. Therefore, when I say that the career of John Newman appears to me to have been more successful than that of Francis, I mean only that he has been a greater influence, a more powerful instrument of his cause than his brother ever has been. The boast was made unjustly for Voltaire that he almost arrested the progress of Christianity in Europe. I think the admirers of John Newman might claim for him that he actually did for a time at least arrest the progress of Protestantism in England. He had indeed the great advantage of passing from one organization to another. Like Coriolanus, when he seceded he became the leader of the enemy's army. It was quite otherwise with his brother, who leaving the English Church was thenceforward only an individual, and for the most part an isolated worker. But indeed, with all his intellect, his high culture, and his indomitable courage, Francis Newman has never been an influential man in English politics. It may be that his keen logic is too uncompromising; and there can be no practical statesmanship without compromise. It may be that there is something eccentric, egotistic (in the less offensive sense), and crotchety in that sharp, independent, and self-sufficing intelligence. Whatever the reason, nine out of ten men in London set down Francis Newman as hopelessly given over to crotchets, while the tenth man, admiring however much his character and his capacity, is sometimes grieved and sometimes provoked that both together do not make him a greater power in the nation. I never remember Francis Newman to have been in accord with what I may call the average public opinion of English political life, except in one instance; and in that case I believe him to have been wrong. He was in favor of the Crimean war; and for this once therefore he found himself on the side of the majority. As if to mark the contrast of views which it has been the fate of these two brothers to present during their lives, it so happened that, so far as John Henry's opinions on the subject could be learned by the public, they were against the war. At least they were decidedly against the Turks. I remember hearing him deliver at that time a course of lectures in an educational institution, having for their subject the origin and the results of the Ottoman settlement in Europe. I well remember how effectively and vividly he argued, with his thin voice and his constrained, ungraceful action, that the Turk had no greater moral right to the territory he occupies, but does not cultivate and improve, than the pirate has to the sea over which he sails. But Francis Newman was then for once mixed up with the majority; and I doubt whether he could have much liked the unwonted position. He certainly took care to explain more than once that his reasons for taking that side were not those of the average Englishman. He thus might have given some of his casual associates occasion to say of him, as Charles Mathews says of woman in general, that even when he is right he is right in a wrong sort of way. For myself I am inclined to reverse the saying, and declare of Francis Newman that even when he is wrong he is wrong in a right sort of way. He was right, and in a very right sort of way, when he came out from his habitual seclusion during the American civil war, and stood up on many a platform for the cause of the Union. Like his brother, he is a poor public speaker. At his very best he is the professor talking to his class, not the orator addressing a crowd. His manner is singularly constrained, ineffective, and even awkward; his voice is thin and weak. There is a certain very small and rare class of bad speakers, which has yet a virtue and charm of its own almost equal to eloquence. I am now thinking of men utterly wanting in all the arts and graces, in all the power and effect of rhetorical delivery, but who yet with whatever defect of manner can say such striking things, can put such noble thoughts into expressive words, can be so entirely original and so completely masters of their subject, that they seem to be orators in all but voice and manner. Horace Greeley always is, to me at least, such a speaker; so is Stuart Mill. These are bad speakers as Jane Eyre or Consuelo may have been an unlovely woman; all the rules declare against them, all the intelligences and sympathies are in their favor. But Francis Newman is not a speaker of this kind. He is feeble, ineffective, and often even commonplace. Nature has denied to him the faculty of adequately expressing himself in spoken words.

He is almost as much out of his element when addressing a public meeting as he would be if he were singing in an opera. Few Englishmen living can claim to be the intellectual superiors of Francis Newman; but you would never know Francis Newman by hearing him speak on a platform. The last time I heard him address a public meeting was on an occasion to which I have already alluded. He was presiding over an assemblage called together to protest against compulsory vaccination. The Government and Parliament have lately made very stringent the enactment for compulsory vaccination, in consequence of the terrible increase of small-pox. There is in London, as in all other great capitals, a certain knot of persons who would refuse to wash their faces or kiss their wives if Government ordered or even recommended either performance. Therefore there was a small agitation got up against vaccination, and Francis Newman consented to become the president of one of its meetings. This meeting was held in Exeter Hall—not indeed in the vast hall where the oratorios are performed, and where once upon a time Henry Ward Beecher pleaded the cause of the Union; but in the "lower hall," as it is called, a little subterranean den. Some eminent classic person, I really forget who, being reproached with the small size of his apartments, declared that he should be only too glad if he could fill his rooms, small as they were, with men his friends. The organizers of this meeting might have been content if they could have filled the hall, small as it was, with men and women their friends. The attendance was not nearly up to the size of the room. There on the platform sat the good, the gifted, and the fearless Francis Newman; and immediately around him were some dozen embodied and living crotchets and crazes. There was this learned physician who has communication with the spirit-world regularly. There was this other eminent person who has long been trying in vain to teach an apathetic Government how to cure crime on phrenological principles. There was Smith, who is opposed to all wars; Brown, who firmly believes that every disease comes from the use of salt; Jones, who has at his own expense put into circulation thousands of copies of his work against the employment of medical men in puerperal cases; Robinson, who is ready to spend his last coin for the purpose of proving that vaccination and original sin are one and the same thing. How often, oh, how often have I not heard those theories expounded! How often have I marvelled at the extraordinary perversion of ingenuity by which figures, facts, philosophy, and Scripture are jumbled up together to convince you that the moon is made of green cheese! We just wanted on this memorable occasion the awful persons who prove to you that the earth is flat, and the indefatigable ladies who expound their claims to the British crown feloniously usurped by Queen Victoria. There sat Francis Newman presiding over this preposterous little conclave, and having of course what seemed to him satisfactory and just reasons for the position he occupied. He spoke rather better than usual, and there was a bewildering bravery of paradox writhing through his speech which must have delighted his listeners. The meeting came to nothing. The papers took hardly any notice of it (London papers were never in my time so entirely conventional, respectable, and Philistinish as they are just now); and Newman's effort went wholly in vain. I have mentioned it only because it was illustrative or typical of so much in the man's whole career. So much of lovely independence; such a disdain of public opinion and public ridicule; such an absence of all perception of the ridiculous! Thus it was that he endeavored to rouse up the English public, who except for the extreme democracy always have had a strong hankering for the Austrian Government, to a sense of the crimes of the House of Hapsburg against its subjects. Thus he was for reform in Parliament when Parliamentary reform was a theme supposed to be dead and buried; when Palmerston had trampled on its ashes, and Disraeli had made merry over its coffin. Thus he came out for the American Union when John Bright stood almost alone in the House of Commons, and Mill and Goldwin Smith and two or three others were trying to organize public opinion outside the House. The same qualities after all which made Newman nearly sublime in these latter instances, were just those which made him well nigh ridiculous in the anti-vaccination business. But in all the instances alike the same thing can be said of Francis Newman. There is a turn or twist of some kind in his nature and intellect which always seems to mar his best efforts at practical accomplishment. Even his purely literary and scholastic productions are marked by the same fatal characteristic. All the outfit, all the materials are there in surprising profusion. There is the culture, there is the intellect, the patience, the sincerity. But the result is not in proportion to the value of the materials. The blending is not complete, is not effectual. Something has always intervened or been wanting. Francis Newman has never done and probably never will do anything equal to his strength and his capacity.

I am not inviting a comparison between these two brothers, so alike in their sincerity, their devotion, their courage, and their gifts—so singularly unlike, so utterly divided, in their creeds and their careers. My own sympathies, of course, naturally go with Francis Newman, who has in a vast majority of instances been a teacher of some opinion, a champion of some political cause of which I am proud to be a disciple and a follower. But I suppose the greater intellect and the richer gifts were those which were given up so meekly and wholly to the service of the dogmatism of the Roman Catholic Church. The career of John Henry Newman may probably be regarded as having practically closed. His latest work of note, "The Grammar of Assent," does not indeed seem to show any falling away of his intellectual powers; but I have heard that his physical strength has suffered severely with years, and he never was a strong man. He is now in his seventieth year, and it is therefore only reasonable to regard him as one who has done his work and whose life is fully open to the judgment of his time. May I be allowed to say that I think he has done some good even to that English Church to which his secession struck so heavy a blow? Newman was really the mainspring of that movement which proposed to rescue the Church from apathy, from dull easy-going quiescence, from the perfunctory discharge of formal duties, and to quicken her once again with the spirit of a priesthood, to arouse her to the living work, physical and spiritual, of an ecclesiastical sovereignty. The impulse indeed overshot itself in his case, and was misdirected in the case of Dr. Pusey, plunging blindly into Romanism with the one, degenerating into a somewhat barren symbolism with the other. But throughout the English Church in general there has been surely a higher spirit at work since that famous Oxford movement which was inspired by John Henry Newman. I think its influence has been more active, more beneficent, more human, and yet at the same time more spiritual, since that sudden and startling impulse was given. For the man himself little more needs to be said. Every one acknowledges his gifts and his virtues. No one doubts that in his marvellous change he sought only the pure truth. His theology, I presume, is not that of the readers of "The Galaxy" in general, any more than it is mine; but I trust there is none of us so narrowed to his own form of Christianity as to refuse his respect and admiration to one so highly lifted above the average of men in goodness and intellect, even though his career may have been sacrificed at the shrine of a faith that is not ours. For me, I am sometimes lost in wonder at the sacrifice, but I can only think with respect and even veneration of the man.

The younger brother needs no apology or vindication, in the United States especially. He is, be it understood, a thoroughly religious man. He has never sunk into materialism or frittered away his earnestness in mere skepticism. He is not orthodox—he has gone his own way as regards church dogma and discipline; but except in the vulgarest and narrowest application of the word, he is no "infidel." The United States owe him some good feeling, for he was one of the few eminent men in England who never were faithless to the cause of the Union, and never doubted of its ultimate triumph. I have now before me one of the most powerful arguments addressed to an English audience for the Union and against secession that reason, justice, and eloquence could frame. It is a pamphlet published in 1863 by "F. W. Newman, late Professor at University College, London," in the form of a "Letter to a Friend who had joined the Southern Independence Association." How wonderful it seems now that such arguments ever should have been needed; how few there were then in England who regarded them; how completely time has justified and sealed them as true, right, and prophetic. I read the pages over, and all the old struggle comes back with its rancors and its dangers, and I honor anew the brave man who was not afraid to stand as one of a little group, isolated, denounced, and laughed at, confiding always in justice and time.

The story of these two brothers is on the whole as strange a chapter as any I know in the biography of human intellect and creed. I think it may at least teach us a lesson of toleration, if nothing better. The very pride of intellect itself can hardly pretend to look down with mere scorn upon beliefs or errors which have carried off in contrary directions these two Newmans. The sternest bigot can scarcely refuse to admit that truthfulness and goodness may abide without the limits of his own creed, when he remembers the high and noble example of pure, true, and disinterested lives which these intellectually-sundered brothers alike have given to their fellow-men.

ARCHBISHOP MANNING

St. James's Hall, London, is primarily a place for concerts and singers, as Exeter Hall is. But, like its venerable predecessor, St. James's Hall has come to be identified with political meetings of a certain class. Exeter Hall, a huge, gaunt, unadorned, and dreary room in the Strand, is resorted to for the most part as the arena and platform of ultra-Protestantism. St. James's Hall, a beautiful and almost lavishly ornate structure in Piccadilly, is commonly used by the leading Roman Catholics of London when they desire to make a demonstration. There are political classes which will use either place indifferently; but Exeter Hall has usually a tinge of Protestant exclusiveness about its political expression, while the ceiling of the other building has rung alike to the thrilling music of John Bright's voice, to the strident vehemence of Mr. Bradlaugh, the humdrum humming of Mr. Odger, and the clear, delicate, tremulous intonations of Stuart Mill. But I never heard of a Roman Catholic meeting of great importance being held anywhere in London lately, except in St. James's Hall.

Let us attend such a meeting there. The hall is a huge oblong, with galleries around three of the sides, and a platform bearing a splendid organ on the fourth. The room is brilliantly lighted, and the mode of lighting is peculiar and picturesque. The platform, the galleries, the body of the hall alike are crowded. This is a meeting held to make a demonstration in favor of some Roman Catholic demand—say for separate education. On the platform are the great Catholic peers, most of them men of lineage stretching back to years when Catholicism was yet unsuspicious of any possible rivalry in England. There are the Norfolks, the Denbighs, the Dormers, the Petres, the Staffords; there are such later accessions to Catholicism as the Marquis of Bute, whose change created such a sensation, and Lord Robert Montagu, who "went over" only last year. There are some recent accessions of the peerage also—Lord Acton, for instance, head of a distinguished and ancient family, but only lately called to the Upper House, and who, when Sir John Acton, won honorable fame as a writer and scholar. Lord Acton not many years ago started the "Home and Foreign Review," a quarterly periodical which endeavored to reconcile Catholicism with liberalism and science. The universal opinion of England and of Europe declared the "Home and Foreign Review" to be unsurpassed for ability, scholarship, and political information by any publication in the world. It leaped at one bound to a level with the "Edinburgh," the "Quarterly," and the "Revue des Deux Mondes." But the Pope thought the Review too liberal, and intimated that it ought to be suppressed; and Lord Acton meekly bowed his head and suppressed it in all the bloom of its growing fame. Some Irish members of Parliament are on the platform—men of station and wealth like Munsell, men of energy and brains like John Francis Maguire; perhaps, too, the handsome, brilliant-minded O'Donoghue, with his picturesque pedigree and his broken fortunes. But in general there is not a very cordial *rapprochement* between the English Catholic peers and the Irish Catholic members. Of all slow, cold, stately Conservatives in the world, the slowest, coldest, and stateliest is the English Catholic peer. Only the common bond of religion brings these two sets of men together now and then. They meet, but do not blend. In the body of the hall are the middle-class Catholics of London, the shopkeepers and clerks, mostly Irish or of Irish parentage. In the galleries are swarming the genuine Irishmen of London, the Paddies who are always threatening to interrupt Garibaldian gatherings in the parks, and who throw up their hats at the prospect of any "row" on behalf of the Pope. The chair is taken by some duke or earl, who is listened to respectfully, but without any special fervor of admiration. The English Catholics are undemonstrative in any case, and Irish Paddy does not care much about a chilly English peer. But a speaker is presently introduced who has only to make his appearance in front of the platform in order to awaken one universal burst of applause. Paddy and the Duke of Norfolk vie with each other; the steady English shopkeeper from Islington is as demonstrative as any O'Donoghue or Maguire. The meeting is wide awake and informed by one spirit and soul at last.

The man who has aroused all this emotion shrinks back almost as if he were afraid of it, although it is surely not new to him. He is a tall thin personage, some sixty-two years of age. His face is bloodless—pale as a ghost, one might say. He is so thin as to look almost cadaverous. The outlines of the face are handsome and dignified. There is much of courtly grace and refinement about the bearing and gestures of this pale, weak, and wasted man. He wears a long robe of violet silk, with some kind of dark cape or collar, and has a massive gold chain round his neck, holding attached to it a great gold cross. There is a certain nervous quivering about his eyes and lips, but otherwise he is perfectly collected and master of the occasion. His voice is thin, but wonderfully clear and penetrating. It is heard all through this great hall—a moment ago so noisy, now so silent. The words fall with a slow, quiet force, like drops of water. Whatever your opinion may be, you cannot choose but listen; and, indeed, you want only to listen and see. For this is the foremost man in the Catholic Church of England. This is the Cardinal Grandison of Disraeli's "Lothair"—Dr. Henry Edward Manning, Roman Catholic Archbishop of Westminster, successor in that office of the late Cardinal Wiseman.

It is no wonder that the Irishmen at the meeting are enthusiastic about Archbishop Manning. An Englishman of Englishmen, with no drop of Irish blood in his veins, he is more Hibernian than the Hibernians themselves in his sympathies with Ireland. A man of social position, of old family, of the highest education and the most refined instincts, he would leave the Catholic noblemen at any time to go down to his Irish teetotallers at the East End of London. He firmly believes that the salvation of England is yet to be accomplished through the influence of that religious devotion which is at the bottom of the Irish nature, and which some of us call superstition. He loves his own country dearly, but turns away from her present condition of industrial prosperity to the days before the Reformation, when yet saints trod the English soil. "In England there has been no saint since the Reformation," he said the other day, in sad, sweet tones, to one of wholly different opinions, who listened with a mingling of amazement and reverence. No views that I have ever heard put into living words embodied to anything like the same extent the full claims and pretensions of Ultramontanism. It is quite wonderful to sit and listen. One cannot but be impressed by the sweetness, the thoughtfulness, the dignity, I had almost said the sanctity of the man who thus pours forth, with a manner full of the most tranquil conviction, opinions which proclaim all modern progress a failure, and glorify the Roman priest or the Irish peasant as the true herald and repository of light, liberty, and regeneration to a sinking and degraded world.

Years ago, Henry Edward Manning was one of the brilliant lights of the English Protestant Church. Just twenty years back he was appointed to the high place of Archdeacon of Chichester, having also, according to the manner in which the English State Church rewards its dignitaries, more than one other ecclesiastical appointment at the same time. Dr. Manning had distinguished himself highly during his career at the University of Oxford. His father was a member of the House of Commons, and Manning on starting into life had many friends and very bright prospects. Nothing would have been easier, nothing seemingly would have been more natural than for him to tread the way so plainly opened before him, and to rise to higher and higher dignity, until at last perhaps the princely renown of a bishopric and a seat in the House of Lords would have been his reward. But Dr. Manning's career was cast in a time of stress and trial for the English State Church. I have described briefly in a former article the origin, growth, and effects of that remarkable movement which, beginning within the Church itself and seeking to establish loftier claims for her than she had long put forward, ended by convulsing her in a manner more troublous than any religious crisis which had occurred since the Reformation. Dr. Manning's is evidently a nature which must have been specially allured by what I may be allowed to call the supernatural claims put forward on behalf of the Church of England. He was of course correspondingly disappointed by what he considered the failure of those claims. As Coleridge says that every man is born an Aristotelian or a Platonist, so it may perhaps be said that every man is born with a predisposition to lean either on natural or supernatural laws in the direct guidance of life. I am not now raising any religious question whatever. What I say may be said of members of the same sect or church— of any sect, of any church. One man, as faithful and devout a believer as any, is yet content to go through his daily duties and fulfil his career trusting to his religious principles, his insight, and his reason, without requiring at every moment the light of spiritual or supernatural guidance. Another must always have his world in direct communion with the spiritual, or it is no world of faith to him. Now it is impossible to look in Dr. Manning's face without seeing that his is one of those sensitive, spiritual, I had almost said morbid natures, which can find no endurable existence without a close and constant communion with the supernatural. Keble, Newman, Time and the Hour, called out for the assertion of the claim that the Church of England was the true heir of the apostolic succession. Such a nature as Manning's must have delightedly welcomed the claim. But the mere investigation sent, as I have already explained, one Newman to Catholicism and the other to Rationalism. Dr. Manning, too, felt compelled to ask himself whether the Church could make good its claim, and whether, if it could not, he had any longer a place within its walls. The change does not appear to have come so rapidly to fulfilment with him as with John Henry Newman. Dr. Manning seems to me to have a less aggressive temperament than his distinguished predecessor in secession. There is more about him of the quietist, of the ecstatic, so far as religious thought is concerned, while it is possible that he may be a more practical and influential guide in the mere policy of the church to which he belongs. There is an amount of scorn in Newman's nature which sometimes reminds one of Pascal, and which I have not observed in Dr. Manning or in his writings. I cannot imagine Dr. Manning, for example, pelting Charles Kingsley with sarcasms and overwhelming him with contempt, as Dr. Newman evidently delighted to do in the famous controversy which was provoked by the apostle of Muscular Christianity. I suppose therefore that Dr. Manning clung for a long time to the faith in which he was bred. But his whole nature is evidently cast in the mould which makes Roman Catholic devotees. He is a man of the type which perhaps found in Fénelon its most illustrious example. I think it is not too much to say that to him that light of private judgment which some of us regard as man's grandest and most peculiarly divine attribute, must always have presented itself as something abhorrent to his nature. I am judging, of course, as an outsider and as one little acquainted with theological subjects;

but my impression of the two men would be that Dr. Newman joined the Roman Catholic Church in obedience to some compulsion of reason, acting in what must seem to most of us an inscrutable manner, and that Dr. Manning never would have been a Protestant at all if he had not believed that the Protestant Church was truly all which its rival claims to be.

Dr. Manning in fact did not leave the Church. The Church left him. He had misunderstood it. It became revealed at last as it really is, a church founded on the right of private judgment, and Manning was appalled and turned away from it. Something that may almost be called accident brought home to his mind the true character of the Church to which he belonged. Many readers of "The Galaxy" may have some recollection of the once celebrated Gorham case in England—a case which I shall not now describe any further than by saying that it raised the question whether the Church of England can prescribe the religion of the State. Had the Church the right to decide whether certain doctrine taught by one of its clergy was heretical, and to condemn it if so declared? In England, Church and State are so bound up together, that it is practically the State and not the Church which decides whether this or that teaching is heresy or true religion. A lord chancellor who may be an infidel, and two or three "law lords" who may be anything or nothing, settle the question in the end. We all remember the epigram about Lord Chancellor Westbury, the least godly of men, having "dismissed Hell with costs," and taken away from the English Protestant "his last hope of damnation." The Gorham case, twenty years ago, showed that the Church, as an ecclesiastical body, had no power to condemn heresy. This, to men like Stuart Mill, appears on the whole a satisfactory condition of things so long as there is a State Church, for the plain reason which he gives— namely, that the State in England is now far more liberal than the Church. But to Dr. Manning the idea of the Church thus abdicating its function of interpreting and declaring doctrine was equivalent to the renunciation of its right to existence. He strove hard to bring about an organized and solemn declaration and protest from the Church—a declaration of doctrine, a protest against secular control. He became the leader of an effort in this direction. The effort met with little support. The then Bishop of London did indeed introduce a bill into the House of Lords for the purpose of enacting that in matters of doctrine, as distinct from questions of mere law, the final decision should rest with the prelates. Dr. Manning sat in the gallery of the House of Lords on that memorable night. The Bishop of London wholly failed. The House of Lords scouted the idea of liberal England tolerating a sort of ecclesiastical inquisition. Every one admitted the anomalous condition in which things then were placed; but few indeed would think of enacting a dogma of infallibility in favor of the bishops of the Church. Lord Brougham spoke against the bill with what Dr. Manning himself admits to be plain English common sense. He said the House of Lords through its law peers could decide questions of mere ecclesiastical law, and the decisions would carry weight and authority; but neither peers nor bishops could in England decide a question of doctrine. Suppose, he asked, the bishops were divided equally on such a question, where would the decision be then? Suppose there was a very small majority, who would accept such a decision? Or even suppose there was a large majority, but that the minority comprised the few men of greatest knowledge, ability, and authority, what value would attach to the judgment of such a majority? The bill was a hopeless failure. Dr. Manning has himself described with equal candor and clearness the effect which the debate had upon him. He mentally supplemented Lord Brougham's questions by one other. Suppose that all the bishops of the Church of England should decide unanimously on any doctrine, would any one receive the decision as infallible? He was compelled to answer, "No one." The Church of England had no pretension to be the infallible spiritual guide of men. Were she to raise any such pretension, it would be rejected with contempt by the common mind of the nation. Hear then how this conviction affected the man who up to that time had had no thought but for the interests and duties of the English Church. "To those," he has himself told us, "who believed that God has established upon the earth a divine and therefore an unerring guardian and teacher of his faith, this event demonstrated that the Church of England could not be that guardian and teacher."

While Dr. Manning was still uncertain whither to turn, the celebrated "Papal aggression" took place. Cardinal Wiseman was sent to England by the Pope, with the title of Archbishop of Westminster. All England raged. Earl Russell wrote his famous "Durham Letter." The Lord Chancellor Campbell, at a public dinner in the city of London, called up a storm of enthusiasm by quoting the line from Shakespeare, which declares that

Under our feet we'll stamp the cardinal's hat.

Protestant zealots in Stockport belabored the Roman Catholics and sacked their houses; Irish laborers in Birkenhead retorted upon the Protestants. The Government brought in the Ecclesiastical Titles Bill—a measure making it penal for any Catholic prelate to call himself archbishop or bishop of any place in England. Let him be "Archbishop Wiseman" or "Cardinal Wiseman, Archbishop of Mesopotamia," as long as he liked—but not Archbishop of Westminster or Tuam. The bill was powerfully, splendidly opposed by Gladstone, Bright, and Cobden, on the broad ground that it invaded the precincts of religious liberty; but it was carried and made law. There it remained. There never was the slightest attempt made to enforce it. The Catholic prelates held to the titles the Pope had given them; and no English court, judge, magistrate, or policeman ever offered to prevent or punish them. So ludicrous, so barren a proceeding as the carrying of that measure has not been known in the England of our time.

Cardinal Wiseman was an able and a discreet man. He was calm, plausible, powerful. He was very earnest in the cause of his Church, but he seemed much more like a man of the world than Newman or Dr. Manning. There was little of the loftily spiritual in his manner or appearance. His bulky person and swollen face suggested at the first glance a sort of Abbot Boniface; he was, I believe, in reality an ascetic. The corpulence which seemed the result of good living was only the effect of ill health. He had a persuasive and an imposing way. His ability was singularly flexible. His eloquence was often too gorgeous and ornamental for a pure taste, but when the occasion needed he could address an audience in language of the simplest and most practical common sense. The same adaptability, if I may use such a word, was evident in all he did. He would talk with a cabinet minister on terms of calm equality, as if his rank must be self-evident, and he delighted to set a band of poor school children playing around him. He was a cosmopolitan— English and Irish by extraction, Spanish by birth, Roman by education. When he spoke English he was exactly like what a portly, dignified British bishop ought to be—a John Bull in every respect. When he spoke Italian at Rome he fell instinctively and at once into all the peculiarities of intonation and gesture which distinguish the people of Italy from all other races. When he conversed in Spanish he subsided into the grave, somewhat saturnine dignity and repose of the true Castilian. All this, I presume, was but the natural effect of that flexibility of temperament I have attempted to describe. I had but slight personal acquaintance with Cardinal Wiseman, and I paint him only as he impressed me, a casual observer. I am satisfied that he was a profoundly earnest and single-minded man; the testimony of many whom I know and who knew him well compels me to that conviction. But such was not the impression he would have left on a mere acquaintance. He seemed rather one who could, for a purpose which he believed great, be all things to all men. He impressed me quite differently from the manner in which I have been impressed by John Henry Newman and by Archbishop Manning. He reminded one of some great, capable, worldly-wise, astute Prince of the Church of other generations, politician rather than priest, more ready to sustain and skilled to defend the temporal power of the Papacy than to illustrate its highest spiritual influence.

The events which brought Cardinal Wiseman to England had naturally a powerful effect upon the mind of Dr. Manning. It was the renewed claim of the Roman Church to enfold England in its spiritual jurisdiction.

For Dr. Manning, who had just seen what he regarded as the voluntary abdication of the English Church, the claim would in any case have probably been decisive. It "stepped between him and his fighting soul." But the personal influence of Cardinal Wiseman had likewise an immense weight and force. Dr. Manning ever since that time entertained a feeling of the profoundest devotion and reverence for Cardinal Wiseman. The change was consummated in 1851, and one of the first practical comments upon the value of the Ecclesiastical Titles Act was the announcement that a scholar and divine of whom the Protestant Church had long been especially proud had resigned his preferments, his dignities, and his prospects, and passed over to the Church of Rome. I cannot better illustrate the effect produced on the public mind than by saying that even the secession of John Henry Newman hardly made a deeper impression.

Dr. Manning, of course, rose to high rank in the church of his adoption. He became Roman of the Romans—Ultramontane of the Ultramontanes. On the death of his friend and leader, Cardinal Wiseman, whose funeral sermon he preached, Henry Manning became Archbishop of Westminster. Except for his frequent journeys to Rome, he has always since his appointment lived in London. Although a good deal of an ascetic, as his emaciated face and figure would testify, he is nothing of a hermit. He mingles to a certain extent in society, he takes part in many public movements, and he has doubtless given Mr. Disraeli ample opportunity of studying his manner and bearing. I don't believe Mr. Disraeli capable of understanding the profound devotion and single-minded sincerity of the man. A more singular, striking, marvellous figure does not stand out, I think, in our English society. Everything that an ordinary Englishman or American would regard as admirable and auspicious in the progress of our civilization, Dr. Manning calmly looks upon as lamentable and evil-omened. What we call progress is to his mind decay. What we call light is to him darkness. What we reverence as individual liberty he deplores as spiritual slavery. The mere fact that a man gives reasons for his faith seems shocking to this strangely-gifted apostle of unconditional belief. Though you were to accept on bended knees ninety-nine of the decrees of Rome, you would still be in his mind a heretic if you paused to consider as to the acceptance of the hundredth dogma. All the peculiarly modern changes in the legislation of England, the admission of Jews to Parliament, the introduction of the principle of divorce, the practical recognition of the English divine's right of private judgment, are painful and odious to him. I have never heard from any other source anything so clear, complete, and astonishing as his cordial acceptance of the uttermost claims of Rome; the prostration of all reason and judgment before the supposed supernatural attributes of the Papal throne. In one of the finest passages of his own writings he says: "My love for England begins with the England of St. Bede. Saxon England, with all its tumults, seems to me saintly and beautiful. Norman England I have always loved less, because, although majestic, it became continually less Catholic, until the evil spirit of the world broke off the light yoke of faith at the so-called Reformation. Still I loved the Christian England which survived, and all the lingering outlines of diocese and parishes, cathedrals and churches, with the names of saints upon them. It is this vision of the past which still hovers over England and makes it beautiful and full of the memories of the kingdom of God. Nay, I loved the parish church of my childhood and the college chapel of my youth, and the little church under a green hillside where the morning and evening prayers and the music of the English Bible for seventeen years became a part of my soul. Nothing is more beautiful in the natural order, and if there were no eternal world I could have made it my home." To Dr. Manning the time when saints walked the earth of England is more of a reality than the day before yesterday to most of us. Where the ordinary eye sees only a poor, ignorant Irish peasant, Dr. Manning discerns a heaven-commissioned bearer of light and truth, destined by the power of his unquestioning faith to redeem perhaps, in the end, even English philosophers and statesmen. When it was said in the praise of the murdered Archbishop of Paris that he was disposed to regret the introduction of the dogma of infallibility, Archbishop Manning came eagerly to the rescue of his friend's memory, and as one would vindicate a person unjustly accused of crime, he vindicated the dead Archbishop from the stigma of having for a moment dared to have an opinion of his own on such a subject. Of course, if Dr. Manning were an ordinary theological devotee or fanatic, there would be nothing remarkable in all this. But he is a man of the widest culture, of high intellectual gifts, of keen and penetrating judgment in all ordinary affairs, remarkable for his close and logical argument, his persuasive reasoning, and for a genial, quiet kind of humor which seems especially calculated to dissolve sophistry by its action. He is an English gentleman, a man of the world; he was educated at Oxford with Arthur Pendennis and young Lord Magnus Charters; he lives at York Place in the London of to-day; he drives down to the House of Commons and talks politics in the lobby with Gladstone and Lowe; he meets Disraeli at dinner parties, and is on friendly terms, I dare say, with Huxley and Herbert Spencer; he reads the newspapers, and I make no doubt is now well acquainted with the history of the agitation against Tammany and Boss Tweed. I think such a man is a marvellous phenomenon in our age. It is as if one of the mediæval saints from the stained windows of a church should suddenly become infused with life and take a part in all the ways of our present world. I can understand the long-abiding power of the Catholic Church when I remember that I have heard and seen and talked with Henry Edward Manning.

Dr. Manning is not, I fancy, very much of a political reformer. His inclinations would probably be rather conservative than otherwise. He is drawn toward Gladstone and the Liberal party less by distinct political affinity, of which there is but little, than by his hope and belief that through Gladstone something will be done for that Ireland which to this Oxford scholar is still the "island of the saints." The Catholic members of Parliament, whether English or Irish, consult Archbishop Manning constantly upon all questions connected with education or religion. His parlor in York Place—not far from where Mme. Tussaud's wax-work exhibition attracts the country visitor—is the frequent scene of conferences which have their influence upon the action of the House of Commons. He is a devoted upholder of the doctrine of total abstinence from intoxicating drinks; and he is the only Englishman of real influence and ability, except Francis Newman, who is in favor of prohibitory legislation. He is the medium of communication between Rome and England; the living link of connection between the English Catholic peer and the Irish Catholic bricklayer. The position which he occupies is at all events quite distinctive. There is nobody else in England who could set up the faintest claim to any such place. It would be superfluous to remark that I do not expect the readers of "The Galaxy" to have any sympathy with the opinions, theological or political, of such a man. But the man himself is worthy of profound interest, of study, and even of admiration. He is the spirit, the soul, the ideal of mediæval faith embodied in the form of a living English scholar and gentleman. He represents and illustrates a movement the most remarkable, possibly the most portentous, which has disturbed England and the English Church since the time of Wyckliffe. No one can have any real knowledge of the influences at work in English life to-day, no one can understand the history of the past twenty years, or even pretend to conjecture as to the possibilities of the future, who has not paid some attention to the movement which has Dr. Manning for one of its most distinguished leaders, and to the position and character of Manning himself.

JOHN RUSKIN

Any one who has visited the National Gallery in London must have seen, and seeing must have studied, the contrasted paintings placed side by side of Turner and of Claude. They will attract attention if only because the two Turners are thus placed apart from the rooms used as a Turner Gallery, and containing the great collection of the master's works. The pictures of which I am now speaking are hung in a room principally occupied by the paintings of Murillo. As you enter you are at once attracted by four large pictures which hang on either side of the door opposite. On the right are Turner's "Dido Building Carthage," and Claude's "Embarkation of the Queen of Sheba." On the left are a "Landscape with the Sun Rising" by Turner, and "The Marriage of Isaac and Rebecca" by Claude. Nobody could fail to observe that the pictures are thus arranged for some distinct purpose. They are in fact placed side by side for the sake of comparison and contrast. They are all eminently characteristic; they have the peculiar faults and the peculiar merits of the artists. In the Claudes we have even one of those yellow trunks which are the abomination of the critic I am about to speak of, and one might almost suppose that the Queen of Sheba was embarking for Saratoga. I do not propose to criticise the pictures; but in them you have, to the full, Turner and Claude.

Now in the contrast between these pictures may be found, symbolically at least, the origin and motive of John Ruskin's career. He sprang into literary life simply as a vindicator of the fame and genius of Turner. But as he went on with his task he found, or at least he convinced himself, that the vindication of the great painter was essentially a vindication of all true art. Still further proceeding with his self-imposed task, he persuaded himself that the cause of true art was identical with the cause of truth, and that truth, from Ruskin's point of view, enclosed in the same rules and principles all the morals, all the politics, all the science, industry, and daily business of life. Therefore from an art-critic he became a moralist, a political economist, a philosopher, a statesman, a preacher—anything, everything that human intelligence can impel a man to be. All that he has written since his first appeal to the public has been inspired by this conviction—that an appreciation of the truth in art reveals to him who has it the truth in everything. This belief has been the source of Mr. Ruskin's greatest successes and of his most complete and ludicrous failures. It has made him the admiration of the world one week, and the object of its placid pity or broad laughter the next. A being who could be Joan of Arc to-day and Voltaire's Pucelle to-morrow would hardly exhibit a stronger psychical paradox than the eccentric genius of Mr. Ruskin commonly displays. But in order to understand him, or to do him common justice—in order not to regard him as a mere erratic utterer of eloquent contradictions, poured out on the impulse of each moment's new freak of fancy—we must always bear in mind this fundamental faith of the man. Extravagant as this or that doctrine may be, outrageous as to-day's contradiction of yesterday's assertion may be, yet the whole career is consistent with its essential principles and belief.

Ruskin was singularly fitted by fortune to live for a purpose; to consecrate his life to the cause of art and of what he considered truth. As everybody knows, he was born to wealth so considerable as to allow him to indulge all his tastes and whims, and to write without any regard for money profit. I hardly know of any other author of eminence who in our time has worked with so complete an independence of publisher, public, or paymaster. I do not suppose Ruskin ever wrote one line for money. Some of his works must have brought him in a good return of mere pounds and shillings; but they would have been written just the same if they had never paid for printing; and indeed the author is always spending money on some benevolent crotchet. He was born in London, and he himself attributes much of his early love for nature to the fact that he was "accustomed for two or three years to no other prospect than that of the brick walls over the way," and that he had "no brothers nor sisters nor companions." I question whether anybody not acquainted with London can understand how completely one can be shut in from the pure face of free nature in that vast city. In New York one can hardly walk far in any direction without catching glimpses of the water and the shores of New Jersey or Long Island. But in some of the most respectable middle-class regions of London, you might drudge away or dream away your life and never have one sight of open nature unless you made a regular expedition to find her. Ruskin speaks somewhere of the strange and exquisite delight which the cockney feels when he treads on grass; and every biographical sketch of him recalls that passage in his writings which tells us of the first thing he could remember as an event in his life—his being taken by his nurse to the brow of one of the crags overlooking Derwentwater, and the "intense joy, mingled with awe, that I had in looking through the hollows in the mossy roots over the crag into the dark lake, and which has associated itself more or less with all twining roots of trees ever since." Ruskin travelled much, and at a very early age, through Europe. He became familiar with most of the beautiful show-places of the

European Continent when a boy, and I believe he never extended the sphere of his travels. About his early life there is little to be said. He completed his education at Oxford, and, more successful than Arthur Pendennis, he went in for a prize poem and won the prize. He visited the Continent, more especially Switzerland and Italy, again and again. He married a Scottish lady, and the marriage was not a happy one. I don't propose to go into any of the scandal and talk which the events created; but I may say that the marriage was dissolved without any moral blame resting on or even imputed to either of the parties, and that the lady afterwards became the wife of Mr. Millais. Since then Mr. Ruskin has led a secluded rather than a lonely life. His constitution is feeble; he has as little robustness of *physique* as can well be conceived, and no kind of excitement is suitable for him. Only the other day he sank into a condition of such exhaustion that for a while it was believed impossible he could recover. At one time he used to appear in public rather often; and was ready to deliver lectures on the ethics of art wherever he thought his teaching could benefit the ignorant or the poor. He was especially ready to address assemblages of workingmen, the pupils of charitable institutions for the teaching of drawing. I cannot remember his ever having taken part in any fashionable pageant or demonstration of any kind. Of late he has ceased to show himself at any manner of public meeting, and he addresses his favorite workingmen through the medium of an irregular little publication, a sort of periodical or tract which he calls "Fors Clavigera." Of this publication "I send a copy," he announces, "to each of the principal journals and periodicals, to be noticed or not at their pleasure; otherwise, I shall use no advertisements." The author also informs us that "the tracts will be sold for sevenpence each, without abatement on quantity." I doubt whether many sales have taken place, or whether the reference to purchase in quantity was at all necessary, or whether indeed the author cared one way or the other. In one of these printed letters he says: "The scientific men are busy as ants, examining the sun and the moon and the seven stars; and can tell me all about them, I believe, by this time, and how they move and what they are made of. And I do not care, for my part, two copper spangles how they move nor what they are made of. I can't move them any other way than they go, nor make them of anything else better than they are made." This might sound wonderfully sharp and practical, if, a few pages on, Mr. Ruskin did not broach his proposition for the founding of a little model colony of labor in England, where boys and girls alike are to be taught agriculture, vocal music, Latin, and the history of five cities—Athens, Rome, Venice, Florence, and London. This scheme was broached last August, and it is rather soon yet even to ask whether any steps have been taken to put it into execution; but Mr. Ruskin has already given five thousand dollars to begin with, and will probably give a good deal more before he acknowledges the inevitable failure. Ruskin lives in one of the most beautiful of London suburbs, on Denmark Hill, at the south side of the river, near Dulwich and the exquisite Sydenham slopes where the Crystal Palace stands. Here he indulges his love of pictures and statues, and of rest—when he is not in the mood for unrest—and nourishes philanthropic schemes of eccentric kinds, and is altogether about the nearest approach to an independent, self-sufficing philosopher our modern days have known. Of his life as a private citizen this much is about all that it concerns us to hear.

Twenty-eight years have passed away since Mr. Ruskin leaped into the critical arena, with a spring as bold and startling as that of Edward Kean on the Kemble-haunted stage. The little volume, so modest in its appearance, so self-sufficient in its tone, which the author defiantly flung down like a gage of battle before the world, was entitled "Modern Painters: their Superiority in the Art of Landscape Painting to all the Ancient Masters. By a Graduate of Oxford." I was a boy of thirteen, living in a small provincial town, when this book made its first appearance, but it seems to me that the echo of the sensation it created still rings in my ears. It was a challenge to all established beliefs and prejudices; and the challenge was delivered in the tones of one who felt confident that he could make good his words against any and all opponents. If there was one thing that more than another seemed to have been fixed and rooted in the English mind, it was that Claude and one or two other of the old masters possessed the secret of landscape painting. When, therefore, this bold young dogmatist involved in one common denunciation "Claude, Gaspar Poussin, Salvator Rosa, Ruysdael, Paul Potter, Cavaletto, and the various Van-Somethings and Koek-Somethings, more especially and malignantly those who have libelled the sea," it was no wonder that affronted authority raised its indignant voice and thundered at him. Affronted authority, however, gained little by its thunder. The young Oxford graduate possessed, along with genius and profound conviction, an imperturbable and magnificent self-conceit, against which the surges of angry criticism dashed themselves in vain. Mr. Ruskin, when putting on his armor, had boasted himself as one who takes it off; but in his case there proved to be little rashness in the premature fortification. For assuredly that book overrode and bore down its critics. I need not follow it through its various editions, its successive volumes, its amplifications, wherein at last the original design, the vindication of Turner, swelled into an enunciation and illustration of the true principles of landscape art. Nor do I mean to say that the book carried all its points. Far from it. Claude still lives, and Salvator Rosa has his admirers, among whom most of us are very glad to enroll ourselves; and Ruskin himself has since that time pointed out many serious defects in Turner, and has unsaid a great deal of what he then proclaimed. But if the Oxford graduate had been wrong in every illustration of his principal doctrine, I should still hold that the doctrine itself was true and of inestimable value, and that the book was a triumph. For, I think, it proclaimed and firmly established the true point of view from which we must judge of the art of painting in all its departments. In plain words, Ruskin taught the English public that they must look at nature with their own eyes, and judge of art by the help of nature. Up to the publication of that book England, at least, had been falling into the way of regarding art as a sort of polite school to which it was our duty to endeavor to make nature conform. Conventionality and apathy had sunk apparently into the very souls of men and women. Hardly one in ten thousand ever really saw a landscape, a wave, a ray of the sun as it is. Nobody used his own eyes. Every one was content to think that he saw what the painters told him he saw. Ruskin himself tells us somewhere about a test question which used to be put to young landscape painters by one who was supposed to be a master of the craft: "Where do you put your brown tree?" The question illustrates the whole theory and school of conventionality. Conventionality had decreed first that there are brown trees, and next that there cannot be a respectable landscape without a brown tree. Long after the teaching of Ruskin had well-nigh revolutionized opinion in England, I stood once with a lover of art of the old-fashioned school, looking on one of the most beautiful and famous scenes in England. The tender autumn season, the melancholy woods in the background, the little lake, the half-ruined abbey, did not even need the halo of poetic and romantic association which hung around them in order to render the scene a very temptation, one might have thought, to the true artist. I suggested something of the kind. My companion shook his head almost contemptuously. "You could never make a picture of that," he said. I pressed him to tell me why so picturesque a scene could not be represented somehow in a picture. He did not care evidently to argue with ignorance, and he even endeavored to concede something to my untutored whim. "Perhaps," he began with hesitation, "if one were to put a large dark tree in there to the left, one might make something of it. But no" (he had done his best and could not humor me any further), "it is out of the question; there couldn't be a picture made out of *that*." How could I illustrate more clearly the kind of thing which Ruskin came to put down and did put down in England?

Of course Mr. Ruskin was never a man to do anything by halves, and having once laid down the canon that nature and truth are to be the guides of the artist, he soon began to write and to think as if nature and truth alone were concerned. He seemed to have taken no account of the fact that one great object of art is simply to give delight, and that however natural and truthful an artist may be, yet he is to bear in mind this one purpose of his work, or he might almost as well let it alone. Nature and truth are to be his guides to the delighting of men; to show him how he is to give a delight which shall be pure and genuine. A single inaccuracy as to fact seems at one time to have spoiled all Mr. Ruskin's enjoyment of a painting, and filled him with a feeling of scorn and detestation for it. He denounces Raphael's "Charge to Peter," on the ground that the apostles are not dressed as men of that time and place would have been when going out fishing; and he makes no allowance for the fact, pointed out by M. Taine, that Raphael's design first of all was to represent a group of noble, serious men, majestic and picturesque, and that mere realism entered little into his purpose. It may seem the oddest thing to compare Ruskin with Macaulay, but it is certain that the very kind of objection which the former urges against the paintings of Raphael the latter brings forward against one of the poems of Goldsmith. "What would be thought of a painter," asks Macaulay, "who would mix January and August in one landscape, who would introduce a frozen river into a harvest scene? Would it be a sufficient defence of such a picture to say that every part was exquisitely colored; that the green hedges, the apple trees loaded with fruit, the wagons reeling under the yellow sheaves, and the sunburned reapers wiping their foreheads, were very fine; and that the ice and the boys sliding were also very fine? To such a picture the 'Deserted Village' bears a great resemblance." Now it would indeed be an incomprehensible mistake if a painter were to mix up August and January as Macaulay suggests, or to depict the apostles like a group of Greek philosophers, as in Ruskin's opinion Raphael did. But I venture to think that even the extraordinary blunder mentioned in the first part of the sentence would not necessarily condemn a picture to utter contempt. It was a great mistake to make Dido and Iulus contemporaries; a great mistake to represent angels employing gunpowder for the suppression of Lucifer's insurrection; a great mistake to talk of the clock having struck in the time of Julius Cæsar. Yet I suppose Virgil and Milton and Shakespeare were great poets, and that the very passages in which those errors occur are nevertheless genuine poetry. Now Ruskin criticises Raphael and Claude on precisely the principle which would declare Virgil, Milton, and Shakespeare worthless because of the errors I have mentioned. The errors are errors no doubt, and ought to be pointed out, and there an end. Virgil was not writing a history of the foundation of Carthage. Shakespeare was not describing the social life of Rome under Julius Cæsar. Milton was not a gazetteer of the revolt of Lucifer and his angels. Mr. Ruskin might as well dispose of a sculptured group of Centaurs by remarking that there never were Centaurs, or of the famous hermaphrodite in the Louvre by explaining that hermaphrodites of that perfect order are unknown to physiology. The beauty of color and contour, the effect of graceful grouping, the reach of poetic imagination, the dignity of embodied thought, outlive all such criticism even when in its way it is just, for they bear in themselves the vindication of their existence. But Ruskin's criticism is the legitimate result of the cardinal error of his career—the belief that the morality of art exactly corresponds with the morality of human life; that there is a central law of right and wrong for everything, like Stephen Pearl Andrews's universal science, of which when you have once got the key you can open every lock—which is the solving word of every enigma, the standard by which everything is finally to be judged. I need not show how he followed out that creed and gave it a new application in "The Seven Lamps of Architecture" and the "Stones of Venice." In these masterpieces of eloquent declamation, the building of houses was brought up to be tried according to Mr. Ruskin's self-constructed canons of æsthetic and architectural morality. No one, I venture to think, cares much about the doctrine; everybody is carried away by the eloquence, the originality, and the feeling. Later still Mr. Ruskin applied the same central, all-pervading principle to the condemnation of fluttering ribbons in a woman's bonnet. The stucco of a house he set down as false and immoral, like the painting of a meretricious cheek. His æsthetic transcendentalism soon ceased to have any practical influence. It would be idle to try to persuade English house-builders that the attributes of a building are moral qualities, and that the component parts of a London residence ought to symbolize and embody "action," "voice," and "beauty." It may be doubted whether a single architect was ever practically influenced by the dogmatic eloquence of Mr. Ruskin. In fact the architects, above all other men, rebelled against the books and scorned them. But the books made their way with the public, who, caring nothing about the principles of morality which underlie the construction of houses, were charmed by the dazzling rhetoric, the wealth of gorgeous imagery, the interesting and animated digressions, the frequent flashes of vigorous good sense, and the lofty thought whose only fault was that which least affected the ordinary reader—its utter inapplicability to the practical subject of the books.

It was about the year 1849 that that great secession movement in art broke out to which its leaders chose to give the title of pre-Raphaelite. The principal founder of the movement has since been almost forgotten as an artist, but has come into a sort of celebrity as a poet—Mr. Dante Gabriel Rossetti. With him were allied, it is almost needless to say, the two now famous and successful painters, Holman Hunt and Millais. Decidedly that was the most thriving controversy in the world of art and letters during our time. It was the only battle of schools which could tell us what the war for and against the Sturm-und-Drang school in Germany, the Byron epoch in England, the struggle of the Classicists and Romanticists in France, must have been like. The pre-Raphaelite dispute has long ceased to be heard. Years ago Mr. Ruskin himself, the prophet and apostle of the new sect, described the defection of its greatest pupil as "not a fall, but a catastrophe." Rossetti's sonnets are criticised, but not his paintings. "Are not you still a pre-Raphaelite?" asked an inquisitive person lately of the sonneteer. "I am not an 'ite' of any kind," was the answer; "I am an artist." John Everett Millais is among the most fortunate and fashionable painters of the day. Those who saw his wonderful "Somnambulist" in last season's exhibition of the London Royal Academy would have found in it little of the harsh and "crawling realism" which distinguished the "Beauty in Bricks Brotherhood," as somebody called the rebellious school of twenty years ago. A London comic paper lately published a capital likeness of Mr. Millais, handsome, respectable, tending to stoutness and baldness, and described the portrait as that of the converted pre-Raphaelite. The progress of things was exactly similar to that which goes on in the English political world so often. A fiery young Radical member of Parliament begins by denouncing the Government and the constitution. He wins first notoriety, and then, if he has any real stuff in him, reputation; and then he is invited to office, and he takes it and becomes respectable, wealthy, and fashionable; and his rebellion is all over, and the world goes on just as before. Such was, so far as individuals are concerned, the course of the pre-Raphaelite rebellion; undoubtedly the movement did some good; most rebellions do. It was a protest against the vague and feeble generalizations and the vapid classicism which were growing too common in art. Ruskin himself has happily described the generalized and conventional way of painting trees and shrubs which was growing to be common and tolerated, and which he says was no less absurd than if a painter were to depict some anomalous animal, and defend it as a generalization of pig and pony. Anything which teaches a careful and rigid study of nature must do good. The pre-Raphaelite school was excellent discipline for its young scholars. Probably even those of Millais's paintings which bear on the face of them least evident traces of that early school, might have been far inferior to what they are, were it not for the slow and severe study which the original principles of the movement demanded. The present interest which the secession has for me is less on its own account than because of the vigorous, ingenious, and eloquent pages which Ruskin poured forth in its vindication. He gave it meanings which it never had; found out truth and beauty in its most prosaic details such as its working scholars never meant to symbolize; he explained and expounded it as Johnson did the meaning of the word "slow" in the opening line of the "Traveller," and in fact well-nigh persuaded himself and the world that a new priesthood had arisen to teach the divinity of art. But even he could not write pre-Raphaelitism into popularity and vitality. The common instinct of human nature, which looks to art as the representative of beauty, pathos, humor, and passion, could not be talked into an acceptance of ignoble and ugly realisms. It may be an error to depict a Judean fisherman like a stately Greek philosopher; but error for error, it is far less gross and grievous than to paint the exquisite heroine of Keats's lovely poem as a lank and scraggy spinster, with high cheek bones like one of Walter Scott's fishwives, undressing herself in a green moonlight, and displaying a neck and shoulders worthy of Miss Miggs, and stays and petticoat that bring to mind Tilly Slowboy.

The pre-Raphaelite mania faded away, but Ruskin's vindication endures; just as the letters of Pascal are still read by every one, although nobody cares "two copper spangles" about the controversy which provoked them. Mr. Ruskin's mental energy did not long lie fallow. Turning the bull's-eye of his central theory upon other subjects, he dragged political economy up for judgment. Who can forget the whimsical sensation produced by the appearance in the "Cornhill Magazine" of the letters entitled "Unto this Last"? I need not say much about them. They were a series of fantastic sermons, sometimes eloquent and instructive, sometimes turgid and absurd, on the moral duty of man. They had literally nothing to do with the subject of political economy. The political economists were talking of one thing, and Mr. Ruskin was talking of another and a totally different thing. The value of an article is what it will bring in the market, say the economists. "For shame!" cries Mr. Ruskin; "is the value of her rudder to a ship at sea in a tempest only what it would be bought for at home in Wapping?" So on through the whole, the two disputants talking on quite different subjects. Mr. Ruskin might just as reasonably have interrupted a medical professor lecturing to his class on the effects and uses of castor oil, by telling him in eloquent verbiage that castor oil will not make men virtuous and nations great. Nobody ever said it would; but it is important to explain the properties of castor oil for all that. It would be a grand thing of course if, as Mr. Ruskin prayed, England would "cast all thoughts of possessive wealth back to the barbaric nations among whom they first arose," and leave "the sands of the Indus and the adamant of Golconda" to "stiffen the housings of the charger, and flash from the turban of the slave." This would be ever so much finer than opening banks, making railways (which Mr. Ruskin specially detests), and dealing in stocks. But it has nothing to do, good or bad, with the practical exposition of the economic laws of banking and exchange. It is about as effective a refutation of the political economist's doctrines as a tract from the Peace Society denouncing all war would be to a lecture from Von

Moltke on the practical science of campaigning. But Mr. Ruskin never saw this, and never was disconcerted. He turned to other missions with the firm conviction that he had finished off political economy, as a clever free-thinking London lady calmly announced a few years back to her friends that she had abolished Christianity. Then Mr. Ruskin condemned mines and factories, railways and engines. With all the same strenuous and ornate eloquence he passed sentence on London pantomimes and "cascades of girls," and the too liberal exposure of "lower limbs" by the young ladies composing those cascades. Nothing is too trivial for the omniscient philosopher, and nothing is too great. The moral government of a nation is decreed by the same voice and on the same principles as those which have prescribed the length of a lady's waist-ribbon and the shape of a door-scraper. The first Napoleon never claimed for himself the divine right of intermeddling with and arranging everything more complacently than does the mild and fragile philosopher of Denmark Hill. Be it observed that his absolute ignorance of a subject never deters Mr. Ruskin from pronouncing prompt judgment upon it. It may be some complicated question of foreign, say of American politics, on which men of good ability, who have mastered all the facts and studied the arguments on both sides, are slow to pronounce. Mr. Ruskin, boldly acknowledging that until this morning he never heard of the subject, settles it out of hand and delivers final judgment. Sometimes his restless impulses and his extravagant way of plunging at conclusions and conjecturing facts lead him into unpleasant predicaments. He delivered a manifesto some years ago upon the brutality of the lower orders of Englishmen, founded on certain extraordinary persecutions inflicted on his friend Thomas Carlyle. Behold Carlyle himself coming out with a letter in which he declares that all these stories of persecution were not only untrue, but were "curiously the reverse of truth." Of course every one knew that Ruskin believed them to be true; that he half heard something, conjectured something else, jumped at a conclusion, and as usual regarded himself as an inspired prophet, compelled by his mission to come forward and deliver judgment on a sinful people.

Mr. Ruskin's devotion to Carlyle has been unfortunate for him, as it has for so many others. For that which is reality in Carlyle is only echo and imitation in Ruskin, and the latter has power enough and a field wide enough of his own to render inexcusable the attempt to follow slavishly another man. Moreover, Carlyle's utterances, right or wrong, have meaning and practical application; but when Ruskin repeats them they become meaningless and inapplicable. Mr. Ruskin endeavoring to apply Carlyle's dogmas to the business of art and social life and politics often reminds one of the humorous Hindoo story of the Gooroo Simple and his followers, who went through life making the most outrageous blunders, because they would insist on the literal application of their traditional maxims of wisdom to every common incident of existence. When a self-conceited man ever consents to make another man his idol, even his very self-conceit only tends to render him more awkwardly and unconditionally devoted and servile. The amount of nonsense that Ruskin has talked and written, under the evident conviction that thus and not otherwise would Thomas Carlyle have dealt with the subject, is something almost inconceivable. I never heard of Ruskin taking up any political question without being on the wrong side of it. I am not merely speaking of what I personally consider the wrong side; I am alluding to questions which history and hard fact and the common voice and feeling of humanity have since decided. Against every movement to give political freedom to his countrymen, against every movement to do common justice to the negro race, against every effort to secure fair play for a democratic cause, Mr. Ruskin has peremptorily arrayed himself. "I am a Kingsman and no Mobsman," he declares; and this declaration seems in his mind to settle the question and to justify his vindication of every despotism of caste or sovereignty. To this has his doctrine of æsthetic moral law, to this has his worship of Carlyle, conducted him.

For myself, I doubt whether Mr. Ruskin has any great qualities but his eloquence, and his true, honest love of Nature. As a man to stand up before a society of which one part was fashionably languid and the other part only too busy and greedy, and preach to it of Nature's immortal beauty and of the true way to do her reverence, I think Ruskin had and has a place almost worthy the dignity of a prophet. I think, too, that he has the capacity to fill the place, to fulfil its every duty. Surely this ought to be enough for the work and for the praise of any man. But the womanish restlessness of Ruskin's temperament, combined with the extraordinary self-sufficiency which contributed so much to his success when he was master of a subject, sent him perpetually intruding into fields where he was unfit to labor, and enterprises which he had no capacity to conduct. No man has ever contradicted himself so often, so recklessly, so complacently, as Mr. Ruskin has done. It is absurd to call him a great critic even in art, for he seldom expresses any opinion one day without flatly contradicting it the next. He is a great writer, as Rousseau was—fresh, eloquent, audacious, writing out of the fulness of the present mood, and heedless how far the impulse of to-day may contravene that of yesterday; but as Rousseau was always faithful to his idea of Truth, so Ruskin is ever faithful to Nature. When all his errors and paradoxes and contradictions shall have been utterly forgotten, this his great praise will remain: No man since Wordsworth's brightest days ever did half so much to teach his countrymen, and those who speak his language, how to appreciate and honor that silent Nature which "never did betray the heart that loved her."

CHARLES READE

A few days ago I came by chance upon an old number of an illustrated publication which made a rather brilliant start in London four or five years since, but died, I believe, not long after. It sprang up when there was a sudden rage in England for satirical portraits of eminent persons, and it really showed some skill and humor in this not very healthful or dignified department of art. This number of which I speak has a humorous cartoon called "Companions of the Bath," and representing a miscellaneous crowd of the celebrated men and women of the day enjoying a plunge in the waves at Havre, Dieppe, or some other French bathing-place. There are Gladstone and Disraeli; burly Alexandre Dumas and small, fragile Swinburne; Tennyson and Longfellow; Christine Nilsson and Adelina Patti, the two latter looking very pretty in their tunics and *caleçons*. Most of the likenesses are good, and the attitudes are often characteristic and droll. Mr. Spurgeon flounders and puffs wildly in the waves; Gladstone cleaves his way sternly and earnestly; Mario floats with easy grace. One group at present attracts very special attention. It represents a big, heavy, gray-headed man, ungainly of appearance, whom a smaller personage, bald and neat, is pushing off a plank into the water. The smaller man is Dion Boucicault; the larger is Mr. Charles Reade. This was the time when Reade and Boucicault were working together in "Foul Play." The insinuation of the artist evidently was that Boucicault, always ready for any plunge into the waves of sensationalism, had to give a push to his hesitating companion in order to impel him to the decisive "header."

The artist has been evidently unjust to Mr. Reade. Indeed, one can hardly help suspecting that there must have been some little personal grievance which the pencil was employed to pay off, after the fashion threatened more than once by Hogarth. Mr. Reade is not an Adonis, but this attempt at his likeness is cruelly grotesque and extravagant. Charles Reade is a big, heavy, rugged, gray man; a sort of portlier Walt Whitman, but with closer-cut hair and beard; a Walt Whitman, let us say, put into training for the part of a stout British vestryman. He impresses you at once as a man of character, energy, and originality, although he is by no means the sort of person you would pick out as a typical romancist. But the artist who has delineated him in this cartoon, and who has dealt so fairly, albeit humorously, with

254 | Modern Leaders Being A Series Of Biographical Sketches

Tennyson and Swinburne and Longfellow, must surely have had some spite against the author of "Peg Woffington" when he depicted him as a sort of huge human gorilla. It is in fact for this reason only that I have thought it worth while to introduce an allusion to such a caricature. The caricature is in itself illustrative of my subject. It helps to introduce an inevitable allusion to a weakness of Mr. Charles Reade's which makes for him many enemies and satirists among minor authors, critics, and artists in London. To a wonderful energy and virility of genius and temperament Charles Reade adds a more than feminine susceptibility and impatience when criticism attempts to touch him. With a faith in his own capacity and an admiration for his own works such as never were surpassed in literary history, he can yet be rendered almost beside himself by a disparaging remark from the obscurest critic in the corner of the poorest provincial newspaper. There is no pen so feeble anywhere but it can sting Charles Reade into something like delirium. He replies to every attack, and he discovers a personal enemy in every critic. Therefore he is always in quarrels, always assailing this man and being assailed by that, and to the very utmost of his power trying to prevent the public from appreciating or even recognizing the wealth of genuine manhood, truth, and feeling, which is bestowed everywhere in the rugged ore of his strange and paradoxical character. I am not myself one of Mr. Reade's friends, or even acquaintances; but from those who are, and whom I know, I have always heard the one opinion of the sterling integrity, kindness, and trueheartedness of the man who so often runs counter to all principles of social amenity, and whose bursts of impulsive ill-humor have offended many who would fain have admired.

I said once before in the pages of "The Galaxy," when speaking of another English novelist, that Charles Reade seems to me to rank more highly in America than he does in England. It is only of quite recent years that English criticism of the higher class has treated him with anything like fair consideration. There was a long time of Reade's growing popularity during which such criticism declined altogether to regard him *au sérieux*. Even now he has not justice done to him. But if I cannot help believing that Mr. Reade rates himself far too highly, and announces his opinion far too frankly, neither can I help thinking that English criticism in general fails to do him justice. For a long time he had to struggle hard to obtain a mere recognition. He had during part of his early career the good sense, or the spirit, or the misfortune, according as people choose to view it, to write in one of the popular weekly journals of London which correspond somewhat with the "New York Ledger." I think Charles Dickens described Reade as the one only man with a genuine literary reputation who at that time had ventured upon such a performance. There are indeed men now of undoubted rank in literature who began their career with work like this; but they did not put their names to it, and the world was never the wiser. Reade worked boldly and worked his best, and put his own name to it; and therefore the London press for some time regarded or affected to regard him as an author of that class whose genius supplies weekly instalments of sensation and tremendously high life, to delight the servant girls of Islington and the errand boys of the City. Long after the issue of some of the finest novels Reade has written, the annual publication called "Men of the Time" contained no notice of the author. The odd thing about this is that Reade is an author of the very class which English criticisms of the kind I allude to ought to have delighted to encourage. In the reaction against literary Bohemianism, which of late years has grown up in England, and which the "Saturday Review" may be said to have inaugurated, it became the whim and fashion to believe that only gentlemen with university degrees, only "blood and culture," as the cant phrase was, could write anything which gentlemanly persons could find it worth their while to read. The "Saturday Review" for a long time affected to treat Dickens as a good-humored and vulgar buffoon, with a gift of genius to delight the lower classes. It usually regarded Thackeray as a person made for better things, who had forfeited his position as a gentleman and a university man by descending to literature and to lectures. Now Charles Reade is what in the phraseology of English *caste* would be called a gentleman. He is of good English family; he is a graduate of Magdalen College, Oxford. He is a man of culture and scholarship. His reading, and especially his classical acquirements, I presume to be far wider and deeper than those of Thackeray, who, it need hardly be said, was as Porson or Parr when compared with Dickens. Altogether Reade seems to have been the sort of man whom the "Saturday Review," for example, ought to have taken promptly up and patted on the back and loftily patronized. But nothing of the sort occurred. Reade was treated merely as the clever, audacious concocter of sensational stories. He was hardly dealt with as an artist at all. The reviews only began to come round when they discovered that the public were positively with the new and stirring romancist. What renders this more curious is the fact that the earlier novels were incomparably more highly finished works of art than their successors. "Peg Woffington" and "Christie Johnstone"—the former published so long ago as 1852—seem almost perfect in their symmetry and beauty. "The Cloister and the Hearth" might well-nigh have persuaded a reader that a new Walter Scott was about to arise on the horizon of our literature. All the more recent works seem crude and rough by comparison. They ought to have been the vigorous, uncouth, undisciplined efforts of the author's earlier years. They ought to have led up to the "Cloister and the Hearth" and "Peg Woffington," instead of succeeding them. Yet, if I am not greatly mistaken, it was while he was publishing those earlier and finer products of his fresh intellect that Charles Reade was especially depreciated and even despised by what is called high-class English criticism. He never indeed has had much for which to thank the English critics, and he has never been slow to express his peculiar sense of obligation; but assuredly they treated with greater respect the works which will be soonest forgotten than those on which he may perhaps rest a claim to a more enduring reputation.

The general public, however, soon began to find him out. "Peg Woffington" was a decided success. Its dramatic adaptation is still one of the favorite pieces of the English stage. "It is Never Too Late to Mend" set everybody talking. Reade began to devote himself to exposing this or that social and legal grievance calling for reform, and people came to understand that a new branch of the art of novel-writing was in process of development, the special gift of which was to convert a Parliamentary blue-book into a work of fiction. The treatment of criminals in prisons and in far-off penal settlements, the manner in which patients are dealt with in private lunatic asylums, became the main subject and backbone of the new style of novel, instead of the misunderstandings of lovers, the trials of honest poverty, or the struggles for ascendancy in the fashionable circles of Belgravia. Mr. Reade undoubtedly stands supreme and indeed alone in work of this kind. No man but he can make a blue-book live and yet be a blue-book still. When Dickens undertook some special and practical question, we all knew that we had to look for lavish outpouring of humor, fancy, and eccentricity, for generous pathos, and for a sentimental misapplication or complete elimination of the actual facts. Miss Martineau made dry little stories about political economy; and Disraeli's "Sibyl" is only a fashionable novel and a string of tracts bound up together and called by one name. But Reade takes the hard and naked facts as he finds them in some newspaper or in the report of some Parliamentary commission, and he so fuses them into the other material whereof his romance is to be made up that it would require a chemical analysis to separate the fiction from the reality. You are not conscious that you are going through the boiled-down contents of a blue-book. You have no aggrieved sense of being entrapped into the dry details of some harassing social question. The reality reads like romance; the romance carries you along like reality. No author ever indulged in a fairer piece of self-glorification than that contained in the last sentence of "Put Yourself in his Place": "I have taken a few undeniable truths out of many, and have labored to make my readers realize those appalling facts of the day which most men know, but not one in a thousand comprehends, and not one in a hundred thousand realizes, until fiction—which, whatever you may have been told to the contrary, is the highest, widest, noblest, and greatest of all the arts—comes to his aid, studies, penetrates, digests the hard facts of chronicles and blue-books, and makes their dry bones live." To this object, to this kind of work, Reade seems to have deliberately purposed to devote himself. It was evidently in accordance with his natural tastes and sympathies. He is a man of exuberant and irrepressible energy. He must be doing something definite always. He did actually bestir himself in the case of a person whom he believed to be unjustly confined in a lunatic asylum, as energetically as he makes Dr. Sampson do in "Hard Cash," and with equal success. Most of the scenes he describes, in England at least, have thus in some way fallen in to be part of his own experience. Whatever he undertakes to do he does with a tremendous earnestness. His method of workmanship is, I believe, something like that of Mr. Wilkie Collins, but of course the object is totally different. Wilkie Collins collects all the remarkable police cases and other judicial narratives he can find, and makes what Jean Paul Richter called "quarry" of them—a vast accumulation of materials in which to go digging for subjects and illustrations at leisure. Charles Reade does the same with blue-books and the reports of official inquiries. The author of the "Dead Secret" is looking for perplexing little mysteries of human crime; the author of "Hard Cash" for stories of legal or social wrong to be redressed. I need hardly say, perhaps, that I rank Charles Reade high above Wilkie Collins. The latter can string his dry bones on wires with remarkable ingenuity; the former can, as he fairly boasts, make the dry bones live.

Meanwhile, let us follow out the progress of Mr. Charles Reade as a literary influence. He grows to have a distinct place and power in England quite independently of the reviewers, and at last the very storm of controversy which his books awaken compels the reviewers themselves to take him into account. "It is Never Too Late to Mend" raised a clamor among prison disciplinarians. Years after its publication it is brought out as a drama in London, and its first appearance creates a sort of riot in the Princess's Theatre. Hostile critics rise in the stalls and denounce it; supporters and admirers vehemently defend it; speeches are made on either side. Mr. Reade plunges into the arena of controversy a day or two after in the newspapers, assails one of the critics by name, and charges him with having denounced the piece in the theatre, and applauded his own denunciation in the journal for which he wrote. Some friend of the critic replies by the assertion that one of Mr. Reade's most enthusiastic literary supporters is Mr. Reade's own nephew. All this sort of thing is dreadfully undignified, but it brings an author at all events into public notice, and it did for Mr. Reade what I am convinced he would have disdained to do consciously—it "puffed" his books. An amusing story is told in connection with the production of this drama. An East End manager thought of bringing it out. (The East End, I need hardly say, is the lower and poorer quarter of London.) This manager came and studied the piece as produced at the West End. One of the strong scenes, the sensation scene, was a realistic exhibition of prison discipline. The West End had been duly impressed and thrilled with this scene. But the East End manager shook his head. "It would never do for *me*," he said despondingly to a friend. "Not like the real thing at all. *My* gallery would never stand it. Bless you, my fellows know the real thing too well to put up with *that*."

In this, as in other cases, Mr. Reade's hot temper, immense self-conceit, and eager love of controversy plunged him into discussions from which another man would have shrunk with disgust. He went so far on one occasion as to write to the editor of a London daily paper, threatening that if his books were not more fairly dealt with he would order his publisher to withdraw his advertisements from the offending journal. One can fancy what terror the threat of a loss of a few shillings a month would have had upon the proprietors of a flourishing London paper, and the amount of ridicule to which the bare suggestion of such a thing exposed the irritable novelist. But Reade was, and probably is, incurable. He would keep pelting his peppery little notes at the head of any and everybody against whom he fancied that he had a grievance. I remember one peculiarly whimsical illustration of this weakness, which found its way into print some years ago in London, but which perhaps will be quite new in the United States, and I cannot resist the temptation to reproduce it. Once upon a time, it would seem from the correspondence, Mr. Reade wrote a play called "Gold," which was produced at Drury Lane Theatre. Except from this correspondence I own that I never heard of the play. Subsequently, Mr. Reade presented himself one night at the stage-door of Drury Lane Theatre, and was refused admittance. Mr. Charles Mathews was then performing at the theatre, and Mr. Reade evidently supposed him to have been the manager and responsible for all the arrangements. Therefore he addressed his complaint to the incomparable light comedian, who is as renowned for easy sparkling humor and wit off the stage as for brilliant acting on it. Here is the correspondence; and we shall see how much Mr. Reade took by his motion:

Garrick Club, Covent Garden, November 28.

Dear Sir: I was stopped the other night at the stage-door of Drury Lane Theatre by people whom I remember to have seen at the Lyceum under your reign.

This is the first time such an affront was ever put upon me in any theatre where I had produced a play, and is without

Modern Leaders Being A Series Of Biographical Sketches | 259

precedent unless when an affront was intended. As I never forgive an affront, I am not hasty to suppose one intended. It is very possible that this was done inadvertently; and the present stage-list may have been made out without the older claims being examined.

Will you be so kind as to let me know at once whether this is so, and if the people who stopped me at the stage-door are yours, will you protect the author of "Gold," etc., from any repetition of such an annoyance?

I am, dear sir, yours faithfully,

Charles Reade.

To this imperious demand Mr. Reade received next day the following genial answer:

T. R., Drury Lane, November 29.

Dear Sir: If ignorance is bliss on general occasions, on the present it certainly would be folly to be wise. I am therefore happy to be able to inform you that I am ignorant of your having produced a play at this theatre; ignorant that you are the author of "Gold"; ignorant of the merits of that play; ignorant that your name has been erased from the list at the stage-door; ignorant that it had ever been on it; ignorant that you had presented yourself for admittance; ignorant that it had been refused; ignorant that such a refusal was without precedent; ignorant that in the man who stopped you you recognized one of the persons lately with me at the Lyceum; ignorant that the doorkeeper was ever in that theatre; ignorant that you never forgive an affront; ignorant that any had been offered; ignorant of when, how, or by whom the list was made out, and equally so by whom it was altered.

Allow me to add that I am quite incapable of offering any discourtesy to a gentleman I have barely the pleasure of knowing, and moreover have no power whatever to interfere with Mr. Smith's arrangements or disarrangements; and, with this wholesale admission of ignorance, incapacity, and impotence, believe me

Faithfully yours,

C. T. Mathews.

Charles Reade, Esq.

The correspondence got into print somehow, and created, I need hardly say, infinite merriment in the literary clubs and circles of London. Not all disputes with Charles Reade ended so humorously, for the British novelist is as fond of actions at law as Fenimore Cooper used to be. Thus more than one critic has had to dread the terrors of an action for damages when he has ventured in a rash moment to disparage the literary value of Mr. Reade's teaching. Lately, however, in the case of the "Times," and its attack on "A Terrible Temptation," Mr. Reade adopted the unexpected tone of mild and even flattering remonstrance. Whether he thought it hopeless to alarm the "Times" by any threat of action, or feared that if he wrote a savage letter the journal would not even give him the comfort of seeing it in print, I do not know. But he certainly took a meek tone and endeavored to propitiate, and got rather coarsely rebuked for his pains. People in London were amused to find that he could be thus mild and gentle. I do remember, however, that on one occasion he wrote a letter of remonstrance, which was probably intended to be a kind of rugged compliment to the "Saturday Review," a paper which likewise cares nothing about actions for damages. Usually, however, his tone of argument with his critics is perfervid, and his estimate of himself is exquisitely candid. In one of his manifestoes he assured the world that he never allowed a publisher to offer any suggestions with regard to his story, but simply sold the manuscript in bulk—"*c'est à prendre ou à laisser.*" In another instance he spoke of one of his novels as "floating" the serial publication in which it was making its appearance, and which we were therefore given to understand would have sunk to the bottom but for his coöperation. In short, it is well known in London that Mr. Charles Readers character is disfigured by a self-conceit which amounts to something like mania, and an impatience of criticism which occasionally makes him all but a laughing-stock to the public. Rarely, indeed, in literary history have high and genuine talents been united with such a flatulence of self-conceit.

Probably Reade had reached his highest position just after the publication of "Hard Cash." This remarkable novel, crammed with substance enough to make half a dozen novels, appeared in the first instance in Dickens's "All the Year Round." Dickens himself, if I remember rightly, felt bound to publish a note disclaiming any concurrence in or personal responsibility for the attacks on the private madhouse system, and the whole subject aroused a very lively controversy, wherein, I think, Reade certainly was not worsted. The "Griffith Gaunt" controversy we all remember. I confess that I have no sympathy whatever with the kind of criticism which treats any of Mr. Reade's works as immoral in tendency, and I think the charge was even more absurd when urged against "Griffith Gaunt" than when pressed against the "Terrible Temptation." To me the clear tendency of Reade's novels seems always healthy, purifying, and bracing, like a fresh, strong breeze. I cannot understand how any man or woman could be the worse for reading one of them. They are always novels with a purpose, and I, at least, never could discern any purpose in them which was not honest and sound. I feel inclined to excuse all Reade's vehemence of self-vindication and childish frankness of self-praise when I read some of the attacks against what people try to paint as the immorality of his books. But I need not go into that controversy. Enough to say for my own part that I found "Griffith Gaunt" a grim and dreary book—a tiresome book, in fact; but I saw nothing in it which could with any justice be said to have the slightest tendency to demoralize any reader. I have indeed heard people who are in general fair critics condemn "Adam Bede" as immoral because Hetty is seduced; and I have even heard poor Maggie Tulliver rated as unfit for decent society because she ever allowed even a moment's thought of her cousin's engaged lover to enter her mind. On this principle, doubtless, "Griffith Gaunt" is immoral. There are people in the book who commit sin, and yet are not eaten by lions or bodily carried down below like Don Juan. But if we are to have novels made up only of good people who always do right and the one stock villain who always does wrong, I think the novelist's art cannot too soon be delegated to its only fitting province—the amusement of the nursery. "Griffith Gaunt," however, I regard as a falling off, because it is a sour, unpleasant, and therefore inartistic book. "Foul Play" was a clever *tour de force*, a brilliant thing, made to sell, with hardly more character in it than would suffice for a Bowery melodrama. "Put Yourself in his Place" was a wholesome return to the former style, a marrowy, living blue-book, instinct with power and passion. "A Terrible Temptation" I do not admire. I do not think it immoral, but it hardly calls for any deliberate criticism. Since "Hard Cash" Mr. Reade has, in my opinion, written only one novel which the literary world will care to preserve, and even that one, "Put Yourself in his Place," can hardly be said to add one cubit to his stature.

Mr. Reade has, I believe, rather a passion for dramatic enterprise, and a characteristic faith in his power to turn out a good drama. A season or two back he hired, I am told, a London theatre, in order to have the complete superintendence of the production of one of his novels turned into a drama. I have been assured that the dramatic version was accomplished entirely by himself. If so, I am sure no enemy could have more cruelly damaged the original work. All the character was completely sponged out of it. The one really effective and original personage in the novel did not appear in the play. A number of the most antique and conventional melodramatic situations and surprises were crammed into the piece. All the silly old stage business about mysterious conspiracies carried on under the very ear of the identical personage who never ought to have been allowed to hear them are called in to form an essential feature of the drama. The play, of course, was not successful, although the novel had in it naturally all the elements of a stirring and powerful drama. If Charles Reade really with his own hand converted a vigorous and thrilling story into that limp, languid, and vapid play, it was surely the most awful warning against amateur dramatic enterprise that ever self-conceit could receive undismayed.

Of course we won't rank Mr. Reade as one of the most popular novelists now in England. But his popularity is something very different indeed from that of Dickens, or even from that of Thackeray. In Forster's "Life of Dickens" there is a letter of the great novelist's in which he complains of having been treated (by Bentley, I think) no better than any author who had sold but fifteen hundred copies. I should think the occasions were very rare when Mr. Reade's circulation in England went much beyond fifteen hundred copies. The whole system of publishing is so different in England from that which prevails in America, our fictitious prices and the controlling monopoly of our great libraries so restrict and limit the sale, that a New York reader would perhaps hardly believe how small a number constitute a good circulation for an English novelist. I assume that, speaking roughly, Reade, Wilkie Collins, and Trollope may be said to have about the same kind of circulation—almost immeasurably below Dickens, and below some such abnormal sale as that of "Lothair" or "Lady Audley's Secret," but much above even the best of the younger novelists. I venture to think that not one of these three popular and successful authors may be counted on to reach a circulation of two thousand copies. Probably about eighteen hundred copies would be a decidedly good thing for one of Charles Reade's novels. Of the three, I should say that Wilkie Collins has the most eager readers; that Trollope's novels take the highest place in what is called "society"; and that Reade's rank the best among men of brains. But there is so wide a difference between the popularity of Dickens and that of Reade that it seems almost absurd to employ the same word to describe two things so utterly unlike. It is, indeed, a remarkable proof of Reade's power and success that, setting out as he always does to tell a story which shall convey information and a purpose of some practical kind, he can get any sort of large circulation at all. For one great charm and excellence of our library system is that it creates a huge class of regular, I might almost say professional, novel-readers, who subscribe to Mudie's by the year, want to get all the reading they can out of it, and instinctively shudder at the thought of any novel that is weighted by solid information and overtaxing thought. This is the class for whom and by whom the circulating libraries exist, and Mr. Reade deserves the full credit of having utterly disregarded them, or rather boldly encountered them, and at least to some extent compelled them to read him.

Mr. Reade's position as a novelist may be adjudged now as safely as ever a novelist's place can be fixed by a contemporary generation. He is nearly sixty years old, and he has written about a dozen novels. It is not likely that he will ever write anything which could greatly enhance the estimate the public have already formed of him; and no future failures could affect his past success. I think his career is, therefore, fairly and fully before us. We know how singularly limited his *dramatis personæ* are. He marches them on and off the stage boldly ever so often, and by a change of dresses every now and then he for a while almost succeeds in making us believe that he has a very full company at his command. But we soon get to know every one by sight, and can swear to him or her, no matter by what name or garb disguised. We know the sweet, impulsive, incoherent heroine, who is always contradicting herself and saying what she ought not to say and does not mean to say; who now denounces the hero, and then falls upon his neck and vows that she loves him more than life. This young woman is sometimes Julia and sometimes Helen and sometimes Grace; she now is exiled for a while on a lonely island, and even she is carried away by a flood; but in every case she is just the same girl rescued by the same hero. That hero is always a being of wonderful mechanical and scientific knowledge of some kind or other, whether as Captain Dodd he makes love to Lucy Fountain, or as Henry Little he captivates Grace Carden, or as the gentleman in "Foul Play" he cures the heroine of consumption and builds island huts better than Robinson Crusoe. Then we have the rough, clever, eccentric personage, Dr. Sampson or Dr. Amboyne, whose business principally is to act a part like that of Herr Mittler in Goethe's novel, and help the characters of the book through every difficulty. Then we have the white-livered sneak, the villain of the book when he is bad enough for such a part; the Coventry of "Put Yourself in his Place"; I forget what his name is in "Foul Play." These are the puppets which principally make up the show. Very vigorously and cleverly do they dance, and capitally do they imitate life; but there are so very few of them that we grow a little tired of seeing them over and over again. Indeed, Charles Reade's array of characters sometimes reminds us of the simple system of Plautus, in which we have for every play the same types of people—the rather stingy father, the embarrassed lover, the clever comic slave, and so forth. It cannot be said that Reade has added a single character to fiction. He understands human nature, or at least such types of it as he habitually selects, very well, and he draws vigorously his figures and groups; but he has discovered nothing fresh, he has rescued no existence from the commonplace and evanescent realistics of life, to be preserved immortal in a work of art. Not one of his characters is cited in ordinary conversation or in the writings of journalists. Nobody quotes from him unless in reference to some one of the stirring social topics which he has illustrated, and even then only as one would quote from a correspondent of the "Times." Every educated man and woman in England is assumed, as a matter of course, to be familiar with the works of George Eliot; but nobody is necessarily assumed to have read Charles Reade. That educated people do read him and do admire him is certain; but it is quite a matter of option with them to read him or let him alone so far as society and public opinion are concerned. There are certain tests and evidences of a novelist's having attained a front-rank place in England which are unmistakable. They are purely social, may be only superficial, and will neither one way nor the other affect the views of foreign critics or of posterity; but they are decisive as far as England is concerned. Among them I shall mention two or three. One is the fact that writers in the press allude to some of his characters without feeling bound to explain in whose novel and what novel the characters appear. Another is the fact that artists voluntarily select from his works subjects for paintings to be sent to the Royal Academy's annual exhibition or elsewhere. A third is the fact that articles about him, not formal reviews of a work just published, appear pretty often in the magazines. Now, whatever may be the genius and merits of an author, I think he cannot be said to have attained the front rank in English public opinion unless he can show these evidences of success; and, so far as I know, Mr. Reade cannot show any of them. For myself, I do not believe that Mr. Reade ever could under any circumstances have become a really great novelist. All the higher gifts of imagination and all the richer veins of humor have been denied to him. Not one gleam of poetic fancy ever seems to have floated across the nervous Saxon of his style. He is a powerful story-teller, who has a manly purpose in every tale he tells, and that is all. That surely is a great deal. No one tells a story more thrillingly. Once you begin to listen, you cannot release yourself from the spell of the *raconteur* until all be done. A strong, healthy air of honest and high purpose breathes through nearly all the stories. An utter absence of cant, affectation, and sham distinguishes them. A surprising variety of descriptive power, at once bold, broad, and realistic, is one of their great merits. Mr. Reade can describe a sea-fight, a storm, the forging of a horseshoe, the ravages of an inundation, the trimming of a lady's dress, the tuning of a piano, with equal accuracy and apparent zest. I once heard an animated discussion in a literary club as to whether the scrap of minute description was artistic and effective or absurd and ludicrous which makes us acquainted with the fact that when Henry Little dragged Grace Carden out of the raging flood, the force of the water washed away the heroine's stockings and garters and left her barefoot. Some irreverent critics would only laugh at the gravity with which the author detailed this important circumstance. Others, however, insisted that this little touch, so homely, and to the profane mind so exceedingly ridiculous, was necessary and artistic;

that it heightened the effect of the great word-picture previously shown by the force of its practical and circumstantial reality. However this momentous controversy may settle itself in the estimation of readers, it cannot be denied that some at least of Reade's success is due to the courage and self-reliance which will brave the risk of being ridiculous for the sake of being real and effective. Indeed, Mr. Reade wants no quality which is necessary to make a powerful story-teller, while he is distinguished from all mere story-tellers by the fact that he has some great social object to serve in nearly everything he undertakes to detail. More than this I do not believe he is, nor, despite the evidences of something yet higher which were given in "Christie Johnstone" and "The Cloister and the Hearth," do I think he ever could have been. He is a magnificent specimen of the modern special correspondent, endowed with the additional and unique gift of a faculty for throwing his report into the form of a thrilling story. But it requires something more than this, something higher than this, to make a great novelist whom the world will always remember. Mr. Reade is unsurpassed in the second class of English novelists, but he does not belong to the front rank. His success has been great in its way, but it is for an age and not for time.

THE EXILE-WORLD OF LONDON

Leicester Square and the region that lies around it are conventionally regarded as the exile quarter of London. The name of Leicester square suggests the idea of an exile, as surely and readily, even to the mind of one who has never looked on the mournful and decaying enclosure, as the name of Billingsgate does that of fish-woman, or the name of the Temple that of a law-student. Yet, if a stranger visiting London thinks he is likely to see any exile of celebrity, while pacing the streets which branch off Leicester square, he will be almost as much mistaken as if he were to range Eastcheap in the hope of meeting the wild Prince and Poins.

Many a conspiracy has had its followers and understrappers in the Leicester square region; but the great conspirators do not live there any more. The place is falling, falling; the foreign and distinctive character of the population remains as marked as ever, but the foreigners whom London people would care to see are not to be found there any longer. The exiles who have made part of history, whose names are on record, do not care for Leicester square. They are to be found in Kensington, in Brompton, in Hampstead and Highgate; in the Regent's Park district; a few in Bloomsbury, a few in Mayfair. A marble slab and an inscription now mark the house in King street, St. James's, where Louis Napoleon lodged; and there is a house in Belgrave square dear to all true Legitimists, where the Count de Chambord ("Henri Cinq") received Berryer and his brother pilgrims. Only poor exiles herd together now in London. Only poverty, I suppose, ever causes nationalities to herd together anywhere. The men who group around Leicester square are the exiles without a fame; the subterranean workers in politics; the men who come like shadows, and so depart; the men whose names are writ in water, even though their life-paths may have been marked in blood.

Living in London, I had of late years many opportunities of meeting with the exiles of each class. I know few men more to be pitied than the great majority of those who make up the latter or Leicester square section. On the other hand, I should say that few men, indeed, are more to be envied by any of their fellow-creatures who love to be courted and "lionized," than the political exiles of great name who come to London and do not stay too long there.

Far away as the days of Thaddeus of Warsaw and the conventional and romantic type of exile now seem, there is still a fervent yearning in British society toward the representative of any Continental nationality which happens to be oppressed. No man had ever before received such a welcome in London as Kossuth did; but Kossuth stayed too long, became domesticized and familiarized, and society in London likes its lions to be always new and fresh. Moreover, the late Lord Palmerston, a warm patron of exiles when the patronage went no further than an invitation to a dinner or an evening party, set his face against Kossuth from the first; and polite society soon took the hint.

The man who most completely conquered all society, even the very highest, in London, during my recollection, was the man who probably cared least about it, and who certainly never sought to win the favor of fashion—I mean, of course, Garibaldi. To this day I am perfectly unable to understand the demeanor of the British peerage toward Garibaldi, when he visited London for a few days some years ago. The thing was utterly unprecedented and inexplicable. The Peerage literally rushed at him. He was beset by dukes, mobbed by countesses. He could not by any human possibility have so divided his day as to find time for breakfasting and dining with one-fifth of the noble hosts who fought and scrambled for him. It was a perpetual torture to his secretaries and private friends to decide between the rival claims of a Prime Minister and a Prince of the blood; an Archbishop and a Duchess; the Lord Chancellor and the leader of the Opposition. The Tories positively outdid the Whigs in the struggle for the society of the simple seaman, the gallant guerilla. The oddest thing about the business was, that three out of every four of these noble personages had always previously spoken of Garibaldi—when they did speak of him at all—with contempt and dislike, as a buccaneer and a filibuster.

What did it mean? Was it a little comedy? Was it their fun? Was it a political *coup de théâtre*, to dodge the Radicals and the workingmen out of their favorite hero? Certainly some of Garibaldi's friends suspected something of the kind, and were utterly bewildered and confounded by the unexpected rush of aristocratic admirers, who beset the hero from the moment he touched the shore of England.

It was a strange sight, not easily to be forgotten, to see the manner in which Garibaldi sat among the dukes and marchionesses—simple, sweet, arrayed in the calm, serene dignity of a manly, noble heart. There was something of Oriental stateliness in the unruffled, imperturbable, bland composure, with which he bore himself amid the throng of demonstrative and titled adulators. I do not think he believed in the sincerity of half of it, any more than I did, but he showed no more sign of distrust or impatience than he did of gratified vanity.

The thing ended in a quarrel between the Aristocracy and the Democracy, between Belgravia and Clerkenwell, for the custody of the hero, and Garibaldi escaped somehow back to his island during the squabble. But I think Lady Palmerston let the mask fall for a moment, when, growing angry at the assurance of Garibaldi's humbler friends, and perhaps a little tired of the whole business, she told some gentlemen of my acquaintance, that quite too much work had been made about a person who, after all, was only a respectable brigand. This was said (and it *was* said) at the very meridian of the day of noble homage to the Emancipator of Sicily.

Garibaldi has never since returned to England. Should he ever do so, he will find himself unembarrassed by the attentions of the Windsor uniform and Order of the Garter. The play, however it was got up, or whatever its object, was played out long ago. But the West End is, as a rule, very fond of distinguished exiles, when they come and go quickly; and Lord Palmerston's drawing-room was seldom without a representative of the class. No man ever did less for any great cause than Lord Palmerston did; but he liked brilliant exiles, and, perhaps, more particularly the soldierly than the scholarly class. Such a man as the martial, dashing, adventurous General Türr, for example, was the kind of refugee that Lord and Lady Palmerston especially favored.

Many English peers have, indeed, quite a *spécialité* in the way of patronizing exiles; but, of course, in all such cases the exile must have a name which brings some gratifying distinction to his host. He must be somebody worth pointing out to the other guests. I know that many Continental refugees have chafed at all this, and some have steadily held aloof from it, and declined to be shown off for the admiration of a novelty-hunting crowd. Many, too, have been deceived by it; have mistaken such idle attention for profound and practical sympathy, and have thought that two or three peers and half a dozen aristocratic petticoats could direct the foreign policy of England. They have swelled with hope and confidence; have built their plans and based their organizations on the faith that Park Lane meant the British government, and that the politeness of a Cabinet Minister was as good as the assistance of a British fleet; and have found out what idiots they were in such a belief, and have gone nigh to breaking their hearts accordingly. Indeed, the readiness of all classes in England to rush at any distinguished exile, and become effusive about himself and his cause is very often—or, at least, used to be—a cruel kindness, sure to be misunderstood and to betray—a love that killed.

Nothing could, in its way, have been more unfortunate and calamitous than the outburst of popular enthusiasm in England about the Polish insurrection four years ago. Some of the Polish leaders living in London were completely deceived by it, and finally believed that England was about to take up arms in their cause. An agitation was got up, outside the House of Commons, by an earnest, well-meaning gentleman, who really believed what he said; and inside the House by a bustling, quickwitted, political adventurer, who certainly ought not to have believed what he said. This latter gentleman actually went out to Cracow, in Austrian Poland, and was received there with wild demonstrations of welcome as a representative of the national will of England and the precursor of English intervention. The Polish insurrection went on; and England wrote a diplomatic note, which Russia resented as a piece of impertinence; and there England's sympathy ended. "I think," said a great English Liberal to me, "that every Englishman who helped to encourage these poor Poles and give them hope of English help, has Polish blood on his hands." I think so, too.

I have always thought that Felice Orsini was in some sort a victim to the kind of delusion which English popularity so easily fosters. I met Orsini when he came to England, not very long before the unfortunate and criminal attempt of the Rue Lepelletier; and I was much taken, as most people who met him were, by the simplicity, sweetness, and soldierly frankness of his demeanor. He delivered some lectures in London, Manchester, Liverpool, and other large towns, on his own personal adventures—principally his escape from prison—and though he had but a moderate success as a lecturer, he was surrounded everywhere by well-meaning and sympathizing groups, the extent of whose influence and the practical value of whose sympathy he probably did not at first quite understand. He certainly had, at one time, some vague hopes of obtaining for the cause of Italian independence a substantial assistance from England. A short experience cured him of that dream; and I fancy it was then that he formed the resolution which he afterward attempted so desperately to carry out. I think, from something I heard him say once, that Mazzini had endeavored to enlighten him as to the true state of affairs in England, and the real value of the sort of sympathy which London so readily offers to any interesting exile. But I do not believe Mazzini's advice had much influence over Orsini. Indeed, the latter, at the time I saw him, had but little respect for Mazzini. He spoke with something like contempt of the great conspirator. It would have been well for Orsini if he had, in one thing at least, followed the counsels of Mazzini. People used to say, some years ago, that odious and desperate as Orsini's attempt was, it at least had the merit of frightening Louis Napoleon into active efforts on behalf of Italy. There was so much about Orsini that was worthy and noble that one would be glad to regard him as even in his crime the instrument of good to the country he loved so well. But documentary and other evidence has made it clear since Orsini's death that the negotiations which ended in

Solferino and Villafranca were begun before Orsini had ever planned his murderous enterprise. The fact is, that, during the Crimean war, Cavour first tried England on the subject, through easy-going and heedless Lord Clarendon—who hardly took the trouble to listen to the audacious projects of his friend—and then turned to France, where quicker and shrewder ears listened to what he had to say.

I have spoken of Orsini's contempt for Mazzini. Such a feeling toward such a man seems quite inexplicable. Many men detest Mazzini; many men distrust him; many look up to him as a prophet, and adore him as a chief; but I am not able to understand how any one can think of him with mere contempt. For myself, I find it impossible to contemplate without sadness and without reverence that noble, futile career; that majestic, melancholy dream. But it must be owned that an atmosphere of illusion sheds itself around Mazzini wherever he goes. I believe the man himself to be the very soul of truth and honor; and yet I protest I would not take, on any political question, the unsupported testimony of any devotee of Mazzini to any fact whatsoever. Mazzini's own faith is so sublimely transcendental, so utterly independent of realities and of experience, that I sincerely believe the visions of the opium-eater are hardly less to be relied on than the oracles and opinions of the great Italian. And yet the force of his character, the commanding nature of his genius, are such that his followers become more Mazzinian than Mazzini himself. There is something a good deal provoking about the manner of the minor followers of Mazzini. I mean in England. I do not speak of such men as my friend, Mr. Stansfeld, now a Lord of the Treasury, or my friend, Mr. P. A. Taylor, M. P. These are men of ability and men of the world, whose enthusiasm and faith, even at their highest, are under the control of practical experience and the discipline of public life. But I speak of the minor and less responsible admirers, the men and women who accept oracle as fact, aspiration as experience, the dream as the reality. The calm, self-satisfied way in which they deal with contemporary history, with geography, with statistics, with possibilities and impossibilities, in the hope of making you believe what they firmly believe—that Italy could, if only she had proclaimed herself Republican, have driven the Austrians into the sea in 1859, and the French across the Alps in 1860, while at the same time quietly kicking Pope, Bourbon, and Savoy out of throned existence. The confident and imperturbable assurance with which they can do all this—and I have never met with any genuine devotee of Mazzini who could not—is something to make one bewildered rather than merely impatient. For it is true in politics as in literature or in fashion, the admiring imitator reproduces only the defects, the weaknesses, the mannerisms and mistakes of the original. Mazzini himself is, I need hardly say, a singularly modest and retiring man. While he lived in London, he shrank from all public notice, and was seen only by his friends and followers. He sought out nobody. "Sir," said Mr. Gladstone, addressing the Speaker of the House of Commons, one night, when a fierce and factious attack was made on Mr. Stansfeld as a follower of the great exile, "I never saw Signor Mazzini." Yet Gladstone was by far the most prominent and influential of all the English sympathizers with the cause of Italian liberty. One would have thought it impossible for such a man as Mazzini to live for years in the same city with Gladstone without the two ever chancing to meet. But for the modest seclusion and shrinking way of Mazzini, such a thing would, indeed, have been impossible.

Louis Blanc is, perhaps, the only Revolutionary exile who, in my time, has been everywhere and permanently popular in London society. The fate of a political exile in a place like London usually is to be a lion among one clique and a *bête noir* in another. But Louis Blanc has been accepted and welcomed everywhere, although he has never compromised or concealed one iota of his political opinions. I think one explanation, and, perhaps, *the* explanation of this somewhat remarkable phenomenon, is to be found in the fact that Louis Blanc never for an hour played the part of a conspirator. He seems to have honorably construed his place in English society to be that of one to whom a shelter had been given, and who was bound not to make any use of that shelter which could embarrass his host. In London he ceased to be an active politician. He refused to exhibit himself *en victime*. He appealed to no public pity. He made no parade of defeat and exile. He went to work steadily as a literary man, and he had the courage to be poor. When he appeared in public it was simply as a literary lecturer. He was not very successful in that capacity. At least, he was not what the secretary of a lyceum would call a success. He gave a series of lectures on certain phases of society in Paris before the great Revolution, and they were attended by all the best literary men in London, who were, I think, unanimous in their admiration of the power, the eloquence, the brilliancy which these pictures of a ghastly past displayed. But the general public cared nothing about the *salons* where wit, and levity, and wickedness prepared the way for revolution; and I heard Louis Blanc pour out an *apologia* (I don't mean an apology) for Jean Jacques Rousseau in language of noble eloquence, and with dramatic effect worthy of a great orator, in a small lecture-room, of which three-fourths of the space was empty. Since that time he has delivered lectures occasionally at the request of mechanics' institutions and such societies; but he has not essayed a course of lectures on his own account. Everyone knows him; everyone likes him; everyone admires his manly, modest character and his uncompromising Republicanism. Lately he has lived more in Brighton than in London; but wherever in England he happens to be, he lives always as a simple citizen; has never been raved about like Kossuth, or denounced like Mazzini; and has occupied himself wholly with his historical labors and his letters to a Paris newspaper.

Another exile of distinction who lived for years in London apart from politics and heedless of popular favor was Ferdinand Freiligrath, the German poet. Freiligrath had to leave Prussia because of his political poems and writings. He had undergone one prosecution and escaped conviction, but Prussia was not then (twenty years ago) a country in which to run such risks too often. So Freiligrath went to Amsterdam and thence to London. He lived in London for many years, and acted as manager of a Swiss banking-house. His life was one of entire seclusion from political schemes or agitations. He did not even, like his countryman and friend, Gottfried Kinkel, take any part in public movements among the Germans in London—and he certainly never went about society and the newspapers blowing his own trumpet, and keeping his name always prominent, like the egotistical and inflated Karl Blind. Indeed, so complete was Freiligrath's retirement that many Englishmen living in London, who delighted in some of his poems—his exquisite, fanciful, melodious "Sand Songs" his glowing Desert poems, his dreamy, delightful songs of the sea, and his burning political ballads—were quite amazed to find that the poet himself had been a resident of their own city for nearly half a lifetime. Freiligrath has now at last returned to his own country. His countrymen invited him home, and raised a national tribute to enable him to give up his London engagement and withdraw altogether from a life of mere business. In a letter I lately received from Freiligrath's daughter (a young lady of great talent and accomplishments, recently married in London), I find it mentioned that Freiligrath expected soon to receive a visit from Longfellow in Germany—the first meeting of these two old friends for a period of some five-and-twenty years.

Alexander Herzen, the famous Russian exile, the wittiest of men, endowed with the sharpest tongue and the best nature, has left us. For many years he lived in London and published his celebrated *Kolokol*—"The Bell," which rang so ominously and jarringly in the ears of Russian autocracy. He has now set up his staff in Geneva, a little London in its attractiveness to exiles; and his arrowy, flashing wit gleams no longer across the foreign world of the English metropolis. I do not know how long Herzen had lived in London, but I fancy the difficulties of the English language must have proved insurmountable to him—a strange phenomenon in the case of a Russian. Certainly he never, so far as I am aware, either spoke or wrote English.

The latest exile of great mark whom we had among us in London was General Prim. When his attempt at revolution in Spain failed some two years ago, Prim went into Belgium. There some pressure was brought to bear upon him by the Ministry, in consequence, no doubt, of certain pressure brought to bear by France, and Prim left Brussels and came to live in London. He lived very quietly, made no show of himself in any way, and was no doubt hard at work all the time making preparation for what has since come to pass. To all appearance he had an easy and careless sort of life, living out among his private friends, going to the races and going to the opera. But he was incessantly planning and preparing; and he told many Englishmen candidly what he was preparing for. There were many men in London who were looking out for the Spanish Revolution months before it came, on the faith of Prim's earnest assurances that it was coming. So much has of late been written about Prim that his personal appearance and manner must be familiar to most readers of newspapers and magazines. I need only say that there is in private much less of the *militaire* about him than one who had not actually met him would be inclined to imagine. He is small, neat, and even elegant in dress, very quiet and perhaps somewhat languid in manner, looking wonderfully young for his years, and without the slightest tinge of the Leicester square foreigner about him. He is rather the foreigner of Regent street and the stalls of the opera house—any one who knows London will at once understand the difference. Prim impressed me with a much greater respect for his intellect, even from a literary man's point of view, than I had had before meeting and conversing with him. I think those who regard him as a mere *sabreur*, the ordinary Spanish leader of a successful military revolution, are mistaken. His animated and epigrammatic conversation seemed to me to be inspired and guided by an intellectual depth and a power of observation and reflection such as I at least was not prepared to find in the dashing soldier of the Moorish campaign.

There is one class of the obscure exiles, different from both the favored and the poorest, whose existence has often puzzled me. A political question of moment begins to disturb the European continent. Immediately there turns up in London, and presents himself at your door (supposing you are a journalist with acknowledged sympathies for this or that side of the question) a mysterious and generally shabby-looking personage, who professes to know all about it, and volunteers to supply you with the most authentic information and the most trustworthy "appreciation" of any events that may transpire. He wants no money; his information is given for the sake of "the cause." You ask for credentials, and he produces recommendations which quite satisfy you that his objects are genuine, although, oddly enough, the persons who recommend him do not seem to have anything whatever to do with the cause he represents. He comes, for example, to talk about the affairs of Roumania, and he brings letters and vouchers from literary friends in Paris. He professes to be an emissary from the Cretans, and his recommendations are from a Manchester cotton-firm. Anyhow, you are satisfied; you ask no explanations; you assume that your Paris or Manchester friends have enlarged the sphere of their sympathies since you saw them last, and you repose confidence in your new acquaintance. You are right. He brings you information, the most rapid, the most surprising, the most accurate. Such a man I knew during the Schleswig-Holstein agitation, which ended in the Danish war of four years since. He was a Prussian—a waif of the Berlin rising of 1848. Was he in the confidence of Von Beust, and Bismarck, and Palmerston, and all the rest of them? I venture to doubt it; yet if he had been, he could hardly have been more quick and accurate in all the information he brought me. Evening after evening he brought a regular minute of the proceedings of the day at the Conference of London, which was sitting with closed doors, and pledged to profoundest secrecy. Perhaps this was only guesswork! Here is one illustration. The Conference was held because some of the European Great Powers, England and France especially, desired to save Denmark from a struggle against the immeasurably superior force of Prussia and Austria. A certain proposal was to be made to the Conference by England and France on the part of Denmark. So much we all knew. One evening my friend came to me, and bade me announce to the world that the proposal had been made that day, and indignantly rejected—by Denmark! The story seemed preposterous, but I relied on my friend. Next day I was laughed at; my news was denounced and repudiated. The day after it was proved to be true—and Denmark went to war.

The last time I saw my friend was in the spring of 1866. He came to tell me that Prussia had resolved—at least that Bismarck had resolved—on war with Austria. "Stick to that statement," he said, "whatever anybody may say to the contrary—unless Bismarck resigns." I took his advice. At this time I am convinced that the English government had not the least idea that a war was really coming. The war came; but I never saw my friend any more.

Another of my mysterious acquaintances was an old, white-haired, grave, placid man who turned up in London during the early part of the French occupation of Mexico. He was a passionate Republican and anti-Bonapartist. He was a friend and apparently a confidant of Juarez, and was thoroughly identified with the interests of the Republicans in Mexico, although himself a Frenchman. I doubt whether I have ever met with a finer specimen of the courtly old gentleman, the class now beginning to disappear even in France, than this mysterious friend of the Mexican Republic. He might have been fresh from the Faubourg St. Germain, such was the grave, dignified, and somewhat melancholy grace of his courtly bearing. Yet he had evidently lived long in Mexico, and he was an ardent Republican of the red tinge; there was something of the old *militaire* about him, too, which lent a certain strength to his bland and placid demeanor. I never quite knew what he was doing in London. He was not what is called an "unofficial representative" of Juarez (at this time diplomatic relations between England and Mexico were of course broken off) for he never seemed to go near any of our ministers or diplomatists, and his only object appeared to be to supply accurate information to one or two Liberal journals which he believed to be honestly inclined toward the right side of every question. His information was always accurate, his estimate of a critical situation was always justified by further knowledge and the progress of events, his predictions always came true. He looked like a poor man, indeed, like a needy man; yet he never seemed to want for money, and he neither sought nor would have any compensation for the constant and valuable information he afforded. His knowledge of European and American politics was profound; and though he spoke not one word of English he seemed to understand all the daily details of our English political life. He was a constant visitor to me (always at night and late) during the progress of the Mexican struggle. When the Mexican Empire was nearly played out he came and told me the end was very, very near, and that in the event of Maximilian's being captured it would be impossible for Juarez to spare his life. He did not tell me that he was at once returning to Mexico, but I presume that he did immediately return, for that was the last I saw or heard of him.

During the quarrels between the Prussian Representative Chamber and Count von Bismarck (before the triumph of Sadowa had condoned for the offences of the great despotic Minister), I had a visit, one night, from a mysterious, seedy, snuffy old German. He came, he said, to develop a grand plan for the extinction of the Junker or Feudal party. Why he came to develop it to me I do not know, as it will presently be seen that I could hardly render it any practical assistance. It was, like all grand schemes, remarkably simple in its nature. Indeed, it was literally and strictly Captain Bobadil's immortal plan; although my German visitor indignantly repudiated the supposition that he had borrowed it, and declared, I believe, with perfect truth, that he had never heard of Captain Bobadil before. The plan was simply that a society should be formed of young and devoted Germans who should occupy themselves in challenging and killing off, one by one, the whole Junker party. My friend made his calculations very calmly, and he did not foolishly or arrogantly assume that the swordsmanship of his party must needs be always superior to that of their adversaries. No; he counted that there would be a certain number of victims among his Liberal heroes, and made, indeed, a large allowance, left a broad margin for such losses. But this, in no wise affected the success of his plan. The Liberals, were many, the Junkers few. It would simply be a matter of time and calculation. Numbers must tell in the end. A day must come when the last Junker would fall to earth—and then Astrea would return. Now the man who talked in this way was no lunatic. He had nothing about him, except his plan, which denoted mental aberration. His scheme apart, he was as steady and prosy an old German as you could meet under the lindens of Berlin or on the Lutherplatz of Königsberg. He was, moreover, as earnest, argumentative, and profoundly wearisome over his project as if he were expounding to an admiring class of students the relations of the Ego and Non-Ego. I need hardly add that one single beam, even the faintest, of a sense of the ridiculous, never shone in upon him during his long and eloquent exposition of the patriotic virtue, the completeness and the mathematical certainty of his ingenious project.

Let me close my random reminiscences with one recollection of a sadder nature. Some three or four years ago there came to London from Naples an Italian of high education and character—a lawyer by profession; a passionate devotee of Italian unity, and filled naturally with a hatred of the expelled Bourbons. This gentleman had discovered in one of the Neapolitan prisons a number of instruments of torture—rusty, hideous old iron chairs, and racks, and screws, and "cages of silence," and such other contrivances. He became the possessor of these, and he obtained from the new government a certificate of the genuineness of his treasure-trove—that is to say, a certificate that the things were actually found in the place where the owner professed to have found them. The Italian authorities, of course, could say nothing as to whether they had or had not been used as instruments of torture in any modern reign. They may have lain rusting there since hideous old days when the Inquisition was a fashionable institution; they may have been used—public opinion and Mr. Gladstone said things as horrible had been done—in the blessed reign of good King Bomba. The Neapolitan lawyer firmly believed that they had been so used; and he became inspired with the idea that to take these instruments, first to London and then to the United States, and exhibit them, and lecture on them, would arouse such a tempest of righteous indignation among all peoples, free or enslaved, as must sweep kingcraft and priestcraft off the earth. This idea became a faith with him. He brought his treasure of rusty iron to London, and proposed to take a great hall and begin the work of his mission. I endeavored to dissuade him (he had brought some introductions to me). I told him frankly that, just at that time, public opinion in London was utterly indifferent to the Bourbons. The fervor of interest about the Neapolitan Revolution had gone by; people were tired of Italy, and wanted something new; the Polish insurrection was going on; the great American Civil War was occupying public attention; London audiences cared no more about the crimes of the Bourbons than about the crimes of the Borgias. He was not to be dissuaded. He really believed at first that he could induce some great English orator, Gladstone or Bright, to deliver lectures on those instruments and the guilt of the system which employed them. Then he became more moderate, and applied to this and that professional lecturer—in vain. No one would have anything to do with a project so obviously doomed to failure—he himself spoke no English. At last he induced a lady who was somewhat ambitious of a public career, to lecture for him; and he took a great hall for a series of nights, and advertised largely, and went to great expense. I believe he staked all he had in money or credit on the success of the enterprise; and the making of money was not his object; he would have cheerfully given all he had to create a flame of public indignation against despotism. Need I say what a failure the enterprise was? The London public never manifested the slightest interest in the exhibition. The lecture-hall was empty. I believe the poor Neapolitan tried again and again. The public would not come, or look, or listen. He spent his money in vain; he got into debt in vain. His instruments of torture must have inflicted on their owner agonies enough to have satisfied Maniscalco or Carafa. At last he could bear it no longer. He wrote a few short letters to some friends (I have still that which I received—a melancholy memorial), simply thanking them for what efforts they had made to assist him in his object, acknowledging that he had been over sanguine, and intimating that he had now given up the enterprise. Nothing more was said or hinted. A day or two after, he locked himself up in his room. Somebody heard an explosion, but took no particular notice. The lady who had endeavored to give voice to my poor friend's scheme came, later in the day, to see him. The door was broken open—and the poor Neapolitan lay dead, a pistol still in his hand, a pistol bullet in his brain.

THE REVEREND CHARLES KINGSLEY

I wonder how many of the rising generation in America or in England have read "Alton Locke"? Many years have passed since I read or even saw it. I do not care to read it any more, for I fear that it would not now sustain the effect of the impression it once produced on me, and I do not desire to destroy or even to weaken that impression. I know the book is not a great work of art. I know that three-fourths of its value consists in its blind and earnest feeling; that the story is heavily constructed, that many of the details are extravagant exaggerations, and that the author after all was not in the least a democrat or a believer in human equality. I have not forgotten that even then, when he braved respectable public opinion by taking a tailor for his hero, he took good care that the tailor should have genteel relations. Still I retain the impression which the book once produced, and I do not care to have it disturbed. Therefore I do not read or criticise "Alton Locke" any more; I remember it only as it struck me long ago—as a generous protest against the brutal indifference, literary and political, which left the London artisan so long to toil and suffer and sicken, to run into debt, to drink and fight and pine and die, in the darkness. Is it necessary—perhaps it is—to explain to some of my readers the story of "Alton Locke"? It is the story of a young London tailor-boy who has instincts and aspirations far above his class; who yearns to be a poet and a patriot; who loves and struggles in vain; who is supposed to sum up in his own weakly body all the best emotions, the vainest pinings, the wildest wishes, the most righteous protests of his fellows; who joins with the Chartist movement for lack of a better way to the great end, and sees its failure, and himself utterly broken down goes out to America to seek a new life there, and only beholds the shore of the promised land to die. Here at least was a grand idea. Here was the motive of a prose epic that ought to have been more thrilling to modern ears than the song of Tasso. The effect of the work at the time was strengthened by the fact that the author was a clergyman of the Church of England, who was believed to be a man of aristocratic family and connections. The book was undoubtedly a great success in its day. The strong idea which was in the heart of it carried it along. The Rev. Charles Kingsley became suddenly famous.

"Alton Locke" was published more than twenty years ago. Then Charles Kingsley was to most boys in Great Britain who read books at all a sort of living embodiment of chivalry, liberty, and a revolt against the established order of baseness and class-oppression in so many spheres of our society. The author of "Alton Locke" about the same time delivered a sermon in the country church where he officiated, so full of warm and passionate protest against the wrongs done to the poor by existing systems, that his spiritual chief, the rector or dean or some other dignitary, arose in the church itself— morally and physically arose, as Mrs. Gamp did—and denounced the preacher. Need it be said that the report of so unusual and extraordinary a scene as this excited our youthful enthusiasm into a perfect flame for the minister of the State Church who had braved the public censure of his superior in the cause of human right? For a long time Charles Kingsley was our chosen hero—I am speaking now of young men with the youthful spirit of revolt in them, with dreams of republics and ideas about the equality of man. If I were to be asked to describe Charles Kingsley now, having regard to the tendency of his writings and his public attitude, how should I speak of him? First, as about the most perverse and wrong-headed supporter of every political abuse, the most dogmatic champion of every wrong cause in domestic and foreign politics, that even a State Church has for many years produced. I hardly remember, in my practical observation of politics, a great public question but Charles Kingsley was at the wrong side of it. The vulgar glorification of mere strength and power, such a disgraceful characteristic of modern public opinion, never had a louder-tongued votary than he. The apostle of liberty and equality, as he seemed to me in my early days, has of late only shown himself to my mind as the champion of slave-systems of oppression and the iron reign of mere force. Is this a paradox? Has the man undergone a wonderful change of opinions? It is not a paradox, and I think Charles Kingsley has not changed his views. Perhaps a short sketch of the man and his work may reconcile these seeming antagonisms and make the reality coherent and clear.

I was present at a meeting not long since where Mr. Kingsley was one of the principal speakers. The meeting was held in London, the audience was a peculiarly Cockney audience, and Charles Kingsley is personally little known to the public of the metropolis. Therefore when he began to speak there was quite a little thrill of wonder and something like incredulity through the listening benches. Could that, people near me asked, really be Charles Kingsley, the novelist, the poet, the scholar, the aristocrat, the gentleman, the pulpit-orator, the "soldier-priest," the apostle of muscular Christianity? Yes, that was indeed he. Rather tall, very angular, surprisingly awkward, with thin, staggering legs, a hatchet face adorned with scraggy gray whiskers, a faculty for falling into the most ungainly attitudes, and making the most hideous contortions of visage and frame; with a rough provincial accent and an uncouth way of speaking, which would be set down for absurd caricature on the boards of a comic theatre; such was the appearance which the author of "Glaucus" and "Hypatia" presented to his startled audience. Since Brougham's time nothing so ungainly, odd, and ludicrous had been displayed upon an English platform. Needless to say, Charles Kingsley has not the eloquence of Brougham. But he has a robust and energetic plain-speaking which soon struck home to the heart of the meeting. He conquered his audience. Those who at first could hardly keep from laughing; those who, not knowing the speaker, wondered whether he was not mad or in liquor; those who heartily disliked his general principles and his public attitude, were alike won over, long before he had finished, by his bluff and blunt earnestness and his transparent sincerity. The subject was one which concerned the social suffering of the poor. Mr. Kingsley approached it broadly and boldly, talking with a grand disregard for logic and political economy, sometimes startling the more squeamish of his audience by the Biblical frankness of his descriptions and his language, but, I think, convincing every one that he was sound at heart, and explaining unconsciously to many how it happened that one endowed with sympathies so humane and liberal should so often have distinguished himself as the champion of the stupidest systems and the harshest oppressions. Anybody could see that the strong impelling force of the speaker's character was an emotional one; that sympathy and not reason, feeling rather than logic, instinct rather than observation, would govern his utterances. There are men in whom, no matter how robust and masculine their personal character, a disproportionate amount of the feminine element seems to have somehow found a place. These men will usually see things not as they really are, but as they are reflected through some personal prejudice or emotion. They will generally spring to conclusions, obey sudden impulses and instincts, ignore evidence and be very "thorough" and sweeping in all their judgments. When they are right they are—like the young lady in the song—very, very good; but like her, too, when they happen to be wrong they are "horrid." Of these men the author of "Alton Locke" is a remarkable illustration. It seems odd to describe the expounder of the creed of Muscular Christianity as one endowed with too much of the feminine element. But for all his vigor of speech and his rough voice, Mr. Charles Kingsley is as surely feminine in his way of reasoning, his likes and dislikes, his impulses and his prejudices, as Harriet Martineau is masculine in her intellect and George Sand in her emotions.

Mr. Charles Kingsley is a man of ancient English family, very proud of his descent, and full of the conviction so ostentatiously paraded by many Englishmen, that good blood carries with it a warrant for bravery, justice, and truth. The Kingsleys are a Cheshire family; I believe they date from before the Conquest—it does not much matter. I shall not apply to them John Bright's epigram about families which came over with William the Conqueror and never did anything else; for the Kingsleys seem to have been always an active race. They took an energetic part in the civil war during Charles the First's time, and stood by the Parliament. I am told that the family have still in their possession a commission to raise a troop of horse, given to a Kingsley and signed by Oliver Cromwell. One of the family emigrated to the New World with the Pilgrim Fathers, and I believe the Kingsley line still flourishes there like a bay-tree. Irrepressible energy, so far as I know, seems to have always been a characteristic of the household. Charles Kingsley was born near Dartmouth, in Devonshire; every one who has read his books must know how he revels in descriptions of the lovely scenery of Devon. He was for a while a pupil of the Rev. Derwent Coleridge, son of the poet, and he finally studied at Magdalene College, Cambridge. Mr. Kingsley was originally intended for the legal profession, but he changed his mind and went into the church. He was first curate and soon after rector of the Hampshire parish of Eversley, the name of which has since been so constantly kept in association with his own. I may mention that Mr. Kingsley married one of a trio of sisters—the Misses Grenfell—a second of whom was afterwards married to Mr. Froude, and is since dead, while the third became the wife of one of the foremost English journalists. Passing away from these merely personal facts, barely worth a brief note, we shall find that Kingsley's real existence, if I may use such a phrase, began and developed under the guidance of a remarkable man and under the inspiration of a strange movement. The man to whose leadership and teaching Mr. Kingsley owed so much was the Rev. Frederick Denison Maurice, who died in the first week of last April.

It would not be easy to explain to an American reader the meaning and the extent of the influence which this eminent man exercised over a large field of English society. The life of Mr. Maurice contains nothing worthy of note as to facts and dates; but its spirit infused new soul and sense into a whole generation. He was not a great speaker or a great thinker; he was not a bold reformer; he had not a very subtle intellect; I doubt whether his writings will be much read in coming time. He was simply a great character, a grand influence. He sent a new life into the languid and decaying frame of the State Church of England. He quickened it with a fresh sense of duty. His hope and purpose were to bring that church into affectionate and living brotherhood with modern thought, work, and society. An early friend and companion of John Sterling (the two friends married two sisters), Maurice had all the sweetness and purity of Carlyle's hero, with a far greater intellectual strength. Mr. Maurice set himself to make the English Church a practical influence in modern thought and society. He did not believe in a religion sitting apart on the cold Olympian heights of dogmatic theology, and looking down with dignified disdain upon the common life and the vulgar toils of humanity. He held that a church, if it is good for anything, ought to be able to meet fair and square the challenge of the skeptic and the infidel, and that it ought to concern itself about all that concerns men and women. One of the fruits of his long and valuable labor is the Workingmen's College in Red Lion Square, London, an institution of which he became the principal and to which he devoted much of his time and attention. Only a few weeks before his death he presided at one of the public meetings of this his favorite institution. He was the parent of the scheme of "Christian socialism," which sprang into existence more than twenty years ago and is bearing fruit still—a scheme to set on foot coöperative associations among working men on sound and progressive principles; to help the working men by advances of capital, in order that they might thus be enabled to help themselves. One of Mr. Maurice's earliest and most ardent pupils was Charles Kingsley; another was Thomas Hughes. In helping Mr. Maurice to carry out these schemes Kingsley was brought into frequent intercourse with some of the London Chartists, and especially with the working tailors, who have nearly all a strong radical tendency. Kingsley's impulsive sympathies took fire, and flamed out with the novel "Alton Locke, Tailor and Poet."

That extraordinary Chartist movement, so long in preparation and so suddenly extinguished, how completely a thing of the past it seems to have become! Only twenty-four years have passed since its collapse. Men under forty can recall, as if it were yesterday, all its incidents and its principal figures. People in the United States know that my friend Henry Vincent is still only in his prime; he was one of its earliest and foremost leaders. But it seems as old and dead as a peasant-war of the Middle Ages. It was a strange jumble of politics and social complaints. It was partly the blind, passionate protest of working men who knew that they had no right to starve and suffer in a prosperous country, but who hardly knew where the real grievance lay. It was partly the protest of untaught and eager intelligence against the brutal apathy of government which would do nothing for national education. Its political demands were very modest. Some of them have since been quietly carried into law; some of them have been quietly dismissed into the realm of anachronisms. Chartism was indeed rather a wild cry, a passionate yearning of lonely men for combination, than any definite political enterprise. One looks back now with a positive wonder upon the savage stupidity of the ruling classes which so nearly converted it into a rebellion. Of course it was in some instances seized hold of by selfish and scheming politicians, who played with it for their own purposes. Of course it had its evil counsellors, its false friends, its cowards, and its traitors. But on the whole there was a noble spirit of manly honesty pervading the movement, which to my mind fills it with a romantic interest and ought to secure for it an honorable memory. It found leaders in many cases outside its own classes. There was, for example, "Tom Duncombe," a sort of Alcibiades of English Radicalism; a brilliant talker in Parliament, a gay man of fashion, steeped deep in reckless debt and sparkling dissipation; hand and glove with the fast young noblemen of the West End gambling houses, and the ardent Chartist working men of Shoreditch and Clerkenwell. There was Feargus O'Connor—huge, boistering, fearless—a burlesque Mirabeau with red hair; a splendid mob-speaker, who could fight his way by sheer strength of muscle and fist through a hostile crowd; vain of his half-mythical descent from Irish kings, even when he delighted in being hail fellow well met with tailors and hod-carriers; revelling in the fiercest struggles of politics and the wildest freaks of prolonged debauchery. O'Connor tried to crowd half a dozen lives into one, and the natural result was that he prematurely broke down. For a long time before his death he was a mere lunatic. A strange fact was that as his manners were always eccentric and boisterous, he had become an actual madman for months before those around him were fully aware of the change. In the House of Commons the freaks of the poor lunatic were for a long time supposed to be only more marked eccentricities, or, as some thought, insolent affectations of eccentricity. He would rise while Lord Palmerston was addressing the House, walk up to the great minister, and give him a tremendous slap on the back. One night he actually assaulted a member of the House, and the Speaker ordered his arrest. Feargus sauntered coolly out into the lobbies. The sergeant-at-arms was bidden to go forth and arrest the offender. Lord Charles Russell (brother of Earl Russell), then and now sergeant-at-arms, is a thin, little, feeble man. I have been told by some who witnessed it that the scene in the lobbies became highly amusing. Lord Charles went with reluctant steps about his awful task. By this time everybody was beginning to suspect that O'Connor was really a madman. Anyhow, he was a giant, and at his sanest moments perfectly reckless. Now it is not a pleasant task for a weak and little man to be sent to arrest even a sane giant; but only think of laying hands on a giant who appears to be out of his senses! The dignity of his office, however, had to be upheld, and Lord Charles trotted quietly after his huge quarry. He cast imploring looks at member after member, but it was none of their business to interfere, and they had no inclination to volunteer. Some of them indeed were deeply engrossed in speculations as to what would happen if Feargus were suddenly to turn round. Would the sergeant-at-arms put his dignity in his pocket and actually run? Or, if he stood his ground, what would be the result? Happily, however, just as Feargus and his unwilling pursuer reached Westminster Hall, the eager eye of Lord Charles Russell descried a little knot of policemen; he hailed them; they came up, and the sergeant-at-arms did his duty and the capture was effected. I can well remember seeing O'Connor, somewhere about this time, sauntering through Covent Garden market, with rolling, restless gait; his hair, that once was fiery red, all snowy white; his eye gleaming with the peculiar, quick, shallow, ever-changing glitter of madness. The poor fellow rambled from fruit-stall to fruit-stall, talking all the while to himself, sometimes taking up a fruit as if he meant to buy it, and then putting it down with a vacant laugh and walking on. It was a pitiable spectacle. His light of reason soon flickered out altogether, and death came to his relief.

I must not omit to mention, when speaking of the Chartist leaders, the brave, disinterested, and highly-gifted Ernest Jones, who sacrificed such bright worldly prospects for the cause of the People's Charter. Long after the Charter and its agitation were dead, Jones emerged into public life again, still comparatively a young man, and he seemed about to enter on a career both brilliant and valuable. An immature and unexpected death interposed.

However, I have wandered away from the subject of my paper. Charles Kingsley came to know the principal working men among the Chartists, and his impulsive nature was greatly influenced by their words and their lives. Most of their leaders drawn from other classes, O'Connor especially, he distrusted and disliked. But the rank and file of the movement, the working men, the sufferers, the "prolétaires" as they would be called nowadays, attracted his kindly heart. Chartism had fallen. It collapsed suddenly in 1848; died amid Homeric laughter of the public. It fell mainly because it had come to occupy a false position altogether. Partly by ignorance, partly by the selfish folly of some of its leaders, and partly by the severity of the government measures, the movement had been driven into a dilemma which it never originally contemplated. It must either go into open rebellion or surrender. It was jammed up like MacMahon at Sedan. Chartism had no real wish to rebel, although of course the flame of the recent revolution in Paris had glared over it and made it wild; and it had no means of carrying on a revolt for a single day. So it could only surrender; and the surrender took place under conditions which made it seem utterly ridiculous. Kingsley was seized with the idea of crystallizing all this into a romance. He had as a further stimulant and guide the work which Henry Mayhew was then publishing, "London Labor and the London Poor," a serial which by its painful and startling revelations was working a profound impression on England. Mayhew's narratives were often inaccurate, for he could not conduct the whole enterprise himself, and had sometimes to call in the aid of careless and untrustworthy associates, who occasionally found it easier to throw off a bit of sentimental or sensational romance than to pursue a patient inquiry. But the general effect of the publication was healthful and practical, and it became the parent of nearly all the efforts that followed to lay bare and ameliorate the condition of the London poor. There can be no doubt that it had a great influence on the impressionable mind of Charles Kingsley. He wrote "Alton Locke," and the book became a great success. The Tailor and Poet was the hero of the hour. "Blackwood" at once christened Alton Locke "Young Remnants;" but Young Remnants survived the joke. The novel is full of nonsense and extravagance; and with all its sympathy for tailors, it has a great deal of Kingsley's characteristic affection for rank and birth. But it had a really great idea at its heart, and struck out one or two new characters—especially that of the old Scotch bookseller—and it made its mark. The peculiarity, however, to which I wish now especially to direct attention is its utter absence of practical thinking-power. Nowhere can you find any proof that the author is able to think about anything. An idea strikes him; he seizes it, and, to use Hawthorne's expression, "wields it like a flail." Then he throws it down and takes up something else, to employ it in the same wild and incoherent fashion. This is Kingsley all out, and always. He is not content with developing his one only gift of any literary value—the capacity to paint big, striking pictures with a strong glare or glow on them. He firmly believes himself a profound philosopher and social reformer, and he will insist on obtruding before the world on all occasions his absolute incapacity for any manner of reasoning on any subject whatsoever. Wild with intellectual egotism, and blind to all teaching from without, Kingsley rushes at great and difficult subjects head downwards like a bull. Thus he tackled Chartism, and society, and competition, and political economy, and what not, in his "Alton Locke"; and thus he has gone on ever since and will to the end of his chapter, always singling out for the display of his powers the very subjects whereof he knows least, and is by the whole constitution of his intellect and temperament least qualified to judge.

I am writing now rather about Kingsley himself than about his books, with which the readers of "The Galaxy" are of course well acquainted. I therefore pass over the many books he produced between "Alton Locke" and "Westward Ho!"—and I dwell upon the latter only because it illustrates the next great idea which got hold of the author after the little fever about Chartism had passed away. I suppose "Westward Ho!" may be regarded as the first appearance of the school of Muscular Christianity. Mr. Kingsley started for our benefit the huge British hero who could do anything in the way of fighting and walking, and propagated the doctrines of the English Church. To read the Bible and to kill the Spaniards was the whole duty of the ideal Briton of Elizabeth's time, according to this authority. The notion was a success. In a moment our literature became flooded with pious athletes who knocked their enemies down with texts from the Scriptures and left-handers from the shoulder. All these heroes were of necessity "gentlemen." One of the principal articles of the new gospel according to Kingsley was that truth, valor, muscle, and theological fervor were only possessed in their fulness by the scions of good old English county families. Other nations seldom had such qualities at all; never had them to perfection; and even favored Britain only saw them properly illustrated in country gentlemen of long descent. Of course this sort of thing, which was for the moment a sincere idea with Kingsley, became a mere affectation among his followers and admirers. The fighting-parson pattern of hero was for a while as great a bore as the rough and ugly hero after Jane Eyre's "Rochester," or the colossal and corrupt guardsman whom "Guy Livingstone" sent abroad on the world. Certainly Kingsley's hero was a better style of man than Guy Livingstone's, for at the worst he was only an egotistical savage, and not a profligate. But I think he did a good deal of harm in his day. He helped to encourage and inflate that feeling of national self-conceit which makes people such nuisances to their neighbors, and he fostered that odious reverence for mere force and power which Carlyle had already made fashionable. Kingsley himself appears to have become "possessed" by his own idea as if by some unmanageable spirit. It banished all his chartism and democracy and liberalism, and the rest of it. Under its influence Kingsley out-Carlyled Carlyle in the worship of strong despotisms and force of any kind. He went out of his way to excuse slavery in the Southern States. He became the fervent panegyrist of Governor Eyre of Jamaica. When two sides were possible to any question of human politics, he was sure to take the wrong one. Nothing for long years, I think, has been more repulsive, and in its way more mischievous, than the cant about "strength" which Kingsley did so much to diffuse and to glorify.

Meanwhile his irrepressible energy was always driving him into new fields of work. It never allowed him time to think. The moment any sort of idea struck him, he rushed at it and crushed it into the shape of a book or an essay. He wrote historical novels, philosophical novels, and theological novels. He wrote poetry—yards of poetry—volumes of poetry. There really is a great deal of the spirit of poetry in him, and he has done better things with the hexameter verse than better poets have done. There was for a long time a fervid school of followers who swore by him, and would have it that he was to be the great English poet of the century. He published essays, tracts, lectures, and sermons without number. He seems to have made up his mind to publish in book form somehow everything that he had spoken or written anywhere. He inundated the leading newspapers with letters on this, that, and the other subject. He was appointed professor of modern history at the University of Cambridge on the death of Sir James Stephen, and he launched at once into a series of lectures, which were almost immediately published in book form. Why he published them it was hard for even vanity itself to explain, because with characteristic bluntness he began his course with the acknowledgment that he really knew nothing in particular about the subjects whereon he had undertaken to instruct the University and the world. He made up in courage, however, for anything he may have lacked in knowledge. He went bravely in for an onslaught on the positive theory of history—on Comte, Mill, Buckle, Darwin, and everybody else. He made it perfectly clear very soon that he did not know even what these authors profess to teach. He flatly denied that there is any such thing as an inexorable law in nature. He proved that even the supposed law of gravitation is not by any means the rigid and universal sort of thing that Newton and such-like persons have supposed. How, it may be asked, did he prove this? In the following words: "If I choose to catch a stone, I can hold it in my hands; it has not fallen to the ground, and will not till I let it. So much for the inevitable action of the laws of gravity." This way of dealing with the question may seem to many readers nothing better than downright buffoonery. But Kingsley was as grave as a church and as earnest as an owl. He fully believed that he was refuting the pedants who believe in the inevitable action of the law of gravitation, when he talked of holding a stone in his hand. That an impulsive, illogical man should on the spur of the moment talk this kind of nonsense, even from a professor's chair, is not perhaps wonderful; but it does seem a little surprising that he should see it in print, revise it, and publish it, without ever becoming aware of its absurdity.

In the same headlong spirit Mr. Kingsley rushed into his famous controversy with Dr. John Henry Newman. I have already, when writing of Dr. Newman, alluded to this controversy, which for a time excited the greatest interest and indeed the greatest amusement in England. I only refer to it now as an illustration of the surprising hotheadedness and lack of thinking power which characterize the author of "Alton Locke." Dr. Newman preached a sermon on "Wisdom and Innocence." Mr. Kingsley went out of his way to discourse and comment on this sermon, and publicly declared that its doctrine was an exhortation to disregard truth. "Dr. Newman informs us that truth need not and on the whole ought not to be a virtue for its own sake." Of course this was as grave a charge as could possibly be made against a great religious teacher. It was doubly odious and offensive to Dr. Newman because it was the revival of an old and familiar charge against the church he had lately entered. It was made by Kingsley in an oft-hand, careless sort of way, as if it were something acknowledged and indisputable—as if some one were to say, "Horace Greeley informs us that a protective tariff is often useful," or "Henry Ward Beecher is in favor of early rising." Newman wrote with a cold civility to ask in what passage of his writings any such doctrine was to be found. Of course nothing of the kind was to be found. If it were possible to conceive of any divine in our days holding such a doctrine, we may be perfectly certain that he would never put it into print. Newman was known to all the world as the purest and most austere devotee of what he believed to be the truth. He had sacrificed the most brilliant career in the Church of England for his convictions, and, strange to say, had yet retained the admiration and the affection of those whose religious fellowship he had renounced. Kingsley had but one course in fairness and common sense open to him. He ought to have frankly apologized. He ought to have owned that he had spoken without thinking; that he had blurted out the words without observing the gravity of the charge they contained; and that he was sorry for it. But he did not do this. He published a letter, in which he said that Dr. Newman having denied that his doctrine bore the meaning Mr. Kingsley had put upon it, he (Kingsley) could only express his regret at having mistaken him. This was nearly as bad as the first charge. It distinctly conveyed the idea that but for Dr. Newman's subsequent explanation and denial, certain words of his might fairly have been understood to bear the odious meaning ascribed to them. Dr. Newman returned to the charge, still with a chill urbanity which I cannot help thinking Kingsley mistook for weakness or fear. He pointed out that he had never denied anything; that there was nothing for him to deny; that Mr. Kingsley had charged him with teaching a certain odious doctrine, and he therefore asked Mr. Kingsley to point to the passage containing the doctrine, or frankly own that there was no such passage in existence. Kingsley thereupon took the worst, the most unfair, and as it proved the most foolish course a man could possibly have pursued. He went to work to fasten on Newman by a constructive argument, drawn from the general tendency of his teaching, a belief in the doctrine of which he was unable to find any specific statement. Then opened out that controversy, which was quite an event in its time, and set everybody talking. Newman's was an intellect which must be described as the peer of Stuart Mill's or Herbert Spencer's. He was a perfect master of polemical science. He could write, when he thought fit, with a vitriolic keenness of sarcasm. When he had allowed Kingsley to entangle himself sufficiently, Newman fairly opened fire, and the rest of the debate was like a duel between some blundering, wrong-headed cudgel-player from a village green, and some accomplished professor of the science of the rapier from Paris or Vienna. Not the least amusing thing about the controversy was the manner in which it put Kingsley into open antagonism with his own teaching. He endeavored gratuitously and absurdly to convict Dr. Newman of a disregard for the truth, because Newman believed in the miracles of the saints. For, he argued, a man of Newman's intellect could not believe in such things if he inquired into them. But he did not inquire into them; he taught that they were not to be questioned but accepted as orthodox. Thereby he showed that he preferred orthodoxy to truth—"truth, the capital virtue, the virtue of virtues, without which all others are rotten." Now, that sounds very well, and we all agree in what Kingsley says of the truth. But Kingsley had not long before been assailing Bishop Colenso for his infidelity. Kingsley declared himself shocked at the publication of a work like Dr. Colenso's, which claimed and exercised a license of inquiry that seemed to him "anything but reverent." He distinctly laid it down that the liberty of religious criticism must be "reverent," and "within the limits of orthodoxy!" Now, I am not challenging Mr. Kingsley's doctrine as to the limit of religious inquiry. That forms no part of my purpose. But it is perfectly obvious that if to limit inquiry within the bounds of orthodoxy shows a disregard for truth in John Henry Newman, the same practice must be evidence of a similar disregard in Charles Kingsley. Of course Kingsley never thought of this—never thought about the matter at all. He disliked Colenso's teaching on the one hand and Newman's on the other. He said the first thing that came into his mind against each in turn, and never heeded the fact that the reproach he employed in the former case was utterly inconsistent with that which he uttered in the other. I do not believe, however, that the controversy did Kingsley any harm. Nobody ever expected consistency or rational argument from him. People were amused, and laughed, and perhaps wondered why Dr. Newman should have taken any trouble in the matter at all. But Kingsley remained in popular estimation just the same as before—blundering, hot-headed, boisterous, but full of brilliant imagination, and thoroughly sound at heart.

Thus Charles Kingsley is always at work. Lately he has been describing some of the scenery of the West Indies, and proclaiming the virtues of Australian potted meats. He has thrown his whole soul into the Australian meat question. The papers have run over with letters from him intended to prove to the world how good and cheap it is to eat the mutton and beef brought in tin cans from Australia. I believe Mr. Kingsley acknowledges that all his energy and eloquence have been unequal to the task of persuading his servants to eat the excellent food which he is himself willing to have at his table. He has also been lecturing on temperance, and delivering a philippic against Darwin. He has also written a paper condemning and deprecating the modern critical spirit. There is one rule, he insists, "by which we should judge all human opinions, endeavors, characters." That is, "Are they trying to lessen the sum of human misery, of human ignorance? Are they trying, however clumsily, to cure physical suffering, weakness, deformity, disease, and to make human bodies what God would have them?... If so, let us judge them no further. Let them pass out of the pale of our criticism. Let their creed seem to us defective, their opinions fantastic, their means irrational. God must judge of that, not we. They are trying to do good; then they are children of the light." This is not, perhaps, the spirit in which Kingsley himself criticised Newman or Colenso. But if we judge him according to the principle which he recommends, he would assuredly take high rank; for I never heard any one question his sincerity and his honest purpose to do good. Of course he is often terribly provoking. His feminine and almost hysterical impulsiveness, and his antiquated, feudal devotion to rank, are difficult to bear always without strong language. His utter absence of sympathy with political emancipation is a lamentable weakness. His self-conceit and egotism often make him a ludicrous object. Still, he has an honest heart, and he tries to do the work of a man; and he is one of those who would, if they could, make the English State Church still a living, an active, and an all-pervading influence. As a preacher and a pastor he often reminds me of the Rev. Henry Ward Beecher. Of course he is far below Mr. Beecher in all oratorical gifts as well as in political enlightenment; but he has the same perfervid and illogical nature, the same vigorous, self-sufficient temperament, the same tendency to "slop over," the same generous energy in any cause that seems to him good.

It will be inferred that I do not rate Mr. Kingsley very highly as an author. He can describe glowing scenery admirably, and he can vigorously ring the changes on his one or two ideas—the muscular Englishman, the glory of the Elizabethan discoverers, and so on. He is a scholar, and he has written verses which sometimes one is on the point of mistaking for poetry, so much of the poet's feelings have they about them. He can do a great many things very cleverly. He belongs to a clever family. His brother, Henry Kingsley, is a spirited and dashing novelist, whom the critics sneer at a good deal, but whose books always command a large circulation, and have made a distinctive mark. Perhaps if Charles Kingsley had done less he might have done better. Human capacity is limited. It is not given to mortal to be a great preacher, a great philosopher, a great scholar, a great poet, a great historian, a great novelist, an indefatigable country parson, and a successful man in fashionable society. Mr. Kingsley seems never to have quite made up his mind for which of these callings to go in especially, and being with all his versatility not at all many-sided, but strictly one-sided, and almost one-ideaed, the result of course has been that, touching success at many points, he has absolutely mastered it at none. His place in letters has been settled this long time. Since "Westward Ho!" at the latest, he has never added half a cubit to his stature. The "Chartist Parson" has, on the other hand, been growing more and more aristocratic, illiberal, and even servile in politics. His discourse on the recovery of the Prince of Wales was the very hyperbole of the most old-fashioned loyalty—a discourse worthy of Filmer, and utterly out of place in the present century. Muscular Christianity has shrunk and withered long since. The professorship of modern history was a failure, and has been given up. Darwin is flourishing, and I am not certain about the success of Australian beef. All this acknowledged, however, it must still be owned that, failing in this, that, and the other attempt, and never probably achieving any real and enduring success, Charles Kingsley has been an influence and a name of mark in the Victorian age. I cannot, indeed, well imagine that age without him, although his presence is sometimes only associated with it as that of Malvolio with the court of the fair lady in "Twelfth Night." Men of far greater intellect have made their presence less strongly felt, and imprinted their image much less clearly on the minds of their contemporaries. He is an example of how much may be done by energetic temper, fearless faith in self, an absence of all sense of the ridiculous, a passionate sympathy, and a wealth of half-poetic descriptive power. If ever we have a woman's parliament in England, Charles Kingsley ought to be its chaplain; for I know of no clever man whose mind and temper more aptly illustrate the illogical impulsiveness, the rapid emotional changes, the generous, often wrong-headed vehemence, the copious flow of fervid words, the vivid freshness of description without analysis, and the various other peculiarities which, justly or unjustly, the world has generally agreed to regard as the special characteristics of woman.

MR. JAMES ANTHONY FROUDE

Mr. Froude, I perceive, is about to visit the United States. *Reddas incolumem!* He is a man of mark—with whatever faults, a great Englishman. It will not take the citizens of New York and Boston long to become quite as familiar with his handsome, thoughtful face as the people of London. Mr. Froude rarely makes his appearance at any public meeting or demonstration of any kind. He delivers a series of lectures now and then to one of the great solemn literary institutions. He is a member of some of our literary and scientific societies. He used at one time occasionally to attend the meetings of the Newspaper Press Fund Committee, where his retiring ways and grave, meditative demeanor reminded me, I cannot tell why, of Nathaniel Hawthorne. He has many friends, and mingles freely in private society, but to the average public he is only a name; to a large proportion of that average public he is not even so much. I presume he might walk the Strand every day and no head turn round to look after him. I presume it would not be difficult to get together a large public meeting of respectable and intelligent London rate-payers of whom not one could tell who Mr. Froude was, or would be aroused to the slightest interest by the mention of his name. Who, indeed, is generally known or cared about in London? I do not say universally known, for nobody enjoys that proud distinction, not even the Prince of Wales—nay, not even the Tichborne claimant. But who is ever generally known? Gladstone and Disraeli are; and Bright is. Dickens was, and, to a certain extent, Thackeray. Archbishop Manning and Mr. Spurgeon are, perhaps; and I cannot remember anybody else just now. Palmerston, in his day, was better known than any of these; and the Duke of Wellington was by far the most widely known of all. The Duke of Wellington was the only man who during my time was nearly as well known in London as Mr. Greeley is in New York. "How can you, you know?" as Mr. Pecksniff asks. We have four millions of people crowded into one city. It takes a giant of popularity indeed to be seen and recognized above that crowd. As for your Brownings and Spencers and Froudes and the rest, your mere men of genius—well, they have their literary celebrity and they will doubtless have their fame. But average London knows and cares no more about them than it does about you or me.

Therefore, let not any American reader, when I describe Mr. Froude as a man of mark and a great Englishman, assume that he is a man of mark with the crowd. Let no American visitor to London be astonished if, finding himself in the neighborhood of Mr. Froude's residence, and stepping into half a dozen shops in succession to ask for the exact address of the historian, he should hear that nobody there knew anything about him. Nobody but scholars and literary people knew anything about the late George Grote, one of the few great philosophic historians of the modern world. Compared with the influence of Mr. Grote upon average London, that of Mr. Froude may almost be described as sensational; for Froude has stirred up literary and religious controversy, and has been denounced and has personally defended himself, and in that way must have attracted some attention. At all events, when New York has seen and heard Mr. Froude, she will have seen and heard one of the men of our time in the true sense; one of the men who have toiled out a channel for a fresh current of literature to run in, and whose name can hereafter be omitted from no list of celebrities, however select, which pretends to illustrate the characteristics of the Victorian age in England.

Mr. Froude is a Devonshire man, son of a Protestant archdeacon. He was educated in Westminster School, and afterward at the famous Oriel College, Oxford. He is now some fifty-four or fifty-five years of age, but seems, and I hope is, only in his prime. Froude is a waif of that marvellous Oxford movement which began some forty years ago, and of which the strange, diversely operating influence still radiates through English thought and society. That movement was a peculiar theological *renaissance*, which partly converted itself into a reaction and partly into a revolt. It began with the saintly and earnest Keble; its master spirits were John Henry Newman and Dr. Pusey. It proposed to vindicate for the Protestant Church the true place of spiritual heir to the apostles and universal teacher of the Christian world. Newman, Pusey, and others worked in the production of the celebrated "Tracts for the Times." The results were extraordinary. The impulse of inquiry thus set going seemed to shake all foundations of agreement. It was an explosion which blew people various ways, they could hardly tell why or how. It made one man a ritualist, another an Ultramontane Roman Catholic, a third a skeptic. Like the two women grinding at the mill in the Scripture, two devoted companions, brothers perhaps, were seized by that impulse and flung different ways. Before the wave had subsided it tossed Mr. Froude, then a young man of five or six and twenty, clear out of his intended career as a clergyman of the Church of England. He had taken deacon's orders before the change came on him, which drove him forth as the two Newmans had been driven; but his course was more like that of

Francis Newman than of John Henry. He seemed, indeed, at one time likely to pass away altogether into the ranks of the skeptics. Skepticism is in London attended with no small degree of social disadvantage. To be in "society," you must believe as people of good position do. Dissent of any kind is unfashionable. A shrewd friend of mine says a dissenter can never enter London. Dissent never gets any further than Hackney or Clapham, a northern and a southern suburb. Allowance being made for a touch of satirical exaggeration, the saying is very expressive, and even instructive. Probably, however, the odds are more heavily against mere dissent than a bold, intellectual skepticism, which may have a piquant and alluring flavor about it, and make a man a sort of curiosity and lion, so that "society" would tolerate him as it does a poet. There was, however, nothing in exclusion from fashionable society to frighten a man like Froude, who, so far as I know, has never troubled himself about the favor of the West End. His first work of any note (for I pass over "The Shadows of the Clouds," a novel, I believe, which I have never read nor seen) was "The Nemesis of Faith." This work was published in 1848, and is chiefly to be valued now as an illustration of one stage of development through which the intellect of the author and the tolerance of his age were passing. "The Nemesis of Faith" was declared a skeptical and even an infidel book. It was sternly censured and condemned by the authorities of the university to which Mr. Froude had belonged. He had won a fellowship in Exeter College, Oxford; the college authorities punished him for his opinions by depriving him of it. "The Nemesis of Faith" created a sensation, an excitement and alarm, which surely were extravagant even then and would be impossible now. Its doubts and complaints would seem wild enough to-day. Men of any freshness and originality so commonly begin—or about that time did begin—their career with a little outburst of skepticism, that the thing seems almost as natural as it seemed to Major Pendennis for a young peer to start in public life as a professed republican. Besides, we must remember that "The Nemesis of Faith" was published in what the late Lord Derby once called the pre-scientific age. It was the time when skepticism dealt only in the metaphysical or the emotional, and had not congealed into the far more enduring and corroding form of physical science. As well as I can remember, "The Nemesis of Faith" —which I have not seen for years—was full of life and genius, but not particularly dangerous to settled beliefs. However, a storm raged around it, and around the author; and finally Mr. Froude himself seems to have reconsidered his opinions, for he subsequently withdrew the book from circulation. Its literary success, however, must have shown him clearly what his career was to be. He was at this time drifting about the world in search of occupation; for he found himself cut off from the profession of the Church, on which he had intended to enter, and yet he had, if I am not mistaken, passed far enough within its threshold to disqualify him for admission to one of the other professions. He began to write for the "Westminster Review," which at that time was in the zenith of its intellectual celebrity, and for "Fraser's Magazine." His studies led him especially into the history of the Tudor reigns, and most of his early contributions to "Fraser" were explorations in that field. Out of these studies grew the "History of England," on which the fame of the author is destined to rest. Mr. Froude himself tells us that he began his task with a strong inclination toward what may be called the conventional and orthodox opinions of the character of Henry VIII.; but he found as he studied the actual records and state papers that a different sort of character began to grow up under his eyes. I can easily imagine how his emotional and artistic nature gradually bore him away further and further in the direction thus suddenly opened up, until at last he had created an entirely new Henry for himself. Of course the old traditional notion of Henry, the simple idea which set him down as a monster of lust and cruelty, would soon expose its irrationality to a mind like that of Froude. But, like the writers who, in revolt against the picture of Tiberius given by Tacitus, or that of the French Revolution woven by Burke, have painted the Roman Emperor as an archangel, and the Revolution as a stainless triumph of liberty, so Mr. Froude seems to have been driven into a positive affection and veneration for the subject of his study. In 1856 the first and second volumes appeared of the "History of England from the Fall of Wolsey to the Death of Elizabeth." There has hardly been in our time so fierce a literary controversy as that which sprang up around these two volumes. Perhaps the war of words over Buckle's first volume or Darwin's "Origin of Species" could alone be compared with it. Mr. Froude became famous in a moment. The "Edinburgh Review" came out with a fierce, almost a savage attack, to which Mr. Froude replied in an article which he published in "Fraser" and to which he affixed his own signature. Mr. Froude, indeed, has during his career fought several battles in this open, personal manner—a thing very uncommon in England. He has had many enemies. The "Saturday Review" has been unswerving in its passionate hostility to him, and has even gone so far as to arraign his personal integrity as a chronicler. Rumor in London ascribes some of the bitterest of the "Saturday Review" articles to the pen of Mr. Edward A. Freeman, author of "The History of Federal Government," "The History of the Norman Conquest of England," and many historical essays—a prolific writer in reviews and journals. Then as the successive volumes of Froude's work began to appear, and the historian brought out his famous portraiture of Elizabeth and Mary, it was but natural that controversy should thicken and deepen around him. The temper of parties in Great Britain is still nearly as hot as ever it was on the characters of Mary and Elizabeth. Not many years ago Thackeray was hissed in Edinburgh, because in one of his lectures he said something which was supposed to be disparaging to the moral character of Mary of Scotland. Then the whole question of Saxon against Celt comes up again in Mr. Froude's account of English rule in Ireland. Everybody knows what a storm of controversy broke around the historian's head. He was accused not merely of setting up his own personal prejudices as law and history, but even of misrepresenting facts and actually misquoting documents in order to suit his purpose. I do not mean to enter into the discussion, for I am not writing a criticism of Mr. Froude's history, but only a chapter about Mr. Froude himself. But I confess I can quite understand why so many readers, not blind partisans of any cause, become impatient with some of the passages of his works. He coolly and deliberately commends as virtue in one person or one race the very qualities, the very deeds which he stigmatizes as the blackest and basest guilt in others. "Show me the man, and I will show you the law," used to be an old English proverb, illustrating the depth which judicial partisanship and corruption had reached. "Show me the person, and I will show you the moral law," might well be the motto of Mr. Froude's history. But I believe Mr. Froude to be utterly incapable of any misrepresentation or distortion of facts, any conscious coloring of the truth. Indeed, I am rather impressed by the extraordinary boldness with which he often gives the naked facts, and still calmly upholds a theory which to ordinary minds would seem absolutely incompatible with their existence. It appears to be enough if he once makes up his mind to dislike a personage or a race. Let the facts be as they may, Mr. Froude will still explain them to the discredit of the object of his antipathy. His mode of dealing with the characters and actions of those he detests, might remind one of the manner in which the discontented subjects of the perplexed prince in "Rabagas" explain every act of their good-natured ruler: "Je donne un bal—luxe effréné! Pas de bal—quelle avarice! Je passe une revue—intimidation militaire! Je n'en passe pas—je crains l'esprit des troupes! Des pétards à ma fête—l'argent du peuple en fumée! Pas de pétards—rien pour les plaisirs du peuple! Je me porte bien—l'oisivite! Je me porte mal—la débauche! Je bâtis—gaspillage! Je ne bâtis pas—et le prolétaire?"

However that may be, it is certain that the "History" placed Mr. Froude in the very front rank of English authors. He had made a path for himself. He refused to accept the thought of what is commonly called a science of history, although his own method of evolving his narrative is very often in faithful conformity with the principles of that science. He had written about political economy, in the very opening of his first volume, in a manner which, if it did not imply an actual contempt for the doctrines of that science, yet certainly showed an impatience of its rule which aroused the anger of the economists. He claimed a reversal of the universal decision of modern history as to the character of Henry VIII. He assailed one of the English Protestant's articles of faith when he denied the virtue of Anne Boleyn. He made mistakes and confessed them, and went to work again. The opening of the Spanish archives in the castle of Simancas flooded him with new lights and required a reconstruction of much that he had done. The progress of his work became one of the literary phenomena of the age. All eyes were on it. The rich romantic splendor of the style, the singular power and impressiveness of the historical portraits, fascinated everybody. Orthodox Protestants looked on him as a sort of infidel or pagan, despite his admiration for Queen Bess, because, with all his admiration, he exposed her meannesses and her falsehoods with unsparing hand. Catholics insisted on regarding him as a mere bigot of Protestantism, although he condemned Anne Boleyn. Mr. Froude has always shown a remarkable freedom from prejudice and bigotry. Some of his closest friends are Catholics and Irishmen. I remember a little personal instance of liberality on his part which is perhaps worth mentioning. There was an official in the Record or State Paper Office of England who had become a Roman Catholic, and was, like most English Catholics, especially if converts, rather bigoted and zealous. This gentleman, Mr. Turnbull, happened to be employed some years ago in arranging, copying, and calendaring the Elizabethan State papers. The Evangelical Alliance Society got up a cry against him. They insisted that to employ a Roman Catholic in such a task was only to place in his hands the means of falsifying a most important period of English history, and they argued that the temptation would be too strong for any man like Mr. Turnbull to resist. There sprang up one of those painful and ignoble disputations which are even still only too common in England when religious bigotry gets a chance of raising an alarm. I am sorry to say that so influential a journal as the "Athenæum" joined in the clamor for the dismissal of Mr. Turnbull, who was not accused of having done anything wrong, but only of being placed in a position which might perhaps tempt some base creatures to do wrong. Mr. Turnbull was a gentleman of the highest honor, and, unfortunately for himself, an enthusiast in the very work which then occupied him. Mr. Froude was then engaged in studying the period of history which employed Mr. Turnbull's labors. The opinions of the two men were utterly at variance. Mr. Turnbull must have thought Froude's work in the rehabilitation of Henry VIII., and the glorification of Elizabeth positively detestable. But Mr. Froude bore public testimony to the honor and integrity of Mr. Turnbull. "Mr. Turnbull," Froude wrote, "could have felt no sympathy with the work in which I was engaged; but he spared no pains to be of use to me, and in admitting me to a share of his private room enabled me to witness the ability and integrity with which he discharged his own duties." Bigotry prevailed, however. Mr. Turnbull was removed from his place, and died soon after, disappointed and embittered. But Froude the man is not Froude the author. The man is free from dislikes and prejudices; the author can hardly take a pen in his hand without being suffused by prejudices and dislikes. Take for example his way of dealing with Irish questions, not merely in his history, but in his miscellaneous writings. Mr. Froude has some little property in the west of Ireland, and resides there for a short time every year. He has occasionally detailed his experiences, and commented on them, in the pages of "Fraser." I shall not give my own view of his apparent sentiments toward Ireland, because I am obviously not an impartial judge; but I shall take the opinion of the London "Spectator," which is. The "Spectator" declares that "it may be not unfairly said that Mr. Froude simply loathes the Irish people; not consciously perhaps, for he professes the reverse. But a certain bitter grudge breaks out despite his will now and then. It colors all his tropes. It adds a sting to the casual allusions of his language. When he wants a figure of speech to express the relation between the two islands, he compares the Irish to a kennel of fox-hounds, and the English to their master, and declares that what the Irish want is a master who knows that he is a master and means to continue master." In his occasional studies of contemporary Ireland from the window of his shooting lodge in Kerry, Mr. Froude exhibits the same strange mixture of candor as to fact and blind prejudice as to conclusion which so oddly characterizes his history. He recounts deliberately the most detestable projects—he himself calls them "detestable;" the word is his, not mine—avowed to him by the agents of great Irish landlords, and yet his sympathy is wholly with the agents and against the occupiers. He tells in one instance, with perfect delight, of a mean and vulgar exhibition of triumphant malice which he says an agent, a friend of his, paraded for the humiliation of an evicted and contumacious tenant. The "Spectator" asks in wonder whether it can be possible that "Mr. Froude, an English gentleman by birth and education, an Oxford fellow, is not ashamed to relate this act as an heroic feat?" Indeed, Mr. Froude seems to associate in Ireland only with the "agent" class, and to take all his views of things from them. His testimony is therefore about as valuable as that of a foreigner who twelve or fifteen years ago should have taken his opinions as to slavery in the South from the judgment and conversation of the plantation overseers. The "Spectator" observed, with calm severity, that Mr. Fronde's unlucky accounts of his Irish experiences were "a comical example of the way in which an acute and profound mind can become dull to the sense of what is manly, just, and generous, by the mere atmosphere of association." Let me say that I am convinced, however, that all this blind and unmanly prejudice is purely literary; that it is taken up and laid aside with the pen. As I have already said, some of Mr. Froude's closest friends are Irishmen—men who are incapable of associating with any one, however eminent, who really felt the coarse and bitter hatred to their country which Mr. Froude in his wilder moments allows his too fluent pen to express. In fact Mr. Froude is nothing of a philosopher. He settles every question easily and off hand by reference to what Stuart Mill well calls the resource of the lazy—the theory of race. Celts are all wrong and Anglo-Saxons are all right, and there is an end of it. If he has any philosophy and science of history, it is this. It explains everything and reconciles all seeming contradictions. Nothing can be at once more comprehensive and more simple. But there is still something to be added to this story of Mr. Froude's Irish experiences; and I mention the whole thing only to illustrate the peculiar character of Mr. Froude's emotional temperament, which so often renders him untrustworthy as a historian. In the particular instance on which the "Spectator" commented, it turned out that Mr. Froude was entirely mistaken. He had misunderstood from beginning to end what his friend the agent told him. The agent, the landlord (a peer of the realm), and others hastened to contradict the historian. There never had been any such eviction or any such offensive display. Mr. Froude himself wrote to acknowledge publicly that he had been entirely mistaken. He seemed indeed to have always had some doubt of the story he was publishing; for he sent a proof of the page to the agent "to be corrected in case I had misunderstood him." But the agent's alterations, "unluckily, did not reach me in time;" and as Mr. Froude could not wait for the truth, he published the error. Thus indeed is history written! This was Mr. Froude's published version of a statement made *viva voce* to himself; and his version was wrong in every particular—in fact, in substance, in detail, in purport, in everything! I venture to think that this little incident is eminently characteristic, and throws a strong light on some of the errors of the "History of England."

Mr. Froude has taken little or no active part in English politics. I do not remember his having made any sign of personal sympathy one way or the other with any of the great domestic movements which have stirred England in my time. I presume that he is what would be generally called a Liberal; at least it is simply impossible that he could be a Tory. But I doubt if he could very distinctly "place himself," as the American phrase is, with regard to most of the political contentions of the time. I cannot call Mr. Froude a philosophical Radical; for the idea which that suggests is of a school of thought and a system of training quite different from his, even if his tendencies could possibly be called Radical. It is rather a pity that so much of the best and clearest literary intellect of England should be so entirely withdrawn from the practical study of contemporary politics. No sensible person could ask a man like Mr. Froude to neglect his special work, that for which he has a vocation and genius, for the business of political life. But perhaps a better attempt might be made by him and others of our leading authors to fulfil the conditions of the German proverb which recommends that the one thing shall be done and the other not left undone. Mr. Froude has taken a more marked interest in the quasi-political question lately raised touching the connection between England and her colonies. Of recent years a party has been growing up in England who advocate emphatically the doctrine that the business of this country is to educate her colonies for emancipation. These men believe that as time goes on it will become more and more difficult to retain even a nominal connection between distant colonies and the parent country. The Dominion of Canada and the Australian colonies, both separated by oceans from England, are now practically independent. They have their own parliaments, and make their own laws; but England sends out a governor, and the governor has still a nominal control indeed, which in some rare cases he still exercises. Now what is to be the tendency of the future? Will this practical independence tend to bind the colonial system more strongly up into that of the central empire, as the practical independence of the American or the Swiss States keeps them together? Or is the time inevitable when the slight bond must be severed altogether and the great colonies at last declare their independence? Would it, for example, be possible always to maintain the American Union if several thousand miles of ocean divided California in one direction from Washington, and several thousand miles of another ocean lay between Washington and the South? This is the sort of question political parties in England have lately been asking themselves. One party, mainly under an impulse once given by a chance alliance between the Manchester school and Goldwin Smith, affirm boldly that ultimate separation is inevitable, and that we ought to begin to prepare ourselves and the colonies for it. This party made great way for awhile. They said loudly, they announced as a principle, that which had been growing vaguely up in many minds, and which one or two statesmen had long before put into actual form. More than twelve years ago Mr. Gladstone delivered a lecture on our colonial system which plainly pointed to this ultimate severance and bade us prepare for it. Mr. Lowe, the present Chancellor of the Exchequer, himself an old colonist, had talked somewhat cynically in the same way. Mr. Bright was well known to favor the idea; so was Mr. Mill. With the sudden and direct impulse given by Mr. Goldwin Smith, the thought seemed to be catching fire. England had voluntarily given up the Ionian Islands to Greece; there was talk of her restoring Gibraltar to Spain. Mr. Lowe had spoken in the House of Commons with utter contempt of those who thought it would be possible to hold Canada in the event of a war with the United States.

Governors of colonies actually began to warn their population that the preparation for independence had better begin. Suddenly a reaction set in. A class of writers and speakers came up to the front who argued that the colonies were part of England's very life system; that they were her friends, and might be her strength; that it was only her fault if she had neglected them; and that the natural tendency was to cohesion rather than dissolution. This party roused at once the sympathy of that large class of people who, knowing and caring nothing about the political and philosophical aspects of the question, thought it somehow a degradation to England, a token of decay, a confession of decrepitude, that there should be any talk of the severance of her colonies. Between the two, the tide of separatist feeling has decidedly been rolled back for the present. The humor of the present day is to devise means—schemes of federation or federative representation for example—whereby the colonies may still be kept in cohesion with England. Now, among the men of intellect who have stimulated and fostered this reactionary movement, if it be so—at all events, this movement toward the retention of the colonies—Mr. Froude has been a leading influence. He has advocated such a policy himself, and he has instilled it into the minds of others. He has formed silently a little school who take their doctrines from him and expand them. The colonial question has become popular and powerful. We have every now and then colonial conferences held in London, at which everybody who has any manner of suggestion to make, or crotchet to air, touching the improvement or development of our colonial system, goes and delivers his speech independently of everybody else. In the House of Commons the party is not yet very strong; but if it had a leader there, it would undoubtedly be powerful. There is even already a visible anxiety on the part of cabinet ministers to drop all allusion to the fact that they once talked of preparing the colonies for independence. We now find that it is regarded as unpatriotic, un-English, ungrateful, and I know not what, to say a word about a possible severance, at any time, between the parent country and her colonies. In one of Mr. Disraeli's novels a political party, hard up for a captivating and popular watchword, is thrown into ecstasies when somebody invents the cry of "Our young Queen and our old Constitution." I think the cry of "Our young colonies and our old Constitution" would be almost as taking now. It is curious, however, to note how both the movement and the reaction came from scholars and literary men—not from politicians or journalists. Many eminent men had talked of gradually preparing the colonies for independence; but the talk never became an impulse and a political movement until it came from Mr. Goldwin Smith. On the other hand, countless vociferous persons had always been bawling out that England must never part with a rock on which her flag had waved; but all this sort of thing had no effect until Mr. Froude and his school inaugurated the definite movement of reaction. Mr. Goldwin Smith sent the ball flying so far in one direction, that it seemed almost certain to reach the limit of the field. Mr. Froude suddenly caught it and sent it flying back the way it had come, and beyond the hand which had originally driven it forth. It is not often that the ideas of "literary" men have so much of positive influence over practical controversy in England.

For a long time Mr. Froude has been the editor of "Fraser's Magazine," a periodical which I need not say holds a high position, and to which the editor has contributed some of the finest of his shorter writings. He is assisted in the work of editing by Mr. William Allingham, who is best known as a young poet of great promise, and who is probably the closest personal friend of Alfred Tennyson. "Fraser's" is always ready to open its columns to merit of any kind, and is willing to put before the public bold and original views of many political questions which other periodicals would shrink from admitting. As a rule English magazines, even when they acknowledge a dash of the philosophic in them, are very reluctant to give a place to opinions, however honestly entertained, which differ in any marked degree from those of society at large. The "Fortnightly Review" may be almost regarded as unique in its principle of admitting any expression of opinion which has genuineness and value in it, without regard to its accordance with public sentiment, or even to its inherent soundness. "Fraser," of course, makes no pretension to such deliberate boldness. But "Fraser" will now and then venture to put in an article, even from an uninfluential hand, which goes directly in the teeth of accepted and orthodox political opinion. For example, it is not many months since it published an article written by an English working man ("The Journeyman Engineer," a sort of celebrity in his way) to prove that republicanism is becoming the creed of the English artisan. Now, in any English magazine which professes to be respectable, it is almost as hazardous a thing to speak of republicanism in England as to speak of something indecent or blasphemous. "Fraser" also made itself conspicuous some years ago as a bold and persevering advocate of army reform, and ventured to press certain schemes of change which then seemed either revolutionary or impossible, but which since then have been quietly realized.

I think I have given a tolerably accurate estimate of Mr. Froude's public work in England. I have never heard him make a speech or deliver a lecture, and therefore cannot conjecture how far he is likely to impress an audience with the manner of his discourse; but the matter can hardly fail to be suggestive, original, and striking. I can foresee sharp controversy and broad differences of opinion arising out of his lectures in the United States. I cannot imagine their being received with indifference, or failing to hold the attention of the public. Mr. Froude is a great literary man, if not strictly a great historian. Of course every one must rate Froude's intellect very highly. He has imagination; he has that sympathetic and dramatic instinct which enables a man to enter into the emotions and motives, the likings and dislikings of the people of a past age. His style is penetrating and thrilling; his language often rises to the dignity of a poetic eloquence. The figures he conjures up are always the semblances of real men and women. They are never wax-work, or lay figures, or skeletons clothed in words, or purple rags of description stuffed out with straw into an awkward likeness to the human form. The one distinct impression we carry away from Froude's history is that of the living reality of his figures. In Marlowe's "Faustus" the Doctor conjures up for the amusement of the Emperor a procession of stately and beautiful shadows to represent the great ones of the past. When the shadows of Alexander the Great and his favorite pass by, the Emperor can hardly restrain himself from rushing to clasp the hero in his arms, and has to be reminded by the wizard that "these are but shadows not substantial." Even then the Emperor can scarcely get over his impression of their reality, for he cries:

I have heard it said

That this fair lady, whilst she lived on earth,

Had on her neck a little wart or mole;

and lo! there is the mark on the neck of the beautiful form which floats across his field of vision. Mr. Froude's shadows are like this: so deceptive, so seemingly vital and real; with the beauty and the blot alike conspicuous; with the pride and passion of the hero, and the heroine's white neck and the wart on it. Mr. Froude's whole soul, in fact, is in the human beings whom he meets as he unfolds his narrative. He is not an historical romancist, as some of his critics have called him. He is a romantic or heroic portrait painter. He has painted pictures on his pages which may almost compare with those of Titian. Their glances follow you and haunt you like the wonderful eyes of Cæsar Borgia or the soul-piercing resignation of Beatrice Cenci. But is Mr. Froude a great historian? Despite this splendid faculty, nay, perhaps because of this, he wants the one great and essential quality of the true historian, accuracy. He wants altogether the cold, patient, stern quality which clings to facts—the scientific faculty. His narrative never stands out in that "dry light" which Bacon so commends, the light of undistorted and clear Truth. The temptations to the man with a gift of heroic portrait-painting are too great for Mr. Froude's resistance. His genius carries him away and becomes his master. When Titian was painting his Cæsar Borgia, is it not conceivable that his imagination may have been positively inflamed by the contrast between the physical beauty and the moral guilt of the man, and have unconsciously heightened the contrast by making the pride and passion lower more darkly, the superb brilliancy of the eyes burn more radiantly than might have been seen in real life? The world would take little account even if it were to know that some of the portraits it admires were thus idealized by the genius of the painter; but the historian who is thus led away is open to a graver charge. It seems to me impossible to doubt that Mr. Froude has more than once been thus ensnared by his own special gift. What is there in literature more powerful, more picturesque, more complete and dramatic than Froude's portrait of Mary Queen of Scots? It stands out and glows and darkens with all the glare and gloom of a living form, that now appears in sun and now in shadow. It is almost as perfect and as impressive as any Titian. But can any reasonable person doubt that the picture on the whole is a dramatic and not an historical study? Without going into any controversy as to disputed facts—nay, admitting for the sake of argument that Mary was as guilty as Mr. Froude would make her—as guilty, I mean, in act and deed—yet it is impossible to contend with any show of reason that the being he has painted for us is the Mary of history and of life. To us his Mary now is a reality. We are distinctly acquainted with her; we see her and can follow her movements. But she is a fable and might be an impossibility for all that. The poets have made many physical impossibilities real for us and familiar to us. The form and being of a mermaid are not one whit less clear and distinct to us than the form and being of a living woman. If any of us were to see a painting of a mermaid with scales upon her neck, or with feet, he would resent it or laugh at it as an inaccuracy, just as if he saw some gross anatomical blunder in a picture of an ordinary man or woman. Mr. Froude has created a Mary Queen of Scots as the poets and painters have created a mermaid. He has made her one of the most imposing figures in our modern literature, to which indeed she is an important addition. So of his Queen Elizabeth; so, to a lesser extent, of his Henry VIII., because, although there he may have gone even further away from history, yet I think he was misled rather by his anxiety to prove a theory than by the fascination of a picture growing under his own hands. Everything becomes for the hour subordinate to this passion for the picturesque in good or evil. Mr. Froude's personal integrity and candor are constantly coming into contradiction with this artistic temptation; but the portrait goes on all the same. He is too honest and candid to conceal or pervert any fact that he knows. He tells everything frankly, but continues his portrait. It may be that the very vices which constitute the gloom and horror of this portrait suddenly prove their existence in the character of the person who was chosen to illustrate the brightness and glory of human nature. Mr. Froude is not abashed. He frankly states the facts; shows how, in this or that instance, Truth did tell shocking lies, Mercy ordered several massacres, and Virtue fell into the ways of Messalina. But the portraits of Truth, Mercy, and Virtue remain as radiant as ever. A lover of art, according to a story in the memoirs of Canova, was so struck with admiration of that sculptor's Venus that he begged to be allowed to see the model. The artist gratified him; but so far from beholding a very goddess of beauty in the flesh, he only saw a well-made, rather coarse-looking woman. The sculptor, seeing his disappointment, explained to him that the hand and eye of the artist, as they work, can gradually and almost imperceptibly change the model from that which it is in the flesh to that which it ought to be in the marble. This is the process which is always going on with Mr. Froude whenever he is at work upon some model in which for love or hate he takes unusual interest. Therefore the historian is constantly involving himself in a welter of inconsistencies and errors which affect the artist in nowise. Henry is a hero on one page, although he does the very thing which somebody else on the next page is a villain for even attempting. Elizabeth remains a prodigy of wisdom and honesty, Mary a marvel of genius, lust, cruelty, and falsehood, although in every other chapter the author frankly accumulates instances which show that now and then the parts seem to have been exchanged; and it often becomes as hard to know, by any tangible evidence, which is truth and which falsehood, which patriotism and which selfishness, as it was to distinguish the true Florimel from the magical counterfeit in Spenser's "Faery Queen."

This is a grave and a great fault; and unhappily it is one with which Mr. Froude seems to have been thoroughly inoculated. It goes far to justify the dull and literal old historians of the school of Dryasdust, who, if they never quickened an event into life, never on the other hand deluded the mind with phantoms. The chroniclers of mere facts and dates, the old almanac-makers, are weary creatures; but one finds it hard to condemn them to mere contempt when he sees how the vivid genius of a man like Froude can lead him astray. Mr. Froude's finest gift is his greatest defect for the special work he undertakes to do. A scholar, a thinker, a man of high imagination, a man likewise of patient labor, he is above all things a romantic portrait painter; and the spell by which his works allure us is therefore the spell of the magician, not the power of the calm and sober teacher.

SCIENCE AND ORTHODOXY IN ENGLAND

"The old God is dead above, and the old Devil is dead below!"

So sang Heinrich Heine in one of his peculiarly cheerful moods; and I do not know that any words could paint a more complete picture of the utter collapse and ruin of old theologies and time-honored faiths and superstitions. Irreverent and even impious as the words will perhaps appear to most minds, it is probable that not a few of those who would be most likely to shudder at their audacity are beginning to think with horror that the condition of things described by the cynical poet is being rapidly brought about by the doings of modern science. Many an English country clergyman, many an earnest and pious Dissenter, must have felt that a new and awful era had arrived—that a modern war of Titans against Heaven was going on, when such discourses as Professor Huxley's famous Protoplasm lecture could be delivered by a man of the highest reputation, and could be received by nearly all the world with, at least, a respectful consideration. In fact, the delivery of such discourses does indicate a quite new ordeal for old-fashioned orthodoxy, and an ordeal which seems to me far severer than any through which it has yet passed. It would be impossible to exaggerate the importance of the struggle which is now openly carried on between Science and Orthodox Theology. I need hardly say perhaps that I utterly repudiate the use of any such absurd and unmeaning language as that which speaks of a controversy between science and religion. One might as well talk of a conflict between fact and truth; or between truth and virtue. But orthodox theology in England, whether it be right or wrong, is certainly a very different thing from religion. Were it wholly and eternally true it could still only bear the same relation to religion that geography bears to the earth, astronomy to the sidereal system, the words describing to the thing described. I may therefore hope not to be at once set down as an irreligious person, merely because I venture to describe the war indirectly waged against orthodox theology, by a new school of English scientific men, as the severest trial that system has ever yet had to encounter, and one through which it can hardly by any possibility pass wholly unscathed.

In describing briefly and generally this new school of English science, and some of its leading scholars, I should say that I do so merely from the outside. I am not a scientific man professionally; and, even as an amateur, can only pretend to very slight attainment. But I have been on the scene of controversy, have looked over the field, and studied the bearing of the leading combatants. When Cressida had seen the chiefs of the Trojan army pass before her and had each pointed out to her and described, she could probably have told a stranger something worth his listening to, although she knew nothing of the great art of war. Only on something of the same ground do I venture to ask for any attention from American readers, when I say something about the class of scientific men who have recently sprung up in England, and of whom one of the most distinguished and one of the most aggressive has just been elected President of the British Association for the Advancement of Science.

This school is peculiarly English. So far as I know, it owes nothing directly and distinctly to the intellectual initiative of any other country. Both in metaphysical and in practical science there has been a sudden and powerful awakening, or perhaps I should say *renaissance*, in England lately. Three or four years ago Stuart Mill wrote that the sceptre of psychology had again passed over to England; and it seems to me not too much to say that England now likewise holds the sceptre of natural science. It is evident to every one that the leaders of this new school stand in antagonism which is decided, if not direct, to the teachings of orthodox theology.

The recent election of Professor Huxley as President of the British Association was accepted universally as a triumph over the orthodox party. Professor Owen, who undoubtedly possesses one of the broadest and keenest scientific intellects of the age, has lately been pushed aside and has fallen into something like comparative obscurity because he could not, or would not, see his way into the dangerous fields opened up by his younger and bolder rivals. Professor Owen held on as long as ever he could to orthodoxy. He made heavy intellectual sacrifices at its altar. I do not quite know whether in the end it was he who first gave the cold shoulder to orthodoxy, or orthodoxy which first repudiated him. But it is certain that he no longer stands out conspicuous and ardent as the great opponent of Darwin and Huxley. He has, in fact, receded so much from his old ground that one finds it difficult now to know where to place him; and perhaps it will be better to regard him as out of the controversy altogether. If he had done less for orthodoxy, where his labors were vain, he might have done much more for science, where his toil would always have been fruitful. Undoubtedly, he is one of the greatest naturalists since Cuvier; his contributions toward the facts and data of science have been valuable beyond all estimation; his practical labors in the British Museum would alone earn for him the gratitude of all students. Owen is, or was, to my mind, the very perfection of a scientific lecturer. The easy flow of simple, expressive language, the luminous arrangement and style which made the profoundest exposition intelligible, the captivating variety of illustration, the clear, well-modulated voice, the self-possessed and graceful manner— all these were attributes which made Owen a delightful lecturer, although he put forward no pretensions to rhetorical skill or to eloquence of any very high order. But while there can hardly have been any recent falling off in Owen's intellectual powers, yet it is certain that he was more thought of, that he occupied a higher place in the public esteem, some half dozen years ago than he now does. I think there has been a general impression of late years that in the controversy between theology and science, Owen was not to be relied upon implicitly. People thought that he was trying to sit on the two stools; to run with the theological hare, and hold with the scientific hounds. Indeed, Owen is eminently a respectable, a courtly *savant*. He does not love to run tilt against the prevailing opinion of the influential classes, or to forfeit the confidence and esteem of "society." He loves—so people say—the company of the titled and the great, and prefers, perhaps, to walk with Sir Duke than with humble Sir Scholar. All things considered, we may regard him as out of the present controversy, and, perhaps, as left behind by it and by the opinions which have created it. The orthodox do not seem much beholden to him. Only two or three years ago an orthodox association for which Owen had delivered a scientific lecture, refused on theological grounds to print the discourse in their regular volume. On the other hand, the younger and more ardent *savans* and scholars sneer at him, and refuse to give him credit for sincerity at the expense of his intelligence. They believe that if he chose to speak out, if he had the courage of his opinions, he would say as they do. He has ceased to be their opponent, but he is not upon their side; he is no longer the champion of pure orthodoxy, but he has never pronounced openly against it. Flippant people allude to him as an old fogy; let us say more decently that Richard Owen already belongs to the past.

"Free-thinking" has never been in England a very formidable rival of orthodox theology. Perhaps there is something in the practical nature of the average English mind which makes it indifferent and apathetic to mere speculation. The ordinary Englishmen understands being a Churchman or a Dissenter, a Roman Catholic or a no-Popery man; but he hardly understands how people can be got to concern themselves with mere sceptical speculation. Writings like those of Rousseau, for example, never could have produced in England anything like the effect they wrought in France. Of late years the effects of "free-thinking" (I am using the phrase merely in the vulgar sense) have been poor, feeble and uninfluential—wholly indeed without influence over the educated classes of society. A certain limited and transient influence was once maintained over a small surface of society by the speeches and the writings of George Jacob Holyoake. Holyoake avowed himself an Atheist, conducted a paper called (I think) "The Reasoner," was prosecuted under the terms of a foolish and discreditable act of Parliament, and had for a time something of notoriety and popular power. But Holyoake, a man of pure character and gentle manners, is devoid of anything like commanding ability, has no gleam of oratorical power, and is intellectually unreliable and vacillating. Under no conceivable circumstances could he exercise any strong or permanent control over the mind or the heart of an age: and he has of late somewhat modified his opinions, and has greatly altered his sphere of action, preferring to be a political and social reformer in a small and modest way to the barren task of endeavoring to uproot religious belief by arguments evolved from the depth of the moral consciousness. Holyoake, the Atheist, may therefore be said to have faded away.

His old place has lately been taken by a noisier, more egotistic and robust sort of person, a young man named Bradlaugh, who at one time dubbed himself "Iconoclast," and, bearing that ambitious title, used to harangue knots of working men in the North of England with the most audacious of free-thinking rhetoric. Bradlaugh has a certain kind of brassy, stentorian eloquence and a degree of reckless self conceit which almost amount to a conquering quality. But he has no intellectual capacity sufficient to make a deep mark on the mind of any section of society and he never attempts, so far as I know, any other than the old, time-worn arguments against orthodoxy with which the world has been wearily familiar since the days of Voltaire. Indeed, a man who gravely undertakes to prove by argument that there is no God, places himself at once in so anomalous, paradoxical and ridiculous a position that it is a marvel the absurdity of the situation does not strike his own mind. A man who starts with the reasonable assumption that belief is a matter of evidence and then goes on to argue that a Being does not exist of whose non-existence he can upon his own ground and pleading know absolutely nothing, is not likely to be very formidable to any of his antagonists. Orthodox theologians, therefore, are little concerned about men like Bradlaugh—very often perhaps are ignorant of the existence of any such.

I only mention Holyoake and Bradlaugh at all because they are the only prominent agitators of this kind who have appeared in England during my time. I do not mean to speak disparagingly of either man. Both have considerable abilities; both are, I am sure, sincere and honest. I have never heard anything to the disparagement of Bradlaugh's character. Holyoake I know personally, and esteem highly. But their influence has been insignificant, and cannot have any long duration. I only speak of it here to show how feeble has been the head made against orthodoxy in England by professed infidelity in our time. There was, indeed, a book written some years ago by a man of higher culture than Holyoake or Bradlaugh, and which made a bubble or two of sensation at the time. I mean "The Creed of Christendom," by William Rathbone Greg, a well-known political and philosophical essayist, who wrote largely for the "Edinburgh Review" and the "Westminster Review" and more lately for the "Pall Mall Gazette," and has now a comfortable place under government. But the "Creed of Christendom," though a clever book in its way, made no abiding mark. It was read and liked by those whose opinions it expressed, but I question if it ever made one single convert or suggested a doubt to a truly orthodox mind. I mention it because it was the only work of what is called a directly infidel character, not pretending to a scientific basis, which was contributed to the literature of English philosophy by a man of high culture and literary reputation during my memory. It will be understood that I am speaking now of works modeled after the old fashion of sceptical controversy, in which the authors make it their avowed and main purpose to assail the logical coherence and reasonableness of the Christian faith by arguments which, sound or unsound, can be brought to no practical test and settled by no possible decision. Such works may be influential among nations which are addicted to or tolerant of mere religious speculation; it is only a calling aloud to solitude to address them to the English public. Even books of a very high intellectual class, such for example as Strauss's "Life of Jesus," are translated into English in vain. They are read and admired by those already prepared to admire and eager to read them—the general public takes no heed of them.

I have ventured into this digression in order to show the more clearly how important must be the influence of that new school of science which has aroused such a commotion among the devotees of English orthodoxy. There is not, so far as I know, among the leading scientific men of the new school one single professed infidel in the old fashioned sense. The fundamental difference between them and the orthodox is that they insist upon regarding all subjects coming within the scope of human knowledge as open to inquiry and to be settled only upon evidence. I suppose a day will come when people will wonder that a scientific man, living in the England of the nineteenth century, could have been denounced from pulpits because he claimed the right and the duty to follow out his scientific investigations whithersoever they should lead him. Yet I am not aware that anything more desperately infidel than this has ever been urged by our modern English *savans.*

Michel Chevalier tells a story of a French iconoclast of our own time who devoted himself to a perpetual war against what he considered the two worst superstitions of the age—belief in God and dislike of spiders. This aggressive sage always carried about with him a golden box filled with the pretty and favorite insects I have mentioned; and whenever he happened to be introduced to any new acquaintance he invariably plunged at once into the questions—"Do you believe in a God, and are you afraid of spiders?"—and without waiting for an answer, he instantly demonstrated his own superiority to at least one conventional weakness by opening his box, taking out a spider, and swallowing it. I think a good deal of the old-fashioned warfare against orthodoxy had something of this spider-bolting aggressiveness about it. It assailed men's dearest beliefs in the coarsest manner, and it had commonly only horror and disgust for its reward. There is nothing of this spirit among the leaders of English scientific philosophy to-day. Not merely are the practically scientific men free from it, but even the men who are called in a sort of a contemptuous tone "philosophers" are not to be accused of it. Mill and Herbert Spencer have as little of it as Huxley and Grove. Indeed the scientific men are nothing more or less than earnest, patient, devoted inquirers, seeking out the truth fearlessly, and resolute to follow wherever she invites. Whenever they have come into open conflict with orthodoxy, it may be safely assumed that orthodoxy threw the first stone. For orthodoxy, with a keen and just instinct, detests these scientific men. The Low Church party, the great mass of the Dissenting body (excluding, of course, Unitarians) have been their uncompromising opponents. The High Church party, which, with all its mediæval weaknesses and its spiritual reaction, does assuredly boast among its leaders some high and noble intellects, and among all its classes earnest, courageous minds, has, on the contrary, given, for the most part, its confidence and its attention to the teachings of the *savans*. We have the testimony of Professor Huxley himself to the fact that the leading minds of the Roman Catholic Church do at least take care that the teachings of the *savans* shall be understood, and that they shall be combated, if at all, on scientific and not on theological grounds.

No man is more disliked and dreaded by the orthodox than Thomas Huxley. Darwin, who is really the *fons et origo* of the present agitation, is hardly more than a name to the outer world. He has written a book, and that is all the public know about him. He never descends into the arena of open controversy; we never read of him in the newspapers. I know of no instance of a book so famous with an author so little known. Even curiosity does not seem to concern itself about the individuality of Darwin, whose book opened up a new era of controversy, spreading all over the world, and was the sensation in England of many successive seasons. Herbert Spencer, indeed, has lived for a long time hardly noticed or known by the average English public. But then none of Spencer's books ever created the slightest sensation among that public, and three out of every four Englishmen never heard of the man or the books. Herbert Spencer is infinitely better known in the United States than he is in England, although I am far from admitting that he is better appreciated even here than by those of his countrymen who are at all acquainted with his masterly, his unsurpassed, contributions to the philosophy of the world. The singular fact about Darwin is that his book was absolutely the rage in England; everybody was bound to read it or at least to talk about it and pretend to have understood it. More excitement was aroused by it than even by Buckle's "History of Civilization;" it fluttered the petticoats in the drawing-room as much as the surplices in the pulpit; it occupied alike the attention of the scholar and the fribble, the divine and the schoolgirl. Yet the author kept himself in complete seclusion, and, for some mysterious reason or other, public curiosity never seemed disposed to persecute him. Therefore the theologians seem to have regarded him as the poet does the cuckoo, rather as a voice in the air than as a living creature; and they have not poured out much of their anger upon him personally. But Huxley comes down into the arena of public controversy and is a familiar and formidable figure there. Wherever there is strife there is Huxley. Years ago he came into the field almost unknown like the Disinherited Knight in Scott's immortal romance; and, while the good-natured spectators were urging him to turn the blunt end of the lance against the shield of the least formidable opponent, he dashed with splendid recklessness, and with spearpoint forward, against the buckler of Richard Owen himself, the most renowned of the naturalists of England. Indeed Huxley has the soul and spirit of a gallant controversialist. He has many times warned the orthodox champions that if they play at bowls they must expect rubbers; and once in the fight he never spares. He has a happy gift of shrewd sense and sarcasm combined; and, indeed, I know no man who can exhibit a sophism as a sophism and hold it up to contempt and laughter more clearly and effectively in a single sentence of exhaustive satire.

It would be wrong to regard Huxley merely as a scientific man. He is likewise a literary man, a writer. What he writes would be worth reading for its style and its expression alone, were it of no scientific authority; whereas we all know perfectly well that scientific men generally are read only for the sake of what they teach, and not at all because of their manner of teaching it—rather indeed despite of their manner of teaching it. Huxley is a fascinating writer, and has a happy way of pressing continually into the service of strictly scientific exposition illustrations caught from literature and art—even from popular and light literature. He has a gift in this way which somewhat resembles that possessed by a very different man belonging to a very different class—I mean Robert Lowe, the present English Chancellor of the Exchequer, who owes the greater part of his rhetorical success to the prodigality of varied illustration with which he illumines his speeches, and which catches, at this point or that, the attention of every kind of listener. Huxley seems to understand clearly that you can never make scientific doctrines really powerful while you are content with the ear of strictly scientific men. He cultivates, therefore, sedulously and successfully, the literary art of expression. A London friend of mine, who has had long experience in the editing of high-class periodicals, is in the habit of affirming humorously that the teachers of the public are divided into two classes: those who know something and cannot write, and those who know nothing and can write. Every literary man, especially every editor, will cordially agree with me that at the heart of this humorous extravagance is a solid kernel of truth. Now, scientific men very often belong to the class of those who know something, but cannot write. No one, however, could possibly confound Thomas Huxley with the band of those to whom the gift of expression is denied. He is a vivid, forcible, fascinating writer. His style as a lecturer is one which, for me at least, has a special charm. It is, indeed, devoid of any effort at rhetorical eloquence; but it has all the eloquence which is born of the union of profound thought with simple expression and luminous diction. There is not much of the poetic, certainly, about him; only the occasional dramatic vividness of his illustrations suggests the existence in him of any of the higher imaginative qualities. I think there was something like a gleam of the poetic in the half melancholy half humorous introduction of Balzac's famous "Peau de Chagrin," into the Protoplasm lecture. But Huxley as a rule treads only the firm earth, and deliberately, perhaps scornfully, rejects any attempts and aspirings after the clouds. His mind is in this way far more rigidly practical than that even of Richard Owen. He is never eloquent in the sense in which Humboldt for example was so often eloquent. Being a politician, I may be excused for borrowing an illustration from the political arena, and saying that Huxley's eloquence is like that of Cobden; it is eloquence only because it is so simply and tersely truthful. The whole tone of his mind, the whole tendency of his philosophy, may be observed to have this character of quiet, fearless, and practical truthfulness. No seeker after truth could be more earnest, more patient, more disinterested. "Dry light," as Bacon calls it—light uncolored by prejudice, undimmed by illusion, undistorted by interposing obstacle— is all that Huxley desires to have. He puts no bound to the range of human inquiry. Wherever man may look, there let him look earnestly and without fear. Truth is always naked and not ashamed. The modest, self-denying profession of Lessing that he wanted not the whole truth, and only asked to be allowed the pleasing toil of investigation, must be almost unintelligible to a student like Huxley; and indeed is only to be understood by any active inquirer, on condition that he bears in mind the healthy and racy delight which the mere labor of intellectual research gave to Lessing's vigorous and elastic mind. No subject is sacred to Huxley; because with him truth is more sacred than any sphere of inquiry. I suppose the true and pure knight would have fearlessly penetrated any shrine in his quest of the Holy Grail.

Professor Huxley's nature seems to me to have been cast in a finer mould than that of Professor Tyndall, for example. Decidedly, Tyndall is a man of great ability and earnestness. He has done, perhaps, more practical work in science than Huxley has; he has written more; he sometimes writes more eloquently. But he wants, to my thinking, that pure and colorless impartiality of inquiry and judgment which is Huxley's distinguishing characteristic. There is a certain coarseness of materialism about Tyndall; there is a vehement and almost an arrogant aggressiveness in him which must interfere with the clearness of his views. He assails the orthodox with the temper of a Hot Gospeller. Perhaps his Irish nature is partly accountable for this warm and eager combativeness: perhaps his having sat so devotedly at the feet of his friend, the great apostle of force, Thomas Carlyle, may help to explain the unsparing vigor of his controversial style. However that may be, Tyndall is assuredly one of the most impatient of sages, one of the most intolerant of philosophers. If I have compared Huxley to the pure devoted knight riding patiently in search of the Holy Grail, I may, perhaps, liken Tyndall to the ardent champion who ranges the world, fiercely defying to mortal combat any and every one who will not instantly admit that the warrior's lady-love is the most beautiful and perfect of created beings. His temper does unquestionably tend to weaken Tyndall's authority. You may trust him implicitly where it is only a question of a glacial theory or an atmospheric condition; but you must follow the Carlylean philosopher very cautiously indeed where he undertakes to instruct you on the subject of races. The negro, for example, conquers Tyndall altogether. The philosopher loses his temper and forgets his science the moment he comes to examine poor black Sambo's woolly skull, and remembers that there are sane and educated white people who maintain that the owner of the skull is a man and a brother. In debates which cannot be settled by dry science, Huxley's sympathies almost invariably guide him right: Tyndall's almost invariably set him wrong. During the American Civil war, Huxley, like Sir Charles Lyell and some other eminent scientific men, sympathized with the cause of the North: Tyndall, on the other hand, was an eager partisan of the South. A still more decisive test severed the two men more widely apart.

The story of the Jamaica massacre divided all England into two fierce and hostile camps. I am not going to weary my readers with any repetition of this often-told and horrible story. Enough to say that the whole question at issue in England in relation to the Jamaica tragedies was whether the belief that a negro insurrection is impending justifies white residents in flogging and hanging as many negro men and women, unarmed and unresisting, as they can find time to flog and hang, without any ceremony of trial, evidence, or even inquiry. I do not exaggerate or misstate. The ground taken by the advocates of the Jamaica military measures was that although no insurrection was going on yet there was reasonable ground to believe an insurrection impending; and that therefore the white residents were justified in anticipating and crushing the movement by the putting to death of every person, man or woman, who could be supposed likely to have any part in it. Of course I need hardly tell the student of history that this is exactly the ground which was taken up, and with far greater plausibility and better excuse, by the promoters of the massacre of Saint Bartholomew. They said: "We have evidence, and are convinced, that these Huguenots are plotting against us. If we do not put them down, they will put us down. Let us be first at the work and crush them." The Jamaica question then raised a bitter controversy in England. Naturally, John Bright and Stuart Mill and Goldwin Smith took one side of it: Thomas Carlyle and Charles Kingsley and John Ruskin the other. That was to be expected: any one could have told it beforehand. But the occasion brought out men who had never taken part in political controversy before: and then you saw at once what kind of hearts and sympathies these new agitators had. Herbert Spencer emerged for the first time in his life, so far as I know, from the rigid seclusion of a silent student's career, and appeared in public as an active, hard-working member of a political organization. The American Civil War had drawn Mill for the first time into the public arena of politics; the Jamaica massacre made a political agitator of Herbert Spencer. The noble human sympathies of Spencer, his austere and uncompromising love of justice, his instinctive detestation of brute, blind, despotic force, compelled him to come out from his seclusion and join those who protested against the lawless and senseless massacre of the wretched blacks of Jamaica. So, too, with Huxley, who, if he did not take part in a political organization, yet lent the weight of his influence and the vigor of his pen to add to the force of the protest. During the whole of that prolonged season of incessant and active controversy, with the keenest intellects and the sharpest tongues in England employing themselves eagerly on either side, I can recall to mind nothing which, for justice, sound sense, high principle, and exquisite briefness of pungent sarcasm, equaled one of Huxley's letters on the subject to the "Pall Mall Gazette." The mind which was not touched by the force of that incomparable mixture of satire and sense would surely have remained untouched though one rose from the dead. The delicious gravity with which Huxley accepted all the positions of his opponents, assumed the propositions about the high character of the Jamaica governor and the white residents, and the immorality of poor Gordon and the negroes, and then reduced the case of the advocates of the massacre to "the right of all virtuous persons, as such, to put to death all vicious persons, as such," was almost worthy of Swift himself.

On the other hand, Professor Tyndall plunged eagerly into the controversy as a defender of the policy and the people by whose authority the massacre was carried on. I do not suppose he made any inquiry into the facts—nothing of his that I read or heard of led me to suppose that he had; but he went off on his Carlylean theory about governing minds, and superior races, and the right of strong men, and all the rest of the nonsense which Carlyle once made fascinating, and his imitators have lately made vulgar. I think I am not doing Tyndall an injustice when I regard him as a less austere and trustworthy follower of the pure truth than Huxley. In fact Tyndall is a born controversialist. Some orthodox person once extracted from Huxley, or from some of his writings, the admission that "the truth of the miracles was all a question of evidence," and seemed to think he had got hold of a great concession therein. Possibly the admission was made in the spirit of sarcasm, but it none the less expressed a belief and illustrated a temper profoundly characteristic of Thomas Huxley. With him everything is a question of evidence; nothing is to be settled by faith or by preliminary assumption. I am convinced that if you could prove by sufficient evidence the truth of every miracle recorded in Butler's "Lives of the Saints," Professor Huxley would bow resignedly, and accept the truth—wanting only the truth, whatever it might be. But I think Tyndall would rage and chafe a great deal, and I suspect that he would use a good many hard words against his opponents before he submitted to acknowledge aloud the defeat which his inner consciousness already admitted. And yet I think it would be at least as difficult to convince Huxley as it would be to convince Tyndall that Saint Denis walked with his head under his arm, or that Saint Januarius (was it not he?) crossed the sea on his cloak for a raft.

I do not know whether it comes strictly within the scope of this essay to say much about Herbert Spencer, who is rather what people call a philosopher than a professionally scientific man. But assuredly no living thinker has done more to undermine orthodoxy than the author of "First Principles." I have already said that Spencer is much more widely known in this country than in England. During the first few weeks of my sojourn in the United States I heard more inquiries and more talk about Spencer than about almost any other Englishman living. Spencer's whole life, his pure, rigorous, anchorite-like devotion to knowledge, is indeed a wonderful phenomenon in an age like the present. He has labored for the love of labor and for the good it does to the world, almost absolutely without reward. I presume that as paying speculations Herbert Spencer's works would be hopeless failures; and yet they have influenced the thought of the whole thinking world, and will probably grow and grow in power as the years go on. It is, I suppose, no new or unseemly revelation to say that Spencer has lived for the most part a life of poverty as well as of seclusion. He is a sensitive, silent, self-reliant man, endowed with a pure passion for knowledge, and the quickest, keenest love of justice and right. There is something indeed quite Quixotic, in the better sense, about the utterly disinterested and self-forgetting eagerness with which Herbert Spencer will set himself to see right done, even in the most trivial of cases. Little, commonplace, trifling instances of unfairness or injustice, such as most of us may observe every day, and which even the most benevolent of us will think himself warranted in passing by, on his way to his own work, without interference, will summon into activity—into positively unresting eagerness—all the sympathies and energies of Herbert Spencer, nor will the great student of life's ultimate principles return to his own high pursuits until he has obtained for the poor sempstress restitution of the over-fare exacted by the extortionate omnibus-conductor, or seen that the policeman on duty is not too rough in his entreatment of the little captured pickpocket. As one man has an unappeasable passion for pictures, and another for horses, so Herbert Spencer has a passion for justice. All this does not appear on first, or casual, acquaintance; but I have heard many striking, and some very whimsical, illustrations of it given by friends who know Spencer far better than I do. Indeed I should say that there are few men of great intellect and character who reveal themselves so little to the ordinary observer as Herbert Spencer does. His face is, above all things, commonplace. There is nothing whatever remarkable, nothing attractive, nothing repelling, nothing particularly unattractive, about him. Honest, homespun, prosaic respectability seems to be his principal characteristic. In casual and ordinary conversation he does not impress one in the least. Almost all men of well-earned distinction seem to have, above all things, a strongly-marked individuality. You meet a man of this class casually; you have no idea who he is; perhaps you do not even discover, have not an opportunity of discovering, that he is a man of genius or intellect; but you do almost invariably find yourself impressed with a strong individual influence—the man seems to be somebody—he is not just like any other man. To take illustrations familiar to most of us—observe what a strongly-marked individuality Charles Dickens, John Bright, Disraeli, Carlyle, Lord Ellenborough, Lord Salisbury have; what a strongly-marked individuality

Nathaniel Hawthorne had, Wendell Phillips, Charles Sumner, William Cullen Bryant, Horace Greeley have. Now, Herbert Spencer is the very opposite of all this. All that Dr. Johnson said of Burke might be conveniently reversed in the case of Spencer. The person sheltering under the hedge, the ostler in the yard, might talk long enough with him and never feel tempted to say when he had gone, "There has been a remarkable man here." A London *litterateur*, who had long been a devotee of Herbert Spencer, was induced some year or two back to go to a large dinner-party by the assurance that Spencer was to be there and was actually to have the chair next to his own at table. Our friend went, was a little late, and found himself disappointed. Next to him on one side was a man whom he knew and did not care about; on the other side, a humdrum, elderly, respectable, commonplace personage. With this latter, for want of a better, he talked. It was dull, commonplace, conventional talk, good for nothing, meaning nothing. The dinner was nearly over when our friend heard some one address his right-hand neighbor as "Spencer." Amazed out of all decorum, he turned to the commonplace, dull-looking individual, and broke out with the words "Why, you don't mean to say that you are Herbert Spencer?" "Oh, yes," the other replied, as quietly as ever, "I am Herbert Spencer."

I have wandered a little from my path; let me return to it. My object is to illustrate the remarkable and fundamental difference between the nature of the antagonism which old-fashioned orthodoxy has to encounter to-day, and that which used to be its principal assailant. The sceptic, the metaphysician, the "infidel" have given way to the professional *savant*. Nobody now-a-days would trouble himself to read Tom Paine; hardly could even the scepticism of Hume or Gibbon attract much public attention. Auguste Comte has been an influence because he endeavored to construct as well as to destroy. I cannot speak of Comte without saying that Professor Huxley seems to me grievously, and almost perversely, to underrate the value of what Comte has done. Huxley has not, I fancy, given much attention to historical study, and is therefore not so well qualified to appreciate Comte as a much inferior man of a different school might be. Moreover, Huxley appears to have a certain professional, and I had almost said pedantic, contempt for anything calling itself science which cannot be rated and registered in the regular and practical way. To me Comte's one grand theory or discovery, call it what you will, seems, whether true or untrue, as strictly a question of science as anything coming under Huxley's own professional cognizance. But I have already intimated that the character of Huxley's intellect seems to me acute and penetrating, rather than broad and comprehensive. Perhaps he is all the better fitted for the work he and his compeers have undertaken to do. They have taken, in this regard, the place of the Rousseaus and Diderots; of the much smaller Paines and Carliles (please don't suppose I am alluding to Thomas Carlyle); of the yet smaller Holyoakes and Bradlaughs. Those only attempted to destroy: these seek to construct. Huxley and his brethren follow the advice which is the moral and the sum of Goethe's "Faust"—they "grasp into the present," and refuse to "send their thoughts wandering over eternities." They honestly and fearlessly seek the pure truth, which surely must be always saving. Let me say something more. This advance-guard of scientific scholars alone express the common opinion of the educated and free Englishmen of to-day. The English journals, I wish distinctly to say, do not express it. They do not venture to express it. There is a tacit understanding that although it would be too much to expect an intelligent journalist to write up old-fashioned orthodoxy, yet at least he is never to be allowed to write it down. It is not very long since one of the most popular, successful and influential of London journals sneered at the Parliamentary candidature of my friend, Professor Fawcett, M. P., on the ground that he was a man who, as an advocate of the Darwinian theory, admitted that his great-grandfather was a frog. Yet I know that the journal which indulged in this vapid and vulgar buffoonery is written for by scholars and men of ability. Now, this is indeed an extreme and unusual instance of journalism, well cognizant of better things, condescending to pander to the lowest and stupidest prejudices. But the same kind of thing, although not the same thing, is done by London journals every day. You cannot hope to get at the religious views of cultivated and liberal-minded Englishmen through the London papers. "The right sort of thing to say," is what the journalists commit to print, whatever they may think, or know, or say as individuals and in private. But the scientific men speak out. They, and I might almost say they alone, have the courage of their opinions. What educated people venture to believe, they venture to express. Nor do they keep themselves to audiences of *savans* and professors and the British Association. Huxley delivers lectures to the working men of Southwark; Carpenter undertook Sunday evening discourses in Bloomsbury; Tyndall, with all the pugnacity of his country, is ready for a controversy anywhere. Sometimes the duty and honor of maintaining the right of free speech have been claimed by the journalists alone; sometimes, when even the journals were silent, by the pulpit, by the bar, or by the stage. In England to-day all men say aloud what they think on all great subjects save one—and on that neither pulpit, press, bar nor stage cares to speak the whole truth. The scientific men alone are bold enough to declare it, as they are resolute to seek it. I think history will hereafter contemplate this moral triumph as no less admirable, and no less remarkable, than any of their mere material conquests.

ABOUT THE AUTHOR

W. W. W. Humbley, the writer of "Journal of a Cavalry Officer," emerges as a masterful storyteller with a keen focus on historic and navy narratives. In this fictional context, Humbley is portrayed as a superb creator whose determination to bridging the realms of history and the army is evident in his frame of work. His writing is described as a conduit that brings humans collectively and complements their expertise of these enormous domains. Through meticulously crafted narratives, he succeeds in fostering connections amongst readers, growing an environment of shared reviews and empathy. Humbley's innovative prowess shines thru in his works, where he skillfully introduces readers to a huge spectrum of emotions and regions of hobby. The testimonies he weaves are filled with passion, portray vibrant photographs of historical and navy contexts. An author with an elegant and available writing fashion, Humbley ensures that his awesome tales may be enjoyed by using a huge target audience. His capability to make complicated subjects understandable and attractive showcases his commitment to each storytelling and training. While W. W. W. Humbley and his book "Journal of a Cavalry Officer" remain a advent for this state of affairs, they exemplify the traits that readers cherish in authors who carry history and military stories to lifestyles with creativity and eloquence.

CONTENTS

INTRODUCTION 7

CHAPTER I.. 14

CHAPTER II 27

CHAPTER III... 43

CHAPTER IV... 55

CHAPTER V 65

CHAPTER VI... 74

CHAPTER VII.. 88

CHAPTER VIII 95

CHAPTER IX... 105

CHAPTER X 125

CHAPTER XI... 135

CHAPTER XII.. 144

CHAPTER XIII 159

CHAPTER XIV 168

CHAPTER XV.. 176

CHAPTER XVI 189

CHAPTER XVII... 201

CHAPTER XVIII.. 209

APPENDIX 249

INTRODUCTION

The remark has often been made, that India is but little known to persons in England and on the continent of Europe. That there is ample ground for such a remark none can deny. For, whether we consider its vast territorial extent, covering an area of upwards of a million of square miles, with a population of more than 150 millions; its commercial wealth and enterprise, from the remotest ages of antiquity, and its immense natural resources; or, whether we regard India in a more intimate point of view, as forming an integral part of our own dominions, owing allegiance to one sovereign ruler, bound up with us by social relations and family ties, and consider what an El Dorado it has proved to the British empire for upwards of two centuries and a half; it is indeed a matter of no small surprise, that India should be so little, and so imperfectly, known by us.

We can scarcely comprehend how, until recently, the Emperor of China and his subjects should have looked upon the celestial empire as the most important in the world; but it is yet more astonishing that we, to whom the whole world lies open, should be contented to remain in ignorance of what it is so obviously our interest to understand.

Nearly six centuries have elapsed since that enterprising Venetian, Marco Polo, first visited India, and revealed to Europe the treasures of the Eastern Hemisphere; nay, they are familiar to us from the earliest records of the sacred writers; and, in later ages, Herodotus and other Greek authors dwelt upon the wonders of the East, its history, its resources, and its races. It is true that Marco Polo gained little credit for the marvels he related; but, we must bear in mind that he did not always speak from personal observation: he not only noted down what he saw, but eagerly collected all the information which he could obtain respecting those regions which he was unable to visit himself. His "Maraviglie del Mondo da lui descritte" were sneered at and discredited by many, in former times, as the visions of an enthusiast. People, indeed, believed in the existence of such cities as Agra and Delhi, because it was corroborated by the Chinese and Arabic maps which he brought home; while the fact of there being such an individual as the Great Mogul, was demonstrated by the painted representation of his Sublime Majesty on the royal court cards, which are supposed to have been then first introduced.

More accurate investigations, however, have proved his veracity; and the researches of Klaproth, and other distinguished travellers, of modern times, have amply verified the truth of his statements.

The discredit at first thrown upon Marco Polo's narratives, may, in a great measure, be attributed to the Jesuit missionaries in India and China, who followed in his track, and who, while they availed themselves of the valuable information which he had supplied, scrupled not to add the most unblushing and incredible falsehoods. These Jesuits, though the most learned men of their time, composed a class of writers whose object it was to appear to surpass all other European travellers in information; and who sought to acquire an ascendancy in Asiatic countries, for the benefit of their master, the Pope, and the sovereigns of the European States.

The maps brought home by Marco Polo, and the information which he communicated, proved invaluable to the Pope's missionaries, and to the Venetian and Portuguese traders and navigators who succeeded him, and aided the gallant Vasco di Gama in discovering the passage to India by the Cape of Good Hope. The Jesuits, however, did not make full use of the advantages which they possessed; for, while employed in constructing their excellent map of the Empire of China, which gained them free access to every part, they lost an opportunity for investigating and describing its natural productions, which might never have occurred again, but for the present movement in China. In the reign of Kang-hi they obtained permission to establish a college for the promotion of Christianity; but his successor regarded the institution with different feelings; and, being jealous of the influence which it was calculated to produce, ordered it to be broken up, and thus deprived us of the means of obtaining much valuable information.

Among the few Oriental works which modern scholars have been able to obtain, the only one that has as yet been translated into English, from the Sanscrit, is, a History of the Kings of Cashmere, down to the Mahomedan conquest, entitled, "Raja Tarengini," published in 1835.

It was not till about seventy years ago, during the war with Hyder Ali, and the subsequent hostilities between the sovereigns of Mysore, from 1792 to 1799, that the English became acquainted with the state of Southern India; when (to our shame be it spoken) the capture at Seringapatam of the Sultan's library, revealed the fact of an extensive political correspondence with Napoleon Bonaparte, the Directory, and the French governor of the Isle of France; also with the Shah of Persia, with Shah Zeman of Affghanistan, the Maharattas, and many other native princes of India.

With so many salient points of tangible danger to defend, it might have been expected that the Government of India would have employed—

as Russia does, and as France has ever done—competent officers in their service to travel in Persia, Afghanistan, and, in fact, in all the countries from whence the danger of an invasion was to be apprehended: especially as it was well known that Zeman Shah of Affghanistan had, in 1796, '97, and '98, made attempts to invade India.

Foreigners have asked the question: "How is it that you English, who have so long possessed a considerable portion of India, know so little of that country, that, in our day, Baron Humboldt, a foreigner, should contemplate a visit to India, to explore the Himalaya mountains?" It is true, that nearly forty years ago, Lieutenant Webb and others had ascertained that the highest peak was about 27,000 feet above the level of the sea, and that it was the loftiest in the world; but doubts were expressed as to the amount of scientific knowledge possessed by a Bengal subaltern. Captain Fraser and other Englishmen have since visited those snowy regions; but it still remains to be seen what enterprising nation will equip an expedition to explore the character and resources of India.

That the English, as a commercial nation, have not as yet ascertained all the products of India, is a matter of yet greater astonishment to all foreign travellers. It is a fact, that the existence of that useful article, coal, has only been known within the last few years; and the same may be said in regard to other natural productions. The truth is, that, till the year 1814, the East India Company, who possessed the exclusive right of trade within the limits prescribed by their Charter of 1660, were the chief merchants of India; and their investments were almost wholly confined to the exportation of silk, and the usual cargoes of tea from China. It is to private enterprise that we are indebted for the commerce in indigo, sugar, and other articles of modern exportation; till the free trade with China, since the year 1834, opened up a more extended commerce.

Since that period, both India and China have become better known to us; and the wars in the latter country have naturally made us acquainted with the eastern portions of its vast dominions.

It cannot, however, be expected that persons pursuing commercial speculations should have leisure or inclination to write on Indian subjects, beyond the facts relating to their own traffic. Some men will not even take the pains to learn the language of the people, but trust to such natives as speak English. Though some of these gentlemen have certainly acquired a colloquial knowledge of the language, and made themselves acquainted with the localities in their immediate vicinity—yet, as they have never travelled much in India, their statements are of course imperfect and superficial. It is from the pen of the civil, military, and other servants of the East India

Company, and from officers in Her Majesty's service, that we must look for accounts descriptive of different parts of India, and of the various tribes and races of its inhabitants.

The removal of the army from place to place, affords an observant officer not only an opportunity of investigating the geological formation, natural history, and productions of the country, but also gives him great facilities for studying the history, religion, and civilization of the people, from the various monuments and inscriptions, both ancient and modern, which lie on his route.

The rapid extension of our Eastern empire since our first occupation of Hindoostan may, in some measure, account for our imperfect acquaintance with the productions and natural resources of the several great Presidencies under our jurisdiction at the present day. Great Britain, in self-defence, rather than from choice, or from a policy of self-aggrandizement, such as she might reasonably be excused in adopting, has been forced to extend her sway, and to annex numerous native territories; for a long time, indeed, she only assumed a passive military tenure of dominions thus acquired, while her natural reluctance to obtrude or infringe upon the rights and prerogatives of others has not only influenced her general policy, but even led her subjects invariably to observe the same caution in indulging their natural bent for investigation and discovery. This, coupled with an apprehension for personal safety, and a want of confidence in native integrity and honour, has greatly impeded a free and frequent intercourse, and damped the ardour of enterprising and scientific enquiry.

The well-known faithlessness of the native character, and the internal disaffection existing among various tribes, have also tended to interrupt or preclude the possibility of travelling about among the people, for the purpose of investigating their manners and customs, and the general state of the country.

The wars with the Sikhs afforded many opportunities of becoming practically acquainted with the perfidy and duplicity of the natives. The treachery of Tej Singh at the battle of Ferozeshah, the artful and wily conduct of Goolab Singh, in his negotiations with the Maharannee and the British, and the subsequent perfidy of our professed friend and ally, Shere Singh, at the siege of Mooltan, where he caused the defection of the Sikh army from the British to Moolraj, and thereby prevented our taking the fortress, are indisputable proofs of this trait. It is a painful peculiarity in the Oriental character, which will ever stamp it in the eyes of a European with an indelible stigma. This inherent vice, and our cognizance of it, have hitherto checked, and will continue to check, the ardour of all enquiry and enterprise, even where pecuniary gain, and still more, scientific information, are the objects in view.

We may also refer to the history of Moolraj, his confederates, and their diabolical schemes; but, thanks to an over-ruling Providence, the arch-traitor and his base accomplices were defeated; their designs were marred, and fell upon themselves. Truly it is said, "Man proposes, but God disposes." Who could have foreseen or anticipated the results of the deliberations within the walls of Mooltan? Who could have foretold that Moolraj would be dethroned and immured in a British prison, and his rich and extensive territories revert to a British Queen? His treachery, however, led to the wanton murder of two of our officers, and to an immense sacrifice of the lives, both of natives and Europeans.

Our unwillingness to invade, or to annex to the British dominions, even partial portions of frontier countries, virtually in our possession before, has proved, as we have seen, a great barrier to enterprising researches; and our officers, generally speaking, had more work upon their hands, than allowed of much leisure or inclination for scientific expeditions into adjacent, and still less into more distant localities. We feel justified in offering this explanation, in order to do away with the reproaches to which the civil and military officers in India, have been subjected in regard to this question.

With respect to the Punjaub, our Government was perfectly justified in its annexation; and the act was quite consistent with wise policy, and compatible with our previous and general mode of dealing with Indian rulers. No other power except Great Britain would so long have abstained from punishing a local authority, which had so shamefully and recklessly disregarded and violated its own solemn pledges and engagements, upon the faith of which, and which only, the rule of the Sikhs rested and eventually depended. Great Britain ought to have annexed this country long before, even as early as 1845. She relied on the gratitude and fidelity of the Sikh rulers, and was betrayed and disappointed.

What is applicable in one case, as in that of the Punjaub, may apply equally to all or any of our Indian acquisitions, and account, in a great measure, for our still imperfect knowledge of the products and vast resources of India.

We will not conceal from ourselves, nor leave the public in ignorance of the fact, that while all classes at home are unanimous as to the benefit and vast importance of steam communication, the case is far otherwise in India. The imperative necessity for improvement in facilitating the means of communication in the interior of India, by means of roads, bridges, canals, railways and river navigation, has not obtained that fair share of attention and support which the past and future wants of India, her products, resources, and trade demand. These reforms are only in their infancy. India, strange to say, is still as backward as Turkey in these respects. It is extraordinary that in a country like India, and under such a rule as the British, no line of railway should have been laid down till the year 1851, when the attempt was made in the short line from Bombay.

Any contributions, however scanty, respecting India will be better appreciated now that a more judicious system has been adopted with regard to the qualification of candidates for Indian affairs. There are few families who have not friends and relations in some part of India, and these are now beginning to give their attention to subjects bearing upon its history, its people, products, institutions, and religion.

If we have been remiss in the past, and of this there is no question, we must endeavour, in the future, to regain our credit as a nation by progressive reform, and the promotion of civilization. India and her riches, her mountains of light and her hills of gold, must not blind us to our duties, nor cause us to forget the true though trite saying, that, "Property and its possession have their duties as well as their rights." We must not lose sight of the well-being of the country and her people, in the pursuit of personal aggrandizement, and thus expose ourselves to the world's obloquy, our children's detriment, and our disgrace as a nation whose glorious destiny it was to elevate India to a high and proud position, compared with that state in which we found her.

It must not be supposed, from the foregoing remarks, that the author of these pages intends to write a history of India; all he presumes to do is to give information respecting that part of the country in which his regiment was on active service, and which is perhaps the most imperfectly known, namely, the vast district in the north west of India, where the Sikh battles were fought. Moreover they are not written for the scrutinizing eye of the public, but only for the amusement of his friends, and of those who have a personal interest in the war.

The author left England in the year 1836, and served with H.M.'s 4th (Queen's own) Light Dragoons for seven years. He studied both the Oordoo and Maharatta languages, passed his examination, and became Interpreter to the regiment, and was therefore able to converse with the natives. Returning to England in 1842, he joined the 9th Queen's Royal Lancers, and was engaged in the Sikh campaign in 1845-46, which prostrated the power of that people, and exhibits a series of the most triumphant successes ever recorded in the military history of India.

The author has endeavoured to delineate scenes presented in a time of war, which could not be familiar to the general traveller, because the presence of two hostile armies exhibits the people in their native character, calling forth their hopes and fears as to the issue of the combat. In times of peace, the minds of the inhabitants repose upon the prospects of a good harvest and a fruitful season. The grand features of an Indian life are comprehended in the expressive phrase: "āb aur hawa humaree bustee kee achchha huen; mi khoob khata aur khoob sota hon:" i.e.; "The climate (air and water) of our village is good; I eat well and sleep well." If the Indian has plenty of good water and food, his family share it with him, and he is content; he is no politician, but when war rages between hostile parties close to his own door, he can be no longer indifferent, and all his energies are aroused in estimating the issue. In losing his old masters, the English, he would fall under the iron rule of the Sikhs; or should the Sikhs suddenly attack his village and carry off his grain, he would have reason to apprehend that this act might be construed into "aiding the enemy," while a refusal to give up his corn to the Sikhs would involve the burning of his village.

In this way I shall, therefore, endeavour to represent the character of these people as I myself observed them in peace and in war, that the reader may judge whether there exists among the natives of her north-western provinces any peculiarity of character, or whether we have any reason to conclude that the actions of human nature there are much the same as in similar countries in the East; for we must not judge them by those of the West.

It is to be hoped that better days are in store for the East; and, in that comprehensive term, I would include China, and countries nearer home, Asiatic Turkey, Persia, etc. I am sanguine that the bright dawning of a happy future is awaiting these interesting countries. If the British people have conquered India, it is their imperative obligation to promote the welfare of their possessions; and we are glad to notice a laudable spirit in recent legislative measures to promote many desirable improvements. India, under an improved system, and with greater facilities of intercourse, will more than recompense any effort, or application of capital, on our part. Its internal resources are beyond our conception, and its people will unquestionably advance and improve in proportion to its elevation as an empire. Schools, industry, and commerce, if based on a solid foundation, will be the quick harbingers of peace, good-will, and prosperity to the people and their rulers, both native and European.

May this happy era be expedited in the good Providence of God!

Eynesbury, St. Neots,
Huntingdonshire,
May, 1, 1854.

CHAPTER I

Voyage to India—Advantages of Sailing with Troops on Board—Regulations at Sea—March from Cawnpore to Meerut—Return from Nougawa Ghât to Meerut—March to Ferozepore—Cantonments at Kurnaul—Colonel Campbell's Force—Number of Cattle required on a March—Sunday—Rev. W.J. Whiting, M.A.—Distribution of Prize-Money—Advanced Guard—Governor-General— Major Broadfoot and Captain Nicolson—Suspicions of the Sikhs—Sir David Ochterlony—The Sikh Army—The Battle of Moodkee—Tej Singh.

The circumstances of a voyage to or from India are so well known, from their frequent occurrence, that I will not even allude to them. Our voyage, however, offered some variety to the usual monotony of a mere passenger ship, from our having troops on board. This naturally gave rise to numerous incidents which afford topics of interest, especially to military men. We, of course, had regular parades both for the sake of discipline, and to ascertain that the men were sober and clean. The men had, too, specific duties assigned to them—keeping watch, etc.

The object of placing the troops in watches, in time of peace, is, that they may assist in pulling and easing the ropes. They are confined to duties on deck only. If there should be an old sailor among them he may, of course, occasionally reef and unfurl sail. It is obvious that the addition of some fifty or sixty men to the crew of a merchant vessel of 600 or 700 tons burthen, is a great advantage in bad weather, as it enables almost the whole of the ship's crew to be employed aloft. In case of necessity a soldier or two will also assist the man at the wheel, or those at the pumps, by order of the quarter-master, or of the officer on duty, or of the captain himself.

Another advantage from having soldiers on board is in the case where the crew might be inclined to mutiny; when they would be restrained by the military. The troops being told off in watches, those on the morning watch assist in cleaning, or, what is called *swabbing*, the quarter-deck; but the rules for merchant ships are very imperfect in this respect.

Having troops on board necessarily adds much to the safety of the vessel.

It will probably be in the recollection of many of my readers, that two ships taken up in Australia as transports, were wrecked on the Great Andamans, islands on the east side of the Bay of Bengal, in the year 1844. These vessels would have been totally lost, but for the assistance rendered by the officers and men of the 80th Foot, the regiment which so nobly distinguished itself, the following year, at the battle of Ferozeshah, where many of those brave fellows who helped to save these vessels, yielded up their lives for their country.

To ensure regularity and a perfect understanding between the commanding officers of troops and captains of ships, a copy of rules for the guidance of the commanders of merchant-ships, should be given to the officer commanding the troops; and a copy of the regulations for troops of Her Majesty's forces, and the East India Company's service, given to the commander of the ship. The captain of a free-trader is not allowed to flog his men; but he may stop a sailor's grog and his pay for any crime of which he has been guilty. He may also put a culprit in irons, and lose the man's services.

Without stopping to describe my first impressions of India, or the countries which I traversed, after landing upon its far-famed shores, I will proceed at once to Cawnpore, where I found that my regiment was quartered, and where I first joined it.

On the 17th of October, 1845, my regiment, the 9th Queen's Royal Lancers, set out on its march from Cawnpore to Meerut, a distance of 266 miles. The Artillery received orders, at the same time, to hold themselves in readiness to proceed to the north-west. We reached Meerut on the 12th of November, and encamped near the lines of the 16th Lancers, to await further orders. We stayed only a few days in this place, which is situated in the province of Delhi. It is a very large town, of some antiquity, lying about forty miles to the north-east of the city of Delhi, and is one of our principal civil and military stations.

On the 23rd, our corps received orders to march the next day to Umballa, a large military station, a distance of 126 miles. We accordingly set out on the morning of the 25th, and marched to Sirdhana, eleven miles. On the 26th we encamped on the right bank of the river Hindon, at Nougawa Ghât, nineteen miles from Meerut. On the 27th, just as the corps was about to proceed onwards—for the trumpet to boot and saddle had already been sounded—we received a sudden order, by an express camel, to return and encamp on our old ground at Meerut. On the 28th, the regiment halted; the following day it re-crossed the river, and encamped at Sirdhana; and on the 30th returned to Meerut.

Here we were quartered till the 10th of December, when the Queen's Royal Lancers received an unexpected and peremptory order, at half-past eight P.M., to march immediately to Umballa. We accordingly again set out for Sirdhana, which we reached the next morning; and whilst at Shamlee, four marches from Meerut, and twenty-eight miles from Kurnaul, we received, between three and four o'clock P.M., an express direct from the Commander-in-Chief, with the following important intelligence:—

"That the 9th Lancers were to proceed at once to Ferozepore, agreeably to an enclosed route; and that the 43rd and 59th regiments of Native Infantry, which were to leave Meerut the same day as the Lancers, were to proceed thither also: the whole to be under the command of Colonel Campbell, of the latter corps."

SKETCH OF THE PRINCIPAL ROADS
approaching the SUTLEJ.

On reaching Kurnaul, we halted on the 18th, in order to make preparations for forming a depôt at Umballa; to which place all the superfluous heavy baggage, and the young horses, were immediately sent, under the charge of Cornet R.W. King, with instructions to rejoin head-quarters as soon as he had reported himself to the officer commanding at Umballa.

At this time, it was not yet known at Kurnaul that the Sikhs had crossed the Sutlej—an event which took place as early as the 13th of this month.

I may here remark, that the extensive cantonments of Kurnaul had been abandoned about three years before, by order of Lord Ellenborough, then Governor-General. The officers' bungalows were now nearly all roofless, and the neat little church going to decay. In 1852 it was entirely dismantled, and the materials conveyed to Umballa, to assist in building a station-church there. The immense parade-ground, large enough to allow for the exercise of 12,000 men, is about the best in India.

The route of the 9th here changed; for instead of proceeding to Umballa, we marched as follows:—

On the 19th of December to Suggah, 10 miles.
" 20th " Khol, 14½ "
" 21st " Pehoah 14 "

These three villages were in the protected Sikh states: the two former are small and insignificant; the latter is larger, and of more importance.

The whole tract of country, on either side of our line of march, was one continued jungle, and as level as a bowling-green.

The force under the personal command of Colonel Campbell, exclusive of officers, amounted at this time to 2,833 men, with twelve iron twelve-pounders, each drawn by an elephant. Brass guns of this description are usually drawn by ten, or even twelve, bullocks; brass eighteen-pounders by fourteen bullocks; and brass twenty-four-pounders by eighteen bullocks. An iron twenty-four-pounder is drawn by twenty-six bullocks; an iron eighteen-pounder by twenty-two bullocks; and an iron twelve-pounder by eighteen bullocks. Singly, therefore, that noble animal, the elephant, will draw a gun for which ten or even more bullocks are allowed.

These and the following remarks regarding cattle, are given for the purpose of showing the number used in dragging guns and carrying loads. By the regulations of the service in Bengal, it is directed that no elephant shall be taken into the service under twelve years of age, nor under seven feet in height. A committee is appointed to examine and report whether the animals are fit for service; but it not unfrequently happens that infantry or cavalry officers, or both, are put upon these committees, who know nothing at all of the matter. Sometimes, however, the animals are so palpably inefficient and diseased, that, as one of the committee-officers exclaimed, "This camel speaks for itself." No elephant is employed unless the committee can report that he is capable of carrying at least 20 maunds of 80 sicca weight, or 1,600 pounds = 14 cwt. 32 lbs.

Camels admitted into the service by a committee, must never be under five, nor more than nine, years old; and capable of carrying a load of at least 6 maunds, or 480 lbs. Bullocks are admitted into the service not under five, nor above eight, years of age. Draught-bullocks must be fifty inches in height; those for carriage, not under forty-eight inches. The former must be capable of carrying 210 lbs. avoirdupoise weight, besides the gear. The comparative value of these animals will be seen by the following scale:—

> An elephant carries 1,600 lbs.
> A camel   "   480 "
> A bullock   "   210 "

In wet weather a camel, which, in dry weather, carries six maunds of tents, etc., will carry only four maunds, one-third being allowed for the difficulty which the camel finds of keeping on his legs in wet ground.

A six-pounder gun is drawn by six horses, and when bullocks are used, by six of these animals. This shows the relative value as to draught. Now a single elephant pulled along by himself one of the iron twelve-pounder guns, or, as they were more properly styled, "nine-pounders *reamed* up to twelves," which may be thus explained. Knowing that the Sikhs used guns of large calibre, the Government had ordered that these guns should be sent to the Delhi magazine, to be re-cast and reamed up for the occasion; and they did good service. They were a fraction lighter by this process than the nine-pounders were before.

On the 21st of December our troops halted at Pehoah. It is a large town, containing a succession of brick-built houses, the high walls of which, without any apertures, face the back streets, being evidently intended as a defence against marauders.

It will be seen, by reference to the map, that the original route by which the troops were ordered to march to Umballa, would have caused us to make a considerable *détour*, indeed, one of about thirty or thirty-five miles, for Umballa is nearly direct north of Kurnaul, while Ferozepore is north-west.

The Sunday at Pehoah was not kept as is customary on the Lord's-day in cantonments. We had no chaplain with us; and hence divine service was not performed. It would appear proper that, in the absence of the chaplain, some officer should take his place. This is the case in several European regiments, where the commanding or some superior officer reads the service to the troops. As on board of ship, when there is no chaplain, the purser reads the service, so I think, in the army, the paymaster should discharge this duty. A graduate of either University, if there be one in the corps, would be, from his education and training, the most desirable person to read a selection of prayers from the church service. A chaplain accompanied the Bengal and Bombay columns, which went to Afghanistan in 1838-39.

We have a noble instance of voluntary dedication to the duties of chaplain to an army on active service, in the case of the Rev. W.J. Whiting, M.A., during the second Sikh campaign. The arduous and invaluable services which this excellent clergyman rendered during that campaign called forth the grateful thanks of the Governor-General, the Commander-in-Chief, the Bishop of Calcutta, and the Court of Directors. He has left an indelible impression, on all engaged in that war, of the importance of his benevolent, as well as spiritual ministrations.

By the warrant for prize-money for the navy, dated 1846, naval chaplains share in the prize money. There appears to be no positive regulation for army chaplains; but the analogy between the two services will point out the propriety of its existing in the latter case; and the warrant being by royal authority, no doubt ought to exist on the subject. It is pleasing to hear that the Rev. George Robert Gleig, M.A., Chaplain-General to the Forces, formerly a subaltern during the Peninsular war, and author of several entertaining and instructive military works, has not only received his medal, with two bars, but has worn it at Court over his canonicals, and does wear it at all times in the pulpit.

By the navy warrant, passengers on board a man-of-war, if they desire to join in an action, receive a share of the prize money. The navy prize rules are fairer than those of the army. The army rules were made—I am speaking of India—by the Prize Committees, assembled at Seringapatam, Agra, etc., in 1799 and 1803; and, being composed of senior officers, they took good care of their own grade, while the juniors got a very disproportionate share.

I return from this digression to the bellicose signs of the times. Colonel Campbell's detachment marched, on the 22nd December, to Goelah, sixteen miles distant. Here, in consequence of rumours that the Sikhs had crossed the Sutlej, and having heard, in the afternoon, a distant noise resembling the sound of cannon (which subsequently turned out to be the explosion of mines), Colonel Campbell ordered all the troops under his immediate command to join and march together.

On the following morning the advanced guard consisted of a troop of the Royal Lancers—the light companies of the 43rd and 59th regiments of Native Infantry—some sappers and miners—and four 12-pounders.

The main body consisted of the 9th Lancers—43rd and 59th regiments of Native Infantry—and six 12-pounders. The rear-guard consisted of a troop of the 9th—one company from each of the Infantry regiments—and two 12-pounders: Captain Spottiswoode, 9th Lancers, an able and most intelligent officer, acting as major of brigade. Here was a respectable force of nearly 3,000 men and twelve guns, or four to each thousand men, being above Napoleon's proportion, which was only three to 1,000.

It will be seen that we began the campaign with an artillery very inferior to that of the Sikhs. In fact, if calibres are reckoned, we, probably, were in the minority as one to three. I shall, in the sequel, prove these facts. But to proceed:

It will appear strange to the European reader when he hears that the whole tract of country between the Sutlej and the Jumna, including the protected Sikh states, which were under our control, as well as our protection, had been in the possession of the East India Company since the year 1809, or for thirty-six years before this period; and that, nevertheless, troops marching to join the army, in a direct line, sixty miles off, were not even aware that the Sikhs had crossed the Sutlej; and that, moreover, two battles had been fought, that of Moodkee, on the 18th, and that of Ferozeshah on the 21st and 22nd of December, the latter being one of the most deadly contested actions ever fought in India. I have before stated that the 9th Lancers had been ordered from Meerut, and did march on the 25th of November; that this line corps, being unfortunately ordered back, did not leave Meerut the second time until the 11th of December. Here was a loss of sixteen days: hence it is clear, that, as the regiment heard firing, or sounds arising from the explosion of powder mines on the 21st of December, it would have been present in the battles of Moodkee and Ferozeshah, had not its march been countermanded.

Now the order to return to Meerut was received on the 27th of November. To what circumstance was this to be attributed? The Sikhs did not cross the Sutlej until the 13th of December, or sixteen days after the 27th of November; and, allowing the order for the return to be dated the 25th of November, there certainly was not any crossing of the Sikhs at that time. It is positively stated, by a staff officer, that Lord Hardinge did not send the order. Although a Governor-General can send such an order direct, yet all military men here know that the Commander-in-chief is the channel for transmitting such orders. At the same time it is an established rule in the Indian army that a Commander-in-chief cannot order any troops on service without the sanction of the Governor-General, or of the government. Even in the common biennial or triennial relief the order is prefaced with the words: "With the sanction of government." The Governor-General being, in the present instance, on the field, was, de facto, the government. As Louis XIV. said: L'état? C'est moi.

Great uncertainty if not mystery prevailed in our army as to the probability of the Sikhs crossing the Sutlej. The Blue Book comes to our aid in deciding upon such a probability. It was argued that in 1843 the Sikhs did threaten to cross, but thought better of it and forebore; and therefore they might do the same now. But all the politicals knew well enough that the Punts and Punchees were no longer under the control of the Durbar as they were in 1843, but were more likely than not, to act in open defiance of it.

There were two officers, however, of great political talent, whose official position enabled them to know more of the feelings of the Sikhs, and of the probability of such a step than most others; one was Major G. Broadfoot of the 34th Madras Native Infantry, who had held the office of British Agent for Sikh affairs since November 1844, and who had acted as engineer in the celebrated defence of Jellalabad, the heroes of which obtained the well merited Roman distinction of a mural crown; the other was Captain P. Nicolson, 28th Bengal Native Infantry who had been appointed his assistant. Captain Nicolson was in Affghanistan in 1838-39, and was deputed to conduct the traitor Dost Mahomed Khan to Calcutta, and afterwards to Saharunpore. This officer had had seven years' experience of the politics of the Affghans and the Sikhs. At this juncture he was with Major General Sir John H. Littler at Ferozepore. He was in the daily receipt of intelligence from Lahore, and knew that the Sikhs would cross, for he wrote to Calcutta on the 9th of October, 1845, that "he believed the Sikhs would cross." What! because Major Broadfoot knew that the Sikhs had made an empty threat to cross in 1843, was it therefore improbable, that, being encamped for a long time, on the right bank of the Sutlej, menacing the Durbar at Lahore, from whence they marched in defiance of their government and of their chief, whom they compelled to join them, they would execute their threat under these circumstances?

Major Broadfoot was the Governor-General's agent, and as such was the officer to whom he looked for intelligence, Captain Nicolson was his subordinate; the Major doubted the Captain's intelligence, because he had received no other information to induce him to believe that the rebellious and infatuated Khalsa (or royal) troops would dare to cross. If they threatened to cross in 1843 without carrying that threat into execution, why might they not do the same in 1845? But this was not good logic; the inference was against him; because in 1843 they were obedient to the Durbar, and in 1845 they acted in defiance of it.

It would be useless at this distant period to enter into the discussion which arose in India, and was afterwards taken up with much warmth in England, as to the correctness of the views entertained by these officers on the crossing of the Sutlej by the Sikhs. The relative views of those two officers were then and are still sustained by their respective friends; but as far as we can individually offer an opinion, and as it seemed to many at the time, there is great difficulty in arriving at a decision as to the rights of the question at issue. It is true that Major Broadfoot, as the superior officer, might be presumed to be in a position for obtaining access to sources of information from which his subordinate was debarred. In a military point of view, this position must always carry its due weight in the scale of probable authentic intelligence, and should have a preponderating influence in ultimate proceedings, especially in such a country as India, and among such a people as we were then dealing with.

On the other hand, it is by no means uncommon for a subordinate in an important position, to have access directly, and indirectly, to authentic intelligence from which his superior may be shut out, and such a subordinate, knowing his duties and his means of intelligence, can constantly elicit facts in a variety of ways, especially from a hostile source, from which his superior is excluded.

Now, in reference to the position of Captain Nicolson at this juncture, and for a long period antecedent, we are decidedly of opinion that his information and impressions were correct: at the same time we do not consider that the admission of this circumstance can warrant any one to seek, or in justice desire, to disparage the opinions of Major Broadfoot. He, no doubt, had strong grounds for arriving at the conclusion that he did, as the information upon which he acted coincided with his own predilections, and for persisting in these views, even in the face of equally strong opinions on the part of Captain Nicolson.

Officers will, and must, differ on points like the one at issue; but we do not hesitate to say, that Major Broadfoot's views have subjected him to no small share of obloquy and censure. It is, however, important to bear in mind, that in no country, and among no class of people in the world, is there so much cause for a difference of opinion as among military men in India, especially on such a question as that under consideration. The character of the Sikhs, their former empty and vacillating tactics, made the crossing of the Sutlej a matter of uncertainty, even up to a few days of their actual transit; and, to the very last moment, some of their own people were doubtful on the point. This has always been a piece of oriental policy.

It cannot be denied, that the Sikhs had considerable cause for provocation. The sequestration of the two Sikh villages near Loodianna, by the British government, early in November, was the culminating point, and left no doubt of our aggressive intentions on the minds of the Sikhs. Their suspicions had long been awakened by our proceedings—by the rumours of boats preparing at Bombay, to form pontoons across the Sutlej—of our equipping troops in Scinde, for a march on Mooltan—and reinforcing our frontier stations with men and ammunition. They persuaded themselves that the policy of our government was territorial aggrandizement, and that war was inevitable. This feeling was shared by the mass of the Sikh population. The Durbar sitting at Lahore, however, knew well enough that the British government would not take the initiative; but it had completely lost the confidence and allegiance of the army by its internal dissensions, and the supine weakness and luxurious indolence of the chiefs of the Punjaub. The Sikh soldiery used to assemble in groups round the tomb of Runjeet Singh, vowing to defend with their lives all that belonged to the commonwealth of Govind—that they would never suffer the kingdom of Lahore to be occupied by the British strangers, but stand ready to march, or give the invaders battle on their own ground.

Thus, led on from one step to another, the Sikhs declared war on the 17th of November, and by an overt act broke the solemn treaty of alliance with our government; they crossed the Sutlej on the 13th of December, and on the 14th took up a position in the immediate vicinity of Ferozepore.

This treaty of alliance between the British government and the Maharajah had been concluded in April, 1809; being occasioned by the aggressions of Runjeet Singh upon the territories of the chiefs of the Cis-Sutlej provinces, who claimed the British protection.[1]

In Sir David Ochterlony's proclamation,[2] which was issued at the same time, it was especially stated, "That the force of cavalry and infantry which may have crossed to this side of the river Sutlej, must be recalled to the other side, to the country of the Maharajah. This communication is made solely with the view of publishing the sentiments of the British, and of ascertaining those of the Maharajah. The British are confident that the Maharajah will consider the contents of this precept as redounding to his real advantage, and as affording a conspicuous proof of their friendship; that with their capacity for war, they are also intent on peace."

There can be no question, that so long as Runjeet Singh held the government, this and subsequent treaties would have remained inviolate. He knew the power and influence of the English well enough to desire their friendship, rather than their enmity. But this was not the case with his successors, whose policy was guided by views of self-aggrandizement, rather than by the weal of their people, by which they lost their hold over them.

Up to this time, the British had adopted only precautionary measures for the protection of their frontier states. The Governor-General, Lord Hardinge, had joined the Commander-in-Chief, Sir Hugh Gough, at Umballa, early in December; and as soon as the rumour gained ground, that the Sikh forces were marching towards the Sutlej, the troops in the upper provinces received marching orders, and all were speedily on the move. The corps stationed at Umballa, Loodianna, and Ferozepore, amounted to about 30,000 men, with 70 field-guns; and as Ferozepore, which was then occupied by Sir John Littler, was the most exposed, the troops from Umballa were sent to his support, and only a small garrison was left at Loodianna, in order that as large a body of available men as possible, should be placed at the disposal of Sir H. Gough to give battle to the Sikhs, should they carry out their threat of crossing the Sutlej.

This, as we have seen, they actually did on the 13th; but so great was the influence which Captain Nicolson exercised over some of their chiefs, that he prevailed upon Lall Singh to divide his forces; and it was only a division of the Sikhs which fought at Moodkee on the 18th of December.

The Sikh army numbered from 35,000 to 40,000 men, with 50 pieces of heavy artillery, besides a reserve force stationed near Loodianna, to act according to circumstances. The army of invasion consequently more than doubled that of the British. Notwithstanding the jealousy, mistrust, and treachery which prevailed in the Sikh army, in one thing they were agreed, that they would rid the commonwealth of Govind, of their hated British allies; and that in order to accomplish this, it behoved every individual to act as if the result depended upon himself alone. The Sikhs were commanded by Tej Singh, an officer of considerable talent. They took up an entrenched position at Ferozeshah, an inconsiderable village about 10 miles from Ferozepore and the same distance from Moodkee.

General Sir John Littler was, as we have stated, lying at Ferozepore with a garrison of about 10,000 men. As the Sikhs appeared to threaten the town, the gallant general immediately led out his men, and offered them battle; this they declined, mainly it would appear, from the double dealing and artful conduct of Lall Singh and Tej Singh, who, uncertain as to the result of the present movement, were anxious to remain friends with both parties.

The head-quarters of the Commander-in-Chief were at Umballa about 150 miles from Moodkee. His Excellency[3] broke up his camp on the 11th, and by forced marches arrived at the village of Moodkee on the 18th. The

Governor-General was a little in advance of his Excellency, and rode over to Loodianna to inspect the troops. Finding that post secure from an attack, he dispatched about 5,000 of the garrison to guard the important grain depôt of Bussean.

On the 18th of December, the Commander-in-Chief, with the Umballa division of the army arrived at Moodkee, and was immediately joined by the Loodianna division. On reaching Moodkee there was no longer any doubt as to the whereabouts of the Sikh forces. Orders were immediately issued by the deputy adjutant-general to a brigadier, that he should be ready for duty next day; in other words, that he should command the advance guard. This was about twelve o'clock in the day, when the officers were in the mess tent at tiffin. Two young officers of the 16th Native Grenadiers overheard the order: "You are brigadier for to-morrow; the army will march early in the morning to attack the Sikhs, who are known to be ten miles off." They were still discussing the glorious prospect of an encounter with the Sikhs, when orders arrived in camp for "all hands to turn out," Major Broadfoot having received intelligence that the Sikhs were near. The order had been sent by Lord Hardinge,—every inch a soldier, but who at that time had not yet been appointed second in command to the Commander-in-Chief.

The cavalry and horse artillery darted off to the right front; the infantry followed; it was a short affair. Lord Gough did not at first credit the report: "The Sikhs are coming!" Like a true Irish soldier, he would have a view of them before he could make up his mind—but he was soon convinced of the reality of the rumour. Major Broadfoot, galloping up to their position, was fired on; both the Governor-General and the Commander-in-Chief were, it is said, at one time nearly captured. The Governor-General, on the other hand, promptly put the troops in motion: being himself an old Peninsular officer, he was an excellent judge of the matter. His Excellency the Commander-in-Chief could not have done otherwise, but there was not time to send to him: the urgency of the occasion satisfies the mind of all military men; by a delay the Sikhs might have attacked the British.

Napoleon and other great generals "always anticipated the attack." They who attack have the advantage of deciding on the form of attack; those who await it, have no certainty where it may be made.

The battle of Moodkee was, as we have said, a short affair. The Sikhs headed by Lall Singh, opened with a heavy cannonade, but were answered by a brisk fire from the English; the enemy's rear was then attacked by a brilliant cavalry movement which routed him; and night put a stop to the carnage. The Sikhs were defeated with a loss of 17 guns. That of the British was very great; they had 215 killed, and 657 wounded. Among the killed were Sir Robert Sale and Sir John McCaskill. It is doubtful whether the addition of the 9th Lancers would have been of service at the battle of Moodkee, because there was no extended field for cavalry movements: at Ferozeshah, however, they would have been of eminent use, for on the the second day (December 22nd,) Tej Singh advanced with a large force of horse artillery; and I have heard it deeply regretted by officers present in this action, that we were not at hand to complete the rout of the brave Sikhs.

FOOTNOTES:

[1] See Appendix I.

[2] See Appendix, II.

[3] The Commander-in-Chief is always so styled; the Governor-General never.

CHAPTER II

Colonel Campbell's Advance—Provisions required—Camp
Followers—Samana—The Doabs—Gooroo Govind—
The Akalees, their quoits—Sikhs attack Ahmed Shah—
Maha Singh—Maharattas—General Thomas—Runjeet
Singh—Holcar—Sir Charles Metcalfe—Ochterlony's
Proclamation—The Akalees routed—Generals Allard and
Ventura—Treaty with Runjeet—Runjeet's Army—Runjeet's
Death—Shere Singh Murdered—Dhuleep Singh—Ajean
Khan—Battle of Moodkee.

In the meanwhile the force under Colonel Campbell was rapidly advancing to the scene of action. It was as we have stated, nearly 3,000 strong, and attended by about 10,000 or 11,000 camp followers, so that we were in all 13,000 or 14,000 assembled in camp, besides numerous elephants, camels, bullocks, horses, ponies, &c. I will here remark for what purposes camp followers are allowed. Every officer, according to his rank, will have from ten to twenty or twenty-five servants; the Bengal officers and others have more than those of Madras and Bombay; but the latter servants cost as much as the Bengalese. If a polki (or palanquin) be kept, then six bearers well be required; for every horse two servants, namely a groom and a grass-cutter;[4] for every elephant, two; for camels, one to every three is the usual number; for every two bullocks, one servant is allowed. Besides these there is a host of tent pitchers, store Lascars, etc.

Let us next consider the quantity of provisions required for our force; calculating the 9th Lancers at 800 horses (including officers' chargers,) the consumption of gram, a kind of vetch, daily would be, $800 \times 5 = 4,000$ seers, or 8,000 lbs. = 71 cwt. 48 lbs. The reader may hence form some idea of the quantity of corn required for 3,000 or 4,000 cavalry horses, or including horse artillery, waggon and private horses, say 5,000, and there would be a consumption of about 440 or 450 cwt. of gram daily. Then each elephant consumes 30 lbs. of atta (flour) cakes;[5] each camel public and private is allowed 6 lbs. of gram, and a bullock 5 or 6 lbs. daily. The elephant likewise gets forage, such as the leaves of trees; and if he can meet with the branch of a tree he is all the happier, for with it he gracefully fans away the flies from himself or his driver: the poor animal suffers greatly from the mosquito bite. The Mahāwat, or elephant-keeper puts the rice in a whisp of rice straw, making a kind of bowl for the food, which is boiled. The camels, too, get bhoosa, or split straw, when it can be procured, otherwise the leaves of trees: they prefer those of the Imlee, Peepul, Babool, and Burh (fig-tree). The bullocks eat bhoosa or karbi, the stalk of Joar or Bajra (the Holcus Sorgum and Spicatus). If we calculate the quantity of grain consumed in an army of 10,000, 30,000, or 40,000 men, the result will be enormous, and we can only marvel where such supplies are obtained.

The Duke of Wellington[6] when in India, often marched with 30,000, or 40,000 bullock-loads of grain, or 600,000, or 800,000 lbs. or 53,571, or 71,428 cwt. His grace's plan was never to open these grain bags so long as he could get supplies from the villages.

Let the reader imagine an Indian army of 20,000 men with its 60,000, 70,000, or even 80,000 camp followers, all of whom must be fed daily. Again, the number of hackeries, or carts, with an army of 20,000 or 25,000 men, varies from 700, to 12,000 or more, (for much depends upon whether there is a siege train), drawn by two, three, or four bullocks each, carrying shot, shells, and stores, and moving at the rate of two miles an hour, the whole line of march from the old to the new ground. Allowing 10 doolies, or light palanquins, for every European troop or company, for the conveyance of the sick or wounded men, there would be 80 required for the 9th Lancers, and as each dooly needs 6 bearers we had 480 bearers in our corps alone. In a European infantry regiment of 10 companies there will be $10 \times 10 = 100$; $100 \times 6 = 600$ bearers. A native corps is allowed only one for a troop or company, but some extra ones accompany the field hospital. Now such an army would have at least 5,000 dooly bearers, besides those which are required for luxurious officers, who have been seen, though, I am happy to say, rarely, to ride in palanquins.

The English waggon train establishment is said not to be good. A veterinary surgeon has published a work on the use of a light cart, with cross seats on springs; but before it can be generally adopted, the roads must be improved. In the Affghan war they used Kajawahs, that is a frame-work on each side of the camel, for two men.

On the 23rd of December, our force marched to Samana, a large old town, now completely in ruins, in the province of Delhi. It is in the Rajah of Pattiala's country, and is about seventeen miles distant from Pattiala, and seventy miles from Kurnaul. It was a very fatiguing march; the road during the last few miles being bad, rough and sandy; this greatly impeded the elephants who dragged the guns, and our progress was very slow; so slow indeed that at six o'clock in the afternoon the men had not dined.

In cantonments one o'clock is the usual hour, but in marching to meet an enemy the dinner hour is uncertain. Yesterday and to-day we were obliged to breakfast upon what chance threw in our way.

On service with Lord Lake, it is said that frequently neither officers nor men got any breakfast at all, but broke their fast at sunset; similar privations no doubt often occurred in the Peninsula; but this is very undesirable when it can be obviated, for especially in hot countries, European soldiers require more nourishment than in colder climates.

Samana contains a large brick-built fort; it appears at one time to have been very strong, but is now falling to decay. There are many of these forts, and their origin is long anterior to 1809, when the British obtained possession of the protected Sikh states. They were built by Runjeet Singh, when he was lord and master of the country on the left bank of the Sutlej, governing, in fact, the whole district between the Jumna and the Sutlej. At that time he fortified all the towns and villages, to defend not only the inhabitants against the attacks of their neighbours, but also to prevent the cattle sheltered under the walls, from being carried off by marauders.

Before proceeding further on our route, we will take a brief survey of the territory of the Sikhs, and of the history of the singular race whom we were marching to encounter.

The Punjaub, or country of five waters, from *punj*, "five," and *āb*, "water," forms the northern portion of the plain of the Indus. It covers an area of 6,000 geographical miles, and extends from the lower ranges of the Himalaya mountains to the confluence of the Chenāb with the Indus. The four streams or arms of the Indus which rise in the Himalayas, namely, the Jelum, the Chenāb, the Rāvee and the Sutlej, intersect the country, and, with the Indus, divide it into four Doabs or Provinces.

The first Doab ("country between two rivers"), lying between the Indus and the Jelum, is 147 miles in breadth; this Doab is intersected with defiles and mountain chains, and covered with thickets. It is the worst cultivated, the most barren and thinly peopled of all the Doabs.

The second Doab is formed by the rivers Jelum and Chenāb. At its narrowest breadth it is forty-six miles across; this country is flat, except the low range of hills terminating the beds of rock salt that run through the Jelum. It is capable of very improved cultivation.

The third Doab lies between the Chenāb and the Rāvee. This Doab might with the greatest ease be converted into a most fertile country, were the land irrigated by the mountain streams, which could be conveyed in artificial canals. It is seventy-six miles in breadth at its widest part.

The fourth Doab is considerably the smallest, being only forty-four miles in breadth. It, however, comprises some of the most important cities, namely, Lahore, Umritsur and Kussoor. It lies between the Rāvee and the Sutlej.

Besides this fine country, the rule of the Sikhs at this time extended over the rich Province of Mooltan, on the right bank of the Indus. The territory under the sway of the Maharajah might be estimated at 8,000 geographical square miles, with a population of about 5,000,000 inhabitants, and an annual revenue of between £2,000,000 and £3,000,000 sterling.

The Sikhs, or "Disciples," were originally a religious sect, which arose among the inhabitants of the Punjaub as late as the close of the fifteenth century. Their leader was Nānak, who succeeded in drawing thousands of enthusiasts after him. He was a disciple of Kahir, and consequently a Hindoo deist; he upheld the principle of universal toleration, calling upon his followers to worship the one invisible God, and to lead a virtuous life. He died at the age of seventy, in 1539. His doctrines and writings tended greatly to elevate the mind, and reform the morals of his disciples. The Sikhs believe that the soul of Nānak has transmigrated into the body of each succeeding Gooroo, or teacher.

The spirit of religious toleration adopted by the Sikhs, was odious in the eyes of the bigoted Mahomedans, and Arjoon, their chief, who was celebrated not only for his piety, but for his wisdom and skill as a legislator, was falsely accused, and put to death, by the Mogul, in 1606. Arjoon converted the obscure hamlet of Umritsur into a city of great importance, by making it the seat of his disciples, and the place of the Sikhs' pilgrimage. His cruel death transformed the quiet and peaceable Sikhs into a warlike nation; their spirit was roused, and, led on by Hur Govind, the son of their murdered priest, they determined to avenge themselves upon his assassins. The Mogul, however, was too mighty for them; and they were forced to retreat into the mountain districts beyond Lahore.

After a series of sanguinary engagements, in which the Mahomedans were successful, a powerful opponent to the infidel faith and arms, was raised up, in the person of Gooroo Govind, grandson of Hur Govind, in 1675. He effected a radical change in the character, laws, and institutions of the Sikhs, by the abolition of caste, and the introduction of religious, social and military reforms. Amidst the surrounding spiritual darkness, Govind had comparatively enlightened views of the Deity; he abhorred idol worship, and declared that there was but one Lord, and that the invisible God, the Creator of heaven and earth, could not be represented by any painted or graven image; and that as He could be seen only by the eye of faith, He must be worshipped in sincerity and truth. Fearful that he himself might hereafter become an object of religious adoration, Govind denounced all who should regard him as a divinity, alleging that it was his highest ambition that his spirit should return to God after his death.

In the full persuasion, that the only hope of successfully opposing the Mahomedan power was by throwing open the ranks of the army to men of every grade and profession, he adopted the wise and politic measure of abolishing the system of caste. This step was at first highly offensive, especially to the Brahmins, and many quitted the community; but the majority of the Sikhs rejoiced at the breaking down of this barrier to all social and religious intercourse. His expectations, however, were more than realized; vast multitudes joined his ranks, he caused each of his followers to wear a peculiar dress, to adopt the name of Singh, or soldier, and to suffer their beard and hair to grow; he completely reorganized the army, divided his followers into troops and bands, and placed them under the command of able and confidential men.

A special corps was formed of the "Akalees," the Immortals, or Soldiers of God, they wore a blue dress and steel bracelets, and were provided with a quoit, which they carried either round their pointed turbans or at their side; this quoit is a flat iron ring, from eight to fourteen inches in diameter, the outer edge is extremely sharp; they twirl this weapon round their finger or on a stick, and fling it to a distance with such dexterity and precision, that the head of the destined victim is often severed from his body.

In proportion as the Mahomedan power declined, that of the Sikhs rose into importance. They were bound together by the strong ties of a fervid common faith; and this gave them unity of purpose, and consequent strength in operation.

After various struggles for independence, in which they displayed heroism amounting even to martyrdom, they boldly attacked Ahmed Shah, the king of Affghanistan on his first invasion of India, in 1747. They were, however, dispersed by Mere Munroo, and expelled from Umritsur by Timoor, the son of Ahmed Shah, who was appointed governor of the Punjaub. Strong in the faith of Govind, and in his all-prevailing name they rallied their forces, drove out the Affghans, and re-occupied Lahore in 1756.

About this time they called in the aid of the Maharattas, gained several victories, and fortified their towns. In 1762, they were again attacked by Ahmed Shah, who completely routed them, but with their native energy and warlike prowess, they once more gathered their scattered forces, and in 1763 slew the Affghan governor, and defeated his army in the plains of

Sirhind, when they took undisputed possession of the country from the Sutlej to the Jumna, and partitioned it among their chiefs.

They successfully defeated a seventh attack made by Ahmed Shah; and after ejecting the governor of Lahore, they took possession of the territory from the Jelum to the Sutlej. Like the former acquisition, it was divided among their chiefs.

During the brief period of peace which now intervened, the Sikhs settled the boundaries of their respective districts, and more firmly established their federal government, which, properly speaking, may be styled a theocratic feudal confederation, inasmuch as they considered God as the Head and Leader of their confraternity. They held stated councils, or conclaves, which they called "gooroo-moottas," in which they settled their civil and religious affairs. The nation was divided into twelve confederacies or "misls," from an Arabic word signifying "equal," each "misl" being under the control of a sirdar or chief.

Their respite from war was not, however, of long duration; for in 1767, Ahmed Shah made an eighth and last attempt to reconquer the Punjaub. Being, however, deserted by 12,000 of his own troops, he was compelled to retire, and had scarcely re-crossed the Indus when he was besieged at Rhotas, by the grandfather of Runjeet Singh; and the Sikhs took possession of this stronghold in 1768.

Timoor, the son of the veteran Shah, had various conflicts with the Sikhs; and in 1779 reconquered the city of Mooltan, which they had taken seven years before. He died in 1793, leaving the Sikhs undisputed masters of the Upper Punjaub.

Maha Singh, though originally an obscure sirdar, soon rose by his military skill to be the most influential chief in the Punjaub. With the view of cementing his power, he espoused his only son, Runjeet Singh, to the daughter of Sudda Kour. Maha Singh died at the early age of twenty-seven, leaving Runjeet Singh to succeed him in the government. He was a boy of only eleven years of age, having been born in 1792, at Gujeranwalla, forty-seven miles from Lahore.

From a very early age, Runjeet Singh began to display that wisdom and valour, combined with prompt decision and firmness of character, which distinguished him through life. He carved out with his sword his own colossal position in the Punjaub; and, at the age of twenty, expelled the Sikh chiefs, Ischet Singh, Muhuc Singh and Sahib Singh, who opposed him. On the second invasion and retreat of Shah Zeman, king of Cabool, Runjeet Singh acquired the object of his ambition—the wealthy kingdom of Lahore, with the royal investiture and title of Maharajah.

About this time the star of the Maharattas again rose in the Northern Provinces, under their able leader, Madhajee Sindhia, who, in 1785, formed an alliance with the Sikhs, and threatened the kingdom of Oude, then under the protection of the British. Runjeet, however, soon became jealous of his allies; and finding that they were likely to prove troublesome, he had recourse to the strongest measures to check their growing influence.

One of the generals of the Maharatta forces was an English adventurer, named George Thomas. He came to India in 1781, in a British man-of-war; he was originally a common sailor, but rose to be quarter-master, and on his arrival in India entered the service of the native chiefs. He was sent to oppose the combined forces of the Sikhs. Leaving a competent force for the defence of Jeypore, which was then threatened with an attack from another quarter, he marched to Kurnaul, where the Sikhs lay encamped. Here four successive engagements took place, in which the Maharattas lost 500 men, and the Sikhs about 1,000. Both parties at last inclining to peace, a treaty was concluded, by which the Sikhs agreed to evacuate the Province. In 1800, General Thomas again entered the Sikh country, with a body of 5,000 men and sixty pieces of artillery. He was now opposed by the youthful Maharajah, Runjeet Singh; but the issue was adverse to the Sikhs. Nor was it surprising that General Thomas with a well disciplined army of 5,000 men, and sixty guns[7] should defeat a young chief of twenty-two years of age.

The British government was not ignorant of the warlike character and growing power of the Sikhs. As far back as the year 1784, Warren Hastings placed a British agent at the court of Delhi, in order to watch the Sikhs, and deter them from making any attempt upon the kingdom of Oude.

The Sikhs, however, finding the Maharattas too powerful for them, applied to the British Resident, to enter with them into a defensive alliance against their common foe, at the same time placing at the disposal of the British a body of 30,000 men, whom they had stationed at Delhi to watch the Maharattas.

In the year 1805, the ambitious spirit of Holcar, the enterprising Mahomedan leader of the Maharatta forces, determined him to invade Upper India, and to invest Delhi. He met with a powerful resistance from Lord Lake, who drove him beyond the Sutlej, where he expected to find support from the Sikhs. Runjeet Singh had penetrated the Doab, between the Chenāb and the Indus. He had a meeting with Holcar at Umritsur, but finding it more to his interest to make friends with the English, the wily Maharajah put Holcar off, under the pretext that he must first reduce the Pathans of Kussoor. Friendly relations were then established with the British;[8] Runjeet Singh visited Lord Lake's camp in disguise, and a treaty was concluded, by which the English agreed not to encroach upon the Sikhs' territories so long as the chiefs of the Punjaub continued to maintain friendly relations.

Runjeet Singh, speaking of this circumstance some time afterwards to Sir John Malcolm, remarks, that he "was very glad to get rid of two such troublesome guests," namely, Holcar and the British. It was a curious coincidence that both Runjeet Singh and Holcar had each but one eye, but those eyes were piercing, nor were they disliked by the fair sex, if report speak true.

The news of the intended invasion of India by Napoleon, in 1808, spread a panic through the country, and the British government took instant measures to ascertain how far they could rely on the support of the various native princes. The most powerful and important of these was Runjeet Singh; and Sir Charles Metcalfe was accordingly despatched to the court of Lahore as British Envoy. The Maharajah was at that time engaged in the subjugation of some of the petty independent Sikh princes. His continued aggressions upon the Cis-Sutlej states, several of which he had made tributary, induced the princes of Sirhind to place themselves under British protection, and the envoy was charged with a remonstrance to Runjeet Singh upon this subject.

He received the envoy at Kussoor, which he had just conquered, and seemed more intent upon the enlargement and defence of his own borders, than alive to the dangers of a French invasion. So far from entering into the views of the British government on the necessity of a defensive alliance between them and the Sikhs and Affghans, in order to oppose the ambitious designs of Napoleon, Runjeet Singh replied, that, as the head of the whole Sikh population, and as master of Lahore, he had an indisputable right to the enlargement of his own territories, and scorned the attempts of the British to confine him to the right bank of the Sutlej. He abruptly broke off the negotiation, and made a third invasion into the Cis-Sutlej territory; the British envoy remonstrated against these open acts of hostility, and remained on the banks of the Sutlej until the Maharajah returned victorious from the conquest of Fureedkot and Umballa.

The British government hereupon again remonstrated, and declared to him, through Sir Charles Metcalfe, that they would not tolerate any superior authority in these parts, as the whole country, from the Jumna to the Sutlej, was under their protection. To give efficacy to this remonstrance, they despatched a corps under Colonel Ochterlony, and a reserve corps under Colonel St. Leger. The former advanced to the Sutlej, and in the beginning of February, 1809, he issued a proclamation declaring the Cis-Sutlej states to be under British protection.[9] The proclamation ordered that the fortresses on the left bank of the Sutlej should be razed, and the lands restored to their ancient possessors: that all the troops which had crossed the Sutlej should be recalled by the Maharajah to his side, and that in future they should never advance into the countries of the chiefs situated on the left bank of the river, who had placed themselves under the protection of the British government. That the British government would maintain perpetual friendship with the government of Lahore, and have no concern with the territories and subjects of the Rajah to the north of the Sutlej; but that in the event of any violation of these stipulations, the treaty should be null and void.

An apparently trivial circumstance, coupled with the apprehension lest the remaining independent states might break their allegiance with him for that of the British, favoured the demands of the envoy, and convinced the Maharajah that the British soldiers far surpassed his own. Sir Charles was at this time in the Sikh camp at Umritsur, and was attended by an escort of only two companies of native troops and sixteen horsemen. The festival of the Muharram was being celebrated by his Mahomedan attendants. The Akalees looked upon this as an insult, collected a body of the Sikhs, and attacked the envoy's camp with a round of musketry. The small escort immediately seized their arms; and, though their assailants were ten times more numerous than themselves, they completely routed them with considerable loss. Runjeet Singh was attracted by the uproar, and arrived just as the little band of brave Sepoys had gained the victory. Their valour had a great effect upon him; he apologized to the envoy for the insult offered by his people, expressed his high admiration of the discipline and courage of the British troops, and declared himself ready to sign the wished for treaty, which he accordingly did on the 5th of April, 1809.

Two years after, in 1811, when the Goorkhas threatened to invade his dominions, and asked the British to aid them in their attempt, Runjeet Singh obtained permission from the Governor-General, not only to cross the Sutlej and fight the enemy in their mountain recesses, but received the assurance, that, if the Goorkhas should descend into the plains of Sirhind, he should receive the assistance of British troops, in maintaining inviolate the passage of the Sutlej.

This assurance allayed his apprehensions and jealousy, of the influence and power of the British. He continued incessantly engaged in extending his dominions and increasing his army. Sword in hand, he conquered Mooltan and Cashmere; while his warfare with his formidable foes, the Affghans, was unabated, till he finally succeeded in obtaining possession of Peshawur, through the treachery of the brother of Dost Mahomed, whom Runjeet had bribed with the large promise of an annual pension of two lakhs. The continued intestine disputes of the minor states, induced the British government to issue the proclamation of 1811.[10]

It was in 1822, that Runjeet first received into his service two foreign officers, MM. Allard and Ventura; the former being a Frenchman, the latter an Italian. After the fall of Napoleon, these officers had in vain sought an honourable employment in Persia, and, therefore, turned to the warlike chief of Lahore. He gave them a most cordial and brilliant reception, and commissioned them to organize his army on the French system; which they did with great success. Each of these officers had a salary of 50,000 rupees, or £5,000. sterling annually. Four years afterwards, they were followed by Generals Court and Avitabile. It was to these officers that the Sikh chief owed the highly efficient state of his army, which consisted of a well disciplined body of 50,000 men, besides 100,000 Irregulars. Lahore and Umritsur were made the depôts of arms; and here cannon foundries, powder magazines and arsenals were established.

At times Runjeet, and still more his chiefs, felt jealous, lest too much authority should be given to these European officers; for which reason he rather wished them to instruct than to command,[11] fearing they might prove dangerous to the state.

In the summer of 1831, his late Majesty King William IV. despatched Sir Alexander Burnes to Lahore, to take charge of a splendid present of horses from His Britannic Majesty to the Maharajah. Runjeet Singh was then at the height of his power; respected by his friends, and dreaded by his foes. The veteran hero was flattered by receiving this distinguished honour from the monarch of a nation which he highly venerated, and whose superiority in every respect he acknowledged. He gave Sir Alexander Burnes a brilliant reception; and the esteem which he thus manifested for the English, led to several interviews between himself and the Governor-General, Lord William Bentinck, at Rooper, in October, 1831.

The result of these interviews was a treaty of commerce and navigation, to which a supplementary treaty was afterwards added, between Runjeet Singh and the British, by which it was agreed, that the merchants and traders should pay a certain fixed duty, in lieu of the former arbitrary exactions.[12]

The meeting at Rooper, in October, 1831, between the Governor-General and Runjeet Singh, caused a great display of British and Sikh troops. An officer who was present on this occasion, told me that the movements of the Sikh battalions were very slow, and to the beat of drum: the cavalry, mostly wearing bright cuirasses, looked glittering and showy; whilst many of the gun carriages seemed as if a long march over a rough road would break them down. The word of command was always given in French.

In March, 1837, the Commander-in-Chief, General Sir Henry Fane, G.C.B., visited Lahore, on the occasion of the marriage of Runjeet's grandson, Nou Nehal Singh. The entertainment was on a magnificent scale, and cost between ten and eleven lakhs of rupees, or between £100,000 and £110,000 sterling. Here there was again a grand military display, and feats of arms. On this occasion, Runjeet Singh established an order of Knighthood, called "the Star of the Punjaub." He bestowed the Order upon Colonels Torrens, Churchill, Lumley, and Dunlop; the Adjutants-General, and Quartermasters-General, of the Queen's and Company's armies respectively. The investiture, with the Order, took place afterwards at Simla, at the head-quarters of Sir Henry Fane. All these individuals, donor and receivers, are now dead. It was the setting star of Runjeet Singh, for he died about two years after, in June, 1839.

The appearance and discipline of Runjeet's army, was the admiration of all military beholders. In December, 1838, before the Bengal column marched from Ferozepore to Cabool, *viâ* Scinde and Candahar, there was a review of the British troops under the Commander-in-Chief, Sir Henry Fane. Several Sikh soldiers who were present, were heard to make very insolent remarks, and twisted their moustachoes, a gross affront to any one, especially to an officer. They asserted that their troops could manœuvre much better, etc. A day or two afterwards the Sikhs gave a review, and actually copied all the British evolutions, with the greatest accuracy and precision. The infantry movements were also more rapid than at Rooper, in 1831.

Lord Auckland, Governor-General of India, in the same month, visited Runjeet Singh, at Lahore, when another display of English and Sikh troops took place. It was on the occasion of the review of our troops, that his Lordship, who was a bad rider, had a serious fall from his horse. His death would have been a great blow.

Lord Auckland, at that time, asked permission of the Maharajah to allow the British troops a free passage through his territory, on their march to Cabool, and to join his forces with those of the British, in this expedition into Affghanistan. This Runjeet Singh acceded to rather as a matter of necessity than of choice. Though only 59 years of age, his mind and body had become so enfeebled by his irregular course of life, that during his interview with Lord Auckland, his speech was already affected. He sank rapidly, from dropsy, and was finally carried off by paralysis.

When the death of their great chief was approaching, the army was drawn up in a line, and the dying monarch was carried in a litter through the ranks. As the procession moved slowly along, his favourite minister, Dhean Singh, appeared, to receive orders from his expiring sovereign, and informed the army, that Runjeet Singh declared, that his son, Khurruk Singh, should succeed him, and that Dhean Singh should be the chief minister of the kingdom. The soldiers received this intimation in perfect silence. According to the custom of the Sikhs, the body of the Maharajah was burnt the next day, before the gates of his palace, in the presence of all the great persons of the kingdom, and of the assembled troops. Four of his wives, two of whom were only sixteen years of age, and endowed with great personal beauty, together with seven of his concubines, committed themselves to the flames with his body. Dhean Singh also made a semblance of profound grief, and appeared to be in the act of throwing himself upon the funeral pile, but was forcibly withheld by the family of the Maharajah.

The death of Runjeet Singh occasioned considerable difficulty in the management of the auxiliary Sikhs under Colonel Wade, the British agent at Lahore who was now with the British army, and had the command of the column that was to force the Khyber pass. This glorious achievement he accomplished from the 22nd to the 27th of June, when he made himself master of Ali Musjid. He was nobly sustained in this campaign by the troops of Runjeet Singh; and on the 6th of August, the army of the Indus entered Cabool and forced Dost Mahomed to fly to Bokhara.

Runjeet Singh was succeeded by his son Khurruk Singh, then thirty-seven years of age. He was a weak and luxurious prince, and was totally incompetent to the affairs of government. Soon after his accession he was seized with a severe illness, of which he died, in November, 1840. His son, Nou Nehal Singh, and the chief minister, Dhean were supposed to have been not altogether innocent of his death.

Nou Nehal Singh, who was nineteen years of age, inherited his grandfather's ambitious spirit, and could scarcely conceal his joy, even at his father's funeral pyre, on finding himself sovereign of Lahore. He hated the English, and dreaded the effect of their policy in procuring a clear passage for their troops through the Punjaub, and thus, by a chain of consecutive alliances, effecting a union between the southern provinces of India and the West of Europe. He was determined to give proof of this on the first favourable opportunity that might present itself; but the royal sceptre which had so long fired his youthful breast soon passed to another, for the same day that elevated him to the throne, saw him a corpse! On leaving the pile he thought to wash away his sins in the Rāvee, and as he was riding through the outer gateway of the palace, a large portion of the archway fell upon him, killed the friend who was riding at his side, and so severely wounded the young prince in the head, that he expired in three hours. For several days his death was kept a secret; by some, in order to give his mother time to come up, and by others, to secure the succession to Shere Singh, the reputed, and afterwards adopted, son of Runjeet Singh. After a fierce contest between the queen mother and Shere Singh, the latter ascended the throne.

Shere Singh, though he had compelled the troops to recognise him as king, was incapable of commanding them. They soon became insubordinate and committed the most violent excesses; and their lawless conduct gave rise to apprehensions of a general insurrection.

This so intimidated the merchants and wealthy inhabitants on both sides of the Sutlej, that they appealed to the English for protection. The Maharajah was fully sensible of the critical state of his position, and though he deprecated the interference of the British power, he considered it best to yield to the necessities of the case and listen to the advice of the British. For though educated at the most magnificent and warlike court in India, amid events which were calculated to call forth a chivalrous spirit, Shere Singh never manifested either valour or firmness of character, but was carried along by the tide of events, and swayed by the dominant minds of the age. He felt his own incapacity as a ruler, and for a long time was completely under the control of Dhean Singh.

During the disastrous campaign of Cabool in 1842, Shere Singh rendered great services to the English in the relief of the distressed garrison of Jellalabad, and provided more than the stipulated corps of 5,000 men on payment of the sum of two lakhs of rupees.

The Governor-General, in consequence of the state of Affghanistan, determined to place an army of reserve at Ferozepore, and took this occasion for proposing an interview with Shere Singh. The Maharajah, however, apprehensive of the result of such an interview, declined the proposed honour. Lord Ellenborough took offence at this, and Shere Singh despatched Dhean Singh and his own son, Perthaub Singh, to make an apology in person, which was accepted; and his Lordship returned the visit of the young prince.

The military Sikh escort which accompanied, them crossed the Sutlej, which was much swollen at the time by the late heavy rains, with a rapidity and skill that excited the admiration of the British officers. The prince was permitted to review the British forces, soon after which the Governor-General broke up the encampment, and Shere Singh was relieved from his dreaded foe.

Shere Singh was addicted to drunkenness and vice, and succumbed to the influence of unworthy favourites. He had become suspicious of Dhean Singh, and, at their instigation, was induced to sign a royal warrant for his execution. This order was shewn to Dhean Singh by the very men who had procured it. Incensed at the treachery and ingratitude of the man whom he had raised to the royal power, Dhean Singh, as prime minister, immediately signed an order for the assassination of Shere Singh himself, and placed it in the hands of Ajeet Singh, the favourite who had supplanted him, and who had before threatened to kill Shere Singh.

Both Shere Singh and his hopeful son, Perthaub Singh were treacherously murdered on the next day, September the 15th, 1843, by Ajeet and Lena Singh; and the wily minister, Dhean Singh, who had joined with them in the conspiracy, met with the same fate, at their hands, before the close of that very day.

Heera Singh, the son of Dhean Singh, called upon the army to avenge his father's murder. Ajeet and Lena Singh were surrounded the same night, and both met with their well-merited fate before the morning's dawn.

Dhuleep Singh, the reputed son of Runjeet Singh, who was only a few months old at the time of his father's death, and, consequently, now only four years of age, was proclaimed Maharajah. His mother, Chunda, appointed her brother, Jowahir Singh, prime minister; but he was disliked by the army, and cruelly murdered by them. The military were now masters of the state, and sought to make Goolab Singh, the oldest of Runjeet's favourites, vizier. Goolab being fully aware that his great wealth was the bait, kept them in a state of uncertainty as to his resolve; but, in the meantime, instigated them to march upon the British territories, with the intent of invasion.

Deceived by the promised support of Goolab, and buoyed up by exalted notions of their own military prowess and discipline, as well as animated by the desire of pillage, the Sikhs made sure of success. Though they had never seen the British troops in battle, the Khalsa soldiers considered themselves fully equal to contend against them. There is no doubt, and it is necessary to make the remark in order to account for the presumptuous conduct of the Sikhs, that our sad reverses at Cabool in 1841, and our retreat in 1842, had greatly affected the prestige of the British military character. Just as the failure of Lord Lake before Bhurtpore, in 1805, even after his victories in 1803 and 1804, had left the impression on the minds of the native princes, that we could not take forts.

Now the Sikhs under Runjeet Singh had defeated the Affghans under Ajean Khan, the elder brother of Dost Mahomed Khan, at Noushera (half way between Attock and Peshawur), in 1823. They imagined themselves superior, as soldiers, to the Affghans, and knew that the latter had defeated the British. They did not, however, bear in mind that our troops were destroyed in the retreat by the frost and snow. Lady Sale says, the first snow fell on the 26th of November. They, therefore, argued thus:—They had beaten the Affghans, and the Affghans had beaten the British; therefore the British were not invincible, and might be overcome by Sikh troops.

The disturbed state of the Lahore government during the latter part of the reign of Runjeet Singh, up to the present moment, had compelled the British government to introduce various precautionary measures for the protection of the British frontier, on a scale which was opposed to the terms of the treaty of 1809. It is true that the British government had recognised their boy-king, Dhuleep Singh, who had been proclaimed by the army, but being of a naturally suspicious character, the Sikhs considered themselves in danger of invasion, and resolved to anticipate the British, and wage war, by crossing the Sutlej. They appointed Lall Singh, prime minister, or vizier, and Tej Singh, an officer of considerable talent and experience, commander-in-chief of the Sikh forces.

The British government demanded an explanation of this movement, but none being given, the Governor-General issued a proclamation,[13] declaring all the possessions and territories of the Maharajah Dhuleep Singh on the left bank of the Sutlej to be confiscated and annexed to the British dominions; calling upon the inhabitants and their rulers to second the British government, he assured all who were peaceably disposed, of the protection of that government.

Thus the war was begun. The Sikhs, as we have seen, crossed the Sutlej with their heavy artillery on the 13th, on the 14th, marched to Ferozeshah, and, on the 18th, met the British forces, under the command of Sir Hugh Gough.

The battle of Moodkee, on the 18th of December, was their first battle with the English. This engagement they themselves allowed to be a defeat; but in that of Ferozeshah, three or four days later, they claimed the victory. Indeed many British officers have told me that it was a very desperate affair, and that it was fortunate the Sikhs were ignorant of their own power and resources. If this fact be held in recollection, when the reader comes to the battle of Sobraon, seven weeks later, he will see the necessity for a grand effort on their part; for another defeat or retreat would have been ruin to the Sikh cause.

Colonel Campbell's force was, as we have stated, nearly 3,000 strong, but the loss of the English in the battles of Moodkee and Ferozeshah, amounted to 3,291 men killed and wounded, and 804 horses; so that the arrival of this force would not replace the numbers lost. It was, therefore, necessary to draw troops from other quarters also, and concentrate them at the place of action.

FOOTNOTES:

[4] In the Dragoons, one groom is allowed by Government for every two horses, the other being paid by the soldiers themselves.

[5] In Bengal Proper, rice. These cakes are made just like those eaten by the men, but thicker and of coarser flour. No bad food on a pinch.

[6] Vide Despatches.

[7] See Appendix III.

[8] See Appendix IV.

[9] See Appendix V.

[10] See Appendix VI.

[11] In 1845, Allard was dead; Ventura, Court and Avitabile were in Europe; Cortland, son of Lieut.-Colonel Cortland, late of H.M. 31st Foot, who had entered the service of the Sikh leader, came over to the British. Colonel Hurbon, a Spanish officer, erected the works at Sobraon; still he was not a regular officer in the pay of the Sikh government, but was employed for the occasion by the troops.

[12] See Appendix VII.

[13] See Appendix VIII.

CHAPTER III

Nidampore—Christmas-day—Munsorepore—Kotla Mullair—Phurawallee—Bussean—Surrender of Wudnee—Cession of Ferozepore—Bhaga Poorana—False Alarms—Roree Bukkur—Sir John Littler—Sir H.M. Wheeler—Ferozeshah—Aliwal—Sikh Forces—British Forces—Sikh Entrenchment—Returns of Killed and Wounded—Sir H. Hardinge—Battle of Ferozeshah—Sudden Attack by Tej Singh—His Blunder—Appearance of a field of Battle—Fate of the Wounded.

To resume our route. On December the 24th, Colonel Campbell's force marched to Nidampore, a small village; a distance of nine miles. Here we halted, with the prospect of spending a quiet Christmas Day. On this day, however, we received intelligence, in camp, of the battle of Ferozeshah, which had taken place on the 22nd of December; and that the Sikhs, driven from the field, had retired across the Sutlej. This day, therefore, instead of breathing peace and love, was employed in preparations for war with our determined foes: unlike the Romans at the siege of Jerusalem, when no operations were undertaken against the Jews on their Sabbaths and Holy days. In Europe, however, and indeed all over the world in the present age, all days are alike in regard to war. The heathen Sikhs, who keep sacred no day in the week, might attack us on any day, and at any hour; so that it was necessary in self-defence that we should be prepared for the enemy. Accordingly the services of the armourer-sergeant and his men were put in requisition to sharpen swords and lances, and all was ready for starting the next morning.

On the 26th, our troops began their march to the village of Munsorepore, a distance of ten miles, through a country abounding in jungle, which rendered it necessary to observe great caution on the march; and flanking parties were sent out to prevent a surprise. Our route lay through two villages, which appeared to be thinly peopled: the walls of the houses were in a state of decay, and altogether they presented a desolate and deserted appearance. This, however, was not extraordinary; for as the Sikhs had been located on the south side of the Sutlej for fourteen days, it was to be expected that the people would abandon their homes and fly to the desert.

On the 27th of December, our troops marched to Kotla Mullair, a distance of sixteen miles. This town is very long and densely built; the main street being peculiarly narrow.

On the 28th we marched to Phurawallee, the country of the Nabah Rajah, twelve miles over a flat country, and by an unmade road, but by no means bad. This was Sunday; and still no public service. Last night, a private of the Lancers shot himself dead; such an event is happily of rare occurrence, and it produced a deep impression upon both men and officers.

There was a report abroad in the bazaar to-day, that another battle had taken place; but there was no foundation for the rumour. The Sikhs, it will be seen, did not meditate fighting again so soon.

On the 29th, we proceeded to Bussean, a long twelve miles' march through a flat and open country. The detachment had under its charge 4,300,000 rounds of ball (musketry) cartridges. This would give for 20,000 infantry, 215 rounds per man; and, as it is said that one shot in 100 kills, there were rounds sufficient to destroy 43,000 of the enemy. Independently of this, we had round-shot, shrapnell, canister and grape.

Our next march was to Wudnee or Budnee, fifteen miles and a half, by a very sandy route, which was consequently quite unfit for hackeries.

On the road, the commanding officer received an Express from the Governor-General, ordering us to take the fort of Wudnee, should we find it occupied by Sikh troops. Captain Rose, of the Lancers, was accordingly sent in advance of our force, to surround the Avails with his troop. To his great regret, the garrison offered no resistance, and about 5,000 rupees, and a few half-starved horses were given up to us. Two companies of the 59th Regt. of Native Infantry were left in charge of the fort.

Only a few days before, the whole of this district had been under the sway of the Maharajah of Lahore; but by the proclamation of the Governor-General it was now incorporated with the British dominions.

About ten years previous to these events, the demise of the female chief of Ferozepore without issue, gave us possession of that place; the rule in such cases being, that the estates of those chiefs who die without heirs become escheats. Thus this city fell to the East India Company. Runjeet Singh had previously objected to cede to us any of the ferries; but we had now for some time past been permitted to make use of them, both here and along the course of the river. On the cession of Ferozepore, however, his jealousy was aroused anew, and studiously fostered by his officers, at our occupation of a territory so near his own capital; and his chiefs constantly urged upon him the necessity of excluding us. Thus, with the possession of Ferozepore, we had gained the ferry at that place, and subsequently also secured one opposite to Loodianna.

This was an important point, for by it we obtained the right to cross whenever we chose. The Sikhs, however, as we have seen, were not prevented from crossing over to us. It was a very anomalous position for the British rule to be placed in, for, while we were protectors of the estates of four Sikh Rajahs, the estates of other chiefs were under the government of the Lahore Durbar. It is obvious that the circumstance of the Sikhs having a right to visit the estates of those chiefs who owed allegiance to the Durbar, and none to the British government, must have been a source of considerable inconvenience and annoyance, to say the least of it. Hence there is no doubt, that they sent over guns and ammunition to the left or south bank of the Sutlej, long before they crossed themselves, and when they did venture over, we confiscated the said estates.

To return to our narrative. On the 31st of December, the detachment under Colonel Campbell marched twelve miles to Bhaga Poorana, a small native village in the possession of the Alloo-walla Rajah, who held lands on both sides of the Sutlej. Here the Colonel received an order from the Commander-in-Chief to proceed to Loodianna, instead of to Ferozepore, the object of which change we could not in the least understand. In the evening, while we were at mess, we were suddenly disturbed by the report that some thousands of Sikhs were approaching our camp, and indeed had actually entered it. Our dessert was left untouched upon the table; the whole regiment was soon mounted, and drawn up at the head of their lines. After waiting about half an hour, and seeing no enemy, all retired to bed. In less than half an hour after, we had a second false alarm, from the firing of some sentries, belonging to the picquets of the Native Infantry corps. Such mistakes, with all their concomitant annoyances, are by no means unfrequent. An alarm has been occasioned by a few bullocks crossing a nullah near a camp during a dark night. In such a case, a Sepoy sentry receiving no answer to his challenge, "Who come dare?" (who goes there?), fires his piece, and the whole camp taking this as a signal of danger, is instantly in motion.

A false alarm of this kind occurred at Roree Bukkur, in Scinde, when the Bengal column under Major-general Sir Willoughby Cotton, was *en route* to Candahar, in February, 1839. The musket of one of the sentries went off by accident; the others immediately fired, whereupon the whole of the troops turned out.

Looking at the map, it would seem as if the recent "Express" to move on Loodianna had in view to command the road from Delhi, though just then no convoy was, it is believed, on the road from that city. Again, troops had been marched from Loodianna, and Runjoor Singh had not then crossed. The sudden appearance of the Sikhs in the neighbourhood of our frontier, threatened the two advanced posts at Ferozepore and Loodianna, both on the south bank of the Sutlej, and distant from each other about seventy miles. Major-General, now Sir John Littler, commanded at the former place; and, when summoned on the 23rd of December, 1845, to join the Commander-in-Chief, had about 10,000 troops. He left a small force at that post, and joined head-quarters at about 1 o'clock, P.M. At Loodianna, Colonel, now Sir Hugh Massy Wheeler, K.C.B., commanded. At Subathoo, fourteen miles up the hills, the Honourable Company's 1st European regiment was stationed. Loodianna is about equi-distant from Subathoo and Moodkee.

The battle of Ferozeshah, on the 21st and 22nd of December, 1845, has been the subject of discussion both as to the time and form of making; the attack. In regard to time, it is the opinion of the French marshal, Marmont, in his "L'Esprit des Instructions Militaires," p. 151, that "it is best to begin a battle early in the morning if certain of success; but if uncertain, in the middle of the day." Some assert that it was not necessary to commence the attack on the 21st, and that it would have been far better to have deferred it till early the next morning. Then again it is maintained, that had the attack been deferred till the morning of the 22nd, Tej Singh would have joined the main body of the Sikhs. However, early next morning the attack was renewed, and the rest of the entrenchments soon taken. It also appears that Tej Singh did actually come up before Ferozeshah at nine o'clock in the morning—at an hour when the British had possession of the place—and Major-General Littler was ordered to hold it at all risks.

I have before said that the cavalry were taken off in the direction of Ferozepore, with the exception of the 3rd Dragoons. Here, again, I may remark on the absence of the 9th Lancers, which was a general subject of regret among the officers present in the battle; a regret which I have heard repeatedly expressed both at the time and since. It is not possible to calculate the value of the services which this strong corps might have rendered in the hour of need; instead of which they were marching backwards and forwards between Ferozepore and Loodianna. Yet it is very probable that Tej Singh may have been aware that the 9th and 16th Lancers, and other corps, were on their march to join the main army, and hence have hastened his retreat.

Another objection to delay was the great scarcity of water; there being, it is said, no water at Ferozeshah, except in the village held by the enemy, and but little in the villages near it. Others, again, assert, that had the troops fallen back a little they would have found a supply of water, and that the Sikhs, moreover, would then most probably have come out of their entrenchments, and attacked the English on even ground.

At the battle of Aliwal, which took place subsequently, namely, on the 28th of January, 1846, the Sikhs did leave the little entrenchment which they had thrown up, and took up a position, their right resting on a village of the same name; their left on a circular entrenchment; and their centre on some heights. Again, it is whispered that the Governor-General and the Commander-in-Chief were desirous of making an immediate attack, in order to prevent the Sikhs from marching upon Ferozepore or Loodianna. Of Loodianna, however, there was no danger, because they would naturally attack that place by crossing at Philoor; there was far more reason to have expected an attack upon Ferozepore, for three good reasons.

1st. Because the Sikhs had fallen back to Ferozeshah, only a few miles from Ferozepore.

2ndly. Because, as has been before stated, Runjeet Singh's Chiefs were very averse to the English having possession of Ferozepore, from which there is a direct road to Lahore, their capital; and

3rdly. Because, by their retrograde movements from Moodkee, the Sikhs joined the other infantry.

The object in not attacking till the next morning, would have been to gain information respecting the nature and strength of the enemy's entrenched position at Ferozeshah. The late Captain P. Nicolson, the assistant political agent, is said strongly to have recommended an attack on the rear of the enemy's entrenchment. Major Broadfoot, when he reached the spot, where Major-General Littler joined about noon, exclaimed, "We will now drive them out of that entrenchment."

It is said that there was a great deal of jungle about Ferozeshah, but that the ground immediately around was open. By a brief delay, it might have been ascertained that the rear was undefended by guns. It is not to be supposed that the Sikhs would have thought of an advance beyond their then position, until they had gained a victory.

Again, it is broadly asserted that the Sikhs would never have left their entrenchments, and might have strengthened them, had any delay taken place.

The Sikh force is said to have been as follows:

	Battalions.		Corps.	Guns.
French Brigade Infantry,	4	Regular Cavalry,	2	26
Buhadoor Singh's do.	4	do.	1	16
Mertab Singh's do.	4	do.	1	18
	—		—	—
	12		4	60

The Infantry were 7,200 men.

	Irregular Cavalry.		
Charaganee Horse	4,500		
Orderly do.	3,500		
Lall Singh's do.	1,800	Heera Singh's do.	3,500
Moolraj's do.	550		
Bala Singh's do.	200		
Nehing's do.	1,000		
Utter Singh's do.	700		
Pindeewalas	900		
Dogras[14]	200		
	————		
	16,850		
	————		

4 Corps of Regular Cavalry,	about 2,000
Irregular Horse,	16,850
	———
	18,850
Infantry	7,200
	———
Total	26,050
	———
Artillery Field Guns	60

Heavy Guns	28
	—
	88
	—
Zumbooruks (Camel Guns)	250
	—

The above force, with 3,000 detached Infantry, and the greater part of the Irregular Horse, marched to Ferozeshah, for the purpose of holding Moodkee; reaching this place in the evening, they fought the battle of the 18th of December, with a force of 17,000 or 18,000 men.

The British force at Moodkee was about 13,000 men, and 48 guns, 36 of which were horse artillery: the action was sudden, and there was no regularity; the corps moved off in echelon, but owing to the dust, confusion, and lateness of the day, some infantry corps fired into each other. I have heard that a native infantry corps fired by mistake into H.M. 50th foot. Many of the officers, and all those of the staff who were killed, were shot by Sikh soldiers from the branches of trees, where they had stationed themselves. The Horse Artillery and Cavalry opened the encounter; but the dust which these troops raised, caused the Infantry, which came up last, to grope as it were in the dark, and to make serious mistakes.

The Sikhs having been defeated at Moodkee, called upon the troops before Ferozepore, and the Nuggur Ghât to join them, which made their force as under:

Battalions.		Infantry.		Cavalry.		Guns.
10 Additional,	6,000	Additional,	500	Additional,	55	
12 Before	7,200	Before	2,000	Before	60	
	——			——	Heavy Guns	28
	13,200		2,500		——	
	——			——	143	
					——	

This, including the 16,850 Irregular Cavalry, gives 32,550 men, of whom the Regular troops were 15,700 men; and, deducting the seventeen guns taken at Moodkee, the enemy ought to have had 126 guns at Ferozeshah, besides the 250 Zumbooruks. These were not very great odds against the British as to numbers.

The number of British killed and wounded was 2,419; namely, 2,269 non-commissioned officers and privates, and 150 officers, which gives one officer to every fifteen men; and as the usual proportion is one to twenty, or twenty-five, this was the greatest proportional loss in the four battles.

At Ferozeshah, including the Sikh force detached to Moodkee, there were 13,200 infantry; deducting, say 1,200 killed and wounded at Moodkee, there remained, say 12,000 men; to these add an additional reinforcement of 6,000 men and we have 18,000 infantry, which appears to have been the amount of the Sikh forces in the entrenchments at Ferozeshah on the 21st of December 1845; also 126 guns, of which twenty-eight were heavy guns, which likewise agrees with the returns; the enemy's cavalry could scarcely have exceeded 8,000 or 10,000 men. The entrenchment was about a mile in length, and half a mile in breadth, but as there was a village within those limits, the space for the troops was of course greatly diminished by it.

It will be for the military reader to form his own judgment, as my experience does not warrant me in giving an opinion of the motives and actions of my superiors. I have trusted a great deal throughout my accounts, to officers who were actually present in this remarkable campaign. It is curious to note the opinions of others. One thing however seems tolerably clear, that the only mode by which a really true account of any battle can be given, is to obtain a statement from some competent officer of each corps, troop, or company of artillery, etc., actually present in the field.

The practice, in this respect in the Indian army is this: each brigadier reports to the major-general commanding his division, upon the efficiency and prominent services of each regiment in his brigade, noting also the disposition of each corps; the major-general in a similar manner makes a report to the Adjutant-General for the information of the Commander-in-Chief, of the state of each of his brigades, and the particular services rendered. It is from these divisional reports that the Commander-in-Chief draws up his despatches.

It is obvious, that after a great battle, particularly if there be a pursuit of the enemy, no correct return of the killed and wounded can be given for two, three, or four days; for those who are killed lie on the field, and those who are wounded will get into a village, if near, and remain concealed there.

The Sikhs having thus, as we have stated, drawn their various forces from Moodkee, Ferozepore, and Nuggur Ghât, concentrated them at Ferozeshah, and formed their entrenchments, which in several places they threw up breast high.

Lieutenant-General Sir Henry Hardinge, the Governor-General, who was second in command, shared all the fatigues and dangers of the army with the Commander-in-Chief. Orders had been despatched to Sir John Littler to join head-quarters immediately. He accordingly left only a small garrison at Ferozepore, and, with a body of about 5,000 men and twenty-one guns, effected the junction, about noon on the 21st of December. Measures for a general attack were at once planned; but a considerable delay occurred, and much time was lost, as we have stated, in consequence of the conflicting views of competent officers, as to whether it was desirable to make an immediate attack, or to defer it till the following morning. The former was ultimately resolved upon.

The British marched in even ranks, and commenced the action with a brisk fire of artillery at a distance of about a mile from the enemy. The Sikhs made a gallant defence. The British artillery advanced steadily till they were within a few hundred yards of the entrenchment; but the Sikhs kept up an incessant fire from their heavy guns; in consequence of which our infantry were ordered to advance, and, in the face of a murderous fire, to take the batteries. Night put a stop to the carnage, but not to the awful state of confusion which prevailed in the British camp, which arose partly from the severe losses and the scattering of the different regiments, with the uncertainty as to whether any advantage had been gained, and partly from the incessant firing kept up during the whole night by the Sikhs upon the wretched soldiers who were lying wounded upon the field of battle, or who were cowering around their scanty fires, worn out with cold, fatigue and excruciating thirst.

Sir Henry Hardinge, finding that a large Sikh gun occasioned much annoyance to our troops, brought up the 80th Foot, who soon took it. He then passed among the different European corps, which greatly cheered and reanimated them under their intense sufferings. It was a night of terrific suspense and anxiety to the two British Chiefs, both of whom nobly resolved to fight and conquer, or perish in the attempt. The British lion was roused, and his vast strength was all centred in one final attempt. The die was cast. The Governor-General gave the word, and Britons struck home the death-blow.

The village of Ferozeshah appears to have been held during the night of the 21st of December, partly by the British and partly by the Sikhs. One of our divisions under the gallant Major-General, Sir Harry Smith, kept up a fire during the greater part of the night. The other divisions bivouacked at some distance, no one knows where. Had a concerted movement been necessary, it would have been quite out of the question; for, by some mistake or oversight, no place of rendezvous had been fixed on. I am told that the men belonging to two or three of the European corps got clubbed together, and were so found the next morning; nay, even the whereabouts of the

Commander-in-Chief himself could not be found. A certain Major-General was anxious to communicate with him, and an engineer officer, who had just been with Sir Hugh Gough, offered to shew him the road; but, to his surprise, he could not find it: either His Excellency had moved his position, or the night was too dark to enable the officer to trace his way back.

The morning light revealed the fact that the Sikhs were still masters of a large portion of their entrenchments; the British retaining only that part where they had bivouacked during the night.

The Commander-in-Chief now drew up his forces; the Infantry forming into a line supported on either side by the horse artillery. His Excellency took the command of the left wing, the Governor-General of the right. The engagement opened with a brisk cannonade from the centre. The Sikhs renewed the deadly fire from their heavy guns, screened by their masked batteries, scattering death and destruction among the British troops. Both the left and right wings of infantry advancing under their able commanders, charged the Sikhs at the point of the bayonet, and took possession of the village of Ferozeshah.

At this juncture, when victory seemed to be decided for the British, Tej Singh, the commander-in-chief of the Sikh army, suddenly appeared on the field with his army of reserve, consisting of 30,000 men, and a large park of light guns. He charged into the midst of the British troops, and attempted to recover the entrenchment, but without success. He then opened a fire upon us from his guns, but, unhappily, all our shot were expended. It was one of those unexpected cases which demand the greatest promptitude and judgment; and our artillery are said to have fired blank ammunition.[15]

The British cavalry had been ordered by a certain staff officer, in the Adjutant-General's department, to move off to Ferozepore. This, I suppose, must have been before Tej Singh came up. It is also reported that Tej Singh conceived that this move was made in connection with some deeply concerted plan, with the intention of getting into his rear. Whatever may have been his opinion, he contented himself with firing a few shots from his light guns— none other had he—by which a few of the British were killed and wounded. Had the cavalry not been ordered off, the whole of which, I understand, moved away, with the exception of that noble regiment the 3rd Light Dragoons, who had previously, in this same action, performed prodigies of valour in charging batteries and entrenchments,—acts unparalleled in cavalry tactics,—Tej Singh might have been attacked to advantage. Thus much is certain; that the officer above alluded to was allowed to retire from the service. The whole affair of the morning of the 22nd cannot be either unravelled or explained; and I have discussed the matter with many officers who were present on that occasion, but have never met with one who could solve its mysteries. It savours more of romance than of reality. "Truth is strange—stranger than fiction." Goolab Singh, now Maharajah of Cashmere, speaking to a European officer, of Tej Singh's advance, as above described, observed that: "Tej Singh committed a great blunder; he should never have gone near you, but should have marched at once upon Delhi!"

Many, however, are of opinion, that the sudden attack of Tej Singh, with his 30,000 troops, was a mere feint. It was well known that he was in correspondence with Captain Nicolson; and it is even affirmed, that he had privately furnished an officer with a plan of the intended operations of the Sikh army. It was his object to ingratiate himself with both parties. His position as leader of the army demanded that he should make the attack; while at the same time he foresaw that the British would ultimately triumph in the Punjaub, and that it would be for his interest to make friends of them. Therefore, after firing a few shots, the Commander-in-Chief of the Sikhs fled from the field of battle, at the very moment when the failure of the enemy's ammunition, and the departure of their cavalry to Ferozepore, gave him an advantage which might have turned the tide of victory in his favour. After the desertion of their general, the Sikhs made several ineffectual attempts, to recover the entrenchment, but before night-fall, were compelled to retreat across the Sutlej.

The view of a field of battle awakens the noblest sympathies of our nature. Even the stern Napoleon has had his cold heart touched by such a scene. The first survey is overwhelming; and the heart of even the stoutest soldier shrinks within him, and sickens at the sight. On a nearer inspection, we find the dead and the dying, friend and foe, lying side by side; their furious contest suddenly cut short by the cold hand of death—while the cries and moans of the wounded till our ears with sounds of lamentation and woe, and our hearts with pity and commiseration.

We lament the fate of the slain, and grieve that his career is ended; yet it is the death of the brave soldier who has gloriously discharged his duty to his country, and whose fame remains imperishable, that calls forth our deepest grief, admiration and gratitude. "*Dulce et decorum est pro patria mori.*" Well did Lord Hutchinson, in reporting the death of the brave and lamented Abercrombie, express the feelings of a soldier, when he said: "His name shall be embalmed in the memory of a grateful country."

Thoughts of a future state are powerfully impressed upon the mind, as the eye wanders over the battle-field of the slain. As we gaze upon those who have distinguished themselves, not only as the liege soldiers of their king, but as the faithful soldiers of the King of kings, our heart insensibly finds relief. While the spark of life yet flickers in the mortal tenement, we watch by the side of our wounded comrade, and, like king David, we fast and weep, and say: "Who can tell whether God will be gracious to me that he may live;" but when the dread fiat has gone forth, and the spirit no longer dwells within its house of clay, like David we restrain our grief, and looking beyond the grave, exclaim in faith: "Wherefore should I weep? Can I bring him back again? I shall go to him, but he shall not return to me."

Before quitting the field of slaughter, I would make a few remarks respecting the wounded. The fate of the private soldier is often very hard: by the loss of limbs he is rendered useless for life as a soldier, his means of subsistence are curtailed, and what is yet dearer to him, his military career is blighted for ever. The officer may do duty again if he lose an arm, or what is almost the same thing, if he be wounded and unable to have the ball extracted. This was the case with my father, who, having been hit in both shoulders at the battle of Waterloo, did duty in his most gallant regiment the old 95th, now the Rifle Brigade, for nearly three years after, although, as the ball remained in the shoulder, the left arm was rendered useless.[16] Some officers even continue in the service after they have lost a leg, and receive a good pension. This is the case with Field-Marshal the Marquis of Anglesey.

The disabled rank and file are what is styled "invalided," that is to say, they are sent to England and elsewhere, where they obtain a pension, fixed and determined by a board of officers.

The late Queen's Inspector-General of Hospitals in Bengal, states a fact which ought to be generally known, "The number of those who are wounded and die in consequence, cannot be ascertained fully under the lapse of a year, because there are cases in which a gun-shot through the lungs has superinduced affections of the brain, fevers, etc." It is likewise worthy of remark that gun-shot wounds are more dangerous than sabre cuts.

FOOTNOTES:

[14] The Jummoo Chief is called Dogra.

[15] When Sir Archibald Campbell, who commanded the expedition against Ava, in 1824-26, headed a Portuguese brigade of infantry in the Peninsular war, he was informed upon one occasion, that only a few rounds of shot were left. He immediately ordered a charge in line, his object being to conceal his want of ammunition.

[16] See Appendix IX.

CHAPTER IV

Return to Bussean—Sir John Grey's Detachment—Battle of
Assaye—Sindiah's Troops—Generals Allard and Ventura—
General Lloyd's Observations on the Art of War—Tactics
of the Sikhs—Runjeet Singh's Discipline—Sikh Artillery—
Goojerat—Moodkee—Sir Joseph Thackwell—Bootawalla—
Pontoons—Their Value to an Army—Great Rise in the Price
of Food.

On the 2nd of January, 1846, Colonel Campbell's force marched
to Bussean, a retrograde movement; but in times of war, such counter
movements are occasionally unavoidable, and their utility can be known
only to the superintending eye of the Commander-in-chief.

In the course of the day, soon after we had finished our long and
fatiguing march, we were surprised to find that we were to return in the
direction of Ferozepore, in company with Major General Sir John Grey's
detachment, which, at this time, was a march or two in our rear. This
detachment consisted of three troops of horse artillery, H.M. 16th Lancers,
3rd Light Cavalry, H.M. 10th Foot, three regiments of Native Infantry, a
company of Sappers and Miners, and the 4th Irregular Horse. This formed a
force of about 7,500 men. There were besides, twelve twelve-pounders and
eighteen horse artillery guns; in all thirty guns, or four to every thousand
men, a force as large as that with which the Duke of Wellington fought the
battle of Assaye, on the 23rd of September, 1803; for, excluding the 3,000
Mysore, etc., cavalry, he had only 4,500 men. The enemy was defeated with
the loss of 120 guns taken, destroyed, or lost; the captured guns amounted
to above 100.

It may be asked, why, when the Duke of Wellington, with a mere
handful of soldiers, attacked some 35,000 men and gained such an action,
we could not utterly eradicate even the very name of Sikh? The reasons
are threefold. The battles of Moodkee and Aliwal were field actions; those
of Ferozeshah and Sobraon were storming entrenchments. The strength of
the entrenchments at Ferozeshah was not equal to those at Sobraon. The
number of killed and wounded at Ferozeshah amounted to 2,419, and at
Sobraon 2,383. At the former battle, the enemy had more than one hundred,
at the latter sixty-seven guns, and two hundred camel-swivels; besides, at

Sobraon, the Sikhs had two strong batteries in the rear of the right and left flanks of the entrenchment; for there were entrenchments and works within one another. We made three good attacks. The attack in front by Major-General Gilbert's division was not originally designed. There was a bank or mound of earth between this division and the entrenchment. The brigade, of which the 29th Foot composed a part, got jammed up, and formed into a wedge, something like the Roman form. It was at first intended that this division should wait as a reserve, and act if required, There was a failure in the right attack on the enemy's left.

Secondly, the troops of Sindiah and of the Berar Rajah, at the battle of Assaye had indeed been drilled, but they had not then had the advantage of having French officers; besides which, they, the Sirdars, were unable to act by themselves; nor had their men, like the Khalsa troops, been disciplined by such distinguished officers as were in the service of Runjeet Singh. The older French officers had died off, and the others were mere adventurers, very different from Ventura and Allard, who had served in the wars of the great Napoleon; the former having been in the retreat from Moscow. Sindiah's European officers were simply drill-sergeants; the merely being able to advance in line, or to execute some common evolutions will not gain a battle. A practised military eye for planning a battle, and marking out the details, is the indispensable requisite for such an achievement. As General Lloyd truly observes, in his able work on the Art of War: "No art or science is more difficult than that of war. It may be divided into two parts: the one mechanical, which may be taught by precepts; the other has no name, nor can it be either defined or taught. It consists in a just application of the principles and precepts of war in all the numberless circumstances and situations which occur; no rule, no study or application however assiduous, no experience however long, can teach this part; it is the effect of genius alone. As to the first, it may be reduced to mathematical principles; its object is to prepare the materials which form an army, for all the different operations which may occur: genius must apply them, according to the ground, number, species, and quality of the troops, which admit of infinite combinations. In this art, as in poetry and eloquence, there are many who can trace the rules by which a poem or an oration should be composed, and even compose according to the exactest rules, but, for want of that enthusiastic and divine fire, their productions are languid and insipid: so in our profession, many are to be found who know every precept of it by heart; but alas! when called upon to apply them, are immediately at a stand. They then recall their rules, and want to make everything, the rivers, woods, ravines, mountains, etc., subservient to them; whereas, their precept should, on the contrary, be subject to these, which are the only rules, the only guide we ought to follow. Whatever manoeuvre is not formed on these is absurd and ridiculous. These form the Great Book of War, and he who cannot read it, must for ever be content with the title of a brave soldier, and never aspire to that of a great general."

The discipline and training of the Sikh army had, as I have observed before, undergone a complete transformation and improvement under Runjeet Singh, so that the troops under Sindiah, in 1803, could not bear comparison with those of 1845, who had been disciplined by Ventura and Allard. Runjeet Singh himself was a great warrior; and from the time that he visited Lord Lake's camp, in 1805, he became convinced of the superiority of the discipline of the British army, and at once resolved on re-forming his own. He had a good material to work upon in the native hardihood, bravery and energy of the Sikh character. His primary attention was given to the formation of a regular infantry; and in this he was greatly aided by some deserters from the British service, to whom he confided the drilling of his troops. After that, he enlisted the Goorkhas, whose able resistance to the English had given him great confidence in their mode of discipline.

The opposition of his officers and troops, especially in the adoption of a new dress, would have daunted a less resolute character; but Runjeet Singh, conscious of the power of example, took part in all the military exercises and drill, and even wore the unaccustomed dress of a British foot-soldier; thus making himself master de facto, and not merely de verbo, of the new principles of war. After this, Ventura, Allard, and other European officers, carried out and perfected that discipline, which made the Sikh army what it was, when led under Tej Singh against the British forces, in 1845.

Let the reader bear in mind how fatal the trap, laid by the Sikhs for our troops at Ramnuggur, had proved to those gallant cavalry officers, Colonel Cureton,[17] Lieutenant-Colonel Havelock, and Captain Fitzgerald; the two latter were my brother officers in the 4th Queen's Own Light Dragoons, at Bombay. At the battle of Goojerat, on the 21st of February, 1849, the Sikhs moved more than once to try and turn our flank. Was such an attempt ever made in 1803? No! It was at Assaye that the Duke of Wellington fought his hardest and best battle (I am speaking of India), for he had five to one as odds against him. In guns, the enemy had seven times the number, besides several 16-pounders and heavy guns. The Duke had none but 17 pop-guns; for 6-pounders, when brought into action against 16 and 12-pounders, deserve no better name.

Thirdly, The Sikhs fired their guns in the ratio of thrice to our twice, which multiplies most fearfully the battering power of artillery, and raises the calibre of a six into a nine-pounder. At the battle of Ferozeshah, the Sikh guns were served with extraordinary rapidity and precision. The infantry stood between and behind the batteries, and lay on the ground behind their artillery, priming their muskets, and actively discharging their pieces in the face of the British force, thus forming an almost unprecedented shower of balls, carrying destruction and death with irresistible force. Recollecting that in 1845 and 1846, the enemy's artillery was double that of the British, we might rather ask how it came that so many escaped its deadly effects, than wonder how it was that so many were destroyed.

At Goojerat, where we had the greatest number of guns, the victory was complete; for after three hours' constant firing, our troops advanced, the enemy's guns were taken, and they fled.

Referring to the history of the battles in India in earlier times, from 1780 to 1792, we find that Hyder Ali Khan and Tippoo Sultan, used 18-pounder guns as field-guns. Sir Eyre Coote was obliged to use the same, which taught the British the necessity of having large guns; but, till very recently, we had departed from the practice of using guns equal in calibre to those of our enemies. It is a curious fact, that the British had 2,419 killed and wounded at Ferozeshah, and 2,383, or 36 less, at Sobraon: also, at the former battle, 694 killed, and at the latter, only 460, being a difference of 50 per cent. less. How can we account for this, but from the circumstance of our having had more guns at Sobraon? At Goojerat, the British loss was 807, out of which number 96 were killed, or not one-eighth. At Moodkee, the English lost 872 killed and wounded, of which number 215 were killed, or nearly one-fourth. At Goojerat, nearly 90 guns had been playing for three hours upon the Sikhs, before they gave way and the British advanced to take their guns. At Moodkee, the 36 Horse Artillery guns were the only ones brought into play. Except at the battle of Aliwal, where the loss was 589, the British suffered less at Goojerat than in any other battle with the Sikhs.

Lord Gough, in his Despatch,[18] says that the enemy had 60,000 men (perhaps overrated), and 59 guns. His lordship had 84 guns, according to the return, and these were of heavier metal than those of the enemy.

Surely, after these proofs, and when we have lost 10,788 men, killed and wounded, and 1,899 horses, in seven battles and one siege, viz., Moodkee, Ferozeshah, Aliwal, Sobraon, Ramnuggur, Chillianwallah, Goojerat, and the fort of Mooltan, we ought to be prepared on every point on our North-West frontier.

When I left India, in 1846, after the decisive battle of Sobraon, it was the general opinion that not another shot would be fired again in India for many years to come, whereas, in little more than two years after, we had, instead of a campaign of two months' duration, that is from the 18th of

December, 1845, to the 10th of February, 1846, an uninterrupted warfare of ten months' continuance.

To resume our narrative. On the 3rd of January, Colonel Campbell's force marched for the third time to Wudnee, a distance of seventeen miles. The fatigue and tedium of marching to and fro, began to be sensibly felt, and many of our camp followers deserted. Among them was my Bihishti, or water-carrier, who had accompanied me on the march from Cawnpore. Then, too, there was so much heavy baggage, that instead of the indispensable refreshment of an ablution at the end of a dusty march, our officers could not get their towels and soap till a late hour in the afternoon.

On Sunday, the 4th of January, we marched back to Bhaga Poorana. Here we experienced a scarcity of water; and what little there was, was very bad. On the 5th, we marched at a quarter to five, A.M., on Moodkee, fifteen miles distant.

Here we encamped on the battle-field, which was still covered with the fragments of soldiers' clothing and appointments, carcases of camels and horses, and the bodies of friends and enemies, who had been slaughtered here on the 18th of December. The atmosphere all round was greatly tainted, which, combined with the horrible sight before us, made our hearts sick, and our heads faint.

About a month ago, this large village, containing about 4,000 inhabitants, belonged to the Lahore Rajah. It was now in the possession of the English: the scene before us proclaimed the price at which it had been bought. But even amid the ruins, the soldier as well as the Christian, looks forward with hope to the future: the one to the promotion of his country's glory, the other to the spread of the Gospel among the heathen.

In the evening, we received an unexpected order to join the "army of the Sutlej"; our Horse Artillery and Cavalry to proceed together; the Infantry and Elephant Battery to halt. On the 6th, we made a forced march of about twenty miles, to Aurufkee. On the road, we saw several corpses of British and Sikh soldiers, in a state bordering on decomposition, and plundered of their clothing.

Colonel Campbell[19] having been appointed to a brigade of Cavalry, as also Colonel Scott, Major and Brevet Lieutenant-Colonel Fullerton[20] assumed the command this day, of the Queen's Royal Lancers.

Our camp was pitched at a distance of four miles from the river Sutlej.

On the 8th, I called on Major-General Sir Harry G.W. Smith, K.C.B., commanding the first division of the army of the Sutlej, an old brother rifleman, and friend of my father's.

The cavalry was commanded by Major-General Sir Joseph Thackwell, K.C.B. (now Colonel of the 16th Lancers), who is very much liked by all who have the honour of knowing him. He is considered one of the ablest officers in the British service; and his experience of military operations in India has always rendered his advice and assistance indispensable in all the late campaigns. Sir Joseph, I am happy to find, has been invested with the highest class of the Bath, and never did a braver or kinder man receive this distinction. His services during the campaign of which I am now treating, were most invaluable, none more so; and yet his reward was slow. Colonel Campbell, having, as I said before, been made a Brigadier of Cavalry, was appointed to the 2nd Brigade, consisting of the 9th Lancers, 11th Light Cavalry, and 2nd and 8th Irregular Cavalry.

On the 9th of January, about 10 a.m., we distinctly heard the roar of the Sikh guns. During the greater part of the previous day, the Sikhs, who were encamped in great apparent regularity, on the right, or opposite side of the river Sutlej, were practising their guns. They were evidently preparing for another encounter. In the course of the day, I called on Major-General Sir Joseph Thackwell, Major-General Sir Robert H. Dick, K.C.B., Lieutenant-Colonel Gough, Acting Quarter-Master-General to H.M. forces, since then Colonel and Aide-de-Camp to the Queen, and Lieut.-Colonel Havelock, Persian Interpreter to the Commander-in-Chief.

On the 10th, the cold was intense, when we were out at a general watering parade, at eight o'clock in the morning. Encamped on an arid plain, we found the dust extremely troublesome, the west wind, which usually prevails at this season, blowing very hard.

Sunday, January 11th. This morning at two o'clock there was an alarm. Every man of the 9th immediately turned out, and, having saddled and bridled, stood by his horse until the reveillé. I sent off all my superfluous baggage to the house of Lieutenant Fullerton, 14th Regiment Bengal Native Infantry, at Ferozepore, distant fourteen miles. He is a cousin of Lieut.-Colonel Fullerton, my commanding officer, and he had kindly offered to give it shelter. The Lieutenant, who had acted as aide-de-camp to Major-General Littler, at the battle of Ferozeshah, was at this period in charge of the Sudder (chief) Bazaar, at Ferozepore. The weather about this time was still intensely cold.

On the 12th of January, we changed ground to Bootawalla, less than two miles distant from the Sutlej: our position was on the left of the army. It is usual to change ground every now and then, because an encampment becomes dirty in a few days, and likewise because it is desirable to be nearer to the forage. When an enemy is close, however, these changes are made with much caution, since it is highly expedient not to give up a good position in exchange for a bad one. Such niceties are reserved for marches in times of peace, or where no enemy is at hand.

January 13th. We marched at two p.m. about three miles out from camp, in the direction of the bridge of boats, erected by the Sikhs; when, after a little cannonading on both sides, we returned by six o'clock p.m. The object of such a movement was this, to try our rockets in the enemy's camp, and to ascertain the range of his guns. But, suppose we had found our enemy off his guard, that there were but few sentries, and no battery to defend the bridge on our side, our plan would then have been to destroy the bridge, and station a guard to prevent its reconstruction.

The advantage of a pontoon bridge consists in your being able to place it at any part of the river. When Major-General Littler heard that the Sikhs were likely to cross, he sunk our pontoon bridge.

And here I may be permitted to digress a little, to give some account of this pontoon bridge, which was made at Bombay. The Duke of Wellington, in 1803, ordered forty boats, each twenty-one feet in length, to be made at Bombay, and transported on a carriage with four wheels. This step was taken with a view to the operations of our army on the river Toombuddra against the Maharatta territory, and to enable him to cross and re-cross the river whenever he chose.[21] The Ferozepore pontoon bridge was sent thither in 1844. My object in mentioning this bridge is, that it forms an argument why the Sikhs expected us to attack them, for they said that the bridge of boats was a clear proof of our design. It is not a little singular, that in all the wars from 1803 to 1844, or for above forty years, the British had never used a pontoon bridge; none have ever been seen in the Delhi magazine. When opposite to Ramnuggur, in 1848, on the Chenāb, the Commander-in-Chief detached a large force to operate against the right flank of the Sikh army, it was found necessary to proceed twenty-five miles up the river, before this force could cross. Thus making a march of fifty miles before it came up with the enemy, and when ranged on the opposite bank, nearly in face of the British camp, that single division stood completely isolated, without the possibility of being supported in case of need. Whereas, had the army of the Punjaub possessed a pontoon train, this force might have crossed above the Sikh entrenchment, and been in a position to receive support from the main army. The Commander-in-Chief could easily have received prompt intelligence of their advance and progress, and instantly on hearing that they had engaged the enemy, transported his army across the ford, or, by means of a second pontoon train, he might have defeated Shere Singh's army at once, and deprived him of all his guns. The moral effect of an attack carried on under such circumstances is incalculable; the chances are that it would have decided the campaign.

Besides, had the British possessed a pontoon train they might have destroyed all the enemy's boats, and prevented him from crossing, except at fords, which are few and often imperfectly known.

But it is not every one who is gifted with the genius of a Wellington; at the battle of Assaye his Grace sent some staff-officers to find a ford at a place where there was a village on each side of the river; and when a ford was found, he remarked: "I thought it probable that the people would not have built villages there unless a ford existed."

The want of a pontoon train caused a complete stand-still of the whole army at Ramnuggur. The artillery, cavalry, and infantry might be said to have been immovable, and therefore, useless, because they could not cross an ordinary river.

Let us consider how they act on the continent of Europe. Windischgrätz crossed the Danube to Vienna, with 150,000 men, by means of a pontoon train. The French army have a special corps of pontoniers. The Russian guards have a movable force of 50,000 men, complete in every branch, with a magnificent pontoon train, exclusive of the other pontoon trains, attached to the other divisions of the mighty army of that vast empire.

Every military man knows that the transport of an army, with its immense quantity of artillery and baggage, across the rivers which intersect its line of march, is one of the most difficult as well as the most important operations in military tactics, especially in India, where the camp followers are so numerous.

History, both modern and ancient, teaches us that the success of a campaign often depends on the rapid conveyance of troops across the rivers that intersect their march. As far back as the days of Darius a floating bridge was thrown across the Bosphorus, and afterwards across the Danube, while Xerxes threw one over the Hellespont at the time of his ill-starred expedition to Europe. The most celebrated pontoon of modern times, was that constructed by the engineers of the British army across the Adour, in the south of France, in 1814, the river being 110 feet across.

During the retreat of Napoleon from Moscow, the whole of his immense army must have been captured or destroyed on the banks of the Beresina, had it not been for the extraordinary care and vigilant forethought of the principal French engineer, in preserving the materials required in the formation of a pontoon.

A pontoon train, such as the Duke of Wellington employed in India, in 1803, composed of forty boats, would require forty carts and 160 to 170 bullocks. The Duke, in his Despatches,[22] states that for some streams he had basket boats ten feet in diameter and three feet deep, and covered with double leather.

When the Duke of Wellington's bridge of boats was brought to Ferozepore in the autumn of 1845, Major Broadfoot, who was charged with its transport, aroused the suspicion of the Sikhs, and in their opinion, virtually acknowledged that hostilities existed between them and the British, by manifesting extraordinary vigilance for its safe keeping, placing it under the escort of a strong guard of soldiers, and by employing the pontoniers to construct it, on the arrival of the boats at Ferozepore.

To return to my journal. On the 14th of January, 1846, the cavalry received orders to hold themselves in readiness to march at a moment's notice. We remained in this state of suspense from eight in the morning till one o'clock in the afternoon, when we again marched towards the Sikh bridge, and did the like execution with our guns as yesterday. The Sikhs having crossed over to our side of the bridge, were busily employed in making an entrenched camp.

On the 15th gram sold at sixteen seers or thirty-two lbs. for the rupee, a rather dismal prospect for a large army. The 9th Lancers had 600 fighting men, and the camp followers amounted to 3,600 men which gives six to every fighting man. After deducting 1,600, the number of followers required for 800 horses, including officers' chargers, and 480 dooly bearers, there would still remain 1,520 followers to be accounted for, and if we again allow the officers about forty in number, say 500 servants, — a very fair portion, — there would then be left 1,020 whom we must conclude to have been elephant and camel drivers, tent lascars, cooks, bazaar people, etc.

On the 18th the Lancers again held themselves in readiness to turn out at a moment's notice, owing to the enemy's crossing the river in large numbers. On the 19th we changed our ground, five miles to the right, and on our arrival the troop of the 9th, to which I belonged, was sent on picquet to a distance of nearly two miles to our right front, and pretty close to the Sutlej; indeed a picquet of the enemy was clearly seen on the other side. Had the enemy crossed, or rather, attempted to cross, the officer in command would have sent information to the camp, and in the meanwhile made arrangements to retard the force in the best manner he could, so as to allow the army time to come up to his support. To gain time is an officer's chief object, under such circumstances; nor must he in any case retire, unless driven in.

FOOTNOTES:

[17] See Appendix X.

[18] See Blue Book, p. 597.

[19] Colonel Campbell, C.B., and K.H., died suddenly in London, of quinsy, March, 1850, a few days after his arrival from India.

[20] Lieutenant-Colonel Fullerton, C.B., died on the 28th of April, 1850, on his way to visit Cashmere, whither his body was conveyed on the following day, and deposited in the Royal Gardens. By his death, the regiment was deprived of a most just, warm-hearted, and honourable man. A simple tablet marks the spot where he is interred.

[21] See Despatches, vol. iii. p. 64, 10th of April, 1803.

[22] Vol. i. p. 136, April 8th, 1803.

CHAPTER V

Hurrekee Ghât—Chain Bridles—Sir Thomas Dallas—
Victory of Sir Harry Smith at Aliwal—Umballa—
Preparations of the Sikhs—Capture of Dhurmkote—
Loodianna—Runjoor Singh—Buddiwal—Sirdar Ajeet
Singh—Invalids at Loodianna—The Pattiala Rajah—
Alarm at Loodianna—Siege-train in Danger—Convoy
inadequately protected—Sikh Artillery at Aliwal—Major
Lawrenson—Singular Formation of the Sikh Infantry at
Aliwal—16th Lancers—Desperation of the Sikhs—Colonel
Cureton—Charge of Lancers—Marshal Marmont's
Opinion—Sikhs evacuate Buddiwal—Rapid Movements of
the Sikhs—Brigadiers Godby and Hicks.

The Governor-General and the Commander-in-Chief inspected the 9th
Lancers on the morning of the 21st of January. An incessant report of guns
of a heavy calibre was heard all day, from the other side of the river. This
afternoon I rode in company with my commanding officer to the Hurrekee
Ghât, near which was our picquet, to enquire about two boats, said to have
been captured by the enemy. We, however, saw only a couple of old boats
and a great many unarmed people near them.

On the 23rd a false alarm caused the Commander-in-Chief to order us
out, and we all stood to our horses at the head of our lines, from twelve till
four o'clock, P.M.

On the 25th several of our officers had chain reins made for their
regimental bridles, because in the last action the enemy had cut some of the
bridles of the 3rd Light Dragoons, with their swords, by which their riders
became powerless, having lost all command over their horses.

This brings to my recollection an anecdote told me of the late Lieutenant-
General Sir Thomas Dallas, of the Madras Cavalry, well known in the wars
with Hyder Ali Khan and Tippoo Sultan, as the best horseman and most
experienced swordsman, in the Madras army, having often proved himself
the victor in single combat, and killed his man. One of the enemy was noted
for possessing a scimitar of the first quality; Sir Thomas, then a Captain, and
this man made an agreement to this effect, that they were to fight together,
and that the native was not to cut the Captain's reins, nor he to use his

pistols. After a long encounter the man violated the engagement and cut the Captain's reins, which were not of steel, upon which the latter drew his pistol and shot his opponent dead on the spot.

In a country like India every officer should go on service, furnished with a chain rein, for without it many a man has lost his life; besides, it is neither heavy nor inconvenient. The dragoons and troopers should also be supplied with them. The natives use them as well as coats of chain armour, and many of the Sikhs, as I myself witnessed, wore even breast plates and back pieces of steel. I picked up a steel helmet in the Sikh camp at the battle of Sobraon, which now serves to decorate my father's dining-room.

On the 28th of January, the Royal Lancers were in readiness the whole day to turn out at a moment's notice, as the Sikhs shewed themselves in great force, and appeared as if bent upon mischief.

January 29th. Intelligence was received in Camp of the splendid victory gained by Major-General Sir Harry Smith over the Sikhs under the command of Runjoor Singh, at Aliwal, on the 28th. The force under Sir Harry having captured the whole of the enemy's guns, forty-eight in number, and put to rout their army of 24,000 men, our whole line turned out at sunrise, when a royal salute was fired in honour of the day. After the salute, the Governor-General and Commander-in-Chief passed up the line, and the former addressed each regiment separately. These addresses are not unusual in India.

The battle of Ferozeshah, it will be remembered, was fought on the 21st and 22nd of December, 1845, so that about five weeks had elapsed since the last feat of arms. More troops were now advancing to the frontier, and several hundred hackeries, laden with shot, shells, powder, and stores of all kinds, were coming up. Engineer officers, too, were in great request; for it now became known that our assiduous enemy was fortifying Sobraon, on the left bank of the Sutlej, between Loodianna and Ferozepore. In fact the Sikhs were working hard at their entrenchments day and night.

We had not as yet received our military stores and supplies from Delhi. A well-stocked magazine, was apparently much needed. Many considered that Umballa was the most advantageous spot for establishing such a depôt, being 150 miles from Ferozepore, and seventy-one from Loodianna. Ferozepore was thought too isolated; delay, therefore, was imperative, and it was of no use to anticipate events.

The reader may easily conclude that the Sikhs, seeing our additional troops, guns and stores moving up to the army, did not remain idle, for they had a great game at stake, being no less than the future fate of a kingdom. They were buoyed up by their success at Buddiwal; the whole army under Tej Singh had re-crossed the Sutlej. The bridge-head, which secured so important an advantage, was enlarged; and, in the very face of the British army, they unremittingly carried on their warlike preparations. They seemed confident of victory, and ready to carry war and destruction into the very heart of their enemy's country, when our unlooked-for and glorious victory at Aliwal, proved to them that they were not invincible.

The announcement in our camp, on the 29th, of Sir Harry Smith's victory at Aliwal, caused considerable sensation. As for myself, I must confess that it was a great disappointment to me not to have taken a part in this engagement. I had written just before to Sir Harry Smith, who, as I have already observed, had been in the Rifle Brigade with my father, during the Peninsular war, expecting that he would have some fighting, and asking to be employed as his aide-de-camp. It was now too late. The news of the brilliant victory came, and put an end to all chance of my witnessing a battle in that quarter.

The object of Sir Harry in moving from our camp was doubtless to prevent the Sikhs from marching towards Delhi and intercepting our supplies. He succeeded in taking the little town and fort of Dhurmkote, which was filled with grain, and thus secured the regular supplies of the army. Having accomplished the reduction of the place, he received intelligence from head-quarters, that Runjoor Singh had crossed the Sutlej with 40,000 Sikhs, and had taken up a position on the road to Loodianna, for the purpose of intercepting our supplies from that town, which he threatened with an attack. This was accompanied by an order to Sir Harry Smith to proceed immediately to Loodianna.

Four regiments of infantry, three of cavalry, and eighteen guns composed the whole of the detachment under the command of this brave general, when on the 21st of January he proceeded to Buddiwal, a small garrison close to Loodianna, which was occupied by Runjoor Singh, and 10,000 of his men. Sir Harry Smith endeavoured by a détour to reach Loodianna, and effect a junction with the Brigade stationed there, before undertaking any engagement with the Sikhs. The latter, however, relying upon their superior numbers, provoked an attack by a brisk fire from their formidable artillery. A severe contest followed, and the British General after sustaining heavy losses, deemed it prudent to fall back upon Loodianna. This he effected by a very skilful evolution, and succeeded in holding the place.

Dr. M'Gregor, in his history of the Sikhs,[23] states that Runjoor Singh, younger brother of Lena Singh Mujetheea,[24] commanded the division of the Sikh army destined to act against Loodianna, as well as to seize the siege-train in progress to join our army, which were the two objects to be held in view by Sir Harry Smith. Dr. M'Gregor says: "Had he (Sir Harry) stopped to return the fire of the Sikhs at Buddiwal, all fear for Loodianna might have been removed; but then there was the risk, that if discomfited, Runjoor Singh might have crossed the country, and captured the siege train, which was escorted by only a Native Infantry regiment, and the 11th Light Cavalry, with a few Artillerymen. The condition of Sir Harry Smith was such, that he could not hope effectually to drive Runjoor Singh across the Sutlej that day, and he probably considered—like a good general, brought up in the school of Wellington, and disciplined in a corps like the immortal old 95th—that half measures were worse than useless. Besides, though making a great sacrifice of baggage, and even of lives, there was the hope that his forbearance would be construed into fear by the Sikhs, who might, in consequence, be induced to meet him in a fair field, where he would have an opportunity of accomplishing the two objects which he had in view; namely, the defence of Loodianna, and the safety of the train, closing all, perhaps, with the entire discomfiture of the Sikhs, when his troops should be a little refreshed." The whole of the Sikh force was not, it was believed, at Buddiwal, therefore the apprehension of Sir Harry Smith, doubtless, was that the other division might get to Loodianna. Buddiwal was at the time in the possession of Sirdar Ajeet Singh, a chief under our protection, who, after the operations at Moodkee and Ferozeshah, burnt a portion of the barracks of H.M. 50th Foot, at Loodianna, and then took possession of Buddiwal, where he made prisoner Assistant-Surgeon R.G.D. Banon, 62nd Foot (now Surgeon of the 96th Foot), and kept him in confinement for twenty-five days,—twelve of which in irons. The Sikhs in vain tried to induce him and the other Europeans who were in the fort, to join their army. They were released after the battle of Sobraon.

It is said, that though Sir Harry Smith was ordered not to fight before he had made a junction with Colonel Wheeler's detachment, yet that as the Sikhs had been moving to the south of Buddiwal, an action must inevitably have ensued, to prevent their advance towards our convoy. There were said to be three roads from Buddiwal to Loodianna. Buddiwal lies to the south-east of Aliwal and between it and Sirhind. Runjoor Singh's force was double that of Sir Harry Smith, besides which he had a large number of guns.

The fort at Loodianna contained all the sick of H.M. and the H.C. troops, which had marched from thence to join the army, as well as the ladies, women, and children belonging to those regiments. The only troops left there were the two Goorkha corps, the Nusseeree and Sirmoor Battalions,[25] but they were afterwards increased by the arrival of the 30th Native Infantry, the 1st Light Cavalry, and about 1,500 of the Pattiala Horse. The Pattiala Rajah was under our protection, and was one of those chiefs who early rendered assistance to our army, both in men, money, and supplies. He died very suddenly, soon after the battle of Ferozeshah, not without suspicion of having been poisoned, which is by no means an unusual method of securing the succession to a Rajahship. It is not impossible that he may have been killed by some of the true Sikhs, for his strenuous support of the British. A mystery hangs over this affair; and if we were to discard mystery from the records of Indian narratives, we should have little left to relate. The deceased Rajah's successor more than fulfilled the expectations of the Governor-General, and was, at the close of the campaign, confirmed in the possession of his estates, and invested by Lord Hardinge with the style and title of Maharajah, in consideration of his important services.

The alarm at Loodianna was natural, for a Sikh force having burnt down part of the cantonments, the appearance of a second, and more powerful force would be conclusive in the minds of most persons as to the fate of the station. It fama per urbes Subathoo et Simla. At Umballa the alarm was still greater. Dr. M'Gregor, in his History of the Sikhs, p. 136, writes: "We may smile at the fears which prompted this fugacious movement,[26] but had Sir Harry Smith not advanced to Loodianna, there is every reason to believe that the siege-train might have been lost, Loodianna pillaged and burnt, the hill stations destroyed, and Umballa, and even other places in the Provinces, sacked and occupied; so that the movement of the 1st division was one of the utmost importance, and not only prevented such sad disasters, but was followed by one of the best managed actions on record." That the train was in some danger is evident, from the fact that the Commander-in-Chief despatched for its security the 3rd Infantry Brigade, under the command of Brigadier Taylor, towards Dhurmkote, which lies to the west of Aliwal, and about half way between Loodianna and Ferozepore. On the 30th of January, this Brigade returned to camp.

Now, if we look at the map we shall see, that on the 28th, the day of the battle of Aliwal, the convoy would have been but a short distance south-west from Dhurmkote, perhaps twenty miles. And, again, if we suppose a line to be drawn from Dhurmkote, in a direction twenty miles to the south-east, which extreme point is called Bussean, we shall find that the Sikh troops at Buddiwal were very near to the convoy, on the night of the 27th of January. The escort for the convoy was extremely weak; for a corps of Native Infantry, and another of Native Cavalry, would not (after the late actions), have been above 1,200 men strong. This convoy was very inadequately protected, and such as our brave Commander-in-Chief would not have sent. Until joined by Taylor's brigade, from the neighbourhood of Kurnaul, it was in imminent danger. Had the Sikhs seized the convoy, the battle of Sobraon could not have taken place when it did; moreover, from delay, the season would have been sickly; and great loss must have ensued from this cause alone.

There are some circumstances which occurred at the battle of Aliwal, deserving of prominent notice. The enemy had a great many guns, which were playing with considerable effect upon the British troops. Major, now Lieutenant-Colonel G. S. Lawrenson, C.B., who commanded the Brigade of Horse Artillery, finding his men and horses falling, to save the delay of waiting for orders, instantly galloped up his brigade of guns to within a short distance of the Sikhs, wheeled round, unlimbered, and, by a brisk cannonade soon forced their gunners to quit their guns for a time. Had the cavalry charged at the same moment, I am assured they would have taken the guns. It was one of those exhibitions of decision and promptitude in war, which well merits, and did receive its reward. It was probably the suddenness of the movement which prevented the immediate support by troops.

The Sikhs made a singular disposition of their infantry in this battle for receiving the charges of the British cavalry. Instead of forming in squares they were arranged into triangles, the apex being in front and opposed to the British, the men also in the rear, or base line, knelt down, so that when the 16th Lancers broke through the front face they were received by fixed bayonets. The French system was followed in these dispositions; and a few French officers were alone wanting to animate the enemy with hopes of success, however futile such hopes must have proved. For, opposed to a force commanded by one of our ablest and most experienced generals, nothing but ruin and utter destruction could, under any circumstances have fallen to the lot of our rash, though brave foe.

The 16th Lancers suffered greatly, for the Sikhs fought with the most obstinate bravery. Preferring a voluntary death, even when all hope of resistance was at an end, they determined that their lives should be purchased at a high cost. Captain Bere of that gallant regiment was most successful in his efforts, having been seen to charge through the wedge of Sikhs, and back again more than once. And cordially do I congratulate a brother officer, Lieutenant T.J. Francis, on having had the good fortune to be present in this glorious action. He had but lately returned from England, and, at the commencement of the campaign, was on his way to the upper provinces with a detachment of recruits. Being anxious not to lose the opportunity of seeing service with Sir Harry Smith's division, Lieutenant Francis hastened up, and arriving opportunely for the battle, obtained permission to accompany the 16th Lancers to the field. After the action, Brigadier Cureton, who commanded the cavalry, thanked Lieutenant

Francis for his valuable services, which commendation I had the pleasure of reading from a copy of an extract from the brigade orders a day or two after.

The late Colonel Cureton of the 16th Lancers, who was unfortunately killed at Ramnuggur, had been known to say that Lancers should never be employed in charges with the enemy in less than a squadron, and from the results of this battle many cavalry officers have questioned whether the lance is the best weapon for cavalry in India. In the charges at Aliwal the Sikhs have been known to receive the point into their bodies and then to kill their adversary by cutting him down. The Sikh could not extract the lance, nor had the Lancer time to draw his sword.

There is no doubt that Lancers should never charge in small parties. Nothing less than a wing should attempt to break squares of infantry.

The charge in line, of a broken enemy is another thing. Marshal Marmont, in his "Esprit des Instructions Militaires," p. 45-50, says: "Cavalry should have one pistol; heavy cavalry, with lances and sabres and some few carbines, should be employed to fight infantry, the light cavalry to finish. The hussar or light cavalry soldier will, single-handed, beat the lancer. Cuirassiers should be armed with the lance and straight sword. The first rank should charge with the lance couched, and the second rank with the sabre in hand. As soon as the shock is effected, and the ranks are mingled, the sabres must do their duty. Lancers are equally successful against cavalry in line, especially if the enemy have only sabres. The cavalry in line should have lances chiefly, the sabre as an auxiliary."

Though Marmont was educated as an artillery officer, his great military experience entitles his opinion to be received with due respect, no matter to which branch of the profession he may refer. The Lancers were not employed in the Peninsular war, nor yet at Waterloo, consequently the 16th is the first Lancer regiment which has had the honour of testing the lance in open conflict, and against bodies of hostile infantry.

After the engagement at Buddiwal on the 22nd of January 1846, the Sikh troops under Runjoor Singh suddenly evacuated that place, and proceeded in the direction of Loodianna, keeping close to the river, where they secured a number of boats with the apparent intention of re-crossing to the right bank to join the main army. Whether this was a feint, or whether Runjoor Singh, having received intimation of the advance of reinforcements with whom his forces might not be equal to cope, desired to secure the means of a hasty retreat; or, whether he was following the example of Tej Singh, and acting a double part, remains uncertain. However this may be, Sir Harry Smith lost no time in taking possession of the place which had been evacuated by the Sikhs, who were soon after joined by a large reinforcement of their own body. The troops under Runjoor Singh, amounting to between 15,000 and 16,000 men, were immediately on the move, and preparing for fresh aggressions.

Sir Harry Smith saw that a collision was inevitable, and his own strength having been reinforced from head-quarters, he proceeded, on the morning of the 28th to reconnoitre the enemy's troops, and, if compelled, to give him battle. Sir Harry encountered them near the village of Aliwal, on their way to Jugraon, with the intention of occupying that town. The Sikhs, finding that Sir Harry was about to out-flank them, suddenly changed their position, and drew up along a ridge with their right flanking the village of Aliwal, and their left resting on their own entrenched camp. With the extraordinary agility and rapidity of action which characterized the Sikhs throughout their engagements with the army of the Sutlej, the centre division of the Khalsa troops instantly threw up entrenchments, behind which they hastily placed their strong artillery, and opened a murderous fire upon the British.

Sir Harry's force amounted to only 11,000 men, being a fourth less than that of the enemy, but like an able tactician, knowing that by the superior activity and disposition of his troops he could bring more men into action against the different salient points of attack, than the enemy who opposed him, he overcame the odds of numbers.

Notwithstanding the sharp fire of the Sikhs, he ordered a halt while he took a rapid survey of the nature of the country, and the position of the troops. His quick eye instantly recognised and decided on the mode of attack. He saw that by carrying the village of Aliwal, he should be able to throw himself upon the enemy's left and centre. This was effected with great promptitude and valour, by Brigadiers Godby and Hicks, who captured two guns. The general then made a skilful and effective charge upon the right wing, where the enemy was worsted; but the contest with the left was for some time doubtful, and the onslaught deadly. Three times did our British Lancers charge into the midst of the closely serried ranks of their brave opponents, whom they literally cut to pieces. To the very last their indomitable spirit did not forsake the Sikhs, they fell back in a body to a distance of a few paces, discharged a full volley into the faces of their conquerors, and then retreated towards the ford on the Sutlej. Although beaten, they were not dismayed; and although their leader, Runjoor Singh, was the first to fly and basely quit the field, leaving his brave followers to conquer or die, their courage never quailed. Again they rallied and made one last and vigorous effort. Though defeat had made them desperate, and they fought like men who jeoparded all, it was a defeat, and they were compelled to give way.

It was a magnificent and hard-fought battle: as ably conducted as it was skilfully planned.

FOOTNOTES:

[23] Vol. ii., p. 133.

[24] Lena Singh had left the Punjaub before the Sikhs crossed the Sutlej, and went to Benares, and subsequently to Calcutta. At one time he was placed under surveillance, after his brother's attack on Loodianna. Lena Singh, no doubt, hoped to prevent the confiscation of his estates on this side of the Sutlej.

[25] These corps were raised in May, 1815, soon after the late Sir David Ochterlony's victories at Malown. The Goorkhas are the bravest and most active native troops in India. They are also excellent shots at game.

[26] No smiling affair, we should think! Ladies, women and children, flying to Meerut, Saharunpore, and Mussooree.

CHAPTER VI

Richard Bond, the Messman—Sikh Grass-cutters—Choice
of Camps—General Lloyd's Opinions—Lieut.-Colonel
Irvine and Sir H. Maddock—Position at Sobraon—
Brigadier E. Smith's Plan—Colonel Irvine's Plan—Goolab
Singh's Policy—Sir Robert Dick's Division—Major-General
Gilbert's Division—Sir Harry Smith's Division—Brigadier
A. Campbell—Sir Joseph Thackwell—Brigadier Scott—
British Batteries—Rockets—Sikh Batteries—Assault on
the Sikh Entrenchments—Brigadier Stacey—Captain
Cunningham's Account—The 10th Foot—Lieut.-Colonel
Franks—Sikh Entrenchments stormed—Sirdar Sham Singh
destroys the Pontoon—Sikh Retreat cut off—Great Loss of
the Sikhs—Peace Principles inapplicable to India—Sikhs
driven across the Sutlej—Tej Singh.

On the 30th of January, 1846, about noon, we moved out and proceeded a distance of two miles, expecting to meet the Sikh cavalry, who were encamped by the bridge of boats, but after having waited for two or three hours we were doomed to be again disappointed.

On the 1st of February, our mess-waiter, Richard Bond, died, he had been for some weeks past in bad health, yet, being anxious not to be separated from his regiment, in which he had served for many years, the poor man accompanied us from Cawnpore, and though apparently of an Herculean frame, an insidious malady gained upon him; and on the 1st of February poor Bond was numbered among those who have been. Mors sola fatetur quantula sint hominum corpuscula. He was an old and meritorious servant: and as a member of the Mess Committee at this period, I feel happy in paying this passing tribute to his memory.

Whilst on an out-line picquet on the 2nd, I heard most distinctly the Sikh drums from the camp in our right front, about six o'clock in the afternoon. During the day also my patrols brought in five grass-cutters in the employ of the enemy. After having questioned them I released them with a warning not to appear near our camp again. This was by no means an uncommon ruse de guerre, while pretending to cut grass they were in fact spying out the land.

On the 7th of February, our regiment again changed ground, from the right to the extreme left. The whole army was encamped in a line nearly parallel to the river Sutlej, from which it was distant not more than a mile and a quarter, and in some parts even less. It is a rule in forming a camp, not to make it within reach of the fire of the enemy's guns; and at the same time to shew as extended a front as possible, both for the purpose of overawing the adversary, and of watching his movements. The same rule applies on having crossed a river, to avoid exposure to the fire of the enemy who occupies the bank which you have quitted.

In reference to the choice of camps, I may perhaps be excused if I again refer to the able and very scarce work on the Art of war by the well known author of the "Seven Years' War in Germany."

"The choice of camps," he says, "depends on two principles: the one geometrical and the other the effect of genius. The first consists in calculating the distance relative to the number and species of troops which compose the army; the other in seeing all the combinations that may be formed on a given piece of ground, with a given army, and in the choice of that precise combination which is most advantageous. This unacquirable and sublime talent is much superior to the other, and independent of it. Great geniuses have a sort of intuitive knowledge; they see at once the cause and its effect, with the different combinations which unite them—they do not proceed by common rules successively from one idea to another, by slow and languid steps. No, the whole with all its circumstances and various combinations is like a picture, all together present to their mind: these want no geometry, but an age produces few of this kind of men; and, in the common run of Generals, geometry and experience will help them to avoid gross errors.

"The perfection of our art would be, no doubt, to find a construction or an order of battle equally proper for all kinds of ground. But this being impossible, the only thing remaining for them to do is to find such a construction and such a formation of the troops as may, with the greatest simplicity, and, consequently velocity, be adapted to those numberless circumstances which occur. This should be the constant subject of their studies, but can never be obtained without geometry."

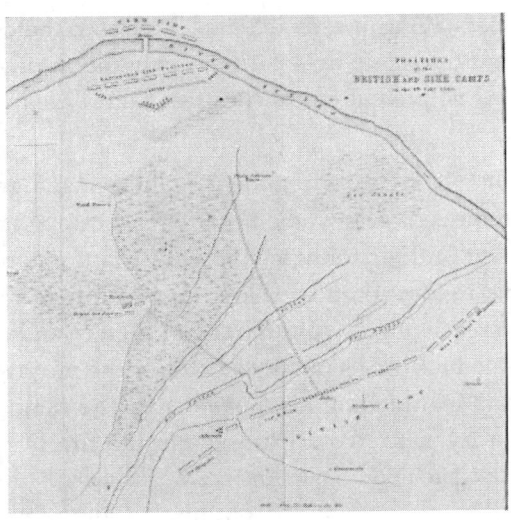

POSITIONS of the BRITISH and SIKH CAMPS on the 4th Feb. 1846

February the 8th. Sunday. Dined at half-past six, with my brother officers, at the mess of the 3rd Light Dragoons. They are encamped on our right, at the distance of about a quarter of a mile. As in the field, so at the mess-table, the Lieutenant-Colonel of this fine corps, Colonel White, C.B. (now aide-de-camp to the Queen), appeared to be beloved by his officers; indeed they have no small reason to be proud of one, so universally esteemed and respected by the cavalry division of the army of the Sutlej.

The battle was at hand: already were preparations making to meet those gallant men, the Sikhs, in mortal combat. On the evening of the 9th, Lieutenant-Colonel Irvine, of the engineers, came into the camp, having been sent to the frontier at the recommendation of Sir Herbert Maddock, Deputy-Governor of Bengal. Troops had been detached from the army to meet the large convoy coming from Delhi, with ammunition and stores; for the operations against the enemy at Moodkee, Ferozeshah, and Aliwal, had exhausted the greater part of our gun ammunition. Indeed, as I have already observed, that on the 22nd of December, 1845, when Tej Singh came before Ferozeshah, the British had no shot left. The force under Brigadier Campbell, however, brought up 4,300,000 rounds of musket ball cartridges, and twelve 12-pounders, with shot and other missiles, otherwise my gallant friend, Sir Harry Smith, would not have had the means of fighting the splendid battle of Aliwal.

And now we come to the 10th of February, the day on which the memorable battle of Sobraon, the crowning battle of the Sikh campaign of 1845-46 was fought, and which most persons expected would be the last.

The fate of the Punjaub seemed to hang by a thread; from the 22nd of December, 1845, to the 28th of January, 1846, no military operations had occurred till Sir Harry Smith gained the battle of Aliwal. The Sikhs' strongly entrenched position at Sobraon still remained to be taken; defended as it was by 30,000 regular troops, besides being equally strong by nature and art. By nature, as situated on the banks of the river, in the form of a half moon, having many and great impediments in its front; by art, the triple form of the entrenchments, bristled with a triple row of guns, which must be silenced before an entrance could be effected; a bridge of boats in its rear, by which the besieged might retire if they chose; and, moreover, batteries commanding the rear of the flanks of the entrenchment, which enabled them to fire upon any troops attempting to storm the works: added to which, the men could come over the pontoon bridge to assist in serving the guns in the works; and this they actually did.

Major-General, Sir Harry Smith, after the battle of the 28th of January, in which he had lost 589 killed and wounded, joined His Excellency, the Commander-in-Chief, on the 8th of February. It was judged expedient to wait for his arrival before the attack on Sobraon could be safely made. Part of the siege train, too, had arrived, to ensure the safety of which, it may be recollected, was the principal object in detaching Sir Harry Smith.

A plan had been proposed by the late Brigadier E. Smith, C.B., Chief Engineer, but when the nature of the proposed attack was explained to Lieutenant-Colonel Irvine, a senior officer, who had been sent by Sir T. Herbert Maddock, to join the army, which he had only reached on the 9th, the day before the battle, he is said to have taken a different view.

It is recorded, that in the year 1776, Sir W. Howe, in a despatch on the American entrenchments, wrote: "If I could have made approaches I could easily have taken the enemy's entrenchments."[27]

Whether Colonel Irvine proposed to make approaches I cannot say; certain it is, that it was agreed to follow the plan laid down by Brigadier Smith, Colonel Irvine being of opinion that it would be better to leave the conduct of the affair in the hands of the officer who had formed a digested plan. Had Brigadier Smith been superseded, a delay of two or three days at least must have ensued. Now, without knowing the exact cause for the delay, it is stated in the "Blue Book" that certain proposals had been made by the Lahore Durbar, or by some of the principal chiefs. Some say, that the celebrated Goolab Singh of Cashmere had made certain offers, to which an answer was required in three days. An officer of artillery remarked to the Commander-in-Chief, that the remainder of the supplies, stores, etc., from Delhi, would reach camp in two days. Lord Gough, in his Despatch of the 13th of February, says:—"Part of my siege train having come up with me, I resolved, on the morning of the 10th, to dispose our mortars and battering guns," etc.[28] This waiting of two days or more would have consumed more time than it was thought politically right to expend. We must remember that an answer was required in three days. Now, if Goolab Singh was the real proposer of these terms, it would seem that it could not answer to grant them. Perhaps he undertook to pay us the expenses of the war, to reduce the Sikh army, and to accept a British Resident at Lahore; these conditions, or something like them, must have been proposed.

Such offers could not have satisfied the government of India, because, when after the treaty of 1846, we took a slice of the Punjaub (Jullundur), and allowed the Sikh Durbar to keep up an army of 32,000 men, they raised more, either openly or covertly; hence, if they acted thus under our own eye, while holding the reins of government at Lahore, it is not unreasonable to conclude that they would follow up the plan *in extenso* in our absence, for a Resident would have been no adequate check.

Goolab Singh was evidently playing a game for himself: if he could be the means of saving the country, then Cashmere ought to be his reward; but, when affairs went in a contrary direction, he was forced to be no longer an actor on the scene. But, distrusting Goolab Singh, and supposing him to have been a traitor to his country, yet might he not be meditating the destruction of the English? He had his own troops with which he could turn the scale against us. Thus, whatever were the terms, or the nature of the terms, they were clearly less than we could accede to.

Colonel Irvine, as I have remarked, instead of acting as Chief Engineer, became an aide-de-camp, and partly a spectator.

The reader will doubtless imagine, and justly so, that we had more shot and shell on the road to join us; but time—that important element in our lives, which when once lost cannot be recalled—time, in military matters is everything. This was a well-known saying of Napoleon's, and the truth of it is evident to less able soldiers. The old plan, therefore, and not the new mode of attack, was the order of the day.

Owing to the peculiar form of the enemy's entrenchment, it was decided that the battering-train and disposable field-artillery should be put in position in an extended semi-circle, embracing within its fire the works of the Sikhs. On the morning of the 10th, a heavy mist prevented the intended cannonade from beginning at daybreak as was proposed. It must be borne in mind, that, strictly speaking, the attack on a strong entrenched position is usually made in the same way as upon a fort or outwork: for forts are, sometimes, surrounded by entrenchments, thus making the fort a kind of citadel, as it were, though it may not be so called technically.

This mist, though unfavourable for artillery is often favourable for troops, for enabling them to form under cover near such works and entrenchments.

Major-General Sir Robert Dick's division was placed on the margin of the river Sutlej, ready to commence the assault. The 7th Brigade belonging to this division, and led by Brigadier Stacey, was to head the attack, supported by the 6th Brigade of the same division, at a distance of two hundred yards. A reserve which was entrenched at the village of Rodawalla, was in readiness to move forward if required.

In the centre, Major-General Gilbert's division was deployed for support or attack, with its right resting on Little Sobraon. With regard to this division, it has been stated by an officer of an infantry corps, that it was not intended that it should attack in the first instance, but it so happened that Major-General Gilbert[29] with that decided conduct which marked all his actions, finding that the left attack on the enemy's right had not succeeded, determined at once to make his attack in front.

As I have before observed, there were impediments in the front, of which we were ignorant; they were in the nature of an embankment, and when our troops came up, this embankment, lying between them and the entrenchment, prevented the British from easily mounting it and entering the enclosure; the only means, therefore, by which they could effect this, was by moving to the right and left of this impediment. It will not be a matter of surprise therefore, that a little confusion occurred, and that our troops were in some slight degree jammed together. But we must defer the result to its proper place, and proceed with the order for the movements of the other troops.

Major-General Sir Harry Smith's Division was formed near the village of Guttah, with its right thrown up towards the Sutlej. It was determined to threaten by feigned attacks, the enemy's horse, under Rajah Lall Singh Misr, which was stationed on the other side of the river. There was a ford at Hurrekee Ghât at which were drawn up the 16th Lancers, who would thus have been enabled to cross over and attack the Sikh cavalry, if circumstances had called for aid. Besides, as there was a ford there, the enemy might have thought of crossing himself, for the purpose of attempting to turn our left flank.

Brigadier A. Campbell took up an intermediate position, between the divisions of Major-General Gilbert's right, and Major-General Sir Harry Smith's left. Campbell's brigade was to the rear of Sir Harry's division, the better to effect this object, for it is desirable, on occasions like these, not to place the cavalry within reach of cannon shot.

Major-General Sir Joseph Thackwell, K.C.B. commanding the cavalry division, had under him Brigadier Scott, C.B.,[30] who held a reserve in the first brigade on our left, ready to act as circumstances might render necessary. Brigadier Scott, as well as the Major-General, had commanded cavalry in the Affghan campaign, when Ghuznee was taken, in July 1839, and proceeded to Cabool; so that, should the presence of Sir Joseph Thackwell have been required in any other part of the field of action, he had as his second in command, an officer whom he well knew, and in whom he could place the most implicit confidence, for it must always be recollected that it is of great advantage to have an officer in the field, who has had experience in Indian warfare. It cannot be supposed that an officer just come from Europe can all at once, be prepared to command a brigade composed of Lancers, Dragoons, and native Cavalry. Surely a little experience is requisite. Besides in India, from the nature of the service, a Lieutenant-Colonel often commands a Brigade; while in Europe that command would generally devolve upon a Major-General.

Our battery of 9-pounders, twelve of which had been reamed up to 12-pounders, opened their fire near Little Sobraon, a village a short way in advance, between Major-General Gilbert's and Major-General Sir Harry Smith's divisions. Our artillery was thus placed,—five 24-pounder howitzers on our right, three 12-pounders (reamed) on the right of the 29th Foot, No. 19 battery on the left of Major-General Gilbert's right brigade; then between General Gilbert's left and the 62nd Foot there were six 8-inch howitzers, and six 5½-inch howitzers; on the left of the 62nd Foot there were eight 8-inch howitzers and five 18-pounders flanked by the 9th Foot and the 26th regiment of Native Infantry. On the extreme right there were forty-eight guns and howitzers, besides twelve guns, etc. on the right and left of Major-General Sir Robert Dick's division. In fact Major-General Sir Harry Smith's division was wheeled up to its left, so as to throw a flanking fire into the enemy's left. Also, Major-General Sir Robert Dick's division on the left, wheeled up to its right, so as to fire into the enemy's right.

Owing to the mist before mentioned, it was half-past-six A.M. before the whole of our artillery fire was brought into full play; the object of this fire was to silence the enemy's guns and to destroy their works before we assaulted the place. There was also a rocket battery. It must be remembered that the enemy had upwards of a hundred guns to fire against our sixty-two guns and the rocket battery. Rockets, the reader must be aware, were formerly much used in Indian warfare among the native armies. They were tried at Hattrass in 1817, with the force under the command of the late Major-General Sir W.S. Whish, K.C.B., but there was too much wind. On the present occasion the wind was not unfavourable. As the enemy's camp on the other side of the river was set on fire, the means by which that important service was effected may be disputed.

We must bear in mind that the Sikh guns were like those of a fortress, protected by walls, not *en barbette*, *i.e.* open all round. Besides this there was a triple line of trenches. The Sikhs also had two batteries on the other side of the river. When these batteries were silenced, the gunners came over by the bridge of boats, to the works on our side, to aid and to replace the gunners who had been killed or wounded. The bridge was said to be mined in case of accident, that is to say, if they were pursued in the retreat they could have blown it up to prevent our pursuing them.

It is clear that the mist had delayed the practice of the batteries, but still the artillery played upon the enemy's works for two hours. A more powerful battery would have been desirable; and it is said that this was Colonel Irvine's reason for proposing the delay. However, in all battles, there are two main points of consideration; first the military delays, and then the political delays, we know are sometimes dangerous. No doubt a casual observer would have exclaimed, "Why not wait for more guns? Recollect Ferozeshah; you tarried fifty days for this attack, during which time the enemy strengthened his position. You have more guns, more shot and shell coming up. Recollect also, you fell short of shot on the 22nd of December at Ferozeshah!" The late Captain J.D. Cunningham, of the Engineers, who was present at the battles of Aliwal and Sobraon, wrote thus: "The officers of artillery naturally desired that their guns, the representatives of a high art, should be used agreeably to the established rules of the engineers; or that ramparts should be breached in front and swept in flank, before they were stormed by defenceless battalions; but such deliberate tediousness of process did not satisfy the judgment or the impatience of the commanders, and it was arranged that the whole of the heavy ordnance should be planted in masses opposite particular points of the enemy's entrenchments, and, that when the Sikhs had been shaken by a continuous storm of shot and shells, the right, or weakest part of the position, should be assaulted in line, by the strongest of the three investing divisions, which, together mustered nearly 15,000 men," the enemy being 30,000 men.[31]

A military friend of mine, Major W. Hough, of the Bengal establishment, formerly a deputy Judge-Advocate, and author of some most valuable works on Military Law, and other subjects, has suggested that the attack in column is the more usual mode of assault, and has adduced many proofs that such a system has been at different periods acted upon, both in ancient and modern warfare.

Now let us look at the other side of the picture. Proposals had been made by the Sikh Sirdars, some say by Goolab Singh, which were refused. Had Goolab Singh's troops mutinied and refused to obey his orders, he would have said that he was helpless; it was possible that these same troops might be anxious to join Sham Singh in the entrenchments, a movement which it was the great object of the British chiefs to prevent.

As to the artillery, which is not surpassed by any artillery in the world, in celerity of movement, in precision of fire, or in any of the qualities which render this branch of the service illustrious, they could not perform impossibilities. They were deficient in that indispensable desideratum, shot. To have continued firing till all our shot was expended, and thus have exposed our want of it to the enemy, would have been very unwise; for, had the infantry failed in the attack, they might have retired, and our artillery resumed their fire. Hence it was that the British artillery ceased for a while to send forth its missiles of death.

After two, or two and a half hour's firing, and at about nine o'clock, Brigadier Stacey's Brigade, supported on either flank by two batteries of Foot and a troop of Horse Artillery, moved to the attack in good order, with Brigadier Stacey at their head. This gallant officer was armed with sword and buckler, the most effective weapons for such an attack, where you may come into personal contact with men who, after the custom of their country, are armed in this peculiar manner.

> Ἀμφὶ σὰρ 'ὤμοισιν βάλετο ξίφος ἀργυρόηον,
> — —αὐτὰρ ἔπειτα σάκος μέγα τε στιβαρόν τε.
> Homer. Iliad III. lines 334-5.

The troops marched in line. Captain Cunningham[32] says:—

"The left division of the British army, advanced in even order, and with a light step to the attack; but the original error of forming the regiments in line instead of in column, rendered the contest more unequal than such assaults need necessarily be. Every shot from the enemy's lines told upon the expanse of men, and the greater part of the division was driven back by the deadly fire of muskets and swivels and enfilading artillery.

"On the extreme left, the regiments effected an entrance amidst the advanced banks and trenches of petty out-works, where possession could be of little avail, but their comrades on the right were animated by the partial success; they chafed under the disgrace of a repulse, and forming themselves instinctively into wedges and masses, and headed by an old and fearless leader, they rushed forward in wrath." Major-General Sir Robert H. Dick, K.C.B. and K.C.H., was mortally wounded close to the trenches whilst cheering on his men; but we must reserve to a future page a further mention of this brilliant and noble officer.

The artillery took up positions to aid these divisions at a gallop. Brigadier Stacey's Brigade drove the Sikhs in confusion before them, within the area of their encampment. The 10th Foot, headed by their dauntless leader, Lieut.-Colonel T.H. Franks, entered; and here the work of carnage commenced, for now it was that hundreds of our indomitable foe fell under the withering fire of this gallant corps, Lieut.-Col. Franks having particularly cautioned his men not to fire until within the works of the enemy.

Let the reader pause and imagine the thunder of 120 guns on both sides reverberating for a length of time

"As if the clouds their echo did repeat,"

and he will have but a very faint conception of the mighty grandeur of those awe-inspiring sounds. Never shall I forget the majesty of the whole scene.

"No pen can write, no pencil trace the sound."

Seeing that Brigadier Stacey's Brigade might incur the whole weight of the attack, the centre and right divisions were ordered to advance. The centre division experienced great difficulty, for the mound in front was a very serious impediment. The Sikhs, sword in hand, strove to regain the points of the entrenchments which they had lost: it was not until the cavalry of the left wing under Major-General Sir Joseph Thackwell advanced and dashed into the entrenchments, in single file, through the openings effected by the pioneers in the mound, re-forming as they passed; and finally the full weight of three divisions of infantry with every available field-gun had been brought to bear against the resolute enemy, that victory crowned our efforts. The work was gloriously achieved. The insult offered to the British arms was avenged; and England stood triumphant.

For the important services which Brigadier Scott rendered in this action in leading his brigade into the enemy's entrenchment, he was honoured with the gratifying distinction of being appointed aide-de-camp to Her Majesty the Queen. At the taking of Ghuznee, July 23rd, 1839, Sir Joseph Thackwell and Brigadier Scott were employed in destroying the enemy who had escaped from the fort; they were, therefore, not novices at their work.

At Sobraon, our cavalry could not pursue the enemy as he retreated across the river; and, to have proceeded by Hurrekee Ghât, the nearest ford, would have been too late. The veteran Sirdar, Sham Singh, who commanded in the entrenchments, was engaged at his devotions when he first heard of the attack. As he must have known that our stores had not all arrived, for the Sikhs had accurate intelligence of our movements, he did not anticipate an attack from us so soon. Summoning his chiefs, Sham Singh reminded them of the great stake at issue, and bade them fight nobly and exterminate the infidel Feringhees (English). He assured his officers and men that the way of glory lay before them; and, to prevent their retreating, boldly commanded the two centre boats of the bridge to be cut away, so that his army could not pass over the pontoon. The order was obeyed; and, when forced to fly, the enemy in vain attempted the bridge, and were constrained to take to the river. Encumbered with arms, many attempted to swim across the river, which had risen seven or eight inches a day or two before; but all their efforts were unavailing. Hundreds and hundreds were drowned, or fell under the fire of our guns.

The press in England have condemned this general slaughter of our defenceless foe; but the answer, in extenuation, is, I believe, that the Sikhs had cruelly and relentlessly cut to pieces our wounded men at Ferozeshah.

If we regard the morality of the measure, we must not, at the same time, overlook the consequences which would have ensued from our sparing this resolute foe; for, at this time, we had yet to cross this river; and we were by no means certain but that we should have to fight another battle.

Messrs. Cobden and Co. must discover some golden rule for keeping the peace in India; for it would be a hard matter to find a single Sikh chief who is not ready to fight. The Rajpoot would laugh and say: "Sirs, it is my trade, as the calico line is yours; we were born soldiers." This universal Peace Association is, I have no doubt, a very amiable fraternity; yet let not its members, being deceived themselves, try to deceive others. The world still lieth in wickedness. Some divines understand the words of our Saviour, when he said, "I came not to send peace upon the earth, but the sword," to signify, there are very many religions in the world, and these will give rise to fighting. The Sikh would say: "You English have come and conquered the best and fairest portions of India, and now you are trying to annex the rest of the country; can you wonder that every man's hand is lifted up against you?"

Even Mr. Cobden must allow that to fight pro aris et focis, is not a very despicable employment. Until all nations and lands are prepared to join the league—until the time that all standing armies shall be dispensed with—

and until right and might can keep their place—away with such empty talk! We must fraternize at home before we can hope to do so abroad. The natives of India do not understand those fine-drawn distinctions of our European policy. They know that the strongest will attack them if they can, and that the only plan of defence is to maintain armies.

The continent of Europe may be likened to India in one respect. Comprising various sovereignties, as in India, there are many independent princes. The native chief, like Alexander the Great, sighs when no more conquests are to be made! India, besides, is not a commercial country, like Europe; and all its inhabitants cannot plough or work at a trade. India has been, for centuries, the arena of strife. From the year 1187, when Delhi was seized by a Mahomedan conqueror, to the present year, anarchy, rapine, and war, have been stalking over the land. Thrice three thousand times blessed will be that period when every man of every nation shall have "turned his sword into a ploughshare, and his spear into a pruning-hook!" Until then, in order to ensure peace, let us be armed for war.

In Europe a sovereign loses a portion of his dominions, when it is taken by a monarch more powerful than himself. The league of the Holy Alliance contracted by four kings, in 1815, has not been able to preserve peace. The principle of uti possidetis, or, "as you are," of 1815, is not recognised in 1854. The Russians and Austrians have attacked Hungary, and Hungary has fought for her independence. The Neopolitans have sent an expedition to Sicily, and the Sicilians have sighed for independence. The French are masters of Rome, and Rome has longed for a republic, and thus we might multiply examples. Independence, the natural right of all countries, cannot generally be obtained except by war.

But *revenons à nos moutons*, the Sikhs again succumb. The battle of Sobraon has been fought and lost by them: at noon on the 10th of February, not a living Sikh remained on the left bank of the Sutlej.

At about two o'clock P.M., I rode leisurely through the enemy's entrenchments, and witnessed the horrible slaughter that had taken place; even at that time, a few determined artillerymen occasionally sent a ball across the river, to the dismay of our plundering camp followers. A mine, too, would now and then explode, and hurl the heedless and inquisitive into eternity, for the entrenchment was completely undermined; and during the following night and morning, explosions were every now and then heard in the camp.

During the action, the 9th Lancers advanced at about eleven o'clock A.M., under a heavy fire, in two lines, for the purpose of charging the enemy, when I commanded the left troop of the second squadron; after a time, however, as no opportunity to charge was allowed, we again fell back. The 9th Lancers left their camp at four o'clock A.M., and returned to it between five and six o'clock P.M., not a little tired, as the reader may imagine.

Thus the day, which rose so bright upon the landscape, after the mists of the early morning had been dispelled by the brilliant rays of the sun, was darkened by a battle and slaughter and death, ere the shades of evening closed upon it. The indomitable Sikhs, whose bravery was but the more aroused by the defeat at Aliwal, and whose feelings had been harrowed by the sight of the corpses of their unavenged comrades slain in that battle, who were still borne along the stream, and who had entered upon the contest with the resolve to conquer or die, these brave fellows were now lying in hundreds, or rather in thousands upon thousands, on the field of carnage, or floating along the sweeping flood of the Sutlej, while others fled in wild confusion before their victorious foe. But where were now their leaders?— the men who had instigated the revolt, and who with dastardly duplicity sought their private interests by simulated friendship with both parties? Where was Tej Singh, the chief commander of the Sikh forces? When the British opened the assault, Tej Singh commanded the entrenchment, but as soon as we had effected breaches in the mound, and the fire from his batteries began to slacken, when his followers were falling thick around him, when the British, led on by their gallant commanders, fought resolutely for every inch of ground, Tej Singh, instead of manfully leading on fresh troops, and animating them by his example, like a base traitor, again deserted his post; he fled at the first brush, and, as at the battle of Ferozeshah, abandoned his troops, and, in their destruction, sought, and effected his own escape; Goolab Singh, who had played his cards so well, was at the side of the Maharannee, counselling the adoption of such measures as would virtually promote his own interests; while the intriguer, Lall Singh, lay with his cavalry higher up the river in a careless, unmilitary position, conscious of being closely watched by the English.

Far different was the conduct and deportment of Sirdar Sham Singh, of Attaree. In accordance with the vow so solemnly made to his men that he would die in the conflict, and thus offer up himself as a propitiatory sacrifice for his country's weal to appease the wrath of Govind, he clothed himself in a white garment, as one who had devoted himself to death, and calling upon all around to follow him, he unflinchingly led on his rapidly thinning ranks, with the assurance of the Gooroo's eternal reward to those who should fall in defence of their country; and, at last, covered with wounds, the fine old veteran sunk down a lifeless corpse, amidst the slaughtered bodies of his brave followers.

The Commander-in-Chief estimated the loss of the Sikhs in this decisive battle at from 12,000 to 15,000 men; while that on the side of the British was, 320 killed, and 2,063 wounded, making our total loss 2,383.[33]

FOOTNOTES:

[27] Field of Mars, 1801.

[28] War in India, Despatches of Lords Hardinge and Gough. Second Edition. London, 1846; p. 116.

[29] Afterwards, Major-General Sir Walter Raleigh Gilbert, Bart., G.C.B. (since deceased).

[30] Lieutenant-Colonel, 9th Lancers, and formerly Lieutenant-Colonel in the 4th Light Dragoons, from which, like the author, he was removed into his present corps, when the 4th was put on the English establishment, on its return from Bombay in 1842. Colonel and A.D.C. to the Queen.

[31] History of the Sikhs, p. 319.

[32] History of the Sikhs, p. 325.

[33] See Appendix XI.

CHAPTER VII

The Advanced-guard cross the Sutlej—Burial of Sir Robert Dick—Bridge of Boats—Kussoor—Surrender of the Sikhs—Dhuleep Singh—Lulleanee—Lahore—Runjeet Singh's Monument—The Summer Palace—The Governor-General's Address.

On the night of the victory of Sobraon, some of our advanced brigades crossed the Sutlej, opposite Ferozepore: they met with no resistance on landing, the whole place was abandoned, and not an enemy was visible. They hastened on to Kussoor, where they took possession of the fort.

Early on the morning of the 11th of February, we were once more on the move. The Commander-in-Chief appointed one division to remain behind and take charge of the sick and wounded, with orders to bring them on to Ferozepore; together with all the guns, etc., which we had taken from the enemy. These amounted to sixty-seven cannon, and 200 camel-swivels, or, as they are generally called, "zumbooruks;" together with immense quantities of ammunition and stores, and many of the Sikh standards.

The 9th Lancers accordingly started for Attaree, a distance of fourteen miles. On the 12th, we left our old encamping ground at Attaree at four o'clock A.M., and at eight o'clock A.M., we reached our new halting-place at Khoonda Ghât, about two miles distant from Ferozepore.

Soon after eight o'clock this morning, we heard the discharge of eleven guns, in the direction of Ferozepore, which we were informed were being fired over the grave of the late lamented Major-General Sir Robert Dick.

Not a month before the battle of Sobraon, I had called upon poor Sir Robert in his tent. He was then all life and animation, highly pleased with the Division to which he was about to be appointed, and which he asserted was the finest in the army. Not having had the opportunity of seeing a hostile shot fired in India, this noble soldier was in ecstasy at the thoughts of meeting the Sikhs in actual warfare. Conspicuous for his gallantry, when commanding the 42nd during the Peninsular War, Sir Robert was determined not to be out-shone; and placing himself at the head of his Division, the 3rd Infantry, he fell gloriously whilst mounting the enemy's entrenchments, in the very moment of victory. Never fell a General more regretted by his troops, nor one who in life was more beloved. The coolness of his temper in the battle-field, was only surpassed by the warmth of his hospitality in quarters; thus adding one more proof to the many on record, that the noblest and bravest heart is ever united with the gentlest and kindliest spirit.

To testify the estimation in which Sir Robert was held by his brother officers, a subscription was immediately set on foot among the officers throughout the army, and a large sum was collected for the purpose of erecting a monument to his memory, in the church of his native village of Tullymet, in Perthshire. The officers and men who have had the honour of serving under him, will not forget him; and the only consolation we could feel was, that he died, as I really believed he wished to die, fighting for his country, exegit monumentum ære perennius.[34]

Our bridge of boats having been completed, the Commander-in-Chief, with the whole of the army, crossed the Sutlej on the 13th. We passed over in single file; and after a tedious march of about eleven miles, arrived at Kussoor.

In the immediate vicinity of the Sutlej, the country is in a high state of cultivation, the valley being covered with a rich, soft verdure, but scarcely a tree is visible till within three miles from the banks; then the scene changes completely, and for miles and miles the eye rests upon nothing but immense tracts of jungle, interspersed with bushes, low tamarisks and tamarinds, with here and there the picturesque view of some ancient mosque or tomb. Close to Kussoor, lie the ruins of a large city scattered about in wild confusion; here mosques, domes, minarets and columns, tell of the departed glory of the Mahomedan era, when the arts and civilization were in their prime. The road runs through the town, which stands on a lofty eminence, and completely commands the place, and the ancient citadel of Kussoor. The town was formerly divided into twelve parts, each surrounded by a wall; and tradition says, that the founder gave one of these divisions to each of his twelve sons. Major Hough states that an army might make a good stand here, because there are not only heights, but each division of the town could be converted into a fortified position. But I am of opinion, that in the event of a hostile attack, it would not be capable of standing either a lengthened siege or a vigourous defence; it consists of a low wall, surrounded by narrow moats and projecting bulwarks. The town itself is surrounded by a very high wall, flanked with towers, and is densely built of brick. We encamped under the walls of the ancient town. The Governor-General joined the army early on the morning of the 14th. Kussoor is situated about sixteen miles from Ferozepore, and thirty-two from Lahore.

On the following morning, after some previous negotiation, the Maharannee of Lahore, who had appointed the Rajah Goolab Singh and some of the council to confer with the British army, sent her embassy to our head-quarters. They were intrusted by the queen mother with full powers, upon the condition that the treaty should embrace the continuance of the Sikh government at Lahore. The Governor-General surrounded by a brilliant staff of officers, received the Lahore embassy in his own tent. The deputation was then referred to Major Lawrence, now Sir Henry Lawrence, K.C.B., and since President of the Board of Administration for the affairs of the Punjaub, and Mr. Currie, now Sir Frederick Currie, Bart., and late Member of the Supreme Council of India, with whom they had a conference which lasted several hours. The Sikh chiefs being at first extremely reluctant to enter into the terms proposed by the English, their negotiations were prolonged far into the night. The following are the terms which were proposed by the English, and finally agreed to by the Sikhs.

The complete surrender of the whole of the territorial possessions of the Sikhs, lying between the Sutlej and the Beas: the payment of a million and a half sterling, as a partial indemnity for the expenses of the war; the disbandment of the Sikh army, and its reorganization on the footing established by Runjeet Singh; the surrender of all the guns used against the British, and the assumption of full powers by the Governor-General to settle the frontiers and to fix the internal government of Lahore. The youthful Maharajah, Dhuleep Singh, the son of the Maharannee, being still regarded as an Ally, was required to meet the British army on its entering Lahore, and tender his submission. It was further stipulated, that the Sikhs should not have the power of raising any armed force, without the consent of the British government.

On the 18th of February, the 9th Lancers reached the little mud-walled village of Lulleanee, a distance of ten miles, during which I was on baggage guard. It stands in the midst of corn fields and jungle. It is about thirty-four miles from Ferozepore, and about midway between that place and Lahore.

This evening, agreeably to the stipulation, the infant Maharajah, Dhuleep Singh, came into the camp of the Governor-General. His council sought forgiveness for the late act of aggression on the part of the army. The Maharajah did not receive any military honours from the Governor-General until he had made his submission; but after having done so, he was treated with the style becoming the rank of a prince, and remained in camp till the entry of the army into Lahore.

While we were at Lulleanee, we suffered much from scarcity of water. On the 19th, we reached the village of Kankuch, a distance of ten miles.

Both yesterday and to-day the 9th Lancers were on the advanced guard of the army. On the 20th of February, we marched to Lahore, a distance of ten miles, and encamped on the celebrated Meanmeer, three miles from the city—the ground where the Sikh troops used to be drilled. Through the kindness of Major Lawrence I obtained a pass out of camp, and an escort of two Sikh horsemen, for the purpose of visiting Lahore, the renowned Sikh capital.

The appearance of the city is very imposing at a distance, from its numerous mosques, with their azure domes and sparkling minarets rising majestically above the palaces, houses and gardens, the far distance being bounded by the bold out-line of the snow-capped Himalayas. To the south, lies the ancient city of Lahore, completely in ruins, interspersed with the remains of caravansaries, sepulchral monuments, towers and domes, overshadowed here and there by the lofty crowns of the graceful date-palm.

These splendid buildings carry the mind back to a bye-gone age, when wealth and grandeur reigned in Lahore, under the first Mahomedan conquerors of Hindoostan, before they succeeded in establishing themselves in the central Provinces of India. Lahore was the residence of Humayoon, the father of Akbar, who greatly enlarged and improved the city, which during his reign is said to have been three leagues in length; even to this day it is of considerable extent.

The modern city of Lahore lies close to the R[=a]vee, and contains about 80,000 inhabitants. It is surrounded by a massive brick wall, twenty-five feet in height, and fortified at regular distances with bastions and towers. Runjeet Singh greatly improved and strengthened the fortifications; and, like a good general, carried a moat completely round the outer side of the wall, and circumvallated this moat with a line of strong ramparts, fortified by out-works and heavy artillery, running in a circumference of seven or eight miles round the city. It gives the impression of a once impregnable place, and even now presents an appearance of considerable strength, though many of the bastions and works are going to decay.

The bright illusions which have previously filled the imagination of the stranger with visions of grandeur and magnificence, vanish like a dream the moment he enters the city gate. The principal street is very narrow, and extremely dirty, with a kennel running through the middle of it, into which is thrown the refuse from the neighbouring houses. Here, too, the streets are unpaved, and in such a wretched condition, that they are almost inpassable in wet weather. The houses are chiefly of brick, and though lofty, present a mean appearance. Like most of the Oriental houses, they have flat roofs, where the inhabitants pass the cool of the day. They are surrounded by dead walls, and present nothing of architectural interest; the only redeeming feature being an elegant arabesque carving, which runs along the wooden balconies and windows.

My first visit was to the citadel, which lies to the North-West of the town. It contains the barracks, extensive magazines, and military stores, together with the Hazuree Bagh, the noble winter palace of the late Maharajah, which was commenced by Akbar, and completed by others of the Mogul emperors. At an angle of the Maharannee's apartments, close to the gate, is the magnificent tomb of Runjeet Singh, together with those of the other members of his family. I visited this fine marble mausoleum, which is built in the Arabesque style, and was erected by Shore Singh, on the spot where Runjeet Singh, his son, and his grandson, together with their wives and female slaves, were consumed on the funeral pyre. This monument is just outside the lofty gates of the Hazuree Bagh. It was while passing through the ruins of these gates that Nou Nehal Singh was crushed to death, by the sudden dislodgment of a ponderous stone, as he was proceeding to the R[=a]vee to wash away his sins, immediately after the burning of his father's corpse.

The Hazuree Bagh was, in ancient times, the residence of the Mogul emperors. It is an immense pile, built of red granite, and consists of three large quadrangles, surrounded by arched corridors, magazines, and stores. From each of the four angles rises a lofty minaret, 150 feet in height; while the Western-side of the principal quadrangle is occupied by the Mosque, of red sand-stone, built by the emperor, Aurungzebe. This quadrangle, which is 500 paces in length, leads to the garden court or Hazuree Bagh, which is likewise surrounded by vaulted corridors, now in ruins. A pavilion of white marble stands in the centre.

The fort, or citadel, is in the third quadrangle. It is surrounded by numerous buildings, among which is the palace of the late Maharajah. The appearance is striking and unique, as it has a winding staircase rising above the highest platform.

The bazaars, which in all Eastern cities are the most animated parts of the town, presented nothing of interest; and instead of the varied display of costly oriental manufactures, in gold and embroidery, there was little else but sweetmeats and eatables.

There are some fine buildings in the immediate vicinity of Lahore. The principal is the tomb of the emperor, Jehangeer. It is of white marble, and red sand-stone, and rises in the centre of a beautiful garden. The Arabesques, above the arches of the piazza, which surround the tomb, are executed with great skill, and are in a state of perfect preservation, while the rest is going to decay. The tomb occupies a square building, 66 paces each way, the piazza being 1,800 feet square. I must not forget to mention the summer palace, or Shalemar. It was the residence of the emperor, Shah Jehan in 1627, and bears the inscription, "House of joy." It is constructed of white marble, in the same style as the Shalemar, at Cashmere, and stands in the middle of a lovely garden, tastefully laid out, with flowers, fountains, shrubberies, magnificent trees, and orange groves.

On my visit to the house of the Maharannee's German physician, I was introduced to Colonel Van Cortland, late of the Sikh service. In my rambles, I went over the house of General Ventura, since the residence of the Chief Commissioner, Sir Henry Lawrence. It is a spacious building, and presents a more European character than any in the city. In the gun-sheds, I saw only seven guns. The Infantry barracks were tenantless. The few soldiers, too, whom I saw in the place, had a mortified and disconsolate look.

Great alarm naturally prevailed in Lahore, in consequence of the defeat of the Sikh army, the arrival of our victorious troops, and the occupation of the citadel by an English garrison. The Governor-General, anxious to allay the ferment, issued a proclamation, which had the desired effect.[35]

On the 9th of March, the Governor-General signed the important treaty between the British and Lahore governments.[36]

I was on duty at the Governor-General's tent, with a troop of my regiment as a guard of honour, for the reception of the young Maharajah of Lahore, who had arrived from the capital attended by his principal Sirdars, and a numerous retinue, for the purpose of signing the treaty between the Government of the Company and that of the Lahore Durbar. Three royal salutes were fired from our 12-pounders, namely, one salute on the arrival of the prince, another at the signing of the treaty, and the third on his Highness' departure.

After the treaty was ratified and signed, the Governor-General made the following speech:—

"For forty years it was the policy of Runjeet Singh to cultivate friendly relations between the two Governments; and during the whole of that period, the Sikh nation was independent and happy. Let the policy of that able man towards the British Government, be the model for your future imitation. The British Government in no respect provoked the late war. It had no objects of aggrandizement to obtain by hostilities. The proof of its sincerity is to be found in its moderation in the hour of victory. A just quarrel, followed by a successful war, has not changed the policy of the British Government. The British Government does not desire to interfere in your internal affairs. I am ready and anxious to withdraw every British soldier from Lahore. At the earnest solicitation of the Sikh government, I have reluctantly consented to leave a British force in garrison at Lahore, until time shall have been afforded for the reorganization of the Sikh army, by whose assistance the stipulations of the treaty may be more easily carried into effect. In no case can I consent that the British troops shall remain in garrison for a longer period than the end of this year. I state this publicly, that all the world may know the truth, and the motives by which I am actuated in this matter."

At the conclusion of this address, the young Maharajah, who had thus been virtually recognised as the Sovereign of Lahore, under the protection of the English, was re-conducted to his palace by British regiments, under a royal salute.

FOOTNOTES:

[34] See Appendix XII.

[35] See Appendix XIII.

[36] See Appendix XIV.

CHAPTER VIII

Review of the Army—Eastern Mode of Adoption—
Cashmere assigned to Goolab Singh—Defeat of Affghan
Cavalry—Major John Cameron Campbell—Security
of the North-west Frontier—Fertility of the Punjaub—
Infantry introduced into the East—Hyder Ali's Notion of
English Power—Runjeet's Craftiness—Improvement in
the Punjaub—Dhuleep Singh professes Christianity—Dr.
Login—Dhuleep baptized by the Rev. W.J. Jay—Dhuleep
Singh's Sincerity.

On the 10th of March, the whole army was reviewed by the Governor-General, the Commander-in-Chief, the Governor of Scinde (the late Lieutenant-General Sir Charles J. Napier, G.C.B.), the Maharajah Dhuleep Singh, Goolab Singh, and many of the Sikh Sirdars. The troops formed line in masses of brigades; the second Brigade of Cavalry, being on the extreme left in open column of squadrons, at quarter distance: there were about 22,000 men on the ground. The conqueror of Scinde, having left behind his 16,500 men and fifty guns, had joined the head-quarters of the army, and was present at this review. The Sikh chiefs also were present, more humble than in former days. They, poor men, with few exceptions, were only the forced actors in the late drama. The Punts and Punchees[37] having decided upon fighting, the chiefs and Sirdars were constrained to gird up their loins for action.

The Governor-General, Sir Henry (now Viscount Hardinge, G.C.B.), was well aware that there were 20,000 Khalsa troops under arms in another part of the Punjaub. Conversing with a field officer, and looking at our European troops, the Governor-General remarked, "See those men, there are only 3,200 fit for duty;" which observation was at the time interpreted somewhat thus: "Out of 7,000 or 8,000 Europeans at first employed in this army, see the reduced remnant; had I not made the treaty, I could not at this season have continued the war."

The young and handsome Maharajah gazed upon the magnificent spectacle before him, with a kind of childish indifference, little concerned about the slice carved out by our swords from the dominions of his putative father; he is ignorant of his paternity, neither does he know whether he can legally call the Maharannee his mother. The Eastern mode of adoption is a very easy mode of providing a successor, for if a Rannee has no sons, others have, who may supply the place. Child-stealing, moreover, is very common in the Punjaub. Report assigns Jummoo as the place of his Highness' birth. The Rajah had a brother. I must leave the unravelling of the mystery, however, to those of my readers who feel an interest in tracing genealogies, with as much likelihood of success, at least, as the Sikh chiefs who tried the puzzle.

On the 10th of March I was on escort duty with my regiment, from half-past two to six in the afternoon, accompanying the Governor-General to and from a visit to the Maharajah, in the palace at Lahore.

On the 12th of March, the army of the Sutlej was broken up, and our kind-hearted Commander-in-chief bade it farewell.

Let us consider our position at the present time, with respect to our late enemy. A treaty has been concluded: we garrison Lahore with our troops, and form a government of Sikh chiefs, superintended by a British officer, namely, Sir Henry Lawrence. We declare that we must withdraw our force from Lahore by the end of the year. The Sikh chiefs entreat us to remain, which we at last agree to, and enter into another treaty to govern until Dhuleep Singh shall be of age, which will be in September, 1854.[38] This period was fixed, because as the Company's charter expires on the 30th of April, 1854, an act of indemnity would otherwise have been required from Parliament.

We first of all take possession of the Jullundur Doab; assign to Goolab Singh the rich and fertile valley of Cashmere,[39] whose productions are those of the temperate zone. The Sikhs are to disband their present army and organize a new one, which is not to exceed 32,000 men, 20,000 of which shall be infantry; and furthermore, we compel them to pay to the British government 22 lakhs of rupees, or £220,000 sterling per annum. Next, a deep conspiracy is discovered at Lahore, and two British officers are murdered at Mooltan. The Sikhs, under Moolraj, Chutter Singh and Shere Singh, raise large armies. The Maharannee is at the bottom of this conspiracy. We send troops in December, 1848, and take Mooltan in February, 1849. We fight at Ramnuggur, and fall into a trap. At Chillianwallah, we take the bull by the horns, but at Goojerat, on the 21st of February, 1849, with eighty-four guns against the enemy's fifty-nine, we gain a victory complete in every point, the Sikhs being battered by our overwhelming force of artillery for three hours. The Affghan Horse, under the command of a son of Dost Mahomed Khan, of Cabool, are routed after a noble charge, by a squadron of the 9th Lancers, and a party of the Scinde Irregular Horse, under the command of Captain J.C. Campbell,[40] of the Lancers, in which he was ably supported by Lieutenant F.J. M'Farlane, of the same corps, a stalwarth and powerful officer; and the whole army of the enemy having been put to flight and pursued for many miles, we finally annex the Punjaub to the British dominions.[41]

Now how would the leader of the British Anti-War Association have acted? The Sikhs cross the Sutlej and attack us. Would that gentleman have reasoned with them, or would he have attacked them? Whatever he may make of Europe, we cannot at present rule India otherwise than by the sword. India has to look to a possible invasion from the North, but none from the South. It is true, Admiral Suffrien did, in 1783, tell the King of France that the French might invade India from the Burmese territory; and he was right. But in 1826, we secured ourselves against such an event by Treaties. The Queen of England is ruler of the Mauritius, and the Cape is subject to her sway. On our North-West lie Scinde and the Punjaub, which two countries protect us against invasion from Candahar direct; and from an attack by the circuitous route of Cabool, we can always secure the Bolan and Khyber Passes; and those of Dhera Ghazee Khan and Dhera Ismael Khan are in our hands whenever we choose, for Mooltan would cover the operation.

Thus has the last Sikh campaign rendered our North-West frontier as safe as we could desire. Time will make the conquest valuable, and it must be our aim to conciliate a new people. Francklin (p. 66) says: "The Punjaub yields to no part of India in fertility of soil; it produces in the greatest abundance, sugar-cane, wheat, barley, rice, pulse of all sorts, tobacco, and various fruits, and it is also well supplied with cattle. The principal manufactures of this country are swords, matchlocks, cotton-cloths, and silks, both fine and coarse."

This description was written in 1802: it is useful to compare the past with the present. The Punjaub still (1854) supplies all the necessaries of life, and the district between the Indus and the Jelum contains salt-mines. In regard to commerce, as well as to manufactures, such as those of cotton-cloths, various stuffs, curious carpets, etc., the Sikhs are behind the other nations of India; yet, considering they are a military people, they shew less contempt for the occupations and amusements of civil life, and the peaceful cultivation of the soil, than might have been expected.

There can be no doubt that this country will become very flourishing under British rule. European art and science will be applied to the improvement of trade and agriculture, and above all, afford that greatest of incentives to industry, the certainty that, "what a man soweth, that shall he also reap." The Sikhs were more anxious to acquire other lands than to improve those which they already held; besides, in the constant scenes of anarchy and warfare, which have desolated this fine country, no man could ever feel certain that he should gather all his produce. Francklin, speaking of the Sikh army, in 1802, says (p. 67): "It has been remarked, that the Sikhs are able to collect from 50 to 60,000 horse; but to render this number effective, those who do not take the field, or who remain at home to guard their possessions, must be included."

The following is Francklin's statement, which comprehended the districts from the Attock to Sirhind:

	Cavalry.
The districts South of the Sutlej	15,000
The Doab, or country between the Sutlej and the Beyah (Beas)	8,000
Between the Beyah and Rowee (Ravee)	11,000
Force of Buyheel Singh, Chief of Pattiala	12,000
The countries above Lahore, the inhabitants of which are chiefly under the influence of Runjeet Singh	11,000
The Force of Nizam-ud-deen Khan	5,000
Ditto of Roy Elias	1,300
Ditto of other Pathan Chiefs in pay of the Sikhs	800
	— — —
Grand total	64,100

The Chief of most consequence was Runjeet Singh. If we suppose that two-thirds of this force might take the field, there would be 42,730 horsemen.

The above writer also says, that the repeated invasion of the Punjaub by small armies, of late years, affords a convincing proof, "that the national force of the Sikhs cannot be so formidable as has been represented." "It was successfully invaded by the Maharatta armies of Ambajee, Bala Row and Nana Furkiah, who drove the Sikhs repeatedly before them." No mention is made of the Sikh artillery.

It is to be remarked of the Sikhs, as of other native states (indeed, it is an old remark, and has been made by some of the best informed natives themselves), that Hyder Ali Khan, and Tippoo Sultan, of Mysore, Sindiah, Holcar, in fact, all the native Chiefs of India, were victorious over their native enemies by means of large masses of horse. Infantry of some description they had; but the regular battalions, drilled by Europeans, were only introduced as a system about 60 years ago, by French, German, and Italian officers.

The principal use of Infantry was to defend their forts. Seeing the advantage of regular and well-disciplined Infantry, under the British and French, the leading princes and chiefs adopted the same plan, and at length resolved to have Brigades of Infantry; as, for example, Sindiah's Brigades, under Duboignie, and the Nizam's, etc., etc.

Before this period and until the chiefs had regular corps, the British marched over the country for hundreds of miles, the enemy flying before them. But, in 1803, Sindiah brought many disciplined brigades of infantry into the field, perhaps 8,000, 10,000, or even 12,000 infantry, and seventy, eighty, or one hundred guns, besides horse. Our losses were sustained in taking the guns. Thorn, in his "History of the Maharatta War, 1803," says; "the Maharatta armies in three of their greatest battles were as follow:—

	Infantry.	Cavalry.	Guns.
At Delhi	8,000	6,000	68
Assaye	10,500	30,000	100
Leswarree	7,000	4,500	72

It will be seen that except at Assaye, they had more infantry than cavalry. While the enemy mustered the above numbers, and always had about one fourth of their guns of large calibre, the British only brought seventeen, twenty-five, and thirty small guns into the field. Runjeet Singh's views were different from those of the native princes. Captain Meadows Taylor, in his "Life of Hyder Ali," says; "In December, 1782, just before his death, Hyder Ali Khan of Mysore, called for his confidential adviser and said, 'What signifies the loss of Colonel Baillie's detachment of 3,000 or 4,000 troops? The English can get more by sea; unless I can build a navy to compete with the Feringhees, and stop them from landing, I cannot destroy them. They come as fast as you cut them down.'"

The Maharatta Chiefs thought differently. The power of the English, whose ascendancy in India dates from about the year 1803, had supplanted that of France. The French having rejected the application for European troops, made by Tippoo Sultan in 1799, a brief pause followed upon Napoleon's expedition to Egypt, but on the renewal of the war with England in 1803, Napoleon, in his projected invasion of India, engaged the assistance of the powerful Maharatta chiefs, who entered warmly into the war, and Sindiah's troops were placed under the direction of French officers sent out for the purpose.

M. Perron, in 1803, had 43,000 Infantry and a powerful Artillery, with which he held Allygurh, Agra, and Delhi. He designed, moreover, by degrees, to supersede Sindiah's authority, but Lord Lake's and Sir Arthur Wellesley's battles defeated the scheme. The Maharattas, or rather their troops under French officers, governed Delhi at this time, the Emperor Shah Allum being a captive prince and blind. Runjeet Singh, although a young man, knew all these facts, he therefore, caused his troops to be disciplined by European officers, for the purpose of fighting his battles against the Affghans, and other native enemies; but he never desired to lead them against the English, nor did he much like to entrust his European officers with commands in his wars. General Avitabile had charge of Peshawur, as civil, not as military, governor.

In 1825, when the British attacked Bhurtpore, the Rajah wished Runjeet to aid him, but the crafty fox refused. Some time after, asking Captain Wade (now Lieutenant-Colonel Sir Claudius M. Wade, C.B.) "what the English would have done had he joined the Rajah:" Captain Wade replied, "We should have attacked you first, and then have gone to undertake the siege." "Indeed!" said Runjeet, "I thought so. I shall not quarrel with the English; they are my friends."

Thus the Punjaub, which had been for centuries the tempting lure of a succession of invading hordes, and a prey to anarchy, rapine, and oppression, has passed, like its far-famed "Mountain of Light," into the possession of Queen Victoria; and from the marvellous success which has already crowned the efforts of the British Government to improve this new domain, I have no doubt that it will soon shed as much lustre on the British name, as this brilliant jewel over the royal brow.

When the Punjaub, paralysed and withered under the military authority of Runjeet Singh, first became ours, it never entered into the imagination of the most sanguine, to conceive the change which a few short years of wise and enlightened rule would produce in the outward face of the country. Whole tracts of forest and jungle have been cleared and brought under cultivation; canals, hundreds of miles in extent, and at an outlay of millions of rupees, are in course of excavation; commerce and agriculture are encouraged, and every possible facility is afforded to the native mind to develop the resources which nature has placed within the reach of its inhabitants.

We cannot but feel that it is only a Christian power, which could have exercised this happy influence; for Christianity has been in all ages, and under all circumstances, the pioneer of enlightenment and civilization. Circumstanced as the British government were, they could not well make any direct efforts to establish Christianity among the Sikhs, and indeed their usual caution and feeling rather lean to the reverse. And yet without any such efforts or encouragement on their part, and no one can tell exactly how, the first fruit of the Gospel among the native sovereigns of India, is the young Maharajah, Dhuleep Singh, the son and successor of the mighty Runjeet Singh.

As this event, so important and significant under any circumstances, but doubly so under the present shaking and waning attachment of the Sikh population to their own religious rites, is deeply interesting to the British public, I will here give an extract from a speech delivered by Archdeacon Pratt, in Calcutta:

"The baptism of Dhuleep Singh is an encouraging event, and although perhaps the less said about it the better, for the young convert's own mind, yet as so many false accounts have gone abroad regarding him, it is well briefly to state the circumstances which led him to seek baptism. His desire to become a Christian has generally been attributed to the influence of Dr. Login, who has charge of the young prince. But this is altogether a mistake. Dr. Login has acted the part of a wise and consistent Christian, in the delicate and responsible charge committed to him, but no overtures were made by him to induce the youth to become a Christian. It is believed that an early disgust of his own countrymen, was created in his mind by the horrible assassinations which he witnessed as a child at the Court of Lahore; and the personal kindness which he afterwards met with from Lord Dalhousie and the officials, up to the time of his quitting the Punjaub, gave him a favourable impression of the English.

"But the first impulse in his mind in favour of Christianity, was occasioned by his Brahmin attendant reading the Scriptures to him, during Dr. Login's absence in Calcutta.

"The Brahmin had learnt English in a missionary school, and like many of his countrymen, was himself convinced of the truth of the Word of God, but had not courage to stem the torrent of opposition, which an open avowal of his convictions would have created. His reading, however, awakened the young prince's mind to the value of the Bible; and Dhuleep Singh wrote to Dr. Login that he must have a copy of the Scriptures; and also, that he intended forthwith to break his caste. From this last step he was wisely dissuaded, till he should be better informed.

"The whole matter was made known to the Governor-General and to the Court. It was determined, that if he finally desired to become a Christian, no impediment should be placed in his way, when he was perfectly prepared for the rite. The chaplain of the Station was directed to give him the necessary instruction, should the prince desire it; and his mind has been growing and maturing under the wise superintendence of Dr. Login, and the instructions of his English tutor and the chaplain; but no more progress in advance has been made without his own desire. His attending divine service, both in private and afterwards in public, in the Mussouree church, was of his own seeking and urging.

"I have seen a good deal of the youth, and feel persuaded that he has been led by a higher hand than human, and that the work is of God. He is only a youth; but his character in every respect is a most interesting one; more especially when we remember who he is, and the darkness out of which he has come. If God keep him steadfast, and to this we should direct our prayers, his conversion may have an important influence on missionary prospects."

After a careful examination into his knowledge of those truths which he professed to believe, the Maharajah was formally admitted into the Christian church by baptism, on the 8th of March, 1853, by the Rev. W.J. Jay, Chaplain of Futtyghur. At this interesting ceremony, which took place in the Maharajah's own house at the station, were present all the civil and military authorities, and the American missionaries, as well as a number of his own attendants, on whom the solemnity of the occasion appeared to make a deep impression.

The "Friend of India," in its notice of this event, remarks:—

"It will, of course, be observed, particularly in England, that it would have been more advisable to postpone this irrevocable renunciation of Hindooism, until matured age should have given the young Maharajah the knowledge and experience necessary to enable him to make a permanent decision; but according to Major Smyth's 'Reigning Family of Lahore,' Dhuleep Singh was born in 1837, and he is therefore already sixteen. A lad of this age in India is a man, with as great a capacity for estimating the merits of different creeds, as he is ever likely to possess. From the time that he was placed under the charge of Dr. Login, his education has been most carefully provided for; and the boy who, when rescued from Lahore, could not even read, is now almost English in language, ideas, and feelings. His conduct, with reference to the ceremonial salutes, and his visit to the Governor-General, are sufficient proofs that his judgment is not beneath his acquirements, and that he has been fairly rescued from those influences which warp the minds of the Porphyrogeniti of the East. Sixteen is the age at which the Law Courts acknowledge the right of a native youth to judge for himself; and this last act of the Maharajah has been performed entirely of his own free will. He has been neither coaxed nor frightened into Christianity. Indeed, the Government had every motive for retaining him in his old creed. An Asiatic Christian prince, with £40,000 a year, might excite an interest in England, which it has hitherto been the policy of the home authorities to avoid, but they doubtless felt that it was not for them to interpose obstacles in his way. He was simply left to his own discretion; and that he has chosen rightly will, we think, be allowed even by those who are not given to 'Missionary fanaticism.' His conversion, will, at least, save the palace of Futtyghur from becoming like that of Delhi, a place where all evil naturally seeks shelter; and a native Christian noble, with his vast wealth, may accomplish far more good than a hundred ordinary converts.

"With the exception of 'Prester John,' in whom, despite Marco Polo, our faith is exceedingly limited, and a Roman Catholic Ziogoon of Japan, Dhuleep Singh is the first of his rank in Asia who has become a Christian. His example may, perhaps, give confidence to many who remain in Hindooism, rather from a vague dread of the consequences of abandoning it, than from any belief in its tenets; and we may see Christianity reverse its ordinary course, and descend from the highest to the lowest ranks. We have little hope of such a result; but it requires no religious belief to prove that it would be of the highest advantage to themselves and the people. The mere fact that there then would exist oaths by which they could be bound, and principles which they would scruple to violate, would bind their subjects to them, with a chain stronger than any which the ablest of their number have yet been able to forge."

The editor of the "Oriental Christian Spectator," observes: "From the persuasion which we have of the Christian judgment and prudence of Dr. Login, whose instructions have been blessed to this great result, we have every confidence that this conversion is of the most satisfactory character.

"The Sikh Prince, in the path he has pursued, appears before us, as no inappropriate specimen of his nation, and of what may be expected from them, if only at the present juncture suitable opportunities be presented. Their national discomfiture has been the overthrow of that fanaticism, under the standard of which they hoped to find themselves invariably the conquerors, and progressing rapidly to universal dominion. It has disappointed them; its prestige is gone; it has lost all hold upon them. If we neglect to meet adequately the present crisis, they will become rapidly absorbed in Hindooism, or Mahomedanism, and infusing a new and energetic element into those decayed systems, may re-invigorate them, and prolong their existence for a season. But if we go forward on a liberal and comprehensive scale of action, to the improvement of the remarkable opportunities now presented to us, there is hope that, as a nation, they may follow the example of the young ex-Maharajah, whose profession of

Christianity, at the present moment, is calculated to exercise upon them a very important influence."

FOOTNOTES:

[37] See Appendix XV.

[38] See Appendix XVI.

[39] See Appendix XVII.

[40] For this gallant charge, Captain Campbell obtained the brevet rank of Major, since which time he has, however, retired from the army, by the sale of his commission, after a long period of service.

[41] See Appendix XVIII.

CHAPTER IX

The Army of the Sutlej broken up—Set out on a Tour—
Dhool—Ferozepore—Grandeur of the Himalayas—
Misri-Wala—Ferozeshah—Moodkee—Bhaga
Poorana—Bussean—Phurewallee—Kotla Mullair—
Munsorepore—Samana—Goelah—The River Cuggur—
Pehoah—Khol—Kurnaul—Military Stations—Transport
of Artillery—Ali Merdan's Canal—English Church—
Malaria—Sir David Ochterlony—Gurounda—Minarets—
Somalka—Paniput—Battles of Paniput—Baber—Ibrahim
Lodi—Ahmed Shah—Defeat of the Maharattas—Nadir
Shah—Capture of Delhi—Mahomed Shah—Troops
engaged—Native Armies—Sunput—Change in the
Weather.

The army of the Sutlej being broken up, the different corps took their departure for the various stations assigned to them, my own regiment, the 9th Lancers, being ordered to Meerut. I set out on the 14th of March, 1846, and commenced a march of 704 miles, intending to ride quietly to Allahabad, and thence proceed by steam to Calcutta. I had obtained leave of absence to England for a period of two years, from the day of embarkation, and four months to Calcutta, from the date of leaving my regiment.

On the 14th, therefore, as I said, I bade "adieu" to my regiment, and commenced my journey attended by my own servants fourteen in number, two camels, and two three-bullock hackeries, my Khidmutgar having engaged to supply me with my meals. On the first day I rode to Kankuch, a distance of ten miles. On the 15th there was a violent storm of wind, rain, thunder and lightning, from four to six o'clock in the morning, which made it unadvisable for me to proceed, as my only tent, a hill-tent, was completely saturated.

On the 16th, I rode to Dhool, about sixteen miles; through Lulleanee, and left Kussoor on my right hand. The next day I made a longer journey, and rode twenty miles to Ferozepore. On my way thither, I met a train of 500 hackeries and 4,000 camels, laden with provisions for the force which was to garrison Lahore. Ferozepore was distant about ten miles from the bridge of boats, by which I crossed the Sutlej. There were formerly two of these pontoons, each nearly 300 yards long, the boats themselves being of the ordinary flat-bottomed sort, with very broad ends, called "dandy boats," which are used in the navigation both of the Indus and Ganges, as well as of the Sutlej. The two bridges consisted respectively of fifty-nine and forty-seven such boats, but Sir J. Littler sank the smaller of them. They are, or rather were, so strong, that the heaviest weight might pass over them with the greatest ease and security. It was interesting to watch the elephants; they put down their proboscis, and then successively each of their fore-feet with extreme caution, to try the strength of the bridge, and when they had satisfied themselves that it would bear their weight, they crossed without the least hesitation.

Ferozepore is one of our large military stations; it derives its present improved state from our occupation; for it was formerly a desolate and ruinous place, the houses deserted and dilapidated, and the country round waste and uncultivated. Now all is animation and progress. The dismal-looking town stands on a rising ground in an immense plain, a couple of miles from the river. Like nearly all the Indian towns, it is surrounded with walls, which were erected chiefly as a protection to their cattle, against the predatory hordes that infested the vicinity, the animals being driven out in the morning, and brought home at night. It contains a very handsome tank, close to an elegant pagoda surrounded with trees. The great detriment here, is the want of water; there are plenty of ditches and a dry arm of the Sutlej, and if the inhabitants would only dig twenty-five or thirty feet for water, the whole face of things would be changed at once.

The cantonments are about three miles to the south of the town. They are divided into streets, which cross at right angles. The officers' bungalows are picturesquely situated in the midst of pretty gardens which combine the flora of the eastern and the western hemispheres; the barracks, both for the European and native regiments, are not particularly good; the magazines and stores are built of stone and have a very durable appearance.

But to the lover of nature, the great attraction is the distant range of the snow-capped Himalaya mountains. Neither pen nor pencil can describe their splendour amid the gorgeousness of an eastern sunset. Earth and sky are covered with a veil of liquid gold; the clouds, as they traverse the deep blue vault, gradually assume the most varied and brilliant tints, and the majestic Himalayas, girdled round their base with a robe of gold and crimson, rear their silvered crests in line relief against the bright effulgence that surrounds them. How different are the feelings inspired by gazing upon such a scene, and those aroused by the din of battle, the sight of slaughter and death which I had so recently witnessed!

"Aye, there they stand, as in creation's prime,
Above the mouldering wrecks of sin and time!
Man's fatal fall, which all beneath them cursed,
Hath left them standing as they stood at first:
Unchallenged, still they keep their place in heaven,
And wear the diadem their God hath given;
And change and death sweep on o'er sea and land,
And find, and leave them changeless: there they stand!"

On the 19th I journeyed to Misri-Wala, ten miles. On my arrival there, I rode over to Ferozeshah, which is only about a mile and a half off, as I was anxious to see the battle-field. It was a horrid sight. After an interval of three months it was still covered with the unburied bodies of the Sikhs, on whom hundreds of Pariah dogs and birds of prey were feasting; dead camels, horses, and bullocks also seemed to invite them to a plentiful repast. The odour was dreadful, even more so than on my former visit.

20th. Proceeded to Moodkee, ten miles and a half, and pitched my tent on the edge of the battle-field, close by the fort, which was then occupied by a company of the 51st regiment of Native Infantry. Three months had just elapsed since the battle, which was fought here on the 18th of December, the first of the four engagements between the army of the Sutlej and the Sikhs. Within that short period no less than 1,449 of our troops had fallen, and 4,926 had been wounded, many of whom have since died; while the destruction of the Sikhs is fearful to contemplate. In round numbers they are said to have lost about 20,000 men.

On the 21st I went to Bhaga Poorana, a distance of fifteen miles. On my route, I again met a train of 400 hackeries laden with stores for the troops at Lahore. Next day I marched to Wudnee. On my arrival, I examined the square brick-built fort; the battlements command a fine view of the surrounding country. The eye wandered over a vast extent, without hill or mountain to intercept its wide spread range. All nature seemed to be at peace, and the Sutlej, which had so lately been stained with the blood of the slain, now flowed down in a pure and silvery current, bearing along with it health and refreshment from its rise in the table land of Thibet, to its junction with the Indus at Mithunkote.

On the morning of the 23rd I made an early start, and was on the move at a quarter to three for Bussean, fifteen miles and a half distant: it lies midway between Lahore and Umritsur, and is about twenty miles from each place. On the 24th I rode to Phurewallee, fourteen miles. On the 25th to Kotla Mullair, ten miles. Here the Dewan, or steward, of the Rajah of Nabah called upon me for a certificate that I had been well treated on my way through his master's territories, a request with which I willingly complied.

On reaching Munsorepore, a distance of sixteen miles, on the next day, I found my tent pitched close to a mosque; yesterday it had been placed near a Hindoo temple—and I was sadly disturbed at sunset by some barbarous sounds on a horn, made by a Brahmin. On the 27th I started, at two o'clock A.M., for Samana, a distance of nineteen miles, which I was desirous to make that day. I was, however, no gainer by my early start, for my guide lost his track in the dark, and I was delayed more than half-an-hour before we found our way. The road, moreover, was exceedingly heavy, neither more nor less than a bed of sand, in consequence of which, part of my establishment did not come up till two o'clock P.M. The Thanadar[42] of Samana furnished me, at his own particular request, with four chokedars, or watchmen, for I had only asked for one.

On the 28th, I rode to Goelah, a distance of twelve miles, and forded the Guggur or Cuggur River, about half way on my journey. After passing the towns of Bunnoor, Seyfabad, Pattiala, Jowhana, and Jomalpore, the Guggur enters the country of the Bhatties at the town of Arwah, formerly the capital of the district.[43]

About sixty miles south of the Sutlej, the Cuggur flows parallel with it, till opposite to Loodianna, where it runs in a straight direction, and is lost in the sands of the desert. It might easily be restored. Mr. Thomas, whilst residing at Bhatneer, could perceive but little vestige of what was called the ancient bed of the river. The natives declared that it formerly extended as far as the Sutlej, which it joined in the vicinity of Ferozepore; now the Sutlej runs south-west of Loodianna.

There is another river which formerly ran from the Jumna to the Sutlej; I understand that the Government intends to open its channel, which would indeed prove an immense benefit.

29th March. Rode to Pehoah, sixteen miles. Travelling alone as I now did, I found the appearance of the country very different to that which it presented when I marched along this same route with the troops. Then all was life and animation—the measured tread of the soldiery—the tramp and neighing of the horses—the heavy step and snort of the elephants and camels—the confused jargon of the immense rabble of camp-followers— the motley sight—the picturesque dresses—the clouds of dust; and, in the midst of all this apparent confusion, the loud, peremptory orders putting all in motion, and keeping all in order, presented an almost inconceivable contrast, to the calm repose of a solitary traveller passing noiselessly along, with his small retinue of twelve or fourteen attendants.

On the 30th, I rode to Khol, fourteen miles, and on the 31st to Suggah, fourteen and a half miles. I have already spoken of these several places, and shall therefore pass them without further mention.

April 1st. Rode to Kurnaul, ten miles. This town is about seventy-eight miles north-west of Delhi. It appears that it was first made a military station in 1806, when a corps of native infantry was quartered here. In 1807, it became the head-quarters of the third or north-west frontier division; Saharunpore and Loodianna being dependent commands. A depôt was also formed here; and in July, 1809, four large platform boats of 700 maunds (25 tons) were established at Khoonda Ghât, for the ferry across the river Jumna. Meerut is seventy miles distant by the road; the Cawnpore road being on the other side of the river. In 1831, H.M. 31st Foot, was sent to Kurnaul, where they encamped till the barracks were built, they being the first European corps stationed there. In 1840, Kurnaul contained a troop of Horse Artillery, a light or horse field-battery, having six guns each, one European regiment of Foot, two regiments of Light Cavalry, and three regiments of Native Infantry, being an establishment of about 5,000 men. It was for many years the head-quarters of the Sirhind division.

A troop of Horse Artillery, on the Bengal system, musters 169 horses, but on detachment the number has been as high as 230. A 6-pounder gun and carriage, with ammunition and stores, loaded and packed ready for service, weighs 23 cwt., not including the wheels, which weigh 238 lbs. each. Each horse carries seven stone of harness, besides the man. The horses are told off as follows, by regulation:

	Horses.		Total Horses.
6 Pieces of Ordnance	14	each.	84
6 Ammunition Carriages	8	"	48
4 Spare ditto	7	"	28
Staff of the troop	.		9
			——
			169

Their actual distribution, however, is about as under; the four spare waggons being drawn by bullocks.

	Horses.
1 Staff-Sergeant.	1
6 Sergeants.	6

2 Trumpeters, 2 Rough-Riders, 2 Farriers, 1 Saddler, and 1 Native Doctor	8
6 Guns, at 13 each.	78
6 Waggons, at 12 each	72
Spare	4
	— —
	169

Six horses to a gun, and four to a waggon, was the order laid down some years ago as the draught power; but of late the weight of the carriages has been so much increased as to equal that of the guns. On the line of march, both guns and waggons have latterly been worked with teams of eight horses, which, although not giving the horses daily relief, answers extremely well, as I am assured by my informant, Major E.J. Pratt, 9th Lancers, Assistant-Adjutant-General of the Cavalry in the Sikh campaign of 1848-49. A 6-pounder takes into action, on its own limber and waggon, 128 rounds in horse draught, besides 96 rounds on its spare waggon, in bullock draught; making 224 rounds present in troop-park.

The remaining stations were: Hansi, 84 miles distant from Kurnaul, where, on the 1st of January, 1849, was the Hurrianah Light Infantry; Loodianna, 120 miles from Kurnaul, containing a Company of Foot Artillery, head-quarters and right wing of 34th Regiment of Native Infantry, and the Sirmoor Rifle Battalion. Ferozepore, 70 miles from Loodianna, to the West, where were stationed, a troop of Horse Artillery, and the 32nd Native Infantry; and lastly, Subathoo in the hills, where there was also, in the same year, a Detachment of the Nusseeree Rifle Battalion.

All these stations had just supplied troops for the Punjaub, and were consequently, at the period of which I am writing, very ill-garrisoned. In the month of January 1840, there were above 13,000 men in the Sirhind division.

At Kurnaul there is a canal, called Ali Merdan Khan's canal, running from the Jumna, which is within three miles of Delhi, and, passing close to the right flank of the old cantonments, near the house built by the late Major-General Sir David Ochterlony; this officer likewise erected a house at Loodianna, and another at Neemuch.

The barracks for the European Infantry are at right angles with the old cantonments. A Church was also built here in 1836; a neat little structure, with a singular tower, close to the parade ground. In 1828, this station was considered very unhealthy, in consequence, it was said, of malaria, generated by the grass growing on the banks of the canal, yet from 1829 to 1836, it was as salubrious as Meerut. In proof of this, it may be stated that H.M. 31st Foot, lost fewer men at Kurnaul, than at Meerut, their next quarters. Now Meerut is reckoned one of the healthiest military stations in the Bengal Presidency.

Whether the malaria which appeared at Kurnaul, in the autumn of 1842, was owing to the clearing out of the great canal, which runs through the city, or whether it was merely a passing evil, confined to a particular quarter, is still an open question; so much is certain, that it broke out among the European troops, and was confined to one locality, precisely where their barracks were situated. Kurnaul has now, unfortunately, ceased to be a military station.

The extensive cantonments, as well as numerous elegant bungalows and villas, in the midst of parks and gardens, stretch in a semi-circle of three miles around the town, and present a unique and extremely picturesque *tout ensemble*. The cantonments are traversed in every direction by good roads, shaded by avenues of trees.

At the time of my visit, in April 1846, the barracks were deserted; the roofs, in many instances, had fallen in, the frame-work with the doors and windows had been removed, and the compounds were overgrown with weeds and jungle. The only exceptions are the houses built by Sir David Ochterlony, both of which are the property of Brigadier-General Thomas Palmer, commanding the Cawnpore division of the army. These two houses are in fine preservation; one, called the banqueting-house, is a noble building, situated in the midst of English park-like grounds, with coach-houses, etc., in good taste and perfect keeping. The other, the dwelling-house, is built somewhat after the Eastern style; the garden surrounding it is most delightful, being filled with a luxuriance of the richest shrubs and flowers I ever saw, its gallant owner being one of the best botanists in India.

The town of Kurnaul is dirty and closely built. The houses are chiefly of brick; and, like most of the old Indian towns, it has a dingy look, and is surrounded by a high wall.

During the time of the Earl of Ellenborough's government, the station was so sickly, that his lordship, ever alive to the well-being and comfort of the army, peremptorily ordered it to be abandoned.

Being situated so near to the frontier, only fifty-three miles from Umballa, it was the practice, during the Sikh campaign of 1845-46, for reinforcements, marching up from Meerut, Delhi, and other stations, to assemble at Kurnaul for the purpose of forming depôts, etc., and then to march forward in a body.

Officers were frequently sent up by Dâk, at the expense of government (at a cost, it is said, of about £20,000), to join their corps, from every part of the Bengal presidency, particularly from Calcutta. They were often detained here twelve or fourteen days, waiting for a convoy for protection.

A re-mount depôt was established at Kurnaul, about nine years ago, by Viscount Gough, which imparted some signs of re-animation to this station, which, in my estimation, is one of the most pleasant quarters in India. The head-quarters of the Sirhind division have been removed to Umballa.

On the 3rd of April I struck my tent and rode to Gurounda, a distance of twelve miles, in a dense jungle, through which a road had been cut. After leaving Kurnaul, the distance was marked at every two miles by the celebrated ancient minarets, which were erected by Akbar the Great, from Delhi to Cashmere. These elegant mile-stones, tapering from their circular pediments to a height of twenty feet, are, notwithstanding their age, kept in a tolerable state of preservation by the inhabitants, from a religious feeling. After a ride of six miles, I came to a handsome bridge, which was built over the canal by the emperor Humayoon. It is lofty, and arched; and looks all the more picturesque from a remarkably large cotton-tree which grows close beside it, and seems to have had its origin about the same time as the bridge. Gurounda itself is an insignificant place, presenting nothing of interest, except the ancient caravansary. It is large, and has lofty turreted gates, which are in fair preservation.

On the 4th I rode to Somalka, twenty-two miles, having passed through Paniput, the scene of two of the fiercest encounters which this country ever witnessed. Paniput is about ten miles from Gurounda, and, like the majority of the cities and towns in this part, a mass of ruins. The road again lay through a tract of jungle, and the greater part was ankle deep in sand. I pitched my tent in the area of a large and once elegant serai; but now, alas! in a state of dilapidation. These serais are public buildings, erected for the convenience of Eastern travellers, where they may eat, drink, and repose, and then go on their way with a thankful heart.

Paniput is a spot of too much celebrity to be silently passed over; for both in a military and political point of view, it fills an important place in the annals of India. It is about forty-eight miles from Delhi, the capital of the emperor of Hindoostan. It was formerly surrounded by a brick-wall, and at its greatest extent is little more than four miles in circumference. Paniput is famous as the scene of two great battles, which were attended with most decided effects upon the fate of Hindoostan. The first took place in the year 1525, between the Sultan—more usually called the Emperor Baber—and the Delhi Pathan emperor, Ibrahim Lodi; the latter was slain, and his army totally routed, which put an end to the Pathan dynasty of Lodi, and introduced the Mogul empire of Timoor, of whom Baber was the great grandson.

The life of the Emperor Baber was written by himself, a beautiful translation of which has been made by Mr. Erskine, formerly of Bombay. This illustrious conqueror was king of Cabool, and equally famous as a warrior, poet, and historian. At the battle of Paniput Baber's army consisted of only 12,000 men, including followers; whereas Ibrahim had 100,000. The former, however, had guns, the latter had none; and we must conclude that the artillery greatly contributed to secure the victory for Baber.

I must not omit the mention of Nadir Shah's invasion of India, in 1739, which preceded the second great battle to which I have alluded. Nadir Shah, having plundered Delhi of several millions sterling of property, retired through the Khyber Pass, where he paid a lakh of rupees as a security against plunder. Being assassinated by one of his attendants, Ahmed Shah Abdallah seized a convoy of treasure on its way to Candahar, and, raising the standard of rebellion, proclaimed himself king of Affghanistan.

It appears, that about A.D. 1720, the Affghans conquered Persia, but were expelled by Nadir Shah, who in turn subjugated their dominions; and in 1739, after the capture of Delhi, annexed Affghanistan to the Persian empire. Ahmed Shah Abdallah, in 1748, occupied the Punjaub and invaded India, but being repulsed, renewed his attempt in the year 1751. In the declining state of their empire, the Moguls called in the Maharattas, a sure sign of weakness in a Mahomedan government, when it craves the aid of the Hindoos to assist in settling its disputes.

Ahmed Shah again invaded India, in 1756, when he took Delhi. He invaded India for the fourth time in 1759, which brings us to the second great battle of Paniput; which was fought on the 6th of January, 1761, between the Maharattas and the army of Ahmed Shah. The Maharatta cavalry, commanded by the Bhow, consisted of 55,000 troops, in regular pay, with at least 15,000 predatory Maharatta cavalry,—the Pindarries,— and 15,000 infantry, of whom 9,000 were disciplined Sepoys, under the command of Ibrahim Khan Gardee, a Mussulman deserter from the French service. He had besides 200 guns, numerous wall pieces, or "zumbooruks," fired from the backs of camels, and a great supply of rockets, the rocket being a favourite weapon with the Maharattas. This army of 85,000 men, with its innumerable followers, made the number within his lines amount to 300,000 men.[44]

Ahmed Shah, on the other hand, had about 40,000 Affghans and Persians, 13,000 Indian Horse, and a force of Indian Infantry, estimated at

38,000, of which the division, consisting of Rohilla Affghans,[45] would be very efficient; but the great majority consisted of the usual rabble of Indian foot soldiers. He had also thirty guns, of different calibre, chiefly belonging to his Indian allies, and a number of wall pieces.

Now, if we reckon the Maharatta force at 70,000 regular troops and 200 guns, and the Dooranees[46] at 44,000 regulars and thirty guns, there will appear great odds against the Dooranees. The Dooranees estimated the number of the army that crossed the Indus at 63,000 men; but Mr. Elphinstone thinks this force is exaggerated, considering that there were only 40,000 Affghans, and 2,000 horse and 2,000 infantry, furnished by the Indian allies.

The camp followers were in overwhelming numbers.

The Shah pitched his camp eight miles from the enemy, and his small red tent was placed at the head of the army, in order that he might see every movement in the enemy's front. At night he surrounded his camp with an abattis of felled trees. At one time flour sold in the Shah's camp for two rupees, or 4s. a seer (2 lbs.), owing to the Maharattas having intercepted the supplies.

The Maharattas, as usual, took the field after the Dusserah,[47] the 17th of October, in 1760; and three actions, of partial success, were fought before the great battle. The two armies daily turned out in battle array; but at length the Hindoostanee allies of Ahmed became impatient and urged him to engage. Then it was that Ahmed Shah gave them the memorable rebuke, "This is a matter of war with which you are unacquainted. Military operations must not be precipitated. At a proper time I will bring the affair to a successful termination."[48] He was resolved to have no councils of war, and used to say to his Hindoostanee allies, "Do you sleep; I will take care that no harm befalls you."

Ahmed Shah was a cautious and vigilant general. Taking with him forty or fifty horsemen, he used, in company with his son, Timoor Shah, to visit daily every part of his army, and reconnoitre the enemy's camp. At night, a body of 500 horse advanced as near as possible to the enemy's position; remaining under arms till daybreak; whilst other bodies went the rounds of the whole encampment. On the day of the great battle, the Dooranees marched from their camp to the attack, when objects were only just visible. The Maharatta army was drawn up facing the east, a great mistake on their part, as they thus had the sun in their eyes; whilst the Dooranees fronted the west.

The Maharattas entered the field with determined courage, each having taken a betel-leaf in the presence of all his comrades, and sworn to fight to the last extremity.

The Shah ordered his trumpets to sound to battle. Breast works of sand had been thrown up, under cover of which the Nawab Vizier's troops advanced; upon which the bildars, or pioneers, proceeded half musket-shot in advance of the cover and threw up another; and in this manner the troops progressed about two miles, until they were within long musket-shot of the enemy. The Rohillas fired volleys of rockets,[49] as many as 2,000 at a time, which not only terrified the horses by their dreadful noise, but did so much execution, that the Maharattas could not advance to charge them. The Mussulmans did not make much use of their guns.

The Dooranees were men of great bodily strength, and their horses, which were of the Toorkee breed,[50] were rendered hardy by constant exercise.

Casi Rai Pundit, who was an eye-witness and attached to Ahmed Shah's allies, says: "About noon, the Shah received advice that the Rohillas and the Grand Vizier's division had the worst of the engagement, upon which he sent for the Nesuckchees—a corps of horse, wearing a peculiar dress and arms, and who were always employed in executing the Shah's immediate commands—2,000 being assembled, he sent 500 of them to his own camp to drive out all the armed people and fugitives whom they should find there, that they might take part in the action; the remaining 1,500 he ordered to meet the fugitives from the battle, and to kill every man who should refuse to return to the charge. This command they executed so effectually that, after killing a few, they compelled 7,000 or 8,000 men to return to the field."

Meanwhile the Shah sent for the reserve corps, of these he despatched 4,000 to cover the right flank, and 10,000 to support the Grand Vizier, with orders to charge the enemy sword in hand, in close order, and at full gallop; at the same time he gave directions to Shah Pussund Khan and Nujeeb-ud-Dowlah that as often as the Grand Vizier should charge the enemy, those two chiefs should at the same time attack him in flank. The advantage still inclined to the side of the Maharattas, when Ahmed, after successfully rallying the fugitives, gave orders for an advance of his own line, at the same time ordering the division on his left, to take the enemy in flank. The manœuvre was decisive, and a terrible conflict ensued, especially in the centre, commanded by the Bhow and Biswas Row. The latter was wounded and unhorsed, which being reported to the Bhow he ordered him to be taken up, and placed upon his elephant,[51] when the Bhow himself continued the action at the head of his men. They fought fiercely on both sides with spears, swords, battle-axes, and even daggers; when Biswas Row expired from his wounds. Suddenly, as if by enchantment, the whole Maharatta army turned and fled at full speed, leaving the battle-field covered with heaps of the dead and dying.

The victors pursued the flying Maharattas with the utmost fury; and, as they gave no quarter, the slaughter was terrific, the pursuit being continued in every direction for fifteen or twenty miles. According to Grant Duff, the whole number of the slain is said to have amounted to 200,000 men, which must have included the losses in both armies, as well as the followers; for the highest numbers given were 176,000 fighting men, which we find reduced to 114,000, including both sides. Never was a defeat more complete. Grief, despondency, and despair spread over the whole Maharatta people. The wreck of the army retired beyond the river Nerbudda, evacuating all their acquisitions in Hindoostan.[52]

The battle lasted about nine hours. Besides the loss in slain and wounded, 40,000 were taken prisoners, and the plunder was enormous. In front of the door of each tent, except that of the Shah and those of his principal officers, an immense pile of heads was placed as a trophy.

Ibrahim Khan Gardee, the Mussulman General of the Maharattas, having, on one occasion during the action, ordered his men and musketry to cease firing, advanced with seven battalions of disciplined Sepoys, to attack Doondy Khan and Hafiz Rahmut Khan's divisions with fixed bayonets. The Rohillas received the charge with great resolution, and fought hand to hand. About 8,000 Rohillas were killed or wounded; and the attack told so severely upon them that a few only remained with their chiefs. Their force originally consisted of 15,000 foot and 4,000 horse. In this action, however, six of the seven battalions of Ibrahim Khan were entirely cut to pieces. This gallant general was covered with wounds, and being taken prisoner, afterwards fell a sacrifice to Ahmed Shah's vengeance, for fighting against his own faith.

Nearly all the great chiefs were either killed or wounded. Malhar Rao Holcar, who was accused of too early a retreat, was wounded. Sindiah, afterwards the founder of a great state, was lamed for life; and Nana Furnavese, who long averted the downfall of the Peishwah's government, narrowly escaped by flight.

The confederacy of the Mahomedan powers dissolved on the cessation of these common dangers. Ahmed Shah returned to Cabool without attempting to profit by his victory; nor did he ever afterwards take any share in the affairs of India. This victory, however, put an end to the Mogul empire.

"Most of the Maharatta conquests," says Mr. Elphinstone, "were recovered at a subsequent period; but it was by independent chiefs, with the aid of European officers and disciplined Sepoys."

The Mogul empire, which had now received its death-blow, had been in a tottering state for more than half a century; for its decline commenced with the death of Aurungzebe, in 1707. Having been viceroy in the Deccan, which he left to proceed to Agra, for the purpose of dethroning his father, Shah Jehan, he assumed the royal authority in 1661, with the arrogant title of "Alumgeer," or "Conqueror of the World." From the death of this crafty and cruel man, in 1707, till 1760, no less than six emperors of Delhi had been dethroned, assassinated, or poisoned, besides two children, who reigned only a few months. This proves the state of the Delhi empire at that period; and it was this internal weakness which allured Nadir Shah, in 1739, to advance to the capital and plunder Delhi. Elphinstone[53] says, "The divided government would have fallen an easy prey to the Maharattas, had not circumstances procured it a respite from the encroachments of these invaders."

The Maharattas, whose early history is involved in much obscurity, were a warlike race, inhabiting the mountain provinces as far as Guzerat and the Nerbudda, a large tract of country on the west coast, between Surat and Canara. In 1720, they were invited by the governor of the Deccan, who aimed at the establishment of an independent monarchy in India, to ravage the territories of the Mogul, and attack the city of Delhi. This predatory race gladly undertook a task which offered such a prospect of booty. They committed great ravages throughout the country, and finally attacked the city of Delhi. Although they sustained a defeat, they so far succeeded in spreading the terror of their name, that the generals of the Mogul army, concluded a dishonourable treaty with them. The Governor of the Deccan, disappointed in his expectations, readily found cause for a quarrel with the Court of Delhi, and induced the disaffected nobles, who were disgusted at the treaty concluded with the Maharattas, to call in the aid of Nadir Shah, the usurper of the throne of Persia.

Nadir Shah, one of the most distinguished, but at the same time most atrocious, men recorded in history, was born in 1687. While General of the Persian forces, he quitted the military service, and became leader of a formidable band of robbers. His military talents, however, were so distinguished, that the king of Persia, not only pardoned this audacious step, but took him again into his service, and gradually raised him to the office of Commander-in-Chief of the Persian forces, with the title of Khan, being the highest dignity he could bestow.

By his intrigues, Nadir Shah soon succeeded in gaining the whole army, and when the Shah of Persia concluded a peace with the Turks without his advice, Nadir basely dethroned his sovereign, seized the regency in the name of the infant prince, who was still in his cradle, and, after a sanguinary victory over the Turks, he was, on the death of his Ward, chosen king of Persia, in 1735. From that day he adopted the name of Nadir Shah. His arms were everywhere victorious; but he shed torrents of blood, and inflicted even upon his own subjects, the most unheard-of cruelties. His soldiers, whom he had enriched with the splendid spoils of many a victory, were so devoted to him, that none of his disaffected subjects, durst place himself at their head. Even the priests, who were incensed at his oppression and cruelty to their own body, and at his attempt to establish the Soonie creed instead of the Shiah form of Mahomedanism, which was the national religion, were utterly powerless, and every conspiracy that was formed to hurl the usurper from the throne, was crushed in its birth. His greatest, but at the same time his most cruel, campaign, was that against the Great Mogul, in 1739, of which we have already spoken.

Being invited by the Grand Vizier, and by those nobles who were indignant at the ignominious treaty concluded by their sovereign with the Maharattas, whom he had induced by a large bribe to retire from the capital, and the promise of an annual tribute in money and treasure, on condition of their not renewing their assault, or plundering the territories of the Great Mogul, Nadir Shah, who was bent upon revenge for the protection afforded to some of his Affghan enemies, lost no time in obeying the summons. He placed himself at the head of his army, and crossed the Indus before Mahomed Shah, the emperor of Delhi, had even heard of his impending approach. Mahomed immediately collected his army, and fortified his camp, near Paniput, but hearing of Nadir's approach, he went out to meet him, and offered him battle in open field. It was a bloody contest. Both sides fought with desperate valour, but Mahomed Shah was beaten; 20,000 of his valiant men were wounded or slain, and Mahomed, to stop the sanguinary strife, went with his chief men, and offered himself and his treasures to appease the conqueror.

Nadir received his fallen foe, with more compassion than might have been expected. He promised to reinstate him in his dominions, on condition that he should give up his treasures and jewels, and that his nobles and people should pay an enormous sum, as some indemnity for the expenses incurred in this inglorious war. The dejected sovereign, glad to be reinstated in his kingly power, had neither the heart nor the means to resist the dictates of the conqueror, and returned with him to his capital. Little did he anticipate the horrible scenes about to be enacted there, in levying the cruel exactions of Nadir, whereby he lost thousands of his subjects, and his already shattered power received a blow which prevented it from ever rallying again. Victor by the power of arms, and by the treachery of Mahomed's nobles, Nadir Shah, sacked and devastated the conquered empire, fired and destroyed the city of Delhi, and slew 200,000 inhabitants. This fearful slaughter was occasioned by a false report of the death of Nadir, which caused the inhabitants to rise en masse, and fall upon the soldiery. Nadir immediately gave orders for a general massacre, which were instantly obeyed. The carnage commenced at sunrise, and lasted till noon, when it was at length put a stop to at the earnest entreaty of the Emperor of Delhi. Nadir Shah carried off the imperial treasures which had been accumulated by the Mogul rulers for upwards of two centuries.

Thus the arrival of Nadir Shah, preserved for a short time longer the existence of the Mogul Empire, by the restoration of Mahomed Shah to the imperial dignity; otherwise it must have succumbed to the Maharattas. When Ahmed Shah first invaded India in 1748, the Vizier of the Emperor of Delhi had recourse, as I have already remarked, to the humiliating expedient of calling in the Maharattas. The state of the Mogul Empire in 1756, was much the same as that of Calcutta when it was attacked by Suraj-ud-Dowlah, the Subahdar of Bengal, in June of the same year. No mandate of the Emperor was obeyed: the Nawab of Oude, the actual Vizier of the Empire, had raised the standard of independence: the power of the Maharattas was at its zenith, and that of the Mogul Empire at its lowest ebb.

Now the proper country of the Maharattas is the south of India. When Aurungzebe left the Deccan about 1658, he appointed a deputy, who, however, was unable to control the Maharattas. Even Aurungzebe himself when he went in pursuit of Sevajee, the founder of the Maharatta Empire, was often baffled by the wily chief who would suddenly retire into his hills and mountain fastnesses.

On the decline of the Delhi power at the death of Aurungzebe, the Maharattas began to extend their operations to the north of the Nerbudda; they gradually threatened all parts of Hindoostan, and even visited Calcutta. At that time, what is called the Maharatta ditch was thrown up to protect the city against these invaders, an ingenious device of the Calcutta factory, and well enough for a body of merchants. The origin of the term "ditchers," as applied to them, is derived from this Maharatta ditch; though it would be as difficult to determine its locality, except on paper, as that of the Black Hole.

The number of elephants and camels with the two armies, is not stated. Elphinstone says, "that the force ascribed to the Indian kings is probably

Journal Of A Cavalry Officer | 119

exaggerated. Porus, one of the princes who occupied the Punjaub, is said to have had 200 elephants, 300 chariots, 4,000 horse, and 30,000 efficient infantry, which, as observed by Sir Alexander Burnes, is, substituting guns for chariots—exactly the establishment of Runjeet Singh, who is master of the whole Punjaub, and several other territories." Burnes must have referred to the year 1831, when he was in the Punjaub; in 1848 Runjeet Singh's force was supposed to be 50,000 men, besides irregulars for garrisons. Neither Polybius nor Arrian's history of Alexander's expedition, mentions the number of elephants or cattle with any of the armies. Humboldt in his "Cosmos"[54] writes: "According to the testimony of Polybius, when African and Indian elephants were opposed to each other in fields of battle, the sight, smell, and cries of the larger and stronger Indian elephants drove the African ones to flight. The latter were probably never employed as war elephants in such large numbers as in Asiatic expeditions, when Chundragupta had assembled 9,000, the powerful King of the Prasii 6,000, and Akbar an equally large number. These armies must have been much larger than those engaged at the battle of Paniput in 1761."

We read that the elephants were placed in the front of the army, and that they often turned back and killed more friends than foes. Now 9,000 elephants in a single line, allowing each to take up 12 feet would reach 20 miles, and 6,000 elephants would extend 13 miles and 1,120 yards. It is said there were 50,000 camels with the army of the Indus[55] in 1838 and 1839.

It may be interesting to the reader, to see the following statement of the native armies in the time of Akbar, in 1582, as given in the Ayeen Akbaree, by Abul Fazel, Prime Minister:—

Province of	Cavalry.	Infantry.	Elephants.	Boats.
Agra	50,600	477,570	221	—
Allahabad	11,375	237,870	323	—
Bahar	11,415	149,350	—	100
Delhi	18,275	125,400	—	—
Oude	1,340	31,900	—	23
Ajmere	8,000	38,000	—	—
Bengal	1,100	142,920	1,100	—
Total	102,105	1,203,010	1,644	123

Thus we find that the cavalry and infantry in the seven Soobahs of Agra, Ajmere, Allahabad, Bahar, Bengal, Delhi, and Oude amounted to 1,305,115;

and if to these we add two others, viz., Lahore and Mooltan, the number of men will be increased to 1,965,116, or of cavalry alone, to 170,370, for

Province of	Cavalry.	Infantry.
Lahore	54,480	426,086
Mooltan	13,785	165,650
	— — —	— — —
Total	68,265	591,736

Making about 2,000,000 of fighting men from Lahore to Bengal: and if we estimate the population at that time (1582) at 35,000,000, there would have been one soldier out of every seventeen inhabitants.[56]

At present the population of the

North Western Provinces is	23,199,668
Punjaub	1,75,0000
Bahar and Bengal	24,000,000
	— — — — —
Total	48,949,668

According to Diodorus, Alexander heard that he was to be opposed on the banks of the Ganges by 20,000 cavalry, 200,000 infantry, 2,000 chariots and 4,000 elephants. Megasthenes mentions Alexander's visit to Sandrocottus, monarch of the Prasii, when encamped with an army of 400,000 men. When Aurungzebe died, in 1707, two of his sons took the field with 300,000 men each, which appear to have been the largest armies assembled within the last 150 years in India.

Sultan Baber, as I have before observed, in 1525, with 12,000 men and guns, defeated Ibrahim Lodi, the emperor of Delhi, who had 100,000 men and no guns. In the battle of Paniput, in 1761, when the Maharattas strove for the ascendancy over the Mahomedans, there were not above 150,000 men on either side. The infantry in Akbar's time were very indifferent soldiers. Elphinstone says:[57] "that it is mentioned in the Akbarnama that the chiefs of Scinde employed Portuguese soldiers in this war; and had also 200 natives dressed as Europeans." These were, therefore, the first Sepoys in India. The same learned author states,[58] under the year 1692, only about fifteen years prior to the death of Aurungzebe, that: "In spite of all Aurungzebe's boasted vigilance, the grossest abuses had crept into the military department. Many officers only kept up half the number of their men, and others filled their ranks with their menials and slaves."

Whatever credit, therefore, may be due to the statement of the number of troops in each Province in 1582, it is evident that in the year 1692, we should, by the like reasoning, have to reduce the royal standing army from 2,000,000 to 1,000,000 men. The cavalry was the most efficient force. The infantry, though ten times more numerous, yet we may reckon that not one-fourth were of much use in action. The cavalry in Akbar's time amounted to 170,000 men, and the infantry to about 1,800,000: but if 500,000 could take the field, it was probably the maximum; wherefore, if we were even to allow 700,000 men for all Hindoostan, from Cabool (for it had been made a Province) to Cape Comorin, the force would not greatly exceed many of the Continental armies. The East India Company's armies at one period numbered 302,797 men, including the royal regiments.[59]

Folard, and many other judicious writers observe, that in proportion as infantry is bad, and the military art declines, the number of horse increases in our modern armies; because, say they, "An able general at the head of a good infantry, can do anything, and wants but a small cavalry." It is certain that when the infantry is good, much may be done with it; and if it is bad you must increase your cavalry to keep the enemy at a distance, as you must have a great quantity of heavy artillery for the same purpose.

I must now take leave of Paniput with the remark, that formerly a treasury was established there, Kurnaul furnishing the necessary guards.

About this time there was a considerable change in the weather. The days for the most part were hot and oppressive, and towards noon even sultry. On the 5th of April I rode to Sunput, about seventeen miles. On the 6th I started, at half past two in the morning, in the midst of a complete hurricane, and proceeded to Barah Duree, a Chokey, or Police Station, near Alepore. The road was excessively sandy and fatiguing, the distance being sixteen miles and a half. On the 7th I rode to Delhi, eleven miles and a half, and encamped outside the walls of this famous royal city of the Moguls, close to the Cashmere gate.

I had now travelled 313 miles and a half, since I quitted Lahore, a distance which I accomplished in twenty-two marches.

FOOTNOTES:

[42] Thanadar, keeper of a public station. The word likewise means commandant of a military post.

[43] Francklin's Life of George Thomas, p. 66.

[44] Grant Duff, in his History of the Maharattas, agrees with Casi Rai in making the paid horse and infantry as in

the text, and estimates the predatory horse and followers at 200,000. Casi Rai makes the whole number to have been 500,000. Asiatic Researches, vol. iii. p. 123.

[45] Roh means a hill; the Rohillas are the Affghans, who settled in Rohilkund on the return of Ahmed Shah to Cabool.

[46] The Dooranees were so called from Ahmed Shah Abdallah, who assumed the name of Dooree Dooraun, "Pearl of the age," when after seizing the sovereignty of Affghanistan, he was crowned king at Candahar, in the year 1747.

[47] A day kept as a holiday by Hindoo Princes, when, if war be intended, the campaign is opened.

[48] Ἀμφί δάρ ωμοισιν βάλετο ξίφος ἀργυρόηλον,
— —αὐτάρ ἔπειτα σάκος μέγα τε στιβαρόν τε.
Homer's Iliad, ii. 204, 205.

[49] The British used rockets on a small scale in 1817, against the Fort of Hattrass; but they have never tried them against troops.

[50] See Appendix XIX.

[51] Chiefs often ride on war elephants to be better seen by their troops. An Indian queen has thus led her van in the battle field. Should the elephant be struck down, or the chief fall wounded from his elephant, the fortune of the day is generally decided.

[52] Hindoostan commences north of the Nerbudda; south of that river the country is called the "South of India," and "The Deccan."—See Malcolm's Malwa. vol. i. pp. 120, 121.

[53] Vol. ii. p. 598.

[54] Vol. ii. p. 540, note.

[55] The return of those lost was 30,000: one commanding officer said 50,000. Lieutenant-Colonel Burlton discredits the amount, but one of his own departmental officers gave

in that number. The Government bought fresh camels in the room of those which died or were lost.

[56] The population of Great Britain and Ireland during the late war, was about 18,000,000; out of which number 1,000,000 were employed in the army, navy, marines, militia, volunteers and yeomanry.

[57] Vol. ii. p. 261.

[58] Vol. ii. p. 494.

[59] Captain Walter Badernach, p. 4, table 1, 1826.

CHAPTER X

Delhi—Mahmood of Ghuznee—Shah Jehan—Gates
of Delhi—Mosques—The Palace—Hall of Audience—
Chapel of Aurungzebe—The Gardens—The Jumma
Musjeed—Khoonee Durwaza—Protestant Church—The
Observatory—Tomb of Zufder Jung—The Cootub Minar—
Allah-ud-Deen—Gheias-ud-Deen—Mahomed Togluk—
Humayoon—Nizam-ud-Deen—The Cantonments—
Mahomedan College—Delhi—Produce of Delhi—Shah
Allum II.—Lord Lake—Monsieur Louis Bourgion—Sir
David Ochterlony—Holcar—Lieutenant-Colonel W.
Burn—Mr. E. Thornton—Allahabad—Marquis Wellesley—
Defence of Delhi—Mahomedan Population—Colonel
Ochterlony's good Generalship.

Delhi, or Dilli, in Sanscrit Indraprastha, an ancient Hindoo city, founded by Delu, was, according to tradition, built more than 300 years before the Christian era. The Rajahs of Dilli, or Indraput, are mentioned by the Mahomedan historians as early as A.D. 1008. In 1011 the city was taken and plundered by Sultan Mahmood, of Ghuznee, but afterwards it was restored to the Rajah as a tributary.[60] It is reported to have covered a space of twenty miles, and the ruins now are very extensive. It is scarcely possible to conceive anything more striking and picturesque than the first appearance of Delhi, situated on its rocky mountain chain, with its mosques, monuments, palaces, and tombs rising in perfect beauty amid the widely scattered ruins of bye-gone days and former greatness, environed with verdant gardens, corn-fields, palms and cypresses; while the silvery Jumna flowing in the luxuriant valley imparts a bright relief to the whole scene. To see the magic grandeur of the tout ensemble the traveller should ascend the lofty Cootub Minar which is about seven miles from the city. The effect produced on the mind by this grand panorama is quite indescribable.

In the year 1631, the Emperor Shah Jehan founded the city of New Delhi, on the west bank of the Jumna, and named it Shahjehanabad, but it did not long retain his name. It is about seven miles in circumference, and is surrounded on three sides by a wall of brick and stone, in most beautiful preservation, with, as far as I could judge, not a stone displaced. The wall is furnished with embrasures, and has been more strongly fortified by the English, who surrounded it with a moat. It has seven gates built of freestone, each indicating by its name the direction in which it lies; thus the Lahore gate points to the city of Lahore; the Ajmere gate to the city of Ajmere. The other five gates are named Agra, Turkoman, Delhi, Mohur, and Cashmere.

The modern city is built on two rocky eminences. It is divided into two parts, the old and the new; the streets are inferior and narrow, except two, the one leading from the palace to the Delhi gate, which is thirty yards broad, and 1,900 yards long, with an aqueduct along the middle of its whole extent, supplied with water from Ali Merdan Khan's canal, and the other leading from the Lahore gate which is still wider and handsomer, being forty yards in width and a mile in length.

Ali Merdan Khan, the Prime Minister, brought the above-named canal from the Jumna, where that river approaches Kurnaul, to Delhi, a distance of more than 100 miles; but it became choked up after the Persian and Affghan invasions; in consequence of which, in 1810, the English undertook to clear and repair it. It was not finished till 1820, and is said to have cost £35,000. It furnishes the inhabitants of Delhi with a supply of fresh water, the water of the Jumna being much impregnated with salt below Kurnaul. And here I would mention, by the way, that it is owing to this circumstance that the overflowing of the Jumna does not improve the soil like the inundation of the Ganges and other Hindoostanee rivers, the deposits of which are of a very fertilizing nature. The restoration of this canal proved an immense benefit, the country around having become scarcely habitable from the deleterious effects of the water.

Delhi contains about forty mosques, and many splendid palaces and residences of rich natives, surrounded with gardens, baths, and other out-buildings. The palace of the Great Mogul, commenced by the Emperor Shah Jehan in 1640, and finished in 1648, has two noble entrances, flanked by massive towers, over the principal of which is the residence of the officer commanding the palace guards, from whom it is necessary to obtain leave for visiting the palace. The palace is all that now remains to the king, of the glory and splendour of his ancestors. It lies on the west bank of the Jumna on some low cliffs; it forms an irregular quadrangle, enclosed by a wall of red sand-stone, between thirty and forty feet high, and about a mile in circumference, with forty-five small bulwarks and towers. Immediately below the wall is a deep moat. A pretty garden extends from the eastern side of the wall to the Jumna.

Passing through the massive portals which I have already named, a long, dimly lighted vaulted passage and gateway, brought me into the first court, which is 300 paces square, enclosed by walls, and traversed by a canal. A large gate led me into another square, containing the hall of audience, which is an open quadrangular terrace of white marble, the façade of the hall being formed by a double row of twenty marble columns, and the sides by eight, in the Arabic-Byzantine style. Here stands the throne, which is also of white marble, ornamented, and, like the hall, adorned with arabesques, Florentine Mosaic, and sculptures in relievo. Here the Great Mogul used to give audiences to the ambassadors and nobles of the empire, who, on these state occasions, always rode on elephants. The docile animals marched in a particular order, and were drawn up in array behind the barrier, which was sufficiently capacious to admit 200 elephants.

Through another white marble court I entered the Khas, or chief hall of audience, which is also of white marble, and the vaulted ceiling supported by thirty-two white marble columns in double file. Here stood the celebrated peacock throne. The throne itself was of gold, covered with diamonds and precious stones, supported on either side by a peacock, whose brilliant outspread tail glittered with jewels, while above the throne was a parrot the size of life, cut out of a single emerald, with wonderful skill. The value of the throne was estimated at between six and seven millions sterling. We all know that Timoor carried off the precious rubies, and that Nadir finished the work of demolition by removing all the other jewels. It is now a simple seat standing on a platform ornamented with gold, and a few worthless jewels, while the canopy which hangs over it bears the following inscription in Arabic: "If a paradise ever existed on earth, it is here, it is here." Alas! for the man who seeks his paradise here below!

Close by this hall is the chapel of Aurungzebe: it is of white marble, very small, but of the most exquisite workmanship. Altogether this pile of building presents a combination of splendour and elegance, with its gardens and fountains, mosques and columns, halls, balconies, corridors and minarets, which awaken feelings of melancholy as we recall to mind its former grandeur, of which the glory is now departed. The gardens are said to have cost Shah Jehan a million sterling; it would have been far too expensive to keep them up in their former style, and they are now rather like a neat park in England than an appendage to an Indian palace.

The Jumma Musjeed is a noble pile, built by the Emperor Shah Jehan, and finished in 1656 at a cost of £100,000; it is raised upon an equilateral foundation, composed of blocks of red sand-stone, about 30 feet above the level of the ground. It is said that the Emperor employed several thousand men for six successive years in its construction. It is, as the word Jumma or "gathering" denotes, the place of worship where all the Mahomedans are expected to meet on Fridays. This building is one of the finest and most perfect specimens of the Arabic-Byzantine style, and is constructed of white marble and red sand-stone, inlaid with arabesques. The massive portico, with an elegant minaret on either side, leads into the marble hall under the principal cupola. In the centre of this hall is a limpid fountain for the ablutions of the worshippers; and the whole is lighted by ever-burning lamps.

Quitting this mosque by the northern gate, I proceeded down the Dureeba Street, in the neighbourhood of which are the principal bankers and jewellers, and issued by the Khoonee Durwaza, or Bloody Gate, so named from the scene that took place during the massacre of 200,000 of the inhabitants by the tyrant Nadir Shah, into the Chandee Chowk, a place where an officer is stationed to receive tolls and customs. Leaving on my left a small mosque called the Roushen-ud-Dowlah, built in 1721, and ornamented with gilt cupolas—where the despot sat unconcerned, while the inhabitants were being slaughtered around him—I traversed the whole length of the street, went out of the Lahore Gate, round the outer wall of the City, and returned to the Cashmere Gate.

Close to this gate, and just inside it, is the Protestant Church, called the Church of St. James. It was built by the late Colonel James Skinner,[61] in 1837, at an expense of £12,000. It is a miniature resemblance of St. Paul's Cathedral, and is certainly a very elegant little place of Divine worship.

I also visited the Observatory, which was built in 1730 by Rajah Jey Singh, of Ambheer, a favourite minister of Mahomed Shah, and a great lover of astronomy. The troublous political events of this period, prevented the completion of this noble work. It is now dilapidated, and is surrounded by buildings, which have shared a similar fate, some more, some less in ruin. I saw, however, enough of the general design, and of the genius of its founder. The sun-dials and quadrants are on an immense scale, and rest upon huge red sand-stone arches.

The fine tomb of Zufder Jung, which was built in 1754 at a cost of £30,000, stands in the midst of an extensive garden. The King of Lucknow caused a suite of apartments in one of the large summer-houses of this garden, to be fitted up at a considerable cost for the convenience of travellers. The Mausoleum, is like many of the Delhi edifices, of white marble and red sand-stone, in alternate perpendicular stripes. The cornices of the building are ornamented with small towers and graceful minarets.

April 8th.—Being anxious to obtain a good panoramic view of the city, I hired a horse and buggy, and went to the celebrated Cootub Minar, which, as I said before, is situated about seven miles from the gates of Delhi. This wonderful and gigantic monument stands in the midst of ancient buildings and temples. Some, dating from the times of the Hindoo dynasty, and dedicated to the service of Buddha, indicate the great prosperity of that era, and the perfection which the arts had attained. The richly sculptured friezes, delineating events descriptive of their history and religion—combats—processions—and ceremonies—are alike interesting and instructive.

The Cootub Minar is so called from Cuttub-ud-deen, "The Pole-Star of religion," the favourite of the emperor Mahomed Gauree. He was originally a slave, and was purchased by that monarch, in whose favour he gradually rose from one office to another, till, on the death of the sovereign, he ascended the throne with the title of Shums-ud-deen Altumsh. He was the first Pathan, or Affghan sovereign. He erected this noble minaret to commemorate his successes over the infidels. It was commenced in 1214 and finished in 1228. It was repaired by Sultan Feroze the Second in 1368, again by Sultan Secunder Ben Lodi in 1503; and, lastly, by the British Government, after the dome had been shattered by an earthquake, in 1803. It is not certain whether the original structure consisted of five stories, as at present, or of only three; for the style of the two upper, does not by any means correspond with the lower portions. It is the loftiest column in the world, being 250 feet (some say 265 feet) in height, with a diameter, at the base, of about 40 feet. A spiral staircase, of 381 steps, leads to the summit of the Cootub Minar, from which I enjoyed a glorious prospect. The late Brigadier Smith, of the Engineers, in repairing the Cootub, restored it, as far as his ingenuity went, to its original appearance. There are various inscriptions, in Persian, on this building. One of these says:—"The prophet, on whom be the mercy and peace of God, has declared, 'he who erects a temple to the true God, on earth, shall receive six such dwellings in Paradise.'"

Close to the Minar are the remains of an old mosque, to which it is supposed to have belonged, the decorations of which are admirably executed. But the most beautiful and interesting object, after the Minar, is the square domed building on the south-east, erected as a gateway; the lofty Saracenic arch of which, coupled with the graceful and beautiful style of ornament, surpasses anything in the neighbourhood. It was built in 1243, by Sultan Allah-ud-Deen, whose now ruinous tomb is close at hand.

The poor emperor, who is now a pensioner upon the British Government, passes some months every year in this vicinity, where he can ruminate in silence on his fallen greatness.

Having spent a considerable time among these noble erections, which immortalize their founders and the era that produced them, I returned to my buggy, and drove a distance of eight miles, to the ancient and long deserted city of Toglukabad, built by Gheias-ud-Deen Togluk in 1321; it is remarkable for the rude and massive grandeur of its fortifications.

In the midst of a small level plain close by, stand the tombs of Gheias-ud-Deen and his son Mahomed Togluk. Near the river is a decayed building, two stories high, deeply imbedded in the terraced roof of which stands the famous pillar, Lath or Monolith, formed of a single stone, which, according to the inscription upon it, as deciphered by the late gifted Mr. James Prinsep, was one of eight similar monuments erected at Allahabad, Hissar, and other places, somewhere about the year B.C. 250, by a sovereign of all India, named Asoka, and was removed from its original site, in the vicinity of Sadowra, by Shah Feroze, to adorn his new residence.

Two miles further is the fort of Deenpunna, built by the emperor Humayoon, in 1531, which contains a highly-ornamented mosque of a peculiar style, built at the same time as the fort. A couple of miles beyond this, is the mausoleum of the emperor Humayoon, son of Baber, whose tomb is at Cabool. This magnificent pile was erected between the years 1565 and 1571, at an expense of £150,000, by his son the famous emperor Akbar. Besides the central dome it contains a number of small chambers, in which are the tombs of members of the royal family, amongst which are those of the Bunoo Begum, mother of the emperor Akbar, and the emperor Alumgeer the Second, who was assassinated in 1756. There is a fine view from the top. Near this Mausoleum is a tomb with a marble screen, to the memory of the poet and historian Ameer Khosroo, who died in 1325. A walled tank, some fifty feet in depth, was dug here by the saint, Nizam-ud-Deen. This is now a place of great public resort for the beggars and idlers of the neighbourhood, who exhibit various feats of diving headforemost, for any coin which the traveller may throw to the bottom for the benefit of the diver.

All these interesting buildings have been so often described, as to render any further account of them unnecessary; but they will long live in my recollection as peculiarly striking and splendid. In them we may read a sad but useful lesson, on the utter nothingness of this world, and learn that the most magnificent creations of puny mortals, are in a world's existence to be compared only to a passing shadow.

Their present imperial master is now a mere pensioner upon the bounty of the British government,[62] and his sway is bounded by the walls of his own palace. The semblance of royalty is all that remains to him. I was told by the sentries at the Cashmere Gate, that as a mark of respect, I must close my umbrella in passing through; no camels or carts are allowed to enter by that particular gate.

At a short distance from the Cashmere Gate, lie the cantonments. Two Native Infantry corps, and a Horse Field-battery are now stationed here. There is also a large magazine for military stores. Close to the cantonments is a bridge of boats across the Jumna, which is in constant use.

Some years ago, there was a Madrissa or Mahomedan college in Delhi; but it is now in disuse, and instead of it there is a college for the instruction of natives in the English language. Mohun Lall, of Cabool celebrity, was educated here.

Delhi is a place of great antiquity and importance, having been the capital of one of the greatest of the Hindoo sovereigns, long before the invasion of India by the followers of the Prophet. In 1011, as I before remarked, it was taken by the Mahomedans, and became the seat of the Affghan monarchs. In 1525, the Mogul dynasty was founded by Baber, when he slew the last of the Affghan kings in battle; and as the deliverer of his people ascended the vacant throne. Under the Mahomedan sway, it became one of the most magnificent cities of Asia; and in the time of the illustrious Aurungzebe, it contained a population of upwards of two millions of inhabitants. According to Shakespear's Statistics for 1848-49, Delhi contained 137,977 inhabitants at that time. It continued under the Mahomedan power till the establishment of the English in India. Since it has been under the British government, it has recovered somewhat of its ancient importance, being one of the principal channels of the Oriental trade with Britain and the Western world.

Delhi is famous for its jewels, shawls, scarfs, medallions, and painted drawings of noted kings, queens, and buildings. I would here venture to offer a word of caution to the traveller, to beware of being duped, for, in the purchase of these articles, there is a vast difference both in the price and value of the materials; and he will often find that what may be considered very good and cheap here, could have been procured in London at a more moderate cost, and of better workmanship.

Ever since the disastrous invasion of Nadir Shah, the emperors of Delhi had been either dethroned or assassinated; in 1761, Shah Allum II. ascended the throne; he attacked the British possessions, but was defeated; and having surrendered himself, remained under their protection till 1771, when he repaired to Delhi under a Maharatta escort. He ascended the throne, and became a puppet sovereign, the Maharattas paying him insulting homage. He remained a prisoner in the hands of the French officers who commanded the Maharatta army till 1804, when Lord Lake defeated the Maharattas, and entered the capital on the 12th of September.[63]

M. Louis Bourgion, who commanded Sindiah's troops, had crossed the Jumna on the night of the 10th of September, with sixteen battalions of regular infantry, 13,000 in number, and 6,000 cavalry, making a total of 19,000 men, and 70 guns. The British had about 7,000 men, and 22 field-pieces. Victory, however, soon declared on the side of the British. General Lake restored Shah Allum to his throne; but his power was merely nominal. He had been deprived of his eye-sight by the Rohilla chief, in 1788. It is not usual among the Mahomedans for a blind sovereign to succeed to the throne; but Shah Allum had previously been emperor for forty-two years. His death occurred in December 1806. The present emperor is his grandson.

The late Major-General Sir David Ochterlony was the Resident at Delhi, at the time when it was found necessary to undertake military operations for its protection against the Maharatta chief, Holcar. He had refused to join the confederation of Sindiah, and the Berar Rajah, and now came forward, single-handed, to fight the English, who had destroyed the armies of two chiefs more powerful than himself. Colonel Ochterlony began to put the defences of the city in order, and planted guns on the ramparts. Holcar, escaping the vigilance of General Lake, appeared before the city of Delhi about the 2nd of October, 1804.

At this time there was only one corps of Native Infantry, the rest being irregulars, not above 2,500 men altogether, at Delhi. Lieut.-Colonel W. Burn, 2nd Battalion 14th Native Infantry,—now 29th Bengal Native Infantry,—commanded the troops; and, when Holcar's army appeared, Lieut.-Colonel Ochterlony made over the command of the city to him. Holcar having erected batteries, the troops made sallies and destroyed them; upon which he constructed others, but more distant. At length the enemy, having made some gaps in the walls, determined to storm the place; for which purpose they brought several ladders. But the British having thrown them down, they did not attempt another assault, but kept up an incessant fire from their guns. General Lake, who had heard of the state of affairs at Delhi, marched towards that city; whereupon Holcar began to retreat on the night of the 8th of October.

Mr. E. Thornton, in his History of British India, intimates, that the Resident did not consider that it was possible to defend the city, but that Colonel Burn took a different and bolder view of the means of defence. A certain Lieut.-General, still living, was then a subaltern in the 14th Native Infantry, and present at the siege; from him, and others, we know that Sir David Ochterlony did plan the defence, and that Colonel Burn thanked him for his ability and advice. Mr. Thornton might have seen Lieut.-Colonel Ochterlony's report to General Lake, stating what he had done for the defence of the imperial city, as well as Colonel Burn's letter of thanks and report of the siege. It is singular, too, that Mr. Thornton was not aware that the Resident was afterwards the celebrated Sir David Ochterlony, G.C.B., the pride of the Bengal army; distinguished no less for his gallantry, than for his political conduct; for he was, when he died, in August 1825, the Governor-General's Agent for the North-west Provinces, an office which has been changed into the designation of Lieut.-Governor of the North-western Provinces.[64]

In 1806, Lieutenant-Colonel Ochterlony was removed from the post of Resident at Delhi to the command of the fortress of Allahabad, in consequence of an order from the Court of Directors, that no military officer should be the Resident at any Native Court. He was, however, granted the allowances of Adjutant-General of the army, as he had, by being Resident, lost his promotion to the head of that department. The Marquis Wellesley had appointed chiefly military men as Residents, which, in a country like India, seems to have been the best arrangement; for a divided authority in an unsettled country has generally proved injurious.

I have thought it right to make the above digression, because Mr. Thornton's omission might lead some to suppose that Colonel Ochterlony had entertained erroneous military notions, and was deficient as a military man. The defence of Delhi depended on two circumstances; firstly, the walls of the city, and secondly, the prevention of an outbreak among the Mahomedan population; for, the people having been under British rule only one year, it was to be apprehended that the disaffected would rise and join Holcar. It was, therefore, Colonel Ochterlony's military skill, together with his knowledge of the native character, his temper, and cool judgment that saved the city of Delhi.

FOOTNOTES:

[60] Ferishta, Rennel, Francklin, etc.

[61] Son of the late Colonel Hercules Skinner of the Bengal Infantry. Colonel James Skinner, for many years commanded the 1st Local Horse, then called Skinner's Horse.

[62] The East India Company allow him an annual pension of £120,000.

[63] Thorn's History of the Maharatta War, p. 110.

[64] As Lieutenant, he accompanied the Bengal force under the late Colonel Pearse, which marched to Madras in 1781, and was present in the battles with Hyder Ali Khan. At the siege of Cuddalore, in 1783, Sir David was wounded; as was also the late King of Sweden, Bernadotte, then a sergeant in the French army.

CHAPTER XI

Ghazenuggur—Secundra—Allyghur—The Fort—The
Church—Monuments—The Gaol—Akbarabad—Meerun-
ke-Serai—Kanoge—Tombs—Ancient Coins—Language
of Kanoge—Supposed Site of Palibothra—Population of
Benares—Streets of Benares—Singers and Musicians—
Productions of Kanoge—Poorah—Cawnpore—Court
Etiquette at Lucknow—Nawab of Oude—His Regal Rank—
Military Depôt at Cawnpore—Saddlery—Sirsole—Dâk
Bungalows—Arapore—Lohunga—-Allahabad.

On the morning of the 11th of April, I bade adieu to the far-famed city of Delhi, after a most agreeable stay of only four days, during which, however, I had made the most of my time.

Quitting the city from my encampment at the Cashmere gate, I set out for Ghazenuggur, a distance of fourteen and a half miles. I passed over the river Jumna, about five miles from Delhi, by the bridge of boats of which I have already spoken. The bed of the river being unusually broad at this time, these boats were exceedingly numerous. Half way en route to Ghazenuggur, or perhaps rather less, I crossed the river Hindon by an iron bridge.

On the 12th, I rode to Secundra, a distance of twenty-three miles, the scenery being very tame and uninteresting. On the 13th, I continued my route as far as Koorjah, seventeen miles and one-eighth; and on the 14th, to Somnagunge, fourteen and a half miles.

On the 15th I reached Allyghur, or Coel, as the town is called. On my arrival, I immediately visited the Great Mosque, with five cupolas, and a large pillar close by it, called the Minar. It is in a ruinous state, and a very poor resemblance of the renowned Cootub Minar, at Delhi. I ascended as high as was practicable by the spiral staircase in the interior, and counted eighty-one steps. An intelligent native, who accompanied me, told me that the founder intended that it should rival the beautiful column at Delhi; but some accident prevented its completion.

I next visited the Fort of Allyghur, taken by Lord Lake, in 1803. It is built of mud, faced with kankar, or limestone, of a square form, and surrounded by a very deep and broad fosse filled with water, and abounding in fish.

Within the gates nothing now remains of this chief stronghold of Sindiah but a few huts, and small bomb-proof magazines; the fortress having been stormed by the British troops under Lord Lake in 1803, and dismantled by Lord William Bentinck.

The church, built at the expence of a liberal and pious civilian, is very small and neat; near it is a monument erected to the memory of seven officers of H.M. 76th Foot, who were killed in action against the army of Sindiah. At no great distance are two low pillars, each encircled by a wall, in memory of two French officers, in the service of Dowlut Row Sindiah; and, close by, a faithful Mussulman Khidmutgar, or butler, lies interred beneath a flat stone. On one side of the church is a European burial ground, nearly covered over with tombs and pillars.

A few minutes' walk conducts the visitor to an enormously large gaol, in which all the culprits in the district of Allyghur, about 700 in number, were at this time confined.

The station appeared to be an exceedingly pleasant one; the bungalows to the north are surrounded with fine tropical trees, which give it a very cheerful appearance. During my stay here, my tent was pitched in an ancient Mahomedan burying ground.

On the 16th of April, I rode to Akbarabad fourteen miles and a half. The hot winds having now set in, and travelling in the day-time being almost insupportable, I started at eleven o'clock the same night, and arrived at Budwas, a distance of twenty miles at half-past-four o'clock on the morning of the 17th. On the 18th I rode to Naia Serai, twenty miles; and on Sunday, the 19th, to Korowlee, thirteen miles and one-eighth; on the 20th, to Bowgong, sixteen miles; on the 21st, to Chiberamow, twenty-one miles; on the 22nd, to Goorsaigunge, fourteen miles.

On the 23rd I rode to Meerun-ke-Serai, a distance of fourteen miles. On my arrival, I visited the ancient city of Kanoge, by diverging two miles from the main road, to my left. An old man of ninety years of age was my guide through the ruins, accompanied by his son apparently as aged as himself. The father's name was Oodee Ram. Kanoge is abbreviated from Kanyacubja.[65] It is a town of great antiquity and celebrity, in the Province of Agra, having been the capital of a powerful kingdom, at the time of the first invasion of the Mahomedans. It is situated on the west of the river Ganges, in Lat. 27° 5′ north, and Long. 79° 52′ east. The Ganges runs about two miles off, and, by means of a canal which makes a bend towards the town, the sacred stream is brought close to the citadel.

The town, at present, consists of only one street, but along an extent of six miles, the fragments of small pieces of brick earth, and the occasional vestiges of a building, point out the site of this ancient capital of Hindoostan. I may mention a peculiarity in the Hindoo buildings, that they are composed of very small bricks, worked in with a great portion of cement, which is harder, and requires more force to break it, than the bricks.

I here saw the tombs of two Mahomedan saints, who lie in state in two Mausolea on an elevation covered with trees. From the terrace which surrounds them I enjoyed a pleasant prospect over the plain, scattered with the ruins of temples and tombs; little images broken into fragments, are lying about in all directions under the trees. Ancient coins of an irregular shape are frequently found among the ruins; they are inscribed with Sanscrit characters, the original language of India, and, sometimes have the figure of a Hindoo deity on one side. We nowhere read of any one having ever collected these coins, much less of having translated the inscriptions upon them. Surely it would be worth the trouble to send some one to dig them up out of the heaps of rubbish which cover them. Coins are the books of antiquity, for the art of printing was not known even in Europe till about 400 years ago. The coins found in the Tope at Munnikala in the Punjaub, have led to the belief, that such structures as those at Kanoge were not raised by the natives of the country. It is true that the search for coins in that district has not always produced genuine ones, for the cupidity of the natives has led them to sell modern copies of ancient coins to Europeans not versed in the knowledge of these antique deposits; they see that they are of Bactrian origin, but cannot distinguish the true from the false coins. General Ventura, who opened the Tope, had the advantage of a first discovery, for spurious ones could not have been originally deposited there.

Kanoge, in the remotest times of Hindoo history, was a place of great renown, and the capital of the powerful kingdom of Hindoostan, which existed down to the period of the Mahomedan invasion, which is about coeval with that of England by William the Conqueror. The name Kanyacubja, has reference to a well-known story related in the Hindoo mythological poems. The language of Kanoge appears to have formed the ground-work of the modern Hindoostanee known also by the appellation of Hindee or Hindivee, it is a graft on the Sanscrit; the Oordoo is a mixture of Hindee and Persian. Oordoo means a camp, hence Oordoo is the Camp or Court language of Delhi and Lucknow, where it is spoken with the greatest purity. Kings formerly often lived in Camp with their troops.

The Rajahs of Kanoge are mentioned by Ferishta as early as 1008. The town was conquered, though not permanently retained, by Mahmood, of Ghuznee, A.D. 1018. The late Lieutenant-Colonel W. Francklin, Bengal army, in his "Enquiry into the Site of the Ancient Palibothra," calls it "Kennouj, or Kanycacubja." The learned Mr. Maurice, in his Indian Antiquities (p.

36), observes, of this city, that it was enclosed by walls fifty coss, or one hundred miles, in circumference; and, in page 42 of the same work, states, on the authority of the Ayeen Akbaree,[66] that, in the beginning of the sixth century, under the reign of Maldeo, it contained 30,000 shops where betel-nut was sold, and 60,000 bands[67] of singers and musicians, who paid a tax to government. The extent of the city might reasonably allow of a population of from two to three millions of souls. If these positions be admissible, we surely need not cavil at the extent of the city of Palibothra, as assigned to it in the Hindoo records. Colonel Francklin writes of Bisnagur (Beejanuggur), "of this city, Cæsar Frederic, a Venetian merchant, who was there in 1567, says, 'that it had a circuit of ninety-four miles, and that it contained within it a number of little hills and pagodas.'" Major Rennel, the well-known Surveyor-general of India, in his Dissertations, agrees with the Venetian, that these hills and pagodas were within the boundaries. Of course, there were many temples at Kanoge; and there seems to be no reason whatever for disbelieving the fact of its having been one hundred miles in circumference, or of there having been 4,000 souls to a square mile.

Now, let us take the city of Benares. The late Mr. James Prinsep,[68] between the years 1824 and 1827, found the population to be 183,491; or, 34,621 to the square mile. The census was taken under peculiar difficulties. Benares, or Kasi, is the most sacred Hindoo city in Hindoostan. In the late census, taken in 1848-49, the population was allowed to stand the same as when taken in 1824-27. The lapse of more than twenty years will give a great increase of population, even supposing that there had been an over-calculation.

Let us test the point by English statistics. In Middlesex[69] they quote 5,590 — 98 souls to a square mile. Now, if we say three millions for Kanoge, it will give about 4,800 souls to a square mile. Then it must be recollected, that the streets of Benares are so very narrow, that if one person enters a street at one end on an elephant, and another comes from the opposite end similarly mounted, neither can pass, but one must back out, which implies that the streets are not twenty feet wide. Besides which, the native houses in Benares are several stories high. It is a fact, that a great portion of the sickness of that city, as of others which I have seen, arises from the circumstance that the sun's rays never penetrate the street. Therefore, if Kanoge were peopled to anything like the extent even of Middlesex, we may believe the number of inhabitants to have been as great as suggested by Maurice. If the Venetian be correct, we may assert that, if Beejanuggur extended ninety-four miles, Kanoge, the most ancient Hindoo city of Hindoostan, was one hundred miles in circumference. It is to be borne in mind, that the population of the world, at the period referred to, was greater than in times before the

Christian era. Lord Lake had his head-quarters at Kanoge before his army took the field in 1803.

The late Lieut.-Colonel Thorn, in his Memoir of the War in India, 1803-6, says: "Kanoge, which modern writers suppose, though certainly on very problematical grounds, to be the site of the celebrated Palibothra;" but this will be noticed again when I speak of Allahabad, which some deem to be the identical site of Palibothra.

The 60,000 bands of singers and musicians is a more puzzling problem: because each band has never less than four persons; two girls and two men. Now, 2,500,000 divided by 60,000, gives a "natch" or dancing set to about every forty-two persons. It proves at least the musical taste of the Hindoos, and their fondness for singing and dancing in those days. We must, however, recollect that singing enters into their religion, and forms a necessary part of their sacred festivals. Again, if we take a brick house to contain six people, and a mud house four, there would be a band for every eight or nine families.

Kanoge is celebrated for its attar of roses, rose-water, and sweetmeats; of the last I purchased fifteen seers, or thirty lbs. for my servants, thus giving two lbs. to each man.

On the 24th of April, I rode twenty-three miles to Poorah; on the 25th, to Kullianpore, nineteen miles and three-quarters. My next stage was to Cawnpore, a distance of seven miles, where I put up at the Bungalow, next to the one I occupied when I was stationed at Cawnpore with my regiment last year. The change from my tent to a Bungalow was exceedingly agreeable, for latterly I had found it almost intolerable, on account of the dust and heat.

Cawnpore is a large military station, situated on the right bank of the Ganges, between Kanoge and Allahabad. The circumstance of its becoming a military station, was the result of a treaty with the Nawab of Oude, by which the British East India Company agreed to keep a Brigade at Cawnpore for the defence of the Nawab's dominions. It is about forty-nine miles from Lucknow, the capital of the King of Oude. About the year 1818, the Governor-General, the late Marquis of Hastings, suggested the title of King in lieu of that of Nawab. The Company, it seems, had borrowed money from his Highness, as he was then called, to pay the expences of the Nepaul war; and as the Nepaul frontier bordered on Oude, there appeared to be some tangible reason for asking for a part of the outlay. His Highness lent two "crores," or two millions sterling: one of which was afterwards repaid, and the other was partly absorbed in the kingly title.

The Nawab, as Vizier, had been the servant of the Emperor of Delhi; and at the time of which I am treating two of the Emperor's sons were living at Lucknow, and used to be supplied with money by the Nawab. Now the court etiquette was such, that whenever his highness met their royal highnesses, the princes of the blood of Delhi, his highness was constrained to make his elephants kneel down, if so mounted; which deportment was considered degrading in the presence of his liege subjects at Lucknow, and called for a remedy. It was therefore, intimated to the Nawab, that he and the Honourable Company might make an amicable agreement, by the government of India conferring upon him the title of Majesty.[70] The Nawab jumped at the proposal, and was dubbed "King and mighty Sovereign." Besides these advantages, he was not only raised in rank above the princes of the blood royal; but he was also king as well as the great Mogul, whose style was "Shahun Shah," or "King of Kings." The Emperor, however, was greatly incensed; what now was to be done? He complained that his income of ten lakhs, or £100,000, was not meet and sufficient to keep up his royal dignity;[71] whereupon the Company, in order to conciliate his majesty, at once raised his pension to £120,000 per annum. Money carries everything in the East, as it does for the most part in the West—it can do anything short of a miracle.

The investiture of the Nawab of Oude with regal dignity is, however, by no means incongruous. Mooltan, for instance, we find from old historians, covered an area of 3,273,932 beegahs, or 1,636,966 acres of measured lands; and again those of Oude were 2,796,206 beegahs, or 1,398,103 acres. Now, as there was formerly a king of Mooltan, the size of which is only 238,863 acres larger than Oude, there seems to be no reason why its ruler should not bear the style and title of King of Oude. Oude is estimated to be 250 miles in length, and 100 in breadth, from which it appears that it is as large as Scotland and much larger than Hanover.

His Majesty has disbanded his disorderly troops, and maintains two corps of Infantry, disciplined and appointed by British officers, stationed at Sultanpore and Seetapore. At Lucknow itself there is a Horse Field-battery and three battalions of East India Company's Sepoys. Visitors to Lucknow should go to the late General Martin's palace and the Dil-Khoosha. The Residency is situated two-and-a-half miles from the cantonments. There is a bridge over the Goomtee river, and an iron bridge near Dil-Khoosha. In the neighbourhood of Lucknow are many fine palaces, which well deserve two or three days' inspection.

At Cawnpore there are two companies of Artillery, a corps of Native Cavalry, a European regiment of Infantry, three corps of Native Infantry, and an Infantry recruiting depôt; whereas formerly, there used to be a troop of Horse Artillery, a regiment of British Dragoons, a corps of Queen's Foot, two companies of Artillery, a corps of Golundaz, a regiment of Native

Cavalry, and three regiments of Native Infantry. The cantonments are of great length and very straggling; the distance from the magazine to the end of the Native Artillery lines being seven miles. Looking from the river, the regiments used to stand thus:—The European Infantry on the left; next to which come the European Foot Artillery, then the Native Infantry; next the Dragoons and Native Cavalry, and, lastly, the Native Artillery. The civilians live chiefly at Nawabgunge, about two or three miles to the left of the cantonments. In the midst of the cantonments are the Church, the Theatre, and the Assembly Rooms, the latter consisting of two rooms parallel to each other and about 100 feet in length, where public meetings are held. Besides the church here spoken of, a neat little chapel was built close to their lines, for the use of the Dragoons, when they were stationed here.

There is an hotel at Cawnpore, kept by a Mr. Duhan, pleasantly situated on the banks of the river. It is a great convenience to travellers, but, owing to the want of sufficient patronage, it will, probably, be soon broken up. Not far from the hotel is the European burial ground, crowded as usual with pillars and slabs, marking out the last resting-place of beloved relatives and friends.

Cawnpore, although very hot and dusty, is, in my opinion, not an unhealthy station; for, during my stay there, from the 28th of April, 1844, to the 17th of October, 1845, I found that, with common prudence, a person might enjoy very tolerable health. There is a fine race-course, which used to afford an exciting amusement during the cold months. The officers' bungalows, pleasantly situated in large compounds,[72] surrounded by walls, are very comfortable. The one which I occupied, while stationed here, and for which I paid only £96 per annum rent, was, perhaps, rather adapted for a general officer than for a captain of Dragoons. The saddlery made at Cawnpore is celebrated throughout India, as particularly good; and the Native Cavalry are chiefly supplied with it. The extension of our frontier has, however, done no small injury to Cawnpore, for it will never again enjoy the large and important commerce which it used to possess. To continue my route:—

On the 30th of April, 1846, I rode to Sirsole, fourteen miles, and put up at the Dâk, or Stage Bungalow. These Dâk Bungalows are stationed along all the principal roads in India, at a distance of about fifteen or twenty miles apart, are a great comfort to the weary traveller; for, as there are few hotels on the route, he thankfully avails himself of such fare as these afford. Here he enjoys the luxury of a bath, accommodation, and attendance, for the trifling sum of 2s. per diem. The traveller must bring his own provisions, which the Dâk Khidmutgar will prepare à son goût. These establishments are under the control of the government post-masters. The word Dâk signifies post;

and the Inland Mail is transferred from one part of India to another not by railway and mail coaches, but by such conveyances as are best adapted for speed in different localities. Thus, in some districts camels are used; in others, horses; and, in others again, mail-carts; while the most ordinary method of transmission is by a runner, who carries the letter-bags, generally at the end of a bamboo pole poised over his shoulder, and shifts it upon those of another runner, who stands, waiting in readiness, at a distance of ten or twelve miles, and who, in his turn, transmits it to another, and so on, till the whole distance is accomplished. These Dâk post runners keep on at a regular speed of four or five miles an hour.

On the 1st of May I rode to Kullianpore, a distance of seventeen miles, and the next day to Futtehpore, sixteen miles. I was on the point of taking my customary ablution this morning, when my Bihishti, or water-carrier, discovered a deadly cobra de capella, partly concealed and asleep, under one of the earthen jars which I was just going to use. I felt very thankful for my escape.

Futtehpore is an extensive Mahomedan city; it is in a lamentable state, and the ruins of tombs, mosques, houses, and walls lie spread over a very large space. It has been a civil station since 1826; and it also contains a very large gaol.

On the third of May, I started for Arapore, a distance of sixteen miles, and proceeded the next morning to Lohunga seventeen miles off. I arrived at Kusseah on the 5th, after a ride of sixteen miles, and having rested till five o'clock in the afternoon, I commenced a long march, but halted for about half-an-hour at the Travellers' Bungalow at Koela, fifteen miles, to allay a burning thirst with some tea, and finally reached Berrill's Hotel at Allahabad at a quarter to one the next morning, being a distance of twenty-nine miles.

Thus I rode the whole way from Lahore to Allahabad, a distance of at least 704 miles in fifty-four days, including the nine days I halted.

FOOTNOTES:

[65] Kanya, a damsel, and cubja, a spinal curve.

[66] A work written by the command of Akbar. It contained a statement of the revenues of all the districts and towns, the amount of the troops, and the number under each commander.

[67] Tyfeeah, "a band," or set of Natch girls.

[68] Statistical Survey of Berar, p. 155, table xxx. Statistics, North-west Provinces. By A. Shakespear, Assistant Surveyor-General.

[69] Shakespear's Statistics, North-west Provinces of India, table ii. p. 172.

[70] Vide Oude, Parliamentary Papers.

[71] See Appendix XX.

[72] From Campaô, a Portuguese word, signifying an enclosure round a house, or bungalow.

CHAPTER XII

Allahabad—Pilgrimages—The River Jumna—Hurdwar—
Akbar—Allum II.—Fortifications—Inscriptions on
Column—Military Depôt—Lieut.-Colonel A. Abbott,
C.B.—Colonel Kyd discovers a Cave—Ancient
Palibothra—Arrian's Account—Megasthenes—Dr.
Adams—Heeren—Chundragupta—Patna—The
Sacred Rivers—Bhaugulpore—The Mandara Hill—The
Chundun—Palibothra—Rajmahal—Antiquity of Kanoge—
Allahabad—Extent of Asiatic Cities—Mahomedan
Invasion—Extent of Hindoostan.

The hotel at which I took up my residence at Allahabad, was very pleasantly situated: my rooms faced the Jumna, whose clear blue water was most refreshing to the eye, the hotel standing on the right bank of that noble stream.

Allahabad, which literally means the "Abode or City of God," is by the Brahmins called Bhat Prayag, or by way of distinction it is designated as "Prayaga," also "Praag," or "Prayagas," or "sacred confluence of rivers."[73] The River Jumna takes its name from Yumna, which in Sanscrit means, meeting, or confluence. Some of the religious ceremonies enjoined upon the Hindoo pilgrims must be performed in a vast subterranean cave, which is situated in the middle of the Fort—it is supported by pillars, and is believed by the vulgar to extend under ground as far as Benares, a distance of fifty-three miles, and to be infested by snakes and poisonous reptiles—granting the cave really to extend thus far, who could possibly live to go through to its termination!

Allahabad is one of the most celebrated places of Hindoo pilgrimage, and the deluded devotees come here by thousands to wash in the sister streams to purify themselves, or to carry some of the precious water to their distant homes. Nay, many annually drown themselves at this celebrated junction of the Ganges and the Jumna; they are conducted into the middle of the stream in a boat, and then sunk by having earthen pots tied to their feet. This reckless sacrifice of life would no doubt have sooner been put a stop to, had not the native governments derived considerable advantage from it, for they used even to levy a tax upon the pilgrims for the privilege of bathing in the sacred stream. The debates in the East India house regarding the tax levied at Juggernauth led to a change in the system; and it has since been abolished.

Allahabad and Hurdwar are the two most noted places of pilgrimage. At the latter city a fair is held annually where thousands of people go to bathe, and although the river Ganges, is very shallow there, many lose their lives. The great fair is held every twelfth year, when several companies of sepoys are generally present both to keep the peace and to prevent accidents. About thirty years since, innumerable lives were lost by the sudden rush of pilgrims down the great ghât leading into the river. Hence the troops have special charge to hinder any large number of persons from congregating together.

Akbar was very partial to Allahabad and founded the modern city, intending it as a stronghold to overawe the surrounding country, for which it was extremely well adapted by its natural position. This enterprising emperor also built Agra, which he styled Akbarabad. Allahabad was taken in 1765, by the British army, under Sir Robert Fletcher; soon after which (1766) the Nawab of Oude, to whom it belonged, having been defeated at Buxar, and in subsequent battles, assigned it by treaty to the East India company.

The Emperor of Delhi, Allum II., who was then a fugitive, had joined the Nawab, and, together with him, made his peace with the British. He was placed under their protection; and they agreed to allow him twenty-six lakhs, or £260,000, per annum. Upon receiving in perpetuity the revenues of Bengal, Bahar, and Orissa, it was agreed that the royal share of those revenues, twenty-six lakhs of rupees, should be annually paid to him by the Company; but when he accepted the aid of the Maharattas to replace him on the throne of Delhi, he was informed that the tribute of those provinces would be no longer granted to him. Mill, vol. iii. p. 579, says:—"The discredit of this transaction belongs to the Directors of the East India Company." It must however, be borne in mind that the Government strongly advised the Emperor not to go to Delhi.

The Emperor of Delhi resided, under the guardianship of the English, in the Fort of Allahabad until the year 1771. In 1765, an imperial grant was issued, constituting the East India Company Dewanny, or receivers of revenue, of Bengal, Bahar, and Orissa, which grant gave the Government the virtual sovereignty of these countries. The Dewanny yielded about two millions sterling a year. The Emperor also confirmed the English in all the titles conveyed to them by the Subahdar, or Viceroy, of Bengal, whose successor is now Nawab only of Moorshedabad.

The city of Allahabad does not present a very striking appearance, as there are only a few brick buildings without any kind of ornament. The fort is placed at some distance, on a tongue of land, the one side being washed by the blue waters of the Jumna, and the other nearly approaching the dull yellow stream of the Ganges. It is lofty and extensive, and completely commands the navigation of the two rivers. Both the river fronts are defended by the old walls, with the addition of some cannon and semi-circular bastions; the third side, near the main land is regular and very strong; it has three ravelines, two bastions, and a half-bastion, and stands higher than any ground in front of it. The gateway is Grecian, and very elegant.

In the centre of the fort rises an ancient granite column, thirty-six feet high, with Pali and Sanscrit inscriptions. The Sanscrit is almost obliterated; it gives the genealogy of Akbar, and states that the column was erected by him. The British have added a third inscription, giving the date of its transfer to them in 1765, and its final cession in 1801, together with the province. In the same line with the fort is another building, which has been modernized and converted into barracks for the garrison staff sergeants. The sums expended upon the fortifications, up to 1803, were something quite enormous, and are said to have amounted to more than twelve lakhs. They have now been rendered quite impregnable against the attacks of a native enemy; and even by a European force its capture would be a matter of no small difficulty.

Allahabad was at one time the grand military depôt of the upper provinces. During the Sikh war of 1848-49, the principal commissary of ordnance was located there, and most of the contents of the arsenal in Fort William, Calcutta, were transferred to Allahabad.[74] The present principal commissary is Lieut.-Colonel A. Abbott, C.B., of the Artillery, distinguished for his services at Bhurtpore, in Affghanistan, and at Jellalabad. The following anecdote will serve to exhibit his energy and promptitude under difficulties. In October, 1848, it was found that the store of musket-ball ammunition at Ferozepore, etc., was damaged; upon which application was made to Colonel Abbott for a fresh supply. By relays of bullocks, he managed daily to send up 100,000 rounds, which reached Umballa, a distance of 529 miles, in fourteen days. He continued this until he was informed that no more were required. This trait of zeal in the public service is given, not only as an instance of the expeditious mode of forwarding supplies, but as an act of justice to Lieutenant-Colonel Abbott, and as shewing the importance of placing in such a post of difficulty, an officer who has seen a great deal of hard service.

There is a place for the manufacture of gunpowder at Papamow, between two and three miles from the cantonments; also another at Isharpore, near Barrackpore. At these two depôts all the Company's gunpowder is made, and a two-years' supply is generally kept in store. The cantonments of Allahabad are about three miles from the fort, and appear very comfortable.

I may here mention an interesting discovery made by Colonel Kyd, of the Engineers, during the restoration of the fort. While forming the glacis, he discovered a cave, which contained a number of images belonging to the tribe of Serawagy, of the sect of the Jains, which were soon after claimed by some persons, who asserted that they had been deposited there by their ancestors, during the persecution of the Hindoos by Aurungzebe in 1680. In the entrance of the cave is a sacred tree, which is said to have flourished there from time immemorial, and is held in great veneration by the Hindoos. There is also a tank of water, which is in high repute among the pilgrims.

The English church is a very neat building, with a light and handsome spire. The rides in the vicinity are numerous and pleasant; and the roads, which extend in various directions for thirty miles, skirted with trees of abundant foliage, are excellent. Indeed there is no other station in the Bengal Presidency which contains so many good roads. They are made by the prisoners, of whom, unhappily, there are always a great number in the Allahabad gaol. It is said, that the allowance of food is so liberal in the gaol, that some contrive to gain admittance there, as into a comfortable asylum; however they are made to work pretty hard, and the government sells the produce of their labours. It has been remarked of Sydney, that if no convicts had been sent thither, there never would have been a road two miles long. The same may be said with equal truth of Allahabad.

The troops now stationed at Allahabad, are a Company of Native Foot Artillery, two regiments of Native Infantry, and a depôt for H.M. regiments of Foot, under the command of a Lieut.-Colonel. Formerly there were two companies of European Artillery in the fort, of which a general officer was always in command. In 1817, just before the Maharatta war, a European Flank Battalion, composed of companies of royal regiments, was quartered in the fortress. At this time a circumstance occurred which created great alarm; for one evening, whilst the officers of the Flankers were at mess, several of them were suddenly taken ill. The cholera had been known in India in 1781 and 1783, but not since; so that it was concluded to be an attack of that fearful and fatal contagion. Upon investigation, however, it appeared that the cooking pots, which it was customary to have fresh tinned every twenty or twenty-five days, were not clean. Many thought it was a premeditated attempt at poisoning; hence it is necessary in India, more particularly on the line of march, to "look before you cook."

Before quitting Allahabad, I must redeem my promise of laying before the reader some statements confirmatory of my view, that the ancient city of Palibothra was the site of Allahabad, and not, as some suppose, Kanoge.

There are many theories in existence respecting the site of ancient Palibothra. Some of them are so improbable as to be unworthy of notice; but others, propounded by learned and ingenious writers, may fairly claim consideration in this place. Before I enter upon the examination of these it will be proper to state such information, with regard to position and other circumstances, as we may gain from early historians.

In the first place we have the statement of Strabo (lib. xv.), that Palibothra was situated at the confluence of the Ganges with another river; but he does not mention the name. Arrian says:[75] "The capital city of India is Palimbothra, in the confines of the Prasii (or Prachi of Sanscrit writers) nigh the confluence of the two great rivers, Erannoboas and Ganges. Erannoboas is reckoned the third river throughout all India, and is inferior to none but the Indus and Ganges, into the last of which it enters." He further states: "Of the two great rivers of India, the Ganges and the Indus, Megasthenes assures us that the first is by far the largest, for it arises great from its very fountains, and receives many great rivers; namely Cainas, Erannoboas, Cassoanes (Coosah?) Sonus,[76] Sitocatis and Solomatis. All these are navigable; and, besides these, the Condochates, Sambus, Magones, Agoranis, and Omalis."

To determine which is this said third river of India, we must premise that the Berhampooter was not known to Alexander the Great, or his successors, nor was it known in Europe until A.D. 1765.

Megasthenes states also "that the length of this city is eighty furlongs, the breadth fifteen, that it is surrounded with a ditch thirty cubits deep, and occupying six acres of ground, the walls being defended with 570 towers and six gates."

Such is the evidence furnished on this subject by early writers, and the question resulting from it is, which of the many rivers flowing into the Ganges are we to consider the third river in India, at the confluence of which Palibothra was situated? It does not appear that Megasthenes has given the rivers in the order of their size; for he omits all mention of some of the largest, and the first river he speaks of, the Cainas, is certainly smaller than the fourth on his list, the Sonus. The only rivers, of any consequence, entering the Ganges on the right bank, are the Jumna and the Sone, of which the former is by far the more considerable.

A very current opinion, entertained and supported by several respectable writers, makes the modern Patna to be the site of the ancient city. Thus Dr. A. Adams[77] says:—"Patna, the capital of Bahar, built along the south bank of the Ganges, an extensive and populous city, supposed to be the ancient Palibothra." Heeren also says: "Palibothra must be sought in, or near the modern town of Patna, where its ancient appellation still survives in the name of a certain district called Patalputhra." Major Rennel also in some places affirms his opinion to be decidedly in favour of Patna, and in others speaks doubtingly to the same purpose,—"S'il est vrai que Palibothra ait été située où est aujourd'hui Patna, et les dernières découvertes rendent cette opinion probable."

Now Patna is situated near the confluence of the Sonus with the Ganges, in a very favourable position for a city of importance: and it appears to be pretty certain that it is the site of a very ancient city, but not that of the city of Palibothra. We must recollect that there is an Upper and Lower Ganges, the latter of which would be below Patna. Now, though the ancient kingdom of Maghada included Patna, it is not probable that there was a capital so low down. Heeren declares that the empire of the Prasii extended beyond the junction of the Jumna with the Ganges, and we may infer from this that the said junction was not much short of the limits of the empire. And, speaking of particular towns, he names Ayodhya, Kanoge, and others. Also mentioning Pataliputra (Patna) the same author says: "The scene of these fables (Hitopadesah, or Pilpay) is laid in the city of Pataliputra, by no means the most ancient in India."

Arrian tells us that Palibothra was in the confines of the Prasii. But Pataliputra was the capital of King Chundragupta, who reigned long before the kingdom of the Prasii was established. Heeren[79] says: "Compare the accounts of Chundragupta given by Wilford in the 'Asiatic Review, vol. v. p. 264.'" In the list of kings arranged by Sir William Jones[80] the reign of Nauda is placed in 1602, and of Chundragupta in 1502 B.C.; the latter, therefore, must have lived 1200 years before Sandrocottus. Will any one pretend that there was another Chundragupta?

Arrian tells us simply that the city of Palibothra is in the confines of the Prasii: he does not say that it had been thus distinguished as the capital of Chundragupta, which he would no doubt have done if the fact had been so, and the very antiquity of Chundragupta destroys the possibility of his capital being Palibothra, which was built so many years after. We conclude, therefore, that Patna, as is generally allowed, is the site of the ancient Pataliputra, the capital of Chundragupta; and that it is not the same as Palibothra, but a much more ancient city.

It has been stated by some, that Pataliputra and Palibothra are one and the same place, and that the latter name is simply a corruption of the former. But Buchanan well remarks on this subject,[81] "This city (Patna) is indeed allowed by the Pundits to be called Pataliputra; but Pataliputra has no great resemblance to Palibothra; nor can Patali be rationally considered as a word of the same origin as Pali, said to be an ancient name of this country, and of its people and language." There is no doubt that the use of the word Pali, in this connection, is derived from the Pali language of the Buddhists, who have a temple at Gya.

And further, as to the derivation of this name, we read that a Brahmin, having married Bhoom Deo (the earth-god), had two sons, one of whom, Bukshun, married Soormut, and had a son called Pootur (or son), who married Patlee, the daughter of the king of the Singhaldees. In the case of Hindoos, the men do not take their fathers' names. Supposing that these joined their names, we have Pootur-patlee, which will not answer, because the young man calls himself Patlee-pootur, taking the wife's name, which is contrary to Hindoo usage. The story states further, that Patlee-pootur planted his staff, and a beautiful city sprang out of the ground, which in honour of his wife he called Patleepoora, or Patleepooturpoora, a name truly royal in its length! The pair died, leaving a son called Puttum, and a daughter named Putnie, from whom the modern name Patna is said to have been derived. In the absence of more definite evidence we may rest a strong presumption on these traditions, and whatever part of them we may accept or reject, they certainly contain some amount of historical evidence to prove that Pataliputra must not be confounded with Palibothra.

In the eleventh century a play is supposed to have been written, the Mudra Rakshasha, the principal scenes in which are laid at Pataliputra, the capital of Chundragupta. Buchanan[82] says, that other traditions preserved in the Skund Poorana derive the name of Patna from the Sanscrit word meaning a cloth; from the circumstance of the goddess Parbuttee having dropt her mantle on the spot, in her flight to Kylas (the sky).

So much with respect to the derivation of the names Patna and Pataliputra. From what has been stated, it may be clearly seen that Palibothra cannot be a corruption or modification of Pataliputra, and that the modern name of Patna is traceable to a very remote period.

To proceed with the proof that Patna is not the ancient Palibothra:—An opinion has been expressed by one who appears to be a competent judge, Mr. E.C. Ravenshaw,[83] that the distance from Patna at which the Sone now runs into the Ganges is so great that it cannot be said to be at the point of confluence, and therefore does not answer to Arrian's description as before quoted.

But a better argument is this,—that the river Sone has no particular sanctity attached to it by the Hindoos; it does not convey sacred water to the district of Patna, such as is supposed to flow in the Ganges, and many other Indian rivers. We know that the most sacred streams issue from the Himalaya mountains, the region of the gods and of Brahma. The Ganges, the Indus, the Jumna, the Gograh, the Coosah, the Gundruk, and others, come from that holy source; but the Sone and the Nerbudda rise in the table-land of Omerkuntuc in Gundwana,—in lat. 22°, 35′ N.; long. 82°, 15′ E.[84] Now it is very certain that the Sone, lacking this sacred character, could not have been reckoned as the third river in India; superior to many streams which take their rise from the Himalaya, and inferior only to the Ganges and the Indus, both of which are regarded with the deepest reverence.

Thus, with regard to Patna, we are led to the conclusion, that, while there is great evidence to prove that it is a most ancient city, and to identify it with the former Pataliputra, the capital of the Gupta dynasty; yet it is quite as clear that it is not the site of Palibothra.

Another opinion, however, would place the ancient city further east, and not far from Bhaugulpore.[85] The late Colonel Francklin took a journey on purpose to examine this subject, and in his preface to the second part of his researches respecting the site of Palibothra, he writes:—"If then my assumption of the Mandara hill as the place recorded in the Puranas,[86] where one of the sovereigns of Palibothra was assassinated, be correct;— if the evidence afforded by the hills which appear in the neighbourhood of the town, and through a very great extent of what formerly constituted the Prasian kingdom, prior to the expedition of Alexander the Great;—if these and other connecting circumstances, as well local and historical, as traditional, be conceded;—it will, I think, be also conceded to me, that they apply in every instance throughout the discussion, as more naturally indicative of the town of Bhaugulpore possessing the site of Palibothra, and the metropolis of the Parsii (Prasii?) than either Rajmahal, Patna, Kanoge, or Allahabad."

The argument drawn from the assassination of this king of Palibothra on the Mandara hill, is really worth nothing. The circumstance that this took place near Bhaugulpore no more proves the site of Palibothra to have been there, than if the sovereign had been assassinated at any other of the places named. For if kings travel, particularly among enemies, and in times of anarchy, they are liable to be killed anywhere. Our first Richard was assassinated in Normandy, and our first Edward had a narrow escape in the Holy Land. Moreover, this murdered king of Palibothra might have been taken to the Mandara hill as a fitting place of execution; so that we can gather from this occurrence no clue whatever, to the actual site of his capital city.

Again, there is no large river flowing into the Ganges at the point where Bhaugulpore is situated. Colonel Francklin states that at Dhurumgunge, five miles N.W. of Bhaugulpore he met with the river Chundun, but the confluence of the Chundun with the Ganges is at Champanuggur, thirteen miles from that town. He assumes this river to have been the Erannoboas of the Greeks; and, because it is to be found thirteen miles from Bhaugulpore and runs into the Ganges, he fixes the Mandara hill as the site of Palibothra. At the end of his journal, he adds, that, "in the words of Arrian, the Erannoboas was a river of the third magnitude among the rivers in India." But here the Colonel mistakes the meaning of his author; for Arrian says, not that it was a river of the third magnitude, but the third river throughout all India. It is thus that historical authority is sometimes falsely cited. The Chundun, even near its mouth, is only seven hundred yards in breadth, and this will not constitute a third-rate river in India. The Gograh, on the left bank, is in some places a mile broad, in many places half-a-mile, and of greater depth even than the Ganges. The Chundun is so inconsiderable, that we hear of no natives, except those of Bhaugulpore, who speak of it at all; and to identify this with a river said to be next in size to the Indus, is plainly absurd.

In a subsequent tour, the Colonel again visited Bhaugulpore, and about four miles south-east of that town, he found a commanding eminence, being 600 yards in circumference, and on which the site of bastions and the outer ditch of a fortification are plainly to be discovered. "The place," he says,[87] "is called by the natives Suffiegur; and here the surface of the ground in the front, as well as the neighbouring grove of mango trees, is overspread with a variety of stones of different kinds, cornelians, agates, flints, and specimens of beautiful veined stone, pieces of crystal and slabs of chalcedony; these evidently indicating the remains of a building of a superior order, at a remote period of time."

The Colonel again remarks—"In my humble opinion, I should assign it as one of the summer palaces of the sovereigns of Palibothra." But since, in that country, ruins are so numerous, and frequently of such a splendid character, we cannot allow this circumstance to be of any weight. Any other hill containing a few stones, and a few relics of ancient fortifications, might, as far as Colonel Francklin has given proof, have been the summer residence of the kings of Palibothra. There are two very singular round towers near the town of Bhaugulpore, in the direction indicated by the Colonel, which he may possibly have mistaken for the summer palace of the king.

We cannot suppose that if Bhaugulpore had been the ancient Palibothra, it would not have been revered as a sacred spot, even though it were in ruins. Kanoge, for example, although no longer in existence, is spoken of with veneration. But it does not appear that any particular sanctity is attached by the natives to Bhaugulpore, nor that they esteem it as more than a common city. And, if it had been what Colonel Francklin claims for it, it would, of course, have been the capital of the Prasii. But we have no evidence whatever that the kingdom of the Prasii extended so far south; and supposing that it did, still it is most improbable that their chief city would be placed at the extremity of their dominions. If the Colonel's opinion were correct, would not Abul Fazel, who wrote in 1582, or some Hindoo writer of prior or subsequent date, have spoken of such a place? Would there not be a pilgrimage to it, as there is now to Allahabad, and other sacred places? Without doubt, such would have been the case; and therefore, taking all these things into consideration, it appears to me that we must reject Colonel Francklin's favourite theory, and that Bhaugulpore could not have been Palibothra.

Another opinion places the site of the lost city at Benares. This is no doubt also an ancient town; it was taken by the Sultan Mahmood of Ghuznee in A.D. 1017, and a mosque with two elegant minarets existing to this day, was built there by Aurungzebe to mortify the Hindoos. The river Birnah runs between the military cantonments and the civil station, across which a small stone bridge was thrown, about fifty years ago, by the late Major-General J. Garstin. This river is situated to the left of the city, where it enters the Ganges. It is a very narrow and inconsiderable stream, and could not bring Benares within the denomination of "a city with two large rivers;" so that we may dismiss this opinion also, as quite improbable.

Rajmahal has likewise been mentioned, as the place where the ancient city stood. But this is at a considerable distance below Patna, and it is not likely that the limits of the Prasii extended so far in this direction. A hundred years ago, Rajmahal was two or three miles inland; and though, by the encroachment of the current upon the land, it is now situated on the bank of the river, yet there is no other river near it, it does not stand at the confluence of any stream with the Ganges, and therefore does not answer to Arrian's description.

Of the opinions on this subject, which I deem erroneous, the only other worthy of mention is that which makes Kanoge the site of Palibothra. This is also a very ancient city, as is clear from the fact that Vicramaditya,[88] who lived in the year B.C. 57, resided alternately at Palibothra and at Kanoge. It is stated by Heeren to have been founded by one of the kings of Ayodhya (Oude) who made it his capital. On the decline of Ayodhya, it rose in importance. Maurice[90] dates its foundation in B.C. 1000. But while we may respect the antiquity of Kanoge, we cannot assign to it the honour claimed for it. The rivers Ramgonga and Gurrah, whose united waters flow into the Ganges near its ruins, are very inconsiderable, and could not by any stretch of the imagination be looked upon as constituting the third river in India.

But now, having, as I hope, clearly shown the great improbability that any of the opinions already quoted are correct, and having proved also, how irreconcilable they are to the historical evidence which we possess on this subject, I will mention my own opinion as to the site of the ancient city of Palibothra. According to Arrian, as we have seen, Palibothra is at the confluence of the Ganges and Erannoboas, which Erannoboas is said to be the third river in India. Now the Ganges is called the first, the Indus the second, and in respect of size, no other river has so great a claim to be ranked the third, as the Jumna. After the two streams just mentioned, the Jumna is certainly the largest in the country. This river and the Ganges may be termed twin-sisters, as their respective sources are within a few miles of each other. Its length is 780 miles, according to Rennel, exceeding by 280 miles that of the Sone.

Coming down to the point at which the Jumna flows into the Ganges, we find the city of Allahabad. And here I would place the site of Palibothra. Its centrical position as to Hindoostan, marks it as being most fitting and convenient for the capital of a kingdom. It is certain also that it was inhabited by the Prasii, and it was most probably in the very centre of their dominions.

The great sanctity of the confluence of the Ganges and the Jumna at Allahabad, as an annual bathing-place, revered by all Hindoos, is well known. The very fact of their being two great rivers, the first and the third in magnitude, would give it a sacredness not attachable to inferior rivers. The second river, the Indus, falls into no other stream. It is joined by the Cabool river at Attock, and after receiving the Punjaub rivers, empties itself into the sea. And the fact that the two greatest rivers are not confluent, tends, no doubt, to add to the high veneration with which the natives regard the confluence of the first and third rivers.

Several of the streams flowing into the Ganges which have been adopted by controversialists, are in reality very insignificant, and are considered by the natives as quite unimportant. But the Jumna is universally known and venerated throughout all India. When water is taken from the Ganges, to a distance, it is invariably either from Hurdwar, Allahabad, or Benares.

The late Maharajah Runjeet Singh always had water from a particular spot, which was considered the best in the Punjaub. A strict Brahmin of Benares, would present his guests with water drawn from the most sacred parts of the Ganges, nor, however hot the weather, would he cool the water with ice, for by so doing, he would mix two waters, the one holy, the other profane: the water of the Ganges, and the water of America.

No native would ever take the Ganges water from near the Chundun; no Brahmin living in Calcutta would ever use it. Allahabad is held in such reverence that a public tax was paid both to the Mahomedan government of the Nawab of Oude, and to the British government, by pilgrims at certain seasons of the year. There are different degrees of sanctity ascribed to the sacred cities of India; all places are not of equal sanctity, Benares is not so sacred as Kanoge, and neither is so sacred as Allahabad. The waters of the Ganges at this confluence are accounted of superior holiness, and special virtue is ascribed to them.

Here then, the description of Arrian, to which I have shown that none of the before-mentioned opinions conformed, is fully answered, and all probability points to Allahabad as the disputed site. The central situation of the city, its position on the right bank of the Ganges, the circumstance of its superior sacredness, and above all, the fact that the Jumna is the third river in India, which no one, who will compare the relative claims of the rivers, can deny; all these together yield more than presumptive proof in its favour. We may fairly conclude then, that the ancient Palibothra is at the junction of the Ganges and the Jumna, and that there appears no just ground for supposing that any other position on the right or left bank of the Ganges can be assigned as its site.

It may now be of interest to state what is known respecting the size of the city. Strabo informs us[91] that "its length is eighty stadia, its breadth fifteen,[92] and its form oblong; that it is environed by a wall of wood, in which are sundry holes to shoot through; also a ditch, both for the defence of the city and the reception of all the filth issuing from it; and that the people are called Prasii." In an appendix to his work, Francklin gives additional notes, extracted from a pamphlet which was printed, but not published, at Calcutta, wherein he says: "For the extent of the city and suburbs of Palibothra, from seventy-five to eighty miles have been assigned, by the Puranas, a distance said to be impossible for a single city." And adds: "so indeed it might, were we to compare the cities of Asia with those of Europe." He next states, that in A.D. 1567, Cæsar Frederic, a Venetian merchant, who was then at Beejanuggur (Bisnuggur), says that it had a circuit of ninety-four miles. Major Rennel makes the city of Gour, the ancient capital of Bengal, to be fifteen miles in length, extending along the old banks of the Ganges, and from two to three miles in breadth. Colonel Francklin (Appendix p. 59) quotes Babylon[93] as extending over 365 furlongs, being the number of days in the year; or forty-five miles and five furlongs. Herodotus allows the city to have been 480 stadia, or sixty miles in circumference.[94] Colonel

Francklin makes Kanoge to have been 100 miles in circuit. London, the largest city in Europe, has been estimated at twenty-five, but at present, with the suburbs, it may be thirty miles round. Now it must be recollected, that in estimating the size of European and Asiatic cities, several distinguishing circumstances are to be borne in mind. For instance, though in London there are numerous churches, they occupy but little space, compared with pagodas, mosques, and mausolea; to which in an Eastern city, much ground and many buildings are usually attached. In Oriental cities too, there are many gardens and granaries, and the stables and studs for elephants occupy a great deal of room. It is calculated that the stabling for one elephant, occupies more space than would afford accommodation for a carriage and four horses.

The Mahomedan invasion of India, which effected so great a change in the character of the country, took place in the first quarter of the eleventh century. The Mahomedan empire was founded there by the Ghorè dynasty in 1157. I may fitly close my remarks on the site of this ancient city, by glancing at the geographical extent and condition of the country at this great era of a mighty change in Indian history. It is said by Rennel and other writers, that according to the testimony of the ancients, India, on the most enlarged scale, divided on the West from Persia by the Arachosian Mountains, bounded on the East by China, on the North by Tartary, and extending South to the Sunda Isles, comprised an area of 40°, including a superficies almost as large as Europe: a statement which appears preposterous. The Mahomedan writers understood Hindoostan, under the sovereigns of Delhi, to include the twelve Soobahs or Provinces into which it was sub-divided in 1582; viz., Lahore, Mooltan, Scinde, Ajmere, Delhi, Agra, Allahabad, Bahar, Oude, Bengal, Malwah, Guzerat; Cabool, and the country west of India, was made a thirteenth Soobah, and again others were added: namely, the Deccan, including Berar, Khandeish, and Ahmednuggur, and afterwards Aurungabad.

According to the geography of the original Hindoos, Hindoostan is bounded on the North by the Himalaya ridge of mountains, including Cashmere, Nepaul, and Bootan; on the South by the Ocean; on the West by the Indus; and on the East by Chittagong. With the exception of Bootan, the primitive Brahminical religion and languages prevail in the above boundaries; nor are they to be found beyond them, save in Assam and Cassey, where Brahminical doctrines still prevail; but in Bootan the people are Buddhists.

The modern name Hindoostan, is a Persian appellation, derived from the word "Hindoo" (black), and "Sthan" (a place). The above limits give 1,020,000 geographical miles. Elphinstone[95] says, "India is bounded by the Himalaya mountains, the river Indus, and the sea. Its length from Cashmere to Cape Comorin is about 1,900 British miles,[96] and its breadth, from the mouth of the Indus to the mountains east of the Berhampooter, is considerably above 1,500 British miles. In its southern boundary it is limited by the Nerbudda."

According to the Hindoo calculation, India extends northward to the thirty-fifth degree of latitude. Cabool, which was included by Akbar in Hindoostan, is reckoned between the thirty-third and thirty-fifth degrees of north latitude. But Hindoostan is bounded on the West by the river Indus, which excludes Cabool and Scinde. Sylhet, and Chittagong are to the East of the Berhampooter, near the mountains, and must be included. The southern boundary is the sea.

FOOTNOTES:

[73] The late Bishop of Lichfield and Coventry, Dr. Samuel Butler, in his Ancient and Modern Geography, p. 267, called it also Helabas. In India some speak of it as "Illahabas."

[74] There is a magazine at Chunar, which serves for Benares and the stations immediately below it. The river from Chunar to Allahabad is not suited for a speedy transmission by boats, because the stream for about thirty miles below Allahabad is full of shoals.

[75] Rooke's Translation of Alexander's Expedition.

[76] Sanscrit, the Sone or Golden River.

[77] Ancient and Modern Geography, p. 522.

[79] note 1.

[80] Works, vol. i. p. 306.

[81] Vol. i. p. 26.

[82] Vol. i. p. 146.

[83] Journal of Asiatic Society. Vol. xiv. p. 137. Part I, Nos. 157-162.

[84] Hamilton's Gazetteer, Rennel, &c.

[85] Wilford, Asiatic Researches. Vol. v. p. 272.

[86] Elphinstone, in his history of India, says: "There are eighteen Puranas composed by different authors between the 8th and 16th centuries." Col. Francklin should have proved his author, and given his date.

[87] Part iv. p. 53.

[88] He was also Lord of Benares, and rebuilt Ayodhya.

[90] Vol. i. p. 36.

[91] Lib. xv. p. 1028.

[92] The eighty stadia long by fifteen broad, would be equal to twenty-three miles and three quarters in circuit.

[93] Diodorus Siculus, vol i. pp. 120, 121.

[94] Francklin (Appendix p. 62.) gives Beejapore as thirty-six miles in circuit, and Nineveh as forty-seven miles. Diodorus Siculus makes Nineveh to have been sixty miles and Babylon only forty-eight.

[95] Vol. i. p. 1.

[96] China has 1,200,000 square miles, and is said to be 1,400 by 1,600 miles.

CHAPTER XIII

Steamers on the Ganges—Native Pilots—Course of the
River—Mr. Sims proposes Shields to the Banks—Shoals—
Tributary Streams—Rapids—The Jumna—Mirzapore—
Benares—Trimbuckjee Danglia—Chunar—Sultanpore.

There is a regular steam communication between Calcutta and
Allahabad; but as the steamers proceed no further than that city, it may
not be out of place to give the reader a few words on Steam Navigation,
at least so far as the Ganges is concerned. Until steamers were introduced,
the only way of proceeding by water from Calcutta to Allahabad, and
the intermediate stations, was by boats, the largest of which are called
budgerows and pinnaces. About twenty years ago, the East India Company
ordered four steamers to be built for the navigation of the Ganges, much
against the advice of many, who urged the impossibility of using steam in
consequence of the shifting sands. They were accordingly built in England,
and shipped in pieces to Calcutta, where they were put together by able
engineers. For many years these government boats were the only steamers
seen on the Ganges; but latterly two Companies have been started, the
one called "the India General Steam Navigation Company," established in
1844, and the other, "the Ganges Company." The control of the government
steamers is under the judicious management of Captain J.H. Johnston, R.N.
The number of boats on the Ganges belonging to government alone, is as
follows:—ten steamers, three accommodation, three cargo, and two troop-
boats. On an average, one steamer leaves Calcutta every ten or fourteen
days, having an accommodation-boat, or sometimes one or two cargo or
troop-boats, in tow. This is a striking and novel sight. Every one is aware
that a ship at sea will take another in tow, which is effected by the ship
to be towed sending out hawsers; but in very bad weather they disengage
themselves by casting off the towing-hawsers. Besides these hawsers for
joining one with the other, there is a plank of wood, twenty-five feet in
length, a foot in width, and six inches in thickness, placed between two
short masts, one at the bow of the accommodation, cargo or troop-boat, the
other at the stern of the steamer, to each of which it is bound by chains.
This plank serves as a mutual convenience to the crews of the two vessels,
without its being requisite to lower a boat; besides, if it were not for this
more solid material, accidents would frequently happen by the vessel in

tow running foul of her leader; whereas, as it is, should the steamer touch ground unexpectedly, the other sheers quietly alongside.

The steamers are of iron, and (I am now speaking only of those belonging to government) are fitted up with two engines of thirty horse power each, and carry sail. The fires are never wholly extinguished, for although the steamers anchor at sunset, yet they are again under steam at the first dawn of day. The fares and prices of the two Companies correspond exactly with those of the government; the charges for the whole trip from Calcutta to Allahabad, being for a first-class cabin, 300 rupees, for a second, 250, and for a third, 200. The charges for the downward passage are only two-thirds those of the upward.

The hours for meals are generally, breakfast at nine, luncheon twelve, dinner four, and tea seven. Anything required between meals, is charged extra. For supplying these, each passenger pays the Commander three rupees per diem. Wines, spirits, etc., are extra, and charged for according to the consumption.

The boats of the two private Companies are differently constructed from those of the Government; for, like the steamers on the American rivers, the steam and accommodation centre in one boat, but some of them, have one or two cargo-boats in tow. The Ganges boats, it is said, draw too much water. The Company's boats draw three feet, and their steamers three-and-a-quarter feet each. Hindoo servants, who are forbidden by caste to cook on board, are landed every evening, if practicable, as soon as the steamer casts anchor. From the Mahomedan servants, one of whom is allowed to each passenger, without cost for the trip, the Commander receives a quarter of a rupee a-day, which each has to pay for his food.

A native pilot is taken on board every twenty or twenty-five miles; he is responsible in some measure, that the vessel does not touch the bottom, or run upon a sand-bank. The poor men, who receive only a scanty pittance for this trouble, are extremely careful; and it is very rare indeed, for any serious accident or interruption to occur. The steamers have a commander, a mate, and about twenty Lascars, or native sailors, and the other boats about the same number. The cabins are generally light and airy, though many of them abound with mosquitoes, cockroaches and ants, and not unfrequently with rats. The dining-room is spacious, being the whole width of the vessel, and would be very comfortable if a punkah could be introduced. The cabins contain no furniture save a bedstead, so that the traveller is required to furnish it with a mattress, table, chair, chillumchee or wash-stand, and mosquito curtains.

The river Ganges is called by the natives "Gunga Jee;" "Gung" signifies river, and "Gunga" the river; "Jee" denotes sir, lord, master, mistress, and is used as a mark of religious respect, the Ganges being pre-eminently the king of rivers—the sacred river. The Hindoos swear by the waters of the Ganges, as we do on the Testament, or the Mahomedans on the Koran. The Ganges has a very uncertain channel, in consequence of its tortuous course; sometimes dashing across from the right to the left bank, and forming a new bed. To obviate this, various clever plans have been proposed; but I shall now merely allude to that of Mr. Sims, Civil Engineer to the East India Company, who was sent out some time back, to select and survey the district which he should consider suitable for a railroad. The scheme fell into abeyance, but is once more revived. A Board was appointed in England, comprising a committee, secretary, engineer, etc.; two of the official staff arrived in Calcutta in February, 1848, for the purpose of collecting the unpaid capital, and the money is fast coming in. Meantime, the Government has desired Mr. Sims to propose a plan for controlling the freaks and sudden changes of this river, which is at the same time one of the most beneficial in the world. The task is a difficult one, and the expense enormous; however, the first sod has been since turned up, and this is some earnest of its completion.

I collect from the Report, that Mr. Sims proposes to form extensive shields at certain points of the banks. Just as in fencing, we guard right and left where the thrust is expected, so the shields are to be erected on the right and left, according as the river rushes in. Brunel used shields in making the Thames tunnel, but they were above, while Mr. Sims's shields are to be perpendicular to the river, and parallel to the banks. Wherever a shoal may be forming, Mr. Sims proposes to make a diversion by means of a channel, which is to be kept open by bamboos and other material, so as to prevent the sand from filling up the excavations. The expense of the operation is not clearly ascertained; but the cost of each shield is £60,000! Until we know how many of these shields are required, we can have no means of estimating the total outlay.

Major Rowland Hill, late 70th Regt. Bengal Native Infantry, and commanding 4th Irregular Cavalry, when at Sultanpore, Benares, tried the following plan, in 1846. Placing several large boats with their prows facing up the river, he cut through the sand-bank, upon which the force of the current drove away the sand to the right and left of the boats.

There are so many points along the Ganges which demand the attention of the engineer, that nothing short of a careful examination of every hundred yards, on both banks, can solve the problem. Thus, having formed a shield in one locality, who can say where the next may be required? or, again, whether the river driving with full force to a new point, the evil may not break out at another? The natives never thought of such schemes in days of yore. Being a sacred river, the Ganges could do no wrong: if a man lost his boat, it was his destiny (nuseeb): the will of God in anger for his sins! Æsop's fables have been translated by a Brahmin; and an Englishman having read, to a Hindoo, the fable of the waggoner's complaint to Jupiter, the man shook his head and laughed.

It would seem possible, that by carefully examining this river during the dry season, from October to April, the channels might be found out. In the Bhauguretty, and smaller Indian rivers, dredging machines are used. The practicability of the plan could be ascertained, and that, too, at no great cost, by buoying off the river, and placing it in sections; this could be done by a native establishment, with some Europeans as supervisors.

The steam-boats often run aground, although they have native pilots, and are frequently not got off for several days. Sometimes, when the river is low, steamers can only reach Sirsah, twenty-six miles below Allahabad.

I must remind the reader, that the first rise of the river is caused by the melting of the snows in the Himalaya mountains during the warm weather, before the rainy season sets in, and that the rains afterwards keep it up to the high-water mark, until the month of October. The fall of rain in Assam, south-east of Calcutta, has been 240 inches in a year. At Bombay, up to the middle of August, 1849, it was eighty-six or eighty-seven inches; which is about the same quantity that falls in Calcutta during the whole of the rainy season.

I must not omit to mention, that some years since, an attempt was made to get a steamer up to Ghurrumkteesur Ghât, on the Ganges, about thirty miles from Meerut. But it proved a failure, for the Ganges from Allahabad to Cawnpore is shoaly, and above the latter place more so than below it, in addition to which hinderance, there was not a sufficient depth of water. By dint of great exertions, Captain Templeton did get the steamer up to Cawnpore; but he first took the precaution to unlade it. The steamers carry freight, as well as the cargo-boats; they are also more capable of enduring bad weather, yet during the rains of 1849, a gale blew so violently that the steamer turned aside, nearly to her opposite gunwale. In the month of August, the river is so rapid opposite Dinapore, that the steamers lose ground, or fall below their starting-point, even in crossing from one side of the river to the other. They go down the river at the rate of twelve or fourteen miles an hour.

There are many rivers that fall into the Ganges below Allahabad. The Ganges, I may remark, rises at Gangoutrie, in the Himalayas, that enormous chain of snow-capped mountains, which extends from Cabool along the north of Hindoostan to China. It flows for more than 1,200 miles through rich fields to the Bay of Bengal, which it enters by a delta of about sixteen miles in extent. In its course, it receives eleven tributary streams, none of which is smaller than the Thames. Below Allahabad, there are on the left bank, the Goomtee, Birnah, Koosee, Dewah, or Gograh, and the Great and Little Gundruk. On the right, at and below Allahabad, the rivers Jumna and Sone, all of which, except the latter, which rises near to the Nerbudda in the Deccan, flow from the Himalaya mountains. As there is no large stream which falls into the Ganges above Allahabad, it will easily be understood, that its greatest width and depth must be below that place.

The next attempt was to steam up the Jumna, but meeting with a shoal at Kulna, the steamer could proceed no further. The rocks which formerly existed in this river, were blasted by the late Lieutenant-Colonel Joseph Taylor, of the Engineers.

The question naturally arises, why the same remedy could not be applied as at Gottenburg, in Sweden, where rapids have been passed by making a canal outside; and why, in India, canals are never resorted to for out-flanking an impediment in a river? This, however, is an enquiry to which no satisfactory reply has ever yet been given.

The Nerbudda[97] offers similar difficulties, having rocks and rapids interspersed at intervals, in quick succession. It has a course of 750 miles, rising at Omercote, and emptying itself below Baroda into the sea. Attempts have been made to navigate the Nerbudda, from the centre downwards, where there are no rocks.

Having referred to Gottenburg, I will quote a passage from the Travels of the late Bishop James, of Calcutta[98]: —

"For the purpose of avoiding the falls or cataracts that for many ages obstructed the communications of the country, a navigable canal had been excavated in the solid rock of granite, which being near two English miles in length, and carried to a depth, in one part, of 150 feet, was a scheme that few minds would have originated, and still fewer even have ventured to put into execution. The great undertaking was completed, after six years' labour, in the year 1830; and it already pays, as we were informed, an interest of 42,000 rix-dollars per annum, upon a capital of 358,988 rix-dollars, originally expended: a return amounting to nearly 12 per cent., and sufficient to afford the most unequivocal testimony both of its success and of its great public utility."

This stupendous work was undertaken by a private Company unaided by the Government. It was necessary to float the timber down the river in order to save the great expense of land carriage. It is true that in the American rivers they contrive to stop the boats short of the rapids, unlade, and then re-ship the goods; but the Swedish plan is preferable. As a commercial speculation, where, the interest of money as in Sweden is two and two-and-a-half per cent., it was a great result. The river Jumna abounds in shoals at certain places, but small canals overcome such impediments; for instance, near Kulna. As the railroad will, probably, not reach that portion of India for many years to come, the Jumna would transport goods thither. The course is estimated at 780 miles. It is fordable at times at Agra, and I believe also at Delhi. It is time, however, that I should resume my narrative.

At noon on the 20th of May, 1846, my servants with the baggage left Berrill's Hotel in a boat for the steamer "Megna," at Sirsah, the water being too low to permit the steamer to proceed higher, than within twenty-six miles of Allahabad, which, as I have before observed, is frequently the case. I left the hotel about 3 P.M., in company with the Commander of the "Soorma," accommodation boat, and reached that vessel in tow of the "Megna," about 9 P.M., at Sirsah. Before leaving the hotel I paid the Commander of the "Soorma" 217 rupees, 10 annas, i.e. 166 rupees, 10 annas, for a cabin to Calcutta; and 51 rupees for seventeen days' messing; being 3 rupees per diem, exclusive of wines, beer, and other extras: or £21 15s.

On the 23rd, at about 3 P.M., we anchored off Mirzapore, nearly ninety miles from Allahabad. It is one of the largest inland trading towns in Hindoostan, and the great mart for cotton. It is noted for its manufacture of carpets, somewhat resembling those of Turkey, and used all over India. I bought a very handsome bedside carpet, entirely made of wool, and as soft as velvet, for only six shillings. Silk is imported into Mirzapore from Bengal, and despatched to the west of India for sale, particularly among the Maharattas, and the central parts of Hindoostan. There are also fabrics of cotton manufacture, plantations of indigo, etc.

The town has many handsome European houses and native dwellings, with clusters of Hindoo temples, crowding the right bank of the Ganges, on which it stands. The appearance from the river is very imposing. Close to the main ghât stand two temples, the top of one of which is most elaborately and beautifully carved. On the other side of the river, which is here not very broad, stands the elegant residence of the Rajah of Benares.

As the steamers stop here to take in coal, as well as to land and receive passengers and goods, I took a stroll on shore. A traveller intending to visit Bombay and the west of India, should take the steamer as far as Mirzapore; this is better than going to Allahabad, which lies too far north; besides which, the navigation is not so pleasant, in consequence, as I have before observed of the shoaly state of the river between Mirzapore and Allahabad.

Mirzapore may be termed central between Allahabad and Benares, the distance from the former, by land, being forty-four miles, and from the latter, thirty-three miles, but situated on the left bank of the Ganges. There are six civilians at this station, and, at the time of which I am writing, a wing of the Shekawattee Battalion—an irregular Infantry corps—was quartered here and at Juanpore, on the opposite side of the river. The Church Missionary Society have a church and chapel here. A beautiful and magnificent Chowk, or Square, was in course of construction; and on my return, in September, 1849, when proceeding up the river, in the India General Steam Navigation Company's steamer, "General Macleod," I had the pleasure of seeing it completely finished. On this latter occasion, I again visited this bustling and thriving place, in company with my friend and fellow-countyman, Lord Frederick Montagu, at this time an officer in the 24th Foot. And here I may be permitted to render a tribute of thanks to Mr. Lord, a resident of Mirzapore, for the sumptuous hospitality with which he received his lordship and myself, both of us having been entire strangers to him previously.

The country around is pretty, and the officers' bungalows are most pleasantly situated on the bank of the river, in the midst of large compounds, or gardens, which are not exuberant with vegetation. The population of Mirzapore is between 70,000 and 80,000, the people are particularly industrious and active, and have great commercial enterprise. On leaving Mirzapore, on Sunday, the 24th, we mustered six in number, at the cuddy table, namely, Mrs. Lushington, Mr. T.A. Lushington, civil service, since deceased, Mrs. Swayne, widow of Major Swayne, killed during the rebellion at Cabool, in 1842, Captain G.R. Siddons, 1st Bengal Light Cavalry, Mr. W.R. Baillie, of the Bengal Secretariat, and myself.

On the 24th of May, at eight o'clock in the evening, we anchored off Benares, forty-nine miles from Mirzapore, having passed Chunar at about two o'clock. Chunar was acquired by the East India Company in 1775, along with the Zumindary of Benares. The fort is erected on a freestone rock several hundred feet in height, and is built of red Chunar-stone (limestone), and fortified after the Indian manner, with walls and towers. It is of considerable strength, and lies on the right bank of the Ganges, which runs close under the very walls and bastions of the fort, thus rendering it secure against the attacks of any native army. On the left, or opposite bank, the water is not very deep. The troops in the garrison are two Companies of European Artillery Invalids, and two of European Infantry Invalids, one European Veteran Company, and a detachment of the Shekawattee Battalion. It also contains a military magazine, which supplies Benares and the other adjacent stations with ammunition, arms, stores, etc. It was formerly used as a kind of state prison, and amongst the names of the compulsory inmates were Trimbuckjee Danglia, a fearful murderer, and the treacherous minister of the ex-Peishwah; and also Hadjee Khan Kakur, who was instrumental in Dost Mahomed's escape, soon after the fall of Ghuznee and Cabool.

There is much treachery in the character of some of the high Hindoos; but the most infamous scheme to destroy an adversary was executed by Sevajee, the founder of the Maharatta Empire. He invited a certain Nawab, under the pretext that he had some urgent and friendly business with him, and requested him to give him a meeting unaccompanied by his suite, or any other person, stipulating that he himself would also be unattended. The Nawab agreed to the proposition. He arrived at the place of rendezvous, at the time appointed. He came unattended, and saw no person but Sevajee, who immediately went up and embraced him with the ardour of a friend; but he had iron claws about his arms. He clasped the Nawab and held him so tight that he could not resist, and then drawing his dagger, stabbed him to the heart. But Sevajee himself did not long go unpunished, for soon after he was seized by the emperor of Delhi and thrown into prison. Cunning and crafty, he determined on a plan of escape. He pretended to become very charitable, and daily gave away large baskets filled with food and sweetmeats. At length he bribed a man to personate him, and having made him lie down in his bed, he crept into one of the baskets, which was accordingly lowered from the window; thus he effected his escape from Delhi, and reached the Deccan or South of India in safety.

The cantonments for invalids at Chunar, are situated outside the fort. The houses are all built of stone, and are generally two stories high; the residence belonging to the stone-cutter, which stands near the crowded cemetry, is a handsome structure. This last resting-place for the dead, is situated on the slope of the hill, which is crowned by the fort; the white monuments contrasting forcibly with the red stone fortress. The Major-General commanding the Division used to reside in the fort, up to the early part of this century, and in 1807, the chaplain, the Rev. Daniel Corrie, afterwards Archdeacon of Calcutta, and lately Bishop of Madras, lived here. There is now a resident chaplain, and some missionaries.

The fortress, as I observed above, fell into the power of the English, in 1775. They had been repulsed in an attempt to assault it by night, but it surrendered shortly after, without a siege. It was formerly a place of great importance, but Allahabad being more north, has superseded it as a military depôt.

In the hills near Chunar, which run parallel to the right bank of the Ganges, and are clothed with heath and brushwood, are to be found some of the largest snakes in India; many of them, it is said, being eighteen feet in length and half the thickness of a man's thigh, but they are not venomous like the cobra de capella, and the short, thin, green snake. The difference between the bite of the snake and the sting of a scorpion, is contained in the following Oriental distich:—

"He that's bitten by a serpent sleeps:
But he that's bitten by a scorpion weeps."

Sultanpore, about four miles from Chunar, is prettily situated; a regiment of Native Cavalry was formerly stationed here.

FOOTNOTES:

[97] "Narmada," Sanscrit, "rendering soft," Colebrooke, Wilks, etc.

[98] See Appendix XXI.

CHAPTER XIV

Benares—Bathing in the Ganges—Water-carrying by
Women—Extent and Population of Benares—Attempted
Tax—Mosque of Aurungzebe—Observatory of Rajah
Jey Singh—Bazaars—Jewellery—Cultivation of Sugar—
Secrole—Murder of Mr. Cherry—State Prisoners—The
Maharannee of Lahore.

We anchored off the ancient and sacred city of Benares, at eight o'clock in the evening. The Sanscrit name of the district of Benares is Varanase, from "Vara" and "Nashi" ("two streams"); it is in the Province of Allahabad, and was ceded to the East India Company by Asophud-Dowlah, the Nawab of Oude, in 1775. Its national appellation was "Kasi," or "the Splendid." It is built upon the left bank of the Ganges, along which it stretches in a semi-circle for six or seven miles. On the outer side of the curve, which is the most elevated, stands the holy city of Benares. Generally speaking, the banks of every river are higher on the side where its course is convex, and they are always high alternately, if the river has a winding course, high on the convex side, and low on the concave of the curve which it forms.

It is customary with the natives to build on rising spots of ground, because such localities are more healthy, and can be easily drained.

Benares is seen to great advantage from Ramnuggur, on the opposite bank of the Ganges. Its appearance is strikingly grand and picturesque; the ground is covered with buildings even to the water's edge, and some of the ghâts, which are constructed of large blocks of red chunar-stone, have a flight of thirty or forty steps leading down to the river. Here a most animated scene generally presents itself. Men and women, boys and girls, may be seen bathing early in the morning, and evening, and, during the cold season, also in the middle of the day; for the cold does not deter even the gentler sex from adventuring into the river. Hither, too, resort the girls and young women of Benares, to fetch water from the sacred stream. Their figures are elegant and their stature erect. They all carry two or three water-pots on their heads, each successive pot being smaller than the one beneath it. Having dipped them into the stream, and filled them with water, they replace them upon their heads, and return homewards. This habit of carrying their gharahs, or jars, filled with water, from their early youth, may account, in a great measure, for their graceful carriage. They balance their pitchers so equally as not even to require any assistance from the hand. The sight of these women, with their water-pots, powerfully recalls to mind passages in Holy Writ;[99] and many of them refer to periods of so ancient a date, that we cannot avoid coming to the conclusion that the Hindoos are a people of great antiquity.

As I ascended into the city, I found the streets so exceedingly narrow that it was difficult to penetrate them, even on horseback. The houses are crowded close to each other, with turrets rising from their terraced roofs. They are built of stone, and some of them are six stories high. The windows are always extremely small, to keep the apartments cool, as the natives suppose, as well as to prevent their neighbours from looking in, for the opposite sides of the street approach very closely to each other, and, in some places, are united by galleries. The natives in eastern countries generally sleep on their flat roofs, in the verandah, or even in front of their dwellings. Here, again, the Bible illustrates the practice of sleeping on the roofs.

According to an old Brahminical legend, Benares was originally built of fine gold; but, owing to the depravity of its inhabitants, the gold was converted into stone; and as they degenerated more and more, the houses were transformed into brick and mud.

The number of stone and brick houses, from one to six stories high, was estimated in the year 1815 to be upwards of 12,000, and the mud houses above 16,000. I find by Shakespear's version of the Statistics of the North-Western Provinces[100] that the Hindoos of the city of Benares amounted to 147,082 persons, and the Mahomedans to 36,409, making a total of 183,491, giving 34,621 inhabitants to a square mile, which is the largest amount of population of any city.

Benares, as I have already observed, is a very crowded city. In speaking of Kanoge, I stated that, according to Mr. Maurice,[101] it was supposed to have been a hundred miles in circumference, with a population of 2,500,000 or 3,000,000. Taking the former number to be correct, there would have been 4,000 souls to every square mile. A country is considered to be well peopled which has 100 inhabitants to every square mile. Certainly, neither London, nor any city in Europe, can have an amount of population equal to one-fourth of Benares. The late Mr. James Prinsep took the census, between the years 1824 and 1827, and it is not called in question now. Recollecting, also, that there are many six-storied houses, not only along the banks, but rising in tiers, closely behind one another, with only a few feet space between them, the European traveller will not be so much surprised at the immense mass of habitations thus congregated together. In 1815, Benares was computed to contain 8,000 houses, occupied by the families of the Brahmins, who receive charitable contributions, and subsist chiefly on the daily offerings of the wealthy inhabitants and pilgrims, although many of them possess private property of their own.

In 1803, the supposed population of the city and suburbs of Benares amounted to 582,000, exclusive of the attendants of the three Mogul princes, who were reported to be 3,000, making an aggregate of 585,000 souls. At that time the Mahomedans were considered to be one to every ten Hindoos. The above return gives 36,409 Mahomedans to 147,082 Hindoos, or a total of 183,491 in the city of Benares, making the Hindoos to exceed the Mahomedans in the ratio of about four to one. Mr. Prinsep took a census in 1824, and gave the returns at 181,482. It is probably now 200,000. Mr. Prinsep's census gives six as the average number of inhabitants to a chowk (yard or court), whether in the city or in the rural outskirts, seven to a pucka (brick) house, and four and a half to a kucha (mud) house.

In the year 1809, the Government resolved to impose a tax on all the houses in the city; upon which thousands of Brahmins and other inhabitants quitted it, and great excitement and uproar prevailed. A serious riot would inevitably have taken place, had not Mr. W.W. Bird, the late Deputy Governor of Bengal, an able and excellent officer, hurried to the spot and promptly quelled the disturbance. The inhabitants hereupon petitioned the Government; and vowed that if the tax were persisted in, they would represent the matter at Calcutta. The authorities, who had not displayed much judgment in the imposition of the tax, had the good sense at once to abolish the obnoxious impost; but in consequence of the émeute, the Government considered it prudent to have a European corps at hand, in the event of any future disturbance; and a royal regiment was accordingly stationed at Ghazepore.

Notwithstanding its dense, close, and crooked streets, taken as a whole, there are few cities that can carry off the palm from Benares, with its gilded pagodas, its temples, and its mosques, their slender minarets, rising in majestic grace amid countless domes and cupolas, all standing out in bold relief, among the varied forms and foliage of groves of mangoes, tamarinds, and plantains, the sombre cypress, and the beauteous palm, beneath the deep blue canopy of heaven, and lighted up by the glorious effulgence of an Eastern sun.

The most celebrated of these mosques is that built by the Emperor Aurungzebe. In order to mortify the Hindoos, he destroyed their most renowned temple, that of Vishnu, and not only raised his mosque upon its site, but, as if to heighten the indignity, caused the materials of their sacred edifice to be used in the construction of this rival temple, which was to celebrate the triumph of the Koran over the laws of Menu. What a contrast to the liberal spirit evinced by Akbar, in the exercise of his power. That great emperor, at the solicitation of his Brahmin prime minister, rescinded a caput tax, which had been imposed upon all his Hindoo subjects. History and experience teach us by many a lesson, how much we lose by harshly opposing the prejudices of others; and how much we gain by the adoption of conciliatory measures—provided no principle be involved—but alas! how slow we all are to learn this important lesson.

This mosque rises in the centre of the noble range of temples, ghâts, and edifices, that run along the left bank of the sacred Ganges. As seen from the river, it presents a most striking appearance. It stands at an elevation of eighty feet above the level of the Ganges, while its graceful minarets, tapering as they rise, tower to a height of 147 feet from their foundation. It is the most conspicuous edifice in the city, being visible for many miles round. The precise date of its erection is not known, but as the emperor died in 1707, we may assign 150 years ago as the period.

I ascended one of the two lofty minarets which flank the principal cupola. It had lately been restored to its original state by the British government, under the able superintendence of Mr. James Prinsep, British Resident at Benares. This was a most critical undertaking; for the minars were more than a foot out of the perpendicular. I enjoyed an extensive and magnificent view of the city and adjacent country, which for ten miles round is held sacred by the Hindoos. Indeed so highly is it venerated, that pilgrims resort to it from all parts of India, and those who, from age, or other circumstances, are unable to perform the lengthened journey themselves, send willing proxies, to whom they pay considerable sums. Many come there to wash away their sins; and not a few to die within its hallowed precincts.

Looking down from this dizzy height, upon the almost miniature world below, such a strange sensation came over me, that I could well conceive the propensity of certain minds to precipitate themselves from a lofty elevation. Several melancholy instances of this kind are said to have occurred here; a few perhaps from impulse, others from despair, and some from mere foolhardiness, with a view of immortalizing their names. Among the last, I was told, was a Fakeer, or devotee, who, whether by accident or design, contrived his fall so cleverly that it was broken by his being caught midway by the matting of a roof, and he alighted almost unscathed upon the floor. The people of course considered this as a miracle; and the Fakeer would doubtless have been idolized by them, had not his cupidity exceeded his love of notoriety, and induced him to make his escape with sundry articles belonging to the good Samaritan who had poured oil and wine into his bruises.

The city of Benares has long been known as the ancient seat of Brahminical learning; and to this day it retains its fame. The arts and sciences still flourish; and the schools and colleges for the training of the priests are yet celebrated, while the laws of Menu continue to be expounded in Sanscrit. But with all his erudition and research, the learned Brahmin is sunk in the most abject ignorance; and with all his wisdom, he degrades the nobler faculties of his mind, by bowing down to worship the most disgusting of monster-idols. Here, as elsewhere in our Indian possessions, the germs of Christianity have been sown under the fostering care of various British Protestant Missionary Societies, especially of the Church Missionary Society. Benares already boasts of fifteen missionary schools, one of them being founded by a wealthy Hindoo. All these schools are more or less frequented by Hindoo children; and the public preaching of the Gospel has been the means of making many of the natives acquainted with the superiority of the Christian religion.

Next to the mosque of Aurungzebe, the most conspicuous object in the city is the celebrated observatory of Rajah Jey Singh, of Jeypore, so renowned as an astronomer. He was likewise the builder of the observatory at Delhi. Here, too, everything is in character with the mind of its great designer, the instruments, etc., being on a grand scale. It is built of large blocks of red sand-stone; and, from its elevated position, commands an extensive prospect over the river and the surrounding country.

Benares is so well known, that I shall not attempt to give any further description of its numerous interesting buildings, nor of the strange sights and scenes which greet you at every turn.

Benares formerly possessed a mint for the coinage of rupees. It was under the direction of the late Mr. James Prinsep, who was the last mint-master. This gentleman was the youngest brother of a family, whose eminent services and varied talents, have identified them with the history of India. Mr. James Prinsep was a good Sanscrit scholar, and deciphered the Sanscrit inscription upon the stone pillar in the fort of Allahabad, as I said before, and which had baffled all previous attempts. In short his was a mind to grasp all things. When the mint at Benares was broken up, Mr. Prinsep was appointed assay-master at Calcutta, and so highly was he esteemed, both as a public servant, and as the liberal patron of everything good and noble, that upon his early death, in 1840, his fellow-citizens erected a splendid landing-place to his memory, one of the first objects of interest which attracts the eye of the traveller on sailing up the Hoogly. It is called Prinsep's Ghât.

I cannot take leave of Benares without saying a word or two about its bazaars, which are most attractive, not only from possessing the usual display of an Oriental mart and rendezvous of the most varied ranks, tribes, and costumes, but also from the extreme beauty and costliness of the native manufactures. Foremost among these, are the jewellery, and the exquisite works in gold and silver. These are made of the pure metal; and though they may not have the same strength and brilliancy as the alloyed, they are more intrinsically valuable, and are held in greater esteem by the natives. Many of these works are elaborate and highly finished. I was particularly struck with the ingenuity and delicacy displayed in the manufacture of a vine leaf, serving the purpose of a tea-ladle; every portion of which was so finely and minutely cut, as to leave only the slender fibres. The value of the labour bestowed upon this little article, was at least a hundred and fifty per cent. upon the cost of the original material. The price of the silver might be four shillings, and the cost of the labour about six. Precious stones, and especially the diamonds from the mines of Bundelkund, form an extensive article in the trade in jewellery which is carried on here, and are much sought after. The beautiful muslins and Benares scarfs, of red and gold, are the admiration and envy both of native and European ladies. The bazaars, too, abound in vessels of various metals, especially copper; and in manufactures in peacocks' feathers, and ingenious toys gaily painted, the colours of which are very durable, and in no danger of being effaced.

The district of Benares is also famous for its growth and manufacture of sugar; indeed, about half the quantity of sugar imported from Calcutta is raised in this neighbourhood. Thus this sacred city presents attractions to those who admire it on account of its antiquity, or sanctity; the richness of its manufactures, or the lucrativeness of its commerce.

The Rajah of Benares has a palace at Ramnuggur, on the right bank of the Ganges, about four miles from the city. It has been the residence of the Rajahs ever since the flight of Cheyte Singh from the city, in 1781.

The cantonments which are situated at Secrole, about four miles from the river, contain the second company fifth battalion, with No. 4 Light Field-battery, and third company fifth battalion, Foot Artillery, 48th and 65th Regts. Native Infantry; and 3rd Infantry Recruit depôt. The church is a very good one. There is likewise a large theatre, and a fine racket-court. The Society at Secrole is very agreeable; independently of the military, it is the station of five or six civilians, a chaplain, and eleven missionaries. The station is large and very healthy; many of the residences are well built, and surrounded by pleasant compounds and gardens; the best are those belonging to the civilians, which, being situated across the Birnah, are united to it by a bridge.

Benares is the scene of the treacherous murder of Mr. Cherry, the British Resident, and three other gentlemen, in January, 1799, which being well known, I will only briefly allude to. Upon the death of Asoph-ud-Dowlah, Nawab of Oude, in 1797, he was succeeded in the government by his illegitimate son, Mirza Ali; but being much disliked he was deposed, and his uncle, Saadut Ali, placed upon the throne. Mirza was at first permitted to reside at Benares; but as he was suspected of hatching a conspiracy, the Marquis Wellesley determined upon his removal, under strict surveillance, to Calcutta. Mirza Ali was exceedingly indignant at the proposed change, and remonstrated with the government. But as his application did not meet with a favourable reply, he waited upon the British Resident; his bearing and language were so intemperate, that the Resident admonished him to be more careful, which so exasperated Mirza, that he rushed upon Mr. Cherry sword in hand. This was a signal for his attendants to follow his example. They made a general rush, and cruelly murdered him upon the spot. This assassination was followed by that of three other Englishmen; the murderers then made a similar attempt upon Mr. Davis, the Judge; but he made a desperate resistance to save himself, and his family. Armed with a short spear, he stood at the top of the narrow winding staircase, on the roof of his house; like all circular stairs, it only admitted a single person at a time. The first man who came to the top was speared, and his dead body blocked up the passage, and impeded the attack of those behind him. Mr. Davis succeeded in warding off the blows, till the arrival of a body of Native Cavalry, upon which Mirza and his attendants took to flight. The regiment was at that time stationed at Sultanpore, seven miles distant. Saadut Ali, notwithstanding the danger to which the suspected conspiracy against his throne exposed him, was too imbecile to use any efforts in aiding the British to capture the assassins, who successfully eluded the vigilance of the government for some months. Mirza Ali even succeeded in collecting a considerable number of adventurers; but upon some offence they abandoned him, and he took refuge in the court of a petty Rajah, who, however, refused to harbour him, and delivered him up to the British government.

Amid the many strange vicissitudes of Indian history, it is by no means unusual to find deposed sovereigns, and other persons of rank, residing at Benares as state prisoners. Among these I would particularize Bajee Row, the late Peishwah, who, after many changes of fortune, surrendered to the English, in 1818. He agreed to abdicate the throne, and to abandon the Deccan, on condition of his retaining all his treasures, and receiving an annual pension from the British government of eight lakhs of rupees, or £80,000 sterling. I visited his palace, and found that the ex-Peishwah still retained some semblance of royalty, in the person of one or two Sepoys, who were on duty at his gate. He died at Benares, in 1851.

In February 1836, the deposed Rajah of Coorg came to Benares. He had been attacked, in 1834, by a division of the Madras army, and his capital, Mercara, taken. In March 1840, his Highness the ex-Rajah of Sattarah was sent to Benares, on the plea of having attempted to tamper with the loyalty of the British Sepoys. He has since died. Therefore, though Benares is not "a refuge for the destitute," unless he be a high caste Brahmin, it may nevertheless be called the "Asylum of deposed Rajahs." Nor must I omit the name of the Maharannee, the mother of the ex-Maharajah Dhuleep Singh, of Lahore, who in 1848 was sent from the Punjaub to Benares, for causing a disaffection towards the British. After residing here for a short time, her Highness was conveyed to the more secure fort, as the officials thought, of Chunar, but from whence she effected her escape, early in 1849, in the disguise of one of her attendants, not being recognised by the sentries at the gates. She is supposed to have reached Nepaul; but how she was received by the Goorkhas—how she likes the country—where her Highness intends to live—and by what funds supported—must be left to the imagination of the reader. Certain it is, that the East India Government ought not to regret the absence of so expensive a pensioner. She exerted too powerful a control over the Maharajah, her son, to be allowed to remain at Lahore with impunity. Her Highness, like many clever women, is somewhat dangerous, particularly as being the mother of the King of Lahore. But there is now no King of Lahore. The revenues of the Punjaub belong to the East India Company, the territorial supremacy, however, is vested in the crown; the Company being only the Trustees.

The life and adventures of this Queen-mother would form a most extraordinary and amusing volume. So varied have been her vicissitudes, that, while her intrigues and romantic amours might be the subject of a novel, the history of the cruelties and murders which have marked her steps since the death of her husband, Runjeet Singh, would furnish matter for a tragedy.

FOOTNOTES:

[99] See Appendix XXII.

[100] 1848, p. 155, table xxx.

[101] Indian Antiquities, p. 36.

CHAPTER XV

Ghazepore—The Opium Trade—Marquis Cornwallis's
Mausoleum—Sand-banks—Buxar—Cossim-Ali-Khan—
Sir Hector Munro—Battle of Buxar—Nawab of Oude—
Emperor of Delhi—Revelgunge—The Sonus—The Ganges
and Jumna—The Indus—The Berhampooter—Arrian—
Dr. Alexander Adam—Dinapore—Captain Strachan—
Bankipore—H.M. 16th Lancers—Deegah—Grain Golah—
Earl of Munster—Patna—Buildings of Patna—Population
of Benares—Magistrates—E. I. Company's Charter—
Products of Patna—Walter Reinhard—Snowy Mountains—
Tirhoot—Juggernauth—Gyah Proper—Cave of
Nugur-jenee—Sir Charles Wilkins—Futwa—Phoolbarea—
Bar—Beggars.

On the 25th of May we left Benares for Ghazepore. After steaming rapidly along the low banks we came to Saidpore, which is distinguished for a temple crowded with sacred monkeys; and lower down, also on the left bank, passed Chochukpore, where there are two handsome temples.

At seven o'clock in the evening, we anchored off Ghazepore, the "Rose Garden of India." It is a large and populous city, celebrated for its fragrant rose-water, the cultivation of the poppy, and the manufacture of opium. The commercial agent and his deputy reside here. At this season of the year the people were employed in collecting the juice which exudes from the poppy; it is kept in vessels, and when dry and solid, is cut into cakes, a process which requires great care. The Bahar or Patna opium sells at a higher price than that of Benares; the value of each chest being about 300 rupees or £30 sterling. The opium trade is an important monopoly in the hands of the government. It meets with a ready sale in China, although by the laws of the Empire it is a contraband article, and its importation stringently prohibited. In the autumn of 1836 it was generally, and confidently believed that the opium trade was about to be legalized in China; and advices to that effect reached Calcutta prior to the commencement of the sales for the season of 1837. This caused much higher prices to be paid by the usual purchasers than formerly, indeed, much above the sum which the capitalists, both of China and Calcutta, considered prudent, even had the legalization been certain.

To the great dismay of the merchants, it was afterwards ascertained that so far from authorizing, the Chinese government had determined to put a total stop to the importation of opium; meanwhile the stock in Calcutta had been accumulating. What was to be done? The above report had been circulated and credited, and the opium growers had got rid of their stock. The sales of 1837 were expected to yield 25,851,386 rupees; but certain influential merchants represented that the higher prices could not be realized without great loss and distress. The mode of payment was a deposit, a certain sum in so many days, and the remainder in some given days after; but several buyers had not even paid their deposits. After considerable demur it was agreed that rather more than three lakhs should be taken off, so that the total sales only yielded 22,789,986 Company's rupees (or at the exchange of two shillings the rupee, £2,278,998) which was the largest sum ever known to be realized. Soon after this the war broke out in China, when the amount of sales decreased, both in the prices and in the number of chests; but in 1841 it again rose, even during the war.

Much has been mooted about the monopoly of the opium trade; but when it is recollected that the land revenue is only about two-thirds of the revenue of India, and that it is by the sole privilege of the sale of this article, and that of salt, aided by that of the abkarry, or sale of spirits, that the expenses of the country can be paid, we should pause before we judge too harshly. If the people of England denounce the opium trade, let them shut up their gin-palaces before they condemn the growth and sale of opium. The people in China drink shamshoo, which is even more deleterious. It is said that if the trade in opium were thrown open, there would be an unlimited quantity manufactured, which is prevented by its being in the hands of the Government. Opium is eaten by many of the natives of Hindoostan, both Mahomedans and Hindoos; and I may add, that lawyers and other professional men, nay, even ladies, indulge in it. In China they smoke it, and it is whispered that even the Emperor is addicted to it. Now, supposing the population of China to be 360,000,000 souls, of which 125,000,000 are male adults, there would not be above half an ounce yearly to each. In 1837-38, there were 17,244 chests exported from Calcutta; if to this we add the Malwa opium, of which 40,000 chests are now yearly sent to China, still only half an ounce would be the maximum of each person. Many, no doubt, commit excesses; but is not the same done in gin-palaces?

Most of the troops formerly stationed in the cantonments of Ghazepore have been withdrawn to Benares. In 1805, on the raising of the 7th and 8th Regiments of Light Cavalry, they were quartered in these cantonments; but when the disturbances broke out at Benares, in 1809, in consequence of the house-tax, a royal regiment of Infantry was stationed at Ghazepore, which is about forty miles from Benares; indeed, so late as the year 1838, the 44th Foot were located here, the cavalry lines having been converted into barracks for the Europeans. The East India Company have a branch stud at Ghazepore, for the breed of horses, the head-quarters being at Buxar, lower down the river.

There is a magnificent mausoleum erected to the memory of the late Marquis Cornwallis, K.G., who died here October 5th, 1805, whilst on a visit to the Upper Provinces, a few months after his second arrival in India. He had been Governor-General of India from the year 1786 to the end of 1792. In 1805, his Lordship returned in his original capacity of Governor-General and Commander-in-Chief, bent upon changing most of the measures adopted by his predecessor, the Marquis Wellesley, when his own plans were frustrated, by the mighty conqueror, Death, who shows us how futile and insignificant are the vastest designs of man. L'homme propose, et Dieu dispose.

The mausoleum is a most costly building; and Bishop Heber laments that so much money should have been lavished upon such an unmeaning structure; indeed, he is very severe upon the subject, arguing that a church might have been erected at but a little more cost, with a monument to Lord Cornwallis placed within its walls.

The commander of our steamer having taken in three hundred maunds, or nearly eleven tons, of coal, we got under weigh at half-past six on the morning of the 26th of May. At two o'clock in the afternoon our progress was arrested by the boat sticking fast on a sand-bank. We remained in this awkward position till nine the following morning. During that day and the 27th we were constantly on and off sand-banks, making very little progress. About six hours after leaving Ghazepore we were off Buxar, one of the Government stud stations, having passed the palace of Cossim Ali Khan, once a fine building, as its ruins indicate, lying on the very verge of the village.

Buxar is a small town, in the province of Bahar, in the district of Shahabad, and is built on the south-east side of the Ganges. The fort of Buxar, though of inconsiderable size, commands the river; but no attention is now paid to keep it in repair.

On the 22nd of October, 1764, a celebrated victory was gained here by the British forces, under Major (afterwards General Sir Hector) Munro, over the united armies of Sujah-ud-Dowlah, of Oude, and Cossim Ali Khan, of Moorshedabad. Major Munro had no cavalry, but taking up a strong position with his right, close to the river, he allowed the enemy, who had crossed over to Buxar by a bridge of boats, from the Oude side of the river, to commence the attack. A native historian says, "It was not an army, but rather a nation." The battle was of short continuance; the allies were defeated; the power of the Nawab of Oude destroyed; and the Emperor thrown on the protection of the English.

The British army consisted of 856 Europeans, and 6,215 Sepoys, making a total of 7,071, of whom eighty-seven Europeans, and 712 Sepoys were killed and wounded. The combined troops were computed at 40,000, of whom 2,000 are supposed to have been slain in the battle. Their flight was so rapid, that hurrying to cross a small but deep river beyond Buxar, many were drowned, or slaughtered in the attempt. The plunder in the enemy's camp was very great, as they left their tents standing; and their whole train of artillery, consisting of 133 pieces of various sizes, fell into the hands of the English. Cossim made his escape to the Rohillas, and the Emperor of Delhi signed a treaty of peace, highly advantageous to the British government, which became henceforth supreme in Bengal.

The Fort now comprises a station for several detachments of European Artillery and Infantry Invalids; as also a portion of a Native Infantry corps. The superintendent of the stud department has his head-quarters on the other side of the river, at a village called Kurruntadhee; there are several hundred horses and colts in the stables here. At Ghazepore, as I have already remarked, there is a branch, and another at Poosah, at the junction of the little Gundruk with the Ganges, which was formerly the only stud in the central Provinces.

After passing Revelgunge, a very long town, extending for more than a mile along the left bank of the river, and at a distance of twenty-eight miles above Dinapore, we came to the spot where the river Sone flows into the Ganges, seventeen miles from Revelgunge.

The Sone river, called by the Greeks "Sonus," has, with the Nerbudda, its source in the table-land of Omerkuntuc (Omercote), in the Province of Gundwana, 22° 53' N. Lat. and 82° 15' E. Long. It rises on the east side, and flows through Pindarah, when, being joined by numerous other streams from the north-eastern side of this mountain domain, it proceeds in a northerly direction through Sohajepore and Bogulkund, whence, turning eastward, it pursues its course to the Ganges, which it joins in the Province of Bahar, after having performed a winding course of about 500 miles. Near its source, this river is said to be designated by the natives "the Sonabudda," to distinguish it from the Nerbudda, by which, conjointly with the Ganges, the southern point of Hindoostan is insulated.[102]

Under the head of Omerkuntuc, we find it styled "a celebrated place of Hindoo pilgrimage, in the Province of Gundwana." There is no peculiar sanctity attached to this river; the sanctity, such as it is, belongs to Omerkuntuc. In Hindoo mythology, Gunga, or the Ganges, is described as the eldest daughter of the great mountain, Himavata, and is called "Gunga," on account of her flowing through "Gung," the earth. In the Hindoo Pantheon, Himalaya is deified, and described as the father of the Ganges. The Jumna and the Ganges have their sources in the Himalaya mountains, at Jumnoutrie and Gangoutrie peaks; at no great distance from each other. The Jumna enters Hindoostan Proper, in the Province of Delhi, and proceeds south, nearly in a line with the Ganges, at a distance of from fifty to seventy miles apart from each other, until they gradually join at Allahabad. Its length, including its windings, may be estimated at 780 miles. The Ganges and the Jumna may be designated "Sister Rivers."

The Indus, too, takes its rise in the Himalayas, as do all the five rivers of the Punjaub, and likewise all the rivers that enter the Ganges on the left bank. The Berhampooter also rises in the same mountains, and after a course of several hundred miles, enters the Ganges near the sea. There are other rivers coming from the Himalayas; but they are, comparatively speaking, insignificant. The three greatest rivers are—

1. The Ganges, having a course of 1,500 miles.
2. The Indus,   "   about   1,000 "
3. The Jumna,   "   780 "

It is believed that the Berhampooter was not known in the time of Arrian. To return, en passant, to the subject of Palibothra, Arrian says the Erannoboas was the third river of India, which will be the present Jumna. It has been shown that the length of the Sone is only 500 miles. I think that those learned gentlemen who advocate the Sone, as being the Erannoboas of the Greeks, are in error, first, because Arrian distinctly mentions the Erannoboas and the Sonus as two of the six rivers which flow into the Ganges. Now the Sone cannot be the Erannoboas by any ingenuity whatever; for it is clearly called the Sonus. Secondly, it is said that the ancient name of Patna was Pataliputra, making an approach to the word Palibothra, which, however, proves nothing. Thirdly, it is more probable that the Jumna is the Erannoboas, because, having found the Sone to be the Sonus, we require the third river in India to meet the Ganges; whereas the Sone, not being so large as the Jumna, cannot be admitted even as the fourth river of Hindoostan; besides, we expect to find a sacred stream to represent such a river as the Erannoboas. Dr. Alexander Adam, in his "Summary of Ancient and Modern Geography," says, "The Sone (Sone-budda) joins the Ganges twenty-two miles above Patna." Patna is seven miles from Dinapore, and Dinapore is now five miles from the Sone; consequently, the Sone is about twelve miles from Patna, and not twenty-two. But to proceed —

On the 29th of May, we anchored off Dinapore, at five o'clock in the afternoon, having experienced rather stormy weather for the three preceding nights. Dinapore is a considerable town, on the right bank of the Ganges, and is situated in a kind of bay, formed by the river. The cantonments are large, and the area comprised by the barracks and lines of both Queen's and Company's troops, is unusually extensive and imposing. The European barracks face the river, upon the immediate bank of which are the wards or quarters for the officers, opposite to those of the men. At right angles with these two ranges, are two others, likewise for the officers, the four ranges forming a large oblong. Beyond these, higher up the river, and close adjoining, is a smaller oblong, formed of three ranges (one being the back of the large oblong), and the fourth range, the bungalows facing the river. The lines for the two corps of Native Infantry are on the left, looking from the river front. The main guard is on the right of the cantonments, near the town. There are also some bungalows for the officers, in rear of the right, and nigh to these is a bridge over a nullah.

Dinapore has long been a considerable cantonment, a large force having been stationed here in 1786. The extension of the British dominion northwards, gradually diminished the importance of this military station; and under the rule of the Marquis Wellesley, it was intended to do away with the whole of the cantonments, and to erect barracks on the other side of the river. In consequence of this resolve, all the buildings, those occupied by the Europeans, as well as those belonging to the natives, were put up for sale, and purchased at a very low price by an officer named Harriott. Government, however, soon after repented of the step it had taken, and was very anxious to cancel the bargain; but the fortunate purchaser demurred. At last, however, Mr. Harriott re-sold to the Company a part of the cantonments at a higher rate than what he had originally paid for the whole. The Government were forced to rent from him whatever further accommodation was needed; and to this day, a descendant of that gentleman receives a monthly rent of no less than 2,000 rupees, or £200 sterling, for the buildings now occupied by the troops. Besides this, a considerable sum is realized from the numerous merchants and others, who rent various buildings included in the first purchase. Thus Governments, like individuals, will sometimes make mistakes.

Dinapore is the head-quarters of a Division of the army, and is capable of being put into a tolerable state of defence. At present there are a light field-battery of Artillery, a royal regiment of Foot, and three corps of Native Infantry stationed here. The church is a very neat building, and stands in the centre of the large oblong. It contains a tablet to two officers of the 62nd Foot, who were unfortunately drowned in company with a great portion of the right wing of the regiment, in a storm which capsized their boats, near Bhaugulpore, on the 10th of July, 1842.

The 39th Foot being quartered here, I called upon Captain Strachan, of this fine corps, under whom I had acted as Adjutant, in 1844, to a detachment of recruits, consisting of my own corps (the 9th Lancers), the 3rd Buffs, 29th, 50th and 62nd Regiments of Foot.

Beyond the cantonments, and half way to Bankipore are many good houses, some of them being occupied by officers, and others by merchants. The view from the river is extremely pleasing, numerous budgerows, and boats of all descriptions, constantly ply up and down the river, and give great animation to the scene. Dinapore is one of the steam stations; and the vessels coming up and down, stop here to take in coals and wood.

Dinapore is also a place of some trade, and is celebrated for its leather, linen, light hats, and paintings. I bought an excellent pair of boots here, for a couple of rupees—quite equal to some I had purchased at Calcutta for eight.

Having taken in 800 maunds of coals (one maund is 80lbs.), and 200 maunds of wood, there having been a scarcity of the former, we started at five o'clock, on the morning of the 30th of May. During the day we passed H.M. 16th Lancers, in country boats, who had been seven days accomplishing what we had done in seven hours; the poor fellows made no hesitation in complaining of the miserable manner in which they were proceeding to Calcutta. It is a pity that the government should have subjected a set of gallant men, to such unnecessary inconvenience and discomfort, when so many steamers were at the time available for their transport. It is only in the hour of need that a soldier's services are duly appreciated, and thus with the 16th: no other Aliwal was in prospect, or perhaps they would have fared better, and many a brave soldier's life might have been spared from an inglorious death on the river.

At a short distance from Dinapore is Deegah, which with Bankipore, almost unites Patna and Dinapore. Bankipore is called a suburb of Patna; and, as the opium agent for Benares resides at Ghazepore, so the agent for the Bahar opium resides at Bankipore. Here is a great grain Golah, or circular stone building something like a bee-hive. It is black from age, and the effects of the climate. This novel and somewhat absurd building was erected by Governor Hastings. In the year 1770 a terrible famine raged in Bengal and Bahar, and carried off thousands. The Bengal government, in order to secure the inhabitants of Patna and its neighbourhood from starvation, in the event of another similar visitation, built this Golah, for the purpose of containing rice, which is grown very extensively at Patna. But, large as was the building, it was discovered that it would not hold a day's consumption for the people of the extensive Province in which it is situated. For, supposing that there were only two millions of souls, each would require 2lbs. per diem, or about 1,800 tons of grain for the whole population, which was far beyond the capacity of the building. The engineer too contrived to make the entrance door to open inwards; and at the top, an aperture surrounded by a parapet; hence it was self-evident that when this granary was filled, or even if the grain were raised but a few feet above the floor, the door could not be opened; besides which, there was also a further danger that the contents would ferment and explode the building. This first and last attempt to build on such vague calculations, cost between £12,000 and £15,000. It is now used as a store-house for arms, and other purposes.

Outside this Golah, are two winding staircases, one of which the late Earl of Munster ascended on horseback for a wager; another gentleman, a civilian, did more, for he rode down also. The walls at the bottom of the granary are enormously thick, namely, twenty-one feet, but they have given way.

There is a large range of buildings for the manufacture of opium; making it into cakes, and packing them in boxes. The latter is a very delicate process. Thus some of the opium of the year 1848 was deteriorated, because the agent had used fresh planks, of a bad description of wood, for the cases. The price of opium has fallen much of late. In the year 1820-21, the Bahar (Patna) opium sold for 4,303 sicca rupees, or 4,589 Company's rupees; and the Benares opium for 4,276 sicca rupees, or 4,531 Company's rupees per chest. But at that time the amount and value of sales was less, and of course the quantity also. When the market returned to its usual state, Bahar opium sold for 1,960 sicca rupees, and Benares for 1,860: but the sales produced more revenue. Before the above period, in 1819-20, the Bahar opium sold for only 2,463 sicca rupees, and Benares for 2,435. At the sales, the buyers paid a deposit of ten per cent.: thirty per cent. in ten days, and the remainder in one month.

Our next station was Patna, which almost joins Bankipore. It is a large city in the Province of Bahar, of which it is the capital, in Latitude 25° 37' N., and Longitude 85° 15' E. It is situated on the south side of the Ganges, which is here very deep, and in the rainy season sometimes five miles across.

Patna is a city of great antiquity, and is supposed by some to be the site of the ancient Palibothra. Among them are Rennel, Lord Valentia, Colebrooke and Tennant. By the modern Mahomedans, Patna is named Azimabad, which signifies "The Great City"; by the Hindoos it is called "Sri Nugur."

The town of Patna is one continued street, running along the right bank of the river, to the length of four miles by one in breadth. It is surrounded by a fortified wall, in bad condition. The citadel is small, and is now used as a store-house. The contrast between the lofty houses of Benares and this city is very striking; here they are, generally speaking, only one or two stories in height. The residences of the Europeans, chiefly of the civil service, are built of brick, and are very handsome, and extend as far as Bankipore; but the rest of the dwellings are rather mean, and for the most part constructed of mud. There are likewise a few elegant mosques and temples. There was formerly a college of Jews here, and also a Roman Catholic College. The latter was of very early date, probably as remote as the fourth or fifth century; for it is stated in the Asiatic Researches, "That there was, in the fourth century a Christian College at Sirhind, near the Sutlej." From this College, missionaries were sent to the town of Bettiah, ninety miles NNW. of Patna.

The town is very prosperous and populous. Taking the population of the city of Benares at something above 183,000, Patna can scarcely have more than 130,000 souls. Among the inhabitants are several Nawabs and native noblemen, whose income is as low as from 1,000 to 500 rupees a month. Many of them have been thus reduced in their worldly circumstances, in consequence of the British having gained the ascendancy over the former Mahomedan governments. Poor nobility are, however, by no means confined to Patna or to any part of India, but may be found in Poland and Germany; nay, on the Continent generally, and even in favoured England.

There are two Nawabs at Bareilly and at Meerut, holding the offices of Sudder Ameens or magistrates, on salaries of from 700 to 1,000 rupees monthly; and in the Bengal Presidency, there are five Pundits, and several Baboos in the same position, besides forty-two Baboos, one Pundit, and several learned Mahomedans (Moolvees), who are deputy collectors. These are uncovenanted appointments, and are, in addition to the civil servants on the establishment. From the printed lists, it would appear that they are almost as numerous as the covenanted appointments, for there are no less than 402 of the former, and 476 of the latter. The uncovenanted appointments are divided as follows:—

	Europeans.	Mahom.	Hindoos.	Total.
The Deputy Magistrates are	67	6	8	81
Sudder Ameens	20	89	37	146
Deputy Collectors	61	45	69	175
	—	—	—	—
	148	140	114	402

In the North-Western Provinces, the Mahomedans are less than one-sixth, or 3,747,022, out of a population of 23,199,668 souls, so that the Hindoos have not their share of the loaves and fishes. The Chairman of the East India Company animadverted upon this subject a few years since. The Hindoos are usually the most studious, and have often been employed in some of the most responsible and critical posts. Chundoo Lall, a Brahmin, was Prime Minister at the Court of Hyderabad, the Nizam's capital, for many years; and a Hindoo was Prime Minister to the Emperor Akbar. Possibly the Government of India may be desirous of conciliating the Mahomedans, who were for so many years the rulers of Hindoostan. The vacancies in the above appointments are most eagerly sought for; and innumerable are the expectants for preferment. This spirit of emulation has certainly improved the minds of the higher classes, who now study English and the Company's regulations to good purpose. In Calcutta a native has been a Commissioner in the Court of Requests for many years. The subject of the extension of the system of employing natives in high civil offices of responsibility, will very probably be discussed at the end of the East India Company's Charter in 1854; for the question is one of great importance, and immediately connected with the scheme of native education.

Patna is not a large manufacturing town; but there are many cotton and linen factories in the neighbourhood, where chintzes, and various kinds of cotton diaper and damask, are made. There are also manufactories of flannels, and a sort of canvas for sails and other purposes. Linen can be procured in the neighbourhood, and is sent to the metropolis. In fact, almost every article, whether Asiatic or European, may be purchased in the bazaars.

The finest saltpetre and opium are produced in the vicinity; and immense quantities of wheat, sugar, and indigo, are grown here. Provisions are very cheap in Bahar, for instance, gram, a kind of vetch for horses, used to sell at 100 seers, or 200 lbs. for a rupee; but from 1805 to a late period, one or more native cavalry corps have been stationed at Ghazepore, which has raised the market, and the same quantity now costs three rupees. The establishment of the stud, and its branches at Kurruntadhee, Ghazepore, and Buxar, has likewise had an influence upon the price of grain. The opium and saltpetre trade is here, as elsewhere, monopolized by the Government, and exported in immense quantities to Calcutta. But a very considerable trade in all other articles is carried on by merchants from every country. It has always been a place of much commercial importance; and, at a very early period, there were English, French, Dutch, and Danish factories. Patna is the first station at which the East India Company established a factory. This was in the year 1620.

We still see the remains of the old British factory, where the fearful massacre of two hundred prisoners was perpetrated, in 1763, by the German adventurer Summer, pronounced by the natives Somroo, but whose real name was Walter Reinhard, then in the service of Mir Cossim. Much as this atrocious event must be condemned, the English had themselves to blame in the first instance; for the soldiers, who had been stationed at the factory for its protection, scaled the walls of the town, wantonly attacked the inhabitants, and plundered their houses. The native garrison immediately turned out, and succeeded in taking the English soldiers prisoners of war. They were confined in the factory; but the Nawab Cossim, incensed at the various indignities which he had received from the British Government, commissioned Somroo to kill all his prisoners, two hundred in number. This charge the German executed with the greatest barbarity. The prisoners were just seated at dinner, in the hall of the factory, when the myrmidons of Somroo fired upon them from the doors and windows, and butchered them all in cold blood. In revenge for this atrocity, Major Adams stormed the city and captured it. Since that period, Patna has owned the British sway; and it is now the residence of the Provincial Court of Appeal and other civil establishments. A monument to the memory of these wretched victims was erected in the European burial ground, but without any inscription.

The road from Patna to Dinapore is excellent, and marked by mile-stones. The snowy mountains are visible on a clear evening, during the rainy season. I am told that the Himalayas, too, command the most extensive view of the plains during the same period of the year, when the rains prevent the dust from rising into the air.

Nearly opposite Patna, is the district of Tirhoot, famous for the cultivation of indigo and sugar-cane; but the latter suffers greatly from the destructive rats which abound there. Tirhoot is near the Nepaul frontier.

About fifty-five miles south of Patna, in Lat. 24° 49′ N., and Long. 85° 5′ E., in the Province of Bahar, lies the city of Gaya, or Gyah. This ancient city is one of the most holy places of Hindoo pilgrimage, being held by tradition to have been the residence of Buddha, the great prophet and legislator of the nations east of the Ganges; and it is usually termed "Buddha Gyah." The temple is of course had in great veneration. The following extract from an inscription on one of the stones, will shew the estimation in which it was held: "This place is renowned, and it is celebrated by the name of Bhood Gaya. The forefathers of him who shall perform the ceremony of the Sraddha at this place, shall obtain salvation. A crime of a hundred-fold shall undoubtedly be expiated from a sight thereof; of a thousand-fold from a touch thereof; and of a hundred thousand-fold from worshipping thereof." The frightful image of the idol is placed in the temple, and is open to the worship of all pilgrims. A vow of sanctity is often taken here by women, and especially by widows, not unlike the Roman Catholic vow of celibacy; for they shave their heads, and promise to renounce the world. The Bengal government was wont to derive a net annual revenue of £15,000, collected from the pilgrims, a sum even exceeding that gathered from the pilgrims at the famous Juggernauth, being levied at a fixed ratio according to the magnitude of the sins which the individual had come to expiate, and, therefore, of the ceremonies which he was to perform.

The town is divided into two parts, one of which, more holy than the other, is the residence of the Brahmins and their families, called "Gyah Proper"; the other inhabited by the merchants and tradesmen, is called "Sahibgunge." The town lies inland at some distance from the river.

About fourteen miles to the north of Gyah, is a hill, or rather rock, in which a remarkable cavern has been excavated, called "Nugur-jenee" ("Nugur" a town, and "Jenee" the Jains). Being unable to visit it, I will give the account of it as communicated to me by our Captain. The cave, it seems, is about two-thirds distant from the summit of the hill; and the entrance, which is about six feet and a half high, by two and a half wide, leads to a chamber of an oval form, having a vaulted roof: this room is forty-four feet in length, eighteen in breadth, and ten in height in the centre. The whole cavity is dug out of the solid granite rock; altogether the excavation extends full a hundred feet. It was probably made for the purposes of worship by the Buddhists, whose religion differs from that of the Brahmins, and who were subjected to great persecutions on account of their tenets. We know that this was the case with the early Christians, who, in consequence of the ruthless tyranny of their heathen oppressors, were compelled to take refuge in the caves of the earth. The cavern at Gyah has two inscriptions, which have been translated by the late Sir Charles Wilkins, and published in the first volume of the "Asiatic Researches." From these inscriptions, it would appear that it is a place of great antiquity, but no dates are given.

Passing Futwa, which lies near the confluence of the Pompon and the Ganges, and is noted for the manufacture of its table linen, and for the remains of an extensive saltpetre manufactory, we reached Phoolbarea, and sometime after the little town of Bar. The whole place swarms with beggars, many of whom afforded no little amusement to our passengers, by their anxiety to pick up the coppers, which they threw from the steamer to the water's edge.

FOOTNOTES:

[102] Vide Major Rennel.

CHAPTER XVI

Monghyr—Wells of Seetacoond—The Fort of Monghyr—
Storms on the Ganges—Cossim Ali Khan—Monghyr
the Birmingham of India—Employment of Women—
The Gaol—A Sacred Bathing-place—Bhaugulpore—Its
Population—Hill Rangers—The Bheels—Mr. Cleveland—
Lieut.-Colonel Tod—Colonel Francklin—Colgong—The
Jungheera Rocks—The Fakeers—The Rajmahal Hills—
Sickreegullee—Boatmen of the Ganges—Rajmahal—Ruins
of Gour—The Bhauguretty—Soottee—The Sunderbunds—
Bogwangola—Jungepore.

After a very stormy night, we reached Monghyr, and at eight on the
morning of the 31st of May, cast anchor before this once celebrated fortress.
It is about fifty-seven miles from Bar, and 436 from Calcutta. Monghyr is a
town in the Province of Bahar, beautifully situated on the south bank of the
Ganges. It was formerly a place of great importance, and is still celebrated
for the cultivation of grain, and the manufacture of opium. A large portion
of the district around, is hilly and unproductive, but the cultivated lands
are extremely fertile, and yield rich returns. Some fifty years ago, the
government tried the plan of granting certain waste lands, to the invalid
officers and native Sepoys, and the experiment has succeeded beyond all
expectation, some of the reclaimed lands being the best in the place. In the
immediate vicinity, and about a mile from the fort, are some famous wells;
they are called by the natives, "Seetacoond," and are highly venerated by
the Hindoos. Seetacoond is a common appellation for hot springs among
them: Koond in Sanscrit means a spring, hence the meaning would be the
"spring of Seeta," which Seeta was the wife of Ram. Only one of these wells,
however, is really a hot spring, for in the second well, the water is cold,
and in the third chalybeate. They are all situated about half-a-mile from the
Ganges, twenty paces apart from each other, in a plain backed by hills, and
in the midst of rocks. The hot spring is considerable, and the air-bubbles
rise in great quantities, the temperature varying from 90° to 140°. The
water is much used on voyages to Europe, or on the sea, on account of its
extreme purity; indeed it is asserted that it keeps for ever without becoming
putrid. The renowned goddess Seeta pledges herself for its eternal purity.
It certainly is very good, and people going to England, viâ the Cape, would

do well to provide themselves with a few dozen large bottles, and fill them at this spring, for the water on board a ship is often extremely bad.

The Fort of Monghyr is very large and situated on a rising ground. The fortifications were formerly quite in the Indian style, encompassed with a lofty wall flanked with towers and surrounded by a dry ditch, except on the river side. But the government found it too expensive to keep these fortifications in repair, and have suffered them to fall almost into complete decay; and at present, the fort alone would be able to stand a siege. The view from the fort is one of the finest in India. The river, in the rainy season, forms quite a large expanse of water, and the Ganges becomes a rapid stream. Sometimes the violence of the torrent is so impetuous, that it undermines the banks of the river and uproots the largest trees. During the hurricanes, which are frequent here at certain seasons, the Ganges assumes the appearance of the sea; and the water dashes over the boats with such violence, that the men are frequently washed overboard; numerous boats are capsized in an instant, and men and goods swept down the engulphing stream. These storms are always accompanied by thunder, lightning, and fierce winds, against which it is impossible to make head. There is a protruding rock here, which juts out boldly into the stream, and withstands the whole force of the water. This morning the river presented a melancholy spectacle, from the numerous wrecks of vessels which had perished during last night's storm.

From a brass plate that was discovered in the immediate vicinity of the fort, in 1781, it would seem to have been a place of importance before the Christian era, and to have been subject to the Hindoo kings of Bengal, who resided at Gour. There is, however, no mention made of Monghyr by the Mahomedan historians, till the beginning of the sixteenth century, when the kings of Bahar disputed its possession with the kings of Bengal. Cossim Ali Khan, whom the British raised to the throne of Moorshedabad, in supercession of Mir Jaffier, having previously created him Nawab, on dethroning Suraj-ud-Dowlah (ludicrously called Sir Roger Dowler), in 1757, after throwing off all allegiance to the British government, repaired to Monghyr to take up his residence there. He added considerably to the strength of the fortifications, and endeavoured to discipline the natives for its defence. But the English took it after a siege of nine days, and made it a military station. At the time that the government of Bengal raised Cossim Ali Khan to the throne, it recommended him to keep troops like the British Sepoys; to drill and arm them after the English fashion, and to make them wear red coats, in fact, entirely to doff the Oriental costume and training. Cossim took this advice, but turned the weapons against those who had placed them in his hands; and for several years he fought many battles against his quondam counsellors. Had Cossim Ali Khan's plan, to lay siege to Kathmandoo (Kath, wood, the wooden city), succeeded, the British would have been spared the trouble of the Nepaul war of 1814-16; but at that time, there was no shadow of coming events in that direction.

In 1766, a strong brigade of six battalions, and some artillery, used to be in quarters at Monghyr; in short, one-third of the Bengal army was stationed here, while at Patna and Allahabad there were other brigades. It is now a station only for invalids, being a very healthy spot. The Commandant occupies the old palace, the former residence of the Sultan Soojah. It is extremely handsome; and is surrounded by fine gardens, tanks and plantations. The houses of the staff-officers are also convenient.

Monghyr is the Birmingham of India, for the natives excel in the manufacture of guns, pistols and rifles; many of them marked with the names of Manton, Egg, and other celebrated gun-makers. I have seen one or two of them fired off, and perhaps safely with light charges. A sporting engineer belonging to our steamer, bought a Manton for £1 4s., and fired several times successively. These guns are very cleverly made; and a novice could not possibly detect that they had not been manufactured by those whose names they bear. Forks and knives, cork-screws, hammers, and other articles of hardware of very good descriptions, are also made here. Fans, table-mats, straw hats and bonnets, necklaces and bracelets, made of a wood resembling jet, etc.; everything in fact may be purchased, very good, and at reasonable cost. In our visit to the bazaars, indeed all over the place, we were beset by beggars, who are excessively numerous, and in the most piteous and abject condition. All the hard work, it seems, is done by the women. I am told that they work much better than the men, and get but badly paid. About twenty brought the fuel required for our steamer, and put it on board, while the men were looking idly on.

The consumption of coals daily, on board our steamer, averages 400 maunds; but when the current is strong, 500 maunds are expended. Three maunds of wood are only equal to one maund of coals.

I really felt quite mortified at seeing the gentler sex engaged in such masculine work; one of them especially looked quite incapable of undergoing the toil. It is the custom for the men to sit lounging at home, or roaming about begging alms of strangers, while the women work in the open air—a strange perversity of our nature, and one which tends to shew the barbarous state of these people; wherever heathenism or infidelity prevails, woman is degraded. Christianity alone, restores her to her proper sphere.

I visited the gaol, which is a large building, and contains, as one of the chained men informed me, "a hundred as good as himself." I likewise went to the burying-ground, which is crowded with monuments, but they cannot last long—a few more monsoons will assuredly destroy them. There is a chaplain at Monghyr and two missionaries, besides several civilians.

Monghyr is considered a sacred bathing-place; and during the season the throng is immense. There the pilgrims, men, women and children, meet to unite in the worship of the Ganges, by bathing in its hallowed stream, and by pouring out water as libations to the sun and moon, or to the spirits of their departed friends. Sir J. Chardin observed a similar custom in Mingrelia and Georgia, as also in other Eastern countries. He says: "The people, before sitting down to a feast, go out abroad, and with eyes turned up to heaven, pour out a cup of wine on the ground as a libation." This idolatrous practice we likewise find prevalent among the Jews, who, when reproved by Jeremiah, persisted in continuing, not only to burn incense to the queen of heaven, but to pour out their drink-offerings unto her.[103]

We had a fine view of the Kurruckpore hills; and at six o'clock the same day anchored off Bhaugulpore, having passed Sooltangunge, on the right bank of the river. There is an indigo factory and house at Sooltangunge, very prettily situated; the lofty rocks of Jehangeera, crowned with a Mahomedan tomb, are in a most singular position.

Bhaugulpore is a town in the Province of Bahar, situated about two miles from the main branch of the Ganges. A nullah runs past Bhaugulpore; it separates a strip of land from the Ganges, into which it afterwards flows. The Ganges is extremely broad here; and in the rainy season, when the waters are much swollen, is full eight miles across. It is pleasantly situated; and commands a distant view of Mount Mandar, an insulated conical hill, and noted place of Hindoo pilgrimage. There are two very peculiar round towers about a mile north-west of the town, which the Rajah of Jeynugur considers so holy, that he has erected a building to shelter his subjects who frequent them from the burning rays of the sun.

At the entrance of the town is a noble banyan tree, which Lord Valentia also mentions in his travels. This tree is found in most parts of India; but perhaps the largest are to be met with towards the South. Humboldt, in his Cosmos,[104] speaking of the banyan, or Indian fig-tree, says, "The Indian fig-tree, that takes root by its branches, and whose stem has a diameter of twenty-eight feet; and which, as Onesicritus remarked with much truth to nature, forms 'a leafy canopy, similar to a tent supported by numerous pillars.'"

The population of Bhaugulpore is a mixture of Mahomedans and Hindoos. The majority are Mahomedans, who had a college, which existed in 1815, though in a state of great decay.

I must remark that many cities in India, such as Delhi, Benares, Allahabad, and Bhaugulpore, exhibit a mixture of Hindoo and Mahomedan buildings. The former, as having been the seat of the Hindoo and Mahomedan governments, is easily accounted for. At Benares, as I stated, the Mussulman emperor erected the mosque, to insult its inhabitants, who were Hindoos. In the cases of Allahabad, Bhaugulpore, and other cities, we must refer the fact to different circumstances.

At Bhaugulpore there is a corps called the "Hill-rangers": it was raised in 1792, and is composed of men who reside in the hills near the District, and sends detachments to Monghyr, Purneah, Bootan frontier, and to Titalyah. Mr. Cleveland, of the Bengal Civil Service, who died in 1784, early recognised the fact, that the wild hill tribes could only be kept in subjection by a system of strict justice and moderation. He went among them, and brought over their chiefs to a sense of the necessity of promoting peace among their people. In order to create a feeling of unanimity, and to put a stop to the quarrels in which they were continually embroiled with the Lowlanders, he disciplined a party of these men, who were subsequently formed into a corps, denominated the Paharees, or "Hill-rangers." In their mountain homes, these men are not far removed from the savage; they live by the chase, and never go unarmed. They are extremely hospitable and honest, and are remarkable for their probity, as servants. With this naturally good foundation, it will readily be conceived that they make good soldiers. They are kept in a state of admirable discipline; and in place of devastating the country, and plundering their neighbours, they now protect the district from the marauders, and both person and property are secure. The character of these tribes bears a close resemblance to that of the Bheels and Nairs, the latter being peculiar to the Madras Presidency.

The Bheels are considered to be the Aborigines of central India; a bold, daring set of banditti, possessing nevertheless, many virtues. Truth, honesty, and fidelity are their distinguishing features. They are born warriors and despise the tillers of the soil. In 1817, Lieut.-Colonel James Tod offered some of these Bheels four rupees, or eight shillings, a month, if they would cultivate the soil; but they indignantly refused, "because their forefathers had never done so before them." In 1840, two Bheel corps were formed; one at Malwa, and the other at Mewar. The Bheels are a decidedly distinct race, and are divided into numerous tribes: they are Hindoos by religion, but some few of them have become followers of the prophet. They have been deprived of the fairest portions of their land by the Rajahs, and are now confined to the uncultivated tracts of their mountains.

Thus Mr. Cleveland's laudable efforts have been more successful than might have been expected, and the people in the neighbourhood of

Bhaugulpore, instead of being in a state of continual strife, are now living very peaceably. Mr. Cleveland's former residence, a large handsome building, is situated immediately on the banks of the Ganges, and a monument to his memory has been erected in the burial-ground. There are several other very good houses, this being a civil station. A Branch of the Agricultural and Horticultural Society has been flourishing for the last ten years, and the Botanical Gardens are worth visiting. There is a resident chaplain who divides his duties between this place and Monghyr. I may remark, by the way, that all the chaplains are military; and, as in the Navy, are entitled to prize money in war time.

The late Colonel Francklin endeavoured to make Bhaugulpore the site of the ancient Palibothra, because he supposed the Chundun to be the Erannoboas of the Greeks. This subject has, however, been so fully discussed, that it is to be hoped that the mind of the reader has been duly impressed with the conviction that Allahabad is the veritable site, as being the spot where the junction of those two mighty rivers, the Ganges and the Jumna, occurs.

Bhaugulpore is noted for its silk manufacture, particularly for a very light material much used in dishabille, as well as for screens, punkahs, etc. The trade has latterly been much promoted by the facility of exportation by the Calcutta steamers, for this is one of the Company's stations.

On the 1st of June, we started at daybreak, and arrived at Colgong at half-past-seven A.M., having passed three singular and romantic looking rocks, rising to a height of about sixty feet from the bed of the river, and covered with verdure, among which some fanatics have built a few sheds.

We left Colgong at eight, A.M. on the same day. Seven miles below Colgong, the river takes a singular turn, round a hill covered with wood, and where some rocks, with carvings of Hindoo deities, jut out boldly into the stream. These rocks are very dangerous, because in descending the river, you must hug the right bank, so as to keep them on your left hand, for just below the rocks, which rise in the middle of the river, there is a strong back-water. The captain's object is to prevent his boat from getting into this back-water, and thus being carried and lost upon, these rocks. There is moreover a kind of whirlpool near the spot, so that we may call it the "Scylla and Charybdis" of the Ganges. Boats ascending the river keep to the left, where the stream is not rapid; but in descending, the boatmen, in order to meet and overcome this back-water, must pull very hard, and for a sixteen-oared boat at least twelve or fourteen of the crew must row. The back-water is probably caused by the tendency of the water to run to the rocks, in consequence of the turn in the river to the right, the rocks being on the left.

The Jungheera rocks, lower down the river, are very picturesque. A Fakeer resides in a small dwelling, on one of these rocks. The natives furnish him with food; but he sometimes makes an excursion on shore, and supplies himself. The Fakeer pleasantly sleeps in the midst of the howling storm, none the worse for the wind and rain; neither has he any fear of being blown out of his cabin, or of his house being washed down the stream; a few monkeys keep him company, and possibly some fairy queen may visit this presiding deity of the stream, and soothe, what to a stranger, would appear a wretched existence.

Just before passing Peerpointee, on the right bank, the river Koosee flows into the Ganges, and above Sickreegullee, or the dangerous pass, so called from the difficulty I have named, which the steamers and boats have in rounding it, we reached the place where the Teryagullee hills end, and those of Rajmahal commence. They are crowded with fine forest trees, shrubs, and other verdure, most pleasing for the eye to rest upon, after the tameness of the first part of our voyage. The hills abound in game; and the sportsman would be rewarded with a variety not frequently met with.

The Rajmahal hills, are intersected by a line which runs as far south as Balasore, traversing the districts of Nagore and Bishunpore, and the mountain chain between Kimore and the Ganges. Extensive coal-beds have recently been discovered along this line of demarcation, and have greatly enhanced the value and importance of the whole district. This mountain-chain is broken by numerous valleys, defiles, and wide-spreading plains, many of which are very fertile, and well cultivated, especially those which lie at the base of the mountains. The highest part of these ridges may be estimated at 4,000 feet, and some of the plains run along at an elevation of more than 2,000 feet above the level of the Ganges.

This chain is for the most part covered with lofty timber trees, and various kinds of woods, which are much used by the natives in building and in cabinet manufactures. These hills are clothed from the base to the summit, and the trees grow in tiers or terraces, down into the plain of the Ganges. In the northern rear of this chain, run the Rajmahal hills, which are divided from the Kimore range by the narrow valley of the Sone. The mountain-chain runs so close to the Ganges, between Bhaugulpore and the Rajmahal hills, as scarcely to admit of a causeway along the banks of the river. The government has wisely met this difficulty, by constructing a good road between Rajmahal and Colgong, which crosses the narrow defile of Sickreegullee.

We anchored off Rajmahal at a quarter to six in the evening of the 1st of June; and having to take in coal, we waited for the night. As usual, whenever an opportunity occurred, I hastened on shore for a stroll. Rajmahal is in the Province of Bengal, and about seventy miles from Berhampore. The Province of Bengal terminates a little below Sickreegullee, a village cultivated by invalided Sepoys, who have redeemed the land from the wilderness of former times. At Teryagullee, on the borders of the district, is the pass of Sickreegullee, which, during the Hindoo and Mahomedan dynasties, was the commanding entrance from Bahar into Bengal, and was strongly fortified. It runs up a narrow winding road, where the traveller will see a ruined gateway and fort, to tell of days gone by. He will also find a great deal of waste land, and mountainous tracts of country. The people are a wild race, quite distinct from those of the plains. They are low in stature, but stout and well proportioned, many being under four feet ten inches high, and many more under five feet three inches, than above that standard. The women are small indeed. They have flat noses, and lips thicker than those of the Lowlanders. They do not venerate the cow like the Hindoos, and have no knowledge of letters, or of any kind of written characters. They subsist principally on maize—the Indian corn. Nearly all the laborious work is done by the women; and a man is rich in proportion to the number of his wives, and who are indeed so many labourers, or, I may say, domestic slaves. These mountaineers have a great regard for the truth, and an utter abhorrence of lying, which ranks them far above their brothers of the plains, where lying is joined to the other vices.

Their traffic is in bedsteads, wood, planks, charcoal, cotton, honey, plantains, and sweet potatoes, which they barter for tobacco, rice, salt, cloth, iron arrow-heads, hatchets, crooks, and iron implements. Their weapons are the bow and arrow; but some few among them possess swords and matchlocks. Their domestic animals are hogs, goats, fowls, dogs, and cats.

It was among these wild races that Mr. Augustus Cleveland, the judge and magistrate of the district, made a permanent settlement about the year 1780. Unfortunately he died at the early age of twenty-nine, in the year 1784, as I have before observed. A monument, in the form of a pagoda, was erected by the Zumindars, or landholders of the neighbourhood, to commemorate his exemplary conduct, and another was put up at the expense of the Government, in honour of a man, who, though young, had done so much to benefit his fellow-creatures.

The Ganges flows close under the ruins of an old palace, on the brink of its right bank. Previous to the year 1638, it was the residence of Sultan Soojah, the brother of Aurungzebe, but scarcely any vestiges of the building now remain. The Ganges, about 1639, wholly quitted the vicinity of Gour, and approached the rocky bank of Rajmahal, where it still holds its course. The force of the current, on the right or Rajmahal side, is so great in the rainy season, that I am told an officer, who was sailing in a twelve-oared budgerow against the stream, which came rushing down like a torrent, actually had the sides of his boat split. The Dandees (not fops, but the boatmen of the Ganges), in sailing up the river used to call out, "Allah! Allah!" i.e. "God! God!" on entering that strong water, just as the native boatmen are wont to do in crossing the surf at Madras. On the left bank the river is smooth and always safe. The ruins of the palace still extend over a large space of ground. Close to the margin of the river are three arches supported by pillars of the colour of black marble. No doubt the Ganges has washed away much; and, probably, many slabs of beautiful marble, like that with which the ball-room of Government House, in Calcutta, is paved, now lie submerged under the stream. It is supposed that the Ganges, in rushing over these ruins, causes the sound of water running over rocks, which is the effect produced in this place.

The ruins of the palace are quite overspread with low jungle, abounding, as I was informed, with snakes and other reptiles. Broken gateways of beautiful architecture, mosques, and a large hall of audience—as it is reported to have been—still indicate the former importance and grandeur of this place.

In the absence of Hindoo historical dates, we must content ourselves with traditions, till we come to the Mahomedan writers. We are told that Rajmahal was anciently the seat of the Hindoo sovereigns, in whose time it bore the name of Raj Ghur. Its first mention by Mussulman historians, is in 1576; and again in 1592, when, in the reign of the Emperor Akbar, Rajah Maun Singh, governor of Bengal and Bahar, made it his capital, gave it the name of Rajmahal, and fortified it with walls and bulwarks. In 1608, Islam Khan, the Mogul governor, transferred the seat of government to Dacca, in consequence of the invasion of the Portuguese. In 1639, Sultan Soojah, the brother of Aurungzebe, again made it the royal residence, and lavished vast treasures in restoring the fortifications, and erecting the palace, of which I have just spoken.

On the expulsion of this sovereign from his dominions, the Mogul governor again moved the seat of government to Dacca. Since this period the ancient capital of Bengal has rapidly declined, not only from the withdrawal of the government; but in consequence, also, of the frequent ravages committed by those two irresistible elements, fire and water.

In recent times, Rajmahal was sought as a place of refuge by the unhappy Suraj-ud-Dowlah, who concealed himself in an out-building in a lone garden; but he was discovered, and betrayed to his enemies by a wretched Fakeer, whom he had treated with great barbarity on a former occasion, having ordered his ears and nose to be cut off. Suraj-ud-Dowlah was seized, and carried to Moorshedabad, where he was murdered with wanton cruelty.

Not many years ago, Rajmahal was a military station; but now no European resides here. There is a small Christian burial-ground, which has been walled in by some liberal and kind-hearted persons. In it is the last resting-place of many an unfortunate European, who has died near the town in his way up or down the river.

On the 2nd of June, we again proceeded at daybreak, and about noon cast anchor nearly opposite to the ancient city of Gour, and close to a village called Lall Dobree. Gour was built about 2,000 years ago, and is the ancient name of the capital of Bengal Proper: it is a few miles to the south of the town of Malda. The name of Gour is said to be derived from Gur or Goor, which, in the Sanscrit and modern languages of India, signifies raw sugar; and, from the Sanscrit term for manufactured sugar (sarcara) are derived the Persian, Greek, Latin, and many of the European names for the same article.

The ruins of Gour extend fifteen miles along the old banks of the Ganges, and are from two to three miles in breadth, which would give a circuit of thirty-four or thirty-five miles. Several villages now occupy part of the ground on which the ancient Gour stood; the remainder is either covered with thick forests, the resort of tigers and beasts of prey, or else has been converted into arable land, the soil of which contains much brick-dust. The city of Gour is nearly central to the populous parts of Bengal and Bahar, and not far from the junction of the principal rivers which form the excellent inland navigation. It is now about four miles from the Ganges; and this river, with a slip of land of a few miles in width, separates it from Rajmahal. The freak of the Ganges, in 1639, in parting from its old bed and rushing over to Rajmahal, proves that very strong shields, or river-bank defences, will be required to protect the banks of the Ganges.

The ruins of this city of former days have supplied the materials for building the more recent towns of Rajmahal, Moorshedabad, Dacca, and Malda. Enough, however, still remains to prove its former magnificence— broken palaces, mosques, mausolea, and temples, testify to its ancient splendour. Major Rennel says, that Gour is supposed to be the Gangia Regia of Ptolemy.

On re-visiting Gour, in September, 1849, I called at one of Lord Glenelg's indigo factories, the superintendent of which, Mr. R.B. M'Intosh, showed me some old coins, which had been found by his workmen at different periods; some slabs of marble, too, taken from a large Mahomedan temple, had been converted by the same gentleman into a handsome outer doorway to his house.

At a little before sunset, we changed the Ganges for the Bhauguretty river.

On the 3rd of June we were early off Sootee, on the right bank, and 210 miles from Calcutta. In 1757, when Suraj-ud-Dowlah, the Subahdar of Bengal, apprehended an attack from the English, and believed that their ships of war could proceed up the eastern branch of the Ganges to the northern point of the Cossimbazar island, and thence down the Bhauguretty to Moorshedabad, he commanded immense piles to be driven into the river at Sootee. By this act, the river has been rendered unnavigable for any vessels beyond boats, and even for these it is navigable only during the rainy season. The Subahdar remembered that Chandernagore, a French settlement, had been attacked on the 14th of March of the same year, and captured, by Admiral Watson and Colonel Clive, with line of battle ships, which cast anchor before it.

The river at times is not less than six miles broad at Sootee; during the rains, the steamers proceed down the Hoogly to Calcutta. At other seasons they go *viâ* the Bhauguretty and the Sunderbunds, or "the beautiful wilderness," where sportsmen may enjoy themselves by killing "a royal Bengal tiger," ten or twelve feet in length, from the head to the tip of the tail. The Sunderbunds consist of that part of the Delta of the Ganges, which is near the sea, and are in extent equal to the Principality of Wales. Salt is made here; and here also is found a boundless stock of timber, for boat building and other purposes.

About forty miles to the south of Mohungunge, at the head of the Bhauguretty, stands Bogwangola, a large inland trading town, eight miles N.E. of Moorshedabad. It is a great mart for grain. The town has a very poor appearance, being constructed entirely of bamboos, mats, and thatch; it has often been removed on account of the encroachment of the Ganges. It has more resemblance to a temporary fair, or an encampment, than to a town. The designation of town in Hindoostan, does not so much depend upon the nature of the buildings (for villages contain brick houses), as upon the rank of the public officer who superintends the general duties of the place, his rank depending on the extent of his charge. Bogwangola is a very stirring town; and the landing-place is always crowded with country boats of all sizes, and even with budgerows.

At about ten o'clock in the morning, we passed Jungepore, the site of one of the Company's principal silk factories, a portion of which is now conducted by private individuals; for since the loss of the Company's trading charter, their factories here and at other places, have been dismantled. Up to 1833, the East India Company, as is well known, held the monopoly of the trade in India and China; but the Government at home considering such a constitution of affairs incompatible with the position of a supreme legislative body, as well as injurious to the commercial and manufacturing interests, passed an act for the abolition of this monopoly, on the removal of what is commonly termed "the last charter of the East India Company, on the 25th of August, 1833." This act, as was expected, has already produced a vast change in the commercial relations of India. By throwing open the trade to private merchants, a greater stimulus has been given to individual enterprise and energy; and the market prices have been considerably lowered.

FOOTNOTES:

[103] Jer. xliv. 17.

[104] Vol. ii. p. 524.

CHAPTER XVII

Moorshedabad—Cossimbazar—"Eina Mahal"—The Nawab Cowar Krishnath Roy—"Snake-boats"—Population of Moorshedabad—Berhampore—Ivory and Silk Manufactures—Kulna—The Tidal-bore—English Factory at Kulna—Hoogly—Chinsurah—Chandernagore—Ishapore— Barrackpore —Serampore—Dum-Dum—Garden Reach— Calcutta.

At four o'clock on the afternoon of the 4th of June, we lay off Moorshedabad, a large, unwalled town, in the Province of Bengal, of which it was the capital from 1704 until our conquests transferred that distinction to Calcutta, in 1757.

In 1704, when Moorshed Coole Khan transferred the seat of government to this place, he changed its name of Mukhsooabad to Moorshedabad. It extends for eight miles along both sides of the most sacred branch of the Ganges, called Bhauguretty, or Cossimbazar, at a distance of about 120 miles above Calcutta. It is an excessively shabby-looking town; the houses are ill built, and have a mean appearance, most of them being only one story high. Some are of brick with tile roofs, others of mud; others again mere straw huts, all jumbled together without the slightest attention to regularity. The streets, too, like most of those in the East, are narrow and crooked, and seem to bid defiance to cleanliness and order. A redeeming point is the number of fine trees, which impart a picturesque character to this heterogeneous mass of buildings. Close to the brink of the river, however, there are some tolerable houses, mosques and temples, but these, too, are inferior to those of other cities.

The most conspicuous and handsome building in the city, is the palace of the Nawab. It is quite a magnificent place, and is called "Eina Mahal." It was planned and built under the superintendence of Lieutenant-General Duncan M'Leod, of the Bengal Engineers. It is a most chaste and elegant structure, built in the European style, of pure white marble of dazzling brightness. It almost rivals the Government House, at Calcutta. The General took a correct model of it to England for the inspection of the public, who must have admired it greatly, and commended the taste and ingenuity of the architect.

There are also some fine remains of the old palace, built by Aliverdi Khan, about 1750, constructed in the Hindoo style, with the rich black marbles and pillars that once graced the city of Gour.

Cossimbazar, a little town about one mile south of the city, and which, properly speaking, is the port of Moorshedabad, is a place of immense traffic, and great inland trade. Until the days of free trade, there was a silk factory at Cossimbazar, and the late Hon. Andrew Ramsay, uncle of the Marquis of Dalhousie, was the commercial Resident for many years.

Moorshedabad is still the residence of the Nawab of Bengal, who inhabits the Palace which I have described above. The present Nawab, Cowar Krishnath Roy, has been instructed in the English language. He is about thirty years of age; an English education has greatly improved him, and though he has not altogether divested himself of his Mahomedan habits, still those who are personally acquainted with him, inform me, that his manners are those of a well-bred European, and that he is intelligent, and very fond of reading. He sometimes goes to Calcutta, and may be seen there on the course, in his barouche and four, driven by an English coachman. My gentle readers must not be surprised to learn that the young prince has more than one wife; but they may be forgiven for being astonished at being told that European ladies have married Nawabs.

The Prince has many boats, built on the Burmese model, of great length, with short paddles. They are called "snake boats," and shoot along with the rapidity of an arrow. I have seen one of them keep pace with a steamer for several miles. They are generally rowed by twenty men. The Nawab's state barge is very handsome, it is richly painted and gilded, and draped with canopies and carpets of the richest combination of colours, which produce a gorgeous and pleasing effect. It is only used on grand occasions, and is attended by a band of music which follows in another boat.

Moorshedabad is now the residence of the British Civil Establishment, and the head-quarters of a Circuit Court, comprising six of the neighbouring districts. The mint is now under the control of the British.

The population of Moorshedabad has been given at 600,000, nay even at 700,000 persons; but taking Delhi and its suburbs, by the returns, to be 160,279 persons, and recollecting that Benares contains only 183,491, we can scarcely allow more than 200,000 inhabitants. The number of houses, of every kind, was returned, in 1814, at about 30,000; and, according to the computation usual in Bengal, of eleven individuals to every two houses, the population at that time was 165,000. The trade, and especially the inland traffic is very brisk; the staple commodities are silk and indigo; the former is manufactured in the vicinity of the city, into the most beautiful silks and taffetas. The silk goods manufactured here are considered to be of very superior quality. The trade is greatly promoted by facilities of steam and river navigation. This is especially the case during the rainy season, when the river is crowded with boats, bringing and fetching the merchandise. From October to May, the trade is very slack, for at that season the Bhauguretty is almost dry. At its junction with the Jellinghee further down, these two branches of the Ganges form the Hoogly, which runs to Calcutta.

The indigo trade is extremely lucrative; large supplies are sent to Calcutta, whence they are shipped to England, and thence to other parts of Europe. It has long formed an important branch in the East Indian trade, as the Indian indigo is highly prized on account of its superior colour. This beautiful dye, which was not known in Europe till the beginning of the 17th century, when it was first introduced by the Dutch, seems to have been in use more than 2,000 years ago, as we infer from a passage in Pliny.

Six miles from Moorshedabad is Berhampore, on the east bank of the Bhauguretty. It contains very fine barracks for European troops, with an upper story, at the extremities of a magnificent parade ground. The quarters of the officers are much like those at Dinapore, of which I have made mention. Berhampore was formerly the head-quarters of a Division of the army: the commandant's house, pleasantly situated on the bank of the river, is now occupied by an indigo planter. There is a chaplain here and two missionaries, one of whom, however, is a Roman Catholic. A few civilians also reside here; but the place is generally very dull, and much disliked.

Formerly, there used to be a European regiment, a corps of Native Infantry, and a brigade of guns: also recruits, recently arrived from England, were generally stationed here, although a sad mortality was the invariable result, on account of the numerous marshes and superabundant foliage which surround the place; its situation being scarcely above the level of the river at certain periods of the year.

At present the only troops stationed here are—a detachment of Native Foot Artillery, and the 14th Regiment Native Infantry; for owing to the demand for Europeans in our extended North-Western frontier, a regiment of our countrymen can hardly be expected to remain here, except as a temporary measure. When I revisited Berhampore, in August, 1849, I was informed, that the authorities had given orders that a portion of the barracks should be put in readiness, for one of the three regiments which had recently landed at Calcutta from England, the European barracks having been unoccupied for the last seven or eight years. The arrival of three regiments at Calcutta, in addition to those already stationed there, called for some little ingenuity in their disposal; the monsoon not being over, so as to allow of a march, and some hundred recruits in addition, being daily expected to land.

Provisions are very cheap here. Berhampore is noted for its ivory and silk manufactures, specimens of which were brought on board for sale. It is likewise one of the coal depôts for the river steamers, as well as one of the principal stations for embarking goods. The coal depôts are Mirzapore, Benares, Ghazepore, Dinapore, Bar, Monghyr, Colgong, Rajmahal, Berhampore, and Kutwa. There is a great deal of communication between this place and Calcutta, which is only 161 miles distant by the river route, the intercourse being now carried on with great regularity and speed.

Leaving Berhampore we reached Kulna, which is situated on the right bank, sixty-four miles from Calcutta. It is a very inconsiderable place.

The native boatmen, on reaching Kulna on their downward course, "rig out anchors," as it is called; that is to say, they have a frame-work, which they fill with stones, the weight of which chiefly acts as an anchor. These primitive anchors are used by the budgerows, and all the native boats, with the exception of the pinnace, which has its regular iron anchor. On nearing the Hoogly, the boatmen meet the bore, or tide, coming up with great violence against the stream. The banks being extremely narrow here, cause such a swell, that as it crosses from bank to bank, or dashes alongside, it upsets all the boats that come within its influence. By keeping in the middle of the stream, with the prow straight to the bore, a boat may remain safe from an upset.

We made but a short stay at Kulna, and were soon on our way to Hoogly, which is situated on the west side of the river of the same name, or more properly speaking, the Bhauguretty. It is twenty-eight miles from Fort William. Hoogly, like several of the large towns on the Ganges, was for a time the capital of Bengal. It is supposed to have been founded by the Portuguese, about the year 1538. They fortified and greatly improved the city, which soon became so important a mart of commerce, as to excite the jealousy of Shah Jehan, who took it after a siege of three months. During this siege, it is said that more than 5,000 of the Portuguese were killed or taken prisoners, and the most beautiful of the girls were sent to Agra, to grace the imperial harem. Shah Jehan now made it the principal port, and gave permission to the Dutch and English to build some factories, which soon became very prosperous.

The English, whose factory was situated in the town, had a body of about twenty soldiers to protect their property; but some disputes having arisen with the imperial government, the British quietly procured a detachment of 400 soldiers, who were landed from some men-of-war which came from

Madras. The Nawab was alarmed at these proceedings, and brought up a large military reinforcement. A conflict ensued, in which Admiral Nicholson opened a cannonade from his men-of-war, fired the city, and, unfortunately, burnt not only 500 native houses, but destroyed the factory, which contained goods to the amount of about £300,000 sterling. The governor was terrified, and offered to indemnify the English for all the damage which they had sustained; but the Nawab not only refused to give his assent to this, but was so incensed that he issued orders for the confiscation of all the English factories and property. He was at that time at Dacca, and dispatched a body of men to expel the British from Hoogly. Just before their arrival, however, the English had withdrawn to Calcutta with all their property. The Nawab soon after relented, and requested their return, which they refused, but obtained permission to establish the factory at Calcutta.

After continued intestine disputes and constant jarring with the English, the latter took possession of Hoogly in 1757. Since that time various political changes were effected in the local government; but, in 1765, the East India Company were appointed, by the Emperor of Delhi, to be his dewans or collectors of revenues for Bengal, Bahar, and Orissa, on the condition of his receiving from them an indemnity of nine lakhs of rupees, or £90,000 per annum.

Ever since that time the importance of Hoogly has declined. The British government made Calcutta the chief port; in consequence of which all the trade has been concentrated there.

The French, Dutch, Portuguese and Danes, had formerly each a factory here.

In going down the river the tide and the bore are first felt. A mile beyond Hoogly, is Chinsurah, once the principal Dutch settlement in the East Indies; it is also on the right bank of the river, about twenty-four miles above Calcutta. The Dutch had a factory here as early as 1656. More wary than the English, the Dutch, on receiving permission from Shah Jehan to establish a factory, built it at Chinsurah, about a couple of miles from Hoogly; and, as they employed natives as well as Dutch, they soon formed a considerable settlement. In consequence of the rebellion which broke out in Bengal in 1696, the various European factories sought and obtained permission from the Nawab to fortify their several establishments. The fortifications constructed by the Dutch were of a very superior character; and, being on the most amicable terms with the government, they quietly aided the authorities in re-capturing Hoogly, which had fallen into the hands of the rebels. This procured them great favour from the government, which granted them fresh privileges. In 1769, however, Chinsurah was blockaded by the Nawab's forces, to compel payment of arrears of duties. It was subsequently taken by the British, to whom it now belongs.

The appearance of the town, as might be expected from the national character of the Dutch, is extremely neat. The houses, generally speaking, are white, and have Venetians and pretty green verandahs running round them. Some barracks have been erected of late years for European troops. In August, 1849, the 87th Royal Irish Fusiliers were sent here, as there was no room for them at the time, either at Fort William or at Dum-Dum.

Proceeding three miles further, we came to Chandernagore, the principal French settlement in Bengal, on the right bank of the river. Its situation is far preferable to Calcutta in every respect. Like the old Dutch settlement, it forms a striking contrast to the Hindoo and Mahomedan cities. The houses look beautifully clean and white, with green Venetians, and a sort of colonnade in front. The roofs are flat, and the inmates frequently resort there in the cool of the day. The town is surrounded by gardens, and groves of trees. The factory was established a few years later than that of the Dutch, and like it was fortified. It was extremely flourishing; and the fort contained a garrison of about 300 soldiers, and a good train of artillery. At this time, 1757, Admiral Watson and Colonel Clive took it from the French by force of arms, having brought three or four sixty-four and sixty gun-ships before the place, though nothing beyond a large gun-boat can now approach the town.

The French are allowed to have a certain number of chests of opium, at the average of the sales. Should the opium afterwards fall in price, they may return it; but should it advance the profit is theirs. The French Consul does not reside here, but at Calcutta. The local government is carried on by nineteen functionaries; and the stranger generally meets with much hospitality and courtesy.

Three miles further down the river is Ishapore, the site of the government gunpowder works; and about five miles lower still, is Barrackpore, a military station, fifteen miles from Calcutta, with a good road between them. It is the head-quarters of the Presidency Division. At present it contains five regiments of Native Infantry; having formerly six quartered here. The cantonments are on the left bank of the Hoogly, and directly opposite to Serampore. The artillery belonging to this division is stationed at Dum-Dum, about seven miles from Calcutta.

The Governor-General has a country residence here, in the midst of a park and grounds, which are laid out, with much taste, in walks, drives, and gardens. The view from the park is very beautiful, as it comprises a most magnificent reach in the river. It formerly contained a menagerie, abounding in tigers and wild animals of all kinds, snakes, birds, etc.; but this is no longer kept up. There is a fine mausoleum in the park, erected by Lord Minto, while Governor-General, in memory of the officers who fell in Java and the Mauritius. The Marquis Wellesley intended to build a palace at Barrackpore, which was to rival his splendid residence at Calcutta; but he was deterred by the home-government. Lord Auckland established a Native school here, and left funds for its endowment. There is also a neat church.

In 1824, Barrackpore was the scene of a mutiny in the Native Infantry corps stationed there, who refused to march to the Burmese territory, in consequence of a deficiency of draught cattle. At the hour of parade, the 47th Regt. Native Infantry refused to turn out. The European officers tried every art and stratagem to overcome the mutiny, which spread to two other corps. Two regiments which were stationed at Calcutta were instantly summoned. The mutineers were drawn up on parade, and some guns placed in their rear. The officers again made every attempt to reduce them to obedience; but the men remaining obdurate, the guns were opened, and made a sad havoc among them. The ringleaders were put to death; others too were killed; and not a few were drowned in trying to escape by swimming across the river.

Serampore, which lies opposite to Barrackpore, was for many years a Danish settlement; the Danes having established a factory here, about the same time when the English, French and Dutch founded theirs, higher up the river. During the war between England and Denmark, in 1807, Serampore was taken by the Company, who subsequently restored it to its former possessors. On the 22nd of February, 1845, a treaty or deed of sale was signed between the Danish and British East India Company's governments, by which Serampore was conveyed to the latter power for the sum of £125,000; the returns for many years previously had not met the expenses, and it was merely held for commercial purposes. It still carries on an unimportant trade both with Europe and China.

Serampore was long celebrated as a missionary station, when the Danish colony flourished here; for no missionaries were allowed to reside in any part of the Bengal Presidency, except at Serampore. At that time no missionary dared venture to open his lips, or even to shew his face in Calcutta; whereas now there are above fifty missionaries, including those at Bishop's college, Howrah and Dum-Dum; whilst at Serampore there are only three, and one of these is a Roman Catholic. In the whole of the Bengal Presidency, there are one hundred and sixty-three, whose mission it is to teach the Christian religion. Of this number, however, including the Bishop, only seventy belong to the Ecclesiastical establishment, the other ninety-three being Roman Catholics, Armenians, and Greeks. The period of which

I am speaking, is January, 1853. Forty-six years earlier, there were only ten missionaries in Bengal.

Serampore presents a similar appearance to Chandernagore, in regard to the extreme neatness and simplicity of the buildings. In both, the houses are white, with flat roofs, and furnished with verandahs and Venetian blinds. The church is very handsome. The town is not fortified; but a battery is drawn up near the flagstaff.

Midway between Barrackpore and Calcutta, we passed Dum-Dum. The mess-house belonging to the artillery, is considered the finest and largest in India. At present there is only one company of European and three companies of Native Artillery quartered here; this scientific and most efficient branch of the service being much needed on our lately extended frontier. There is here a remarkably fine cannon-foundery, where twelve brass guns may be bored at the same time. The iron guns are brought from Europe. All the arrangements, machinery and works, are of the first order. The Elephant Battery is most ingenious, and these noble animals perform their work with admirable precision and effect.

The young officer, on his arrival from England, receives here a course of instruction not exceeding a twelvemonth in duration, before he joins his regiment. The apartments of the officers are very handsome and comfortable.

There is a monument at Dum-Dum, to the memory of the late Colonel T.D. Pearse, who died here in 1789.

After quitting Dum-Dum, we passed the cannon foundery, which is at Cossipore, about half a mile from the town. It is pleasantly situated on the banks; and there are many fine houses belonging to the merchants of the city, who come here to enjoy some little relaxation, after the fatigues and anxieties inseparable from money-getting.

On the 8th of June, 1846, at ten o'clock in the morning, we anchored off Garden Reach, Calcutta, where I bade adieu to the accommodation-boat, "Soorma," and its civil commander and officers, and by noon was domiciled in Spence's hotel.

During my short stay at Calcutta, I received much kindness and hospitality from the arch-deacon (now Bishop of Madras), and Mrs. Dealtry, Professor and Mrs. Weidemann, Mr. and Mrs. Murray Gladstone, and Mr. William Abbott. I must reserve till the next chapter the fruits of my four several visits to this city, on my passage to and from Europe.

CHAPTER XVIII

Project of a Railway to Calcutta—Calcutta, a Six Months'
Trip from England—The Strand Road—The Mint—
Professor Weidemann—The Strand Mills—The General
Post Office—Custom House—Auditor General's Office—
Military Board—The Commissariat—The Ice House—
Metcalfe Hall—The Public Library—Bank of Bengal—The
Oriental Bank—Indian Failures—Chandpaul Ghât—Baboo
Ghât—Docks of Howrah—Prinsep's Ghât—Kidderpore
Ghât—Fort William—Mir Jaffier—Arsenal—Chowringhee
Road—Ochterlony Monument—Government House—
Entertainments at Government House—Policy of Marquis
Wellesley—Hotels at Calcutta—Theatricals—The Town
Hall—Concerts—Fancy Fairs—The Mayor's Court—
Newspapers—Merchants—Agency Business—Railways—
Asiatic Society—Martinière Charity—College of Fort
William—Haileybury College—Military Seminary at
Addiscombe—Colleges—Schools—Mesmeric Hospital—
Chloroform—Sailors' Home—Alms Houses—Masonic
Lodges—Botanical Garden—Charter of 1834—Lunatic
Asylums—Law Courts—Police Office—Provident Funds.

The stupendous project of bringing Calcutta within seven or eight days
of London, by means of the Euphrates valley railway route, will probably
not take place in our days; but, incredible as it may seem, we yet hope we
may look forward to its being carried out in those of our children. Some
persons may possibly smile, and say, "It is the scheme of a visionary;" but
who, let me ask, in the days of Job Charnock,—only 120 years ago, when he
founded Calcutta—would have dreamt that that wretched, swampy village
would have been converted into a city of palaces, and still less, that instead
of a tedious sea-voyage of six or seven months from the mother country, it
would be brought within the brief limits of forty-five or fifty days! Again
let me ask, who only a few years ago would have conceived the possibility
of a mode of communication whereby intelligence may be transmitted, not
only by land but by sea, with the rapidity of lightning. Nay, that 4,000 miles
of electric wire have already reached Calcutta, soon to connect every large
town in India with the port of Bombay; while at the same time the submarine

telegraph is in progress from Suez to Trieste, and before the expiration of 1855, will enable us to hear from our friends in any part of India in eleven or twelve days.

Calcutta is so well worth a visit, that notwithstanding the numerous and able descriptions which have been given of it by various writers, I would strongly advise all who have it in their power, to become personally acquainted with it. This can now be done in so brief a space of time, and with so much ease and comfort, that many persons will be glad to avail themselves of the opportunities now offered, and desire to know the readiest way to accomplish this object. I shall therefore note down a few data, as to the best mode of spending a pleasant and profitable six months in visiting the chief cities of India.

Persons who do not like the long sea-voyage of ninety or a hundred days, round by the Cape of Good Hope, in the ordinary sailing vessels, may reach Calcutta from England by the overland route in fifty days or under; and in two months may see the great city, as well as a part of the interior. Thus, suppose the traveller arrives at Calcutta on the 6th of November, he may leave it again by the steamer on the 8th of February. Let him leave London on the 20th of September of any year, and he may reach it again on the 25th of March following. Say that he arrives at Calcutta on the 6th of November, in fourteen days he can see all that is worth visiting in Calcutta, and as a river steamer leaves about the 20th of every month, he may go up the country on that day, and in twenty days more he will reach Allahabad, which will be the 10th of December. If he prefer it, he may travel Dâk to Bombay. Arriving at the Western Presidency about the middle of January, he may take another steamer and visit part of Scinde. Again, suppose a traveller proceeds north-west, let him leave Allahabad on the 15th or 16th of November for Lucknow, Agra, and Delhi, and even for Simla.

My calculation would be about as follows:—

To Lucknow (Dâk),	128	miles, requiring	3	days.
" stay at			2	"
" Agra	200	miles, requiring	4	"
" stay at			4	days
" Delhi	112	miles,	2	"

" stay at				6	"
" Kurnaul	78	miles, requiring		1	"
" stay at				1	"
" Umballa	50	miles, requiring		1	"
" Foot of hills				1	"
" Subathoo				1	"
" stay at				1	"
" Simla	23	miles, requiring		1	"
" stay at				3	"
" Kotgurh on the Sutlej				5	"
" stay at				2	"
Back to foot of hills				7	"
To Ferozepore				2	"
" Lahore				1	"
" stay at				3	"
" Ferozepore				1	"
" Kurnaul				3	"
" Meerut				1	"
" Cawnpore				4	"
" Allahabad				2	"

" Calcutta by steam	11	"
	—	
January 28th.	73	"

Thus the traveller may return on the 8th of February, and reach London on the 25th of March; a trip of six months. The longer journey would cost him about £500, and the shorter one from £280 to £300. In this manner he would see two Presidencies, and the best part of the North-Western Provinces, including Lahore.

Calcutta lies on the left or east bank of the Hoogly, or as the natives call it, Bhauguretty, or the "True Ganges," as being the chief of the ten branches which empty themselves into the sea, through their several estuaries in the Sunderbunds. It is distant about 100 miles from the Indian Ocean, in Long. 84° 22′ E., Lat. 22° 23′ N.

A magnificent line of buildings extends for six miles along the bank of the river, from Fort William on the south point, to Chitpore at the northern extremity. The princely residence of the Governor-General stands in the verdant square of the Esplanade, and is flanked on either side by the Chowringhee road, which is two miles in length.

The city is divided into two districts, the north-eastern part being inhabited by the Europeans, and the eastern by the natives. The streets are, for the most part, narrow, and the houses lofty; the lower part is appropriated to the bazaars, and the upper to the dwellings.

I propose describing Calcutta as viewed from the river. Beginning from the right, the spectator will run a line down all the way to the left of what is called the "Strand Road," or "Course," though Calcutta extends beyond the Strand Road. On the extreme right of this line is the Mint, which was planned and erected by Lieutenant-Colonel W.N. Forbes, Bengal Engineers, the present Mint-master. It is a very handsome building, one story high, supported on pillars, and was completed in the year 1830. The Mint is divided into five offices, viz., the Bullion, English, Mechanical, Assay, and Mint Committees, each of which departments gives employment to many persons. Deducting Sundays and holidays, 95 days, there will remain 270 working days.

The standard of the Bengal money is silver. Gold is sometimes coined, but the most considerable part of the currency is silver. The silver is first melted, and then run through a mould and made into long bars; next it is passed under rollers, and flattened, until it is of the thickness of the coin required, say a rupee; it is then cut into round pieces of the size of a rupee, and afterwards stamped and milled by one and the same machine. All these processes are effected by the steam engine. Next comes the weighing of the rupees, when if any be found light, they are re-melted and re-formed into bars.

Old rupees defaced, or those of native coinage, are sent down by the steamers from the Upper Provinces to Calcutta, to be re-coined. Accounts are carried on with their sub-divisions in rupees, annas, and pies; twelve pies make one anna, and sixteen annas make one rupee. The silver coins made at the Mint are rupees, half-rupees, and quarter-rupees, the copper are pice, double pice, and pies.

In the beginning of 1848, Lieutenant-Colonel Forbes, at the request of Her Majesty's Government, was ordered by the Court of Directors to proceed to England, and form part of a Royal Commission to inquire into the working of the London Mint. The Colonel was allowed to draw his Indian salary during his absence, and the expenses of his passage, home and back, were defrayed by Her Majesty's Government. The late Right Honourable R.L. Sheil, the Master of the Mint, on behalf of the Government, paid his acknowledgments for the valuable assistance which the Colonel had rendered, previous to his return to India, in June, 1849.

The Calcutta Mint is said to be more extensive than the Royal Mint. Madras has a mint, and so has Bombay; the former, however, does not appear to be much needed, as the circulation does not extend very far, and Calcutta could supply the demand.

On the occasion of my visit to the Mint, on the 27th of June, 1846, I was accompanied by my friend, the late Professor Weidemann, and his accomplished lady; and had the benefit of being conducted by some of the *employés*, who were desired to explain such parts as were new to me. In the smelting-room, the crucible is capable of containing at one time, silver enough to make 13,000 rupees; and when necessary, 250,000 can be coined in one day. Between 300 and 400 natives, and about twenty-five Europeans are attached to this scientific building, the machinery and fittings-up of which are admirable, more so, I am told, than the Mint in the Metropolis of Great Britain.

On the left of the Mint, is a large five-storied building, called the Strand Mills, belonging to Muttyloll Seal, a rich native. Here any person may have his wheat, or other corn, converted into flour on moderate terms. These mills are worked by steam. The Cossipore mills, situated near the foundry, of which I have made some mention, are similar to these.

To the left of the Strand Mills is another large building, called the Bonded Warehouse. The association was incorporated by act, of March, 1837, and consists of six Directors and a Secretary. The warehouse occupies a large oblong, the smallest front being towards the river. Some merchants at the time objected to the scheme, because having warehouses ("godowns," from the Malay word "gadong") of their own, which were usually rented on lease, they would suffer a pecuniary loss by joining the association until their leases had expired. Moreover it was an advantage to them to have their godowns near their offices.

Next to the Bonded Warehouse, stands the Marine Board Office. The river, or west front, is not very conspicuous, but it runs far back eastward. The marine superintendent is a Captain in the Indian navy. The other departments under its roof, are the master-attendant's and pilots' courts. The members of the latter court are merchants and branch pilots, usually two of each, who discuss such matters as the loss of a ship, the stranding of a vessel, etc.

The General Post Office is the next building. The post is a very important office all over India, particularly during a war, for it is then that every one looks to the arrival of news, and the post-office is literally besieged. Though India does not yet boast of railways, still the post usually travels between five and six miles an hour. An "express" to Bombay has been sent in the dry season from Calcutta in seven days, a distance of 1,300 miles. Besides the Postmaster-General, and Deputy Postmaster-General, there are twenty-seven European clerks, and a very great number of native writers.

The office of the Board of Customs, salt and opium, is of great moment, for as it includes the Abkarry or spirit department, it has the control over a revenue yielding five or six crores (£5,000,000 or £6,000,000) yearly. The Board consists of three members, a secretary, deputy-secretary, thirty-four European clerks, and a large number of natives. The Custom-house, though not on a line with the last-named building, may as well be introduced here. The establishment consists of a collector, deputy-collector, and 136 European clerks, etc., independent of a vast multitude of native writers. No ships can leave Calcutta to go to sea, without first procuring a Custom-house clearance; nor can a vessel discharge her cargo without the custom-house "permit." The importance of this establishment is obvious in a city like Calcutta, not only as regards the merchants, European and native, but thousands of private individuals; for a person cannot even ship or unship a parcel, by the monthly steamer, without a pass from the Custom-house, as I can very well testify.

To the right of the Marine Board is situated the Military Auditor-General's office, though not seen from the river front. When it is stated that the pay of the Army, Ordnance, Commissariat, and Pensioners is audited and checked here to an annual amount of several crores,[105] or millions of money, the importance of this office will be understood; and such is the opinion of the Court of Directors, for the appointment of Military Auditor-General must be confirmed by them. There is a Military Auditor-General, Deputy Military Auditor-General, and first and second Assistants holding commissions in the Company's army, besides twenty-six uncovenanted clerks, and a great many native writers.

With regard to an officer's pay and allowances, if he be retrenched, it is thus effected. The Paymaster of his regiment or Circle receives the retrenchment from the Military Auditor-General's Office, signed by the chief or his deputy. If the officer thinks his charge is not according to the regulations, he writes down his reasons on the back of the paper—if the objection be lengthy, the officer appends a sheet of paper—and sends it back through the Paymaster to the Military Auditor-General's office: who, should he agree, will write in red ink "Passed." If the drawer still demurs, he requests that it may be laid before the Governor-General in council, when the Military Auditor-General is usually called upon to explain. An appeal lies to the Court of Directors; but this is a step which is very rarely resorted to.

The Military Board is near the river side. It is composed of a paid Member, the Commandant of Artillery (ex-officio), the Chief Engineer (ex-officio), and the Commissary-General (ex-officio). There is a secretary and two assistant secretaries, besides forty-three clerks and several native writers, who are employed in the six departments—General and Miscellaneous; Public Works, Roads and Canals; Draftsmen's; Ordnance; Commissariat; and Stud. The arms and accoutrements of a corps which are indented for by the commanding officer, are checked by this board. All Ordnance stores for practice, or service ammunition of the Artillery, or for corps; all estimates and charges for fortifications or military buildings, for civil buildings, roads and canals; in fact every item entering into the operations of war, or required in time of peace, is indented for and checked at this office. Indents are annually forwarded to the Court of Directors so as to keep the arsenals and magazines filled. Sometimes the Court clip the indents. During the Affghan war the Board sent up twelve 9-pounders instead of six

18-pounders, because it is said $9 \times 12 = 108$ and $18 \times 6 = 108$, being the ratio as to calibre, however 18-pounders will breach when 9-pounders will not. The paid member is an exception to Virgil's adage: non omnia possumus omnes.

The new plan which has lately been very judiciously introduced into her Majesty's army, for the education of the officers, which requires them to have some knowledge of mathematics and "that symbolical language, by which alone the laws can be fully decyphered by which God has thought good to govern the universe,"[106] leads me to remark how necessary and important it is that the officers should possess some amount of scientific learning. Thus, the member of this Military board, for instance, has an estimate sent him for erecting a building. The amount of pressure on the foundation, its superficial extent, etc., call for a considerable amount of scientific knowledge.

The Commissariat Department embraces the supplies for armies in the field; for instance, to find 25,000 or 30,000 camels for a campaign, etc. It is said that when the Commander-in-Chief took the field, in October, 1848, the government, not having previously given sufficiently early notice to the Commissariat, were obliged to buy grain at war prices, showing the penny-wise and pound-foolish system of a government, which spent £12,000,000 in the Burmese war, and £7,000,000 in the Affghan war. On the 1st of May, 1838, the Commissariat expenses for the year were, 3,800,000 rupees, or £380,000; before this, they had been £440,000.

The Company's Dispensary is not far from Government House. The reader may form some idea of the quantities of medicine consumed, when he is informed that £50,000 worth is annually sent out to Calcutta from England. The depôts up the country are supplied from this dispensary.

Near to the dispensary is the Ice-house. Ice was first introduced into Calcutta by a Mr. Tudor, of America, a person of enterprising spirit. Previous to this experiment, the good people of this luxurious city, used to cool their wines, beer, water, etc., by the application of saltpetre, but which practice is now discontinued. There was a person called an abdar, whose sole business it was to cool such drink as was required, and who conducted the process in a room built for the purpose; a bottle of wine could be cooled in ten or twelve minutes; but the consumption of saltpetre was great and expensive; the best white, costing three and a half, to four rupees for eighty-two pounds. Most persons still keep an abdar, who now cools the wine with ice. At its first introduction into India, ice was sold at four annas (sixpence) for a seer (two pounds), but now it is to be had for threepence.

Most of the steamers plying between Calcutta and Suez, take in a supply of ice for the outward and return passengers. At Madras—called the

Benighted City—the benefit of Mr. Tudor's exertions have also been felt, for it, too, has now an ice-house. This invaluable article may likewise be procured at Bombay.

The Public Library, or Metcalfe Hall, is in a line beyond the ice-house, and separated from it by a street. It is a very handsome building, and has received its name in honour of the late able and talented Lord Metcalfe. The foundation-stone was laid by Brother J. Grant, the Provincial Grand Master of Bengal, assisted by Brother James Burnes, K.H., Provincial Grand Master of Western India, those masons holding office, and by a convocation of the craft, with masonic honours, on the 19th of December, 1840, in presence of the late Earl of Auckland, G.C.B., Governor-General of India, and a large assemblage of visitors.

The late Lord Metcalfe (then Sir Charles) had, as acting Governor-General, given liberty to the press of India, on the 15th of September, 1835; and there is a metal plate in the Hall, with an inscription to this effect. The funds for the erection of the building were raised chiefly by public subscription, and the valuable piece of ground on which it stands, was the munificent grant of Lord Auckland, as Governor of Bengal. The building was designed by the late Mr. C.K. Robinson, a magistrate of Calcutta, and a gentleman of great architectural taste and judgment. It was built by Messrs. Burn and Co., and cost about 68,000 Company's rupees, of which sum 16,390 rupees were contributed for the Library, and the balance by the Agricultural and Horticultural Society, and other bodies, who had originally intended to do honour to Sir Charles for the emancipation of the press, and for his public and private virtues. Owing to the alterations, the expenses exceeded the estimate, upon which Sir E. Ryan, the Chief Justice of the Supreme Court of Calcutta, liberally gave upwards of £400 sterling towards paying the balance.

The Public Library owes its origin to Mr. J.H. Stocqueler, at one time editor of the "Englishman" newspaper, who, in August, 1835, circulated an address among the principal inhabitants of Calcutta, urging the necessity of this establishment. The nucleus of the Library was formed by donations from private individuals, and by the transfer, from the library of the College of Fort William, of a valuable collection of books, consisting of 4,675 volumes. This transfer was made by the Governor-General, Lord Metcalfe (then Sir Charles), on certain conditions, one of which was, that an establishment should be provided for the reception and care of the books, subject to the approbation of the Honourable Court of Directors, who sanctioned the measure in their letter of the 14th of August, 1839.

It appears, that in 1846 there were 6,821 sets of works, and 15,408 volumes, of which 423 volumes were on East India affairs, and 362 Oriental and Hebrew. There are works in Greek, Latin, French, German, Italian, Spanish, and Portuguese. In fact there are books upon the arts and sciences, and upon almost every subject, in all languages. There are more than ninety proprietors. The subscribers are divided into three classes, enjoying different privileges, as to the number of books to be taken away at any one time. There are three curators, a librarian, two sub-librarians, and an establishment of about ten native servants.

The Agricultural and Horticultural Society here hold their meetings. The building is a great ornament to the city, and is very conspicuous, both in coming up and going down the river. The reading-room is most convenient; newspapers and periodicals are, of course, always found on the table. There are fresh arrivals of books by every steamer; and of some works, more than one copy. The public who are non-subscribers, are permitted to go there and read; but unfortunately books are occasionally lost.

The Bank of Bengal is the next building in order. It has a capital of £1,000,000 sterling; and the Government has many shares in the Bank.

At the time of its formation, there was no Bank; the houses of agents and merchants being quasi bankers: i.e., persons for the convenience of procuring money when wanted, lodged with their agents, sums varying from £300 or £400, to the amount of even £10,000. The insolvency of the great house of Messrs. Palmer and Co., in January, 1830, the first of a series of failures of the leading houses, to the extent of many millions sterling, induced many persons to seek for a more sure plan of deposit.

In the Bank of Bengal, persons can have shares, and obtain a fair annual per centage; or they may have money in deposit for a year, or even a less period; or, if they like, they may have it in deposit with interest. No account is opened for a less sum than 500 rupees; nor are ordinary depositors allowed to draw out less sums than fifty rupees at a time. There are three directors, who are civil servants of the Government.

On the failure of the Agency houses, it was thought necessary to establish another Bank, called the "Union Bank." This establishment was not conducted on banking principles. Loans were made to carry on indigo factories. To recover these advances, the factories became mortgaged. Still the persons who had them, thought that it was necessary to work these factories, instead of adopting the wise course of a favourable sale. The directors also made advances to the Agency houses, which led to the negotiation of bank post-bills, at ten months' sight. The ruin of the Bank became inevitable, if both the factories were unprofitable, and the houses failed. The upshot was that indigo fell to low prices, and as a consequence, the houses found their sales of produce decline below par. The failure took place in the year 1848, and all the Indian world, and the merchants in Great Britain, well know the result. The insolvency of this Bank pulled down, in the crash, all the shareholders, and ruined many widows and orphans, who were living on the interest of their money, which was lodged there, and which was their only income and source of maintenance.

There was another ruinous system, which had lasted for several years. It was thought desirable to give the usual dividends, and having no profits, they actually took from their capital to pay these dividends. A case of this description was brought before the Privy Council, in July, 1849, when Lords Brougham and Campbell declared the practice to be illegal.

Of late years, several branch Banks have been formed, namely, the Agra and United Service, having a capital of 63,64,500 rupees; the North-Western Bank of India, the Delhi, and the Simla, having a capital of 22,05,600 rupees.

The Oriental Bank Corporation has a capital of £2,000,000 sterling: it was incorporated by Royal Charter in 1851. This bank does an immense deal of business, and is more liberal in its transactions than any other bank in India. It has its head office at Bombay. Now the capital of the Bengal Bank is, as I have already remarked, £1,000,000; and it has a charter, so that in case of failure, no one is liable to any loss, beyond the amount of his share. The Union Bank had no charter. The failure of the Union has caused the shareholders not to pay (besides the loss of their capital) pro rata; but a list of the wealthiest shareholders having been made out, one person was assessed £20,000, another £10,000, another £5,000, and others £1,000, and so on, even though the unlucky wight had only one unfortunate share. Thus, under these circumstances, the Bishop of Calcutta, as trustee of the Cathedral, for which his Lordship had subscribed a large sum, was compelled to pay a very considerable amount.

Some of the minor Banks are desirous to procure charters, and to be only liable for double the amount of their shares. These repositories advance money to officers in the civil and military services, on the security of two persons, or other satisfactory pledge. Suppose an officer borrows 4,000 rupees at ten per cent., to be paid in two years, by instalments of so much per month. If he fail to do this, the Bank immediately calls upon the Securities. Thus the Securities sign a paper, to pay so much per month, should the borrower fail to do so! They generally agree, however, that the sum in question shall be deducted by the Paymaster; but in the event of the death of the borrower, before he has refunded the loan, and without having any property, the Securities are liable for the remaining balance, and have to pay the Bank.

To return to the subject of the Houses of Agency. Of the forty-five houses which failed in Great Britain in 1847 and 1848[107] eighteen exhibited balance-sheets, which either actually exceeded, or nearly approached the aggregate of their liabilities, of which only six houses have either paid, or made arrangements to pay, twenty shillings in the pound. Of another house, a bill broker proved, that it had assets nearly triple the amount of its liabilities, the suspension being caused by temporary difficulties, which produced a complete panic. One London house connected with India, showed a schedule of assets amounting to £200,000 beyond their liabilities, still nothing had been paid in July, 1849. Another house has paid 2s. 6d. in the pound; a third, 2s.; a fourth, 1s. 6d.; a fifth, 1s.; and a sixth expects to pay 4d. in the pound!

We next arrive at the Chandpaul Ghât, which is nearly in a line with the Bank of Bengal. It is very old, and is the usual landing-place of the Governor-General.

In succession come the Steam-engine House and the Baboo Ghât, the latter having been built in the time of Lord William Bentinck, Governor-General, by a wealthy native.

We have now described the buildings which run from the extreme right, beginning with the Mint. The Strand extends beyond the Mint, and is not used as a drive, for, strictly speaking, the drive, or Course, begins a little beyond Baboo Ghât, and reaches as far as the Water gate of Fort William. This road may be three-fourths of a mile in length, and a hundred feet in width. From the Course, there is a fine view of the river and shipping, all the way down to Garden Reach. There is generally a breeze in the hot weather, and during the rains it is pretty considerable. The plan usually adopted is to drive gently down the road to the south, and then to return quickly, as the wind is at your back. Thus you best enjoy "the eating of the air," as it is called by the natives.

Besides the view of the river and the shipping, the docks and mills of Howrah give an appearance of great activity, both in ship-building and in commerce. Some years ago, it was proposed to have a steam ferry bridge thrown over the Hoogly at this place; and the plan was so far acted upon, that the bridge was actually sent out from England; but it was sold, and proved to be one of the many abortive schemes for the improvement of Calcutta, which fall to the ground for the want of public spirit. It was said, and perhaps truly, that the plan was opposed by the Dingee-walas, or native boatmen.

Opposite the Water gate at Fort William is a cenotaph, with a dome in the Oriental style, erected by Lord Ellenborough to the memory of the British soldiers who were killed in action at Maharajpore and Punniar, in December, 1843. The drive extends down to Hastings' Bridge, so named after Warren Hastings, the first and once celebrated Governor-General of India. This would extend the drive to the distance of about a mile and a half. Between the two bridges is Prinsep's Ghât, built in honour of James Prinsep, the talented Oriental scholar, of whom I have before made mention.

Beyond the second bridge, are the Kidderpore Docks, and lower still is Garden Reach, a road of about a mile and a half in length. There are some handsome houses at Garden Reach, arranged something in the character of country-seats in the suburbs of London. Here the Peninsular and Oriental Steam Navigation Company have a yard, containing marine stores, coals, and other requisites. The superintendent resides close by, in a very neat and classic building.

Fort William, which next demands our attention, was projected by Lord Clive soon after the Battle of Plassey, in 1757; but it was not finished till the year 1773. It mounts 619 guns, and is said to have cost, from first to last, £2,000,000 sterling, half of which sum was paid by Mir Jaffier, whom the British seated on the throne of Moorshedabad, after the Battle of Plassey. No doubt he was prompted to this generous act, by his gratitude to his benefactors.

Mir Jaffier was a General, in the service of the former Nawab Suraj-ud-Dowlah, who in the preceding year, 1756, took Calcutta and put 146 Europeans into the English prison, since designated by every schoolboy, "the black hole of Calcutta," where 123 were found to have died the next morning from suffocation. Lord Clive played a deep game, but the cruelty of Suraj-ud-Dowlah merited dethronement. He was killed by the son of Mir Jaffier, when taken prisoner, and although it is not proved that the father was implicated, still we know that in Eastern countries, dethronement and death are often contemporaneous.

A Queen's Regiment of Infantry has barracks in the fort. At one time the Artillery, now quartered at Dum-Dum, used to be stationed here, except during the cold, or practice season. The Church is an octagonal building in the centre of the Fort near the Government house. The Fort has several gateways, the principal of which is the Water gate. The quarters for the Staff officers of the Fort are in two ranges, where reside, the principal Commissary of Ordnance, the chief Engineer, the Fort and Town Majors, and the officer commanding the Queen's Corps. Facing the river, on the west side, is a three-storied barrack; a range called the South Barracks, and opposite, or towards the north,—being part of the Staff Row,—is another range, which together form three sides of a square. To the south of this square is the Rampart Range, running south and east, with bomb-proofs. The Arsenal is in front of the North or Staff range.

Some writers have asserted that the Fort would contain 15,000 men; it is surrounded by a dry ditch, but is furnished with two sluices, so that it can be laid under water, if needful, in a few minutes, as it is not many yards from the river. No batteries could effect anything from the other side of the water. A bombardment might destroy the Royal Barracks; but the Fort could only be attacked from the land-side. During the Burmese war, or rather before the British troops landed at Rangoon in 1824, the Burmese threatened to march to Calcutta; upon which the merchants took the alarm, and sent a memorial to government to have their cash and papers lodged in the Fort; certain it is that some of the built-up embrasures were opened. Though the Fort was safe, it is possible that 20,000 Burmese troops might have done some mischief to the lieges of Calcutta.

The Arsenal of Fort William contains a large supply of arms, and vast quantities of stores and ammunition. It is now more of a receiving depôt than formerly. During the second Sikh war of 1848-49, the Fort of Allahabad was the grand depôt, as explained under the head of Allahabad. There are hundreds of iron and brass guns in the Fort, the former garnishing the sides of the roads as if to prove to the natives, "these are the guns taken at Plassey and Seringapatam; these from the Maharattas and Sikhs." Constant exposure to the rain, and all weathers, has caused many of the guns to become "honey-combed," which renders a gun quite unfit for service.

At a short distance from the river, in the back ground to the east, is the Chowringhee Road running north and south; to begin north, or from the right: it is nearly on a line with Cossitollah Street, the northern part of the city, which I will describe afterwards. The best houses are those in the centre and left. Before reaching the Racket-court, the visitor comes to Theatre-street, where, on the north-west angle, stood "Old Drury," which, I am told, was in its glory from 1807 to 1814. The Earl of Minto, father of the present Earl, was then Governor-General, and so great a patron of the drama, that he allowed the performers, who were in the services, to wear his ambassadorial and other dresses on the stage; and Mr. H.H. Wilson, M.A., F.R.S., Sanscrit Professor of Oxford, found time, amid his duties of Assay-master of the Mint, to take part in the performances, and was, it is said, a good actor.

Between the river and the Chowringhee Road, is the Ochterlony Monument, which was raised by subscription, among the officers and admirers of Major-General Sir David Ochterlony, of whose services I have spoken, when treating of Delhi. Sir David arrived in India in the year 1775, and died in 1825. Doorjun Lall, the uncle of the present Rajah, who was a mere boy at his father's death, in the year 1825, usurped the Guddee[108] from his nephew; upon which Sir David, who was then Governor-General's Agent, and as such had the power of putting the troops in motion, assembled an army in the neighbourhood of Muttra. The Government in Calcutta, however, hearing of this, ordered the troops to be countermanded. Sir David (called the "Hero of Malown," for his gallant service in the Nepaul war, in 1814-16, when he accepted from the Government of that country the ratified treaty, which he had taken the field to obtain), was therefore constrained to order the troops back to their several stations. He conceived, as there were two parties in the city of Bhurtpore, that if a force suddenly marched to the place, the party in favour of the injured young Rajah would join the British, and open the city gates. The Government of India, however, did not, for various reasons, approve of the measure. The season of the year was certainly an objection against the marching of troops. They[109] were at that time also "greatly embarrassed by the continual difficulties and heavy disbursements of the war with Ava," which had lasted sixteen months, from April, 1824, to August, 1825; and, "influenced also by the spirit of the injunctions from home, which so decidedly deprecated interference with the internal affairs of the native principalities, the Governor-General was averse to take part in the adjustment of the succession to Bhurtpore, and disallowed the existence of any obligation to uphold the claims of the minor Rajah." However, the majority of the members of Council were of opinion,[110] "that interference might become indispensable for the protection of tranquillity in Hindoostan." The Governor-General's sentiments prevailed: the force was countermanded, and an order sent to Sir David "to retract the hostile declarations which had been published by him."

The consequence of this expressed disapprobation of his conduct, was Sir David's resignation. He was at that time sixty-eight years of age, fifty of which he had passed in the uncongenial climate of India. The mortification, caused by reversing of his arrangements, doubtless accelerated his death, for he died almost immediately after, on the 15th of July, 1825. When his decease was reported to Government, a General Order was issued on the 28th of July, in the Political department, of which the following are extracts:—

"The Right Hon. the Governor-General has learnt, with great sorrow, the demise of Major-General Sir David Ochterlony, Resident in Malwa and Rajputana.... On the eminent military services of Major-General Sir David Ochterlony it would be superfluous to dilate.... With the name of

Ochterlony, are associated many of the proudest recollections of the Bengal army.... The Governor-General is pleased to direct, that minute-guns, to the number of sixty-eight, corresponding with his age, be fired this evening, at sunset, from the ramparts of Fort William."

Sir David was the first Indian officer who obtained the Grand Cross of the Bath; an honour so highly prized, that Sir John Malcolm accepted it in preference to a baronetcy, which Lady Malcolm coveted for her son. The following remark, made by Sir John at a party at Mhow, in 1819, on returning thanks, was communicated to me by a friend who was present:—

"Gentlemen,—I preferred the military to the civil honour; and you will agree with me that I studied the honour of my profession."

Sir David, moreover, was made a baronet. He was, it is believed, an American.

The monument erected to his memory is situated to the east of Government House. Mr. C. K. Robinson, the same who built Metcalfe Hall, and well known for his great taste in civil architecture, was requested to draw a design for the column. He sketched two plans; and the one, which now forms such a conspicuous ornament among the public erections of Calcutta, was selected, as being in the Moslem style, to indicate the preference which Sir David always shewed to the followers of the prophet, over the other native population. Subscriptions were received from all classes in the Bengal Presidency—civil, military, and mercantile—amounting to nearly 40,000 rupees or £4,000. A wealthy Calcutta firm, as it was then considered, were appointed the treasurers; but the building had made only a very little progress when the firm failed, and £2,700 was lost. The committee requested the subscribers to repair the deficiency; but many refused, alleging that the committee were the responsible party, as they might have deposited the money in the Bank of Bengal. The committee excused themselves on the plea that their object was to get as much interest as possible; for, had they vested it in the Bank, they must have deposited a part for a fixed time, while the remainder would have been a floating capital without interest.

The builder had contracted to erect the monument for £3,300, without the platform or the rail around it. A fresh subscription was opened, and £1,000 collected; but the committee had not benefited by their recent experience. They placed this £1,000 with another Calcutta firm, and lost a portion of it by a second failure! Mr. Parker, the public-spirited contractor, however, agreed to finish the column on receiving an assignment of the dividend of both houses.

The monument has a pedestal and a railing. In ascending, I counted 190 steps to the first projecting balcony, and twenty-five steps further led me to the summit. The best view from the top is about sunrise; and especially in the rainy season, when the dust has been laid by the previous rain, and the whole city lies before you, with the Hoogly stretching out right and left.

On the occasion of Her Majesty's birthday, in May 1840, the Court of Directors ordered fireworks, to the amount of £2,000, when the Ochterlony monument was illuminated with variegated lamps, to keep in countenance the Government house, where all the *élite* of Calcutta were assembled. The pyrotechnist, on the occasion, was Colonel Richard Powney, the Commissary of Ordnance in Fort William, whose subsequent fêtes, in honour of many other events, are well known.

Government house was built during the vice-royalty of the Marquis Wellesley, at a cost of £130,000 sterling. It is a fine palace, but the basement is too low, to be in keeping with the superstructure. It has a centre, and four extending wings; so that, looking at it north, south, east, or west, you see the centre flanked by two wings. Above the centre, is a dome, with Britannia standing on a pedestal, armed with the trident. There are two entrances, one towards the north, and another towards the south, the grand entrance to the north, being by a magnificent flight of stone steps. Below, is a covered way for carriages, and an ingress, through the lower hall, to the stairs leading to the second floor, in the centre of which is the dining-room. The wings are appropriated to the private apartments and bedrooms. The third story is likewise used on state occasions, the centre part containing the magnificent ball-room. All the staircases are of stone. The rooms below comprise the military secretaries' offices, and the official apartments of the aides-de-camp. It is here that the visitor goes to enter his name and residence in a book, and this is denominated a call.

There are three gateways to Government House; that to the south is small and private. In front of the palace is a large verdant square, which in this hot climate is peculiarly refreshing to the eye, especially just after the grass has been cut and rolled. The front rooms of Spence's Hotel command a view of this square, and their occupants experience much pleasure in looking upon this green spot.

With regard to parties at Government House, the Governor-General has, what is called, a general list of all persons eligible to the entrée, not to the Queen's Palace entrée, but to the ball and supper, given in honour of Her Majesty's birthday, or other state occasions. Those in the two services are invited by public notice in the following manner:—

"The Governor-General requests the honour of the company of the officers of the Civil Service, and of Her Majesty's and the Honourable

Company's army and navy, at a ball and supper in honour of Her Majesty's birthday."

A dinner was given in 1848, by Lord Dalhousie, on the 24th of May, and a ball on the 26th. At the former were invited all the heads of departments. At the ordinary dinners, which generally take place once a week, gentlemen and ladies are invited according to a list, and dine in turn. Merchants receive the honour of an invitation, and others of a certain class. The οἱ πολλοι only attend the great balls and suppers, when it is possible for an officer to be seated at supper next to his own coach-maker. Not that any of this class are poor, for many have realized ample fortunes. During the government of Lord Auckland, the Misses Eden, his lordship's sisters, introduced weekly soirées at which from 150 to 200 persons were present. His lordship was Governor-General from 1836 to 1842. These parties, I am told, were the most agreeable ever known in Calcutta; for once a week a person met not only his Calcutta friends, but many also from Europe and Upper India. People of all shades of colour were collected here, from the fair blonde of the North, to the Armenian, and even Mahomedan. At first there was a soirée without dancing every alternate week, but the introduction of music, and the presence of fair maidens and young bachelors soon led to the tripping of the light fantastic toe. If not a dancer, the visitor could sit down and converse with some lady, or he might cut in for a game of whist with Lord Auckland. On these occasions the Governor's band was always present, to infuse an equal harmonious temper into men's minds. At dinner parties, a guest might, if so disposed, play at billiards; or he might ask one of the Misses Eden to entreat Mrs. A. or Miss B. to sing; "such a charming creature, and the finest vocalist ever heard!" —always excepting Jenny Lind.

While Lord Metcalfe was Governor-General, he gave splendid concerts in the dancing-room, which is eighty feet long, at which all the professional talent of Calcutta was employed. Lord Auckland, who was decidedly popular as Governor-General, had, occasionally, private theatricals and concerts, his parties were numerous, and without any ostentation or show.

Ideas of grandeur only befit lofty minds. When the Marquis Wellesley sent home an account of the project of a building fit for the residence of the Governor-General of British India, his honourable masters were alarmed at the expense. The reader must look back to that period, when those gigantic measures of the Marquis had not yet prostrated the Maharattas; and he must suppose, as was the case, the Bengal Presidency to have had its northern limit at Futtyghur. If he will now take the map, and look for Peshawur, and cast his eye south-east towards Calcutta, he will find Futtyghur nearly central. He must also recollect that Bundelkund did not then belong to the Company, and that both the Madras and Bombay Presidencies were much smaller than they are at present. Besides, the East India Directors, having determined on not making any territorial acquisitions, could not understand the object of this immense palace. It was a mystery and a political device. But now the East India Company hold a greater extent of country than did Aurungzebe, the emperor, on his death, in 1707; for his successor had certainly very little power in the Deccan or south of India, nor was the Punjaub in a settled state.

We next come to the Racket Court, which is situated nearly at the end of the left of the Chowringhee Road. There are two courts, a wall dividing the north from the south court. The entrance fee is 100 rupees, with a monthly subscription of eight rupees.

I must next mention the Hotels, of which Spence's is decidedly the best. It is situated to the west of Government House, and close to the west gate. It is a long range of buildings, running north and south, having another range inside, running east and west. The latter rooms are preferable, having northern and southern aspects. The hotel can accommodate about 100 persons. A lady and gentleman, occupying a sitting and bed-room, with a separate table, pay 250 rupees, or £25 per month; for each additional room, 100 rupees, or £10. Single gentlemen, who chiefly occupy the range running north and south, having an aspect east and west, pay 100 rupees for board and lodging; that is to say, they have only one room each, and must take their meals at the table d'hôte. In both cases, married or single persons, pay separately for their wines, beer, spirits, soda-water, etc. The proprietors are very civil persons. The only improvement which suggested itself to me, during my frequent stay there, was the appointment of Europeans to superintend the native servants.

The Auckland Hotel, kept by Messrs. Wilson, is opposite the north-east angle of Government House. This, also, is much frequented. Indeed, I was assured that the *table d'hôte* excels Spence's in its *cuisine*. The terms are similar to Spence's.

There are other hotels on a smaller scale, and of less repute. Spence's Hotel was the first ever established in Calcutta, and is an immense concern; for the rent of the buildings alone swallows up £300 a month. Adjoining, and belonging to the hotel, is a large shop, containing ices, creams, and confectionary of all sorts, which is generally a great and favourite lounge for fresh arrivals. In the evening, numbers of carriages may be seen there at the door, waiting to take up their owners, who have gone in to quench their thirst, and recruit their strength, after the heat of the day.

About the year 1812, a theatre was built by some amateurs. Towards the end of 1813, a society of gentlemen bought the theatre, which stood on the south side of the street, near the Racket Court, called Theatre Street, the name it now bears. The manager was Mr. H.H. Wilson, whom I have had occasion to mention; and the secretary, Mr. W. Linton, organist of the old Cathedral, now St. John's Church.

Lord Minto took great pleasure in theatricals, and, as I have observed, gave his diplomatic wardrobe for the use of the performers. Sometimes the officers acted at Barrackpore, where there was a small theatre, and at which Lord Minto was generally present. The Marquis of Hastings, who came out in October, 1813, as Lord Minto's successor, also patronised theatricals.

When the theatre was burnt, in 1835, the Sans Souci, under the management of Mr. Stocqueler, was got up near Wilson's Hotel. A theatre was afterwards built in Park Street, which continued for some time; but within the last few years, a play can only be got up now and then. The Roman Catholic Archbishop has since purchased it for a College, or Seminary for students. This put a termination to the theatricals in Calcutta.

The Town Hall was raised out of the surplus of a lottery; the undertaking originated in a resolution of the British inhabitants of Calcutta, in 1804. The object of the lotteries was the improvement of the city; and twelve per cent. being deducted from all prizes, gave a surplus of about £7,000 per annum. From this fund the Town Hall was built, and is therefore public, *i.e.* government property. It is situated in Esplanade Row, in a line west from the West gate of Government house. It was built under the superintendence of the late Major-General Garstin, of the Engineers, and was finished about the year 1809, at an expense of £70,000. The members of the Lottery Committee formed the Town Hall Committee, and all applications for its use were sent to the secretary. Public meetings were held here and the lottery drawn, until about the year 1841, when Lord Auckland put a stop to these gambling concerns, in distinct compliance with the act of Parliament, which had long before been passed in England.

The length of the Town Hall, from north to south is, inside, 120 feet, its breadth 50 feet, and the height of the lower rooms about twenty-four feet, and the upper thirty-six feet. It is said to exceed the Government House in height. Large dinner-parties are frequently given here in the long room, which is also appropriated to public meetings.

There are also lesser rooms, where smaller parties and meetings are convened. The long upper room is used for balls, concerts, etc. When it was first resolved, in 1812, to have a ball in the upper rooms of the Town Hall, doubts were entertained, as to whether the beams were so situated, to render dancing safe; as the walls rested upon the beams; arches were therefore introduced to support the ceiling, and about 200 coolies were ludicrously made to jump up and down, in imitation of dancing, to test the capabilities of the beams and walls. The report being favourable, dancing was decided on, and as this pastime has now been going on for forty years, it is pretty evident, that the ladies may safely rely on the proof of long experience, that no danger need be apprehended from this quarter. Meetings of every kind are held here; at one time, before regular actresses came out to India, the ladies of the civil and military services, used to act private theatricals at the Town Hall; these are among the things that were.

In 1844 a magnificent public dinner was given here to Lord Ellenborough, prior to his return to England. Meetings have likewise been held here to decide upon testimonials of public approbation, in honour of Lords Auckland, Ellenborough, and Hardinge, of Sir Harry Smith, the hero of Aliwal, and Sir John H. Littler, late Deputy-Governor of Bengal, on his arrival in Calcutta as member of Council.

Local and charitable meetings also take place here; concerts too used to be given at the Town Hall, for many years, but latterly they have not been on the same scale as heretofore; in former times a concert used to yield £200 and even £300 a night; single tickets sold at 16s., double at 24s., and family tickets at 32s. each, whereas now, owing perhaps in some measure to the absence of musical talent in Calcutta, the same tickets fetch respectively 8s. or 10s., 14s. or 16s., 22s. or 24s. In August, 1848, a club was formed, called the "Calcutta Glee Club," and which in October following gave its first concert at the Town Hall, to about 250 friends, all the tickets being free. In January, 1849, the club gave a grand concert in the great room, when 800 tickets are said to have been distributed. During the season of 1849-50 the members had four grand concerts. This club is a great addition to the amusements of Calcutta society. Mr. S. Harraden, the organist of the old church, a gentleman of great talent, is the musical conductor of this Glee Club.

Mr. George Thompson, alias "Grievance Thompson," on his arrival from England with the late Dwarkanath Tagore, used to make speeches in the Town Hall, recommending to the natives of India "steam navigation." He was considered an eloquent and amusing speaker.

The upper part of the Hall, on ascending the long staircases, is ornamented with large pictures, of Lord Lake and his son, Lord Metcalfe, Mr. W.W. Bird, and Dwarkanath Tagore. In the room to the south, are the portraits of Her Majesty Queen Victoria, and of her Royal Consort, the Prince Albert. In the Hall below, is a very fine marble statue of the late Marquis Cornwallis, and in the vestibule, a marble statue of Warren Hastings; on a raised pedestal, facing Warren Hastings, within the distance of about 100 feet, is a bronze statue of Lord William C. Bentinck.

Fancy Fairs are also frequently held in the Town Hall, on which occasions ladies occupy stalls, for the sale of articles made by themselves and other kind persons, for the benefit of different charities and schools.

The Town Hall is certainly a very handsome building; but it is of the Doric order, which looks too heavy a style for the purposes for which it is intended.

The long building called the Supreme Court is in a line with the Town Hall, and about 150 yards from it, in the direction of the river. The Court was established in 1773, with judges appointed by the Crown. It is a dark and dreary-looking building, in which much money is lost and gained. Originally, there was a chief judge and three puisne judges; but now there is only a chief judge and two puisnes, from which it is to be inferred, that litigation was more prevalent in those days than it is at present. The celebrated Sir Elijah Impey was the first Chief Justice. He was also, in 1781, appointed by Warren Hastings judge of the "Sudder Dewanny Adawlut," or the Company's Chief Native Court of Appeal, with a salary of £6,000 per annum; a step which put an end to the disputes between the Supreme Court and the East India Company. Sir Elijah, however, was recalled by the House of Commons in the following year. At present, there are nineteen barristers admitted to the Supreme Court.

When the Company had merely a factory at Calcutta, and lived under the sufferance of the Nawab, this Court was called "the Mayor's Court"; for in the year 1726 a charter was granted, enabling the Company to establish a Mayor's Court in each of the three Presidencies, Calcutta, Madras, and Bombay; also to hold Courts of Quarter Session, to determine all penal causes, save those of high treason.

An Advocate-General and a Standing Counsel are appointed by the Company. Owing to a defect in not having a jury in civil causes, the Judges are both judge and jury. In commercial cases, I am told, they often lament that there are not juries composed of commercial men; just as if the remedy were not in their own hands! There are 254 grand jurors; but including the civilians, there would be at least 270, of whom forty-three are natives. The petty jury list contains 1,586 names, and of these 533 are natives. It is to be presumed that civil juries could be easily formed. The next charter will very probably alter the present law, which is so contrary to the British constitution.

There are fifty-five attorneys; formerly there were only forty, when they were facetiously called "the forty thieves." The Supreme Court includes a "Common Law Court," an "Ecclesiastical Court," a "Court of Equity" (Chancery), and a "Vice-Admiralty Court."

When, in 1835, the Government cancelled the Sicca rupee, and coined a new one, called the "Company's rupee," which is six and two-thirds per cent. of less value than the Sicca rupee, and above two per cent. below the value of the old Sonaut; the Chamber of Commerce addressed a memorial on this subject, setting forth the fact that, while all merchants, shopkeepers, and traders, made their charges in Company's rupees, the attorneys and barristers of the Supreme Court adhered to the Sicca rupee charge. To this memorial no answer was given; but it is to be hoped, that the time is near at hand when this outrageous custom will be put a stop to, and when lawyers will be content to receive the same reductions that others have agreed to.

There are four daily Newspapers published at Calcutta; viz., the "Bengal Hurkaru," the "Englishman," the "Morning Chronicle," and the "Citizen;" the two former take the lead. There is also a talented weekly paper, called the "Friend of India," published at Serampore, sixteen miles distant. When Sir Charles (afterwards Lord) Metcalfe, on the 15th of September, 1835, emancipated the press from the old censorship, many persons thought it a bold measure. The step might have been dangerous thirty years ago; but it is now proved to be extremely useful that measures and systems should be discussed.

About 1821, the "Calcutta Journal," ably conducted by Mr. J.S. Buckingham, was prosecuted by the Civil and Military Secretaries to Government, when the learned editor was obliged to withdraw from India. For many years there was a meeting at the Town Hall, on the anniversary of the 15th of September, to commemorate the "freedom of the press," at which one of the judges usually presided. The remedy for an abuse of privilege is simple; for if an editor publishes a libellous paragraph, an action with all its consequences follows. It must be admitted, that during the commercial distress in 1847-48, and the failure of many mercantile houses, the press was of important service. Likewise during the Affghan war, in 1841-42, when, in consequence of the great distance—more than 1,000 miles from the seat of war—and the serious interruption to all commercial intercourse under the Bengal Presidency, the newspapers published many private communications of much interest from officers, whereas the Government only received intelligence from official sources.

In the Upper Provinces, the "Delhi Gazette," and the "Mofussilite," enjoy about an equal share of patronage. At Lahore, the "Chronicle" has been established, under the auspices of Mr. Cope, for many years the able editor of the "Delhi Gazette," and which bids fair to rival the other two. One of the Subalterns of the army (now Major H.B. Edwardes, C.B.), attracted notice a few years since, by some excellent letters written in the Delhi paper, called "Brahminee Bull." In fact the letters from civilians, officers in the army, merchants, indigo planters, and others, often constitute the life and soul of the Metropolitan papers. There is a great deal of talent in the services, and it is well that it should be called forth, and find a legitimate field for its exercise. The merits of a trial in the Supreme Court are sometimes discussed; and in 1849, the press certainly was in a great measure the cause of the appointment of the commission to inquire into the misconduct of the Calcutta police; and which at once led to the removal of a magistrate, who was proved to be indebted £40,000 to an influential native.

In these public journals, various improvements in the civil administration of the Provinces are often suggested; the best means for the safe navigation of the Ganges, etc. Then there are cases of cure from cholera, or the bites of snakes; letters on the state of Great Britain and our colonies; dissertations on the native languages; poetical effusions, etc. In short, many articles in these papers have led, as it would seem at the East India House, to the formation of an office for the collection of Indian statistics, so long a desideratum, and without which the Court of Directors could not state the number of acres in the North-western Provinces out of cultivation, which is now known to be 9,816,749.

In Calcutta, there are twelve printing presses; besides the daily papers, there are six weekly; also two daily, two tri-weekly, two bi-weekly, four weekly, and five monthly native newspapers. Besides, the presses publish periodicals, Army Lists, the Calcutta Review, etc., so that the lieges of Calcutta have ample means of reading, and becoming acquainted with the state of affairs in the political and social world.

The liberty of the press in India has not been abused. In a case, for instance, which occurred in October, 1849, when a barrister stated,—that if the evidence of a certain examination as to the conduct of a civil servant were published, it would prejudice the case,—the press refrained from the publication. In fact, as regards publication, it is cried down only by those whose conduct is bad; for such shun the light of truth, as a bat does the light of day.

At present there are about seventy European merchants in Calcutta, if we deduct the fallen houses. Forty years ago there were only six or seven. Large fortunes were made in what are called "the good old days;" but the merchant traded, for the most part, with borrowed capital. It will be obvious to any person, that if a merchant gave 8, 10, and at times of pressure 12 per cent., he must have made immense profits to repay the money borrowed, and realize, besides, what a merchant considers a fair profit, namely, 12 per cent. per annum. It was a ruinous system; for, when it was found prudent to speculate, it was evident that the profit, say upon half the usual outlay, would do little more than pay the borrower; whereas, by trading with your own capital, you would acquire smaller profit, but it would be all your own. When the Houses failed, in the years 1829-33, for eight or ten crores of rupees, or, in English money, for eight or ten millions sterling, the shock was dreadful. Though the smaller Houses were left in possession of the field, they could not take up the business of the bankrupt firms without pecuniary aid, and that would be by borrowing. The result would appear to have been this: the small Houses could not raise the necessary funds, but some old firms sent out a merchant to form a new House. Thus the late Capt. Cockerell, R.N. (a connexion of Cockerell and Co., London), established a business on the ruins of Palmer and Co.

It was the Agency business which destroyed many Houses; because, while there were a few wealthy servants of government who had lent money, there were a great many civilians and officers in debt, who had borrowed money from the Agents. In fact, it might happen that a House had advanced more money than it had borrowed. The system was mischievous in another way; for the Agents, to make certain that the lives of the borrowers were insured, paid the insurance themselves, and charged it as an item of account with interest: but, cui bono! they failed, and could not come upon the insurance office till the death of the persons so insured.

Now in the army we reckon the deaths, except in time of war, at three per cent. in Bengal, and at Madras and Bombay nearly four per cent. per annum. Now, if they had a hundred of such constituents, as they were erroneously called, they would not soon recover their advances.

Again, there was another system devised in Calcutta, namely, that of compromise. One civilian, for instance, who owed 300,000 rupees, or £30,000, compromised for £7,000, which he borrowed from a friend. Some made three and four lakhs of rupees, £30,000 or £40,000, in three or four years. Some have wound up in fifteen or twenty years; that is, on the last dividend being paid; say one anna in a hundred rupees, or three half-pence in £10! or the infinitesimal least portion. Those who had lent the Houses money, were losers, minus these dividends; i.e. some Houses paid 8, 10, 15, 25, and even 33 per cent.

Now, those who lent money, got, say 8 per cent., at a time when the Company's paper yielded only 4 or 5 per cent., and the Bengal bank 10 (6 per cent. was the last dividend paid in 1849). Many a man risked his whole fortune in the effort to obtain 3 or 4 per cent., with the chance of losing all; and he not only lost his all, and ruined himself and his family, but, in many cases, took refuge in drink, to drown care.

The failure of the great Houses produced a host of small ones; nearly ten times the number there were forty years ago. On the 1st of January, 1849, there were, deducting defuncts (forty insolvent firms in liquidation), about seventy European merchants, thirteen Armenian merchants and agents, and four Greek firms. Forty years since there were only six English houses, namely, Alexander and Co., Colvin and Co., Downie, Cruttenden, and Co., Fairlie and Co., Mackintosh and Co., and Palmer and Co. There are now above sixty commercial brokers, the system of brokers or middlemen being of modern date.

The Chamber of Commerce, consisting of a President, Vice-President, nineteen members, and a Secretary, was established in April, 1834. The duty of this chamber is to discuss any subject connected with commerce. Thus, in the year 1842, the merchants sent in a memorial to Sir Lawrence Peel, chief justice, complaining that the barristers and attorneys still charged sicca rupees while all the rest of the community were taking Company's rupees, or six and two-thirds per cent. less. Any matter connected with port-dues and pilots, is also considered by this committee, which is a very useful board.

The Calcutta Trade Association, established in July, 1830, is for the purpose of regulating matters of trade, and to represent to Government any grievance injurious to it.

The Indian establishment of the East India Railway Company arrived in Calcutta in November, 1847. The act for the formation of the Company guaranteeing 5 per cent., has been passed by Parliament, and a Staff of Engineers are at work in laying down the projected line of railway.

The great undertaking of a railroad from Calcutta to Delhi, a distance of more than 900 miles, and afterwards to the Sutlej will require some years for its completion. The government will thus be able to move troops, with great rapidity, to any desired spot, at any moment, and incalculable will be the advantages which India must reap on its accomplishment. I must refer the reader to a very sensible letter, written by Lieut.-Colonel Pitt Kennedy, military secretary to the late Sir Charles Napier, at that time Commander-in-Chief, in which he briefly points out the comparatively slow progress which Sir Charles made daily en route from Calcutta to the Upper Provinces, although, as he says, every facility practicable was afforded. He distinctly shows what a saving a railroad would effect, in the cost of the transport of goods from one station to another, and as clearly determines how the traveller may accomplish in weeks, what he now does in months, and in hours, what now occupies days.

The Asiatic Society was instituted in the year 1784. It comprises five scientific sections, as follow:

Section I., Oriental Literature and Philology;

Section II., Natural History;

Section III., Geology and Mineralogy;

Section IV., Meteorology and Physics;

Section V., Geography and Indian Statistics.

The Society meet on the first Wednesday evening in every month, to discuss the various subjects and papers submitted to their notice. The rooms are at the corner of Park-street, Chowringhee. Each member pays sixteen rupees a quarter, or sixty-four rupees a year.

The late Major-General Claud Martine, who was born at Lyons, in France, and died at Lucknow in September, 1800, left by will the sum of 350,000 Sicca rupees, or about £35,000 sterling, to the town of Calcutta, to put out at interest in government paper, on the best security; and the principal and interest to be placed under the protection of Government, or the supreme Court, in order that they might devise an Institution the most necessary for the public good of the town of Calcutta, or establish a school to educate a certain number of children of either sex, to a certain age, after which the boys were to be apprenticed to some profession, and the girls married when of proper age; "and," as the will runs, "every year a premium of a few rupees, or other thing, and a medal be given to the most deserving or virtuous boy and girl."

This was to be done on the anniversary of the General's death, when a sermon was to be preached, the prizes distributed, and a dinner given to the children. This money was most improperly allowed to remain in the hands of a House of Agency; but at length, after a lapse of more than thirty years, on the 22nd of October, 1832, the Advocate-General, having moved the Court against the Agents, the Supreme Court at Calcutta passed a decree, and directed a school to be established, to be called "La Martinière," (agreeably to the twenty-fourth clause of the General's will), and appointed 165,293 Sicca rupees, or about £16,530, for the cost of the building.

The Court nominated Mr. J.P. Parker to be the builder, and Captain George Hutchinson, of the Bengal Engineers, to superintend its erection, receiving six per cent. for his trouble. This arrangement left a large residue, invested in Government Securities. The children were to be selected from amongst the poor Christian population of Calcutta. The girls were to be not under four, nor above twelve years of age, so that there should be twenty girls at the least: well-conducted girls, moreover, were to be permitted to remain until they were sixteen years old, if not before apprenticed or married. The boys were to be not under four, nor above ten years of age, so that there should be at least thirty boys.

The Governors of the Martinière Charity met at the Government House in August, 1835, when it was decided that the religious instruction given to the children of the school should be in conformity with the principles held in common by the English, Scotch, Roman, Greek, and Armenian Churches; but the School was not to be placed under any particular denomination of Christians! There is a library attached, consisting of 4,142 volumes, and a large collection of philosophical instruments, etc.

The Principal of the College is Mr. Henry Woodrow, M.A., Fellow of Caius College, Cambridge.

On the 31st of August, 1848, the Institution contained 100 foundation scholars, 32 boarders, 42 day scholars, and 1 day boarder, making a total of 175 boys; which, with the 70 girls, made a total of 245 children. There were in December, 1849, 270 children on the books of the School. The funds of the Institution now amount to 1,575,000 Company's rupees, or £157,500, which is more than four times the sum originally left by General Martine.

The College of Fort William was established by the late Marquis Wellesley in the year 1802, with various Professors appointed for Arabic, Persian, Hindoostanee, Sanscrit, and Bengalee. The Writers intended for the Civil Service used to reside in the long range called "Writers' Buildings," situated in Tank Square, not far from the north of Government House.

Examinations were formerly held half-yearly, in the presence of the Governor-General. The Professors read their report on the number of terms kept by each student, and their individual proficiency; the students of each class being severally numbered 1, 2, 3, etc., according to the report. The Governor-General then addressed the students, particularly noticing those who had distinguished themselves in the various classes; after which the medals and prizes were distributed.

Among the eminent men who passed at these examinations were the late Lord Metcalfe, Sir Richard Jenkins, G.C.B., Director of the East India

Company, and W.B. Bayley, Esq., also a Director. At that time all the Writers for the Bengal, Madras, and Bombay Presidencies passed at this College; but this system was afterwards given up, and only the Bengal Writers enter the Calcutta College.[111]

On the establishment of the Haileybury College, in England, about the year 1805, for the education of Writers, the Calcutta College became nothing more than a school for the study of the Oriental languages, for the Bengal Writers, on their arrival in Calcutta. The Marquis Wellesley had proposed to the Court of Directors that there should be a Provost; in fact, that it should be placed on the footing of a college in England, with Professors for all languages. The Court of Directors and the Board of Control appear to have thought, and with good judgment, as to general education, that a college in England would be preferable. As far as the Oriental languages are concerned, the young student may learn the rudiments in England; and, in a few cases, bright examples have occurred in the persons of some Writers, who, in a very few months after their arrival, have passed in three languages. These exceptions are the cases of young men of considerable talent. It is said by the natives, that it requires seven years, to master the Arabic language, and twelve to acquire a perfect knowledge of the Sanscrit. Admitting that a profound acquaintance with the Sanscrit, or Arabic, may not be requisite, though the latter is so intimately connected with the Persian, and the former with the Hindoo languages of Hindee and Bengalee, still, great advantages result in those cases where students desire to possess a perfect knowledge of the minor languages.

At present the system in Bengal is this:—The Writers are divided into two classes; one for the Bengal Presidency, and the other for the North-west provinces. For the former, Bengalee and Hindee are the languages studied; and for the latter, Persian and Oordoo. Each Writer must pass in two languages before he can be reported "qualified for the public service." There are now two examiners; one of whom is a subaltern in the 42nd Regiment Bengal Native Infantry. The examinations are held in the College rooms, at Writers' Buildings; but, unlike the examinations of our English universities, they are private and not public. There are at times from twenty to twenty-five, or even more students, in Calcutta, some of whom are allowed, if they have relations or friends in the civil service, in the Mofussil (country), to go into the interior to study.

The usual course is to examine the students monthly; and a report of their proficiency is made quarterly, and published in the "Gazette." The "Gazette" also gives the names of those young men who have obtained prizes; for several read for "honours." It will be evident that the expenses of a college, which is to embrace the European and other languages, as well as other studies, such as general history, mathematics, and geography, would be very considerable. In England, besides, professors can easily be procured; whereas, in India, it is impossible to obtain them without great trouble and expense. The latter consideration weighed with the Court of Directors; and, while they acknowledged the validity of the Marquis's arguments on the necessity of giving a superior education to young men, who, in their progressive rise in the service, would have hundreds, or thousands under them; who would become heads of great departments in the government, and, possibly, members of the Council, still acted wisely in giving that education in England; and this, among other, for the following reasons:—

Because the young men are brought up in a more congenial climate, and do not leave England before they are nineteen or twenty years of age, when they are better able to endure the change of climate; they arrive in India when they have acquired a certain amount of practical knowledge of the world; at a period when young men begin to see the folly of indulging in the expensive habits of youth; and, moreover, have before them the sad warning of Writers getting into debt, who might have quitted the service on a pension of £1,000 a-year, had they not involved themselves in debt in their early career. In fact, they arrive as young men, and not as boys.

It is evident, therefore, that Haileybury is far superior to any College which could be established in India.

Except in a few cases of very talented Writers, it is all lost time to study the Oriental languages in England, beyond the mere grammar and ground-work. To teach a civilian a few words and phrases, in order to enable him to ask some necessary questions and give a few orders, is all that is requisite. It is far better to devote their minds to the study of the history and political economy of the country, in which they are to reside, and to assist in governing. Let them study the laws of England as to crimes, and the civil laws as to obedience and allegiance; the law of contracts; the mode of recovering debts due to the Government, and to individuals. Let them well digest the principal regulations of the government under which they are to serve; and the customs, manners, prejudices and religion of the natives, both Hindoos and Mahomedans. These are ample subjects for the employment of the Writer's mind whilst in England; for as to the Oriental languages, there is great danger of acquiring a bad pronunciation, a point which is of the utmost importance in the colloquial languages, such as Oordoo and Persian.

At the East India Military Seminary, at Addiscombe, the students are taught mathematics and classics, fortification and artillery, military drawing and surveying, landscape drawing, geology and mineralogy, chemistry and French.

It is an important consideration, whether cadets who can now, as in the Royal Army, enter the service at sixteen years of age, should not rather leave England at the age of eighteen; for it is a well-known fact, that recruits for the army are more healthy, and bear the climate of India better, when they arrive at the age of eighteen, nineteen or twenty years. Formerly, indeed, direct cadets were sent out to India at the early age of fifteen years, and Marlow cadets at fifteen and a half.

Bishop's College was founded in 1820, by "The Incorporated Society for the Propagation of the Gospel in Foreign Parts," at the instance of Bishop Middleton. This institution is essentially a religious foundation, and is under the management of a Principal, the Rev. W. Kay, B.D., Lincoln College, Oxford, and three Professors.

Bishop's College is open for the admission of all students of moderate qualifications, who shall conform to its religious ordinances, and its academical instruction and discipline. It has a library of about 6,000 volumes, besides a large and varied collection of manuscripts, chiefly Oriental; namely, Syriac, Zend, Pehlevi, Arabic, Persian, Tibetan and Sanscrit. Among the latter are parts of the first two Vedas, and several Puranas. The Universities of Oxford and Cambridge send copies of all works printed at their presses, to Bishop's College.

The students are required to attend divine service twice daily, after the form of the Common Prayer of the United Church of England and Ireland, in the beautiful little chapel of the College. They have their meals in common, in the hall, which is a spacious and elegant room, adorned with the portraits of the Founder, Bishop Middleton, and of a former distinguished Principal, the late Rev. W.H. Mill, D.D., Trinity College, Cambridge, a man for whom I entertained the greatest respect, as well for his varied and gigantic literary attainments, as for his quiet and unassuming manners.

The students, with the exception of the natives, wear an academical dress; and, with the sanction of their parents or guardians, are expected to embrace the profession of schoolmasters, catechists or missionaries. The usual period of study is five years, after which they are employed at a fixed stipend as catechists, until of age for ordination, when they become missionaries.

There are native teachers for Arabic and Persian, Sanscrit and Bengalee, Cingalese and Tamul. At the College press, translations are made into the Oriental languages of the Holy Scriptures and of the Liturgy, under a revision of the College Syndicate, which consists of seven members. There were, in 1849, seventeen persons studying at the College, who, as soon as they become qualified, will be sent as catechists or missionaries to different parts of India. Two of the chaplains of the Bengal establishment have been ordained from this College.

The Madrissa, or Mahomedan College, is situated in Wellesley Square, Cullinga. Natives are here instructed in the Arabic, the language in which the laws of the Mahomedan Government are written; and the object is to preserve a correct knowledge of that language.

There is another Mahomedan College at Hoogly, about twenty miles from Calcutta, called the College of Mahomed Mohsin, established in August, 1836.

The Hindoo College was established in 1816. It consists of a Principal, a Lecturer on Mathematics, a Professor of Natural and Experimental Philosophy and Civil Engineering, a Surveying Master, and an Assistant Professor of Literature, besides several assistants in the respective departments.

The Sanscrit College consists of eleven Pundits, three English teachers, who are natives, two secretaries, and a librarian. The object of this Institution is to preserve a correct acquaintance with this original and learned Hindoo language, in which the Hindoo sacred books and laws are written.

The Schools in Calcutta are numerous. The Free School is a charitable institution, and its object is not only to educate, but also to apprentice the children, when they have arrived at a suitable age. Parents, whose children are not eligible on the score of poverty, may have them educated in this School, on the monthly payment of a sum, not exceeding ten rupees, or £1 sterling. On the 1st of January, 1849, there were 400 children in this Institution.

The Lower Orphan School, Alipore, is divided into two departments, a boys' and a girls'.

St. Paul's School, Chowringhee, was established in 1845. It is under a Committee of Management, of which the Right Rev. the Lord Bishop of Calcutta is the President.

St. James' School, was established by the Society for Promoting Christian Knowledge. This benevolent Institution, founded in 1809, admits children of both sexes, and is under the control of three Trustees. The Parental Academic Institution was founded in March, 1823.

The Free Church Institution, originally established in August, 1830, under the name of "the General Assembly's Institution," and now supported by the Free Church of Scotland, consists of a College, a Normal and Preparatory School. The number of pupils is about 1,100. In immediate connexion with the Free Church Institution are three Branch Schools, mustering 550 pupils. The General Assembly's Institution, situated in Cornwallis Square, has about 500 pupils.

The Bhowanipore Christian Institution was established by the Church Missionary Society, and contains 475 scholars.

The Indian Free School, situated in Cornwallis Street, was instituted in 1839. Each scholar pays a fee of two rupees, or 4s. a month.

The Anglo-Indian School was established in 1829; the boys pay one and two rupees, or 2s. and 4s. per mensem.

The Patriotic College was established in 1846. The terms are from one and a half to three rupees monthly, and the course of education is the same as that adopted in the Hindoo college, with slight modifications. The Normal Institution has two schools, the one Normal and the other Model. In the former the students are divided into two classes, stipendiary and free, the first of whom receive from Government 12 rupees or £1. 4s. per month.

There is a Baptist Mission School, a European Female Orphan Asylum, and a Ladies' Baptist Missionary Society. In all, there are seventeen Public Seminaries for the instruction of boys, exclusive of the military Upper and Lower Orphan Schools at Kidderpore, and ten private schools for girls, besides two public schools. The military Upper and Lower Orphan Schools at Kidderpore are supported, partly by Government, but chiefly by the subscriptions of the officers of the Bengal army; the Upper Schools are for the children of officers, and the Lower for those of the non-commissioned officers and privates. There are 114 boys and 116 girls, or a total of 230 children. Fifteen of the boys are at St. Paul's school and fifty-seven of the girls at Kidderpore House. Some of the boys are sent to the regimental bands, and others are apprenticed to trades. Each girl, on her marriage, receives 1,500 rupees, or £150, as a marriage portion.

There is a Roman Catholic Cathedral Free School for boys and girls, and a Roman Catholic Seminary, established about the year 1829, for young ladies and boys under ten years of age.

The Armenian Philanthropic School, founded by the Armenian community in April, 1821, numbers sixty-seven pupils.

The Medical College comprises two classes of students, namely, one class who are taught in English, and another in Hindoostanee; the number of the former is 109, and of the latter 128. A few years since four of the students of the college were taken to England by Dr. Goodeve, one of the Professors, where they all passed the London examination with great credit; one of them took the degree of M.D. and was made F.R.C.S., a second became

M.R.C.S. and is now Assistant Demonstrator of Anatomy in the college. The object is to furnish a superior class, in room of the former unscientific, native surgeons. When they have passed the usual course, the students are called Sub-Assistant Surgeons, and are sent to corps and to civil stations.

The General Hospital, situated to the south of the race-course, is for the admission of European soldiers, whose case requires more detailed treatment than they can have in Fort William. European seamen of merchant vessels requiring amputations, and patients from the native troops at Barrackpore, doing duty in Calcutta, are eligible for this hospital.

The Native Hospital is a most useful institution; besides which there is also a good Native Hospital at Howrah, and a Seaman's Hospital, supported by the mercantile community of Calcutta.

In the year 1847 the Government formed an Experimental Mesmeric Hospital, which was to be tried for a year; Dr. J. Esdaile was appointed surgeon in charge. There is no doubt that some of the medical profession at Calcutta did not like the new hospital, for it was utterly foreign to the ideas of most people in India. At the end of the year a Report was given in, and a committee appointed to determine upon its merits; but their decision being unfavourable to the renewal of the hospital for a further term, the experiment was given up. Upon this the natives of rank and influence sent a memorial to Government, who replied, that as the Hospital was chiefly for the benefit of the natives, the Government would allow Dr. Esdaile's services for the institution, on condition that the natives should subscribe to it.

In June, 1848, a meeting took place to consider the matter; when several European and native gentlemen gave donations, and offered monthly subscriptions, for the formation of the hospital. At the request of the Committee, the Government furnished the necessary instruments for operations.

Dr. Esdaile had previously published a work on the subject of Mesmerism; and had, while civil surgeon of Hoogly, privately, and at his own expense, formed a ward in his hospital for mesmeric operations. A report was published of his cases; and the result was highly satisfactory.

The new hospital was opened in August, 1848, since which time people have come from great distances to undergo a "painless operation." If Dr. Elliotson, who is considered, by many, to be one of the most accomplished medical men in Europe, and, luckily, a man of property, lost many of his patients in consequence of his advocacy of the new theory, Dr. Esdaile surely was a bold man to propose Mesmerism in Calcutta, where there are so many "ditch" jobs carried on. Had a Governor-General undergone an operation, under its mild influence, Mesmerism would have been the order of the day; for then all the members of council and secretaries of government would have become converts, as a matter of course.

The objections of the medical members who drew up the unfavourable report, were most singular. Some thought Mesmerism would affect the nervous system; others said that as it had only been tried on natives, they doubted whether Europeans could be influenced by it. Latterly, however, there has been a reaction. It is known that ether and chloroform have been extensively used in England, France, and America; indeed, in one large hospital in London, all surgical operations are effected under the influence of chloroform. Both ether and chloroform may become safe means in process of time; but as yet it cannot be denied that many fatal results have occurred. With a large army on active service, one or the other of the remedies will, doubtless, often be resorted to, after an action. But the mesmeric process would not always answer in such cases, as it frequently requires time. Some patients are altogether incapable of being affected in one day.

As to Europeans, the answer is simply this; if one manipulator be not sufficient, two, three, or more operators must be called in. At Madras, a short time ago, it was proposed to place a lady about to be confined, under the influence of ether, when her husband objected, because it is written in the Bible (Gen. iii. 16) "I will greatly multiply thy sorrow and thy conception; in sorrow thou shalt bring forth children." Upon the same principle a man ought to object to another person's taking medicine to alleviate pain. Such an unchristian perversion of doctrine was never before resorted to; as if it could be displeasing to God, that his creatures should use any means to mitigate the sufferings of humanity.

The Eye Infirmary was established about thirty years since. It is a very useful hospital, for many of the natives suffer from cataract. About twenty years ago it was proposed to establish an Eye infirmary at Meerut, and there certainly appears to be an opening for a second. About two-thirds of the Bengal army is now stationed in the Upper Provinces; and, if one such infirmary be required for the city of Calcutta, it is to be presumed that another would be necessary in a position so distant as 900 miles. The population of the North-Western provinces is, as I have stated, 23,199,668, not including some 60,000 soldiers.

The Sailors' Home was instituted in 1837. Captain T.E. Rogers, I.N., Superintendent of Marine, is President, and the American, Danish, and French Consuls, are Vice-Presidents. The object is to suppress the system of crimping. Before this "Home" was established, seamen, when ill, were obliged to go where they could, and thus they fell into the hands of crimps, who cheated them out of their money, and injured their health and morals. Now both officers and men can go to the "Home," and obtain comfortable board and lodging at reasonable rates. By another admirable rule of the institution, they may deposit their earnings with the Superintendent, during their stay in Calcutta. The Superintendent is also at liberty to provide dinners for parties coming on shore on leave, at fixed rates, on a day's notice being given. "Drunkenness, profane swearing, and inordinate conduct, will be in every way discountenanced; and orderly, sober, and industrious habits encouraged. Medical attendance when required."

The Government make an allowance of 1,100 rupees (£110) yearly for house-rent. On the 31st of January, 1849, it appears from the Report, that "the 'Home' had clothed and maintained, free of expense to the men themselves, eighty shipwrecked and distressed seamen, who, but for the 'Sailors' Home,' would have been destitute."

In the year 1848, the number of inmates was 687. The men on the whole behaved well.

The Calcutta Alms Houses, were erected by the munificence of Lady William Bentinck, about the year 1835.

There are eight Masonic Lodges in Calcutta, and about 1,700 free and accepted Masons. As a Master Mason (Scientific Lodge, No. 105), adhering to the obligations I have entered into, never to reveal any masonic secrets, which have been entrusted to my keeping, I would cautiously shun the present occasion of doing so. Although as a soldier I might be led to expatiate, still I will pass over the allegorical and symbolical science of masonry, only remarking that I never knew a mason who was a bad or troublesome soldier: but, on the contrary, the more perfect the mason, the more noble the soldier.

The Botanical Garden was established about sixty years since, under the superintendence of the late General Kyd, of the Bengal Engineers. In 1794, the late Dr. Roxburgh, of the Madras Medical Establishment, was nominated Superintendent; since that gentleman's retirement, it has been under a Bengal medical officer. The object is to collect trees, plants, and flowers from the different parts of India and adjacent countries, from the Malayan Archipelago, China, Mauritius, Africa, Europe and America. The Garden is situated on the other, or right bank of the river, opposite Garden Reach, and not far from Bishop's College. It is a very favourite resort in the cold season, when parties are made up to visit the Garden, and spend the day there. There is a branch garden at Saharunpore near the hills, under the Himalaya Mountains.

With the renewal of the charter, in 1834, it was thought necessary to appoint a Law Commission, and the President, a legal gentleman who was sent out from England, has a seat in the Council of India. Two members were at the same time appointed, one from Madras, and another from Bombay; together with a secretary. The present President is Mr. Peacock, who appears to be left alone to work out acts for India, the two members having gone. How long this office may continue, it is impossible to say: the next charter will probably introduce a new system. The members were gentlemen of the Civil Service; and if the system of law education at Haileybury should be improved, it may become possible to find one, out of eight or nine hundred civilians, competent to be President.

The Council of Education consists of a President and nine members, three of whom are natives. All Colleges and schools, supported or assisted by the Government with any allowance, are under the superintendence of the Council of Education. This Council directs the course of education for all colleges and schools where English is taught, excepting Bishop's College, and the Medical (strictly so called) College, and selects the works or books to be read. This supervision or control extends to the out-stations, and indeed to all the schools under the Bengal Presidency.

The European Lunatic Asylum, is near the General Hospital. At Benares, there is a similar one for unfortunate natives.

The Small Cause Court, is a Court for the recovery of debts due by Europeans to natives, or by natives to Europeans; in fact any person may be a plaintiff.

The maximum amount of claim or debt, sued for in this court, is 500 rupees or £50 sterling. The amount of decrees probably extends to five or six lakhs of rupees (£50,000 or £60,000) per annum. Poor people can sue in *forma pauperis*, when the judges dispense with the cost of fees. The Act is somewhat similar to the English Small Cause, or County Courts.

Military Courts of Request, are held at every station in the army. All European as well as Native Officers, Non-commissioned Officers and Sepoys are subject to them, except such European and non-commissioned officers as are holding staff appointments away from their regiments.

There is a European Court and a Native Court, in which sums of 400 and 200 rupees (£40 and £20) or under, can be respectively sued for. In certain cases, however, in the Native Courts, sums to any amount may be investigated.

The Police Office, is presided over by a Chief Magistrate and two other Magistrates, one of whom is a Native. The Chief Magistrate superintends the River Police; the Senior Magistrate, the Second or Southern Division; and the Junior Magistrate, the First or Northern Division of Calcutta. There is also a Superintendent of Police. The Native Policemen amount to about 1,900, besides a body of Mounted Police who patrol at night. On my second arrival at Calcutta, in August, 1849, I found the police in a much more efficient state than when I left for England, in July, 1846, both as regards number and general usefulness.

The Bengal Civil Fund, entitles the civil servants of the Government to obtain their pension of £1,000 per annum, by paying 4 per cent. out of their salaries. To become entitled to this pension, a civilian must pay up 50,000 rupees (£5,000); it is taken by seniority.

The Bengal Civil Service Annuity Fund, is to grant pensions to the widows and orphans of deceased civil servants, securing to the widow £300 a year, and so much for each child; if she marries, she forfeits the pension for herself, but the children are kept on the Fund. If the widow has a private income of less than £100 a year, she gets the £300; but if above £100 and under £400, the sum is made up to £400 per annum.

The object of the Bengal Military Fund, is to grant pensions to the widows of officers, after the following scale:

	If in India, per mensen.			In England per annum.		
	Rupees	Annas	Pies.	£.	s.	d.
A Colonel's widow draws	238	6	5	342	3	9
A Lieut.-Colonel's	190	11	6	273	15	0
A Major's	143	0	7	205	6	3
A Captain's	95	5	9	136	17	6
A Lieutenant's	71	3	1	102	3	9
An Ensign's	56	9	8	81	5	0

Children are allowed so much a year; boys up to a certain age, but girls may be kept on the Fund till they are married. A sick officer, provided he does not possess 5,000 rupees (£500), will obtain 1,200 rupees (£120) passage money. Subalterns when sick, if they do not possess £50 per annum above their pay, will be allowed £50 passage money.

Lord Clive's Fund, established in 1776, is now paid by the Court of Directors, and amounts to half an officer's pay, if not possessing as follow:

A Colonel   £4,000

A Lieut.-Colonel	3,000
A Major	2,500
A Captain	2,000
A Lieutenant	1,000
A Surgeon	2,000
An Ensign	750

The object of the Queen's Military Fund, which was raised in 1820, and revised in 1827, is to pay the passage home of widows and children of the Royal Service:

A Field Officer's Widow is allowed 2,000 rupees, or £200
A Captain's and Subaltern's   1,500   "   150

The allowance for each child

Not exceeding three, is 500 rupees, or £50
Exceeding three   300   "   30

A certain sum is also granted to enable widows and children, on landing, to reach their homes, which is called "travelling expenses." Officers, if so disposed, may pay so much monthly: that is to say,

	Rupees		£ s.
Commander-in-Chief	30	or	3 0
General Officer	20	"	2 0
Adjutant-General	12	"	1 4
Deputy ditto	8	"	16
Brigade-Major	6	"	12
Lieutenant-Colonel, if commanding	10	"	1 0
Ditto, if not	8	"	16
Major, if commanding	8	"	16
Do. if not	6	"	12
Captain, Paymaster, or Surgeon	4	"	8
Lieutenant, or Assistant Surgeon	2	"	4
Cornet, Second Lieutenant, or Ensign	1	"	2

FOOTNOTES:

[105] A Crore is 100 lakhs, or 10,000,000 rupees.

[106] Vide "A Discourse on the Studies of the University of Cambridge," by Professor Sedgwick, M.A., F.R.S., etc., Vice-Master of Trinity College, Cambridge.

[107] Atlas for India, July, 1849.

[108] "Guddee" means a "cushion." Let the reader place a cushion for the back, and one on each side, and he will have the Hindoo "Guddee" or throne.

[109] Wilson's Mill's History of India, vol. ix. p. 185.

[110] Ibid, vol. ix. p. 186.

[111] Whilst correcting the press this College has been abolished, and is replaced by a Board of Examiners at Calcutta, consisting of a president, and as many members as the Government may think fit to appoint.

APPENDIX

I.

THE TREATY WITH LAHORE OF 1809.

Treaty between the British Government and the Rajah of Lahore,
(25th of April, 1809.)

Whereas certain differences which had arisen between the British Government and the Rajah of Lahore have been happily and amicably adjusted; and both parties being anxious to maintain relations of perfect amity and concord, the following articles of treaty, which shall be binding on the heirs and successors of the two parties, have been concluded by the Rajah Runjeet Singh in person, and by the agency of C.T. Metcalfe, Esquire, on the part of the British Government.

Article 1.—Perpetual friendship shall subsist between the British Government and the State of Lahore: the latter shall be considered, with respect to the former, to be on the footing of the most favoured powers, and the British Government will have no concern with the territories and subjects of the Rajah to the northward of the river Sutlej.

Article 2.—The Rajah will never maintain in the territory which he occupies on the left bank of the river Sutlej, more troops than are necessary for the internal duties of that territory, nor commit or suffer any incroachments on the possessions or rights of the Chiefs in its vicinity.

Article 3.—In the event of a violation of any of the preceding articles, or of a departure from the rules of friendship, this treaty shall be considered null and void.

Article 4.—This treaty, consisting of four articles, having been settled and concluded at Umritsur, on the 25th day of April, 1809, Mr. C.T. Metcalfe has delivered to the Rajah of Lahore a copy of the same in English and Persian, under his seal and signature; and the Rajah has delivered another copy of the same under his seal and signature, and Mr. C.T. Metcalfe engages to procure within the space of two months, a copy of the same duly ratified by the Right Honourable the Governor-General in Council, on the receipt of which by the Rajah, the present treaty shall be considered complete and binding on both parties, and the copy of it now delivered to the Rajah shall be returned.

II.

SIR DAVID OCHTERLONY'S PROCLAMATION OF 1809.

Precept or "Ittillah Nameh," under the Seal of General St. Leger, and under the Seal and Signature of Colonel Ochterlony; written on the 9th of February, 1809, corresponding to the 23d Zee Hijeh, 1223, Hijree.

The British army having encamped near the frontiers of the Maharajah Runjeet Singh, it has been thought proper to signify the pleasure of the British Government, by means of this precept, in order to make all the Chiefs of the Maharajah acquainted with the sentiments of the British Government, which have solely for their object and aim to confirm the friendship with the Maharajah, and to prevent any injury to his country, the preservation of friendship between the two States, depending on particular conditions which are hereby detailed.

The Thânnahs in the fortress of Khur'r, Khanpore, and other places on this side of the river Sutlej, which have been placed in the hands of the dependents of the Maharajah, shall be razed, and the same places restored to their ancient possessors.

The force of cavalry and infantry which may have crossed to this side of the Sutlej must be recalled to the other side, to the country of the Maharajah.

The troops stationed at the Ghât of Philour must march thence, and depart to the other side of the river as described, and in future the troops of the Maharajah shall never advance into the country of the Chiefs situated on this side of the river, who have called in for their security and protection Thânnahs of the British Government; but if in the manner that the British have placed Thânnahs of moderate number on this side of the Sutlej, if in like manner a small force by way of Thânnah be stationed at the Ghât of Philour, it will not be objected to.

If the Maharajah persevere in the fulfilment of the above stipulations, which he so repeatedly professed to do in the presence of Mr. Metcalfe, such fulfilment will confirm the mutual friendship. In case of non-compliance with these stipulations, then shall it be plain that the Maharajah has no regard for the friendship of the British, but, on the contrary, resolves on enmity. In such case the victorious British army shall commence every mode of defence.

The communication of this precept is solely with the view of publishing the sentiments of the British, and to know those of the Maharajah. The British are confident that the Maharajah will consider the contents of this precept as abounding to his real advantage, and as affording a conspicuous proof of their friendship; that with their capacity for war they are also intent on peace.

III.

I must here observe, that in having so very large an Artillery, General Thomas proved his appreciation of powerful batteries, an experience which he had probably acquired on board a man-of-war, as everything, in a naval action, depends upon the quick application of a powerful broadside of, say thirty, forty, or sixty guns. General Thomas had twelve guns to every thousand men. In Europe, the largest number ever used, was by the Russians, in 1807, namely seven guns to every thousand men. Hyder Ali Khan and Tippoo Sultan always used a great number of guns of a large calibre; in like manner the Maharatta chiefs, Sindiah and Holcar brought eighty and a hundred guns into the field of battle. Except very recently, we have had fewer guns than the Sikhs; the battle of Goojerat (Feb. 21, 1849) being the only one in which we appear to have been superior to the enemy in this respect.

IV.

THE TREATY WITH LAHORE OF 1806.

Treaty of Friendship and Unity between the Honourable East India Company and the Sirdars Runjeet Singh and Futteh Singh.
(1st of January, 1806.)

Sirdar Runjeet Singh and Sirdar Futteh Singh have consented to the following articles of agreement concluded by Lieutenant-Colonel John Malcolm, under the special authority of the Right Honourable Lord Lake, himself duly authorized by the Honourable Sir George Hilaro Barlow, Bart., Governor-General, and Sirdar Futteh Singh, as principal on the part of himself, and plenipotentiary on the part of Runjeet Singh:—

Article 1.—Sirdar Runjeet Singh and Sirdar Futteh Singh Aloowalla, hereby agree that they will cause Jeswunt Rao Holcar to remove with his army to the distance of thirty coss from Umritsur immediately, and will never hereafter hold any further connection with him, or aid or assist him with troops, or in any other manner whatever; and they further agree that they will not in any way molest such of Jeswunt Rao Holcar's followers or troops as are desirous of returning to their homes in the Deccan, but, on the contrary, will render them every assistance in their power for carrying such intention into execution.

Article 2.—The British Government hereby agrees, that in case a pacification should not be effected between that Government and Jeswunt Rao Holcar, the British army shall move from its present encampment, on the banks of the river Beeah, as soon as Jeswunt Rao Holcar aforesaid shall have marched his army to the distance of thirty coss from Umritsur; and that in any treaty which may hereafter be concluded between the British Government and Jeswunt Rao Holcar, it shall be stipulated that, immediately after the conclusion of the said treaty, Holcar shall evacuate the territories of the Sikhs, and march towards his own, and that he shall in no way whatever injure or destroy such parts of the Sikh country as may lie in his route. The British Government further agrees that, as long as the said Chieftains, Runjeet Singh and Futteh Singh, abstain from holding any friendly connection with the enemies of that Government, or from committing any act of hostility on their own parts against the said Government, the British armies shall never enter the territories of the said Chieftains, nor will the British Government form any plans for the seizure or sequestration of their possessions or property.

Dated 1st of January, 1806.

V.

PROCLAMATION OF PROTECTION TO CIS SUTLEJ STATES AGAINST LAHORE. Of 1809.

Translation of an "Ittilah Nameh," addressed to the Chiefs of the Country of Malwa and Sirhind, on this side of the river Sutlej. (3rd of May, 1809.)

It is clearer than the sun and better proved than the existence of yesterday, that the marching of a detachment of British troops to this side of the river Sutlej was entirely at the application and earnest entreaty of the several Chiefs, and originated solely from friendly considerations in the British Government, to preserve them in their possessions and independence. A treaty having been concluded, on the 25th of April, 1809, between Mr. Metcalfe on the part of the British Government, and Maharajah Runjeet Singh, agreeably to the orders of the Right Honourable the Governor-General in Council, I have the pleasure of publishing, for the satisfaction of the Chiefs of the country of Malwa and Sirhind, the pleasure and resolution of the British Government, as contained in the seven following articles:—

Article 1.—The country of the Chiefs of Malwa and Sirhind having entered under the British protection, they shall in future be secured from the authority and influence of Maharajah Runjeet Singh, conformably to the terms of the treaty.

Article 2.—All the country of the Chiefs thus taken under protection shall be exempted from all pecuniary tribute to the British Government.

Article 3.—The Chiefs shall remain in the full exercise of the same rights and authority in their own possessions which they enjoyed before they were received under the British protection.

Article 4.—Should a British force, on purposes of general welfare, be required to march through the country of the said Chiefs, it is necessary and incumbent that every Chief shall, within his own possessions, assist and furnish, to the full of his power, such force with supplies of Grain and other necessaries which may be demanded.

Article 5.—Should an enemy approach from any quarter, for the purpose of conquering this country, friendship and mutual interest require that the Chiefs join the British army with all their force, and, exerting themselves in expelling the enemy, act under discipline and proper obedience.

Article 6.—All European articles brought by merchants from the eastern districts, for the use of the army, shall be allowed to pass, by the Thânnahdars and Sayerdars of the several Chiefs, without molestation and the demand of duty.

Article 7.—All horses purchased for the use of cavalry regiments, whether in the district of Sirhind or elsewhere, the bringers of which being provided with sealed "Rahdaries" from the Resident at Delhi, or officer commanding at Sirhind, shall be allowed to pass through the country of the said Chiefs without molestation or the demand of duty.

VI.

PROCLAMATION OF PROTECTION TO CIS SUTLEJ STATES AGAINST ONE ANOTHER OF 1811.

For the Information and Assurance of the Protected Chiefs of the Plains between the Sutlej and the Jumna. (22nd of August, 1811.)

On the 3rd of May, 1809, an "Ittilah Nameh," comprised of seven articles, was issued by the orders of the British Government, purporting that the country of the Sirdars of Sirhind and Malwa having come under their protection, Rajah Runjeet Singh, agreeably to treaty, had no concern with the possessions of the above Sirdars: That the British Government had no intention of claiming Peishkushs or Nuzerana, and that they should continue in the full control and enjoyment of their respective possessions.

The publication of the above "Ittilah Nameh" was intended to afford every confidence to the Sirdars, that the protection of the country was the sole object, that they had no intention of control, and that those having possessions should remain in full and complete enjoyment thereof.

Whereas several Zumindars and other subjects of the Chiefs of this country have preferred complaints to the officers of the British Government, who, having in view the tenor of the above "Ittilah Nameh," have not attended, and will not in future pay attention to them;—for instance, on the 15th of June, 1811, Delawur Ali Khan of Samana complained to the Resident of Delhi against the officers of Rajah Sahib Singh, for jewels and other property said to have been seized by them, who, in reply, observed, that the "Cusba of Samana being in the Ameeldary of Rajah Sahib Singh, his complaint should be made to him;" and also, on the 12th of July, 1811, Dussowndha Singh and Goormook Singh complained to Colonel Ochterlony, Agent to the Governor-General, against Sirdar Churrut Singh, for their shares of property, etc.; and in reply it was written on the back of their urzee, "that since during the period of three years, no claim was preferred against Churrut Singh by any of his brothers, nor even the name of any co-partner mentioned; and since it was advertised in the 'Ittilah Nameh' delivered to the Sirdars, that every Chief should remain in the quiet and full enjoyment of his domains, the petition could not be attended to,"—the insertion of these answers to complaints is intended as examples, and also that it may be impressed on the minds of every Zumindar and other subject, that the attainment of justice is to be expected from their respective Chiefs only, that they may not, in the smallest degree swerve from the observance of subordination.—It is, therefore, highly incumbent upon the Rajahs and other Sirdars of this side of the river Sutlej, that they explain this to their respective subjects, and court their confidence, that it may be clear to them, that complaints to the officers of the British Government will be of no avail, and that they consider their respective Sirdars as the source of justice, and that, of their free will and accord, they observe uniform obedience.

And whereas, according to the first Proclamation, it is not the intention of the British Government to interfere in the possessions of the Sirdars of this country, it is nevertheless, for the purpose of ameliorating the condition of the community, particularly necessary to give general information, that several Sirdars have, since the incursion of Rajah Runjeet Singh, wrested the estates of others, and deprived them of their lawful possessions, and that in the restoration they have used delays, until detachments of the British army have been sent to effect restitution, as in the case of the Rannee of Terah, the Sikhs of Cholian, the Talookas of Carowley and Chehloundy, and the village of Cheeba; and the reason of such delays and evasions can only be attributed to the temporary enjoyment of the revenues, and subjecting the owners to irremediable losses:—It is, therefore, by order of the British Government, hereby proclaimed, that if any one of the Sirdars or others has forcibly taken possession of the estates of others, or otherwise injured the lawful owners, it is necessary that, before the occurrence of any complaint, the proprietor should be satisfied, and by no means to defer the restoration of the property,—in which, however, should delays be made, and the interference of the British authority become requisite, the revenues of the estate from the date of ejection of the lawful proprietor, together with whatever other losses the inhabitants of that place may sustain from the march of troops, shall without scruple be demanded from the offending party; and for disobedience of the present orders, a penalty, according to the circumstances of the case and of the offender, shall be levied, agreeably to the decision of the British Government.

VII.

INDUS NAVIGATION TREATY OF 1832.

Articles of Convention established between the Honourable the East India Company, and his Highness the Maharajah Runjeet Singh, the Ruler of the Punjaub, for the opening of the Navigation of the rivers Indus and Sutlej. (Originally drafted 26th of December, 1832.)

By the grace of God, the relations of firm alliance and indissoluble ties of friendship existing between the Honourable the East India Company and his Highness the Maharajah Runjeet Singh, founded on the auspicious treaty formerly concluded by Sir T.C. Metcalfe, Bart., and since confirmed in the written pledge of sincere amity presented by the Right Honourable Lord W.C. Bentinck, G.C.B. and G.C.H., Governor-General of British India, at the meeting at Rooper, are, like the sun, clear and manifest to the whole world, and will continue unimpaired, and increase in strength from generation to generation:—By virtue of these firmly established bonds of friendship, since the opening of the navigation of the rivers Indus proper (i.e. Indus below the confluence of the Punjaub) and Sutlej, (a measure deemed expedient by both States, with a view to promote the general interests of commerce),— has lately been effected through the agency of Captain C.M. Wade, Political Agent at Loodianna, deputed by the Right Honourable the Governor-General for that purpose. The following Articles, explanatory of the conditions by which the said navigation is to be regulated, as concerns the nomination of officers, the mode of collecting the duties, and the protection of the trade by that route, have been framed, in order that the officers of the two States employed in their execution may act accordingly:—

Article 1.—The provisions of the existing treaty relative to the right bank of the river Sutlej and all its stipulations, together with the contents of the friendly pledge already mentioned, shall remain binding, and a strict regard to preserve the relations of friendship between the two States shall be the ruling principle of action. In accordance with that treaty, the Honourable Company has not, nor will have any concern with the right bank of the river Sutlej.

Article 2.—The tariff which is to be established for the line of navigation in question is intended to apply exclusively to the passage of merchandise by that route, and not to interfere with the transit duties levied on goods proceeding from one hank of the river to the other, nor with the places fixed for their collection: they are to remain as heretofore.

Article 3.—Merchants frequenting the same route, while within the limits of the Maharajah's Government, are required to show a due regard to his authority, as is done by merchants generally, and not to commit any acts offensive to the civil and religious institutions of the Sikhs.

Article 4.—Any one purposing to go the said route will intimate his intention to the Agent of either State, and apply for a passport, agreeably to a form to be laid down; having obtained which, he may proceed on his journey. The merchants coming from Umritsur, and other parts on the right bank of the river Sutlej, are to intimate their intentions to the agent of the Maharajah, at Hurrekee, or other appointed places, and obtain a passport through him; and merchants coming from Hindoostan, or other parts on the left bank of the river Sutlej, will intimate their intentions to the Honourable Company's Agent and obtain a passport through him. As foreigners, and Hindoostanees, and Sirdars of the protected Sikh States and elsewhere, are not in the habit of crossing the Sutlej without a passport from the Maharajah's officers, it is expected that such persons will hereafter also conform to the same rule, and not cross without the usual passports.

Article 5.—A tariff shall be established exhibiting the rate of duties leviable on each description of merchandise, which, after having been approved by both Governments, is to be the standard by which the superintendents and collectors of customs are to be guided.

Article 6.—Merchants are invited to adopt the new route with perfect confidence: no one shall be suffered to molest them or unnecessarily impede their progress, care being taken that they are only detained for the collection of the duties, in the manner stipulated, at the established stations.

Article 7.—The officers who are to be entrusted with the collection of the duties, and examination of the goods on the right bank of the river shall be stationed at Mithenkote and Hurrekee; at no other places but these two, shall boats in transit on the river be liable to examination or stoppage. When the persons in charge of boats stop of their own accord to take in or give out cargo, the goods will be liable to the local transit duty of the Maharajah's Government, previously to their being landed, as provided in Article 2. The superintendent stationed at Mithenkote having examined the cargo, will levy the established duty, and grant a passport, with a written account of the cargo and freight. On the arrival of the boat at Hurrekee, the superintendent of that station will compare the passport with the cargo; and whatever goods are found in excess will be liable to the payment of the established duty, while the rest, having already paid duty at Mithenkote, will pass on free. The same rule shall be observed in respect to merchandise conveyed from Hurrekee by the way of the rivers towards Scinde, that whatever may be fixed as the share of duties on the right bank of the river Sutlej, in right of the Maharajah's own dominions and of those in allegiance to him, the Maharajah's officers will collect it at the places appointed. With regard to the security and safety of merchants who may adopt this route, the Maharajah's officers shall afford them every protection in their power; and merchants, on halting for the night on either bank of the Sutlej, are required, with reference to the treaty of friendship which exists between the two States, to give notice, and to show their passports to the Thânnahdar, or officers in authority at the place, and request protection for themselves: if, notwithstanding this precaution, loss should at any time occur, a strict enquiry will be made, and reclamation sought from those who are blamable. The Articles of the present treaty for opening the navigation of the rivers above mentioned having, agreeably to subsisting relations, been approved by the Right Honourable the Governor-General, shall be carried into execution accordingly.

Dated Lahore the 26th of December, 1832.

SUPPLEMENTARY INDUS NAVIGATION TREATY OF 1834.

Draft of a Supplementary Treaty between the British Government and Maharajah Runjeet Singh for establishing a Toll on the Indus. (29th of November, 1834.)

In conformity with the subsisting relations of friendship, as established and confirmed by former treaties, between the Honourable the East India Company and his Highness Maharajah Runjeet Singh; and whereas in the 5th Article of the treaty concluded at Lahore on the 26th day of December, 1832, it was stipulated that a moderate scale of duties should be fixed by the two Governments in concert, to be levied on all merchandise on transit up and down the rivers Indus and Sutlej; the said Governments being now of opinion that, owing to the inexperience of the people of these countries in such matters, the mode of levying duties then proposed (viz. on the value and quantity of goods) could not fail to give rise to mutual misunderstandings and reclamations, have, with a view to prevent these results, determined to substitute a toll, which shall be levied on all boats, with whatever merchandise laden. The following articles have therefore been adopted as supplementary to the former treaty; and in conformity with them, each Government engages that the toll shall be levied, and its amount neither be increased nor diminished except by mutual consent.

Article 1.—A toll of 570 Rupees shall be levied on all boats laden with merchandise in transit on the rivers Indus and Sutlej, between the sea and Rooper, without reference to their size, or to the weight or value of their cargo; the above toll to be divided among the different States in proportion to the extent of territory which they possess on the banks of these rivers.

Article 2.—The portion of the above toll appertaining to the Lahore Chief in right of his territory on both banks of these rivers, as determined in the subjoined scale shall be levied opposite to Mithenkote on boats coming from the sea towards Rooper, and in the vicinity of Hurrekee Puttun on boats going from Rooper towards the sea, and at no other place:—

In right of territory on the right bank of the rivers Indus and Sutlej, 155 Rupees 4 annas.

In right of territory on the left bank of the rivers Indus and Sutlej, the Maharajah's share, of 67 Rupees 15 annas. 9 pies.

Article 3.—In order to facilitate the realization of the toll due to the different States, as well as for the speedy and satisfactory adjustment of any disputes which may arise connected with the safety of the navigation and the welfare of the trade by the new route, a British officer will reside opposite to Mithenkote, and a native agent on the part of the British Government, opposite to Hurrekee Puttun. These officers will be subject to the orders of the British Agent at Loodianna; and the Agents who may be appointed to reside at those places on the part of the other States concerned in the navigation, viz. Bhawulpore and Scinde, together with those of Lahore, will co-operate with them in the execution of their duties.

Article 4.—In order to guard against imposition on the part of merchants in making false complaints of being plundered of their property which formed no part of their cargoes, they are required, when taking out their passports, to produce an invoice of their cargo, which, being duly authenticated, a copy of it will be annexed to their passports; and wherever their boats may be brought to for the night, they are required to give immediate notice to the Thânnahdars or officers of the place, and to request protection for themselves, at the same time showing the passports they may have received at Mithenkote or Hurrekee, as the case may be.

Article 5.—Such parts of the 5th, 7th, 9th, and 10th Articles of the Treaty of the 26th of December, 1832, as have reference to the fixing a duty on the value and quantity of merchandise, and to the mode of its collection are hereby rescinded, and the foregoing articles substituted in their place, agreeably to which, and the conditions of the preamble, the toll will be levied.

N.B.—A distribution of the shares due to the British protected States and the feudatories of the Maharajah on the left bank of the Sutlej will be determined hereafter.

VIII.

DECLARATION OF WAR OF 1845.

Proclamation by the Governor-General of India.

Camp Lushkuree Khan ke Serai,
December 13th, 1845.

The British Government has ever been on terms of friendship with that of the Punjaub.

In the year 1809, a treaty of amity and concord was concluded between the British Government, and the late Maharajah Runjeet Singh, the conditions of which have always been faithfully observed by the British Government, and were scrupulously fulfilled by the late Maharajah.

The same friendly relations have been maintained with the successors of Maharajah Runjeet Singh by the British Government up to the present time.

Since the death of the late Maharajah Shere Singh, the disorganized state of the Lahore Government has made it incumbent on the Governor-General in Council to adopt precautionary measures for the protection of the British frontier: the nature of these measures and the cause of their adoption, were, at the time, fully explained to the Lahore Durbar.

Notwithstanding the disorganized state of the Lahore Government during the last two years, and many most unfriendly proceedings on the part of the Durbar, the Governor-General in Council has continued to evince his desire to maintain the relations of amity and concord which had so long existed between the two States, for the mutual interests and happiness of both. He has shown, on every occasion, the utmost forbearance, from consideration to the helpless state of the infant Maharajah, Dhuleep Singh, whom the British Government had recognised as the successor to the late Maharajah Shere Singh.

The Governor-General in Council sincerely desired to see a strong Sikh Government re-established in the Punjaub, able to control its army, and to protect its subjects; he had not, up to the present moment, abandoned the hope of seeing that important object effected by the patriotic efforts of the Chiefs and people of that country.

The Sikh army recently marched from Lahore towards the British frontier, as it was alleged, by the orders of the Durbar, for the purpose of invading the British territory.

The Governor-General's Agent, by direction of the Governor-General, demanded an explanation of this movement, and no reply being returned within a reasonable time, the demand was repeated. The Governor-General, unwilling to believe in the hostile intentions of the Sikh Government, to which no provocation had been given, refrained from taking any measures which might have a tendency to embarrass the Government of the Maharajah, or to induce collision between the two States.

When no reply was given to the repeated demand for explanation, while active military preparations were continued at Lahore, the Governor-General considered it necessary to order the advance of troops towards the frontier, to reinforce the frontier posts.

The Sikh army has now, without a shadow of provocation, invaded the British territories.

The Governor-General must therefore take measures for effectually protecting the British provinces, for vindicating the authority of the British Government, and for punishing the violators of treaties and the disturbers of the public peace.

The Governor-General hereby declares the possessions of Maharajah Dhuleep Singh, on the left or British bank of the Sutlej, confiscated and annexed to the British territories.

The Governor-General will respect the existing rights of all Jaghirdars, Zumindars, and tenants in the said possessions, who, by the course they now pursue, evince their fidelity to the British Government.

The Governor-General hereby calls upon all the Chiefs and Sirdars in the protected territories to co-operate cordially with the British Government for the punishment of the common enemy, and for the maintenance of order in these States. Those of the Chiefs who show alacrity and fidelity in the discharge of this duty, which they owe to the protecting power, will find their interests promoted thereby; and those who take a contrary course will be treated as enemies to the British Government, and will be punished accordingly.

The inhabitants of all the territories on the left bank of the Sutlej are hereby directed to abide peaceably in their respective villages, where they will receive efficient protection by the British Government. All parties of men found in armed bands, who can give no satisfactory account of their proceedings, will be treated as disturbers of the public peace.

All subjects of the British Government, and those who possess estates on both sides of the river Sutlej, who by their faithful adherence to the British Government, may be liable to sustain loss, shall be indemnified and secured in all their just rights and privileges.

On the other hand, all subjects of the British Government who shall continue in the service of the Lahore State, and who disobey the Proclamation by not immediately returning to their allegiance, will be liable to have their property on this side the Sutlej confiscated, and themselves declared to be aliens and enemies of the British Government.

IX.

SERVICES OF CAPTAIN HUMBLEY,

Rifle Brigade.

Captain Humbley served with the 95th (Rifle Brigade) at the siege of Copenhagen, in 1807, and was engaged in some skirmishes near that city, and in the action of Kioge; he was also present at the surrender of Copenhagen, and of the whole of the Danish navy. In 1808, he landed with a detachment in Portugal, and was present at the battles of Roleia and Vimiera, the advance from Lisbon into Spain, the subsequent retreat from Salamanca, the action of Calcavellas, and the battle of Corunna. He served on the Walcheren expedition, in 1809, commanded an advanced outpost before Flushing, on the night of the 31st of July, when he surprised, and took prisoners, an outlying picquet of the enemy; on the following day, while under the fortifications of Flushing, he was severely wounded in the forehead by a musket-ball, which lodged and was extracted, and the head trepanned.

Captain Humbley joined the army in the Peninsula in March, 1810, and served there until the end of that war in 1814, with the exception of four months in 1812.

On the passage to Spain, December the 5th, 1812, he was present at the capture, after a running fight of several miles, of a large, well-armed, American merchant ship.

Captain Humbley was present at the defence of Cadiz and Fort Matagorda, debarked at Tarifa, and was present at the battles of Barrosa, Salamanca, and Vittoria, and, in the last engagement, was severely wounded in the left arm. He took part in the action at Vera Bridge, storming the heights of Vera, and in the battles of the Pyrenees, where he was wounded near the left eye. He was present at the crossing of the Bidassoa, at the battles of Nivelle, Nive, and Orthes, in which last he was severely wounded in the right thigh; he was also in the action of Tarbes, and the battle of Toulouse, besides several minor engagements, skirmishes, and affairs of outposts.

Captain Humbley served also in the campaign of 1815, and was severely wounded at the battle of Waterloo, by a musket-ball in each shoulder. The two balls having lodged, one was extracted two days afterwards, but the other still remains lodged under the scapula in the left shoulder.

Captain Humbley has received the War Medal and Twelve Clasps.

X.

A monument, by R. Westmacott, Junr., R.A., F.R.S., is about to be erected at Shrewsbury, to the memory of Colonel Cureton. The gallant Colonel will be represented at full length, lying on his back, with his hands clasped. The following is the inscription:

SACRED TO THE MEMORY
OF
COLONEL G.R. CURETON,
C.B., AND A.D.C., TO THE QUEEN,
ADJUTANT-GENERAL OF H.M. FORCES IN INDIA,
AND LATE LIEUT.-COLONEL COMMANDING THE 16TH LANCERS
WHO
FELL IN AN ENGAGEMENT WITH THE SIKH TROOPS AT
RAMNUGGUR, ON THE 22ND OF NOVEMBER, 1848,
WHEN COMMANDING THE CAVALRY OF THE BRITISH ARMY
UNDER GENERAL LORD GOUGH, G.C.B.,
THIS MONUMENT IS ERECTED BY HIS COMRADES AND BROTHER
OFFICERS IN INDIA. BY WHOM HE WAS HELD, AS A

SOLDIER, IN UNIVERSAL ADMIRATION AND
RESPECT; AND IN LOVE AND ESTEEM
AS A FRIEND.

XI.

OFFICIAL DESPATCHES.

From the Governor-General of India to the Secret Committee of the East India Company, dated Camp, Ferozepore, Dec. 31st, 1845.

The Sikh army, in large numbers, commenced crossing the Sutlej on the 11th, and, after investing Ferozepore on one side, took up an entrenched position at the village of Ferozeshah, about ten miles in advance of Ferozepore, and about the same distance from the village of Moodkee.

In this camp the enemy had placed 108 pieces of cannon, some of large calibre, with a force exceeding 50,000 men, for the purpose of intercepting the approach of the British force moving up from Umballa, to the relief of Ferozepore, which had been thus treacherously attacked, without provocation or declaration of hostilities.

I had ordered, on the 8th inst., that portion of our army posted at Umballa for defensive purposes, to move up on the 11th; and, after a rapid march of 150 miles, it reached Moodkee on the 18th, where, on the evening of the same day, it repulsed an attack of the Sikh army, and captured seventeen guns. On the following day the army was concentrated at Moodkee, and, on the 21st, moved by its left on Ferozepore; and having, on the march, formed its junction, at half-past one o'clock, with 5,000 men and twenty-one guns, under Major-Gen. Sir John Littler, which had moved from Ferozepore that morning, the Commander-in-Chief formed the army in order of battle, and attacked the enemy's entrenched camp, and, on that evening and the following morning, captured severity pieces of artillery, taking possession of the enemy's camp, with a large quantity of ammunition and warlike stores.

These successful and energetic operations have been followed by the retreat of the Sikh army to the other side of the Sutlej; the British army being now encamped between Ferozepore and the fords of the Sutlej.

You will not fail to observe that these important and brilliant successes have been achieved by that portion of our army posted at and in advance of

Umballa for defensive purposes, and that our forces from Meerut and other stations from the rear, ordered to move up at the same time, are in reserve, and will reach this neighbourhood between the 5th and the 9th of January.

I have the honour to inclose two reports from the Commander-in-Chief, detailing the admirable manner in which these important duties have been performed.

The Commander-in-Chief has successfully accomplished every object I had directed him to effect for the relief of Ferozepore, and the protection of the British States. No accident or failure has occurred during: the complicated operations of a combined movement; and our army, whether for defence or attack, has shewn, as heretofore, that its power is irresistible.

From General Sir Hugh Gough, Bart., G.C.B., the Commander-in-Chief of the Army in India, to the Governor-General of India.

Head Quarters, Army of the Sutlej,
Camp, Moodkee, Dec. 19th, 1845.

Right Hon. Sir,

It would be a superfluous form in me to address to you a narrative of the campaign which has opened against the Sikhs, and the successful action of yesterday, since you have in person shared the fatigues and dangers of our army, and witnessed its efforts and privations, but that my position at its head renders this my duty; and it is necessary, from that position, I should place these events on record, for the information of all Europe, as well as of all India.

You, Sir, know, but others have to be told, that the sudden and unprovoked aggression of the Sikhs, by crossing the Sutlej with the great proportion of their army, with the avowed intention of attacking Ferozepore in time of profound peace, rendered indispensable, on our side, a series of difficult combinations for the protection of our frontier station, so unjustifiably and so unexpectedly menaced.

From the advanced and salient situation of Ferozepore, and its vicinity to the Sikh capital, its defence against a sudden attack became a difficult operation. It was always possible for the Sikh government to throw a formidable force upon it before one sufficiently numerous could on our side be collected to support it; but when, upon the 11th instant, it became known at Umballa, where I had established my head-quarters, that this invasion had actually taken place, the efforts to repel it followed each other in rapid succession; notwithstanding I had the fullest confidence in Major-General

Sir John Littler, commanding at Ferozepore, and in the devotedness and gallantry of the troops occupying it.

The troops from the different stations in the Sirhind division were directed to move by forced marches upon Bussean, where, by a most judicious arrangement, you had directed supplies to be collected, within a wonderfully short space of time.

The main portion of the force at Loodianna was withdrawn, and a garrison thrown into the little fortress there. From this central position, already alluded to, both Loodianna and Ferozepore could be supported, and the safety of both places might be considered to be brought, in some measure, within the scope of the contingencies of a general action to be fought for their relief. All this is soon related; but most harassing have been the marches of the troops in completing this concentration. When their march had been further prolonged to this place, they had moved over a distance of upward of 150 miles in six days, along roads of heavy sand; their perpetual labour allowing them scarcely time to cook their food, even when they received it, and hardly an hour for repose, before they were called upon for renewed exertions.

When our leading corps reached Wudnee, a small jaghire of the late Maharajah Shere Singh, its garrison shut the gates of the fort against them; and, as our battering guns were far in the rear, it was determined to reserve it for future chastisement, and we remained content with compelling the village to furnish supplies (it could, however, provide little, except for our overworked cattle), under pain of enduring a cannonade and assault; this it did, without the necessity of firing a shot.

When we reached Wudnee, it was evident that the force before Ferozepore felt the influence of our movements, as we heard that a very large portion of that force had been detached to oppose our further advance; their feeling parties retired on the morning of the 18th before our Cavalry picquets, near the village and fort of Moodkee.

Soon after mid-day, the division under Major-General Sir Harry Smith, a brigade of that under Major-General Sir J. M'Caskill, and another of that under Major-General Gilbert, with five troops of Horse artillery, and two light field batteries, under Lieutenant Colonel Brooke, of the Horse Artillery (brigadier in command of the Artillery force), and the Cavalry division, consisting of H.M. 3rd Light Dragoons, the body-guard, 4th and 5th Light Cavalry, and 9th Irregular Cavalry, took up their encamping ground in front of Moodkee.

The troops were in a state of great exhaustion, principally from the want of water, which was not procurable on the road, when, about three P.M., information was received that the Sikh army was advancing; and the troops had scarcely time to get under arms, and move to their positions, when the fact was ascertained.

I immediately pushed forward the Horse Artillery and Cavalry, directing the Infantry, accompanied by the field batteries, to move forward in support. We had not proceeded beyond two miles when we found the enemy in position. They were said to consist of 15,000 to 20,000 Infantry, about the same force of Cavalry, and forty guns. They evidently had either just taken up this position, or were advancing in order of battle against us.

To resist their attack, and to cover the formation of the Infantry, I advanced the Cavalry under Brigadiers White, Gough, and Mactier, rapidly to the front, in columns of squadrons, and occupied the plain. They were speedily followed by the five troops of Horse Artillery, under Brigadier Brooke who took up a forward position, having the Cavalry then on his flanks.

The country is a dead flat, covered at short intervals with a low, but in some places, thick jhow jungle, and dotted with sandy hillocks. The enemy screened their Infantry and Artillery behind this jungle, and such undulations as the ground afforded; and whilst our twelve battalions formed from echelon of brigade into line, opened a very severe cannonade upon our advancing troops, which was vigorously replied to by the battery of Horse Artillery under Brigadier Brooke, which was soon joined by the two light field batteries. The rapid and well-directed fire of our artillery appeared soon to paralyse that of the enemy; and as it was necessary to complete our infantry dispositions without advancing the Artillery too near to the jungle, I directed the Cavalry under Brigadiers White and Gough, to make a flank movement on the enemy's left, with a view of threatening and turning that flank if possible. With praiseworthy gallantry, the 3rd Light Dragoons, with the 2nd brigade of Cavalry, consisting of the body guard and 5th Light Cavalry, with a portion of the 4th Lancers, turned the left of the Sikh army, and, sweeping along the whole rear of its Infantry and guns, silenced for a time the latter, and put their numerous cavalry to flight. Whilst this movement was taking place on the enemy's left, I directed the remainder of the 4th Lancers, the 9th Irregular Cavalry, under Brigadier Mactier, with a light field battery, to threaten their right. This manœuvre was also successful. Had not the Infantry and guns of the enemy been screened by the jungle, these brilliant charges of the Cavalry would have been productive of greater effect.

When the Infantry advanced to the attack, Brigadier Brooke rapidly pushed on his Horse Artillery close to the jungle, and the cannonade was resumed on both sides. The Infantry under Major-Generals Sir Harry Smith, Gilbert, and Sir John M'Caskill, attacked in echelon of lines the enemy's Infantry, almost invisible amongst wood and the approaching darkness of night. The opposition of the enemy was such as might have been expected from troops who had everything at stake, and who had long vaunted of being irresistible. Their ample and extended line, from their great superiority of numbers, far outflanked ours; but this was counter-acted by the flank movements of our Cavalry. The attack of the Infantry now commenced, and the roll of fire from this powerful arm soon convinced the Sikh army that they had met with a foe they little expected; and their whole force was driven from position after position with great slaughter, and the loss of seventeen pieces of artillery, some of them of heavy calibre; our infantry using that never failing weapon, the bayonet, whenever the enemy stood. Night only saved them from worse disaster; for this stout conflict was maintained during an hour and a half of dim starlight, amidst a cloud of dust from the sandy plain, which yet more obscured every object.

I regret to say, this gallant and successful attack was attended with considerable loss; the force bivouacked upon the field for some hours, and only returned to its encampment after ascertaining that it had no enemy before it, and that night prevented the possibility of a regular advance in pursuit.

H. Gough, General,
Commander-in-Chief.

From His Excellency the Commander-in-Chief to the Right Hon. the Governor-General of India, dated Camp, Ferozeshah, December 22nd, 1845.

Right Honourable Sir,

I have again to congratulate you on the success of our arms. A grand battle has been fought against the Sikh army at this place, and, by the blessing of Divine providence, victory has been won, by the valour of our troops, against odds and under circumstances which will render this action one of the most memorable in the page of Indian history.

After the combat of the 18th at Moodkee, information was received the following day, that the enemy, increased in numbers, were moving on to attack us. A line of defence was taken up in advance of our encampment, and dispositions made to repel assault; but the day wore away without their appearing, and at night we had the satisfaction of being reinforced by H.M. 29th Foot, and the East India Company's 1st European Light Infantry, with our small division of heavy guns.

I must here allude to a circumstance most favourable to our efforts in the field. On this evening, in addition to the valuable counsel with which you had in every emergency before favoured me, you were pleased yet further to strengthen my hands, by kindly offering your services as second in command in my army. I need hardly say with how much pleasure the offer was accepted.

On the morning of the 21st, the offensive was resumed; our columns of all arms debouched four miles on the road to Ferozeshah, where it was known that the enemy, posted in great force, and with a most formidable artillery, had remained since the action of the 18th, incessantly employed in entrenching his position. Instead of advancing to the direct attack of their formidable works, our force manœuvred to their right: the second and fourth divisions of infantry, in front, supported by the first division and cavalry in second line, continued to defile for some time out of cannon-shot between the Sikhs and Ferozepore. The desired effect was not long delayed, a cloud of dust was seen on the left, and according to the instructions sent him on the preceding evening, Major-General Sir John Littler, with his division, availing himself of the offered opportunity, was discovered in full march to unite his force with mine. The junction was soon effected; and thus was accomplished one of the great objects of all our harassing marches and privations, in the relief of this division of our army from the blockade of the numerous forces by which it was surrounded.

Dispositions were now made for a united attack on the enemy's entrenched camp. We found it to be a parallelogram, of about a mile in length, and half a mile in breadth, including within its area the strong village of Ferozeshah; the shorter sides looking towards the Sutlej and Moodkee, and the longer towards Ferozepore and the open country. We moved against the last-named face, the ground in front of which was like the Sikh position in Moodkee, covered with low jungle.

The divisions of Major-general Sir John Littler, Brigadier Wallace (who had succeeded Major-general Sir John M'Caskill), and Major-general Gilbert, deployed into line, having in the centre our whole force of artillery, with the exception of three troops of horse artillery, one on either flank and one in support, to be moved as occasion required. Major-general Sir Harry Smith's division, and our small cavalry force, moved in second line, having a brigade in reserve to cover each wing.

I should here observe, that I committed the charge and direction of the left wing to Lieutenant-general Sir Henry Hardinge, while I personally conducted the right.

A very heavy cannonade was opened by the enemy, who had dispersed over their position upwards of one hundred guns, more than forty of which were of battering calibre; these kept up a heavy and well-directed fire, which the practice of our far less numerous artillery, of much lighter metal, checked in some degree, but could not silence; finally, in the face of a storm of shot and shell, our infantry advanced and carried these formidable intrenchments; they threw themselves upon their guns, and with matchless gallantry wrested them from the enemy; but, when the batteries were partially within our grasp, our soldiery had to face such a fire of musketry from the Sikh infantry, arrayed behind their guns, that, in spite of the most heroic efforts, a portion only of the entrenchment could be carried. Night fell while the conflict was everywhere raging.

Although I now brought up Major-general Sir Harry Smith's division, and he captured and long retained another point of the position, and her Majesty's 3rd Light Dragoons charged and took some of the most formidable batteries, yet the enemy remained in possession of a considerable portion of the great quadrangle, whilst our troops, intermingled with theirs, kept possession of the remainder, and finally bivouacked upon it, exhausted by their gallant efforts, greatly reduced in numbers, and suffering extremely from thirst, yet animated by an indomitable spirit. In this state of things the long night wore away.

Near the middle of it, one of their heavy guns was advanced and played with deadly effect upon our troops. Lieut.-general Sir Henry Hardinge immediately formed H.M. 80th Foot and the 1st European Light Infantry. They were led to the attack by their commanding officers, and animated in their exertions by Lieut.-col. Wood (aide-de-camp to the Lieut.-general), who was wounded in the outset. The 80th captured the gun, and the enemy, dismayed by this counter-check, did not venture to press on further. During the whole night, however, they continued to harass our troops by fire of artillery, wherever moonlight discovered our position.

But with daylight of the 22nd came retribution. Our infantry formed line, supported on both flanks by horse artillery, whilst a fire was opened from our centre by such of our heavy guns as remained effective, aided by a flight of rockets. A masked battery played with great effect upon this point, dismounting our pieces and blowing up our tumbrils. At this moment Lieutenant-general Sir Henry Hardinge placed himself at the head of the left, whilst I rode at the head of the right wing.

Our line advanced, and, unchecked by the enemy's fire, drove them rapidly out of the village of Ferozeshah and their encampment; then, changing front to its left, on its centre, our force continued to sweep the camp, bearing down all opposition, and dislodged the enemy from their whole position. The line then halted, as if on a day of manœuvre, receiving its two leaders, as they rode along its front, with a gratifying cheer, and displaying the captured standards of the Khalsa army. We had taken upwards of seventy-three pieces of cannon, and were masters of the whole field.

The force assumed a position on the ground which it had won, but even here its labours were not to cease. In the course of two hours, Sirdar Tej Singh, who had commanded in the last great battle, brought up from the vicinity of Ferozepore fresh battalions and a large field of artillery, supported by 30,000 Ghorepurras, hitherto encamped near the river. He drove in our cavalry parties, and made strenuous efforts to regain the position at Ferozeshah; this attempt was defeated; but its failure had scarcely become manifest, when the Sirdar renewed the contest with more troops and a large artillery. He commenced by a combination against our left flank; and when this was frustrated, made such a demonstration against the captured village, as compelled us to change our whole front to the right. His guns during this manœuvre, maintained an incessant fire, whilst our artillery ammunition being completely expended in these protracted combats, we were unable to answer him with a single shot.

I now directed our almost exhausted cavalry to threaten both flanks at once, preparing the infantry to advance in support, which apparently caused him suddenly to cease his fire, and to abandon the field.

For twenty-four hours not a Sikh has appeared in our front. The remains of the Khalsa army are said to be in full retreat across the Sutlej, at Nuggurputhur and Tella, or marching up its left bank towards Hurrekeeputhur, in the greatest confusion and dismay. Of their chiefs, Bahadur Singh is killed; Lall Singh said to be wounded; Mehtab Singh, Adjoodhia Pershad, and Tej Singh, the late governor of Peshawur, have fled with precipitation. Their camp is the scene of the most awful carnage, and they have abandoned large stores of grain, camp equipage, and ammunition.

Thus has apparently terminated this unprovoked and criminal invasion of the peaceful provinces under British protection.

On the conclusion of such a narrative as I have given, it is surely superfluous in me to say that I am, and shall be to the last moment of my existence, proud of the army which I had the honour to command on the

21st and 22nd instant. To their gallant exertions I owe the satisfaction of seeing such a victory achieved, and the glory of having my own name associated with it.

The loss of this army has been heavy; how could a hope be formed that it should be otherwise? Within thirty hours this force stormed an intrenched camp, fought a general action, and sustained two considerable combats with the enemy. Within four days it has dislodged from their positions, on the left bank of the Sutlej, 60,000 Sikh soldiers, supported by upwards of 150 pieces of cannon, 108 of which the enemy acknowledge to have lost, and ninety-one of which are in our possession.

In addition to our losses in the battle, the captured camp was found to be everywhere protected by charged mines, by the successive springing of which many brave officers and men have been destroyed.

I have the honour to be, etc.,
H. Gough, General,
Commander-in-Chief, East Indies.

Extract from a Despatch of His Excellency the Commander-in-Chief to the Right Hon. the Governor-General, dated Feb. 1, 1846.

Head Quarters, Army of the Sutlej.

Meanwhile the Upper Sutlej has become the scene of very interesting operations.

It is a strange feature of this war, that the enemy, pressed for supplies on his own bank, has been striving to draw them from his jaghire estates on this side of the river. In the town and fort of Dhurmkote, which were filled with grain, he had in the second week of January a small garrison of mercenaries—Rohillas, Eusufzies, and Affghans. Major-General Sir Harry Smith was on the 18th sent against this place with a single brigade of his division and a light field battery. He easily effected its reduction, the troops within surrendering at discretion after a few cannon shots. But whilst he was yet in march, I received information of a more serious character. There remained little cause to doubt that Sirdar Runjoor Sing Mujetheea had crossed from Philour, at the head of a numerous force of all arms, and established himself in a position at Baran Hara, between the old and the new courses of the Sutlej: not only threatening the city of Loodianna with plunder and devastation, but indicating a determination to intersect the line of our communications at Bussean and Rackote.

The safety of the rich and populous town of Loodianna had been, in some measure, provided for by the presence of three battalions of Native Infantry, under Brigadier Godby, and the gradual advance of our reinforcements, amongst which was included her Majesty's 53rd regiment, and the position of the Shekawattee brigade, near Bussean, gave breathing time to us in that direction.

But on receipt of intelligence which could be relied on, of the movements of Runjoor Singh and his apparent views, Major-general Sir Harry Smith, with the brigade at Dhurmkote, and Brigadier Cureton's cavalry, was directed to advance by Jugraon towards Loodianna, and his second brigade, under Brigadier Wheeler, moved on to support him.

Then commenced a series of very delicate combinations, the momentous character of which can only be comprehended by reflecting on the task which had devolved on this army of guarding the frontier from Rooper down to Mundote.

The Major-General, breaking up from Jugraon, moved towards Loodianna, when the Sirdar, relying on the vast superiority of his forces, assumed the initiative, and endeavoured to intercept his progress by marching in a line parallel to him, and opening upon his troops a furious cannonade. The Major-General continued coolly to manœuvre; and when the Sikh Sirdar, bending round one wing of his army, enveloped his flank, he extricated himself by retiring with the steadiness of a field-day by echelon of battalions, and effected his communication with Loodianna, but not without severe loss.

Reinforced by Brigadier Godby, he felt himself to be strong; but his manœuvres had thrown him out of communication with Brigadier Wheeler; and a portion of his baggage had fallen into the hands of the enemy. The Sikh Sirdar took up an entrenched position at Buddiwal, supporting himself on its fort, but, threatened on either flank by General Smith and Brigadier Wheeler, finally decamped and moved down to the Sutlej. The British troops made good their junction, and occupied the abandoned position of Buddiwal; the Shekawattee brigade and her Majesty's 53rd regiment also added to the strength of the Major-General, and he prepared to attack the Sikh Sirdar on his new ground. But on the 26th, Runjoor Singh was reinforced from the right bank with 4,000 regular troops, 12 pieces of artillery, and a large force of cavalry.

Emboldened by this accession of strength, he ventured on the measure of advancing towards Jugraon apparently with the view of intercepting our communications by that route.

It is my gratifying duty to announce, that this presumption has been rebuked by a splendid victory obtained over him. He has not only been repulsed by the Major-General, but his camp at Aliwal carried by storm, the whole of his cannons and munitions of war captured, and his army driven headlong across the Sutlej, even on the right bank of which he found no refuge from the fire of our artillery.

I have now the honour to forward the Major-General's report, which has just reached me. It is so ample and luminous, that I might perhaps have spared some of the details into which admiration of the General's conduct, and of the brave army confided to him in these operations, has led me.

Camp, Field of the Battle of Aliwal,
January 30, 1846.

To the Adjutant-General of the Army.

Sir,

My despatch to his Excellency the Commander-in-Chief, of the 23rd instant, will have put his Excellency in possession of the position of the force under my command after having formed a junction with the troops at Loodianna, hemmed in by a formidable body of the Sikh army under Runjoor Sing and the Rajah of Ladwa. The enemy strongly entrenched himself around the little fort of Buddiwal by breastworks and "abattis," which he precipitately abandoned on the night of the 22nd instant (retiring, as it were, upon the ford of Tulwun), having ordered all the boats which were opposite Philour, to that ghât. This movement he effected during the night, and, by a considerable détour, placed himself at a distance of ten miles, and consequently out of my reach. I could, therefore, only push forward my cavalry so soon as I had ascertained he had marched during the night, and I occupied immediately his vacated position. It appeared subsequently he had no intention of re-crossing the Sutlej, but moved down to the Ghât of Tulwun (being cut off from that of Philour by the position my force occupied after its relief of Loodianna), for the purpose of protecting the passage of a very considerable reinforcement of twelve guns and 4,000 of the Regular or Aicen troops, called Avitabile's battalion, entrenching himself strongly in a semi-circle, his flanks resting on the river, his position covered with from forty to fifty guns (generally of large calibre), howitzers, and mortars. The reinforcement crossed during the night of the 27th instant, and encamped to the right of the main army.

Meanwhile his Excellency the Commander-in-Chief, with that foresight and judgment which marks the able general, had reinforced me by a considerable addition to my cavalry, some guns, and the 2nd brigade of my own division under Brigadier Wheeler, C.B. This reinforcement reached me on the 26th, and I had intended the next morning to move upon the enemy in his entrenchments; but the troops required one day's rest after the long marches Brigadier Wheeler had made.

I have now the honour to lay before you the operations of my united forces on the morning of the eventful 28th of January, for his Excellency's information. The body of troops under my command having been increased, it became necessary so to organize and brigade them as to render them manageable in action. The cavalry under the command of Brigadier Cureton, and horse artillery under Major Lawrenson, were put into two brigades; the one under Brigadier Mac Dowell, C.B., and the other under Brigadier Stedman. The 1st division as it stood, two brigades; her Majesty's 53rd and 30th Native Infantry, under Brigadier Wilson of the latter corps; the 36th Native Infantry and Nusseree battalion, under Brigadier Godby; and the Shekawattee brigade, under Major Forster. The Sirmoor battalion I attached to Brigadier Wheeler's brigade of the 1st division, the 42nd Native Infantry having been left at head-quarters.

At daylight on the 28th my order of advance was, the Cavalry in front, in contiguous columns of squadrons of regiments; two troops of Horse Artillery in the interval of brigades; the Infantry in contiguous columns of brigades at intervals of deploying distance; Artillery in the intervals, followed by two eight-inch howitzers on travelling carriages, brought into the field from the fort of Loodianna by the indefatigable exertions of Lieutenant-Colonel Lane, Horse Artillery; Brigadier Godby's brigade, which I had marched out from Loodianna the previous evening, on the right; the Shekawattee Infantry on the left; the 4th Irregular Cavalry and the Shekawattee Cavalry considerably to the right, for the purpose of sweeping the banks of the wet nullah on my right, and preventing any of the enemy's horse attempting an inroad towards Loodianna, or any attempt upon the baggage assembled round the Fort of Buddiwal.

In this order the troops moved forward towards the enemy, a distance of six miles, the advance conducted by Captain Waugh, 16th Lancers, the Deputy Assistant Quartermaster of Cavalry; Major Bradford of the 1st Cavalry, and Lieutenant Strachey, of the Engineers, who had been jointly employed in the conduct of patrols up to the enemy's position, and for the purpose of reporting upon the facility and points of approach. Previously to the march of the troops, it had been intimated to me by Major Mackeson, that the information by spies led to the belief that the enemy would move somewhere at daylight, either on Jugraon, my position of Buddiwal, or Loodianna. On a near approach to his outposts this rumour was confirmed by a spy, who had just left his camp, saying the Sikh army was actually in march towards Jugraon. My advance was steady, my troops well in hand, and if he had anticipated me on the Jugraon road, I could have fallen upon his centre with advantage.

From the tops of the houses of the village of Poorcin, I had a distant view of the enemy. He was in motion, and appeared directly opposite my front on a ridge, of which the village of Aliwal may be regarded as the centre. His left appeared still to occupy its ground in the circular entrenchment; his right was brought forward and occupied the ridge. I immediately deployed the cavalry into line, and moved on. As I neared the enemy, the ground became most favourable for the troops to manœuvre, being open and hard grass land. I ordered the Cavalry to take ground to the right and left by brigades, thus displaying the heads of the Infantry columns, and as they reached the hard ground I directed them to deploy into line. Brigadier Godby's brigade was in direct echellon to the rear of the right; the Shekawattee Infantry in like manner to the rear of my left; the cavalry in direct echelon on, and well to the rear of both flanks of the Infantry; the Artillery massed on the right, and centre, and left. After deployment I observed the enemy's left to out-flank me, I therefore broke into open columns and took ground to my right: when I had gained sufficient ground, the troops wheeled into line; there was no dust, the sun shone brightly. The manœuvres were performed with the celerity and precision of the most correct field-day. The glistening of the bayonets and swords of this order of battle was most imposing, and the line advanced. Scarcely had it moved forward 150 yards, when at ten o'clock the enemy opened a fierce cannonade from his whole line. At first his balls fell short, but quickly reached us. Thus upon him, and capable of better ascertaining his position, I was compelled to halt the line, though under fire, for a few moments, until I ascertained that by bringing up my right and carrying the village of Aliwal, I could with great effect precipitate myself upon his left and centre. I therefore quickly brought up Brigadier Godby's brigade, and with it and the 1st brigade under Brigadier Hicks, made a rapid and noble charge, carried the village, and two guns of large calibre. The line I ordered to advance,—her Majesty's 31st Foot and the Native regiments contending for the front, and the battle became general. The enemy had a numerous body of Cavalry on the heights to his left, and I ordered Brigadier Cureton to bring up the right brigade of cavalry, who, in the most gallant manner, dashed in among them, and drove them back upon their Infantry. Meanwhile a second gallant charge to my right was made by the Light Cavalry and the body-guard. The Shekawattee brigade was moved well to the right, in support of Brigadier Cureton. When I observed the enemy's encampment, and saw it was full of Infantry, I immediately brought upon it Brigadier Godby's brigade, by changing front, and taking the enemy's Infantry en reverse. They drove them before them, and took some guns without a check.

Whilst these operations were going on upon the right, and the enemy's left flank was thus driven back. I occasionally observed the brigade under Brigadier Wheeler, an officer in whom I have the greatest confidence, charging and carrying guns and everything before it, again connecting his line and moving on in a manner which ably displayed the coolness of the Brigadier and the gallantry of his irresistible brigade—her Majesty's 50th Foot, the 48th Native Infantry, and the Sirmoor battalion, although the loss was, I regret to say, severe in the 50th. Upon the left, Brigadier Wilson, with her Majesty's 53rd and 30th Native Infantry, equalled in celerity and regularity their comrades on the right; and this brigade was opposed to the "Aieen" troops, called Avitabile's, when the fight was fiercely raging.

The enemy, well driven back on his left and centre, endeavoured to hold his right to cover the passage of the river, and he strongly occupied the village of Bhoondee. I directed a squadron of the 16th Lancers, under Major Smith and Captain Pearson, to charge a body to the right of the village, which they did in the most gallant and determined style, bearing everything before them, as a squadron under Captain Bere had previously done, going through a square of infantry, wheeling about and re-entering the square in the most intrepid manner with the deadly lance. This charge was accompanied by the 3rd Light Cavalry, under Major Angelo, and as gallantly sustained. The largest gun upon the field and seven others were then captured, while the 53rd regiment carried the village by the bayonet, and the 30th Native Infantry wheeled round to the rear in a most spirited manner. Lieutenant-Colonel Alexander's and Captain Turton's troops of Horse Artillery, under Major Lawrenson, almost dashed among the flying infantry, committing great havoc, until about 800 or 1,000 men rallied under the high bank of a nullah, and opened a heavy, but ineffectual fire from below the bank. I immediately directed the 30th Native Infantry to charge them, which they were able to do upon their left flank, while in a line in rear of the village. This native corps nobly obeyed my orders, and rushed among the Avitabile troops, driving them from under the bank, and exposing them once more to the deadly fire of twelve guns within three hundred yards. The destruction was very great, as may be supposed, by guns served as these were. Her Majesty's 53rd Regiment moved forward in support of the 30th Native Infantry, by the right of the village. The battle was won, our troops advancing with the most perfect order to the common focus, the passage of the river. The enemy, completely hemmed in, were flying from our fire, and precipitating themselves in disordered masses into the ford and boats, in the utmost confusion and consternation. Our 8-inch howitzers soon began to play upon their boats, when the "debris" of the Sikh army appeared upon the opposite and high bank of the river, flying in every direction, although a sort of line was attempted to countenance their retreat, until all our guns commenced a furious cannonade, when they quickly receded. Nine guns were on the verge of the river by the ford. It appears as if they had been unlimbered to cover the ford. These, being loaded, were fired once upon our advance. Two others were sticking in the river; one of them we got out. Two were seen to sink in the quick-sands; two were dragged to the opposite bank and abandoned. These, and the one in the middle of the river, were gallantly spiked by Lieutenant Holmes, of the 11th Irregular Cavalry, and Gunner Scott, of the 1st Troop 2nd Brigade Horse Artillery, who rode into the stream, and crossed for the purpose, covered by our guns and light infantry.

Thus ended the battle of Aliwal, one of the most glorious victories ever achieved in India. By the united efforts of her Majesty's and the Hon.

Company's troops, every gun the enemy had fell into our hands, as I infer from his never opening one upon us from the opposite bank of the river, which is high and favourable for the purpose: fifty-two guns are now in the Ordnance Park, two sunk in the bed of the Sutlej, and two were spiked on the opposite bank—making a total of fifty-six pieces of cannon captured or destroyed.[112] Many jinjalls which were attached to Avitabile's corps, and which aided in the defence of the village of Bhoondee, have also been taken. The whole army of the enemy has been driven headlong over the difficult ford of a broad river; his camp, baggage, stores of ammunition, and of grain—his all, in fact—wrested from him by the repeated charges of cavalry and infantry, aided by the guns of Alexander, Turton, Lane, Mill, Boileau, and of the Shekawattee brigade, and by the eight-inch howitzers, our guns literally being constantly ahead of everything. The determined bravery of all was as conspicuous as noble. I am unwont to praise when praise is not merited; and I here most avowedly express my firm opinion and conviction, that no troops in any battle on record ever behaved more nobly. British and native (no distinction) cavalry all vying with her Majesty's 16th Lancers, and striving to head in the repeated charges. Our guns and gunners, officers and men, may be equalled, but cannot be excelled, by any artillery in the world. Throughout the day no hesitation, a bold and intrepid advance; and thus it is that our loss is comparatively small, though I deeply regret to say severe. The enemy fought with much resolution; they maintained frequent rencontres with our cavalry hand to hand. In one charge of infantry upon her Majesty's 16th Lancers, they threw away their muskets, and came on with their swords and targets against the lance.

Having thus done justice, and justice alone, to the gallant troops his Excellency entrusted to my command, I would gladly, if the limits of a despatch (already too much lengthened, I fear), permitted me, do that justice to individuals all deserve. This cannot be....

The Fort of Goongrana has, subsequently to the battle, been evacuated, and I yesterday evening blew up the fort of Buddiwal. I shall now blow up that of Noorpore. A portion of the peasantry, viz., the Sikhs, appear less friendly to us, while the Mussulmans rejoice in being under our government.

I have, etc.,

(Signed)   H.G. Smith,

Maj.-Gen. commanding.

Camp, Field of Battle of Aliwal, 30th January, 1846.
True copy (Signed) P. Grant, Major,

Dep. Adj.-Gen. of the army.

TO THE RIGHT HON. THE GOVERNOR-GENERAL OF INDIA.

Head-quarters, Army of the Sutlej,
Camp Kussoor, Feb. 13.

Right Hon. Sir,

This is the fourth despatch which I have had the honour of addressing to you since the opening of the campaign. Thanks to Almighty God, whose hand I desire to acknowledge in all our successes, the occasion of my writing now is to announce a fourth and most glorious and decisive victory!

My last communication detailed the movements of the Sikhs, and our counter-manœuvres, since the great day of Ferozeshah. Defeated on the Upper Sutlej, the enemy continued to occupy his position on the right bank, and formidable tête de pont and entrenchments on the left bank of the river, in front of the main body of our army. But on the 10th instant, all that he held of British territory, which was comprised in the ground on which one of his camps stood, was stormed from his grasp, and his audacity was again signally punished by a blow, sudden, heavy, and overwhelming. It is my gratifying duty to detail the measures which have led to this glorious result.

The enemy's works had been repeatedly reconnoitred during the time of my head-quarters being fixed at Nihalkee, by myself, by my departmental staff, and my engineer and artillery officers. Our observations, coupled with the reports of spies, convinced us that there had devolved on us the arduous task of attacking, in a position covered with formidable entrenchments, not fewer than 30,000 men, the best of the Khalsa troops, with seventy pieces of cannon, united by a good bridge to a reserve on the opposite bank, on which the enemy had a considerable camp and some artillery, commanding and flanking his field-works on our side. Major-General Sir Harry Smith's division having rejoined me on the evening of the 8th, and part of my siege-train having come up with me, I resolved, on the morning of the 10th, to dispose our mortars and battering guns on the alluvial land, within good range of the enemy's works. To enable us to do this, it was necessary first to drive in the enemy's pickets at the post of observation in front of Koodeewalla, and at the little Sobraon. It was directed that this should be done during the night of the 9th; but the execution of this part of the plan was deferred, owing to misconceptions and casual circumstances, until near daybreak. The delay was of little importance, as the event showed that the Sikhs had followed our example in occupying the two posts in force by day only. Of both, therefore, possession was taken without opposition. The battering and disposed field-artillery was then put in position in an extended semi-circle, embracing within its fire the works of the Sikhs. It had been intended that the cannonade should have commenced at daybreak; but so heavy a mist hung over the plain and river, that it became necessary to wait until the rays of the sun had penetrated it, and cleared the atmosphere. Meanwhile, on the margin of the Sutlej, on our left, two brigades of Major-General Sir R. Dick's division, under his personal command, stood ready to commence the assault against the enemy's extreme right. His 7th brigade, in which was the 10th Foot, reinforced by the 53rd Foot, and led by Brigadier Stacey, was to head the attack, supported, at 200 yards' distance, by the 6th brigade, under Brigadier Wilkinson. In reserve, was the 5th brigade, under Brigadier the Hon. T. Ashburnham, which was to move forward from the entrenched village of Koodeewalla, leaving, if necessary, a regiment for its defence. In the centre, Major-General Gilbert's division was deployed for support or attack; its right wing resting on, and in the village of the little Sobraon. Major-General Sir Harry Smith's was formed near the village of Guttah, with its right thrown up towards the Sutlej. Brigadier Cureton's cavalry, threatened, by feigned attacks, the ford of Hurrekee and the enemy's horse, under Rajah Lall Singh Misr, on the opposite bank. Brigadier Campbell, taking an intermediate position in the rear, between Major-General Gilbert's right and Major-General Sir Harry Smith's left, protected both. Major-General Sir Joseph Thackwell, under whom was Brigadier Scott, held in reserve on our left, ready to act as circumstances might demand, the rest of the Cavalry.

Our batteries of 9-pounders, enlarged into twelves, opened near the little Sobraon, with a brigade of howitzers, formed from the light field-batteries and troops of Horse-artillery, shortly after daybreak. But it was half-past six before the whole of our artillery fire was developed. It was the most spirited and well-directed. I cannot speak in terms too high of the judicious disposition of the guns, their admirable practice, or the activity with which the cannonade was sustained; but notwithstanding the formidable calibre of our iron guns, mortars, and howitzers, and the admirable way in which they were served, and aided by a rocket-battery, it would have been visionary to expect that they could, within any limited time, silence the fire of seventy pieces, behind well constructed batteries of earth, plank, and fascines; or dislodge troops covered either by redoubts or epaulements, or within a treble-line of trenches. The effect of the cannonade was, as has since proved by an inspection of the camp, most severely felt by the enemy; but it soon became evident that the issue of this struggle must be brought to the arbitrament of musketry and the bayonet.

At nine o'clock, Brigadier Stacey's brigade, supported on either flank by Captains Horsford's and Fordyce's batteries, and Lieut.-Colonel Lane's troop of Horse-artillery, moved to the attack in admirable order. The Infantry and guns aided each other correlatively. The former marched steadily on in line, which they halted only to correct when necessary. The latter took up successive positions at the gallop, until at length they were within three hundred yards of the heavy batteries of the Sikhs; but, notwithstanding the regularity and coolness, and scientific character of this assault, which Brigadier Wilkinson well supported, so hot was the fire of cannon, musketry, and zumbooruks kept up by the Khalsa troops, that it seemed for some moments impossible that the entrenchments could be won under it; but soon, persevering gallantly, we triumphed; and the whole army had the satisfaction to see the gallant Brigadier Stacey's soldiers driving the Sikhs in confusion within the area of their encampment. The 10th Foot, under Lieutenant-Colonel Franks, now for the first time brought into serious contact with the enemy, greatly distinguished themselves. This regiment never fired a shot till it got within the works of the enemy. The onset of her Majesty's 53rd Foot was as gallant and effective. The 43rd and 59th N.I. brigaded with them, emulated both in cool determination.

At the moment of this first success, I directed Brigadier the Hon. T. Ashburnham's brigade to move on in support; and Major-General Gilbert's and Sir Harry Smith's divisions to throw out their light troops to threaten their works, aided by artillery. As these attacks of the centre and right commenced, the fire of our heavy guns had first to be directed to the right, and then gradually to cease; but at one time the thunder of 120 pieces of ordnance reverberated in this mighty combat through the valley of the Sutlej; and as it was soon seen that the weight of the whole force within the Sikh camp was likely to be thrown upon the two brigades that had passed its trenches, it became necessary to convert into close and serious attacks the demonstrations with skirmishers and artillery of the centre and right; and the battle raged with inconceivable fury from right to left. The Sikhs, even when at particular points their entrenchments were mastered with the bayonet, strove to regain them by the fiercest conflict, sword in hand. Nor was it until the cavalry of the left, under Major-General Sir Joseph Thackwell, had moved forward, and ridden through the openings of the entrenchments made by our sappers, in single file, and re-formed as they passed them; and the 3rd Dragoons, whom no obstacle usually held formidable by horse appears to check, had on this day, as at Ferozeshah, galloped over and cut down the obstinate defenders of batteries and field-works, and until the full weight of three divisions of Infantry, with every Field-artillery gun which could be sent to their aid, had been cast into the scale, that victory finally declared for the British. The fire of the Sikhs first slackened and then nearly ceased; and the victors then pressing them on every side, precipitated them in masses over the bridge, and into the Sutlej, which a sudden rise of seven inches had rendered hardly fordable. In their efforts to reach the right bank, through the deepened water, they suffered from our Horse-artillery a terrible carnage. Hundreds fell under this cannonade; hundreds upon hundreds were drowned in attempting the perilous passage. Their awful slaughter, confusion, and dismay, were such as would have excited compassion in the hearts of their generous conquerors, if the Khalsa troops had not, in the early part of the action, sullied their gallantry by slaughtering and barbarously mangling every wounded soldier whom, in the vicissitudes of attack, the fortune of war left at their mercy. I must pause in this narrative, especially to notice the determined hardihood and bravery with which our battalions of Ghoorkhas, the Sirmoor and Nusseree, met the Sikhs wherever they were opposed to them. Soldiers of small stature, but indomitable spirit, they vied in ardent courage in the charge with the Grenadiers of our own nation; and armed with the short weapon of their mountains, were a terror to the Sikhs throughout this great combat.

Sixty-seven pieces of cannon, upwards of two hundred camel-swivels (zumbooruks), numerous standards, and vast munitions of war, captured by our troops, are the pledges and trophies of our victory. The battle was over by eleven in the morning, and in the forenoon I caused our engineers to burn a part and to sink a part of the vaunted bridge of the Khalsa army, across which they had boastfully come once more to defy us, and to threaten India with ruin and devastation.

The loss of the enemy has been immense; an estimate of it must be formed with a due allowance for the spirit of exaggeration which pervades all statements of Asiatics, where their interest leads them to magnify numbers; but our own observation on the river banks and in the enemy's camp combine, with the reports brought to our intelligence department, to convince me that the Khalsa casualties were between 8,000 and 10,000 men killed and wounded in action, and drowned in the passage of the river. Amongst the slain, are Sirdars Sham Singh, Attareewalla, Generals Gholab Singh, Koopta, and Heera Singh, Topee, Sirdar Kishen Singh, son of the late Jemadar Kooshall Singh, Generals Mobaruck Ally, and Illahee Buksh, and Shah Newaz Khan, son of Futteh-ood-deen Khan, of Kussoor. The body of Sham Singh was sought for in the captured camp by his followers; and, respecting the gallantry with which he is reported to have devoted himself to death rather than accompany the army in its flight, I forbade his people being molested in their search, which was finally successful.

The consequences of this great action have yet to be fully developed. It has at least, in God's providence, once more expelled the Sikhs from our territory, and planted our standards on the soil of the Punjaub. After occupying their entrenched position for nearly a month, the Khalsa army had, perhaps, mistaken the caution which had induced us to wait for the necessary material, for timidity. But they must now deeply feel, that the blow which has fallen on them from the British arm, has only been the heavier for being long delayed.

I have, etc.,
(Signed) H. Gough, General,
Commander-in-Chief, East Indies.

XII.

The monument erected to the memory of Sir Robert Dick, at the church of Tullymet, Perthshire, by his brother officers, is of white marble; the main features being a sculptured representation of the veteran soldier, who has just received the deadly shot, whilst animating, by his dauntless example, Her Majesty's 80th Regiment. In the upper portion of the monument is a group of war trophies; and, surrounded by laurel, are inscribed the names of the several battles in which this gallant officer had participated.

SACRED TO THE MEMORY

OF

MAJOR-GENERAL SIR ROBERT HENRY DICK,
K.C.B., K.C.H.,

WHO, AFTER DISTINGUISHED SERVICES IN THE PENINSULA,
IN THE COMMAND OF A LIGHT BATTALION
AT WATERLOO, WITH THE 42ND ROYAL HIGHLAND REGIMENT,
FELL
MORTALLY WOUNDED, WHILST LEADING THE THIRD DIVISION OF
THE ARMY OF THE SUTLEJ TO THE ATTACK ON THE
SIKH ENTRENCHED CAMP, AT SOBRAON,
ON THE
10TH OF FEBRUARY, 1846.

THE OFFICERS WHO HAD THE HONOUR OF SERVING UNDER HIM
IN
HIS LAST BATTLE, AND OTHERS, HIS FRIENDS, IN HER
MAJESTY'S AND THE HONOURABLE EAST INDIA
COMPANY'S SERVICE, IN BENGAL,
HAVE CAUSED THIS MONUMENT TO BE PLACED IN
HIS PARISH CHURCH
IN TESTIMONY OF THEIR RESPECT AND AFFECTION FOR A
GENEROUS, COURTEOUS, AND CONSIDERATE
COMMANDER,
A GALLANT AND DEVOTED SOLDIER.

XIII.

PROCLAMATION OF PEACE.

Foreign Department, Camp, Lahore, Feb. 22nd, 1846.

The British Army has this day occupied the gateway of the citadel
of Lahore the Badshahee Mosque, and the Hazuree Bagh. The remaining
part of the citadel is the residence of his highness, the Maharajah, and
also that of the families of the late Maharajah Runjeet Singh, for so many
years the faithful ally of the British Government. In consideration of these

circumstances, no troops will be posted within the precincts of the palace-gate.

The army of the Sutlej has now brought its operations in the field to a close, by the dispersion of the Sikh army, and the military occupation of Lahore, preceded by a series of the most triumphant successes ever recorded in the military history of India. The British Government, trusting to the faith of treaties, and to long subsisting friendship between the two states, had limited military preparations to the defence of its own frontier.

Compelled suddenly to assume the offensive, by the unprovoked invasion of its territories, the British army, under the command of its distinguished leader, has, in sixty days, defeated the Sikh forces in four general actions; has captured 220 pieces of field artillery; and is now at the capital, dictating to the Lahore Durbar the terms of a treaty, the conditions of which will tend to secure the British provinces from the repetition of a similar outrage. The Governor-General being determined, however, to mark with reprobation the perfidious character of the war, has required and will exact, that every remaining piece of Sikh artillery which has been pointed against the British army during the campaign shall be surrendered. The Sikh army, whose insubordinate conduct is one of the chief causes of the anarchy and misrule which have brought the Sikh state to the brink of destruction, is about to be disbanded.

The soldiers of the army of the Sutlej have not only proved their superior prowess in battle, but have, on every occasion, with subordination and patience, endured the fatigues and privations inseparable from a state of active operations in the field. The native troops of this army have also proved that a faithful attachment to their colours, and to the Company's service, is an honourable feature in the character of the British sepoy. The Governor-General has repeatedly expressed, on his own part and on that of the Government of India, admiration and gratitude for the important services which the army has rendered. The Governor-General is now pleased to resolve, as a testimony of the approbation of the Government of India of the bravery, discipline, and soldier-like bearing of the army of the Sutlej, that all the generals, officers, non-commissioned officers, and privates, shall receive a gratuity of twelve months' batta.

Every regiment which, in obedience to its orders, may have remained in posts and forts between Loodianna and Ferozepore, and was not present in action—as in the case of the troops ordered to remain at Moodkee to protect the wounded, and those left in the forts of Ferozepore and Loodianna—shall receive the gratuity of twelve months' batta. Obedience to orders is the first duty of a soldier; and the Governor-General, in affirming the principle, can never admit that absence caused by the performance of indispensable duties, on which the success of the operations in the field greatly depended, ought to disqualify any soldier placed in these circumstances, from participating in the gratuity given for the general good conduct of the army in the field. All regiments and individuals ordered to the frontier, and forming part of the army of the Sutlej, which may have reached Loodianna or Bussean before the date of this order, will be included as entitled to the gratuity.

By order of the Right Hon. the Governor-General of India,

F. Currie,
Secretary to the Government of India
with the Governor-General.

XIV.

FIRST TREATY WITH LAHORE OF 1846.

Treaty between the British Government and the State of Lahore, concluded at Lahore, on the 9th of March, 1846.

Whereas the treaty of amity and concord, which was concluded between the British Government and the late Maharajah Runjeet Singh, the Ruler of Lahore, in 1809, was broken by the unprovoked aggression on the British provinces, of the Sikh army, in December last: And whereas, on that occasion, by the Proclamation dated the 13th of December, the territories then in the occupation of the Maharajah of Lahore, on the left or British bank of the river Sutlej, were confiscated and annexed to the British provinces; and, since that time, hostile operations have been prosecuted by the two Governments, the one against the other, which have resulted in the occupation of Lahore by the British troops: And whereas it has been determined that, upon certain conditions, peace shall be re-established between the two Governments, the following treaty of peace between the Honourable English East India Company, and Maharajah Dhuleep Singh Bahadoor, and his children, heirs and successors, has been concluded, on the part of the Honourable Company, by Frederick Currie, Esq., and Brevet Major Henry Montgomery Lawrence, by virtue of full powers to that effect vested in them by the Right Honourable Sir Henry Hardinge, G.C.B., one of Her Britannic Majesty's most Honourable Privy Council, Governor-General, appointed by the Honourable Company to direct and control all their affairs in the East Indies; and, on the part of his Highness the Maharajah Dhuleep Singh, by Bhaee Ram Singh, Rajah Lall Singh, Sirdar Tej Singh, Sirdar Chutter Singh Attareewalla, Sirdar Runjoor Singh Mujetheea, Dewan Deena Nath, and Fakeer Noor-ood-deen, vested with full power and authority on the part of his Highness.

Article 1.—There shall be perpetual peace and friendship between the British Government, on the one part, and Maharajah Dhuleep Singh, his heirs and successors, on the other.

Article 2.—The Maharajah of Lahore renounces for himself, his heirs and successors, all claim to, or connection with, the territories lying to the south of the river Sutlej, and engages never to have any concern with those territories, or the inhabitants thereof.

Article 3.—The Maharajah cedes to the Honourable Company, in perpetual sovereignty, all his forts, territories, and rights, in the Doab, or country, hill and plain, situate between the rivers Beas and Sutlej.

Article 4.—The British Government having demanded from the Lahore State as indemnification for the expenses of the war, in addition to the cession of territory described in Article 3, payment of one and a half crores of rupees; and the Lahore Government being unable to pay the whole of this sum at this time, or to give security satisfactory to the British Government for its eventual payment; the Maharajah cedes to the Honourable Company, in perpetual sovereignty, as equivalent for one crore of rupees, all his forts, territories, rights, and interests, in the hill countries which are situate between the rivers Beas and Indus, including the provinces of Cashmere and Hazarah.

Article 5.—The Maharajah will pay to the British Government the sum of fifty lacs of rupees on or before the ratification of this treaty.

Article 6.—The Maharajah engages to disband the mutinous troops of the Lahore army, taking from them their arms; and his Highness agrees to reorganize the regular, or Aieen, or regiments of infantry, upon the system, and according to the regulations as to pay and allowances, observed in the time of the late Maharajah Runjeet Singh. The Maharajah further engages to pay up all arrears to the soldiers that are discharged under the provisions of this article.

Article 7.—The regular army of the Lahore State shall henceforth be limited to 25 battalions of infantry, consisting of 800 bayonets each, with 12,000 cavalry: this number at no time to be exceeded without the concurrence of the British Government. Should it be necessary at any time, for any special cause, that this force should be increased, the cause shall be fully explained to the British Government; and when the special necessity shall have passed, the regular troops shall be again reduced to the standard specified in the former clause of this article.

Article 8.—The Maharajah will surrender to the British Government all the guns, thirty-six in number, which have been pointed against the British troops, and which, having been placed on the right bank of the river Sutlej, were not captured at the battle of Sobraon.

Article 9.—The control of the rivers Beas and Sutlej, with the continuations of the latter river, commonly called the Garrah and Punjnud, to the confluence of the Indus at Mithenkote, and the control of the Indus from Mithenkote to the borders of Beloochistan, shall, in respect to tolls and ferries, rest with the British Government. The provisions of this article shall not interfere with the passage of boats belonging to the Lahore Government on the said rivers, for the purposes of traffic, or the conveyance of passengers up and down their course. Regarding the ferries between the two countries respectively, at the several ghâts of the said rivers, it is agreed that the British Government, after defraying all the expenses of management and establishments, shall account to the Lahore Government for one half of the net profits of the ferry collections. The provisions of this article have no reference to the ferries on that part of the river Sutlej which forms the boundary of Bhawulpore and Lahore respectively.

Article 10.—If the British Government should, at any time, desire to pass troops through the territories of his Highness the Maharajah, for the protection of the British territories, or those of their allies, the British troops shall, on such special occasions, due notice being given, be allowed to pass through the Lahore territories. In such case the officers of the Lahore State will afford facilities in providing supplies, and boats for the passage of rivers; and the British Government will pay the full price of all such provisions and boats, and will make fair compensation for all private property that may be endamaged. The British Government will moreover observe all due consideration to the religious feelings of the inhabitants of those tracts through which the army may pass.

Article 11.—The Maharajah engages never to take, or retain, in his service, any British subject, nor the subject of any European or American State without the consent of the British Government.

Article 12.—In consideration of the services rendered by Rajah Goolab Singh of Jummoo to the Lahore State, towards procuring the restoration of the relations of amity between the Lahore and British Governments, the Maharajah hereby agrees to recognise the independent sovereignty of Rajah Goolab Singh, in such territories and districts in the hills as may be made over to the said Rajah Goolab Singh by separate agreement between himself and the British Government, with the dependencies thereof, which may have been in the Rajah's possession since the time of the late Maharajah Khurruk Singh: and the British Government, in consideration of the good conduct of Rajah Goolab Singh, also agrees to recognise his independence in such territories, and to admit him to the privileges of a separate treaty with the British Government.

Article 13.—In the event of any dispute or difference arising between the Lahore State and Rajah Goolab Singh, the same shall be referred to the arbitration of the British Government; and by its decision the Maharajah engages to abide.

Article 14.—The limits of the Lahore territories shall not be, at any time changed, without the concurrence of the British Government.

Article 15.—The British Government will not exercise any interference in the internal administration of the Lahore State; but in all cases or questions which may be referred to the British Government, the Governor-General will give the aid of his advice and good offices for the furtherance of the interests of the Lahore Government.

Article 16.—The subjects of either State shall, on visiting the territories of the other, be on the footing of the subjects of the most favoured nation.

This treaty, consisting of sixteen articles, has been this day settled by Frederick Currie, Esq., and Brevet Major Henry Montgomery Lawrence, acting under the directions of the Right Honourable Sir Henry Hardinge, G.C.B., Governor-General, on the part of the British Government; and by Bhaee Bam Singh, Rajah Lall Singh, Sirdar Tej Singh, Sirdar Chutter Singh Attareewalla, Sirdar Runjoor Singh Mujetheea, Dewan Deena Nath, and Fakeer Noor-ood-deen, on the part of Maharajah Dhuleep Singh; and the said treaty has been this day ratified by the seal of the Right Honourable Sir Henry Hardinge, G.C.B., Governor-General, and by that of his Highness Dhuleep Singh.

Done at Lahore, this 9th day of March, in the year of our Lord 1846, corresponding with the 10th day of Rubbeeool-awul, 1262, Hijree, and ratified on the same day.

SUPPLEMENTARY ARTICLES TO THE FIRST
TREATY WITH LAHORE OF 1846.

Articles of Agreement concluded between the British Government and the Lahore Durbar, on the 11th of March, 1846.

Whereas the Lahore Government has solicited the Governor-General to leave a British force at Lahore for the protection of the Maharajah's person and of the capital, till the reorganization of the Lahore army, according to the provisions of Article 6 of the Treaty of Lahore, dated the 9th instant: And whereas the Governor-General has, on certain conditions, consented to the measure: And whereas it is expedient that certain matters concerning the territories ceded by articles 3 and 4 of the aforesaid treaty should be specifically determined; the following eight articles of agreement have this day been concluded between the afore-mentioned contracting parties.

Article 1.—The British Government shall leave at Lahore, till the close of the current year, A.D. 1846, such force as shall seem to the Governor-General adequate for the purpose of protecting the person of the Maharajah, and the inhabitants of the city of Lahore, during the reorganization of the Sikh army, in accordance with the provisions of article 6 of the treaty of Lahore; that force to be withdrawn at any convenient time before the expiration of the year, if the object to be fulfilled shall, in the opinion of the Durbar, have been obtained; but the force shall not be detained at Lahore beyond the expiration of the current year.

Article 2.—The Lahore Government agrees that the force left at Lahore for the purpose specified in the foregoing article, shall be placed in full possession of the fort and the city of Lahore, and that the Lahore troops shall be removed from within the city. The Lahore Government engages to furnish convenient quarters for the officers and men of the said force, and to pay to the British Government all the extra expenses in regard to the said force, which may be incurred by the British Government, in consequence of them troops being employed away from their own cantonments, and in a foreign territory.

Article 3.—The Lahore Government engages to apply itself immediately and earnestly to the reorganization of its army, according to the prescribed conditions, and to communicate fully with the British authorities left at Lahore, as to the progress of such reorganization, and as to the location of the troops.

Article 4.—If the Lahore Government fails in the performance of the conditions of the foregoing article, the British government shall be at liberty to withdraw the force from Lahore, at any time before the expiration of the period specified in Article 1.

Article 5.—The British Government agrees to respect the *bonâ fide* rights of those Jaghirdars within the territories ceded by Articles 3 and 4 of the Treaty of Lahore, dated the 9th instant, who were attached to the families of the late Maharajah Runjeet Singh, Khurruk Singh and Shere Singh; and the British Government wall maintain these Jaghirdars in their *bonâ fide* possessions, during their lives.

Article 6.—The Lahore Government shall receive the assistance of the British local authorities in recovering the arrears of revenue justly due to the Lahore Government from their Kardars and managers in the territories ceded by the provisions of Articles 3 and 4 of the Treaty of Lahore, to the close of the Khureef harvest of the current year, viz. 1902, of the Sumbut Bikramajeet.

Article 7.—The Lahore Government shall be at liberty to remove from the forts in the territories specified in the foregoing article, all treasures and state property with the exception of guns. Should, however, the British Government desire to retain any part of the said property, they shall be at liberty to do so, paying for the same at a fair valuation; and the British officers shall give their assistance to the Lahore Government in disposing on the spot of such part of the aforesaid property as the Lahore Government may not wish to remove, and the British officers may not desire to retain.

Article 8.—Commissioners shall be immediately appointed by the two Governments, to settle and lay down the boundary between the two States, as defined by Article 4 of the Treaty of Lahore, dated March the 9th, 1846.

XV.

Puncheess or Punchayets were a jury or assembly of five persons. These assemblies, which were of very ancient origin, obtained, both in the military and civil services of the Sikhs. In the former, five men who had distinguished themselves by their valour, were selected from every battalion or company, and to them were referred for decision, all affairs which brought the army into contact with the Government. In the latter, every tribe had its Punt. The system was also generally adopted in every trade and calling. The decision of the Punchees was definitive.

XVI.

TREATY WITH GOOLAB SINGH OF 1846.

Treaty between the British Government and Maharajah Goolab Singh, concluded at Umritsur on March 16th, 1846.

Treaty between the British Government on the one part, and Maharajah Goolab Singh of Jummoo on the other, concluded on the part of the British Government, by Frederick Currie, Esq., and Brevet Major Henry Montgomery Lawrence, acting under the orders of the Right Honourable Sir Henry Hardinge, G.C.B., one of Her Britannic Majesty's most Honourable Privy Council, Governor-General, appointed by the Honourable Company to direct and control all their affairs in the East Indies, and by Maharajah Goolab Singh in person.

Article 1.—The British Government transfers and makes over, for ever, in independent possession, to Maharajah Goolab Singh, and the heirs male of his body, all the hilly or mountainous country, with its dependencies, situated to the eastward of the river Indus, and westward of the river Ravee, including Chumba and excluding Lahool, being part of the territory ceded to the British Government by the Lahore State, according to the provisions of Article 4 of the Treaty of Lahore, dated March the 9th, 1846.

Article 2.—The eastern boundary of the tract transferred by the foregoing Article to Maharajah Goolab Singh shall be laid down by commissioners appointed by the British Government and Maharajah Goolab Singh respectively, for that purpose, and shall be defined in a separate engagement, after survey.

Article 3.—In consideration of the transfer made to him and his heirs by the provisions of the foregoing Articles, Maharajah Goolab Singh will pay to the British Government the sum of seventy-five lakhs of rupees (Nanukshahee), fifty lakhs to be paid on ratification of this treaty, and twenty-five lakhs on or before the 1st of October of the current year, A.D. 1846.

Article 4.—The limits of the territories of Maharajah Goolab Singh shall not be at any time changed without the concurrence of the British Government.

Article 5.—Maharajah Goolab Singh will refer to the arbitration of the British Government any disputes or questions that may arise between himself and the Government of Lahore, or any other neighbouring State, and will abide by the decision of the British Government.

Article 6.—Maharajah Goolab Singh engages for himself and heirs, to join, with the whole of his military force, the British troops, when employed within the hills, or in the territories adjoining his possessions. Article 7.— Maharajah Goolab Singh engages never to take, or retain, in his service any British subject, nor the subject of any European or American State, without the consent of the British Government.

Article 8.—Maharajah Goolab Singh engages to respect, in regard to the territory transferred to him, the provisions of Articles 5, 6, and 7, of the separate engagement between the British Government and the Lahore Durbar, dated March the 11th, 1846.

Article 9.—The British Government will give its aid to Maharajah Goolab Singh, in protecting his territories from external enemies.

Article 10.—Maharajah Goolab Singh acknowledges the supremacy of the British Government, and will, in token of such supremacy, present annually to the British Government one horse, twelve perfect shawl goats of approved breed (six male and six female), and three pairs of Cashmere shawls.

This treaty, consisting of ten articles, has been this day settled by Frederick Currie, Esq., and Brevet Major Henry Montgomery Lawrence, acting under the directions of the Right Honourable Sir Henry Hardinge, G.C.B., Governor-General, on the part of the British Government, and by Maharajah Goolab Singh in person; and the said treaty has been this day ratified by the seal of the Right Honourable Sir Henry Hardinge, G.C.B., Governor-General.

Done at Umritsur, this 16th day of March, in the year of our Lord 1846, corresponding with the 17th day of Rubbeeool-awul, 1262, Hijree.

XVII.

SECOND TREATY WITH LAHORE OF 1846.

Foreign Department, Camp, Bhyrowal Ghât, on the left Bank of the Beas, the 22nd of December, 1846.

The late Governor of Cashmere on the part of the Lahore State, Sheik Imam Ooddeen, having resisted by force of arms the occupation of the province of Cashmere by Maharajah Goolab Singh, the Lahore Government was called upon to coerce their subject, and to make over the province to the representative of the British Government, in fulfilment of the conditions of the treaty of Lahore, dated the 9th of March, 1846.

A British force was employed to support and aid, if necessary, the combined forces of the Lahore State and Maharajah Goolab Singh in the above operations.

Sheik Imam Ooddeen intimated to the British Government that he was acting under orders received from the Lahore Durbar in the course he was pursuing; and stated that the insurrection was instigated by written instructions received by him from the Vizier Rajah Lall Singh.

Sheik Imam Ooddeen surrendered to the British Agent on a guarantee from that officer, that if the Sheik could, as he asserted, prove that his acts were in accordance with his instructions, and that the opposition was instigated by the Lahore minister, the Durbar should not be permitted to inflict upon him, either in his person or his property, any penalty on account of his conduct on this occasion. The British Agent pledged his Government to a full and impartial investigation of the matter.

A public inquiry was instituted into the facts adduced by Sheik Imam Ooddeen, and it was fully established that Rajah Lall Singh did secretly instigate the Sheik to oppose the occupation by Maharajah Goolab Singh of the province of Cashmere.

The Governor-General immediately demanded that the ministers and Chiefs of the Lahore State should depose and exile to the British provinces the Vizier Rajah Lall Singh.

His Lordship consented to accept the deposition of Rajah Lall Singh as an atonement for the attempt to infringe the treaty by the secret intrigues and machinations of the Vizier. It was not proved that the other members of the Durbar had cognizance of the Vizier's proceedings; and the conduct of the Sirdars, and of the Sikh army in the late operations for quelling the Cashmere insurrection, and removing the obstacles to the fulfilment of the treaty, proved that the criminality of the Vizier was not participated in by the Sikh nation.

The Ministers and Chiefs unanimously decreed, and carried into immediate effect, the deposition of the Vizier.

After a few days' deliberations, relative to the means of forming a Government at Lahore, the remaining members of the Durbar, in concert with all the Sirdars and Chiefs of the State, solicited the interference and aid of the British Government for the maintenance of an administration, and the protection of the Maharajah Dhuleep Singh during the minority of his Highness.

This solicitation by the Durbar and Chiefs has led to the temporary modification of the relations between the British Government and that of Lahore, established by the treaty of the 9th of March of the present year.

The terms and conditions of this modification are set forth in the following Articles of Agreement.

Articles of Agreement concluded between the British Government and the Lahore Durbar, on 16th of December, 1846.

Whereas the Lahore Durbar and the principal Chiefs and Sirdars of the State have, in express terms, communicated to the British Government their anxious desire that the Governor-General should give his aid and his assistance to maintain the administration of the Lahore State during the minority of Maharajah Dhuleep Singh, and have declared this measure to be indispensable for the maintenance of the government: And whereas the Governor-General has, under certain conditions, consented to give the aid and assistance solicited, the following articles of agreement, in modification of the articles of agreement executed at Lahore on the 11th of March last, have been concluded, on the part of the British Government, by Frederick Currie, Esq., Secretary to the Government of India, and Lieutenant-Colonel Henry Montgomery Lawrence, C.B., Agent to the Governor-General, North-West

Frontier, by virtue of full power to that effect vested in them by the Right Honourable Viscount Hardinge, G.C.B., Governor-General, and on the part of his Highness Maharajah Dhuleep Singh, by Sirdar Tej Singh, Sirdar Shere Singh, Dewan Deena Nath, Fakeer Noor-ood-deen, Raee Kishen Chund, Sirdar Runjoor Singh Mujetheea, Sirdar Utter Singh Kaleewalla, Bhaee Nidhan Singh, Sirdar Kan Singh Mujetheea, Sirdar Shumshere Singh, Sirdar Lall Singh Morarea, Sirdar Kher Singh Sindhanwalla, Sirdar Urjun Singh Rungmungleea, acting with the unanimous consent and concurrence of the Chiefs and Sirdars of the State assembled at Lahore.

Article 1.—All and every part of the treaty of peace between the British Government and the state of Lahore, bearing date the 9th day of March, 1846, except in so far as it may be temporarily modified in respect to clause 15 of the said treaty by this engagement, shall remain binding upon the two Governments.

Article 2.—A British officer, with an efficient establishment of assistants, shall be appointed by the Governor-General to remain at Lahore, which officer shall have full authority to direct and control all matters in every department of the State.

Article 3.—Every attention shall be paid in conducting the Administration to the feelings of the people, to preserving the national institutions and customs, and to maintain the just rights of all classes.

Article 4.—Changes in the mode and details of administration shall not be made, except when found necessary for effecting the objects set forth in the foregoing clause, and for securing the just dues of the Lahore Government. These details shall be conducted by native officers, as at present, who shall be appointed and superintended by a Council of Regency, composed of leading Chiefs and Sirdars, acting under the control and guidance of the British Resident.

Article 5.—The following persons shall in the first instance constitute the Council of Regency, viz.—Sirdar Tej Singh, Sirdar Shere Singh Attareewalla, Dewan Deena Nath, Fakeer Noor-ood-deen, Sirdar Runjoor Singh Mujetheea, Bhaee Nidhan Singh, Sirdar Utter Singh Kaleewalla, Sirdar Shumshere Singh Sindhanwalla; and no change shall be made in the persons thus nominated, without the consent of the British Resident, acting under the orders of the Governor-General.

Article 6.—The administration of the country shall be conducted by this Council of Regency in such manner as may be determined on by themselves in consultation with the British Resident, who shall have full authority to direct and control the duties of every department.

Article 7.—A British force, of such strength and numbers, and in such positions, as the Governor-General may think fit, shall remain at Lahore for the protection of the Maharajah, and the preservation of the peace of the country.

Article 8.—The Governor-General shall be at liberty to occupy with British soldiers any fort or military post in the Lahore territories, the occupation of which may be deemed necessary by the British Government for the security of the capital, or for maintaining the peace of the country.

Article 9.—The Lahore State shall pay to the British Government twenty-two lakhs of new Nanukshahee rupees, of full tale and weight, per annum, for the maintenance of this force, and to meet the expenses incurred by the British Government, such sum to be paid by two instalments, or 13 lakhs and 20,000 in May or June, and 8 lakhs and 80,000 in November or December of each year.

Article 10.—Inasmuch as it is fitting that her Highness the Maharannee, the mother of Maharajah Dhuleep Singh, should have a proper provision made for the maintenance of herself and dependents, the sum of one lakh and 50,000 rupees shall be set apart annually for that purpose, and shall be at her Highness's disposal.

Article 11.—The provisions of this engagement shall have effect during the minority of his Highness Maharajah Dhuleep Singh, and shall cease and terminate on his Highness attaining the full age of 16 years, or on the 4th September of the year 1854; but it shall be competent to the Governor-General to cause the arrangement to cease, at any period prior to the coming of age of his Highness, at which the Governor-General and the Lahore Durbar may be satisfied that the interposition of the British Government is no longer necessary for maintaining the government of his Highness the Maharajah.

This agreement, consisting of eleven articles, was settled and executed at Lahore, by the officers and Chiefs and Sirdars above named, on the 16th day of December, 1846.

XVIII.

NOTIFICATION.

Foreign Department, Camp, Ferozepore.
March, 30.

The Governor-General is pleased to direct, that the accompanying Proclamation, by which the Punjaub is declared to be a portion of the British

Empire in India, be published for general information, and that a royal salute be fired at every principal station of the army, on the receipt thereof.

By order of the Right Honourable, the Governor-General of India.

P. Melvill,

Under Secretary to the Government of India, with the Governor-General.

PROCLAMATION OF THE GOVERNOR GENERAL.

Head Quarters, Ferozepore,
March 29, 1849.

For many years, in the time of Maharajah Runjeet Singh, peace and friendship prevailed between the British nation and the Sikhs. When Runjeet Singh was dead, and his wisdom no longer guided the counsels of the state, the Sirdars and Khalsa army, without provocation and without cause, suddenly invaded the British territories. Their army was again and again defeated. They were driven with slaughter and in shame from the country they had invaded, and, at the gates of Lahore, the Maharajah, Dhuleep Singh, tendered to the Governor-General the submission of himself and his chiefs, and solicited the clemency of the British Government. The Governor-General extended the clemency of his Government to the State of Lahore, he generously spared the kingdom which he had acquired a just right to subvert; and the Maharajah having been replaced on the throne, treaties of friendship were formed between the States.

The British have faithfully kept their word, and have scrupulously observed every obligation which the treaties imposed upon them. But the Sikh people and their chiefs have, on their part, grossly and faithlessly violated the promises by which they were bound. Of their annual tribute no portion whatever has at any time been paid, and large loans advanced to them by the Government of India have never been repaid. The control of the British Government, to which they voluntarily submitted themselves, has been resisted by arms. Peace has been cast aside. British officers have been murdered when acting for the State; others engaged in the like employment have treacherously been thrown into captivity. Finally, the whole of the State and the whole Sikh people, joined by many of the Sirdars in the Punjaub who signed the treaties, and led by a member of the Regency itself, have risen in arms against us, and have waged a fierce and bloody war for the proclaimed purpose of destroying the British and their power.

The Government of India formerly declared that it required no further conquest and it proved by its acts the sincerity of its professions. The Government of India has no desire for conquest now; but it is bound in its duty to provide fully for its own security, and to guard the interests of those committed to its charge. To that end, and as the only sure mode of protecting the State from the perpetual recurrence of unprovoked and wasting wars, the Governor-General is compelled to resolve upon the entire subjection of a people whom their own Government has long been unable to control, and whom (as events have now shown) no punishment can deter from violence, no act of friendship can conciliate to peace. Wherefore the Governor-General of India has declared, and hereby proclaims, that the kingdom of the Punjaub is at an end; and that all the territories of Maharajah Dhuleep Singh, are now and henceforth a portion of the British empire in India. His Highness the Maharajah shall be treated with consideration and with honour.

The few chiefs who have not engaged in hostilities against the British shall retain their property and their rank. The British Government shall leave to all the people, whether Mussulman, Hindoo or Sikh, the free exercise of their own religions, but it will not permit any man to interfere with others in the observance of such forms and customs as their respective religions may either enjoin or permit.

The jaghires and all the property of Sirdars, and others who have been in arms against the British, shall be confiscated to the State. The defences of every fortified place in the Punjaub which is not occupied by British troops shall be totally destroyed, and effectual measures shall be taken to deprive the people of the means of renewing either tumult or war.

The Governor-General calls upon all the inhabitants of the Punjaub, Sirdars, and people, to submit themselves peaceably to the authority of the British Government, which has hereby been proclaimed.

Over those who shall live as obedient and peaceful subjects of the State, the British Government will rule with mildness and beneficence. But if resistance to constituted authority shall again be attempted, if violence and turbulence be renewed, the Governor-General warns the people of the Punjaub that the time for leniency will then have passed away, and that their offence will be punished with prompt and most rigorous severity.

By order of the Right Honourable the Governor-General of India.

H.M. Elliott,

Secretary to the Government of India, with the Governor-General.

XIX.

After Shah Soojah of Cabool had lost his throne, the number of Northern horses formerly sent to India became greatly reduced. Hence studs were formed by the East India Company in Bengal. Some of the stud horses have English, some Arab blood. The losses in the Sikh campaign of 1845-46 were 1,300 horses killed and wounded. Now the animal re-mount is equal to about one twentieth of the full complement of Horse Artillery, Dragoons, Light Cavalry, and Field Batteries; so, supposing the complement to be 10,000 horses, the re-mounts yearly are 500. Some time since an officer was sent to Sydney, New South Wales, to procure horses. Many of these horses have heavy shoulders; but it is certain that good and serviceable ones may be bred in New South Wales. A mixture of English and Arab blood is required; and the stud should be there and not in India. Some persons, however, are of opinion that it is best to breed them in the climate in which they are to live. Lord William Bentinck nearly destroyed the central stud at Buxar and Kurruntadhee. The Cape has been tried; but the horses though strong are under size.

XX.

One hundred and twenty thousand pounds seems to be a large sum even as the annual revenue of an Emperor of Delhi, but it must be borne in mind that the Emperor's family, including his seraglio, suite, and dependents, amounted, at least, to 4,000 persons. Just now there is a political difficulty respecting the succession to the throne of Delhi. When Shah Allum died in 1806, he was succeeded by his eldest son, Akbar, although he endeavoured to secure the throne for his third son, Wulli Ahud; but this was refused by the British Government. The present Emperor (1854), desires that his younger son, Prince Jewan Bukht, should succeed him, and has actually invested him with the imperial dignity without waiting for the sanction of the East India Company. Generally speaking, younger sons are more obedient to their fathers; for the eldest often sticks upon his rights, and this doubtless is the case in the family of the Emperor of Delhi.

XXI.

This extract is from the pen of my lamented friend the late Right Reverend Dr. James, Lord Bishop of Calcutta, in his most interesting work, entitled "Journal of a Tour through Germany, Sweden, Russia, and Poland," 1813-1814, third edition 1819, vol. i., pp. 5-6. Poor Dr. James was for some years, and up to the period of his leaving England for India, Vicar of Silsoe, in Bedfordshire, where I resided with my father during my holidays—for I am speaking now of more than twenty years ago, at a period when I was at the school of my most esteemed friend and much valued correspondent, the Rev. John Fell, M.A., Huntingdon—I can remember distinctly Dr. James's kind and excellent advice to me, and the undissembled pleasure which shone in his countenance every time I met him. How very brief was his term of usefulness in his far distant diocese, for he only reached it to die there!

XXII.

There are many customs observed in India which are mentioned in the Old and New Testaments, to wit:—the custom above named of drawing water, "Behold, I stand here by the well of water; and the daughters of the men of the city come out to draw water." Gen. xxiv. 13. "And the damsel was very fair to look upon; and she went down to the well, and filled her pitcher, and came up," verse 16; and in verse 15 we read, "with her pitcher upon her shoulder."—Again "trough for watering cattle." In India there are troughs made of brick and mortar, and sometimes also of earth, whither the camels and horses are taken to drink water.—Cakes, "And make cakes upon the hearth" Gen. xviii. 6. These cakes are placed upon an iron plate and turned often.—Milch Camels, "Thirty milch camels with their colts," Gen. xxxii. 15. The milk of camels is drunk by the natives of India when in a weak state of health; it is more nutritious than asses' milk, and is very fattening.—Earrings, "And all their ear-rings which were in their ears," Gen. xxxv. 4. Men as well as women in India wear ear-rings, nay even many of the native officers of the Sepoy corps.—Wheat in a mortar, "Though thou shouldest bray a fool in a mortar among wheat with a pestle," Prov. xxvii. 22. Wheat is frequently brayed in a mortar to clear it from the chaff.—Not new wine into old bottles, Our Saviour said, "Neither do men put new wine into old bottles; else the bottles break, and the wine runneth out, and the bottles perish: but they put new wine into new bottles: and both are preserved," Matt. ix. 17. Sir J. Chardin, a well-known traveller in India says; compare Joshua ix. 4. "The Arabs and all those who live a wandering life, still keep their milk, water, and other liquors in leathern bottles (mashks) which are generally made of goats' skins." In India water is put into sheeps' skins. "These natives never go a journey without a small leathern bottle of water hanging by their side like a scrip; when these bottles are old, and much used, they mend them, either by sewing on a piece, or by gathering up the broken place, in the manner of a purse." The Bombay Column which went to Affghanistan and Cabool, in 1839, had each man a little keg of wood, painted white, large enough to contain a quart of water; and it is to be regretted that the troops in the Sikh campaign of 1845-6 were not similarly supplied, for they suffered much from want of water. Surgeon Taylor in his report of killed and wounded, in H.M. 29th regiment, with the army of the Sutlej, in 1845-46, says; "during the three days they remained exposed to the powerful heat of the sun by day, and the very disproportionately cold air of the night, many of them suffered from the most agonizing thirst; only a very small quantity of water could be got, and that was very putrid. The excessive thirst of the men, and the impossibility of obtaining water may be judged of by the fact, that on the morning of the 22nd, men of this and other regiments were literally seen to drink their own urine."

Grinding grain, "Two women shall be grinding at the mill; the one shall be taken and the other left," Matt. xxiv. 41. Dr. E. Clarke says; "The two women, seated on the ground, held between them two round flat stones. In the centre of the upper stone was a cavity for pouring in the corn, and by the side of this, an upright wooden handle, for moving the stone. As the operation began, one of the women, with her right hand, pushed this handle to the woman opposite, who again sent it to her companion; thus communicating a rotary and very rapid motion to the upper stone, the left hand being all the while employed in supplying fresh corn, as fast as the bran and flour escaped from the sides of the machine."

The above are large stones, called in India chakkis, sometimes a smaller kind is used by one woman who turns the chakki round with her right hand, from left to right, in the same rotary motion; the women may be heard at this work in the villages before daybreak, singing their monotonous songs to while away the time. They also form an important appendage to a cavalry corps, having to grind all the corn required for the horses.

FOOTNOTES:

[112] Eleven guns since ascertained to be sunk in the river, total sixty-seven; thirty odd jinjalls fell into our hands.